A Practical Guide to the Companies Act 2006
— A guide for busy directors and company secretaries

PriceWaterhouseCoopers 🔳

A Practical Guide to the Companies Act 2006
— A guide for busy directors and company secretaries

Published by

a Wolters Kluwer business

145 London Road
Kingston-upon-Thames
Surrey
KT2 6SR
Tel: +44 (0) 844 561 8166
Fax: +44 (0) 870 247 1184
E-mail: customerservices@cch.co.uk
Web site: www.cch.co.uk

ISBN 978-1-84140-989-4

Typeset by YHT Ltd
Printed and bound in the UK by Hobbs the Printers Ltd

British Library Cataloguing-in-Publication Data.
A catalogue record for this book is available from the British Library.

Editors

Sarah Holmes read law at Cambridge University and is a solicitor and a partner in PricewaterhouseCoopers Legal's corporate team. She has extensive experience and expertise in company law and related regulations at EU and UK level. She advises FTSE 100 and other multinational clients within a wide range of industries on structuring projects and mergers and acquisitions.

Nigel Dealy read Chemistry at Queen Mary College, London University. He is a Fellow of the Institute of Chartered Accountants in England and Wales and is a member of its Financial Reporting and Company Law Committees and the Joint Institutes' Working Party on Distributable Profits. He specialises in advising clients primarily on the interpretation and application of International and UK Financial Reporting Standards and the accounting aspects of UK and EU Company Law.

Jonathan Gibson is a business graduate from the University of Hertfordshire and a Fellow of the Institute of Chartered Secretaries and Administrators. Jonathan leads PricewaterhouseCoopers Legal's company secretarial business which specialises in global governance and compliance issues for multinational clients. He also advises both listed and private companies on the Companies Act 2006 and regulatory requirements and best practice.

The authors of this book are drawn from PricewaterhouseCoopers Legal LLP and PricewaterhouseCoopers LLP. They are practitioners in a range of specialisms including lawyers, company secretaries, accountants, share scheme consultants and corporate governance specialists combining to provide a comprehensive overview of the impact of the new legislation.

Principal authors

Marc Boston
Cynthia Chan
Caroline Cook
Nigel Dealy
Caroline Graham
Margaret Heneghan
Paul Pilkington
Anna Pope
Stephen Quick
Richard Setchim
Mark Smith
Charlotte Thackrah

Editors

Contributors
Georgie Blyth
Richard Brady
Ian Carson
Margaret Cassidy
Roz Crawford
Charlotte Eastwood
Stuart Hatcher
Louise Inward
Veoeani Krishna
Janice Lingwood
Susannah McKay
Tatiana Psaraki
Ajali Shah
Sadaf Shahid
Craig Stevenson
Hugh Thomas
Christine Walser-Sacau
Samantha Wheeler
Nick Willis

Acknowledgments
We greatly appreciate the time and support provided by many of our colleagues around PricewaterhouseCoopers Legal LLP and Pricewaterhouse Coopers LLP. In particular, our thanks to the following colleagues who have assisted in numerous ways with checking technical content and the overall consistency of the text:
Thomas Allen
Rebecca Gifford
Alexandra Harrison-Cripps
Orla Lowe
Sam Newman
Gemma Phillips
Anthony Shaw
Kate Valdar
Carmel Weitzmann

In addition, we thank the following colleagues who were responsible for producing the text:
Pauline Johnson
Hortensia Lawrence
Brooke L'Huillier
Theresa Sabini

and to Faye Graham and Paula Knight for their project management.

Finally, our special thanks go to Alistair Hogarth and Richard Smerdon whose initial conversations led to the production of this book and above all to Nicole Johnson, Mia Kilroy, Claire McDermott, and their colleagues at CCH for their support in what has been a significant undertaking.

Contents

Chapter

Introduction I1001

1   The board and its directors 1001
2   Transactions with directors 2001
3   Setting up and maintaining a company under the Companies
      Act 2006 3001
4   Managing the shareholder relationship 4001
5   The preparation of annual accounts and reports 5001
6   Changes in financial reporting 6001
7   Working with the auditors 7001
8   Share capital and transactions involving shares 8001
9   Returning cash or other assets to shareholders and group
      reorganisations 9001
10   Employee incentive share plans 10001
11   Corporate simplification 11001
12   The process of managing regulatory change 12001

Appendix 1 – Overview of key changes introduced by the Companies
              Act 2006 . . . . A1001
Appendix 2 – Implementation of the Takeovers Directive
              (2004/25/EE) A2001
Appendix 3 – Implementation timetable for secondary legislation . . . A3001
Appendix 4 – Glossary of terms A4001

Table of cases T001
Table of legislation T003
Index I001

Introduction

I.1   The Companies Act 2006 .... I1001

Introduction

The Companies Act 2006

The Companies Act 2006 received Royal Assent in November 2006. It represents a major national overhaul of company law resulting from the Company Law Review which was commissioned by the then DTI and completed in July 2001 to recommend "a simple, efficient and cost effective framework for British businesses in the twenty-first century"[1]. The Act introduces a range of measures designed to modernise and simplify company law and to make it more efficient; it also has an increased focus on corporate governance and accountability and shareholder engagement. The provisions are currently being implemented over a phased period with all provisions required to be in force by 1 October 2009.

Although predominantly deregulatory, the Companies Act 2006 is a very significant piece of legislation; with the phased implementation timetable extending from 1 January 2007 to 1 October 2009 the Act represents substantial challenges for businesses. This book intends to fulfil the function of ensuring compliance as well as taking advantage of the cost savings associated with the Acts deregulatory aspects.

A Practical Guide to the Companies Act 2006 has been written predominantly for finance directors, in house counsel and company secretaries who need to understand how the Act will affect their businesses but should also be of relevance to other specialists who wish to increase their familiarity with the new provisions. As the model for each of the chapters we have therefore taken twelve of the key issues or activities which finance directors, in house counsel and company secretaries typically have to consider in the ordinary course of the financial year of a commercial group and each chapter discusses the company law aspects of those activities. Within each chapter we have endeavoured to present the information in a way which will enable the key changes to be identified swiftly with an emphasis on the practical rather than the esoteric. Each chapter concludes with a section summarising the changes and identifying any actions that need to be taken. We have also based the content on the questions which clients have asked us in the course of specific advisory work as well as those which have been raised in more general terms when explaining the implications of the new Act.

The *Guide* will be relevant to listed and unlisted companies in the UK, companies starting businesses here for the first time and overseas businesses

---

[1]   Explanatory notes to the Companies Act 2006.

with subsidiaries and branches in the UK. It focuses on the Act itself and is not intended to include the whole body of regulation that applies to quoted companies. The regulation of transactions outside the ordinary course of business, such as listings, mergers and acquisitions and third party transactions are also outside the scope of this publication.

The Companies Act 2006 also gives effect to a number of EU Directives although its provisions mainly implement the recommendations resulting from the Company Law Review. Of these the most significant is the Takeovers Directive. In addition to regulating takeovers, the Directive also amends the Companies Act 1985 provisions relating to the special powers for the compulsory acquisition of shares held by minority shareholders which apply to both public and private companies. Although these transactions typically do not arise in the ordinary course of business we have nevertheless, in view of their importance, included a summary of the key provisions in a separate appendix to this book. We have also included for ease of reference in Appendix 1 a quick reference overview of key changes made by the Act and in Appendix 3 a timetable of the implementation dates of the subordinate legislation which is either in force or pending and which is required to give full effect to the Act.

The following websites contain useful further information on the Act:

- The Department of Business Enterprise and Regulatory Reform, *www.berr.gov.uk/bbf/co-act-2006/index.html*

- Companies House, www.companieshouise.gov.uk

- The Office of Public Sector Information, *www.opsi.gov.uk*

- The Institute of Chartered Accountants in England and Wales, *www.icaew.com*

- The Institute of Chartered Secretaries and Administrator, *www.icsa.org.uk*.

All information is correct as at 30 June 2008 but where possible we have updated the information to the latest practicable date prior to publication.

We have greatly enjoyed putting this book together and very much hope that you will find it a very useful addition to existing publications on the subject.

Nigel Dealy   Sarah Holmes
PricewaterhouseCoopers LLP   Jonathan Gibson
                                     PricewaterhouseCoopers Legal LLP

Chapter 1

The board and its directors

1.1	Introduction		1002
	1.1.1	Scope of this chapter	1002
	1.1.2	What is the background to the changes?	1002
	1.1.3	Does the question of directors' duties really arise during the day to day conduct of a business?	1003
	1.1.4	Are directors' duties really an issue for directors of owner-managed companies and/or wholly-owned subsidiaries?	1003
	1.1.5	What are the key changes to directors' duties under the Companies Act 2006?	1003
1.2	What are the codified directors' duties?		1004
	1.2.1	Why have directors' duties been codified?	1004
	1.2.2	What are the seven statutory duties?	1005
	1.2.3	Duty to act in accordance with the company's constitution	1005
	1.2.4	Duty to promote the success of the company	1006
		1.2.4.1 What does 'success' mean for general commercial companies?	1007
		1.2.4.2 What does 'success' mean for non-commercial companies such as charities?	1007
		1.2.4.3 What does the 'benefit for members as a whole' mean?	1007
		1.2.4.4 Are the six statutory factors the only factors that a director needs to consider?	1008
		1.2.4.5 What if the statutory factors present conflicting interests?	1008
		1.2.4.6 Duty to promote the success of the company and the business review	1009
	1.2.5	Duty to exercise independent judgment	1010
	1.2.6	Duty to exercise reasonable care, skill and diligence	1010
	1.2.7	Duty to avoid conflicts of interest	1011
		1.2.7.1 Can a conflict of interest be authorised by the company?	1012
	1.2.8	Duty not to accept benefits from third parties	1014
	1.2.9	Duty to declare interest in a proposed transaction or arrangement	1015
		1.2.9.1 Duty to declare interest in an existing transaction or arrangement	1016
		1.2.9.2 Is there a requirement to keep information continuously updated?	1016
	1.2.10	What if the duties overlap?	1016

1.2.11   Does the codification of directors' duties mean that the common law is superseded? 1017

1.2.12   Does the duty to 'promote the success of the company' extend the previous common law duty? 1017

1.2.13   To whom do the duties apply? 1019

    1.2.13.1   Do the duties apply to statutory/*de jure* directors? 1019

    1.2.13.2   Do the duties apply to shadow directors? 1020

    1.2.13.3   Do the duties apply to *de facto* directors? 1021

    1.2.13.4   Do the duties apply to 'courtesy' or 'associate' directors? 1022

    1.2.13.5   Do the duties apply to alternate directors? 1022

    1.2.13.6   Do the duties apply to both executive and non-executive directors? 1022

1.2.14   To whom are the duties owed? 1023

1.2.15   Do the duties apply to directors who have ceased to hold the office of director? 1023

1.2.16   BERR guidance on directors' duties 1023

1.2.17   What practical steps should be taken in the light of the statutory duties? 1024

    1.2.17.1   Not just a 'box-ticking' exercise – some actions a company can take to support compliance with directors' duties 1025

1.3   Documenting board decisions 1025

    1.3.1   What is the status of board minutes? 1026

    1.3.2   What impact do the statutory duties have on board minutes? 1026

    1.3.3   Could a company be compelled to disclose board minutes in litigation? 1027

1.4   Directors' liability for a breach of duty 1028

    1.4.1   What are the consequences of a breach of directors' duties under the Companies Act 2006? 1028

    1.4.2   What are the consequences if a director acts in breach of the company's constitution? 1029

    1.4.3   What are the consequences for breaching other statutory obligations? 1029

1.5   Derivative claims 1029

    1.5.1   What are derivative claims? 1029

    1.5.2   What are the key provisions of the Companies Act 2006 relating to derivative claims? 1030

    1.5.3   What are the new rules relating to derivative claims? ... 1030

    1.5.4   In what circumstances can a derivative claim be brought under the Companies Act 2006? 1030

    1.5.5   Who can bring a derivative claim? 1031

    1.5.6   Whom can a derivative claim be issued against? 1031

    1.5.7   What process must a shareholder follow when seeking to continue a derivative claim? 1031

1.5.8   When must the court refuse permission to continue a
         derivative claim? 1032
1.5.9   What factors will a court take into account in deciding
         whether permission should be given? 1032
1.5.10 What are the implications of the new derivative claim
         regime for UK boards? 1033
1.5.11 In what kinds of situations in practice might a derivative
         claim be brought? 1034
1.5.12 What was the derivative claim regime prior to 1 October
         2007? 1035
1.5.13 What if the derivative claim relates to an alleged cause of
         action that occurred prior to 1 October 2007? 1036
1.5.14 Practical steps to consider under the new derivative claim
         regime 1036
1.6 Managing the risk to directors of personal liability 1038
1.6.1   Can shareholders ratify the decisions of the directors of the
         company? 1038
1.6.2   Does a director have a defence to a claim if he can show
         that he acted honestly and reasonably? 1038
1.6.3   Can a company or the parent provide directors with an
         indemnity against liability? 1038
         1.6.3.1   Can a company provide insurance for its
                    directors? 1039
         1.6.3.2   Can a company provide an indemnity to a
                    director against third party liability (qualifying
                    third party indemnity)? 1039
         1.6.3.3   Can a company indemnify a director of a pension
                    trustee company (qualifying pension scheme
                    indemnities)? 1041
         1.6.3.4   Does the company need to disclose a qualifying
                    indemnity provision and a qualifying pension
                    scheme indemnity pension? 1041
         1.6.3.5   Can qualifying indemnity provisions be inspected
                    by the company's shareholders? 1041
         1.6.3.6   Summary of changes that were introduced by the
                    Companies Act 2006 1041
1.7 Directors' liability on insolvency of the company 1042
1.7.1   When can a director be found to be liable for wrongful
         trading? 1042
1.7.2   When is a director liable for fraudulent trading? 1043
1.8 Directors as employees 1043
1.9 Common difficulties involving directors' duties in the context of
      group companies 1043
1.9.1   Do directors' duties apply to directors of a UK subsidiary
         of an overseas parent? 1044
1.9.2   Can a director of a subsidiary simply act in the manner in
         which its parent company directs? 1044

1.9.3 A practical example of the operation of directors' duties in a group context 1044

1.10 What is the difference between executive and non-executive directors? 1045

1.10.1 Who is an executive director? 1046

1.10.2 What is the role of a non-executive director? 1046

1.10.3 What are the legal duties and liabilities of a non-executive director? 1047

1.11 What are alternate directors? 1047

1.11.1 What is an alternate director? 1047

1.11.2 How can an alternate director be appointed? 1048

1.11.2.1 Do the 1985 Table A articles allow the appointment of alternate directors? 1048

1.11.2.2 Do the 2006 model articles allow the appointment of alternate directors to private companies? 1048

1.11.3 Who can be appointed as an alternate director? 1048

1.11.4 What rights does an alternate director have? 1048

1.11.5 What liabilities does an alternate director have? 1049

1.11.6 What filings must be made with Companies House in respect of an alternate director? 1049

1.11.7 Are there any restrictions on the period of time for which an alternate can be appointed? 1049

1.11.8 Is an alternate director entitled to receive remuneration in respect of his appointment? 1049

1.11.8.1 Is an alternate director entitled to receive remuneration under the 1985 Table A articles? 1049

1.11.8.2 Is an alternate director entitled to receive remuneration under the 2006 model articles? . . 1050

1.11.9 Does an alternate count when calculating the minimum number of directors that have been appointed? 1050

1.12 How many directors is a company required to have? 1050

1.12.1 What are the relevant Companies Act 2006 provisions? 1050

1.12.2 Is there a minimum number of directors that can be appointed? 1050

1.12.3 Can a sole director also be the secretary of the company? 1051

1.12.4 Is there a maximum number of directors that can be appointed? 1051

1.12.5 What happens if there is an insufficient number of directors? 1051

1.12.6 How does the Combined Code impact upon the composition of the board? 1052

1.13 Are there any restrictions on who can be appointed as a director? 1052

1.13.1 What are the relevant Companies Act 2006 provisions? . . 1052

1.13.2 Can a disqualified director be appointed, or act, as a director? 1052

1.13.3 Can an undischarged bankrupt act as a director? 1053

1.13.4   What are the rules relating to 'phoenix' companies? 1053

1.13.5   Can a company be a director? 1053

1.13.6   Is there a minimum age requirement for natural
directors? 1054

1.13.7   Is there a maximum age requirement for natural
directors? 1054

1.13.8   Is a director required to have minimum academic or
professional qualifications? 1055

1.13.9   Is a director required to live in the UK? 1055

1.13.10 How does the Combined Code apply to the appointment of
directors? 1056

1.13.11 Comparison between the Companies Act 1985 and the
Companies Act 2006 (excluding the Combined Code)
relating to the minimum requirements for directors 1057

1.14 How is a director appointed? 1058

1.14.1   What is the requirement for informed consent? 1058

1.14.2   How are the first directors of a company appointed to the
board? 1058

      1.14.2.1   How are the first directors of the company
appointed under the Companies Act 1985? 1058

      1.14.2.2   How are the first directors of the company
appointed under the Companies Act 2006? 1059

1.14.3   How are subsequent directors appointed to the board? . . 1059

      1.14.3.1   What if there is a restriction on the maximum
numbers of directors? 1059

      1.14.3.2   Can shareholders appoint directors pursuant to
the company's articles of association? 1059

      1.14.3.3   What is a casual vacancy? 1061

      1.14.3.4   What is an additional appointment? 1061

      1.14.3.5   How do existing board members make additional
appointments to the board? 1062

1.14.4   What notification of appointment does the company need
to make to the Registrar of Companies? 1062

1.14.5   What registers does a company need to update when a
director is appointed? 1063

1.14.6   Are there any additional considerations when appointing a
director of a public company? 1063

1.14.7   Are the acts of a director still valid if there is a defect in a
director's appointment? 1063

1.14.8   Is a director required to disclose his residential address? 1064

1.14.9   Checklist of considerations when appointing a director 1065

1.14.10 Checklist of considerations when accepting an
appointment as a director 1065

1.15 How is a director's appointment terminated? 1066

1.15.1   Methods of removal of a director 1066

      1.15.1.1   Removal by resignation 1066

      1.15.1.2   Retirement by rotation 1067

1.15.1.3 Expiry of a fixed term contract 1068
1.15.1.4 Removal by the board 1068
1.15.1.5 Removal by shareholders 1068
1.15.2 Further considerations when removing a director 1069
1.15.2.1 Removal of a director who is also an employee 1069
1.15.2.2 Removal of a director who is also a
shareholder 1069
1.15.3 What are the rules relating to payment for loss of office? 1070
1.15.4 What notification needs to be made to the Registrar of
Companies when removing a director? 1070
1.15.5 What registers need updating when a director is removed
from office? 1070
1.15.6 Checklist of considerations when removing a director ... 1070
1.16 Automatic vacation of office 1071
1.16.1 What are the rules relating to the vacation of office under
the 1985 Table A articles? 1071
1.16.1.1 Disqualification/operation of law 1071
1.16.1.2 Resignation 1071
1.16.1.3 Bankruptcy 1071
1.16.1.4 Loss of mental capacity 1071
1.16.1.5 Absence from board meetings for more than six
months 1071
1.16.2 Automatic vacation pursuant to the 2006 model articles 1072
1.16.2.1 Disqualification 1072
1.16.2.2 Resignation 1072
1.16.2.3 Removal by shareholders 1072
1.16.2.4 Failure to participate in the operation of the
company 1072
1.16.2.5 Termination of service agreement 1072
1.17 Summary of key changes under the Companies Act 2006 1073

Where it is helpful to do so, this chapter refers to the Combined Code, the Higgs Report and the Smith Guidance. These guidance documents only apply to fully listed companies, namely companies listed on the main market of the London Stock Exchange, although it is common for companies listed on the Alternative Investment Market and larger private companies to adopt voluntarily their recommendations. The provisions of these guidance documents are extensive and a full analysis of their application is outside the scope of this book. Therefore, any reference to the Combined Code, the Higgs Report or the Smith Guidance in this chapter should not be considered to be an exhaustive analysis of the recommendations made in these documents[1].

We also refer in this chapter to the 1985 Table A articles and the 2006 model articles. These are the articles of association that will, in the absence of bespoke articles of association being adopted, apply as default articles of association to companies incorporated under either the Companies Act 1985 (in the case of companies incorporated before 1 October 2007) or the Companies Act 2006 (in the case of companies incorporated on or after 1 October 2009). Interim model articles of association have also been published and these apply as default articles of association for companies incorporated on or after 1 October 2007. These interim articles of association do not make significant changes to the 1985 Table A articles and we have not therefore undertaken an analysis of these interim articles of association in this chapter. However, the complete text of the interim articles of association for private companies limited by shares can be found on the Companies House website[2].

It is common for these 'model' articles of association to form the basis of a company's bespoke articles of association.

For companies incorporated before 1 October 2007 their articles of association will remain unchanged unless specifically amended with shareholder approval as the implementation of the Companies Act 2006 will not automatically amend a company's articles of association. A company will therefore need to amend its articles of association should it wish to take advantage of certain provisions of the Companies Act 2006 and/or the 2006 model articles.

At the time of writing, the 2006 model articles are in draft form and the references in this chapter to specific regulations of the 2006 model articles are references to the draft 2006 model articles that were published in April 2008 (but dated March 2008).

---

[1] The text of any of these documents can be accessed using the following links:
- the Combined Code: *www.frc.org.uk/documents/pagemanager/frc/Combined_Code_June_2008/ Combined%20 Code%20(June%202008)%20Web%20;*
- the Higgs Report: *www.berr.gov.uk/files/file23012.pdf;*
- the Smith Guidance: *www.frc.org.uk/documents/pagemanager/frc/Smith%20Report%202005. pdf.*

[2] *www.companies-house.gov.uk/companiesAct/implementations/TableA Private.pdf.*

The board and its directors

"We should remind ourselves that being a company director is a wonderful thing for the person who is a company director. But it is a position of great responsibility which involves running the affairs of a company for the benefit of other people. It is a heavy responsibility we should not water down."

Lord Goldsmith, Lords Grand Committee, 6 February 2006, column 291

1.1   Introduction

1.1.1   Scope of this chapter

This chapter considers some of the most fundamental reforms that have been introduced by the Companies Act 2006 and the practical impact that these will have for companies and their directors. These reforms relate to issues of corporate governance with the key change being the codification of directors' duties, which is the first time that directors' duties have been codified in the UK. This chapter also discusses the management of directors' conflicts of interest, which has become increasingly important in light of the changes made by the Companies Act 2006 to directors' duties.

The codification of directors' duties was one of the most widely debated aspects of the Companies Act 2006 as it is one area where the Companies Act 2006, which is otherwise a largely deregulatory statute, has potentially increased the risks faced by directors. In codifying directors' duties the Companies Act 2006 introduces seven statutory duties that directors must comply with when discharging their functions as a director, which has caused extensive debate on the following issues:

(i)   does the codification of directors' duties change the corresponding common law duties?

(ii)   does the codification of directors' duties increase a directors' liability?

(iii) what impact does the codification of directors' duties have on documenting the board decision making process?

In light of these changes, companies and their directors therefore need to identify any changes to their current policies and practices that may be necessary to comply with the Companies Act 2006 or to mitigate the increased risks it might impose in a particular case.

1.1.2   What is the background to the changes?

The Government wished to clarify the nature of directors' duties and to provide an accessible statement of the law. The codified provisions also encapsulate the concept of 'enlightened shareholder value' by including a non-exhaustive list of statutory factors to be taken into account when directors exercise their duty to promote the success of the company (see section 1.2.4).

1.1.3 Does the question of directors' duties really arise during the day to day conduct of a business?

Yes. Throughout the course of a year directors will need to make a number of decisions that require a detailed consideration of the duties that they owe to the company for whom they act. The discharge of these duties can often involve balancing the competing interests of various stakeholders and can be particularly complicated in a group situation where a transaction is in the interests of the group, but may not necessarily be in the best interests of the particular company for whom the director acts (see section 1.9). Notwithstanding the inherent challenges faced by a director in discharging these duties a breach of duty has significant consequences, both for the company and the individual director concerned in terms of their personal liability.

In practice, the question of directors' duties will arise both in one-off transactions and during the day to day management of the company. By way of example, during the course of a year a company will experience changes to the board composition, it may enter into finance agreements, intra-group reorganisations or transactions with third parties all of which require directors to consider, and act in accordance with, their duties to the company.

1.1.4 Are directors' duties really an issue for directors of owner-managed companies and/or wholly-owned subsidiaries?

Yes. Directors' duties are applicable to all directors, regardless of the ownership of the company for whom they act. The immediate risk is low for owner-managed companies or for wholly-owned subsidiaries where the company remains solvent. Nevertheless, even in this situation, a breach of duty might become apparent in the event of a sale of the company where due diligence is undertaken by the prospective purchaser. Furthermore, a new board (or shareholder) can also review the acts or omissions of the previous directors and take action where it feels it is appropriate to do so.

1.1.5 What are the key changes to directors' duties under the Companies Act 2006?

The most fundamental change is the codification of directors' duties, which are effective from 1 October 2007 (save for those relating to conflicts, which are effective from 1 October 2008). Other key changes for directors under the Companies Act 2006, which are discussed in more detail in this chapter, are:

■ changes to the conflicts of interest regime and in particular the ability of independent directors to authorise conflicts, which are effective from 1 October 2008;

■ the introduction of a statutory derivative claim regime, which is effective from 1 October 2007;

■ the introduction of a new minimum age requirement for directors, which is effective from 1 October 2008;

■ the abolition of the maximum age for directors of public companies, which was repealed on 6 April 2007; and

■ the requirement for every company to have at least one natural, that is not corporate, director, which (subject to a grace period for certain companies that extends until October 2010) is effective from 1 October 2008.

This chapter also considers the procedures for the appointment and removal of directors.

1.2 What are the codified directors' duties?

The Companies Act 2006 has, for the first time, codified directors' duties in the UK. In doing so, the Companies Act 2006 sets out seven statutory duties that directors must comply with (see section 1.2.2) together with six statutory factors that directors must have regard to (as a minimum) when discharging their duty to 'promote the success of the company' (see section 1.2.4). Most of these duties are effective from 1 October 2007; those relating to the management of conflicts of interest and duties are effective from 1 October 2008.

1.2.1 Why have directors' duties been codified?

Prior to 1 October 2007, directors' duties were set out in a patchwork of complex and detailed common law rules and equitable principles. As a result, there was no single statement of duties that directors could refer to.

When drafting the Companies Act 2006, the Government considered that it was unsatisfactory for directors' duties in the UK to continue to be governed almost entirely by common law and without a clear and concise statement of the duties that a director owed to a company. This was especially the case now that companies operate in an increasingly international environment and would often have non-UK directors appointed to the board. It was therefore considered desirable that the Companies Act 2006 codified directors' duties with the intention of making the law in this area clearer and more accessible. Nevertheless common law will remain relevant to the interpretation of these duties.

1.2.2 What are the seven statutory duties?

The Companies Act 2006 sets out seven general duties that a director owes to the company on whose board the directors sits. These seven duties are:

(i)   the duty to act in accordance with the company's constitution;

(ii)   the duty to promote the success of the company;

(iii)   the duty to exercise independent judgment;

(iv)   the duty to exercise reasonable care, skill and diligence;

(v)   the duty to avoid conflicts of interest;

(vi)   the duty not to accept benefits from third parties; and

(vii)   the duty to declare interest in proposed transactions.

Each of these duties is considered in more detail below.

1.2.3 Duty to act in accordance with the company's constitution[3]

The Companies Act 2006 states that:

"A director of a company must –

(a)   act in accordance with the company's constitution, and

(b)   only exercise powers for the purposes for which they are conferred."

The definition of the constitution of the company for this purpose includes[4]:

(i)   the company's articles of association;

(ii)   any special resolutions of the members of the company;

(iii)   any resolution or agreement approved by all the members of a class of shareholders that, if not so agreed, would not be effective for its purpose;

(iv)   any other resolution or decision made in accordance with the constitution; and

(v)   any decision by the members of the company, or a class of members, that is treated by virtue of any enactment of the rule of law as equivalent to a decision by the company.

This duty codifies the common law requirement that directors exercise their powers in accordance with the terms on which they were granted and that such powers are exercised for a proper purpose.

---

[3]   Section 171, Companies Act 2006.
[4]   Sections 17 and 257, Companies Act 2006.

The Companies Act 2006 is introducing a number of changes that may impact upon a company's articles of association. Therefore, to ensure compliance with this duty a director will need to keep the provisions of the company's articles of association under review to ensure that directors do not act under a deregulatory aspect of the Companies Act 2006 where the company's articles have not yet been updated to reflect such a change. In this situation, the company's articles of association may contain more restrictive provisions than the Companies Act 2006 and failure to comply with the provisions of the articles of association will mean that a director is in breach of this duty.

1.2.4 Duty to promote the success of the company[5]

The duty to promote the success of the company has been one of the most widely debated of the seven statutory duties. The Companies Act 2006 provides that a director must:

> "act in the way he considers, in good faith, would be most likely to promote the success of the company for the benefit of its members as a whole and in doing so have regard (amongst other matters) to –
>
> (i)   the likely consequences of any decision in the long term;
>
> (ii)   the interests of the company's employees;
>
> (iii)   the need to foster the company's business relationships with suppliers, customers and others;
>
> (iv)   the impact of the company's operations on the community and the environment;
>
> (v)   the desirability of the company maintaining a reputation for high standards of business conduct; and
>
> (vi)   the need to act fairly as between members of the company."

This duty to promote the success of the company replaces the pre 1 October 2007 common law duty for a director to 'act in good faith in the best interests of the company'. The statutory factors set out in paragraphs (ii) (employees) and (vi) (acting fairly as between members) above reflect existing law but the other statutory factors are new.

The change of language between the pre 1 October 2007 duty for a director to 'act in good faith in the best interests of the company' and the statutory duty set out above to 'promote the success of the company' reflects the language of the Combined Code, and this amendment is thought to be intended to bring all directors within a single governance principle. It also encapsulates the concept of 'enlightened shareholder value', which is one of the major tenets of the Companies Act 2006.

---

[5]   Section 172, Companies Act 2006.

As referred to above, it is this duty and the corresponding six statutory factors to which a director is required to have regard that has attracted the most debate during the passage of the Company Law Reform Bill (as the Companies Act 2006 was then known) through Parliament. We discuss the key concerns that have been raised in respect of this duty below.

1.2.4.1 What does 'success' mean for general commercial companies?

In giving guidance on this question, Lord Goldsmith in his comments to the Lords Grand Committee, said:

> "What is success? The starting point is that it is essentially for the members of the company to define the objective they wish to achieve. Success means what the members collectively want the company to achieve. For a commercial company, success will usually mean long-term increase in value. For certain companies, such as charities and community interest companies, it will mean the attainment of the objectives for which the company has been established."

> *Lord Goldsmith, Lords Grand Committee, 6 February 2006, column 255.*

Accordingly, for most commercial companies success is likely to mean the long-term increase in value of the company. However, no guidance is given as to what constitutes 'long-term', and this may present a challenge, for example, for institutions acquiring corporate investments with a view to restructuring and resale in the shorter term. However, the Government has made it clear that ultimately what constitutes success is a matter for the independent judgment of the directors of the company and a director will not be able to rely on the guidance referred to above to defend an allegation that the director has acted in breach of the duty to promote the success of the company. The courts are, however, unlikely to interfere with the directors' commercial judgment on what constitutes success (provided that the directors' decision is made in good faith).

1.2.4.2 What does 'success' mean for non-commercial companies such as charities?

Where the purpose of the company is, or includes, a purpose other than the benefit of its members (such as a charitable company) then the duty to promote the success of the company for the benefit of its members as a whole has effect as a duty to achieve such an alternative purpose[6].

1.2.4.3 What does the 'benefit for members as a whole' mean?

The directors are required to act, in good faith, in the manner that they consider will promote the success of the company for the benefit of its members

---

[6] Section 172(2), Companies Act 2006.

as a whole. It is clear that in some instances the members will have competing interests. However, it is for the directors to determine 'in good faith' in the exercise of their commercial judgement how best to promote the success of the company for the benefit of its members. Provided the directors act in good faith and comply with their duty to act fairly as between members[7] they are unlikely to be found to be in breach of this duty.

This section of the Companies Act 2006 specifically states[8] that the duty to promote the success of the company for the benefit of its members as a whole is subservient to any enactment or rule of law that requires directors to consider or act in the interests of the creditors of the company in certain circumstances. Therefore, in an actual or potential insolvency situation directors are (as they were before 1 October 2007) required to act in accordance with the interests of the creditors of the company as a group.

1.2.4.4 Are the six statutory factors the only factors that a director needs to consider?

No. Directors are required to have regard to the six statutory factors 'amongst others' when discharging their duty to promote the success of the company.

It is therefore clear that a director will not necessarily have discharged his duty to promote the success of the company simply by demonstrating that he has considered the six factors set out above. It will be for a director to demonstrate that he has considered all factors that are relevant to the issue before him to enable him to argue successfully that he has discharged his duty to promote the success of the company. This issue necessarily raises a question of evidence, namely how does a director demonstrate that he has discharged the duty to promote the success of the company (in addition to the other codified duties)? We consider this question further in section 1.3 below.

1.2.4.5 What if the statutory factors present conflicting interests?

This question actually raises two issues. First, what if the statutory factors represent competing interests and secondly what if the statutory factors appear to conflict with the overriding duty to promote the success of the company?

It is quite probable that, in some circumstances, the statutory factors will present conflicting interests. In this situation the directors will need to consider the matter before them having 'regard' to all six factors (amongst other relevant factors) and ultimately decide, using due care and skill, which course of action they consider will, in good faith, promote the success of the company.

Turning to the second issue, it is apparent that the six statutory factors and the overriding duty to promote the success of the company could also present

---

[7] Section 172(1)(f), Companies Act 2006.
[8] Section 172(2), Companies Act 2006.

conflicting interests. For example, making a large number of employees redundant may not be in the interests of employees (which is one of the six statutory factors) but could ultimately promote the success of the company, namely the long-term increase in value of the company.

In this situation, a director must remember that the overriding duty is the duty to promote the success of the company. In discharging this duty a director is required to have 'regard to' the six statutory factors; this does not preclude a director from acting in a certain way if to do so would be contrary to one of the statutory factors. Nor does the Companies Act 2006 necessarily require a director to take positive steps to remedy the consequences of any action that is contrary to the six statutory factors. Instead, what the Companies Act 2006 does require is that directors, in discharging their duty to promote the success of the company, have regard to the six statutory factors in addition to any other factors that may be relevant to the matter before them.

1.2.4.6 *Duty to promote the success of the company and the business review*

The concept of the duty to promote the success of the company is not limited to the general duties for directors. As noted by Margaret Hodge in her Ministerial Statements, "the new expression of the duties is part of the wider recognition and encouragement of change in the Act". An example of this is the linking of the directors' duty to promote the success of the company to external reporting to members. Specifically, new provisions in the Companies Act 2006 that were implemented on 1 October 2007, link this duty to the purpose of a 'business review'.

All companies (other than small companies) have been required to publish a business review as part of their directors' report for some time. The requirement was introduced in order to implement certain provisions of the EU's Accounts Modernisation Directive, and applied to annual reports for years beginning on or after 1 March 2005.

The Companies Act 2006 specifically states that the purpose of the business review is to "inform members of the company and help them assess how the directors have performed their duty under section 172 (duty to promote the success of the company)"[9].

It is essential that the business review and internal procedures are consistent to avoid inaccurate or contradicting statements being included within the business review. This has become particularly important in light of the new derivative claim regime (see section 1.5).

---

[9]   Section 417(2), Companies Act 2006.

1.2.5   Duty to exercise independent judgment[10]

The Companies Act 2006 provides that:

"A director of a company must exercise independent judgment."

The duty to exercise independent judgment codifies the common law requirement that directors do not subordinate their authority to third parties. This duty reflects the requirement for directors to exercise their own judgment on any given matter and not simply to agree with the majority of the board.

The duty to exercise independent judgment does not prohibit a director from delegating authority where such delegation is authorised by a provision in the company's constitution or where a director is acting in accordance with an agreement entered into by the company that restricts the future exercise of discretion by its directors. However, any such delegation does not absolve the director from complying with the other statutory duties.

In addition, this duty does not prevent a director from acting upon the advice of others (for example relying on the advice of the company's solicitor in certain matters) provided that the director exercises independent judgment when coming to an ultimate decision on any given matter.

1.2.6   Duty to exercise reasonable care, skill and diligence[11]

The Companies Act 2006 states that:

"(1) A director of a company must exercise reasonable care, skill and diligence.

(2) This means the care, skill and diligence that would be exercised by a reasonably diligent person with –

(a)   the general knowledge, skill and experience that may reasonably be expected of a person carrying out the functions carried out by the director in relation to the company; and

(b)   the general knowledge, skill and expertise that the director has."

The Companies Act 2006 therefore codifies the two stage common law test (which has developed in recent years to reflect the test set out in section 214 of the Insolvency Act 1986) that a director must satisfy when discharging his duty to exercise reasonable care, skill and diligence. The first stage of this test involves an objective test and the second a subjective test.

---

[10]   Section 173, Companies Act 2006.
[11]   Section 174, Companies Act 2006.

First, a director will need to satisfy an objective test that the director has exercised the reasonable care, skill and diligence that a reasonably diligent person with the general knowledge, skill and expertise that may reasonably be expected of a person undertaking the functions carried out by the director in relation to the company would exercise. A director should not therefore accept a position, even on a temporary basis, if he does not have the relevant skills that are required by that position.

Secondly, a director will need to satisfy the subjective test that the director has exercised the reasonable care, skill and diligence that the director actually possesses. For example, a HR director with a finance background would be expected to discharge his duties making full use of both his HR and finance knowledge and could not seek to limit his responsibility to HR matters alone.

In both cases directors should ensure that they keep themselves up to date with relevant developments, and thereby address any skills gaps relevant to their role, that they allow sufficient time to read and consider board papers and that they take advice where they are in doubt as to how to proceed.

1.2.7 Duty to avoid conflicts of interest[12]

The Companies Act 2006 provides that:

> "(1) A director of a company must avoid a situation in which he has, or can have, a direct or indirect interest that conflicts, or possibly may conflict, with the interests of the company.
>
> (2) This applies in particular to the exploitation of any property, information or opportunity (and it is immaterial whether the company could take advantage of the property, information or opportunity)."

The duty to avoid conflicts of interest, which is effective from 1 October 2008, does represent a departure from the previous common law duty.

This duty imposes, in contrast to the common law, a positive obligation on a director to avoid a conflict of interest. The duty is expressed to apply in particular to the exploitation of any property, information or opportunity regardless of whether the company could take advantage of the property, information or opportunity referred to. This duty does not apply to a conflict of interest arising in relation to a transaction or arrangement with the company, which is dealt with by section 177 of the Companies Act 2006 and that is discussed in section 1.2.9 below. However, it is feasible that a potential conflict that is caught by the provisions of section 175 develops to become a transaction or arrangement that is caught by the provisions of section 177.

---

[12] Section 175, Companies Act 2006.

Furthermore, this duty imposes an obligation on a director to avoid a situation that not only represents an actual conflict but that 'may' conflict with the interests of the company and the broad scope of this duty arguably extends the corresponding common law rule. For example, an investment bank may acquire shares in a company and appoint a director to the board. This might constitute a conflict of interest and duty at that point; it might also give rise to a potential conflict because it is conceivable that at some point in the future the investment bank may be a lender to the company. It is therefore not clear how far this duty extends although it is evident that the duty has a potentially broad application.

The duty to avoid a conflict of interest includes a conflict of interest and duty together with a conflict of duties[13]. A conflict of interest can arise where a person who is a director of one company proposes to enter into a contract with a company of which the director is a shareholder. A conflict of duties could exist for example where a director is an officer of two companies that are potential competitors.

In accordance with the common law regime, the Companies Act 2006 specifically states that the duty to avoid a conflict of interest is not infringed where a situation cannot reasonably be regarded as likely to give rise to a conflict of interests[14]. Therefore in the above example, if a director sits on the board of two companies that operate in different markets where there is no possibility of a conflict of interest by virtue of the director holding office with both companies, then the director will not need to obtain authorisation from either company in respect of his holding office with the other.

1.2.7.1   Can a conflict of interest be authorised by the company?

In accordance with the existing common law, conflicts of duty and interest are permissible as long as they have been declared to, and approved by, shareholders. The approval mechanism is usually set out in the company's articles of association and commonly enables the board to approve a conflict. Any director acting in a situation where there is a conflict without the requisite approval will be liable to account to the company for any gain made and the contract from which he has benefitted can be set aside by the company.

In an important change from the common law regime, the Companies Act 2006[15] stipulates that the independent directors of the company (namely those directors that are not interested either directly or indirectly in the matter before them) may authorise a conflict of another director that would otherwise be a breach of the duty to avoid a conflict of interest with the company.

---

[13] Section 175(7), Companies Act 2006.
[14] Section 175(4), Companies Act 2006.
[15] Section 175(5), Companies Act 2006.

The ability for independent directors to authorise a conflict differs depending on whether the relevant company is a private company or a public company:

(i)   the independent directors of a private company, which is incorporated on or after 1 October 2008, may authorise a conflict provided there is nothing in the articles of association of the company that would invalidate or prohibit the authorisation being given;

(ii) the independent directors of a private company that was incorporated before 1 October 2008, may only authorise a conflict provided there is no restriction in the articles of association of the company that would invalidate or prohibit the authorisation being given and provided the shareholders of the company have passed an ordinary resolution authorising the independent directors of the company to approve such a conflict (although best practice suggests that it may be appropriate for such a company to also include an express authority in its articles of association as this will enable the company to attach any conditions to such authority that may be desirous, e.g. provisions relating to the management of confidential information); and

(iii) the independent directors of a public company (whether listed or otherwise) may only authorise the conflict concerned provided there is an express provision in the company's constitution enabling the directors to do so.

Any authorisation of a conflict by independent directors is only valid if the quorum at the meeting at which the matter was considered is met without counting the conflicted director or any other interested director, and where the conflict was approved without the conflicted director voting or, if the conflicted director did vote, without his vote having been counted.

If the company does not have sufficient independent directors to authorise the conflict then the conflict can only be authorised by the shareholders of the company. As with the regime that applied prior to the Companies Act 2006 shareholders are able to authorise a conflict by passing an ordinary resolution to this effect (or such higher threshold that may be provided for in the company's articles of association). However, in a change to the previous regime, unless the resolution is passed unanimously, the resolution ratifying the conflict cannot be voted on by either the interested director, or any shareholder connected with that director.

Provided the conflict has been properly authorised by the directors pursuant to the Companies Act 2006, the transaction or arrangement to which the conflict relates is not liable to be set aside by virtue of any common law principle that may otherwise apply.

It would be prudent for all companies to review their articles of association to determine whether any changes are required in readiness for the introduction of the new provisions. For instance, public companies will need to include an express authority in their articles of association to enable the independent directors to authorise a conflict. In addition, both public and private companies may wish to consider including in their articles of association certain conditions that they may wish to attach to any consent given to a conflicted director (such as the management of confidential information or a requirement for the conflicted director to abstain from voting on any matter relating to the conflict). Alternatively, the articles of association could detail that the independent directors may impose any conditions to such approval as they see fit.

1.2.8   Duty not to accept benefits from third parties[16]

The Companies Act 2006 states that:

> "A director of a company must not accept a benefit from a third party conferred by reason of –
>
> (a)   his being a director, or
>
> (b)   his doing (or not doing) anything as a director."

Therefore from 1 October 2008, the Companies Act 2006 imposes a strict prohibition on directors accepting benefits from third parties where those benefits are conferred by reason of a person's position as a director. 'Third party' in this context is defined as any person other than the company, an associated company or an individual acting on behalf of the company or an associated company[17]. An associated company is a subsidiary of the company, the holding company of the company or a sister company[18].

The duty not to accept benefits from a third party is not infringed if the acceptance of a benefit cannot reasonably be regarded as likely to give rise to a conflict of interest[19]. It is thought therefore that the acceptance of corporate hospitality in the usual and reasonable construction of the term would not infringe this duty. It is however advisable for companies to introduce a corporate hospitality policy which articulates the circumstances in which a conflict of interest might arise.

As before, a reference to a conflict of interest with regard to the duty not to accept benefits is also a reference to a conflict of interest and a conflict of duty as well as to a conflict of duties (see section 1.2.7 for an example of when such a conflict may arise).

---

[16]   Section 176, Companies Act 2006.
[17]   Section 176(2), Companies Act 2006.
[18]   Section 256, Companies Act 2006.
[19]   Section 176(4), Companies Act 2006.

Unlike the duty to avoid a conflict of interest, the independent directors of the company are not able to authorise the acceptance of a benefit; only the shareholders of the company will be able to do this.

1.2.9 Duty to declare interest in a proposed transaction or arrangement[20]

The Companies Act 2006 provides that:

> "If a director of a company is any way, directly or indirectly, interested in a proposed transaction or arrangement with the company, he must declare the nature and extent of that interest to the other directors."

This duty, which is effective from on 1 October 2008, does increase directors' disclosure obligations under the Companies Act 1985.

Under the Companies Act 2006 a director is required to disclose the 'nature and extent' of any direct or indirect interest in a proposed transaction or arrangement with the company. It is not therefore sufficient for a director to simply declare that he is interested in a proposed transaction or arrangement without disclosing the nature and extent of that interest.

Disclosure can be made[21]:

(i)   at a meeting of the directors; or

(ii) by written notice, which must be sent to the other directors of the company in hard copy form or, if the recipient has agreed to receive the notice by electronic means, electronically and in either case the notice will be deemed to form part of the next meeting of the directors; or

(iii) by general notice, whereby a director gives notice to his co-directors that he has an interest in a specified entity or person and is to be regarded as interested in any transaction or arrangement that may after the date of the notice be made with that entity or person. A general notice is not effective unless it is given at a meeting of directors or the director takes reasonable steps to secure that the notice is read at the next meeting of directors after the notice is given.

If a director makes a disclosure that subsequently becomes inaccurate then a further disclosure must be made[22]. There is therefore a requirement for a director to keep this information continuously updated and this requirement should be reflected in the company's internal policies on this issue.

The declaration of an interest by a director must be made before the company enters into the transaction or arrangement.

---

[20]   Section 177, Companies Act 2006.
[21]   Section 177(2), Companies Act 2006.
[22]   Section 177(3), Companies Act 2006.

A director is not required to disclose an interest that he is not aware of, or where the director is not aware of the transaction or arrangement in question. However, the Companies Act 2006 provides that a director is deemed to be aware of those matters that he ought reasonably to be aware of and directors should ensure that they make proper disclosure of all situations that represent a potential conflict.

In addition, a director need not disclose an interest that cannot reasonably be regarded as giving rise to a conflict, which the directors are already aware of or if the conflict relates to the director's service contract that has been, or is to be, considered by a meeting or committee of the directors.

1.2.9.1 *Duty to declare interest in an existing transaction or arrangement*[23]

A director is also under an obligation pursuant to section 182 of the Companies Act 2006 to disclose his interest in an existing transaction or arrangement (save where such a disclosure has already been made under section 177). Again, disclosure can be made at a meeting of the directors, by notice in writing or by general notice. If a director fails to make a disclosure under section 182 of the Companies Act 2006 he is guilty of an offence punishable by fine whereas liability for a breach of section 177 is a civil offence only.

1.2.9.2 *Is there a requirement to keep information continuously updated?*

Yes. If a declaration that has been made in respect of an interest in an existing or proposed transaction proves to be, or becomes, inaccurate or incomplete, a further declaration must be made[24]. A company's internal policies should be reviewed and, where necessary, updated to reflect this requirement.

1.2.10 What if the duties overlap?

The Companies Act 2006 specifically acknowledges that, save where otherwise expressly provided, more than one duty may apply to any given case[25]. A director will not be able to rely on compliance with one duty to avoid a breach of another. For example, a director will not be able to rely on an argument that the director was somehow promoting the success of the company when acting in breach of the duty to avoid a conflict of interest.

---

[23] Section 182, Companies Act 2006.
[24] Section 177(3) and 182(3) Companies Act 2006.
[25] Section 179, Companies Act 2006.

1.2.11 Does the codification of directors' duties mean that the common law is superseded?

No. Notwithstanding the codification of directors' duties, the common law is still relevant as the Companies Act 2006 provides that the codified duties will be "interpreted and applied in the same way as common law rules or equitable principles, and regard shall be had to the corresponding common law rules and equitable principles in interpreting and applying the general duties"[26].

In addition, the Companies Act 2006 specifically states that it only codifies "certain common law rules and equitable principles as they apply in relation to directors and have effect in place of those rules and principles"[27] intimating that those rules not so codified survive the implementation of the Companies Act 2006. It appears therefore that, notwithstanding the original aim of the Government in codifying directors' duties it is arguable that the Companies Act 2006 does not in fact provide a fully codified statement of directors' duties.

1.2.12 Does the duty to 'promote the success of the company' extend the previous common law duty?

There has been a significant amount of debate as to whether the codified duties extend the directors' duties that applied prior to 1 October 2007. To assist with the interpretation of the codified duties the Department of Business Enterprise and Regulatory Reform (BERR, formerly the Department of Trade and Industry) issued a collection of Ministerial Statements. These are statements that were made by ministers when discussing the meaning of the codified duties during the passage of the Companies Law Reform Bill (as the Companies Act 2006 was then known) through Parliament. These do not have legal effect but the court can have regard to the intention of Parliament when interpreting legislation. The full text of the Ministerial Statements can be accessed using the following URL: *www.berr.gov.uk/files/file40139.pdf*.

When considering whether the Companies Act 2006 extends the previous common law regime, the Ministerial Statements acknowledge:

> "There are two ways of looking at the statutory statement of directors' duties: on the one the (*sic*) hand it simply codifies the existing common law obligations of company directors; on the other – especially in section 172: the duty to act in the interests of the company – it marks a radical departure in articulating the connection between what is good for a company and what is good for society at large."

> *Margaret Hodge, Introduction, Companies Act 2006, Duties of company directors, Ministerial Statements, June 2007*

---

[26] Section 170(4), Companies Act 2006.
[27] Section 170(3), Companies Act 2006.

Further guidance is given on this question when looking at the rationale provided for the introduction of the duty to promote the success of the company, namely that:

> "This duty codifies the current law and enshrines in statute what is commonly referred to as the principle of 'enlightened shareholder value'."

> *Explanatory notes on the Companies Act 2006, paragraph 325.*

Margaret Hodge, Minister of State for Industry and the Regions, goes on in the Ministerial Statements to state:

> "But compared with most text-book definitions of the common law duties of directors, the new statutory statement captures a cultural change in the way in which companies conduct their business. There was a time when business success in the interests of shareholders was thought to be in conflict with society's aspirations for people who work in the company or in the supply chain companies, for the long-term well-being of the community and for the protection of the environment.

> "I strongly believe that businesses perform better, and are more sustainable in the long term, when they have regard to a wider group of issues in pursuing success. That is a common-sense approach that reflects a modern view of the way in which businesses operate in their community: they interact with customers and suppliers: they make sure that employees are motivated and properly rewarded; and they think about their impact on communities and the environment. They do so at least partly because it makes good business sense."

What is clear is that a company with commercial objects can continue to operate as an economic vehicle designed to deliver benefit for the shareholders. By continuing to make common law relevant to the interpretation of the codified duties it is also probable that, notwithstanding differences in language, the majority of the codified duties largely reflect the law prior to 1 October 2007 (save for the regulation of conflicts).

What is new, however, is the introduction of the statutory factors. These factors reduce the flexibility of directors to determine the issues which they consider relevant to a particular decision and thereby increase the risk that they will be in breach of duty if they fail to take account of a statutory factor and as a consequence, cause loss to the company. Many companies, especially the larger groups, have already been operating within the framework of the statutory factors and for them they represent no change. For others, particularly smaller businesses, including the statutory factors in the board decision-making process represents more of a challenge. The inclusion of a statutory factor on community and environmental issues is also the first time that corporate social responsibility has directly been made a main board issue. Case law will ultimately determine the issue and, as there remains some uncertainty as to how the courts will construe these provisions, companies (if they are not doing so already) will need to take steps to manage their risk.

1.2.13   To whom do the duties apply?

Anyone who occupies the position of director is required to comply with the codified duties. Therefore, to understand who is affected by the provisions of the Companies Act 2006 relating to directors, it is necessary to first determine who is (or can be held to be) a director, which is not as straightforward as it may at first seem. In most cases the board of directors will be formally appointed and the details of the individual directors filed at Companies House.

However, a director also includes any person occupying the position of director, regardless of title[28] and a person does not need to be specifically appointed as a director to be held accountable as such. Whether an individual is a director is determined by reference to a person's conduct in respect of the company, as opposed to his title. An individual who has not been formally appointed as a director (and does not consider it necessary to comply with the duties of a director) can therefore still have the same duties, responsibilities and liabilities of a director who has been formally appointed.

The identification of directors is an essential part of managing risk within a company or group of companies. A company must be able to identify who is subject to the duties and obligations of a director and who may have the authority to enter into contracts on behalf of the company. The risk can then be managed by company's Directors' and Officers' insurance and the provision of indemnities.

There are a number of possible ways in which a person can be found to be a director of a company and therefore be held liable as such which are discussed below.

1.2.13.1   *Do the duties apply to statutory/*de jure *directors?*

Yes. Ordinarily, provided the individual concerned has given his informed consent to hold office, a director will be specifically appointed by the existing board of directors or by the requisite majority of shareholders (see section 1.14 below for the methods by which a director can be appointed and the process that will need to be followed). A director who has been specifically and validly appointed is known as a *de jure* or statutory director.

---

[28]   Section 250, Companies Act 2006.

A *de jure* director has the right (amongst others) to hold himself out as a director of the company, to receive notice of all board meetings and can validly execute contracts on behalf of the company.

1.2.13.2 Do the duties apply to shadow directors?

In the most part, yes. The Companies Act 2006 states[29] that the general duties that a director owes to the company apply to shadow directors where, and to the extent that, the corresponding common law rules or equitable principles also apply to shadow directors.

However, the duty to declare an interest in an existing transaction or arrangement applies in the case of shadow directors with the adaptations that the declaration does not have to be made at a meeting of directors and that a general notice of interest that is given by a shadow director will not be effective unless given in writing in accordance with the provisions of the Companies Act 2006.

A shadow director will not have been appointed as a director (either by the board of directors or shareholders of the company) but is a person in accordance with whose directions and instructions a governing majority of the board of directors has become accustomed to act[30]. When determining whether an individual is a shadow director it is important to be aware of the necessity for the board to 'act' in some way in conformity with the directions and instructions of the shadow director; it is not sufficient for the individual concerned to simply give such directions and/or instructions that are then disregarded by the board.

A shadow director will not normally hold himself out to be a director, and may not therefore be aware that he has assumed the responsibilities and liabilities of a director. A shadow director is required to enter his details on the company's register of directors[31].

In theory, a parent company can be held to be a shadow director of its subsidiary companies. However, the Companies Act 2006 provides that a company is not a shadow director of any of its subsidiaries for the purpose of complying with the provisions of the Companies Act 2006 in respect of:

(i)   the general duties of directors;

(ii)   transactions requiring members' approval; or

(iii) contracts with a sole member who is also a director,[32]

---

[29] Section 170(5), Companies Act 2006.
[30] Section 251(1), Companies Act 2006.
[31] Section 288(6), Companies Act 1985, section 162(6), Companies Act 2006.
[32] Section 251(3), Companies Act 2006.

by reason only that the directors of the subsidiary are accustomed to act in accordance with the parent company's directions.

This makes no change to the Companies Act 1985. However, the most significant potential liability of a parent company as a shadow director is for wrongful trading, which is discussed further in section 1.7.1 below. In managing the parent subsidiary relationship it is therefore prudent to avoid creating shadow directorships as this will create uncertainty as to where legal responsibility lies. Additionally, the operation of a dominant parent company board could expose directors of subsidiaries to potential claims for breach of duty either for failing to act independently or for not discharging their duties with due care especially where a company has minority shareholders.

1.2.13.3 Do the duties apply to de facto directors?

Yes. In most instances, a *de facto* director has the same obligations and liabilities as a statutory director including liability for wrongful trading (see section 1.7.1 below). A *de facto* director can also be disqualified as a director.

A *de facto* director is a person who acts, or is held out, as a director without having been validly appointed as such. Directors' duties apply to *de facto* directors in the same manner that they apply to statutory (or *de jure*) directors. A person is most likely to be found to be a *de facto* director in two situations. First, where the company had intended to appoint the person as a director but there was a defect in the appointment that rendered the purported appointment invalid, or secondly, where a person (whom the company has not attempted to appoint as a director) holds himself out as a director of the company or otherwise acts as if he was a statutory director.

To establish that a person is a *de facto* director it is necessary to demonstrate that the person concerned carried out functions that only a director of the company would carry out. It is not sufficient that the individual merely undertook functions that a senior employee who is not a director would undertake[33].

Although there is no definitive list of factors that will determine whether a person is a *de facto* director the courts are likely to have regard to a number of common factors when deciding this issue, such as whether there was any fetter on the person's authority and whether the person acted on an equal footing with the other directors of the company. Ultimately, whether a person is a *de facto* director will be determined by reference to the facts of a particular case.

---

[33] *Re Hydrodam (Corby) Ltd* [1994] BCC 161.

1.2.13.4 Do the duties apply to 'courtesy' or 'associate' directors?

Some companies grant senior employees titles that include the word 'director', even though it is not the intention of either the company or the employee to appoint the employee as a statutory director. The usual rationale behind the use of such titles is to provide a senior employee with a title that reflects the employee's senior position within the company, albeit that the employee concerned has not yet reached sufficient status within the company to be appointed to the board of directors.

The difficulty with the use of so called courtesy or associate directorships is that a person that holds himself out as a director can be relied upon as such by third parties. It may therefore be possible for an associate director to contract on behalf of the company as if he was a statutory director. If a courtesy director is found to be a statutory director (see 1.2.13.3 above), then he will then face potential liability as a director.

In practice, it is preferable to avoid the use of the word 'director' in the title of any employee who is not a statutory director. However, where an employee already includes 'director' in his title, a change to his title will most likely require the employee's consent under his employment contract. This is due to the fact that a unilateral amendment to an employee's title could amount to a breach of the employee's terms and conditions of employment, which could entitle the employee to issue a claim against the company.

1.2.13.5 Do the duties apply to alternate directors?

Yes. As set out in section 1.11 in more detail, an alternate director has the same obligations as the director that appointed him. If a director needs to appoint a representative to the board, that director should therefore consider appointing a proxy or an attorney, who will not be bound by such duties.

1.2.13.6 Do the duties apply to both executive and non-executive directors?

Yes. A non-executive director owes the same duties to a company as an executive director (see section 1.10). Although it has been suggested that a non-executive director should not be held to the same standard of care as executive directors, case law on this issue has indicated that there should be no difference between the skill required of an executive director and that of a non-executive[34].

---

[34] *Dorchester Finance Co Ltd v Stebbing* [1989] BCLC 498.

1.2.14 To whom are the duties owed?

The directors of a company owe their duties to that company[35] and there is no change to the pre 1 October 2007 position.

However, if a company is nearing insolvency, the duty to act in the interests of the company is superseded by a duty to act in the interests of the company's creditors as a general body.

It is worth noting that although a director is under a statutory duty to have regard to the employees of the company[36] when discharging the directors' duty to promote the success of the company this does not create a direct cause of action between the director and the company's employees.

In certain circumstances shareholders can bring a derivative claim in the name of the company against directors for breach of duty. The Companies Act 2006 has introduced significant changes to the derivative claim regime which are discussed in more detail in section 1.5.

1.2.15 Do the duties apply to directors who have ceased to hold the office of director?

In part, yes[37]. A person who ceases to be a director is still bound by the duty[38] to avoid a conflict of interests that arises in relation to the exploitation of any property, information or opportunity of the company, which the person became aware of at the time he was a director of the company. A director also remains bound by the duty[39] not to accept benefits from third parties as a result of things done or omitted to be done by that director before the director ceased to hold office.

1.2.16 BERR guidance on directors' duties

The Ministerial Statements referred to in section 1.2.12 above also include high level guidance on the directors' duties set out in the Companies Act 2006. This guidance details that directors should:

(i)   act in the company's best interests, taking everything that they think relevant into account;

(ii) obey the company's constitution and decisions taken under it;

(iii) be honest, and remember that the company's property belongs to the company and not to the directors or to its shareholders;

---

35   Section 170(1), Companies Act 2006.
36   Section 172, Companies Act 2006.
37   Section 170(2), Companies Act 2006.
38   Section 175, Companies Act 2006.
39   Section 176, Companies Act 2006.

(iv)   be diligent, careful and well informed about the company's affairs;

(v)   make sure the company keeps records of directors' decisions;

(vi)   remember that directors remain responsible for the work that they give to others;

(vii)   avoid situations where directors' interests conflict with those of the company. When in doubt, directors should disclose potential conflicts quickly; and

(viii) seek external advice where necessary, particularly if the company is in financial difficulty.

1.2.17   What practical steps should be taken in the light of the statutory duties?

Companies should consider the following practical steps to respond to the implementation of the codified duties:

(i)   Review existing Directors' and Officers' insurance to ensure that it covers a breach of the statutory duties and/or a derivative claim brought under the Companies Act 2006 (see section 1.5).

(ii)   Introduce a conflicts policy (or review any existing policy) that includes regular training for directors in their obligations with regard to conflicts including:

- obligations for periodic reporting and updating of directors' interests (and potential conflicts); and

- processes for the proper management of directors' conflicts including the management of confidential information when a director is conflicted.

(iii) Review corporate hospitality policies to take into account the provisions of the Companies Act 2006 relating to the acceptance of benefits from third parties.

(iv) Amend articles of association of public companies to enable the independent directors of a company to authorise a conflict of interest. Some companies have amended their articles of association to include detailed provisions relating to the management of conflicts of interest whilst others are including a general authority for independent directors to approve a conflict. Shareholders of private companies that are incorporated before 1 October 2008 will need to pass a resolution to enable independent directors to authorise a conflict. Technically, private companies will only need to amend their articles of association if they contain a prohibition on directors authorising a conflict (although as a matter of best practice private companies may want to include express provisions in their articles).

(v) Review terms of reference for the board (and other company policies) to ensure that these reflect the changes introduced by the Companies Act 2006.

1.2.17.1 Not just a 'box-ticking' exercise – some actions a company can take to support compliance with directors' duties

- Tone from the top – establish the right tone from the top of the organisation – ensure this is reflected in any articulated terms of reference and statements of culture and values – and importantly in day to day actions.

- Board effectiveness – formally assess how effective the board has been in discharging its duties.

- Stakeholder engagement – understand the significant relationships with stakeholders that are likely to influence the performance of the company and its value in the future through appropriate engagement.

- Broadly framed strategy – establish a broadly framed strategy that addresses the resources and relationships that are essential to achieve the company's goals/aspirations.

- Provision of balanced information – provide directors with balanced information to enable them to fully understand issues as they develop, not just to assess the financial outcomes (discussed more fully in section 1.13).

- Risk analysis – ensure that procedures aimed at identifying risks do not focus simply on financial aspects, but are broad, encompassing sustainability issues, as well as upstream and downstream impacts.

- Training – ensure that all those who act as board members or advise board members (including the preparation of board papers) understand the scope and application of directors' duties.

- Be prepared – put plans in place to manage derivative claims.

- Communication – leverage annual reports and other reporting to shareholders to communicate the company's actions relating to employees, environment etc., where these are relevant to the achievement of long-term goals.

- Consistency – ensure consistency between internal processes and external communication to investors.

1.3 Documenting board decisions

There has been significant debate as to how directors should evidence that they have complied with their statutory duties and, in particular, whether the codification of directors' duties will impact on board minutes. These issues are considered in more detail in this section.

It should be noted that the Companies Act 2006 requires a company to keep minutes of all proceedings at meetings of its directors. These minutes must be kept for ten years from the date of the meeting[40].

1.3.1   What is the status of board minutes?

Minutes recorded in accordance with the Companies Act 2006, if authenticated by the chairman, are evidence of the proceedings at the meeting to which they relate. Until the contrary is proved the meeting to which such minutes relate will be deemed to be duly held and convened, all proceedings at the meeting are deemed to have taken place and all appointments made at the meeting are deemed valid.

1.3.2   What impact do the statutory duties have on board minutes?

One of the key concerns that arose in respect of the statutory duties was how directors could evidence that they have complied with the codified duties. In particular, commentary has concentrated on whether it is now necessary for directors to create verbatim minutes of all board meetings and, specifically, whether board minutes should state that the directors considered the six statutory factors that they must have regard to when discharging their duty to promote the success of the company.

It is important to remember that the Companies Act 2006 does not require companies to create a paper trail of their decision making process. As Margaret Hodge noted:

> "The clause does not impose a requirement on directors to keep records, as some people have suggested, in any circumstances in which they would not have to do so now."

Margaret Hodge, Commons Committee, 11 July 2006, column 592

The purpose of the duty to promote the success of the company is to ensure that directors properly consider the six statutory factors, amongst others, that may be relevant to their decision making process; it is not designed to create a box-ticking exercise. Nevertheless, directors will need to manage their risk to protect themselves against allegations of a breach of duty.

Companies are not currently required to create verbatim minutes of the board decision making process and there is nothing in the Companies Act 2006 that requires companies to change their existing policy on minute taking. It may be that if a particular statutory factor is relevant to a board decision then the consideration of this factor should be documented. However, there is no requirement to make negative statements such as 'the directors considered the impact on employees and concluded that there was no such impact'.

---

[40] Section 248(2), Companies Act 2006.

Nevertheless, directors will require sufficient information to enable them to properly consider the six statutory factors and, policies on the preparation of board papers may therefore change.

Traditionally, board minutes have been brief and the reasoning for a board's decision is often to be found in board papers prepared by management. The general consensus is that board papers should continue to be the primary source of evidence to demonstrate the board's reasoning behind a particular decision. The primary purpose of the actual board minutes should continue to be to record the decision itself. It remains the case therefore that regardless of a board's policy on minute taking, companies should review how they prepare the board papers that are circulated to the directors prior to a board meeting. When preparing board papers, management should ensure that all relevant information is included in the board papers to enable the directors to consider the statutory factors in respect of any particular matter to be discussed at the meeting. This will provide the directors with sufficient information to enable them to properly consider the statutory factors (amongst others) in respect of any decision to be made, which was the intention of the legislation. A company should therefore ensure that not only are the directors aware of the duties set out in the Companies Act 2006 but that the people responsible for producing board papers must also be made aware of the new legal context within which these papers are now prepared. Larger businesses are likely to have sufficient internal resources for this; for smaller companies this may well present difficulties.

Ultimately, the decision on how to document board decisions will be influenced by the board's stance on this issue before the codification of directors' duties. If a board currently adopts a practice of only documenting the decision that was made together with any key considerations that led to such a decision then there is nothing in the Companies Act 2006 to dictate that such a practice should now change. However, if a company produced detailed board minutes prior to 1 October 2007 it is likely that the company will continue with this policy following the codification of directors' duties, unless there is a risk of litigation.

1.3.3 Could a company be compelled to disclose board minutes in litigation?

One question that often arises in respect of board minutes is whether board minutes attract legal advice privilege, which would prohibit their disclosure in litigation. This is a specialist area on which legal advice should be taken on any specific issue. However, the general position is set out below.

If the board minutes simply detail matters that do not themselves attract privilege (for example, they do not contain legal advice) then the minutes themselves will also fail to attract privilege and disclosure of the minutes could be demanded. However, if the board minutes include legal advice, which is in itself privileged, then the minutes themselves will also be privileged. A difficulty arises when the minutes contain a combination of privileged and non-privileged matters as such a hybrid of content may cause the privilege to be lost and therefore render the minutes open to disclosure. In this scenario, it may be possible to disclose the minutes with the privileged aspects redacted, although this is not always possible in which case privilege to the whole document may be waived. Care should also be taken when circulating minutes to individuals other than directors to minimise the risk of an argument that privilege (if any) has been waived.

1.4 Directors' liability for a breach of duty

A breach of a duty may give rise to civil or criminal liability for a director. The liability incurred will depend on the duty that has been breached although the following is a general guide to the potential liability that may be incurred by a director for a breach of duty.

1.4.1 What are the consequences of a breach of directors' duties under the Companies Act 2006?

Interestingly, the remedy for a breach of the codified directors' duties cannot be found in the text of the Companies Act 2006. Instead, the Companies Act 2006 simply states that the remedy for a breach of the codified duties is the same as would apply if the corresponding common law rule or equitable principle applied[41].

This means that in the case of a breach of one or more of the codified duties set out in the Companies Act 2006 (save for a breach of the duty to exercise reasonable care, skill and diligence) a director will find himself liable to account to the company for any profit or other unjust enrichment received by him as a result of the breach. The director may also be required to compensate the company for any loss it has suffered as a result of the breach, an injunction may be granted or the director may be required to restore any company property that he holds. As the duty to exercise due care, skill and diligence is not a fiduciary duty (unlike the other codified duties) the remedy for a breach of this duty is usually damages.

In addition, any contract entered into between the company and a director in breach of a duty may be rescinded by the company. It is also possible that a third party may be held liable as a constructive trustee (on behalf of the company) of any asset received that should be for the benefit of the company, which means that the company will usually have remedies available to it to recover the asset concerned.

---

[41] Section 178(1), Companies Act 2006.

A breach of one or more of the codified duties may also give rise to a derivative claim (see section 1.5).

1.4.2 What are the consequences if a director acts in breach of the company's constitution?

Where a director acts in breach of the memorandum or articles of association of the company, the director may be liable to account to the company for any loss arising as a result of the breach (in the same manner as the director would be liable for a breach of the codified duties referred to above).

1.4.3 What are the consequences for breaching other statutory obligations?

Both the Companies Act 1985 and the Companies Act 2006 impose a range of additional obligations on directors. A failure to comply with such obligations will generally (but not always) attract civil liability for directors. However, a number of criminal penalties are also imposed, which include imprisonment. Persistent failure to comply with certain statutory requirements may also result in disqualification (for example, failure to maintain adequate accounting records).

1.5 Derivative claims

1.5.1 What are derivative claims?

Where a wrong is occasioned to a company then the company is the appropriate entity to issue a claim to remedy that wrong. As such, a tension arises where the company has suffered harm but that harm has been caused by the company's directors who are not therefore willing to take the necessary action on behalf of the company to remedy the harm caused.

In response to this issue the common law developed a regime to enable the shareholders of a company, in very specific circumstances, to issue a claim in the name of the company against the directors at fault (and thereby enable the company to receive recompense for the damage that has been caused). This type of action, issued by shareholders on behalf of the company, is called a derivative claim.

An important element of a derivative claim is that the claim is made on behalf of the company and that therefore any damages awarded by the court pursuant to the claim are awarded to the company and not to the shareholders that have issued the claim in the company's name. As a result, and because the law is uncertain, these actions are costly to bring and the shareholders receive no direct benefit (other than through a possible increase in the value of their shares, or dividends, if successful).

On 1 October 2007 the Companies Act 2006 introduced new provisions relating to derivative claims and in doing so put the derivative claim regime on a statutory footing for the first time. These provisions have removed many of the uncertainties relating to derivative claims but have also increased the circumstances in which such an action can be brought.

1.5.2   What are the key provisions of the Companies Act 2006 relating to derivative claims?

Sections 260 to 264 (sections 265 to 269 for derivative proceedings in Scotland) are the key provisions of the Companies Act 2006 relating to derivative claims and are effective from 1 October 2007. These sections apply to breaches of duty arising on or after 1 October 2007 only.

1.5.3   What are the new rules relating to derivative claims?

With effect from 1 October 2007, the Companies Act 2006 introduced significant changes to the common law by increasing the circumstances in which a shareholder can bring a derivative claim against a director. The changes to the derivative claim regime have been introduced at a time where both shareholder activism and board accountability are increasing.

1.5.4   In what circumstances can a derivative claim be brought under the Companies Act 2006?

The circumstances in which a derivative claim can be brought are now set out in Part 11 of the Companies Act 2006[42]. A derivative claim can now be brought under the Companies Act 2006 in respect of an actual or proposed act or omission involving negligence, default, breach of duty or breach of trust by a director of the company that occurred on or after 1 October 2007. It is clear that the circumstances in which a derivative claim can be brought have been significantly widened from the pre 1 October 2007 regime. Furthermore, unlike the regime that applied before 1 October 2007, there is no longer a requirement for a shareholder bringing a derivative claim to show that the directors concerned are in control of the company or that they have personally benefitted from the alleged wrongdoing (see section 1.5.12).

In particular, a derivative claim may now be brought for negligence and/or a breach of duty by a director. It is therefore possible that an aggrieved shareholder could use the statutory factors under section 172 of the Companies Act 2006 (a director's duty to promote the success of the company), to base a claim that the directors have acted in breach of duty by failing to take into account the relevant factors.

In addition, in some circumstances a claim can be brought in relation to an act which has not yet taken place. It would therefore be possible for a shareholder

---

[42] Sections 260 – 269, Companies Act 2006.

of a company, which was about to make an acquisition of another company, to bring a derivative claim alleging that the proposed transaction was a breach of duty.

It remains the case that any damages recovered as a result of a derivative claim will be paid to the company and not the aggrieved shareholder.

1.5.5   Who can bring a derivative claim?

A derivative claim may be brought by any shareholder of the company and it is irrelevant whether the cause of action arose before or after the shareholder seeking to bring the claim became a shareholder of the company. It is therefore possible for an activist shareholder to acquire a share in the company simply to enable him to issue a derivative claim in respect of events which took place before he became a member. This also means that directors of a wholly-owned subsidiary or owner-managed company are still at risk of a derivative claim. This is due to the fact that on the sale of the company the new shareholders could bring a claim in respect of the acts or omissions of the directors that occurred before the new shareholders acquired the company.

1.5.6   Whom can a derivative claim be issued against?

A derivative claim may be brought against any director or former director (including a shadow director) of the company.

The application of the derivative claim regime to shadow directors could be of concern to third party funders and advisers, such as private equity houses and external consultants. These entities will need to take care that their involvement does not lead to the exercise of an executive function otherwise they may also be a target for disgruntled shareholders where management decisions have resulted in a loss of shareholder value.

1.5.7   What process must a shareholder follow when seeking to continue a derivative claim?

There is a two-stage process for bringing a derivative claim. The first stage is an application by the shareholder to the court without formal notice to the company. However, in practice, the shareholder may well choose to inform the company to bring pressure to bear on the directors. At this stage the shareholder only has to show a *prima facie* case. Most commentators seem to think this is a relatively low threshold which will not be too difficult to achieve. Failure to demonstrate a *prima facie* case will result in the court dismissing the application and making any consequential order that it considers appropriate to make, including a costs order[43].

---

[43]   Section 261(2), Companies Act 2006.

If the court is satisfied that there is a *prima facie* case to answer then the shareholder must apply to the court for permission to proceed with the claim. This is the second stage of the process. The court will invite evidence from the directors and the hearing will take place in open court. In certain situations a court must refuse permission to proceed with the case (see section 1.5.8); in other situations the court has a discretion as to whether to allow the claim to proceed. The intention behind the 'two stage' process is to filter out claims being brought purely for publicity or tactical reasons. Notwithstanding this 'filter' process, even if a claim is rejected by the court the fact that the derivative claim has been issued could cause significant damage to the company's and/or a director's reputation.

1.5.8 When must the court refuse permission to continue a derivative claim?

A court must refuse permission to continue a derivative claim where the court is satisfied that a person acting in accordance with the duty to promote the success of the company would not continue the claim.

Directors will also obtain protection from a derivative claim where the acts or omissions of the directors, whether or not they have yet taken place, have been authorised or ratified by the company. It will therefore be prudent in specific circumstances, where the directors have particular concerns over a course of conduct, to obtain shareholder approval for that conduct. However, it should be noted that (save for a resolution that is passed unanimously) a 'connected' shareholder (see section 2.3.9 of chapter 2 for a definition of 'connected') may not vote on the resolution to ratify (see section 1.6 below). In smaller companies, where the directors concerned are also major shareholders, ratification may not be possible when unanimity is not obtained.

1.5.9 What factors will a court take into account in deciding whether permission should be given?

The Companies Act 2006 provides that the court must take into account certain factors when deciding whether to grant permission for a derivative claim to proceed. These factors are[44]:

(i)   whether the member is acting in good faith in seeking to continue the claim;

(ii) the importance that a person acting in accordance with section 172 of the Companies Act 2006 (duty to promote the success of the company) would attach to continuing the claim;

(iii) where the cause of action results from an act or omission that is yet to occur, whether the act or omission could be, and in the circumstances would be likely to be:

---

[44] Section 263(3), Companies Act 2006

    (a)   authorised by the company before it occurs; or

    (b)   ratified by the company after it occurs;

(iv)   where the cause of action arises from an act or omission that has already occurred, whether the act or omission could be, and in the circumstances would be likely to be, ratified by the company;

(v)   whether the company has decided not to pursue the claim; and

(vi)   whether the act or omission in respect of which the claim is brought gives rise to a course of action that the member could pursue in his own right rather than on behalf of the company.

1.5.10   What are the implications of the new derivative claim regime for UK boards?

One of the key concerns arising out of the changes to the derivative claim regime is whether the new provisions will increase the number of derivative claims brought against directors. At the date of printing there have been no high profile actions. However, litigation against directors usually increases in times of economic retrenchment and corporate failure and it is undoubtedly the case that shareholders can now bring derivative claims in a broader range of situations than was the case under the old common law. The law in this area remains to be tested.

A further concern is whether claims might still be brought by activist shareholders with a political agenda primarily for publicity purposes. This remains a risk notwithstanding the protections that are contained in the two-stage process.

It is quite likely that the reputational damage of such a claim having been made will already have been caused to both the company and the individual directors concerned at the first stage, even if the claim is deferred at the permission stage. It should also be noted that the Claim Form initiating the legal proceedings is open to public inspection. There must also be a risk that, where the merits of the claim are not clear one way or the other, the court will be tempted to allow the claim to proceed so that all the issues can be fully aired at trial, even if the directors oppose this. Furthermore, the second stage of the permission application, which requires an oral hearing, is likely to be held in open court. As a result, there is ample opportunity for shareholder campaigners to generate publicity for their cause. It is therefore possible that, notwithstanding the requirement to demonstrate a *prima facie* case against the company, the new derivative claim regime may still be a tool that is used by activist shareholders, amongst others, to cause damage to a company's reputation or force disclosure of internal documents, rather than as a means of holding directors to account for loss suffered to the company as a result of their negligence.

In addition, the defence of a derivative claim could require a significant amount of senior management time, legal costs and the disclosure of sensitive, confidential information. In particular, where a major commercial decision is being challenged, the court is likely to have to weigh up a wide range of competing factors and comparisons with the performance and policies of other companies.

1.5.11 In what kinds of situations in practice might a derivative claim be brought?

The most obvious situation is where directors have acted in breach of their statutory duties causing loss to the company and existing shareholders bring a derivative action in the name of the company requiring the directors to make good the loss. However the following hypothetical situations are also conceivable:

(i)   Sale of a subsidiary

A subsidiary is sold to a third party who then brings a derivative action against former directors (who may well have resigned on completion of the sale).

(ii)   Future purchase of a company

The board wishes to proceed with a future acquisition. However, shareholders do not consider that the acquisition will promote the success of the company and wish to challenge the directors on whether they are properly exercising their duties and to prevent the purchase from going ahead.

(iii)   Redundancy programme

A company wishes to carry out a redundancy programme. Many of the employees are also shareholders. The employees believe that the rationalisation of staff will not promote the success of the company in the longer term. They also believe that the directors are driven solely by the need to be profitable in the short term and that they have not had regard to the interests of employees or those of the community in approving the redundancies. The employees (in their capacity as shareholders) apply to the court alleging anticipated loss to the company if the directors proceed. They are also hoping to force disclosure at the permission stage of documents showing the underlying reasons for the board's decision.

(iv)   Breach of duty by directors of a wholly-owned subsidiary

There has been a negligent failure by the board of a subsidiary to introduce proper fraud controls and as a result a fraud has been discovered that has caused significant loss to the subsidiary and a resultant decline in the value of the subsidiary to the parent. The parent company sees the issue as an internal matter and takes steps to improve internal controls. A shareholder of the parent brings a derivative action against the parent board for failing to hold the directors of the subsidiary to account for the damage caused to the subsidiary.

It must be emphasised that these are examples only of situations where a claim might be brought. It remains to be seen whether a court would give permission to proceed or whether such actions would be successful.

1.5.12 What was the derivative claim regime prior to 1 October 2007?

Before the right to issue a derivative claim was put on a statutory footing by the Companies Act 2006, the derivative claim regime was set out in the common law. This section contains a brief overview of the common law regime as the common law continues to apply to acts or omissions that occurred on or before 1 October 2007.

In essence two key principles underpinned the common law derivative claim regime[45]:

(i) in the event of a wrongdoing to a company, the company is the proper party to any proceedings and not the shareholders of the company; and

(ii) ordinarily, the court will not interfere with the management decisions of the company when such decisions were made in accordance with the powers of the company.

One of the key aspects of the rule in *Foss v Harbottle* (which is the leading case that established the principles set out above) is that the court should not be concerned with claims that could either be ratified by shareholders at general meeting or where shareholders could remove the directors of the company by passing an ordinary resolution if they disagreed with the management decision that is the subject of the claim (this is the principle of 'majority rule').

However, in some circumstances the majority rule set out above did not offer adequate protection to shareholders. As such, exceptions to the rule in *Foss v Harbottle* developed, primarily where the directors against whom the wrongdoing is alleged are majority shareholders and therefore the removal of, or taking action against, the offending directors was not possible.

In this situation a shareholder would have a right to bring a derivative claim in the name of the company if he can demonstrate, *inter alia*, that:

(i) a wrongdoing had been committed to the company by the directors of the company;

---

[45] *Foss v Harbottle* 1843 2 Hare 461.

(ii)   the directors that the shareholder alleges to have committed the wrongdoing have control of the company; and

(iii) the directors have personally benefited from the wrongdoing complained of.

Any damages recovered would be paid to the company, as the action is taken in the name of the company, and therefore the shareholders would not receive a direct benefit from the claim.

1.5.13   What if the derivative claim relates to an alleged cause of action that occurred prior to 1 October 2007?

For claims where the shareholder has applied to the court for permission to continue with the derivative claim on or before 1 October 2007 the law in force before 1 October 2007 will continue to apply to the claim.

Where an application to continue with the claim has been made after 1 October 2007 but the claim is in relation to an alleged cause of action that arose before 1 October 2007, the court must exercise its powers under the relevant sections of the Companies Act 2006 to ensure that the claim is only allowed to proceed if the law immediately in force prior to 1 October 2007 would have allowed the claim to proceed. In principle therefore the old common law rule discussed in section 1.5.12 above will apply rather than the regime set out in the Companies Act 2006.

1.5.14   Practical steps to consider under the new derivative claim regime

Companies should consider whether they have exposure to possible derivative claims and whether there is a need to introduce an escalation procedure in the event that a derivative claim is made.

In addition, consideration should be given to the following:

(i)   Does the company's Directors' and Officers' insurance cover the defence of a derivative claim?

(ii)   Have directors been briefed on their duties under the Companies Act 2006 and are they aware of their potential liabilities? Provisions should be made to educate directors who join the board in the future. Directors need to be aware that delegation to line managers (although essential in the ordinary course of business) will not absolve them of their ultimate responsibilities. Care needs to be taken to delegate to suitably competent management.

(iii) Care should also be taken to ensure that the content of publicly available documents such as the annual business review is consistent with internal board papers. The credibility of the directors will be at risk if internal documents disclosed in derivative proceedings are inconsistent with previous public statements.

(iv)   In addition to the content of company documents, directors should put in place a clear document retention policy, particularly in relation to matters which may be contentious or controversial. This should include consideration as to the extent of the circulation of any such contentious material both within the company and externally. It should also be noted that internal e-mails will be subject to the same disclosure obligations as formal board papers. See also section 1.3.2 above discussing the extent to which legal advice privilege applies to board papers.

(v)   Effective management of shareholder relations should reduce the risk of a claim. In general, the better informed shareholders are, the more likely they are to understand and accept the board's strategy. Support from the general body of shareholders may also be a crucial part of the defence to a derivative action. The views of other shareholders with no personal interest in the derivative claim is one of the factors influencing the court whether to grant permission for the claim to continue.

(vi)   When a body of shareholders has already made their objections known, it could be useful to monitor their campaign through what is being said on websites and in the media. The company should consider using a professional media relations agency to coordinate the company's response.

(vii)   Before any shareholder challenge reaches the courts, activist shareholders may use the annual general meeting to generate publicity for their cause. In such circumstances, careful forward planning by the company is advisable in terms of briefing the board, security, voting procedures and publicity.

(viii)   For companies whose shares are traded the company's registrars should be asked to notify the company of unusual share activity particularly the acquisition of a small number of shares.

(ix)   The company should identify who within the company will be responsible for coordinating a response to the claim in the first instance.

(x)   Companies should decide which external advisers it will engage to advise it on a derivative claim, as there will be a need to act quickly.

(xi)   Companies should identify who in the first instance will be involved in gathering evidence in respect of the claim (although ultimately this will be dictated by the nature of the claim).

1.6   Managing the risk to directors of personal liability

1.6.1   Can shareholders ratify the decisions of the directors of the company?

Yes. With effect from 1 October 2007, the Companies Act 2006 codifies the common law position that the shareholders of a company may, by ordinary resolution (subject to any higher threshold set out in the company's articles of association), ratify the acts or omissions of the directors that amount to negligence, default, breach of duty or breach of trust in relation to the company[46].

However, in a change to the common law, save where the resolution is passed unanimously, the votes of the director concerned (and any shareholder connected with the director) are to be disregarded when considering whether the resolution has been passed (although any such person can count in the quorum of the meeting at which the resolution is being considered).

As will be seen in chapter 2 the definition of a 'connected person' has been considerably expanded. This may make ratification more difficult for family owned companies than was the case before 1 October 2007.

1.6.2   Does a director have a defence to a claim if he can show that he acted honestly and reasonably?

Both the Companies Act 1985[47] and, with effect from 1 October 2008 the Companies Act 2006[48], enable a director to raise a defence that he should not be liable for negligence, default or breach of trust if it appears to the court that the director has acted honestly and reasonably and that having regard to all the circumstances of the case the director ought fairly to be excused for the negligence, default, breach of duty or breach of trust alleged. In practice, this is a high threshold to satisfy.

1.6.3   Can a company or the parent provide directors with an indemnity against liability?

As a general rule, a UK incorporated company cannot indemnify a director against liability for negligence, default, breach of duty or breach of trust in relation to the company[49]. This prohibition also extends to group companies providing an indemnity to the directors of any other member of the group (although it appears that a non-UK incorporated parent or subsidiary is not caught by this prohibition). As a result of this prohibition, any provision under

---

[46] Section 239, Companies Act 1985.
[47] Section 727, Companies Act 1985.
[48] Section 1157, Companies Act 2006.
[49] Section 232(1), Companies Act 2006.

which a company or any group company provides an indemnity to a director against any such liability is void save in three specific instances[50]:

(i)   the provision of insurance;

(ii)   qualifying third party indemnities; and

(iii) qualifying pension scheme indemnities.

We discuss each of these exceptions in turn.

1.6.3.1   Can a company provide insurance for its directors?

Yes. A company is entitled to purchase and maintain insurance for a director of that company, or a group company, against liability for negligence, default, breach of duty or breach of trust in relation to the company[51]. This exception to the general prohibition therefore enables a company to purchase and maintain Directors' and Officers' insurance.

A company should review the terms of existing Directors' and Officers' insurance to ensure that it covers a breach of the newly codified duties and a derivative claim issued pursuant to the Companies Act 2006.

1.6.3.2   Can a company provide an indemnity to a director against third party liability (qualifying third party indemnity)?

Yes, subject to certain limitations. A company can, but is not required to, provide an indemnity to a director against liability incurred by the director to a person other than the company or a group company[52]. This indemnity is specifically intended to apply to liabilities to third parties (such as class actions). It can apply to the legal costs of defending a claim and to any award made against a director. However, to fall within this exception the indemnity must not indemnify against any liability of the director:

(i)   to pay a fine imposed in criminal proceedings;

(ii)   to pay a sum to a regulatory authority by way of a penalty in respect of non-compliance with any regulatory requirement;

(iii) in defending criminal proceedings in which the director is convicted;

(iv)   in defending civil proceedings brought by the company or a group company in which judgment is given against the director; or

(v)   in connection with an application for relief (in the case of the acquisition of shares by an innocent nominee or in the case of honest and reasonable

---

[50] Section 232(2), Companies Act 2006.
[51] Section 233, Companies Act 2006.
[52] Section 234(2), Companies Act 2006.

conduct) in which the court refuses to grant the director the relief requested[53].

It is possible therefore for a company to pay a director's costs in defending litigation even where the claim is being brought by the company. However, the director would still be required to pay any damages awarded to the company and, if the director failed to successfully defend the claim, would also be required to repay any defence costs paid for by the company.

The reference to a conviction, judgment or refusal of relief referred to in paragraphs (iii), (iv) and (v) above are references to the final decision in respect of any such proceedings. A conviction, judgment or refusal of relief becomes the final decision at the end of the period available for bringing an appeal (if a decision is not appealed against) or, if appealed against, at the time when the appeal is disposed of[54] (being the point at which an appeal is abandoned or, if the appeal is determined, the point at which the period for bringing any further appeal has ended).

1.6.3.3   Can a company indemnify a director of a pension trustee company (qualifying pension scheme indemnities)?

Yes. In extending the regime under the Companies Act 1985, the Companies Act 2006 allows a company, or any group company, to indemnify a director of a company that is a trustee of an occupational pension scheme against liability incurred in connection with the company's activities as trustee of that scheme[55].

In reflecting the restrictions imposed on granting a third party indemnity, the Companies Act 2006 precludes a company from indemnifying a director pursuant to a pension scheme indemnity for any liability:

(i)   to pay a fine imposed in criminal proceedings;

(ii)   to pay a sum to a regulatory authority by way of a penalty in respect of non-compliance with any requirement of a regulatory nature; or

(iii)   incurred by the director in defending criminal proceedings in which he is convicted[56].

Again, the limitation applies to a final conviction, judgment or refusal of relief and for the purposes of determining whether a director has been convicted in criminal proceedings, the conviction becomes final if not appealed against at the end of the period for bringing an appeal or, if appealed against, at the time when the appeal (or any further appeal) is disposed of. An appeal is disposed of

---

[53]   Section 234(3), Companies Act 2006.
[54]   Section 234(5), Companies Act 2006.
[55]   Section 235(2), Companies Act 2006.
[56]   Section 235(3), Companies Act 2006.

if the appeal is determined and the period for bringing any further appeal has ended or if the appeal is abandoned or otherwise ceases to have effect.

1.6.3.4 Does the company need to disclose a qualifying indemnity provision and a qualifying pension scheme indemnity provision?

Yes. A company is required to disclose in the directors' report any qualifying third party indemnity provision and any qualifying pension scheme indemnity provision that was in force at any time during the financial year to which the report relates. The disclosure relates to any such indemnity made by the company either for the directors of the company or of any associated company[57].

1.6.3.5 Can qualifying indemnity provisions be inspected by the company's shareholders?

Yes. Where a third party indemnity or pension scheme indemnity is made in favour of a director then the company of which he is a director and, where the provision is made by a group company, that group company must keep a copy of the qualifying indemnity, or a written memorandum setting out the terms of the indemnity, available for inspection. The indemnity or memorandum must be available for inspection at the company's registered office or at the company's principal place of business provided that it is in the same part of the UK in which the company is registered. The qualifying indemnity or written memorandum must be available for inspection during the term of the indemnity and for at least one year following the termination of the indemnity[58].

Every qualifying indemnity or written memorandum must be open to inspection by any shareholder of the company without charge[59]. Failure to allow such an inspection to be made is a criminal offence by every officer in default and is punishable with a fine.

1.6.3.6 Summary of changes that were introduced by the Companies Act 2006

The Companies Act 2006 largely restates the Companies Act 1985 in respect of indemnifying directors. However, with effect from 1 October 2007 the following changes (which are discussed in more detail above) are new:

(i)   indemnities in favour of trustees of occupational pension schemes;

(ii)   the creation of the right of members to request a copy of a qualifying third party indemnity;

---

[57] Section 236, Companies Act 2006.
[58] Section 237, Companies Act 2006.
[59] Section 238, Companies Act 2006.

(iii) the removal of criminal liability for the company (as opposed to the officers) for failure to make a copy of a qualifying third party indemnity available for inspection;

(iv) provisions for regulations to specify places in addition to the registered office where inspection of indemnities may take place; and

(v) a requirement for all companies to retain a copy of any qualifying third party indemnity for at least a year after they have expired.

Companies will therefore wish to consider whether to provide indemnities in favour of trustees of occupational pension schemes and will need to be aware of their increased obligations under paragraphs (ii) and (v) above.

1.7 Directors' liability on insolvency of the company

The insolvency of a company is one of the circumstances in which a director can be held to account for a breach of duty.

Every administrator, administrative receiver and liquidator is required to report in respect of each person who was a director (or shadow director) of the insolvent company at any time during the three years preceding the company's insolvency where, in his opinion, that director's conduct renders the director unfit to be concerned in the management of the company. Directors should therefore be aware that in an insolvency situation the conduct of the directors will be closely scrutinised as a matter of course, and if there is evidence of a breach of duty, the possibility of a claim being made against directors will arise.

In particular, a director can be held to be personally liable pursuant to the Insolvency Act 1986 where that director is found guilty of either wrongful or fraudulent trading.

1.7.1 When can a director be found to be liable for wrongful trading?

A director is guilty of wrongful trading if the director continues to trade when the director knew, or ought to have known, that there was no reasonable prospect of the company avoiding insolvent liquidation[60].

If a liquidator can prove that before the start of the winding-up of the company a director knew or ought to have known that there was no reasonable prospect of the company avoiding insolvent liquidation, that director may be required to contribute to the company's assets.

The only defence to wrongful trading is that the director took every step available (and which the director ought to have taken) with a view to minimising the potential loss to the company's creditors. This is a very high

---

[60] Section 214, Insolvency Act 1986.

threshold to meet if a director is to raise a successful defence to an allegation of wrongful trading.

If a court makes an order that a director is to contribute to the assets of the company the court can also make an order to disqualify the director from being in any way concerned with the management of a company for a minimum period of two years.

1.7.2 When is a director liable for fraudulent trading?

A director is guilty of fraudulent trading if the director continues to trade with the intention of defrauding creditors when the director knew that there was no reasonable prospect of the creditors being paid by the company[61].

Again, a liquidator can apply to the court for a contribution to the company's assets from any person who was knowingly a party to the carrying on of fraudulent trading. Unlike an allegation of wrongful trading, the fact that the director took steps to minimise the loss to creditors is no defence to an allegation of fraudulent trading.

Under the Companies Act 1985 fraudulent trading is punishable by up to seven years' imprisonment or an unlimited fine or both. The maximum term of imprisonment has been increased to ten years under the Companies Act 2006.

1.8   Directors as employees

Directors are often also employees of the company for which they act. This gives rise to additional issues, such as shareholder approval of service agreements, and these issues are discussed in more detail in chapter 2.

1.9   Common difficulties involving directors' duties in the context of group companies

A tension can sometimes arise between the obligation of directors of UK companies to promote the success of the particular company for whom they act (namely the duty to discharge their duties on an entity by entity basis) and the interests of the group of companies as a whole.

Case law on this issue has made it clear that directors must discharge their duties for the benefit of the company for whom they act. Therefore, even if a transaction is in the interest of other group companies, if the transaction does not promote the success of a particular group company, then the directors of that company will be in breach of their duties as directors if they approve such a transaction.

---

[61]   Section 993, Companies Act 2006; section 213, Insolvency Act 1986.

We address some of the common issues that can arise for directors of group companies below.

1.9.1   Do directors' duties apply to directors of a UK subsidiary of an overseas parent?

Yes, the codified duties set out in the Companies Act 2006 apply to the directors of all UK incorporated companies, regardless of the territory of incorporation of the parent company.

The statutory duties do not apply to the directors of an overseas company carrying on business in the UK.

1.9.2   Can a director of a subsidiary simply act in the manner in which its parent company directs?

A director may be asked to represent the interests of the company on the boards of subsidiary and associated companies. It is important for the directors of such companies to first consider the position of each company as an independent legal entity and not the group as a whole, save to the extent that the interests of the group are also in the interests of the company. As a matter of strict law, a director of a subsidiary must exercise his powers and discharge his duties in the best interests of that company alone.

As a matter of practice, in many cases an action which is in the best interests of the group may also be in the best interests of a specific group company but this is not always the case. In these cases it is essential that a director is satisfied that the action to be approved promotes the success of each of the companies involved of which he is a director or that he obtains shareholder approval to the action concerned (in cases where the company is and will remain solvent).

1.9.3   A practical example of the operation of directors' duties in a group context

We set out below an example of an intra-group transaction where the issue of directors' duties can arise.

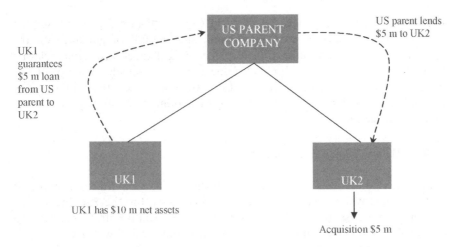

In this example, the US parent company grants UK2 a loan to enable UK2 to make an acquisition for an aggregate consideration of $5 million. It is proposed that UK1, which is a major trading group, guarantees the loan.

There are a number of issues that the directors of UK1 will need to consider before they can proceed with the guarantee, for example:

(i)   where is the corporate benefit for UK1 in guaranteeing the loan?

(ii)   what is the value of the asset that UK2 is acquiring?

(iii)   will the return received by UK2 from the acquisition (for example by way of dividend) be sufficient to cover the loan repayments?

(iv)   what is the financial position of UK2? Is it likely that UK2 will default under the terms of the loan and that therefore the guarantee will be called upon?

(v)   will the giving of the guarantee impact upon the ability of UK1 to enter into other transactions in the future?

These are just some of the issues that the directors of UK1 would need to consider before proceeding with the transaction. It may be that following consideration of such matters the directors of UK1 are satisfied that they are able to proceed. However, failure to consider such issues could result in the directors of UK1 being in breach of their duties to the company.

1.10   What is the difference between executive and non-executive directors?

Directors' duties apply to executive and non-executive directors, and we set out below a brief overview of the differences between these two roles.

In addition to the Companies Act 2006, the Combined Code, the Higgs Report and the Smith Guidance contain a significant amount of guidance on the appointment of non-executive directors, including detailed provisions relating to their independence. These guidance documents are outside the scope of this book but must be considered carefully by companies that adopt their principles, particularly when considering their obligations in respect of non-executive directors.

1.10.1   Who is an executive director?

An executive director is appointed to perform a managerial function on behalf of the company and has day to day responsibility for the running of the company's business (or a particular part of it). An executive director is likely to be either a full- or part-time employee of the company and will therefore owe the company obligations both as a director and as an employee (see chapter 2 for a more detailed discussion of a director's obligations as an employee).

1.10.2   What is the role of a non-executive director?

A non-executive director is ordinarily appointed to provide an objective review of the acts and decisions of the executive board and will not have day to day responsibility for, or involvement in, the operations of the company. A non-executive director is not an employee of the company.

The Higgs Report, which applies only to listed companies, observes that although non-executive directors bring an independent perspective to the company and should scrutinise the performance of management, they are also involved in:

(i)   challenging and helping development proposals on strategy;

(ii)   providing entrepreneurial leadership;

(iii)   setting the company's values; and

(iv)   satisfying themselves on the integrity of financial information and systems of risk management and internal control.

Following the recommendation of the Higgs Report, the Combined Code now includes a definition of the role to be performed by a non-executive director as follows:

> "... non-executive directors should constructively challenge and help develop proposals on strategy. Non-executive directors should scrutinise the performance of management in meeting agreed goals and objectives and monitor the reporting of performance ... and have a prime role in appointing, and where necessary removing, executive directors." (paragraph A.1 of the Combined Code).

Although the Higgs Report and the Combined Code apply to listed companies, AIM listed companies usually apply the principles as a voluntary matter and many private companies adopt elements of such guidance to underpin their governance structures.

1.10.3 What are the legal duties and liabilities of a non-executive director?

A non-executive director has the same legal duties and liabilities as an executive director, although this is an area of law which is developing. A non-executive director is expected to undertake an active role in appraising the decisions of the executive board and failure to identify concerns with the conduct of the executive board, and failure to take steps to respond to such concerns, could render a non-executive director liable for a breach of duty in the same way as an executive director.

Non-executive directors often hold a number of board appointments and therefore will need to have particular regard to the new conflicts regime that is introduced by the Companies Act 2006 (see section 1.2).

Companies applying the Combined Code should also take into account the Combined Code recommendations that:

(i)   the board should not agree to a full-time executive director taking on more than one non-executive directorship of a FTSE 100 company nor the chairmanship of such a company (paragraph A.4.5 of the Combined Code); and

(ii)   non-executive directors should undertake that they have sufficient time to meet what is required of them (paragraph A.4.4 of the Combined Code).

Although it is a requirement of the Combined Code that listed companies appoint non-executive directors it is not unusual for private limited liability companies to also appoint non-executive directors as a matter of best practice.

1.11   What are alternate directors?

1.11.1   What is an alternate director?

An alternate director is a person appointed by an existing statutory director to act in the appointing director's absence from a board meeting. An alternate director has the same duties and liabilities as a statutory director and care should be taken when agreeing to accept such a position. Where an existing statutory director simply wants to grant signing authority to another individual he should consider using a power of attorney instead as this does not impose liability on the attorney in the same way that the position of alternate does.

1.11.2   How can an alternate director be appointed?

A company's articles of association will dictate whether a director can appoint (and remove) an alternate director. The default articles of association of a company incorporated under the Companies Act 1985 and the Companies Act 2006 are discussed below although in practice a company will often tailor the default position to reflect its specific requirements.

1.11.2.1   Do the 1985 Table A articles allow the appointment of alternate directors?

Yes. Regulations 65 to 69 of the 1985 Table A articles authorise a director to appoint (and remove) an alternate. Often a company's articles of association will be amended so that board approval is required to any proposed appointment of an alternate.

1.11.2.2   Do the 2006 model articles allow the appointment of alternate directors to private companies?

No. The 2006 model articles for private companies limited by shares do not authorise the appointment of an alternate director, although this right is retained in the 2006 model articles for public companies.

If a company's articles of association do not authorise the appointment of an alternate director no such appointment may be made. Companies that adopt the 2006 model articles will need to amend them to provide directors with authority to appoint an alternate, if they so wish.

1.11.3   Who can be appointed as an alternate director?

The same restrictions on who can be appointed as a statutory director, which are set out in section 1.13 below, also apply to who can be appointed as an alternate director.

1.11.4   What rights does an alternate director have?

Subject to any restrictions set out in the company's articles of association or in the specific terms of an alternate director's appointment an alternate may receive notice of, attend and vote at all board meetings and committee meetings[62] in the place of his appointing director. Importantly, an alternate director will count in the quorum of the board meeting, which will allow a matter to proceed that may otherwise have been frustrated due to the lack of quorum. However, pursuant to the 2006 model articles, an alternate director that is also a statutory director of the company cannot be counted twice when

---

[62]   Regulation 66, 1985 Table A articles.

determining whether a meeting is quorate. Directors should therefore consider quorum requirements when deciding who to appoint as an alternate.

1.11.5 What liabilities does an alternate director have?

The appointment of alternate directors can be useful to ensure the uninterrupted operation of a company during the absence of one or more directors. However, it is important for the alternate director to understand fully the extent of his liability when accepting the appointment. Unlike a proxy or attorney, who does not incur liability when acting under the power that he has been granted by the statutory director, an alternate director (subject to any provisions of the company's articles of association to the contrary) is subject to the same obligations and liabilities as a statutory director[63].

1.11.6 What filings must be made with Companies House in respect of an alternate director?

A company must file details (currently Form 288a) with the Registrar of Companies in respect of an alternate director in the same way as the company would for a statutory director, unless the alternate director is already a statutory director of the company. The company should also update its register of directors.

1.11.7 Are there any restrictions on the period of time for which an alternate can be appointed?

No. An alternate director may be appointed for a specific time period or indefinitely. In either case the alternate's appointment will automatically terminate when the appointment of the statutory director that made the appointment terminates[64].

1.11.8 Is an alternate director entitled to receive remuneration in respect of his appointment?

1.11.8.1 Is an alternate director entitled to receive remuneration under the 1985 Table A articles?

The 1985 Table A articles provide that although an alternate director is entitled to receive expenses that are properly incurred in connection with the discharge of his duty as an alternate director, the alternate director is not entitled to receive remuneration in respect of his appointment as an alternate. However, an independent agreement as to remuneration may be reached between the appointing director and the alternate.

---

[63] Regulation 69, 1985 Table A articles.
[64] Regulation 67, 1985 Table A articles

1.11.8.2   *Is an alternate director entitled to receive remuneration under the 2006 model articles?*

The 2006 model articles for a public company provide that an alternate director is not entitled to receive any remuneration from the company (other than expenses) save for such part of the remuneration that is payable to the appointing director that the appointing director directs in writing should be paid to the alternate.

1.11.9   Does an alternate count when calculating the minimum number of directors that have been appointed?

No. Both the 1985 Table A articles and the 2006 model articles provide that alternate directors shall not be included when calculating whether the requisite minimum number of directors have been appointed (namely at least one director, in the case of a private company, or at least two directors, in the case of a public company).

All of the above provisions can be varied by shareholder resolution.

1.12   How many directors is a company required to have?

A company is required to appoint a minimum number of directors, which depend on whether the company is a private company or a public company. A company's articles of association can also impose restrictions on the maximum number of directors that can be appointed. We discuss these issues below.

1.12.1   What are the relevant Companies Act 2006 provisions?

Section 154 of the Companies Act 2006 sets out the minimum number of directors that a company must appoint, and this section comes into force on 1 October 2008.

1.12.2   Is there a minimum number of directors that can be appointed?

Yes. Every private company must have at least one director[65] whilst all public companies (whether listed or not) must have at least two directors[66]. This requirement reflects the position under both the Companies Act 1985 and the Companies Act 2006 and therefore companies do not need to change the current composition of their boards.

For most trading companies, the appointment of a sole director will result in practical difficulties at times when the sole director is unavailable, such as the execution of documents and day to day management of the company. Even

---

[65]   Section 154(1), Companies Act 2006.
[66]   Section 154(2), Companies Act 2006.

non-trading companies can experience difficulties when only one director is appointed and consideration should be given to the appointment of an alternate or a second director in appropriate cases.

Under the Companies Act 2006, if a private limited liability company elects to appoint a single director and does not appoint a secretary (see section 1.12.3 below), that single director is duly authorised to execute deeds on behalf of the company by signing the deed in the presence of a witness (which ordinarily would have required the signature of two officers or by affixing the company seal[67]).

1.12.3   Can a sole director also be the secretary of the company?

Under the Companies Act 1985, if a company only had one director this sole director could not also be appointed as the secretary of the company[68].

With effect from 6 April 2008, under the Companies Act 2006, a private limited liability company is no longer required to appoint a secretary. Therefore, the restriction on a sole director being appointed as the secretary of the company is no longer necessary and is not therefore reproduced in the Companies Act 2006. With effect from 6 April 2008 it has therefore been possible for a sole director of a private company to be appointed as the secretary of the company (if the company is electing to retain the role of secretary).

1.12.4   Is there a maximum number of directors that can be appointed?

A company may specify a maximum number of directors in its articles of association although there is no statutory maximum and neither the 1985 Table A articles nor the 2006 model articles impose a maximum number of directors.

1.12.5   What happens if there is an insufficient number of directors?

A board meeting must be quorate, that is, it must have a sufficient number of directors present for the board to make valid decisions. A company's articles usually provide that if the company fails to appoint the minimum number of directors required by the articles of association the board may validly act to appoint additional directors[69] (to rectify the shortfall) but the board will not be able to act for any other purpose. That said, case law on this issue indicates that innocent third parties will not be prejudiced by a breach of this provision, which means that a company may still be bound by its actions in respect of an innocent third party even if such decision was not validly made due to a lack of quorum.

---

[67] Section 44, Companies Act 2006.
[68] Section 283(2), Companies Act 1985.
[69] Regulation 90, 1985 Table A articles / Regulation 11, 2006 model articles.

If a company is in breach of the requirement to appoint a minimum number of directors the Secretary of State may direct the company to remedy the breach within a specified period. Failure to comply with any such direction will render the company and any officer in default liable to a fine together with a daily fine for continued contravention.

The shareholders of the company also have the power to appoint directors (see section 1.14.3.2).

1.12.6 How does the Combined Code impact upon the composition of the board?

Quoted companies should also take into account that:

(i) the appointment process and succession planning of a company should be such to maintain an appropriate balance of skills and experience within the company and the board (paragraph A.4 of the Combined Code). The Higgs report suggested that to do so, companies should broaden their pool of applicants to capture new sources of talent; and

(ii) the board should have a balance of executive and non-executive directors. The Combined Code recommends that except for smaller companies at least half of the board, excluding the chairman, should comprise non-executive directors who are deemed to be independent. A smaller company should have at least two independent non-executive directors (paragraph A.3.2 of the Combined Code). A smaller company is one that is below FTSE 350 throughout the year prior to the reporting year.

1.13 Are there any restrictions on who can be appointed as a director?

There are very few statutory limitations on who can be appointed as a director. However, directors are under a duty to exercise reasonable care, skill and diligence and they may breach this duty if they resolve to appoint a director who is not suitably qualified for the role.

We set out below those limitations that do apply to who can act as a director.

1.13.1 What are the relevant Companies Act 2006 provisions?

The relevant sections of the Companies Act 2006 relating to the appointment of directors are set out in sections 154 to 161 of the Companies Act 2006.

1.13.2 Can a disqualified director be appointed, or act, as a director?

No. An individual who has been disqualified from acting as a director cannot act as a director during the period of his disqualification. The disqualification extends to the individual acting either as a statutory director, shadow director or *de facto* director. A board cannot therefore act in accordance with the instructions of a disqualified individual even if that individual has not been specifically appointed as a director of the company. A detailed analysis of the provisions of the Company Directors Disqualification Act 1986 is outside of the scope of this book.

The Companies Act 2006 grants the Secretary of State the right to make regulations that would prohibit an individual from acting as a director of a UK company where that individual has (amongst other restrictions) been disqualified from acting as a director in another jurisdiction. Such regulations may also provide that a person who acts as a director of a UK company whilst subject to such foreign restrictions will be personally liable for the debts and other liabilities of the UK company.

1.13.3   Can an undischarged bankrupt act as a director?

No. It is a criminal offence for an undischarged bankrupt to act as a director of a company unless he has leave of court to do so[70].

1.13.4   What are the rules relating to 'phoenix' companies?

Where a company has entered insolvent liquidation it is an offence for an individual who was a director (including a shadow director) of that company at any time during the twelve months immediately preceding the insolvent liquidation to become a director, or otherwise be involved with the management, of another company that has the same or similar name as the liquidated company (unless the person concerned has the consent of the court). This prohibition applies for a period of five years from the date of liquidation of the original company[71]. This provision is intended to prevent the use of 'phoenix' companies. It can however also impact on larger groups with an insolvent subsidiary that bears the group's name. In that situation any decision to allow that subsidiary to go into insolvent liquidation should also include consideration of the impact of this restriction on the operation of the group going forward.

1.13.5   Can a company be a director?

Yes. However, the Companies Act 2006 introduces a new requirement from 1 October 2008 that all companies (both public and private) are required to have at least one natural, meaning not corporate, director[72]. The Government has announced that it intends to allow a grace period for compliance with this provision until 1 October 2010 for those companies that did not have a natural director at the time the Companies Act 2006 received Royal Assent on 8

---

[70] Section 11, Company Directors Disqualification Act 1986.
[71] Section 216, Insolvency Act 1986.
[72] Section 155(1), Companies Act 2006.

November 2006. Any companies that have a sole director that is a corporate entity should therefore appoint an additional, natural, director to the board by 1 October 2010.

If a company breaches the requirement of the Companies Act 2006 to have at least one natural director then the Secretary of State may direct the company to rectify the breach within a period of one to three months from the date of the direction. Failure to comply with any such direction is an offence committed by the company and every officer in default. Any person in default is liable to a fine together with a daily fine for continued contravention.

1.13.6 Is there a minimum age requirement for natural directors?

Yes. In a change to the regime under the Companies Act 1985, and with effect from 1 October 2008, every natural director of a company must be at least 16 years old[73]. If a company has a director that is underage on 1 October 2008 that director will automatically cease to be a director of the company on that date[74]. Companies that would have underage directors on 1 October 2008 should, if necessary, appoint a new director prior to this date to ensure that the company continues to have a sufficient number of directors to meet quorum requirements when the underage director ceases to act.

Where a director automatically ceases to act by virtue of the fact that he is underage, the company must update its register of directors to reflect the termination of the director's appointment, although it will not be required to notify the Registrar of Companies of such termination[75].

It is possible for a company to enter into an agreement to appoint an underage individual as a director provided that the appointment does not take effect until after the individual reaches the age of 16.

An underage director will incur civil and criminal penalties if he purports to act as a director after 1 October 2008.

The Companies Act 2006 reserves the right to the Secretary of State to make regulations that would allow an underage director to act in specific situations although at the time of writing no such regulations have been made.

1.13.7 Is there a maximum age requirement for natural directors?

On 6 April 2007 the Companies Act 2006 abolished the requirement under the Companies Act 1985 that directors of public companies or their subsidiaries automatically retire at 70 years of age.

---

[73] Section 157(1), Companies Act 2006.
[74] Section 159(2), Companies Act 2006.
[75] Section 159(3), Companies Act 2006.

The repeal of this statutory restriction will not override any express provisions set out in a contract of employment requiring the automatic resignation of the director upon the director reaching a certain age. If a director's contract of employment does include a requirement that the director resigns upon reaching a certain age this requirement is likely to breach age discrimination legislation and should therefore be reviewed. In addition, any age limit in a company's articles of association continues to apply until amended.

1.13.8 Is a director required to have minimum academic or professional qualifications?

No. There is no requirement under either the Companies Act 1985 or the Companies Act 2006 for a director to have minimum academic or professional qualifications. For a company applying the Combined Code, it should ensure that the board has the balance of skill and experience that is appropriate for the requirements of the business (although this will undoubtedly also be a commercial consideration of the board in any event).

However, when the existing directors of the company are considering the appointment of a new director they must have regard to their duties to promote the success of the company and to exercise due care and skill. They will therefore need to ensure that any director that they appoint has sufficient skill and ability to perform the role for which he or she is being appointed.

Although there is no statutory requirement for a director to have certain qualifications, a company's articles of association can impose a requirement that the directors of the company possess certain minimum qualifications. Companies applying the Combined Code and Smith Guidance should also have regard to the requirements of these guidance documents (see section 1.13.10).

A director, when accepting a position, should also ensure that he has sufficient skill to discharge the role as the standard of care expected of him will be determined by reference to the position he occupies as well as the skills he has (see section 1.2.6).

1.13.9 Is a director required to live in the UK?

No. Subject to an express provision in the company's articles of association to the contrary, there is no requirement for a company director to be resident in a particular territory. However, it is questionable whether a trading company will be able to operate efficiently if it does not appoint any local directors. Therefore when appointing non-resident directors the existing board will need to have regard to the existing composition of the board to ensure that any such appointment is in the best interests of the company.

Directors living abroad will also need to consider whether they can properly perform the duties they are required to undertake, especially if for example this involves responsibility for the day to day running of the business.

1.13.10   How does the Combined Code apply to the appointment of directors?

Companies applying the Combined Code should also appoint a non-executive independent director who should have recent and relevant financial experience to sit on the audit committee. In addition, the Smith Guidance recommends that a director should have a professional qualification from one of the professional accounting bodies. The Smith Guidance also recommends that experience of corporate financial matters is required from all members of the audit committee.

The above requirement will be strengthened when the 8th Directive comes into force via the FSA Rules (for reporting periods starting on or after 29 June 2008), as the Directive specifically requires that the audit committee has at least one person with financial expertise and competence in accounting and auditing. This requirement applies to companies whose securities are traded in a regulated market in the EU and have their registered office in an EU member state.

1.13.11 Comparison between the Companies Act 1985 and the Companies Act 2006 (excluding the Combined Code) relating to the minimum requirements for directors

Minimum requirements for directors			
Provision	**Companies Act 1985**	**Companies Act 2006**	**Is the Companies Act 2006 in force?**
Minimum number of directors	One director is required for a private company and two directors are required for a public company.	No change from the position under the Companies Act 1985.	1 October 2007.
Appointment of corporate directors	A company can have a sole corporate director.	A company must have at least one director who is a natural person.	1 October 2008 although there is a grace period for compliance until 1 October 2010 for companies that did not have at least one natural director on 8 November 2006.
Minimum age for directors	There is no minimum age requirement.	Natural directors must be at least 16 years old.	1 October 2008.
Maximum age for directors	Directors of public companies must retire at 70 years old.	There is no maximum age limit for directors and the requirement for directors of public companies to retire at 70 is repealed.	6 April 2007.
Qualification requirements	None.	None.	None.
Residency requirement	None.	None.	None.

1.14   How is a director appointed?

Once a company has determined that an individual is eligible to be appointed as a director the company must follow an appointment process, which is usually set out in the company's articles of association.

The process of appointment of the first directors of the company and any subsequent directors is different. However, in each instance the director who is being appointed must give his informed consent to accept the appointment.

The Combined Code sets out additional criteria to be met when appointing a director to the board of a listed company. For example, the Combined Code recommends that there should be a nomination committee to lead the process for board appointments. The Combined Code also outlines specific recommendations for the remuneration committee's composition, role and operations. The recommended appointment process includes using an external search consultancy or open advertisement when appointing a chairman or non-executive director (paragraph A.4 of the Combined Code).

1.14.1   What is the requirement for informed consent?

Regardless of whether the appointment is that of an initial or subsequent director the director must first give his informed consent to the appointment.

1.14.2   How are the first directors of a company appointed to the board?

1.14.2.1   How are the first directors of the company appointed under the Companies Act 1985?

The Companies Act 1985[76] applies to the appointment of the first directors of companies that are incorporated before 1 October 2009. Under the Companies Act 1985 the appointment of the first directors of the company is made via the incorporation documents of the company, namely form 10. The directors consent to act by signing form 10, which is then submitted to the Registrar of Companies. This signed statement also includes personal details of the directors such as their residential address (but see 1.14.8 below), date of birth and details of any other directorships that the directors may hold. Upon the incorporation of the company the appointment of the first directors becomes effective. Any other method of purported appointment of the first directors of a company is void.

Since 2001 it has also been possible to incorporate a company electronically, without the requirement for directors to sign form 10. Instead, directors provide a series of information (such as eye colour and their mother's maiden name) which creates a unique 9 digit pin that operates as an electronic

---

[76] Sections 10 and 12, Companies Act 1985.

signature to 'sign' companies forms, therefore precluding the need for the director to actually sign paper forms.

1.14.2.2 How are the first directors of the company appointed under the Companies Act 2006?

With effect from 1 October 2009, the Companies Act 2006 replaces the requirement to file form 10 (as set out above) with a requirement to file an application for registration[77]. This application for registration contains the information that is required to be entered into the company's register of directors and register of residential addresses and also includes the directors' consent to act. As with the regime under the Companies Act 1985, the directors that are named in the application for registration are automatically appointed upon registration of the company. Any other attempt to appoint the initial directors of the company will be void.

In accordance with the regime for companies formed under the Companies Act 1985, a company incorporated under the Companies Act 2006 can also be incorporated electronically (see section 1.14.2.1).

1.14.3   How are subsequent directors appointed to the board?

Once the initial directors of a company have been appointed, any subsequent directors are appointed in accordance with the articles of association of the company. Ordinarily, the articles of association will provide for appointment either by the existing directors of the company or by the shareholders of the company and we examine these two methods of appointment, together with other considerations that apply when appointing additional directors, in more detail below.

1.14.3.1   What if there is a restriction on the maximum number of directors?

If there is a restriction in the articles of association on the number of directors that can be appointed, and this maximum has been reached, then it will be necessary to amend the articles of association by special resolution before any further appointments can be made.

1.14.3.2   Can shareholders appoint directors pursuant to the company's articles of association?

(i)   Appointment by shareholders pursuant to the 1985 Table A articles

The 1985 Table A articles for a private company provide that, save where the director is being reappointed having retired by rotation (which is discussed in more detail in paragraph 1.15.1.2), the shareholders of a company may appoint

---

[77] Sections 9 to 12, Companies Act 2006.

a director by passing an ordinary resolution provided that the proposed director has:

(i)   been recommended by the directors of the company; or

(ii)   notice of the intention to propose the appointment of the new director has been given to the company not less than 14 but no more than 35 clear days before the date of the meeting. This notice must contain the name and any former name of the director, the usual residential address of the director, the country or state in which the director is usually resident, the nationality of the director, the director's business occupation (if any) and the director's date of birth. The notice must also be accompanied by the written consent of the proposed director indicating the proposed director's willingness to be appointed.

The 1985 Table A articles provide that no less than seven, but no more than 28, clear days' notice before the date of the general meeting at which the proposed appointment is to be considered must be given to all who are entitled to receive notice of the meeting. This notice must also include the particulars of the proposed director that would need to be included in the company's register of directors if the person concerned is appointed.

Companies which are subsidiaries commonly amend the provisions of the 1985 Table A articles to provide that a majority shareholder can appoint and remove a director on notice to the company.

(ii)   Appointment by shareholders pursuant to the 2006 model articles

Under the 2006 model articles any person who is willing to act as a director, and who is permitted by law to do so, may be appointed as a director by an ordinary resolution of the shareholders[78].

The 2006 model articles also introduce important changes to the 1985 Table A procedure for the appointment of directors by shareholders. In particular, there is no requirement that a proposed director must first be recommended by the existing board or that notice must be given by a shareholder of the intention to propose an individual for appointment as a director. The procedure for the appointment of the shareholders is therefore simplified by the 2006 model articles and companies adopting the 2006 model articles may consider imposing additional restrictions for appointment of directors by shareholders, if they so wish.

As with current practice, it is likely that subsidiaries will amend the 2006 model articles to allow a majority shareholder to appoint (and remove) a director on written notice.

[78]   Regulation 17, 2006 model articles.

(iii)   Enhanced voting rights (*Bushell v Faith* [1970] AC 1099[79] clauses)

A company's articles of association can provide for certain shareholders (usually existing directors of the company) to have enhanced voting rights on particular resolutions such as a resolution to appoint or remove a director. These enhanced rights are often designed to protect existing directors' positions on the board of the company. A company's articles of association should be reviewed to identify any such provisions when a resolution to appoint a director is proposed.

(iv)   What appointments can the shareholders make?

Subject to the company's articles of association the shareholders of the company may appoint a director to fill either a casual vacancy or to appoint a new director to the board[80].

(v)   Appointments by written resolution

The members of a private company may appoint a director by passing a written ordinary resolution. With effect from 1 October 2007 changes introduced by the Companies Act 2006[81] make it easier for shareholders of a private company to pass a written ordinary resolution by reducing the requirement for the written resolution to be passed unanimously to a requirement (in the case of an ordinary resolution) for a simple majority.

1.14.3.3   *What is a casual vacancy?*

This is usually defined in the company's articles.

In general terms a person is appointed as a director to fill a casual vacancy if the appointment is made to replace a previous director who no longer holds office either by reason of death, resignation, disqualification or for any other reason other than retirement by rotation or the expiry of a fixed term of appointment.

1.14.3.4   *What is an additional appointment?*

An individual is appointed as an additional director if his appointment increases the previous number of directors on the board i.e. the appointment is not being made to fill a casual vacancy.

---

[79] (1970) AC 1099.
[80] Regulation 78 Table A / regulation 17, 2006 model articles.
[81] Sections 281 to 300, Companies Act 2006.

1.14.3.5   *How do existing board members make additional appointments to the board?*

A company's articles of association typically provide that directors (by a majority vote) can appoint other directors to the board.

(i)   Appointments by directors under the 1985 Table A articles

The 1985 Table A articles enable existing directors to appoint another director provided that the appointment does not exceed any maximum set out in the articles[82]. The articles provide that an appointment made by directors needs to be approved by shareholders at the next annual general meeting of the company. Under the 1985 Table A articles, if the appointment is not approved at the next annual general meeting of the company the director so appointed by the board will vacate office at the end of that annual general meeting.

Most companies will amend the provisions of the 1985 Table A articles to enable the directors of the company to appoint additional directors or to fill a vacancy without the need for shareholder approval.

(ii)   Appointments by directors under the 2006 model articles

The 2006 model articles for a private limited liability company authorise the directors of the company to appoint any person who is willing to act as a director and who is permitted by law to do so[83].

Contrary to the 1985 Table A articles there is no requirement under the 2006 model articles for a director who is appointed by the directors of the company to retire at the next annual general meeting of the company.

1.14.4   What notification of appointment does the company need to make to the Registrar of Companies?

A company must notify the Registrar of Companies of the appointment of any director within 14 days of the appointment using Form 288a (note that this form reference will change following the implementation of the relevant Companies Act 2006 provisions), which must be signed by both the director being appointed and any one officer of the company. Note that there is an obligation to notify the Registrar of Companies of the appointment of a shadow director, although in practice this in fact only happens when the board becomes aware that a person is a shadow director. From 1 October 2009 details of other directorships held by a director need not be disclosed. From 1 October 2009 it is also a requirement to disclose any former name by which a director was known for business purposes and the exception for maiden names will be removed.

---

[82] Regulation 79, 1985 Table A articles.
[83] Regulation 17, 2006 model articles.

1.14.5 What registers does a company need to update when a director is appointed?

A company is required to maintain an up to date register of directors (including shadow directors)[84], which must be kept at the company's registered office. The Secretary of State has power to make regulations specifying an alternative place where the register may be kept.

1.14.6 Are there any additional considerations when appointing a director of a public company?

The Combined Code required listed companies to have a 'formal, rigorous and transparent procedure for the appointment of new directors to the board' (paragraph A.4 of the Combined Code) which includes amongst other matters the appointment of a nomination committee. The Combined Code also recommends that a company uses an external search consultancy or open advertisement when appointing a chairman or non-executive director.

When shareholders are appointing a director of a public company (whether listed or not) the appointment of each director must be voted on individually[85] (the relevant provision of the Companies Act 2006 comes into force on 1 October 2008). It is not possible for the appointment of all potential new directors to be approved by one vote (unless a prior resolution has been unanimously passed to authorise such block voting). Any attempt to appoint a director in contravention of this section will be void.

1.14.7 Are the acts of a director still valid if there is a defect in a director's appointment?

Yes. The acts of a person acting as a director are valid notwithstanding that it is afterwards discovered that there was either a defect in his purported appointment, that he was disqualified from acting as a director, that he had ceased to hold office or that he was not entitled to vote on the matter in question[86].

An innocent third party that deals with a person holding himself out to be a director may hold the company responsible for such acts under agency principles (provided that the third party was not aware of the defect in the directors' appointment). In this circumstance, a director holding himself out as such will be a *de facto* director who, as set out in section 1.2.13.3 above, will be bound by the same duties (and subject to the same liabilities) as a director who has been validly appointed.

---

[84] Section 288, Companies Act 1985 / Section 162, Companies Act 2006.
[85] Section 160, Companies Act 2006.
[86] Section 285, Companies Act 1985 / Section 161, Companies Act 2006.

1.14.8 Is a director required to disclose his residential address?

Currently, when a director is appointed he is required to file a residential address with Companies House, using Form 288a, and to notify Companies House of any changes to his residential address using Form 288c.

The only instance in which a director is relieved of the obligation to file a residential address is where a confidentiality order has been granted in favour of the director, in which case a residential address need not be filed. A confidentiality order will only be granted if the director can show that there is a risk of violence or intimidation to the director, or any person residing at the director's residential property, which justifies the grant of the order.

The Companies Act 2006 introduces a significant change to the current requirement for a director to file a residential address. With effect from 1 October 2009, all directors are entitled to file a service address, as opposed to their residential address, without the need to first obtain a confidentiality order. The service address may be the company's registered office or any other address of the director's choosing. Directors are still required to provide Companies House with their residential address but this information will be kept on a separate register that will not be available for public inspection. Where there is a change to the director's service address, the company must file a notice of the change and when doing so must also state whether or not there is any change to the details of the director's residential address.

The amendment to the requirement for directors to file residential addresses means that companies will need to update their register of directors to reflect the service addresses filed by directors.

With effect from 1 October 2009, as a result of the fact that directors are no longer required to file residential addresses, companies are required to maintain a register of directors' residential addresses that will not be made available for public inspection. At the time of printing there is no mechanism for completely removing existing records of residential addresses from public inspection at Companies House.

The Companies Act 2006 provides that the Registrar of Companies must not include a director's address in material that is available for inspection on the register provided that the address is included in those parts of the document filed with the Registrar of Companies that require such disclosure. The Registrar of Companies is not required to check any documents to identify whether a director's residential address is included elsewhere in the document and, if it is, the Registrar of Companies is not under an obligation to omit this information from the public record. Furthermore, the Registrar of Companies may disclose a director's residential address to a public authority specified in regulations made by the Secretary of State on this issue or to a credit reference agency (unless regulations are made to the contrary). The Registrar of

Companies may also disclose this information when required to do so by court order. Finally, the Registrar of Companies may put the director's residential address on public record if communications sent by the Registrar of Companies to the director that require a response in a specified time remain unanswered or if there is evidence that the service address provided for the director is ineffective to bring documents to the director's attention.

1.14.9   Checklist of considerations when appointing a director

- Who has the right to appoint a director?

- Do the company's articles of association set out a procedure that must be followed when appointing a director?

- Do the articles of association contain a restriction on the maximum number of directors that can be appointed?

- Is the director suitably qualified and does the director have the requisite skills and experience for the appointment?

- Has the director been disqualified from acting as a director (or is otherwise prohibited from acting as a director)?

- Has the director provided informed consent to accept the appointment as a director?

- What are the terms of the director's appointment? Is the director to be an employee? Ensure that the terms of engagement or employment are evidenced in a service or employment agreement.

- If the director is being appointed by shareholders, do any shareholders have weighted voting rights?

- Does the director have any interests that may conflict with those of the company?

- Ensure that the appointment is notified to the Registrar of Companies within 14 days.

- Ensure that the company's register of directors is updated to reflect the appointment.

- Should the newly appointed director be added as a signatory to the bank mandate?

1.14.10   Checklist of considerations when accepting an appointment as a director

- Have you investigated the affairs of the company to ensure that you are willing to accept the appointment. In particular, are you familiar with the financial history of the company?

- Are you satisfied that the internal regulation of the company is sound?

- Are you satisfied that the size, structure and make-up of the board will enable you to make an effective contribution?

- Do you hold any existing appointments that may conflict with the appointment that you are considering?

- What will be expected of you in the role that you are considering?

- What are the terms of your appointment?

- What is the company's position in comparison to its competitors?

1.15   How is a director's appointment terminated?

1.15.1   Methods of removal of a director

A director can be removed from office by a number of methods:

(i)   voluntary resignation by the director (1.15.1.1 below);

(ii)   retirement by rotation (1.15.1.2 below);

(iii)   expiry of a fixed term contract (1.15.1.3 below);

(iv)   removal by the board (1.15.1.4 below); and

(v)   removal by a simple majority of the shareholders of the company (1.15.1.5 below)[87].

We discuss each of these methods in turn.

1.15.1.1   Removal by resignation

A director may resign from office at any time (although the director may be liable for any breach of contract if, for example, he resigns prior to the expiry of a fixed term contract and the company suffers a loss as a result).

It is possible for the company's articles of association to stipulate the process that a director must follow to resign validly from office, which may include a requirement for the resignation to be made in writing. Where possible, a company will want a director to confirm in his letter of resignation that he has no outstanding claims against the company.

It is not necessary for the company to accept formally the resignation of a director for the resignation to take effect. The resignation becomes effective from the date of resignation set out in the resignation letter or, if the resignation letter is silent as to the effective date of resignation, from the date of delivery of the letter.

---

[87] Section 303, Companies Act 1985; section 168, Companies Act 2006.

1.15.1.2   Retirement by rotation

(i)   What is the position pursuant to the 1985 Table A articles?

The 1985 Table A articles provide that all directors, save for the managing director and executive directors[88], are required to retire by rotation. All directors are required to retire from office at the first general meeting and thereafter one third of directors that are subject to retirement by rotation (or if there are less than three directors the number nearest to one third) shall retire at each subsequent annual general meeting[89] (with the directors who are required to retire being determined by reference to their length of service). If at the meeting at which a director retires by rotation the vacancy of the retiring director is not filled then the director who has so retired will be deemed to be reappointed unless it is resolved not to fill the vacancy or where the reappointment of the director is put to the meeting and lost[90].

It is common for most companies to stipulate that the executive directors of the company are not required to retire by rotation.

(ii)   What are the proposed changes under the 2006 model articles?

The 2006 model articles for private companies no longer stipulate that a director must retire by rotation. However the requirement for directors to retire by rotation has been retained in the 2006 model articles for public companies.

(iii)   What is the position under the Combined Code?

The Combined Code recommends that all directors should be subject to re-election at the first AGM following the director's appointment and thereafter at three year intervals.

The Combined Code details that, save for smaller companies, at least half of the board (excluding the chairman) of a listed company should comprise independent directors (paragraph A.3.2 of the Combined Code). The Combined Code provides that where independent non-executive directors hold office for a term in excess of six years (e.g. two three-year terms) this should be subject to a rigorous review, while a term of office extending beyond nine years would be considered a factor impairing a non-executive director's independence. However, it is possible for a non-executive director to hold office for nine years or more where the non-executive director is subject to annual re-election (paragraph A.7.2 of the Combined Code).

---

[88]   Regulation 84, 1985 Table A.
[89]   Regulation 73, 1985 Table A.
[90]   Regulation 75, 1985 Table A.

1.15.1.3 *Expiry of a fixed term contract*

If a director is appointed for a fixed term then the director's appointment will automatically terminate upon the expiry of that fixed term.

1.15.1.4 *Removal by the board*

The board may vote to remove a director (by majority vote). However, there will also be employment law considerations if the director is also an employee of the company (see section 1.15.2.1).

1.15.1.5 *Removal by shareholders*

Shareholders have a statutory right to remove a director by passing an ordinary resolution (which is passed by a simple majority of the shareholders of the company)[91]. The relevant provisions of the Companies Act 2006 came into force on 1 October 2007 and did not make any substantive changes to the regime under the Companies Act 1985. This is an absolute right of shareholders and applies notwithstanding anything to the contrary in the company's articles of association, or in any agreement between the company and the director (such as an employment contract). However these rights of a majority shareholder can be overridden in practice where weighted voting rights (known as *Bushell v Faith* clauses) are given to minority shareholders when voting on this issue.

The removal of a director by shareholders in accordance with their statutory right is without prejudice to any rights that the director may have to claim from the company compensation or damages.

To enable a director to have a right to be heard and object to his removal the Companies Act 2006 details a specific procedure that must be followed before shareholders can vote to remove a director. To remove a director (and to appoint a director to fill the vacancy that is created at the same meeting) special notice must be given to the company by the shareholders proposing the removal and such notice must be received by the company at least 28 days before the meeting at which the removal is to be considered. This notice should include a request from the shareholders that a resolution be included at the meeting proposing the removal of the director concerned (and, if required, the appointment of a director in his place).

Notice of the resolution must be given to the director concerned immediately and sent to the shareholders of the company at least 21 days before the meeting.

---

[91] Section 168, Companies Act 2006.

The director whom the shareholders propose to remove is entitled to make written submissions in respect of the resolution, which must be circulated to the shareholders of the company. If the written submissions are received too late to circulate to shareholders then these submissions must be read out at the general meeting before the resolution is voted upon. The director concerned may also attend the general meeting and speak in respect of the proposed removal[92].

A company may include a provision in its articles of association to remove the 28-day notice procedure set out above. To do this the shareholders must pass a special resolution to approve the amendment to the articles.

It is also common for a company to include a provision in its articles of association to enable a majority shareholder to remove a director on notice.

When seeking to remove a director under the statutory right, the shareholders cannot use the written resolution regime (which would otherwise preclude the director concerned from speaking at the general meeting at which the resolution is being considered).

1.15.2   Further considerations when removing a director

1.15.2.1   Removal of a director who is also an employee

Many directors will also be employees, which means that the directors will receive the same statutory protections as any other employees of the company. In addition, it may be a term of the individual's contract of employment that he is a director of the company and removal from office may therefore result in a breach of an express term of the director's contract of employment.

As such, care must be taken when removing a director who is an employee as even though the director may be removed from office as a director in accordance with the provisions of the company's articles of association it may still be possible for the director to bring a claim against the company for constructive or unfair dismissal (in his capacity as an employee).

1.15.2.2   Removal of a director who is also a shareholder

It is common for a director to be a shareholder of the company. Therefore, when removing a director who is also a shareholder of the company the terms of any shareholders' agreement to which the director is a party should be considered as, for example, the termination of the director's office may be a trigger for the automatic sale of the director's shares.

---

[92] Section 169(2), Companies Act 2006.

1.15.3 What are the rules relating to payment for loss of office?

The Companies Act 2006 contains detailed rules relating to payment to directors for loss of office, which are discussed in more detail in chapter 2.

1.15.4 What notification needs to be made to the Registrar of Companies when removing a director?

A company must notify the Registrar of Companies of the removal of a director using Form 288b (or equivalent under the Companies Act 2006) within 14 days of the date of removal.

1.15.5 What registers need updating when a director is removed from office?

Following the removal of a director from office the company must ensure that it updates its register of directors at the earliest opportunity.

1.15.6 Checklist of considerations when removing a director

- Who has the right to remove the director?

- Will the removal result in the company having too few directors (either under the articles of association or otherwise)?

- Does the company's articles of association detail a procedure that must be followed when removing a director?

- Is the director a shareholder of the company? If so, is the director a party to a shareholders' agreement that provides the director with protection against dismissal?

- Does the director have weighted voting rights in respect of any proposed resolution to remove the director?

- Is the director also an employee of the company? If so, is the proposed removal of the director from office going to trigger any employment related issues?

- Is it proposed to make a payment to the director for loss of office? If so, has this payment first been approved by the shareholders of the company (unless the payment relates to a genuine claim that has arisen in respect of a pre-existing legal obligation)?

- Has the Registrar of Companies been notified of the director's removal by filing Form 288b (or equivalent under the Companies Act 2006)?

- Has the register of directors been updated to reflect the director's removal from office?

1.16 Automatic vacation of office

A director may be required automatically to vacate office. The circumstances giving rise to automatic vacation are set out in a company's articles of association (although automatic vacation of office may also occur by operation of law) and therefore may vary from company to company. For example, it is common for a company's articles of association to provide for automatic vacation of a director's office upon conviction of certain offences. We set out below the common provisions for automatic vacation of office.

1.16.1 What are the rules relating to the vacation of office under the 1985 Table A articles?

1.16.1.1 Disqualification/operation of law

If a director is disqualified from acting as a director (or is otherwise prohibited by law from acting as a director) any appointment, or purported appointment, will be ineffective.

1.16.1.2 Resignation

If a director gives notice of his resignation in writing then this is effective to vacate his office.

1.16.1.3 Bankruptcy

If a bankruptcy order is made against a director, or if a director enters into an arrangement with his creditors, then he will automatically vacate office. For the purposes of vacating office, bankruptcy lasts until the discharge of the bankruptcy order.

1.16.1.4 Loss of mental capacity

If a director suffers from a 'mental disorder' and is admitted to hospital pursuant to the Mental Health Act 1983, or an order is made by the court for reasons concerning a mental disorder for the detention of the director or for the appointment of a receiver or other person to exercise powers with regard to the director's property or affairs, then the director will vacate office.

1.16.1.5 Absence from board meetings for more than six months

If a director fails to attend board meetings for more than six months without permission then the remaining board can resolve that the absent director's office be vacated.

1.16.2   Automatic vacation pursuant to the 2006 model articles

The 2006 model articles also include a statement of circumstances in which a director will be deemed to have automatically vacated office. These are:

1.16.2.1   Disqualification

Again, the 2006 model articles stipulate that if a director is disqualified from acting, or is otherwise prohibited from acting pursuant to the Companies Act 2006, that he will automatically vacate office.

1.16.2.2   Resignation

Resignation by the director will be effective from the date set out in the resignation letter.

1.16.2.3   Removal by shareholders

The shareholders may remove a director from office by passing an ordinary resolution to this effect.

1.16.2.4   Failure to participate in the operation of the company

If the other directors of the company determine that the director has repeatedly, and without excuse, failed to participate in the processes by which majority decisions may be taken they can resolve that he should cease to hold office. Note that the provisions of the 2006 model articles are therefore potentially wider than those set out in the 1985 Table A articles, which provide that failure to attend board meetings for six months will constitute a vacation of office.

1.16.2.5   Termination of service agreement

The 2006 model articles provide that if a contract pursuant to which the director was appointed as a director, or personally performs services for the company or of any subsidiary, is terminated the director will cease to hold office (unless the contract is immediately renewed). This resolves the situation whereby a director is no longer an employee of a company but continues to hold office as a director.

1.17   Summary of key changes under the Companies Act 2006

The table below sets out the key provisions of the Companies Act 1985 and the Companies Act 2006 in respect of directors:

Issue	Companies Act 1985	Companies Act 2006	Action Required
Directors' duties (section 1.2)	Directors' duties are primarily derived from common law principles.	With effect from 1 October 2007 (and 1 October 2008 for conflicts of interests) directors' duties are codified.	Consider practical steps to mitigate risk and manage conflicts (see section 1.2.17).
Derivative claims (section 1.5)	No express provisions; governed by common law.	New statutory regime introduced by the Companies Act 2006 on 1 October 2007.	Consider practical steps to mitigate risk (see section 1.5.14).
Ratification of directors' acts (section 1.6.1)	Permitted under the common law.	With effect from 1 October 2007 the Companies Act 2006 provides that independent shareholders (unless the resolution is passed unanimously) can ratify directors' acts (section 1.6.1).	Ensure that independent shareholders ratify directors' acts where necessary (unless the resolution is passed unanimously).
Statutory provisions relating to directors' indemnities (section 1.6.3)	No provision for companies to provide indemnities for pension fund trustees.	New third party indemnity for pension fund trustees.	Consider whether to provide indemnities in favour of trustees of occupational pension schemes (see section 1.6.3.3).
Corporate directors (section 1.13.5)	A company could have a sole corporate director.	With effect from 1 October 2008 all companies must have at least one natural director.	Identify boards consisting solely of corporate directors and appoint at least one natural person as a director.
Minimum age requirement for directors (section 1.13.6)	No minimum age requirement.	With effect from 1 October 2008 all natural directors must be at least 16 years old.	Review board composition and appoint additional overage directors prior to 1 October 2008 if necessary.
Maximum age requirement for directors (section 1.13.7)	Directors of public companies automatically retire at 70.	With effect from 6 April 2007 the maximum age restriction for directors of public companies is repealed.	Review existing articles of association to identify any provision requiring a director to retire at 70.

Issue	Companies Act 1985	Companies Act 2006	Action Required
Use of service addresses (section 1.14.8)	Directors required to file residential address (unless they have the benefit of a confidentiality order).	With effect from 1 October 2009, all directors may file a service address.	Review and amend statutory books (from 1 October 2009) where necessary and maintain a separate list of directors' residential addresses.
Retirement of directors by rotation (section 1.15.1.2)	Governed by a company's articles of association. The 1985 Table A articles detail that directors are required to retire by rotation.	The 2006 interim model articles of association no longer require an executive director of a private limited liability company to retire by rotation.	Consider amending existing articles of association and identify whether any changes are required.

Chapter 2

Transactions with directors

2.1   Introduction 2002
    2.1.1   Scope of the chapter 2002
    2.1.2   What is the background to the changes? 2002
    2.1.3   Is shareholder approval required where the director
         concerned is a majority shareholder? 2003
    2.1.4   In what commercial situations can a breach of the rules
         relating to transactions with directors be identified and
         who can bring an action? 2003
    2.1.5   What are the key changes to transactions with directors
         under the Companies Act 2006? 2004
2.2   Directors' service contracts and letters of appointment 2005
    2.2.1   When did changes introduced by the Companies Act 2006
         come into force? 2005
    2.2.2   What service contracts are caught by the new provisions of
         the Companies Act 2006? 2005
    2.2.3   How do directors' duties apply when considering a
         director's service contract? 2006
    2.2.4   When does a directors' service contract require approval?   2006
    2.2.5   How is the 'guaranteed term' calculated? 2006
    2.2.6   Can the requirement for shareholder approval be
         circumvented by entering into successive contracts with
         terms of less than two years? 2006
    2.2.7   Which shareholders need to approve a director's service
         contract? 2007
    2.2.8   Are there any exemptions to the requirement for
         shareholder approval of a director's service contract? ... 2007
    2.2.9   What procedure needs to be followed when obtaining
         shareholders' approval of a director's long-term service
         contract? 2007
    2.2.10 Is shareholder consent required for service contracts with a
         fixed term of two years or more that were entered into
         before 1 October 2007? 2008
    2.2.11 What are the consequences of failing to obtain shareholder
         approval to a director's long-term service contract? 2008
    2.2.12 Do shareholders have a right to inspect directors' service
         contracts? 2008
    2.2.13 Does the Companies Act 2006 change the requirements
         relating to the inspection of directors' service contracts?   2008
    2.2.14 Can a company charge a shareholder for inspecting a
         director's service contract? 2009

2.2.15 Can a company refuse to allow a shareholder to inspect a director's service contract? 2009

2.2.16 Are shareholders entitled to a copy of a director's service contract? 2009

2.2.17 Does a company need to make shadow directors' service contracts available for inspection? 2009

2.2.18 How do the conflicts of interest rules introduced on 1 October 2008 apply to service contracts? 2009

2.2.19 What are the rules relating to a service contract with a sole member who is also a director? 2010

2.2.20 What are the rules relating to contracts (other than service contracts) with a sole member who is also a director? . . . 2010

2.3 Substantial property transactions 2010

2.3.1 What changes have been introduced by the Companies Act 2006? 2010

2.3.2 What is a substantial property transaction? 2011

2.3.3 What approval is required for a substantial property transaction? 2012

2.3.4 Can a director's service contract or a payment for loss of office constitute a substantial property transaction? 2013

2.3.5 How do the rules relating to substantial property transactions apply to a series of transactions? 2013

2.3.6 Are there any exceptions to the requirement to obtain shareholder approval for a substantial property transaction? 2014

2.3.7 To whom do the rules on substantial property transactions apply? 2015

2.3.8 What changes have been made to the definition of a 'connected person' for the purposes of substantial property transactions? 2015

2.3.9 With whom is a director 'connected'? 2015

2.3.10 Which members of a director's family are 'connected' with him? 2016

2.3.11 Which companies are 'connected' with a director? 2016

2.3.12 What are the consequences of breaching the rules relating to substantial property transactions? 2017

2.3.13 When can a substantial property transaction be rescinded by the company? 2017

2.3.14 Who can be held personally liable? 2018

2.3.15 Can a company affirm a contract that was entered into in breach of the rules relating to substantial property transactions? 2019

2.4 Loans and other credit transactions with directors 2020

2.4.1 What changes have been introduced by the Companies Act 2006? 2020

2.4.2 What types of transactions require shareholder approval? 2021

2.4.3 What is a quasi-loan? 2021

2.4.4   What is a credit transaction? 2021
2.4.5   What is the procedure for obtaining shareholder approval
          for a loan or other credit transaction? 2023
2.4.6   Which shareholders are required to approve the
          transaction? 2023
2.4.7   Can a company avoid the requirement to obtain
          shareholder approval by arranging for a third party to
          make the loan? 2024
2.4.8   In summary, how do the rules relating to loans, security,
          quasi-loans and credit transactions differ for public
          companies and private companies? 2025
2.4.9   Are there exceptions to the requirement for shareholder
          approval for loans, the provision of security, quasi-loans
          and credit transactions? 2026
          2.4.9.1   Expenditure on company business up to
                     £50,000 2027
          2.4.9.2   Expenditure on defending proceedings 2027
          2.4.9.3   Expenditure in connection with regulatory
                     actions or investigations 2028
          2.4.9.4   Expenditure for minor and business
                     transactions 2028
          2.4.9.5   Expenditure for intra-group transactions 2029
          2.4.9.6   Money-lending companies 2029
2.4.10   What is the value of the transaction or arrangement? ... 2029
2.4.11   What are the consequences of breaching the rules relating
          to loans, security, quasi-loans or credit transactions? ... 2030
          2.4.11.1   When can a loan, security, quasi-loan or credit
                     transaction be rescinded? 2030
          2.4.11.2   Personal liability of directors and 'connected
                     persons' 2031
2.4.12   Are there any defences against personal liability for a
          breach of the rules relating to loans, security, quasi-loans
          and credit transactions? 2031
2.4.13   Can shareholders approve a loan, security, quasi-loan or
          credit transaction that has been entered into by the
          company without prior shareholder approval? 2031
2.5   Tax-free payments to directors 2031
2.6   Payments for loss of office 2032
2.6.1   What changes have been introduced by the Companies Act
          2006? 2032
2.6.2   What is a 'payment for loss of office'? 2033
2.6.3   What shareholder approval is required for a payment for
          loss of office? 2034
2.6.4   Are there exceptions to the requirement for shareholder
          approval for payments to directors for loss of office? ... 2034

2.6.5   What are the consequences of failing to obtain shareholder approval for a payment that is made to a director for loss of office? 2035

2.7   What is the position where a transaction requires approval under more than one provision of the Companies Act 2006? 2035

2.8   What are the disclosure requirements where directors have interests in the company's shares? 2035

2.9   Directors' disclosures of interest in shares 2036

2.10 Summary of key changes under the Companies Act 2006 2036

This chapter addresses the provisions of the Companies Act 2006 that apply to transactions by a company with its directors. For fully listed companies, namely companies listed on the main market of the London Stock Exchange, transactions of this nature are commonly also governed by the Listing Rules, an analysis of which is outside of the scope of this book[1].

Companies admitted to trade on the Alternative Investment Market (AIM) or PLUS markets will need to comply with the AIM Rules or relevant PLUS rules[2].

---

[1]   The Listing Rules can be accessed using the following link: *www.fsahandbook.info/FSA/html/ handbook/LR.*

[2]   The AIM rules can be accessed using the following link: *www.londonstockexchange.com/NR/ rdonlyres/91B19E7D-550C-440A-BCCA-52A32F1913DB/O/AIMRULESFORCOMPANIES_ 2007.pdf;* and the PLUS rules can be accessed using the following link: *www.plusmarkets group.com/PLUS_rules.shtml.*

Transactions with directors

2.1 Introduction

2.1.1 Scope of the chapter

This chapter discusses the significant changes introduced by the Companies Act 2006 to the regime that must be complied with when a company is proposing to enter into a transaction with one or more of its directors.

Transactions between a company and its directors have always been highly regulated. The purpose of such regulation is to reduce the ability of directors to commit a company to arrangements or transactions that personally benefit the directors (such as payments for loss of office) to the detriment of the company's shareholders and/or creditors. The Companies Act 2006 is, in some respects, deregulatory in relation to transactions with directors, particularly for private companies. However, in some cases there has been an increase in the types of transactions with directors that will require shareholder approval. Importantly, the provisions of the Companies Act 2006 that regulate transactions with directors also apply to transactions with directors of a holding company and with persons who are 'connected' with a director. The definition of who is 'connected' for this purpose has been expanded.

A failure to comply with the rules relating to transactions with directors attracts substantial penalties. For example, in the event that a company enters into a transaction with a director without following the proper approval process, or without properly managing any conflict of interest, the director concerned can be liable to account to the company for any gain made as a result of the transaction. The transaction is also likely to be a breach of a director's duty and the director who is a party to the transaction, together with the directors who approved the transaction, will be obliged to account to the company for any loss suffered by the company or gain made by the director. In addition, the transaction may be rescinded by the company, which would result in the reversal of the transaction and the parties being put in the position in which they would have been had the transaction never taken place.

In practice, the rules relating to transactions with directors can be complicated to apply, such as those relating to credit transactions and quasi-loans, with the result that the possibility of an inadvertent breach of these provisions is high.

2.1.2 What is the background to the changes?

Corporate governance has increasingly become a matter for government scrutiny and legislative control. The principles that directors should have the ability to exercise independent judgment, not abuse their office to obtain a personal benefit and avoid conflicts of interest (save where a conflict is expressly permitted) are fundamental to effective corporate governance and this is reflected in the Companies Act 2006. Nevertheless, in certain respects changes have been made in this area that are deregulatory which remove unnecessary restrictions and provide more flexibility.

2.1.3 Is shareholder approval required where the director concerned is a majority shareholder?

Yes. In general terms the Companies Act 2006 requires a company to obtain shareholder approval for a transaction with a director and there is no general exemption to this requirement even where the director concerned is a major shareholder (and may properly vote his own shares in favour of the transaction in which he is interested).

Notwithstanding the above, it may well be that the common law principle of unanimous consent will apply to some of these transactions (for example, the approval of substantial property transactions). Under this principle, if all of the shareholders have, in practice, consented to a particular transaction, then a court will treat this as satisfying a requirement under the Companies Act 2006 to obtain formal shareholder approval, but this is not certain in every case and will not apply where provisions of the Companies Act 2006 are designed for the protection of creditors.

2.1.4 In what commercial situations can a breach of the rules relating to transactions with directors be identified and who can bring an action?

A breach of the rules relating to transactions with directors is typically identified in the following situations:

(i) during the due diligence process on the sale of the company or where a company is being prepared for sale;

(ii) during the course of the audit;

(iii) where a company is sold and subsequent shareholders bring a derivative claim[3] against the previous directors;

(iv) where there is a change in the board (with or without a change in ownership of the company itself) subsequent directors could take action to enforce the company's rights against former directors;

(v) if the company goes into liquidation, the liquidator is under an obligation to recover as many assets of the company as possible and this may include unwinding a transaction with a director that is voidable as a result of a breach of the rules relating to transactions with directors; and

---

[3] See chapter 1.

(vi)   minority shareholders might challenge the transaction as constituting conduct which is unfairly prejudicial to their interests[4] and these rights can apply whether or not the transaction has been approved by the majority shareholders.

2.1.5   What are the key changes to transactions with directors under the Companies Act 2006?

The Companies Act 2006 has introduced a number of important changes to transactions with directors. In summary, the key changes are:

(i)   the abolition of the prohibition on making tax-free payments to directors, which came into force on 6 April 2007;

(ii)   the repeal of the requirement for directors to disclose their interests in shares of the company (directors of listed companies are still required to disclose such an interest but the provisions are now contained in the Disclosure and Transparency Rules), which came into force on 6 April 2007;

(iii)   a requirement for shareholder approval for directors' service contracts having a guaranteed term of more than two years (prior to that date, approval was only required for contracts of more than five years), which came into force on 1 October 2007;

(iv)   changes to the rules that apply to substantial property transactions, which came into force on 1 October 2007;

(v)   the repeal of the prohibition on making loans to, and entering into other forms of credit transactions with, directors (instead these will be permitted with shareholder approval), which came into force on 1 October 2007;

(vi)   the repeal of criminal penalties for making loans to, and entering into other forms of credit transactions with, directors, which came into force on 1 October 2007;

(vii)   the expansion of the definition of persons who are 'connected' with a director thereby broadening the range of transactions that will require shareholder approval, which came into force on 1 October 2007; and

(viii)   changes to the requirement for shareholder approval for the payment of compensation to directors for loss of office (which now includes payments relating to a director's loss of employment in connection with the management of the company), which came into force on 1 October 2007.

---

[4]   See chapter 4 for a discussion on the rights of minority shareholders.

A new regime regulating directors' conflicts of interest (which is a fundamental consideration when looking at transactions with directors) is also effective from 1 October 2008 (and this is discussed in more detail in chapter 1).

2.2 Directors' service contracts and letters of appointment

The Companies Act 2006 requires companies to obtain shareholder approval for long-term service contracts with directors.

The key change introduced by the Companies Act 2006 is the requirement for all service contracts with a guaranteed term of more than two years to be approved by shareholders (previously the guaranteed term had to be for more than five years).

If shareholder approval is not obtained then the company will be able to terminate the contract on reasonable notice.

2.2.1 When did changes introduced by the Companies Act 2006 come into force?

Sections 188 and 227 to 230 of the Companies Act 2006 relating to directors' service contracts came into force on 1 October 2007.

2.2.2 What service contracts are caught by the new provisions of the Companies Act 2006?

The Companies Act 2006 applies to service contracts (entered into by both public and private companies with both statutory and shadow directors) under which:

(i)   a director undertakes personally to perform any services (whether as a director or otherwise) for the company or a subsidiary; or

(ii)   the services that a director of the company undertakes personally to perform are made available by a third party to the company or a subsidiary (e.g. an agreement for services with a director's service company).

The Companies Act 2006 also expands the requirement for shareholder approval to letters of appointment and to services provided by a director as an independent contractor[5]. The requirement for shareholder approval is not therefore limited to contracts of employment (non-executive directors, for example, are not typically employees of the company). References in this section to a 'service contract' also apply to these types of agreement.

---

[5]   Section 227, Companies Act 2006.

2.2.3 How do directors' duties apply when considering a director's service contract?

The directors approving a service contract (whether or not the service contract also requires shareholder approval) must comply with their duty to promote the success of the company when doing so (see chapter 1). This means that the directors must believe, in good faith, that the appointment being made pursuant to the service contract, together with the terms of that appointment will promote the success of the company.

2.2.4 When does a director's service contract require approval?

A director's service contract must be approved by the shareholders of the company (by passing an ordinary resolution) when the service contract has a guaranteed term of two years or more. Such approval must be given before the service contract is entered into.

Shareholder approval is also required for a shadow director's service contract that has a guaranteed term of two years or more.

2.2.5 How is the 'guaranteed term' calculated?

The 'guaranteed term' of a director's employment (which includes a term during which a director acts as a consultant) is:

(i)   the period (if any) during which the director's employment is to continue, or may be continued, otherwise than at the instance of the company and that cannot be terminated by the company by notice (or can be terminated by the company giving notice but only in specified circumstances)[6]; and

(ii) where the director's service contract is terminable by notice, the notice period that is required to be given.

If a service contract contains provisions that fall in both paragraphs (i) and (ii) above (for example, where a contract has a fixed term of two years and thereafter it is only terminable on six months' notice) then the guaranteed term of the agreement is the aggregate of these two periods (in the previous example the guaranteed term would therefore be two and a half years).

2.2.6 Can the requirement for shareholder approval be circumvented by entering into successive contracts with terms of less than two years?

No. A company cannot circumvent the requirement to obtain shareholder approval for directors' service contracts by entering into successive contracts that have a guaranteed period of less than two years. If the company enters

---

[6]   Section 188(3), Companies Act 2006.

into an additional contract with a director more than six months before the end of the guaranteed term of that director's existing service contract, then the guaranteed term of any subsequent contract is added on to the term of the preceding contract. A service contract will therefore require shareholder approval if, in aggregate, its term exceeds two years.

2.2.7 Which shareholders need to approve a director's service contract?

Where a company enters into a long-term service contract with one of its own directors then, save where an exception applies (see section 2.2.8), the shareholders of that company must provide informed consent to that service contract (see section 2.2.9).

Where a company enters into a long-term service contract with a director of its holding company, or if the guaranteed employment of a director of a group's holding company exceeds two years, then the shareholders of the holding company must also provide their informed consent to the agreement.

2.2.8 Are there any exemptions to the requirement for shareholder approval of a director's service contract?

Yes. Shareholder consent is not required by shareholders of a company that is not a UK registered company or is a wholly owned subsidiary of another body corporate[7].

2.2.9 What procedure needs to be followed when obtaining shareholders' approval of a director's long-term service contract?

Informed shareholder consent is required. This means that a shareholders' resolution approving the terms of a director's service contract will not be valid unless a memorandum setting out the terms of the proposed contract is first circulated to the shareholders of the company.

In the case of a resolution passed at a general meeting of the shareholders the memorandum must be circulated at least 15 days before the general meeting and must also be available for inspection at the meeting. In the case of a written resolution, the memorandum must be circulated no later than the time that the written resolution is sent to shareholders for approval. This concept of 'informed' shareholder consent also applies to other transactions with directors which require shareholder approval (see section 2.4 relating to loans, security, quasi-loans and credit transactions).

Where approval is being given by written resolution an accidental failure to send the memorandum to one or more shareholders will be disregarded when determining whether the requirement to send the memorandum has been met.

---

[7] Section 188(6), Companies Act 2006.

2.2.10   Is shareholder consent required for service contracts with a fixed term of two years or more that were entered into before 1 October 2007?

No. If a service contract with a guaranteed term of more than two years was entered into before 1 October 2007 it will not need shareholder approval under the Companies Act 2006 (such contracts only required consent under the Companies Act 1985 if they had a guaranteed term of five years or more). However, any renewal of such contracts after 1 October 2007 will require shareholder approval if the renewal carries a guaranteed term of two years or more.

2.2.11   What are the consequences of failing to obtain shareholder approval to a director's long-term service contract?

If a director's service contract is not properly approved by shareholders then the provision of the service contract that guarantees the term of the appointment (and not the contract itself) will be void. In substitution for the void term, the contract is deemed to include a provision that the company can terminate the agreement on giving reasonable notice to the director[8]. This means that the director may not be protected by adequate notice periods in his service contract.

2.2.12   Do shareholders have a right to inspect directors' service contracts?

Yes. A copy of every director's service contract with the company (or a subsidiary) and any variation thereto must be made available for inspection at the company's registered office or any other such place that the Secretary of State may provide in regulations (which have yet to be passed at the date of writing). The Registrar of Companies must be notified of the place of inspection, if the copy is not kept at the registered office, and of any subsequent changes to such place of inspection.

If a director's service contract is not in writing then a written memorandum setting out the terms of the contract must be made available for inspection. In a new requirement, a copy of the service contract (or memorandum of terms) must be kept by the company for at least one year from the date of termination or expiry of the contract concerned and must remain available for inspection during this one year period but copies do not have to be retained thereafter.

2.2.13   Does the Companies Act 2006 change the requirements relating to the inspection of directors' service contracts?

Yes. The Companies Act 1985 only required those service agreements with an unexpired term of 12 months or more, or that could not be terminated by the company within 12 months without paying compensation to the director, to be made available for inspection. Under the Companies Act 2006, companies

---

[8]   Section 189, Companies Act 2006.

must ensure that all directors' service contracts are available for inspection at the company's registered office regardless of the unexpired term of such contracts. These contracts must remain available for inspection for a period of 12 months from the date of termination or expiry of the contract concerned[9].

In addition, the exemption for contracts requiring a director to work outside the UK has also been removed. Breach of the inspection requirements is no longer a criminal offence.

2.2.14 Can a company charge a shareholder for inspecting a director's service contract?

No. Shareholders cannot be charged for inspecting directors' service contracts[10] although a charge may be levied for providing a copy (see section 2.2.16).

2.2.15 Can a company refuse to allow a shareholder to inspect a director's service contract?

No. Failure to allow a shareholder access to a director's service contract will render the company and every officer in default liable to a fine.

2.2.16 Are shareholders entitled to a copy of a director's service contract?

Yes[11]. In a new requirement a company must provide a shareholder with a copy of a director's service contract within seven days of a request for a copy being made. A company may charge such fee as may be prescribed from time to time for providing a copy of a director's service contract to a shareholder.

2.2.17 Does a company need to make shadow directors' service contracts available for inspection?

Yes. A company is required to make available for inspection any service contract, or memorandum of the terms of appointment, of a shadow director[12]. There is the exception to this requirement where a company is unaware that a person is a shadow director[13].

2.2.18 How do the conflicts of interest rules introduced on 1 October 2008 apply to service contracts?

Full details of these rules are contained in chapter 1. In broad terms the duty to avoid a conflict of interests[14] will not apply when the board is considering a

9 Section 228(3), Companies Act 2006.
10 Section 229, Companies Act 2006.
11 Section 229, Companies Act 2006.
12 Section 230, Companies Act 2006.
13 For further information on the duties and liabilities of shadow directors see chapter 1.
14 Section 175, Companies Act 2006.

director's service contract. More specifically, from 1 October 2008 a director is not required to disclose his interest in his service contract (proposed or existing) when such a contract is being considered by the board, provided the service contract is considered at a meeting of the directors or at a committee appointed for the purpose. Before 1 October 2008 a director is under an obligation to disclose such an interest.

Notwithstanding the strict statutory position, a director must nevertheless comply with any procedures or requirements set out in the company's articles of association relating to conflicts.

Regardless of the above, as a matter of best practice (and to avoid the perception of a conflict) a director may wish to abstain from discussions that relate to his service agreement.

2.2.19   What are the rules relating to a service contract with a sole member who is also a director?

The rules relating to the directors' service contracts (see sections 2.2.1 to 2.2.18) also apply to service contracts with a director who is the sole shareholder of the company.

2.2.20   What are the rules relating to contracts (other than service contracts) with a sole member who is also a director?

Where a limited company has only one member who is also a director of the company, and the company enters into a contract with that director (where such contract is not in the ordinary course of business for the company) the terms of that contract (if the contract is not in writing) must be set out in a written memorandum or recorded in the minutes of the first meeting of the directors following the making of the contract.

2.3   Substantial property transactions

The Companies Act 2006 retains the general requirement that a company entering into a 'substantial property transaction' with one of its directors must obtain shareholder approval to the transaction.

2.3.1   What changes have been introduced by the Companies Act 2006?

The Companies Act 2006 changes the previous regime in respect of substantial property transactions by:

(i)   extending the definition of 'connected person';

(ii) increasing the financial thresholds for determining whether a transaction is a substantial property transaction;

(iii) providing for the aggregation of a series of transactions for the purpose of determining whether the relevant thresholds have been reached;

(iv) enabling a company to enter into a substantial property transaction that is conditional upon shareholder approval;

(v) excluding payments under directors' service contracts and payments for loss of office from the substantial property transaction requirements;

(vi) expanding the exemption for transactions with members to include the acquisition of assets from a person in his character as a member of the company; and

(viii) providing an exemption for companies in administration or being wound up (unless it is a members' voluntary winding-up).

These changes are set out in sections 190 to 196 of the Companies Act 2006 and are effective from 1 October 2007.

2.3.2   What is a substantial property transaction?

A substantial property transaction is an arrangement whereby[15]:

(i) a director of the company or of its holding company acquires or is to acquire from the company (directly or indirectly) a substantial non-cash asset; or

(ii) the company acquires or is to acquire a substantial non-cash asset (directly or indirectly) from such a director.

The provisions of the Companies Act 2006 relating to substantial property transactions catch 'arrangements' with directors. This is therefore a broad obligation that is not simply limited to contracts between the company and a director.

Approval is required not only for transactions with a director but also a person 'connected' with him, such as family members and related business interests. The precise meaning of 'connected' is discussed further in section 2.3.9.

The Companies Act 2006 governs substantial property transactions entered into by a UK registered company; it is immaterial whether the transaction or arrangement is governed by UK law or that of another jurisdiction.

A 'substantial' non-cash asset for the purposes of the Companies Act 2006 is an asset with a value that exceeds 10% of the company's asset value and is more than £5,000 (compare this to the £2,000 *de minimis* threshold under the Companies Act 1985) or which exceeds £100,000 (these amounts may be

---

[15]   Section 190, Companies Act 2006.

increased by the Secretary of State from time to time although any such increase will not have retrospective effect). The company's asset value is the value of the company's net assets determined by reference to the company's most recent statutory accounts or, if no statutory accounts have been prepared, the amount of the company's called up share capital. Whether or not an asset is 'substantial' is determined at the time that the transaction is entered into[16].

A 'non-cash asset' is any property or interest in property other than cash[17] (which includes foreign currency). The acquisition of a non-cash asset includes:

(i)   the creation or execution of an estate or interest in, or a right over, any property; and

(ii)   the discharge of a liability of any person, other than a liability for a liquidated sum.

Examples of substantial property transactions

The following transactions are examples of the types of arrangements that may be caught by the provisions of the Companies Act 2006 relating to substantial property transactions (provided they meet the financial thresholds set out in the Companies Act 2006):

(i)   the sale of a business to a director;

(ii)   the licence of intellectual property by a director to the company;

(iii)   the interposing of a new holding company ('H') between shareholders and an existing company ('E') by way of share for share exchange where the directors of H are also shareholders of E; and

(iv)   the sale of new office premises by a director to the company.

2.3.3   What approval is required for a substantial property transaction?

A substantial property transaction must be approved by the shareholders of the company passing an ordinary resolution (or an ordinary written resolution).

In a change to the regime under the Companies Act 1985 (which required prior shareholder approval before the 'arrangement' was entered into), the Companies Act 2006 allows a company to enter into a substantial property transaction that is conditional upon shareholders granting such consent.

Where a subsidiary enters into a substantial property transaction with a director of its parent (or person connected with such a director), then the

---

[16] Section 191, Companies Act 2006.
[17] Section 1163, Companies Act 2006.

transaction must also be approved by an ordinary resolution of the members of the parent.

Shareholder approval is not required from the shareholders of a company that is not a UK registered company or is a wholly-owned subsidiary of another company[18].

2.3.4 Can a director's service contract or a payment for loss of office constitute a substantial property transaction?

No. The Companies Act 2006 provides that the rules relating to substantial property transactions do not apply to anything that relates to an entitlement of a director under the director's service contract (the rules relating to which are discussed in more detail in section 2.2) or to a payment for loss of office (the rules relating to which are discussed in more detail in section 2.6)[19].

2.3.5 How do the rules relating to substantial property transactions apply to a series of transactions?

The Companies Act 2006 has specific provisions that apply where a company enters into a series of transactions which are individually below the *de minimis* thresholds for substantial property transactions but, which taken in aggregate, exceed these financial thresholds.

Under the Companies Act 2006, if a company enters into an arrangement that involves more than one non-cash asset, or is part of a series of arrangements involving non-cash assets, then these arrangements shall be aggregated under the Companies Act 2006 and treated as if they are a single arrangement[20]. What constitutes a series of arrangements will be a matter of fact to be determined in any given situation and which will have to be determined by case law.

In practical terms, if a company is proposing to enter into a substantial property transaction which is below the threshold set out in the Companies Act 2006 then it will also need to consider whether there are any other transactions that should be aggregated with it to determine whether shareholder approval is necessary.

---

[18] Section 190(4), Companies Act 2006.
[19] Section 190(6), Companies Act 2006.
[20] Section 190(5), Companies Act 2006.

> **Example of a series of aggregated transactions for the purpose of the rules relating to substantial property transactions:**
>
> A director sells 10 cars (for £20,000 per car) to the company. Each sale is completed by a separate agreement but each agreement is conditional upon the other. Although each individual transaction fails to meet the financial thresholds for the purpose of the substantial property transactions provisions the 10 sale agreements will be aggregated under the Companies Act 2006 (as they are conditional upon each other and therefore are likely to form a 'series' of transactions). Once taken in aggregate the agreements will exceed the financial thresholds set out in the substantial property transactions regime and will therefore require shareholder approval.

2.3.6   Are there any exceptions to the requirement to obtain shareholder approval for a substantial property transaction?

Yes. Shareholder approval is not required:

(i)   where the transaction is made between a holding company and its wholly owned subsidiary or two wholly owned subsidiaries of the same holding company[21];

(ii)   where the person entering into the transaction is a shareholder of the company and the transaction is being entered into in that person's capacity as a shareholder[22] (as opposed to his capacity as a director), e.g. a distribution *in specie* to a director who is also a shareholder;

(iii)   where the company is being wound up (unless the winding up is a members' voluntary winding up) or the company is in administration[23]; or

(iv)   for a transaction entered into by a director on a recognised investment exchange where the transaction is effected through the agency of a person who acts as an independent broker, e.g. the acquisition of shares in a listed subsidiary of the company (where those shares are listed on a recognised investment exchange such as the main market of the London Stock Exchange) from the company by an independent broker appointed by the trustees of a discretionary trust the beneficiaries of which include the director and his family provided the broker has complete discretion as to the shares that are to be acquired and from whom[24].

---

[21]   Section 192(b), Companies Act 2006.
[22]   Section 192(a), Companies Act 2006.
[23]   Section 193, Companies Act 2006.
[24]   Section 194, Companies Act 2006.

2.3.7 To whom do the rules on substantial property transactions apply?

The rules apply to a transaction entered into by a company with a *de jure* director, a shadow director, and an alternate director (see chapter 1 for a definition of these terms) or any person connected with them (see section 2.3.9).

The rules relating to substantial property transactions also apply to transactions with people who are 'connected' with directors of the company.

2.3.8 What changes have been made to the definition of a 'connected person' for the purposes of substantial property transactions?

The definition of a connected person for the purposes of the Companies Act 2006 has been extended to also apply to:

(i)   the director's parents;

(ii)   the director's children who are over the age of 18;

(iii)   people with whom the director lives as a partner in an enduring family relationship; and

(iv)   children or step-children of a person with whom the director lives in an enduring family relationship and are under the age of 18.

This means that when companies are assessing whether they need to obtain shareholder approval they will have to identify a broader range of connected persons than was formerly the case.

2.3.9 With whom is a director 'connected'?

The complete list of people that are considered to be 'connected persons' for the purpose of a substantial property transaction is[25]:

(i)   a member of the director's family (see 2.3.10 below);

(ii)   a body corporate with which the director is connected (see 2.3.11 below);

(iii)   a person acting in his capacity as a trustee of a trust (including discretionary trusts) the beneficiaries of which include the director, a member of the director's family or a body corporate with which the director is connected (trustees of employee share schemes or pension schemes are not connected persons);

(iv)   a person acting in his capacity as partner of the director or anyone connected with the director; and

(v)   a firm that is a legal person and in which: (a) the director is a partner; (b) a partner of which is a person who is connected with the director; or (c) a

---

[25] Section 252, Companies Act 2006

partner of which is a firm in which the director is a partner or in which there is a partner who is connected with the director.

2.3.10   Which members of a director's family are 'connected' with him?

The members of a director's family who are 'connected' with him are:

(i)   the director's spouse or civil partner;

(ii)   any other person (whether of a different sex or the same sex) with whom the director lives as a partner in an enduring family relationship save that this definition does not include the director's grandparent, grandchild, sister, brother, aunt, uncle, nephew or niece;

(iii)   the director's children or step-children of any age;

(iv)   any children or step-children of a person within paragraph (ii) above who live with the director and are under 18; and

(v)   the director's parents.

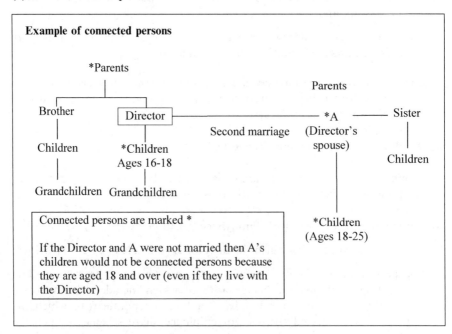

Example of connected persons

Connected persons are marked *

If the Director and A were not married then A's children would not be connected persons because they are aged 18 and over (even if they live with the Director)

2.3.11   Which companies are 'connected' with a director?

A director is connected with a body corporate if he and the persons connected with him together[26]:

---

[26]   Section 254, Companies Act 2006.

(i) are interested in shares representing at least 20% of the nominal value in the equity share capital of that body corporate; or

(ii) are entitled to exercise or control the exercise of more than 20% of the voting power at any general meeting of that body.

The ability to control voting power includes voting power that is controlled by a body corporate that is controlled by the director concerned[27]. The expression 'interested in shares' is also defined by extensive provisions in schedule 1 of the Companies Act 2006.

A 'body corporate' includes non-UK registered companies.

2.3.12 What are the consequences of breaching the rules relating to substantial property transactions?

There are two potential consequences[28]:

(i) rescission: the company can rescind the contract and require the return of any asset that is the subject of the transaction; and

(ii) personal liability of the directors approving the transaction and of the director (and persons who are connected with him) entering into the transaction,

both of which are discussed in more detail below.

2.3.13 When can a substantial property transaction be rescinded by the company?

The arrangement that constitutes the unlawful substantial property transaction can be rescinded by the company unless[29]:

(i) any money or other asset that is the subject of the transaction cannot be returned or the company has been indemnified for the loss or damage it has suffered;

(ii) any rights acquired *bona fide* for value without actual notice of the contravention of the rules (i.e. by an innocent third party who has paid consideration for the asset) and who is not a party to the arrangement would be affected by the company voiding the arrangement; or

(iii) the arrangement is, within a reasonable period, affirmed by the shareholders of the company passing an ordinary resolution to this effect (no guidance is given on what a 'reasonable period' is)[30].

---

[27] Section 254(4), Companies Act 2006.
[28] Section 195, Companies Act 2006.
[29] Section 195(2), Companies Act 2006.
[30] Section 196, Companies Act 2006.

2.3.14 Who can be held personally liable?

In the event of a breach of the rules relating to substantial property transactions the following people may be found personally liable whether or not the transaction is rescinded:

(i)   any director of the company (or of its holding company) who entered into the arrangement;

(ii)   any person who entered into the arrangement and who is connected with a director of the company or of its holding company (unless he can show that at the time the arrangement was entered into he did not know the relevant circumstances constituting the contravention);

(iii)   the director of the company (or of its holding company) with whom any such person is connected; and

(iv)   any other director of the company who authorised the arrangement or any transaction entered into in pursuance of such an arrangement (unless he can show that at the time the arrangement was entered into he did not know the relevant circumstances constituting the contravention).

Example of who incurs personal liability in the event of a breach

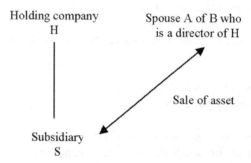

Holding company
H

Spouse A of B who
is a director of H

Sale of asset

Subsidiary
S

A transaction was entered into by S with A in breach of the Companies Act 2006. The individuals who potentially incur personal liability are:

(i)   The spouse (A) unless A can show that she did not know of the relevant circumstances that constituted the breach.

(ii) The director (B) unless he can show that he took all reasonable steps to secure S's compliance with the relevant requirements.

(iii) The directors of S who authorised the transaction unless they can show that they did not know of the relevant circumstances constituting the breach.

Each of the above will be liable to account to the company for any gain that he has made directly or indirectly by the arrangement and will be jointly and severally liable with any others who are liable to indemnify the company for any loss or damage suffered. This individual liability arises regardless of whether the transaction has been avoided by the company[31].

Example of personal liability arising from a breach of the substantial property transaction rules

Company X sells a property to the spouse (A) of one of the directors (B) of X at market value without obtaining shareholder approval. The property is sold by A at a profit two years later to an independent third party (C).

Consequences:

The transaction cannot be rescinded by the company because a third party has since acquired the property for value and had no knowledge of the breach of the Companies Act 2006.

However, as A is 'connected' to one of the directors of company X, A is liable to account to the company for the gain made on the sale to C even though A originally paid market value for the property to X.

B, and any director of company X who authorised the transaction, are also jointly and severally liable to indemnify company X for any loss suffered (in this case for the lost profits arising on the sale of the property).

2.3.15 Can a company affirm a contract that was entered into in breach of the rules relating to substantial property transactions?

Yes. Where a transaction is entered into in breach of the provisions of the Companies Act 2006 the transaction can be affirmed by the shareholders of the company passing an ordinary resolution within a 'reasonable period'. The Companies Act 2006 does not detail what constitutes a 'reasonable period' for this purpose and we will need to wait for case law to develop for guidance on this question.

If the transaction is affirmed by shareholders then it can no longer be avoided by the company[32]. However, notwithstanding the affirmation of the transaction, the directors that have acted in breach of the substantial property transaction provisions will remain liable to account to the company for any profit made or to indemnify the company for any loss suffered as a result of the transaction.

---

[31] Section 195(3), Companies Act 2006.
[32] Section 196, Companies Act 2006.

2.4 Loans and other credit transactions with directors

Under the Companies Act 1985 a company was prohibited from making loans to its directors or from providing security for a loan to a director. For public companies the prohibition also applied to a wide range of other credit transactions and a breach of these provisions was a criminal offence.

With effect from 1 October 2007, the Companies Act 2006 repealed the absolute prohibition on companies entering into loans, providing security or entering into credit transactions with directors. Instead, such transactions are permitted provided that informed shareholder consent is obtained.

The articles of association of a company should still be reviewed to identify any relevant restrictions to such transactions as these are not overridden by the Companies Act 2006. Listed companies will also need to comply with the provisions of the Listing Rules (transactions with related parties) whilst those companies admitted to trade on AIM or PLUS markets will need to comply with the AIM and PLUS rules respectively.

2.4.1 What changes have been introduced by the Companies Act 2006?

The key changes introduced by the Companies Act 2006 are:

(i)   a company can now make a loan and enter into other types of credit transactions with a director, provided that informed shareholder consent is given;

(ii)   an unapproved loan or credit transaction may be affirmed by shareholders within a 'reasonable' time after it has been entered into;

(iii)   certain exemptions to the rules relating to loans and credit transactions have been amended and a new exemption introduced relating to expenditure on regulatory actions or investigations; and

(iv)   the criminal sanctions that previously applied to public companies have been repealed.

These changes are set out in sections 197 to 214 of the Companies Act 2006, which came into force on 1 October 2007.

For public companies (and private companies that are part of a group which comprises a public company) the rules will continue to apply to transactions with persons 'connected' with a director (depending on the type of company concerned) but the definition of 'connected person' has been widened. This has been discussed in section 2.3.9 above in relation to substantial property transactions but the provisions apply equally here.

2.4.2 What types of transactions require shareholder approval?

There are five main types of transactions with directors (which includes shadow directors) which require shareholder approval:

(i)   loans;

(ii)   the provision of security for a loan made to a director;

(iii)   quasi-loans (discussed further in section 2.4.3);

(iv)   credit transactions (discussed further in section 2.4.4) and related guarantees; and

(v)   the provision of security in respect of (iii) and (iv).

A private company requires shareholder approval only for transactions that fall within paragraphs (i) and (ii) above.

A public company, or a private company which forms part of a group which includes a public company, requires shareholder approval for all of the transactions in (i) to (v) above. In addition, approval will be required if the transaction is with a director of a company's parent rather than the company itself and with a person who is 'connected' with the director.

2.4.3 What is a quasi-loan?

A quasi-loan is a transaction by which "one party (the creditor) agrees to pay, or pays otherwise than in pursuance of an agreement, a sum for another party (the borrower) or agrees to reimburse, or reimburses otherwise than in pursuance of an agreement, expenditure incurred by another party for the borrower on terms that the borrower (or a person on his behalf) will reimburse the creditor or in circumstances giving rise to a liability on the borrower to reimburse the creditor[33]".

By way of example, a quasi-loan will arise where a company agrees to discharge a debt that a director has incurred with a third party on the basis that the director will reimburse the company for the payment so made.

2.4.4 What is a credit transaction?

A credit transaction is a transaction whereby one party (the creditor) supplies any goods or sells any land under a hire-purchase agreement or a conditional sale agreement, or leases or hires any land or goods in return for periodical payments, or otherwise disposes of land or supplies goods or services on the understanding that payment is to be deferred[34]. The person for whose benefit a credit transaction is entered into is the person to whom the goods, land or

---

[33]   Section 199, Companies Act 2006.
[34]   Section 202, Companies Act 2006.

services are supplied, sold, leased, hired or otherwise disposed of (as the case may be) under the transaction.

The definition of credit transaction is drafted extremely widely and has the potential to include a considerable number of transactions. In particular 'services' is defined to mean anything other than goods or land.

Examples of loans, security, quasi-loans and credit transactions with directors

There follows examples of transactions that could constitute a loan, security, quasi-loan or credit transaction.

Loans and the provision of security for loans:

The company makes a loan (i.e. advances money on the understanding that such payment will be repaid) to one of its directors instead of paying a dividend. It is intended that repayment of the loan will be waived in due course.

A company guarantees repayment of a loan made by a third party to a director.

Quasi-loans:

The company makes a payment of tax to HMRC on behalf of a director on the basis that the director will, over time, repay the tax paid by the company e.g. where the company pays a tax charge that becomes due in respect of the director's share options where the director's monthly salary is insufficient to cover the tax payable.

A company provides a director with a season ticket (on the basis that the director will repay the cost of the season ticket to the company).

A company pays the director's rent under a tenancy agreement on the basis that the director will repay the company.

Credit transactions:

A company leases a property to the director and the director pays rent to the company on a quarterly basis.

A company issues shares fully paid to a director against his undertaking to pay for them at a future date.

A company sells goods or land to a director on deferred payment terms.

2.4.5 What is the procedure for obtaining shareholder approval for a loan or other credit transaction?

The Companies Act 2006 enables a company to enter into certain transactions with directors provided the company has first obtained 'informed shareholder consent'.

In essence, to obtain informed shareholder consent, the company must comply with the following requirements:

(i)   prepare a memorandum to shareholders setting out:

- the nature of the transaction;

- the amount of the loan, security, quasi-loan or credit transaction (as the case may be) and the purpose for which it is required; and

- the extent of the company's liability under any transaction connected with the loan, security, quasi-loan or credit transaction;

(ii)   in the case of a written resolution, the memorandum must be sent or submitted with (or before) the resolution to every shareholder that is eligible to vote on the resolution. In the case of a resolution to be passed at a general meeting the memorandum must be made available for inspection by shareholders both at the company's registered office for not less than 15 days before the meeting and also at the meeting itself. It does not appear to be possible to shorten this period even where the meeting itself is to be held on short notice; and

(iii) where approval is being given by written resolution an accidental failure to send the memorandum to one or more members shall be disregarded for determining whether the requirement to send a memorandum has been met.

2.4.6 Which shareholders are required to approve the transaction?

The shareholders of the company that is entering into the transaction are required to approve the transaction. Where the transaction is to be made with a director of the holding company the approval of shareholders of the holding company is also required. Shareholder approval is not, however, required for a loan to a director where the company is not a UK-registered company or where it is a wholly-owned subsidiary of another company.

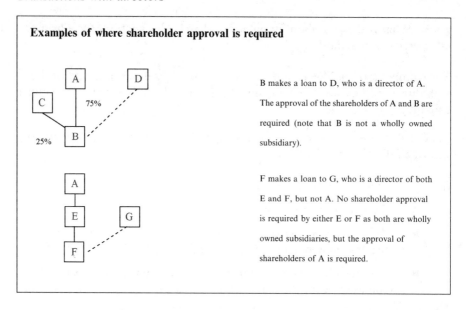

Examples of where shareholder approval is required

B makes a loan to D, who is a director of A. The approval of the shareholders of A and B are required (note that B is not a wholly owned subsidiary).

F makes a loan to G, who is a director of both E and F, but not A. No shareholder approval is required by either E or F as both are wholly owned subsidiaries, but the approval of shareholders of A is required.

2.4.7   Can a company avoid the requirement to obtain shareholder approval by arranging for a third party to make the loan?

No. The Companies Act 2006 prohibits a company from 'taking part' in an arrangement pursuant to which a third party enters into a transaction, which if it had been entered into by the company would have required approval under the provisions of the Companies Act 2006 and[35] where that third party in pursuance of the arrangement obtains a benefit from the company or a body corporate associated with it.

The Companies Act 2006 also prohibits a company from arranging for the assignment to it, or assumption by it, of any rights, obligations or liabilities under a transaction that if it had been entered into by the company would otherwise have required shareholder approval.

However, in both cases a company may enter into such a transaction with shareholder consent. If the party to the transaction is a director of the company's holding company (or a person connected with such a director) then the transaction must be approved by a resolution of the members of the holding company.

---

[35]   Section 203, Companies Act 2006.

Example of the operation of the anti-avoidance provisions:

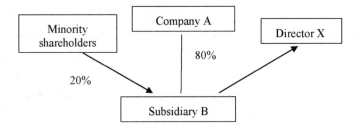

Facts:

A subsidiary 'B' proposes to make a loan to its director 'X'. It arranges for the parent, company 'A', to make the loan and agrees to guarantee repayment of the loan. X is not a director of A and there are no public companies in the group. A receives a benefit because repayment of X's borrowing is guaranteed.

Application of the anti-avoidance provisions:

Under the Companies Act 1985 the loan by subsidiary B to director X would have been prohibited but a loan by company A to director X (when looked at in isolation) permitted. However, as this is part of an arrangement between A and B the making of the loan by A was still prohibited. Under the Companies Act 2006 the loan by subsidiary B, and the entry into the arrangement between A and B are both permitted but only with shareholder approval.

2.4.8 In summary, how do the rules relating to loans, security, quasi-loans and credit transactions differ for public companies and private companies?

The table below sets out a high-level summary of how the rules relating to loans, quasi-loans and credit transactions apply to public and private companies. For this purpose 'public company' includes any private company that is associated with a public company, namely[36] if the private company is a subsidiary of the public company (or vice versa), or if the private company and public company are both subsidiaries of the same body corporate.

---

[36] Section 256, Companies Act 2006.

Transaction	Public company (including a private company associated with a public company)	Private company
Loans and security for such loans.	Permitted with informed shareholder consent. May be affirmed within a 'reasonable period'.	Permitted with informed shareholder consent. May be affirmed within a 'reasonable period'.
Quasi-loans and security for such loans.	Permitted with informed shareholder consent. May be affirmed within a 'reasonable period'.	Permitted – shareholder approval not required.
Credit transactions and security for such transactions.	Permitted with informed shareholder consent. May be affirmed within a 'reasonable period'.	Permitted – shareholder approval not required.
Do the rules apply to transactions with persons who are 'connected' with the director?	Yes.	No.

2.4.9 Are there exceptions to the requirement for shareholder approval for loans, the provision of security, quasi-loans and credit transactions?

Yes. The Companies Act 2006 sets out a number of situations where shareholder approval to such transactions is not required. These exemptions, which are discussed in more detail in sections 2.4.9.1 to 2.4.9.6 below, apply to expenditure incurred as follows:

(i)   on company business;

(ii)   on defending proceedings;

(iii) in connection with regulatory actions or investigations;

(iv)   for minor and business transactions; and

(v)   for intra-group transactions.

There is a further exemption for moneylending companies able to lend money to directors in the ordinary course of business.

2.4.9.1 *Expenditure on company business up to £50,000*[37]

There is an exemption for funds provided to meet expenditure incurred by a director of a company (and persons connected with him):

(i)   for the purposes of the company;

(ii)   for the purpose of enabling the director to properly perform his duties as an officer of the company; or

(iii) to enable such a person to avoid incurring such expenditure.

This exception is subject to an upper limit of £50,000 (this limit has been increased from £20,000 under the Companies Act 1985). In calculating the limit the value of any other relevant transactions or arrangements must also be taken into account. The rules relating to the valuation of such a transaction are set out in section 2.4.10 below[38].

It is no longer a requirement for the loan or any liability incurred by the company to be discharged within six months. The exemption has also been widened to include funds provided by a subsidiary to the directors of a holding company and any connected persons.

2.4.9.2 *Expenditure on defending proceedings*[39]

There is an exemption where a director is provided with funds to meet expenditure incurred (or due to be incurred) in defending any criminal or civil proceedings. The Companies Act 2006 has narrowed this exemption by requiring that these proceedings must be in connection with any alleged negligence, default, breach of duty or breach of trust by a director or in connection with an application for relief from liability. Nevertheless, with the potential increased risks of derivative claims in relation to breaches of duty by directors this provision is of significant benefit for directors. There are, however, certain limitations which provide that:

(i)   the loan is to be repaid, or any liability incurred by the company to be discharged, in the event of:

- the director being convicted in the proceedings;

- judgment being given against the director in proceedings; or

- the court refusing to grant the director relief on the application;

(ii)   the loan is to be repaid or discharged no later than:

- the date when the conviction becomes final;

---

[37] Section 204, Companies Act 2006.
[38] Section 211, Companies Act 2006.
[39] Section 205, Companies Act 2006.

- the date when the judgment becomes final; or

- the date when the refusal of relief becomes final.

A conviction, judgment or refusal of relief becomes final (i) if not appealed against, at the end of the period for bringing an appeal; or (ii) if appealed against, when the appeal (or any further appeal) is disposed of. This is when either the appeal is determined and the period for bringing any further appeal has ended or if the appeal is abandoned or otherwise ceases to have effect.

2.4.9.3 *Expenditure in connection with regulatory actions or investigations*

The Companies Act 2006 has introduced a new exemption enabling a company to fund a director's defence costs in a regulatory investigation or where action is proposed to be taken by a regulator in connection with any alleged negligence, default, breach of duty or breach of trust by the director. This exemption also applies to funding provided to a director of a holding company.

2.4.9.4 *Expenditure for minor and business transactions*

A company may make a loan or quasi-loan (or to give a guarantee or provide security in connection with a loan or quasi-loan) of up to £10,000[40] without obtaining shareholder consent.

A company may enter into a credit transaction (or give a guarantee or provide security in connection with a credit transaction) of up to £15,000[41] without obtaining shareholder consent.

These financial limits were increased by the Companies Act 2006 by £5,000 and it is no longer a requirement that in the case of a quasi-loan the director must have reimbursed his creditor within two months of his expenditure being incurred.

However, in calculating these thresholds other relevant transactions or arrangements are taken into account.

A company can also enter into a credit transaction (or give a guarantee or provide security in connection with a credit transaction) if such transaction is in the ordinary course of the company's business. This exemption only applies if the value of the transaction is not greater, and the terms on which it is entered into are not more favourable, than it is reasonable to expect that the company would have offered to, or in respect of, a person of the same financial standing but unconnected with the company[42].

---

[40] Section 207(1), Companies Act 2006.
[41] Section 207(2), Companies Act 2006.
[42] Section 207(3), Companies Act 2006.

2.4.9.5 *Expenditure for intra-group transactions*

There is a general exemption for intra-group transactions (namely transactions between subsidiaries or between a parent and its subsidiaries), which has been widened by the Companies Act 2006. Subsidiaries do not have to be wholly-owned to qualify for the exemption.

2.4.9.6 *Money-lending companies*

There is a general exemption for money-lending companies, which applies to all of the above transactions other than credit transactions.

A money-lending company is a company whose ordinary business includes the making of loans or quasi-loans, or the giving of guarantees or provision of security in connection with loans or quasi-loans[43].

The transaction must be entered into by the company in the ordinary course of the company's business and the value of the transaction cannot be greater, and its terms cannot be more favourable, than it is reasonable to expect the company would have offered to a person of the same financial standing but unconnected with the company[44].

Home loans (which may often be on preferential terms for employees) may also be made if the company has a home loan scheme for its employees and:

(i) the terms offered to the director are no more favourable than those offered to other staff members;

(ii) the home loans are for the purchase of the only or main residence of the director or to improve a dwelling house or to replace an existing loan which has been taken out for that purpose; and

(iii) such loans are ordinarily made by the company to its employees and the terms of the loan in question are no more favourable than those on which such loans are ordinarily made[45].

The Companies Act 2006 has removed the upper limit of £100,000 on transactions within this exemption.

2.4.10 What is the value of the transaction or arrangement?

The value of a loan, quasi-loan or credit transaction is calculated as follows:

(i) the value of a loan is the value of its principal;

---

[43] Section 209(2), Companies Act 2006.
[44] Section 209(1), Companies Act 2006.
[45] Section 209(3), Companies Act 2006.

(ii)   the value of a quasi-loan is the amount, or maximum amount that the person to whom the quasi-loan is made is liable to reimburse the creditor;

(iii)   the value of a credit transaction is the price that it is reasonable to expect could be obtained for the goods, services or land to which the transaction relates if they had been supplied in the ordinary course of business and on the same terms as the transaction in question;

(iv)   the value of a guarantee or security is the amount guaranteed or secured;

(v)   the value of a related arrangement is the value of the transaction to which the arrangement relates; and

(vi)   if the value of the transaction cannot be expressed as a specific sum of money the value of the transaction is deemed to exceed £50,000.

2.4.11   What are the consequences of breaching the rules relating to loans, security, quasi-loans or credit transactions?

Under the Companies Act 1985 a director who authorised or permitted a public company (or a member of the group which included a public company) to enter into a transaction in breach of the prohibition set out in the Companies Act 1985 faced criminal sanctions, namely a fine, imprisonment or both.

The Companies Act 2006 has abolished the criminal sanctions but the civil remedies that remain are still substantial[46] and are similar in effect to those that apply to substantial property transactions.

2.4.11.1   *When can a loan, security, quasi-loan or credit transaction be rescinded?*

The transaction is voidable at the instance of the company (namely reversible) unless:

(i)   this is no longer possible;

(ii)   the company has been indemnified for any loss or damage resulting from the transaction; or

(iii)   a third party's rights would be affected provided that his rights were acquired in good faith, for value and without actual notice of the contravention.

---

[46]   Section 213, Companies Act 2006.

2.4.11.2   *Personal liability of directors and 'connected persons'*

The director who entered into the transaction, and any director who authorised it, is liable to account to the company for any gain that he has made (directly or indirectly) as a result of the transaction and to jointly and severally indemnify the company for any loss or damage suffered by the company as a result of the transaction. A person who was connected with a director and who enters into a transaction in breach of the requirements is similarly liable.

The implications of this are significant for directors. If, for example, a director has received an unlawful loan from the company and uses it to acquire a property, which he then sells for a significant profit he could be liable to account to the company for the whole of the gain he has made.

2.4.12   Are there any defences against personal liability for a breach of the rules relating to loans, security, quasi-loans and credit transactions?

Yes. A director is not liable if he can demonstrate that he took all reasonable steps to prevent the contravention. In addition, a director will not be liable if he can show that at the time that the transaction was entered into he did not know the relevant circumstances constituting the contravention.

2.4.13   Can shareholders approve a loan, security, quasi-loan or credit transaction that has been entered into by the company without prior shareholder approval?

Yes, unlike the regime under the Companies Act 1985, the Companies Act 2006 enables the shareholders of the company to affirm the transaction within a reasonable period[47]. There is no guidance on what a 'reasonable period' is for this purpose and case law will determine this issue.

If the breach is affirmed by shareholders then the company will no longer be able to avoid the transaction although the personal liability of the directors will remain. A specific waiver and release of that liability will therefore have to be obtained, which may require shareholder approval.

2.5   Tax-free payments to directors

The Companies Act 1985 prohibited a company from making a payment to a director that was "free of income tax or otherwise calculated by reference to or varying with the amount of his income tax, or to or with any rate of income tax"[48]. The prohibition has caused a number of difficulties in the structuring of remuneration packages for directors.

---

[47]   Section 214, Companies Act 2006.
[48]   Section 311, Companies Act 1985.

The rationale behind the prohibition was a concern to ensure that the directors of the company (who controlled the way in which remuneration was presented to shareholders and the wider public) were not able to mislead shareholders and the wider public as to the basis on which directors were remunerated. However, as a company is required to disclose in its annual accounts an estimate of the tax it has undertaken to pay on behalf of a director, it therefore cannot conceal such payments from shareholders or the wider public.

The prohibition was therefore repealed on 6 April 2007.

Examples of payments to directors that are now permitted include:

(i)   tax equalisation provisions for directors working overseas; and

(ii) the discharge of a director's liability for unpaid PAYE.

2.6   Payments for loss of office

The Companies Act 2006 requires companies to obtain shareholder approval for *ex gratia* payments that are made to directors (including shadow directors) for loss of office or employment with the company or its subsidiaries. This requirement extends to payments made by a company to a director of its holding company. Payments made in connection with retirement also require shareholder approval.

2.6.1   What changes have been introduced by the Companies Act 2006?

On 1 October 2006, the Companies Act 2006 made several changes to the regime relating to payments for loss of office that applied under the Companies Act 1985. These are as follows:

(i)   the rules apply not only to payments for loss of office but also to payments made to a director for retirement or loss of any other office or employment in connection with the management of the company;

(ii) payments for loss of office made to people who are connected with a director and to payments to directors of its holding company and their 'connected persons' now also require shareholder approval;

(iii) the requirements for shareholder approval in connection with payments made in respect of the transfer of the undertaking or property of the company is extended to include transfers of the undertaking or property of any subsidiary;

(iv) the requirements in connection with share transfers are extended to include all transfers of shares in a company or a subsidiary resulting from a takeover bid;

(v) the persons making the offer for shares in the company (where relevant) and any associate are excluded from voting on any resolutions to approve a payment for loss of office in connection with a share transfer;

(vi) a new exemption is included where payments are made pursuant to certain legal obligations; and

(vii) a new exemption for small payments is introduced.

The Companies Act 2006 also amends certain provisions relating to the civil consequences of a breach of the rules relating to payments for loss of office.

2.6.2 What is a 'payment for loss of office'?

A payment for loss of office is a payment:

(i) by way of compensation for loss of office as a director;

(ii) by way of compensation for loss (while a director) of any other office or employment in connection with the management of the company or a subsidiary undertaking;

(iii) in connection with the director's retirement from office as a director; and

(iv) in connection with the director's retirement, whilst ceasing to be a director, from any other office in connection with the management of the company or subsidiary undertaking.

Payments in kind and payments to persons 'connected' with a director are also included as payments for loss of office[49].

Where a director is to cease to hold office in connection with a transfer of an undertaking, property or shares and payment is to be made to the director for any shares that he holds in the company in excess of their market value then the excess shall also be treated as compensation for loss of office that will require shareholder approval.

In this context, payment for loss of office also includes a payment for loss of office that is made in connection with the transfer of the whole, or any part, of the undertaking or property of the company[50] or a subsidiary of the company. A payment that is made as part of an agreement for such a transfer is presumed to be a payment for loss of office that requires shareholder approval.

In addition, a payment for loss of office includes a payment for loss of office that is made in connection with a transfer of shares in the company, or any of its subsidiaries, resulting from a takeover bid[51]. The shareholder making the

---

[49] Section 215(3), Companies Act 2006.
[50] Section 218, Companies Act 2006.
[51] Section 219, Companies Act 2006.

offer for the shares is not entitled to vote on the resolution approving the payment for loss of office.

2.6.3 What shareholder approval is required for a payment for loss of office?

Where a company is making a payment for loss of office to one of its directors, it must first obtain the approval of its shareholders (by ordinary resolution). If the payment is to be made to a director of a company's parent then the parent company must also obtain its shareholders' approval.

A company which is a wholly owned subsidiary or not incorporated in the UK is not required to obtain shareholder approval.

A memorandum setting out the particulars of the proposed payment (including its amount) must first be made available to the shareholders of the company whose approval is sought. Where the resolution is to be passed as a written resolution, the memorandum must be sent to the shareholders entitled to vote at or before the time at which the proposed resolution is sent to the shareholders. Where the resolution is to be passed at a meeting of the shareholders of the company the memorandum must be made available for inspection by the shareholders both at the company's registered office for a period of not less than 15 days ending with the date of the meeting and also at the meeting itself.

Where approval is being given by written resolution an accidental failure to send or submit the memorandum to one or more members will be disregarded for the purpose of determining whether the requirement has been met.

2.6.4 Are there exceptions to the requirement for shareholder approval for payments to directors for loss of office?

Yes. In addition to the exemptions for wholly owned subsidiaries and non-UK incorporated entities, a company will not be required to seek shareholder approval where the payment is made in good faith for one of the following reasons[52]:

(i)   in discharge of an existing legal obligation (namely an obligation that was not entered into in connection with, or in consequence of, the event giving rise to the payment for loss of office);

(ii)   by way of damages for beach of an existing legal obligation;

(iii) by way of settlement or compromise of any claim arising in connection with the termination of a director's office or employment; or

(iv)   by way of pension in respect of past services.

[52] Section 220, Companies Act 2006.

It is clear therefore that the exceptions to the requirement for shareholder approval relate to the settlement of a pre-existing obligation (i.e. for a genuine bonus payment that arose out of the director's service agreement) or to compromise or settle a legitimate claim that the director may have in respect of his termination (i.e. for breach of contract). In the event that the proposed payment does not fall within one of these four exceptions then the payment must be approved by the shareholders of the company.

There is also a *de minimis* exception, which is unlikely to be of significant practical benefit, if the total value of the payment does not exceed £200[53].

2.6.5 What are the consequences of failing to obtain shareholder approval for a payment that is made to a director for loss of office?

If shareholder approval is not obtained for a payment for loss of office the recipient will hold the payment on trust for the company (with the resulting obligation to repay the money received). Any director who authorised the payment is also jointly and severally liable with the director who received the payment to indemnify the company for any loss resulting from the payment[54].

2.7 What is the position where a transaction requires approval under more than one provision of the Companies Act 2006?

In the event that a transaction with a director requires approval under different provisions of the Companies Act 2006, the requirements of each provision of the Companies Act 2006 must be met but a separate shareholder resolution for each transaction is not required[55].

In addition to the specific requirements of the Companies Act 2006 relating to certain transactions, directors must comply with their statutory duties (which are set out in chapter 1) and be satisfied that the proposed transaction would promote the success of the company for the benefit of its members as a whole.

2.8 What are the disclosure requirements where directors have interests in the company's shares?

Under the Companies Act 1985 a director was precluded from dealing in share options in the company of which he was a director. The penalty was severe and included imprisonment, a fine or both for the director concerned. This provision was repealed on 6 April 2007.

---

[53] Section 221, Companies Act 2006.
[54] Section 222, Companies Act 2006.
[55] Section 225, Companies Act 2006.

2.9 Directors' disclosures of interest in shares

Under the Companies Act 1985 a director was required to disclose his interest in any shares that he held in the company, its subsidiaries or holding company (or subsidiaries of the company's holding company). The company was also under an obligation to maintain a register of directors' interests.

With effect from 6 April 2007 this general requirement is repealed in line with the implementation of European Directives on this issue. These Directives only required the application of these restrictions to directors of quoted companies and the Government decided not to 'gold-plate' the Directive by applying these provisions to all companies. The rules on disclosure of directors' interests in shares of a listed company are now contained in the Disclosure and Transparency Rules.

2.10 Summary of key changes under the Companies Act 2006

The table below sets out a summary of the key provisions of the Companies Act 1985 and the Companies Act 2006 in respect of transactions with directors.

Issue	Companies Act 1985	Companies Act 2006	Action required
Directors' service contracts (section 2.2)	Shareholder approval is required for service contracts with a guaranteed term in excess of five years.	With effect from 1 October 2007 shareholder approval is required for service contracts with a guaranteed term in excess of two years.	Review and update where necessary policies relating to the approval of directors' service contracts. Ensure that approval is obtained for both letters of appointment and contracts for services.
Substantial property transactions (section 2.3)	Prior shareholder approval required. A *de minimis* threshold of £2,000.	With effect from 1 October 2007 substantial property transactions can be entered into that are conditional upon shareholder consent. Changes to the definition of 'connected person' and the aggregation of transactions will mean that a wider range of transactions will require shareholder approval.	No specific action is required other than to determine whether to take advantage of the deregulatory measure.

Issue	Companies Act 1985	Companies Act 2006	Action required
Loans and other credit transactions to directors (section 2.4)	Public and private companies are prohibited from entering into certain types of loan and other credit transactions with directors.	With effect from 1 October 2007 a company can enter into loans and other credit transactions with a director and connected persons provided they have informed shareholder consent. Criminal penalties have been abolished and the exemptions to the requirement for shareholder approval have also been amended.	No specific action is required other than to determine whether to take advantage of the deregulatory measure.
Tax-free payments to directors (section 2.5)	A company cannot make a tax-free payment to its directors.	With effect from 6 April 2007 a company can make tax-free payments to directors.	No specific action is required other than to determine whether to take advantage of the deregulating measure.
Payments for loss of office (section 2.6)	Shareholder approval is required for compensation payments made to a director for loss of office (subject to certain exemptions).	With effect from 1 October 2007 shareholder approval is required when compensation is paid to a director (or connected person) for loss of office and employment in connection with the management of company affairs. The exemptions have also been amended.	Review company policies in relation to payments for loss of office as a broader range of payments will require shareholder approval.

Chapter 3

Setting up and maintaining a company under the Companies Act 2006

3.1   Introduction   3002
    3.1.1   Scope of the chapter   3002
    3.1.2   What is the background to the changes?   3002
    3.1.3   What are the key changes under the Companies Act
          2006?   3002
3.2   What types of companies are there under the Companies Act
    2006?   3003
    3.2.1   To which companies does the Companies Act 2006
          apply?   3003
    3.2.2   What is the difference between a company that is public,
          private, limited by guarantee or unlimited?   3003
    3.2.3   Can companies not formed under companies' legislation
          register under the Companies Act 2006?   3004
3.3   How does the Companies Act 2006 change company formations?   3005
    3.3.1   What documents must be submitted to the Registrar of
          Companies to incorporate a company?   3005
    3.3.2   Can a company be formed on-line?   3007
    3.3.3   What evidence is there that a company has been validly
          incorporated?   3008
    3.3.4   Can the Registrar of Companies refuse to incorporate a
          company?   3008
    3.3.5   What requirements must be met by a public company for it
          to be able to trade?   3009
    3.3.6   How can a trading certificate be obtained and why is it
          necessary?   3009
    3.3.7   What are the consequences of a public company doing
          business without a trading certificate?   3010
    3.3.8   How many members are required to incorporate a
          company?   3010
3.4   What are the component parts of a company's constitution?   3011
    3.4.1   What is the memorandum of association?   3011
    3.4.2   Is there still a need for an objects clause?   3011
    3.4.3   What are the articles of association?   3012
    3.4.4   What is 1985 Table A?   3012
    3.4.5   What are 1985 Tables B-F?   3013
    3.4.6   How has the Companies Act 2006 impacted on Tables
          A-F?   3013
    3.4.7   Are model articles of association available under the
          Companies Act 2006?   3014

3.4.8　How does the 1985 Table A differ from the 2006 model articles? 3014

3.4.9　Is it possible to entrench provisions in the articles? 3018

3.4.10　How can a company's articles of association be amended under the Companies Act 2006? 3019

3.4.11　What filings must be made with the Registrar of Companies for a change to the articles of association? ... 3019

3.4.12　If a member of a company did not vote in favour of an amendment to the articles is he still bound? 3020

3.4.13　Do existing memorandum and articles need to be changed to provide for a single constitution? 3020

3.4.14　Following the changes introduced on 1 October 2007 is it necessary to amend articles? 3020

3.4.15　Who has the right to obtain copies of the constitutional documents? 3024

3.5　Who has the capacity to bind the company? 3025

3.5.1　If a director breaches a limitation in the constitution is the Act still valid? 3025

3.5.2　Who has power to enter into contracts on behalf of the company? 3025

3.5.3　Is the position any different if the transaction involves a director? 3026

3.5.4　How are company documents validly executed? 3026

3.5.5　Why are certain documents required to be executed as a deed? 3026

3.5.6　Can a company appoint an attorney to execute documents on its behalf? 3027

3.5.7　What is the difference between an alternate director and an attorney? 3027

3.5.8　Can a person sign a contract in the name of the company even if it has not yet been incorporated? 3027

3.5.9　How are Scottish company contracts validly executed? .. 3028

3.6　Can a company choose any name? 3028

3.6.1　What checks should be undertaken before deciding on a company name? 3029

3.6.2　What restrictions are there on the choice of company name? 3029

3.6.3　Is it possible to dispense with the requirement to use 'limited' in a company's name? 3030

3.6.4　Who may object to a company's registered name? 3031

3.6.5　Is there any power to change a name on the grounds it is misleading? 3032

3.6.6　How does a company change its name? 3032

3.6.7　When a company changes its name what other changes need to be made? 3033

3.6.8　Is the company obliged to disclose its company name and other information? 3033

3.7   What are the rules relating to the requirement for a company to
      have a registered office? 3033
3.8   Can a company change its status by re-registration? 3034
      3.8.1   What does a private limited company need to do to
              re-register as a public company? 3034
      3.8.2   Do the articles of association need to be changed on
              re-registration as a public company? 3035
      3.8.3   Does the company need to appoint a company secretary on
              re-registration as a public company? 3035
      3.8.4   Are there any other steps that need to be taken on
              re-registration? 3035
      3.8.5   What share capital requirements must be met to re-register
              as a public company? 3035
      3.8.6   What net asset requirements must be met? 3036
      3.8.7   If there has been an allotment of shares for a non-cash
              consideration since the balance sheet date what additional
              requirements must be satisfied? 3037
      3.8.8   What steps should be taken if the requirements cannot be
              met? 3037
      3.8.9   What documents must be submitted to the Registrar of
              Companies? 3038
      3.8.10 At what date does the re-registration become effective? 3038
      3.8.11 Do I need to apply for a trading certificate once
              re-registered as a public company? 3038
      3.8.12 What does a public company need to do to re-register as
              private limited company? 3039
      3.8.13 Does a public company need to change its articles on
              re-registration as a private limited company? 3039
      3.8.14 Who can object to re-registration? 3040
      3.8.15 What other steps should the company take? 3040
      3.8.16 What does a private limited company need to do to register
              as an unlimited company? 3040
      3.8.17 Why would a private limited company re-register as an
              unlimited company? 3041
      3.8.18 What does an unlimited company need to do to re-register
              as a private limited company? 3041
      3.8.19 What does a public company need to do to re-register as an
              unlimited company? 3042
3.9   What is the role of the company secretary and do companies need
      to appoint a company secretary? 3043
      3.9.1   Is it necessary to appoint a company secretary? 3043
      3.9.2   What do I need to consider when deciding whether to
              dispense with the requirement to appoint a company
              secretary? 3044
      3.9.3   What are the relevant considerations if dispensing with a
              company secretary? 3044

3.9.4   What are the qualifications required for the secretary of a public company? 3044

3.9.5   What are the qualification requirements for the secretary of a private company? 3045

3.9.6   What are the key responsibilities of a company secretary?   3045

3.9.7   On appointment does the secretary need to file details of his home address with Companies House? 3046

3.9.8   What happens if there is a vacancy? 3047

3.9.9   If the company proposes to dispense with the requirement for a company secretary must it notify Companies House? 3047

3.9.10   Does the company have a duty to keep a register of secretaries? 3047

3.10   What has to be disclosed in the annual return? 3047

3.10.1   Has the annual return changed under the Companies Act 2006? 3049

3.11   What procedures should be followed when a company creates a charge over the assets and/or property of a company? 3050

3.11.1   What is the position regarding charges created over property which is situated within the UK? 3050

3.11.2   What is the position regarding charges created over property outside the UK? 3051

3.11.3   What is the position regarding charges created over property which is in another part of the UK? 3052

3.11.4   What happens when a charge is satisfied or released? ... 3052

3.11.5   What are the consequences of failure to register charges created by a company? 3052

3.11.6   What obligations are imposed on companies to keep a register of charges and copies of the instruments under which charges are created? 3052

3.11.7   What are the consequences of failure to maintain a register of charges? 3053

3.11.8   What obligations does the Registrar of Companies have to keep a register of charges? 3053

3.11.9   Are there any changes to the rules relating to the registration of Scottish charges? 3053

3.11.10 How does the Bankruptcy and Diligence etc. (Scotland) Act 2007 fit with the requirements of the Companies Act 2006? 3054

3.12   What are the rules relating to the registration and conduct of overseas companies that wish to open a branch in the UK? 3055

3.12.1   When does an overseas company have to register as having a branch in the UK? 3055

3.12.2   What are the registration requirements on establishing a branch? 3056

3.12.3   What accounts are required to be filed on registration?   3057

3.12.4   Are there restrictions on the use of the name? 3058

3.12.5   What information must be disclosed at the address of an overseas company? 3058

3.12.6   What happens if there is a change in the registered particulars? 3058

3.12.7   What happens if the overseas company changes the location of the branch? 3058

3.12.8   Is a director of an overseas company or a permanent representative of the company required to make their residential address publicly available? 3059

3.12.9   What happens if the overseas company has multiple branches in the UK? 3059

3.12.10 What are the penalties for failure to register? 3059

3.12.11 What accounts are required to be filed on an annual basis? 3059

3.12.12 What must individual accounts for an overseas company comprise? 3060

3.12.13 What must group accounts for an overseas company comprise? 3061

3.12.14 Are there any additional considerations and requirements for overseas companies listed on a regulated market in the UK? 3062

3.13 What is a business name and what restrictions are there on the use of business names? 3062

3.13.1   Are there any sensitive words or expressions that may not be used? 3062

3.14 What are the requirements for the inspection and copying of company records? 3063

3.14.1   What records are companies required to make available for inspection? 3063

3.14.2   Where are these records required to be kept? 3063

3.14.3   Can company records be kept in electronic form? 3063

3.14.4   What are the inspection and copying rights? 3063

3.14.5   Are there any changes to the requirements relating to the register of members? 3065

3.14.6   Are there any changes to the requirements relating to the register of directors and secretaries? 3066

3.14.7   Is there a requirement to maintain a register of substantial interests in shares? 3066

3.14.8   Is there a requirement to maintain a register of directors' interests in shares? 3067

3.14.9   What are the changes relating to the transfer of debentures and related company books? 3067

3.14.10 What changes are there to the requirement to keep records of meetings and resolutions? 3069

3.14.11 When is it necessary to maintain an overseas branch register? 3069

3.14.12 What are the requirements relating to the maintenance of a branch register? 3070

3.14.13 What happens if a company is no longer required to maintain an overseas branch register? 3070

3.15 How can documents be served on a company and when are documents deemed to have been delivered under the Companies Act 2006? 3070

    3.15.1 What happens when there is a change of registered addresses of a director, secretary or other person? 3071

    3.15.2 When does deemed delivery of documents and information occur? 3071

3.16 What is the role of the Registrar(s) of Companies? 3071

    3.16.1 What are the responsibilities of the Registrar of Companies? 3072

    3.16.2 What are the requirements for the proper form, authentication and manner of delivery of documents to the Registrar of Companies? 3072

    3.16.3 What are the obligations of the Registrar of Companies to keep a register and an index of companies? 3073

    3.16.4 What are the rules on the allocation and use of unique identifiers? 3073

    3.16.5 What are the Registrar of Companies' obligations for the preservation of original documents for companies currently on the register or for those that have been dissolved? ... 3074

    3.16.6 What rights do the public have to inspect the register and obtain copies of documents filed with the Registrar of Companies? 3074

    3.16.7 Is any material not available for public inspection? 3074

    3.16.8 Does the Registrar of Companies have the power to remove material from the register or rectify incorrect information or documents on the register? 3075

    3.16.9 What are the language requirements for documents filed with the Registrar of Companies and can the Registrar of Companies require documents to be certified or verified? 3075

    3.16.10 What is the position where a person makes a false statement to the Registrar of Companies? 3076

    3.16.11 What powers does the Registrar of Companies have to enforce a company's filing obligations? 3076

    3.16.12 Does the Registrar of Companies have the power to insist upon the use of electronic filing of annual returns? 3076

3.17 What are a company's annual compliance obligations? 3076

3.18 Summary of key changes under the Companies Act 2006 3078

In this chapter we refer to 1985 Table A, the 2006 model articles and the transitional Table A. The 1985 Table A are the articles of association that will, in the absence of bespoke articles of association being adopted, apply as default to companies incorporated before 1 October 2007 and the 2006 model articles will apply to companies incorporated on or after 1 October 2009. The transitional Table A applies to those companies incorporated between 1 October 2007 and 1 October 2009, however, these transitional articles of association do not make significant changes to 1985 Table A.

At the time of writing, the 2006 model articles are in draft form and the references in this chapter to specific regulations of the 2006 model articles are references to the draft 2006 model articles published in July 2007.

We also refer to listed companies throughout this chapter which means a company that has satisfied the requirements for any class of its securities to be admitted to the Official List maintained by the United Kingdom Listing Authority. Listed companies are subject to the Listing Rules, under which they must have their listed securities admitted to trading on a Recognised Investment Exchange, such requirements are not within the scope of this chapter. For further information relating to the requirements of listed companies see the websites of the Financial Services Authority and the Financial Reporting Council:
www.fsahandbook.info/FSA/html/handbook/
www.frc.org.uk/corporate/combinedcode.cfm.

Setting up and maintaining a company under the Companies Act 2006

3.1 Introduction

3.1.1 Scope of the chapter

In this chapter we discuss the changes introduced by the Companies Act 2006 in relation to setting up and maintaining a company.

3.1.2 What is the background to the changes?

One of the key objectives of the Companies Act 2006 is to make it easier for small businesses to set up and maintain companies going forwards. It is in light of this aim that many of the provisions contained in the Companies Act 1985 have been simplified for private companies with additional legislation for public and listed companies applying where required.

3.1.3 What are the key changes under the Companies Act 2006?

The Companies Act 2006 has introduced a number of changes in this area. Some examples of the key changes are:

(i)   the ability for private companies to dispense with the need to appoint a company secretary which is effective from 6 April 2008;

(ii) the repeal of the requirement for private companies to hold annual general meetings which is effective from 1 October 2007;

(iii) the introduction of a single constitutional document (the articles of association) and new simplified 2006 model articles for private and public companies which is effective from 1 October 2009;

(iv) the right of directors to use a service address rather than their residential address which is effective from 1 October 2009;

(v)   the single registration regime for overseas companies which is effective from 1 October 2009;

(vi) the ability for public companies to re-register directly as an unlimited company which is effective from 1 October 2009;

(vii) the ability to object to the registration of a company name which is effective from 1 October 2009;

(viii) the ability for listed companies not to disclose the addresses of members holding less than 5% of the share capital on the annual return which is effective from 1 October 2009; and

(ix)   the extension of the existing restriction on the use of business names to all overseas companies carrying on business in the UK which is also effective from 1 October 2009.

3.2   What types of companies are there under the Companies Act 2006?

The relevant provisions are contained in sections 3 to 6 of the Companies Act 2006 which, unless otherwise stated, are effective from 1 October 2009.

3.2.1   To which companies does the Companies Act 2006 apply?

The Companies Act 2006 preserves the existing forms of company namely, public and private companies limited by shares, companies limited by guarantee without a share capital and unlimited companies. Community interest companies will continue to be covered by the Charities Act 2006 and are not covered in this book.

For the first time the Companies Act 2006 will regulate all companies formed in the UK, including Northern Ireland which was previously subject to separate legislation.

In addition, a later section of this chapter covers the provisions that apply to companies formed overseas and which are required to register branch offices in the UK regulating the conduct of their business in UK.

3.2.2   What is the difference between a company that is public, private, limited by guarantee or unlimited?

A company may be formed in England and Wales (or Wales), Scotland or Northern Ireland as public, private, limited by guarantee or unlimited.

A limited company is defined as a company whereby the liability of its members is limited by its constitution and may be limited by shares or by guarantee. If the liability is limited to the amount, if any, unpaid on the shares held, then the company is one that is 'limited by shares'. If the liability is limited to such amount as individual members or guarantors have undertaken to contribute to the assets of the company in the event of it being wound up, the company is limited by guarantee.

A company where the members have uncapped liability is an unlimited company. An unlimited company is always classified as a private company.

A public company is defined as a company limited by shares, whose certificate of incorporation states it is a public company and which has registered or re-registered as a public company in compliance with the Companies Act 2006 or previous Companies Acts on the relevant date.

A public company is the only type of company which has shares or debentures that can be acquired by the public. Public companies are not, however, required to have a market in their shares and are sometimes selected in those cases where a business wishes to equate itself to a public company whose securities are traded. A public company must comply with minimum share capital requirements. In accordance with the Companies Act 1985, public companies have been required to have an authorised share capital of £50,000 with each of the company's shares being paid up at least as to one-quarter of the nominal value of the share and the whole of any premium on it. There are some changes to the minimum share capital requirements under the Companies Act 2006 which are described in section 3.3.5.

A private company is a company that is not a public company and which is not allowed to offer its shares to the general public. It can be limited by shares or limited by guarantee.

A company limited by guarantee may not be formed with, or become, a company with share capital. Members undertake to contribute to the assets up to an agreed amount to meet liabilities if wound up, this is usually a nominal amount.

Companies limited by guarantee are frequently used to undertake charitable or 'not for profit' activities. They are able to apply for dispensation from use of the word 'limited' in their title, but only on condition that they do not make distributions to members and that any surplus on liquidation is donated to charity. This is discussed further at section 3.6.3.

3.2.3   Can companies not formed under companies' legislation register under the Companies Act 2006?

Sections 1040 to 1043 of the Companies Act 2006 replace the existing provisions of the Companies Act 1985 with little change other than new provisions allowing the Secretary of State to make regulations in this area. Sections 1040 to 1042 come into force on 1 October 2009 and section 1043 on 6 April 2007.

As is the case under the Companies Act 1985 the provisions of the Companies Act 2006 allow any company that was in existence on 2 November 1862 and any company formed after that date in pursuance of an Act of Parliament other than the Companies Act 2006 or any previous Companies Acts; in pursuance of letters of patent; or that is otherwise duly constituted according to law, to make an application to register under the Companies Act 2006. Such companies may register as an unlimited company, as a company limited by shares or as a company limited by guarantee (see below for exceptions).

For any such company, where the liability of its members is limited by Act of Parliament or letters of patent, it is not possible to register pursuant to these sections of the Companies Act 2006 unless it is a joint stock company but it can not register as an unlimited company or a company limited by guarantee.

3.3 How does the Companies Act 2006 change company formations?

The relevant provisions are contained in Part 2 of the Companies Act 2006 (sections 7-16) which are effective from 1 October 2009.

There are some substantive changes to formation requirements, the most significant being changes relating to the memorandum and articles of association. In addition any type of company may be formed with just one member, not just private companies as is the case under the Companies Act 1985.

3.3.1 What documents must be submitted to the Registrar of Companies to incorporate a company?

The Companies Act 2006 retains the requirement for a memorandum and articles of association signed by the initial subscribers to be filed as part of the formation process. However the memorandum is a one-off filing and all the constitutional powers and internal regulations are instead set out in the articles. The content of the memorandum and articles and practical impact of the change on *ultra vires* laws is discussed in section 3.4 of this chapter.

The forms 10 and 12 filed as part of the formation process under the Companies Act 1985 will be replaced with new forms with effect from 1 October 2009. The new forms are likely to contain a description relating to their functionality together with the relevant reference to the Companies Act 2006.

In addition to the memorandum and articles of association an application to register a company must contain the following information which should be lodged with the relevant Registrar of Companies (i.e. for England and Wales (or Wales), Scotland or Northern Ireland):

(i)   statement of compliance with all requirements of the Companies Act 2006;

(ii)   application for registration of the company covering:

- proposed name (see section 3.6 for more detailed information on choosing a company name);

- country of the registered office (e.g. England and Wales (or Wales), Scotland or Northern Ireland);

- whether the liability of the members is to be limited and if so whether by shares or guarantee; and

- whether public or private;

(iii) if the application is delivered by agents acting on behalf of the subscribers, the agent's name and address, as is currently the case under the Companies Act 1985;

(iv) in the case of a company with a share capital the application must also include a statement of the capital and initial shareholdings, including the name and address of the subscriber. This is a new requirement introduced by the Companies Act 2006;

(v) a statement of the proposed officers, being the first director and company secretary (unless in the case of a private company there is no company secretary); and

(vi) a statement of the intended registered office address.

The statement of capital for a company with share capital must include:

(i) the total number and class of shares;

(ii) the nominal price per share and aggregate nominal value of the shares as a whole and of each class of shares, if more than one class is created;

(iii) any prescribed rights attached to the shares;

(iv) the total number of shares taken on formation by the subscribers to the memorandum of association;

(v) the individual amounts subscribed to by each subscriber and the nominal value and class of shares taken by him on formation and the amount to be paid on formation (for example whether it is purely the nominal amount or includes a premium and if not fully paid up how much is committed but outstanding); and

(vi) if the subscriber to the memorandum has subscribed for more than one class of shares, similar information is required for each class.

A key change made by the Companies Act 2006 is the statement of capital which is limited to details of subscribed capital only as, with effect from 1 October 2009, the concept of authorised share capital is abolished. This is discussed further in section 9.3.

If a company is limited by guarantee, a statement of guarantee must be included with the documents to be submitted to the Registrar of Companies. The statement of guarantee is an undertaking, given by each member of the company, to contribute to the assets of the company up to a specified amount in the event of it being wound up. The statement must include the following prescribed information:

(i)   the name and address of each of the subscribers to the memorandum of association;

(ii)   the amount that each member undertakes to contribute to the assets of the company on winding up whilst he is a member or within one year after he ceases to be a member; and

(iii)   cover the position on:

- payment of the debts and liabilities contracted before he ceases to be a member;

- costs and expenses of winding up; and

- any sums required to adjust the contributions between the members.

The statement of proposed officers must contain the following information:

(i)   particulars of the first director(s) and, in a change to the Companies Act 1985, this includes a married woman's maiden name;

(ii)   particulars of the person or corporate entity being appointed as the first secretary (unless a private company has decided not to appoint a secretary (see section 3.9)). Again, for a married woman this includes her maiden name;

(iii)   a statement of consent to act; and

(iv)   the residential or service address (see 1.14.8).

Under the Companies Act 2006 there is no longer a requirement for directors to register their home address, instead a service address may be registered. However, where a director is a natural person he is also required to file his residential address with the Registrar of Companies which is maintained on a secure register.

With effect from 1 October 2008 all companies are required to have at least one natural person as a director and anyone under the age of 16 will not be permitted to act as a director. These provisions are discussed further in chapter 1.

3.3.2 Can a company be formed on-line?

Yes, on-line formations have been possible for quite some time and the Companies Act 2006 confirms the existing position, which is that formation agents and those with proprietary software systems may continue to form companies on-line.

Where electronic filing is used, agreed identification procedures are established between the company and/or its agent and the Registrar of Companies both for the initial application and also for the electronic filing of subsequent documents. Data protection measures against fraudulent filing are used, for example the colour of a director's eyes, the last three digits of their telephone number or other unique identifying information. This regime has been in existence for some time and the Companies Act 2006 makes no changes to the existing position.

Company formation applications may also continue to be made by filing physical documents with the Registrar of Companies. However, the Registrar is encouraging increased use of electronic filing and the filing fees for electronic formations are expected to be less than those for formations using physical documents.

3.3.3   What evidence is there that a company has been validly incorporated?

Once the Registrar of Companies is satisfied that all formalities have been completed, he will issue a certificate of incorporation under section 15 of the Companies Act 2006.

The certificate will be signed by the Registrar of Companies and is conclusive evidence of compliance with the registration requirements of the Companies Act 2006. The certificate will confirm the following:

(i)   the date of incorporation;

(ii)   the registered name and number;

(iii)   the jurisdiction of the registered office;

(iv)   the status of the company, (limited or unlimited, and if limited whether by shares or by guarantee); and

(v)   whether the company is private or public.

Registration confirms that the company is, from the date of incorporation, an independent legal entity capable of exercising all the functions of an incorporated company and that the subscribers to the memorandum have become the members of the company.

It also confirms that the directors and secretary (if any) have been duly appointed to that office.

3.3.4   Can the Registrar of Companies refuse to incorporate a company?

Yes, a company may not be formed for an unlawful purpose and the Registrar of Companies will refuse to register any company that purports to be set up in contravention of this prohibition.

3.3.5   What requirements must be met by a public company for it to be able to trade?

As required under the Companies Act 1985, a public company is still required to have a trading certificate issued to it before being permitted to trade or borrow money.

The relevant sections of the Companies Act 2006 are sections 761 to 767 which are effective on 6 April 2008.

These provisions state that a public company must not do business or exercise its borrowing powers without first obtaining a trading certificate from the Registrar of Companies, which will only be issued if the Registrar of Companies is satisfied that the share capital requirements for public companies are met, namely that:

(i)   the authorised minimum nominal value of the company's allotted share capital is £50,000 (or the equivalent in Euros rounded to the nearest 100 Euros but not partly in Sterling and partly in Euros); and

(ii)   at least 25% of the nominal value and the whole of any premium on the shares has been paid.

This represents a change to the provisions of the Companies Act 1985, which required the authorised minimum to be denominated in Sterling and did not permit a Euro equivalent.

A trading certificate is not required where a private company re-registers as a public company (see section 3.8.11 for further detail on the procedural requirements of re-registration).

In a further change to the Companies Act 1985, once the Sterling or Euro minimum share capital requirements have been met a company may re-denominate the whole of its share capital to another currency and is no longer required to retain a statutory minimum in Sterling. The simplified process for re-denomination of share capital is discussed further in chapter 9.

In calculating the minimum paid up share capital, any share allotted under an employee share scheme must not be taken into account unless at least 25% of its nominal value and the whole of any premium have also been paid.

3.3.6   How can a trading certificate be obtained and why is it necessary?

A trading certificate has effect from the date on which it is issued and is conclusive evidence that the public company has satisfied the requirements of the Companies Act 2006 listed above and is entitled to do business and exercise any borrowing powers.

The application for a trading certificate must:

(i)   state that the nominal value of the company's allotted share capital is not less than the authorised minimum, and the currency in which the share capital is to be denominated;

(ii)   specify the amount, or estimated amount of the company's preliminary expenses;

(iii)   specify an amount or benefit paid, given or intended to be paid or given to any promoter of the company and the consideration for the payment of such benefit; and

(iv)   be accompanied by a statement of compliance from the directors.

The statement of compliance replaces the requirement under the Companies Act 1985 for a statutory declaration. The statement does not need to be witnessed and may be made in paper or electronic form.

3.3.7   What are the consequences of a public company doing business without a trading certificate?

If a public company carries on business or exercises any borrowing powers without a valid trading certificate, the company and every officer who is in default commits an offence and is liable on conviction on indictment or summary conviction to a fine (section 767).

Contravention of section 767 of the Companies Act 2006 through the company's failure to obtain a trading certificate does not affect the validity of transactions entered into by the company insofar as third parties are concerned.

However, where the company enters into a transaction without a valid certificate having been issued and fails to comply with its obligations to obtain one within 21 days of being called on to do so, then the directors of the company at the time the company entered into the transaction are jointly and severally liable to indemnify any third party to that transaction in respect of loss or damage suffered by him as a result of the company's failure to comply with its obligations under the Companies Act 2006. So, obtaining a trading certificate is an essential element of the formation of a public company.

3.3.8   How many members are required to incorporate a company?

In a change to the provisions of the Companies Act 1985 it will be possible under the Companies Act 2006 for all types of company to be formed as single member companies, whereas under the Companies Act 1985 two members were required to form both a public and an unlimited company.

3.4 What are the component parts of a company's constitution?

The relevant sections relating to a company's constitution are sections 17 to 38 of the Companies Act 2006.

The constitutional documents of a company include the articles of association, and certain resolutions and agreements by members by which the company is bound. For companies formed under the Companies Act 2006 the memorandum of association will no longer form part of a company's constitution. Companies that were incorporated under previous Companies Acts are able to retain constitutional provisions in their memorandum and these will be deemed to be included in their articles. There is no need for such companies to change their constitution on this ground alone although for a number of other reasons this is likely to be desirable (see section 3.4.14).

The provisions of the company's constitution bind the company and its members.

3.4.1 What is the memorandum of association?

Under previous Companies Acts the memorandum of association is a detailed statement containing the objects and powers of the company which frequently imposes restrictions on what the company is empowered to do. A company will be acting *ultra vires* if it acts outside the scope of its objects stated in its memorandum and the directors will be in breach of their duties. The implications of this are discussed in section 3.5.

Under the Companies Act 2006 newly formed companies will have a single constitutional document regulating its powers and internal management called the articles of association. Certain provisions, such as the name and the type of company, which have previously been contained in the memorandum of association, will instead be set out in the application for registration and there is no longer a requirement for an objects clause.

The memorandum of association will therefore look very different for companies formed under the Companies Act 2006, consisting only of a statement that the founders wish to form a company and details of subscriber shares (if the company has a share capital). The memorandum cannot be altered and will be purely an historical document filed on incorporation.

3.4.2 Is there still a need for an objects clause?

No, the Companies Act 2006 provides a company's objects are unrestricted unless a company's articles specifically provide for restrictions. There is no need for a company formed under the Companies Act 2006 to have an objects clause. The starting position is that it has all the powers it needs to conduct any activities save to the extent that it is restricted by the articles.

For companies incorporated under previous Companies Acts the existing restrictions in the memorandum will remain valid and a company will have to obtain shareholder approval if it wishes to have unrestricted objects. Such a change may also require third party consent under material contracts.

The ability to have unrestricted objects will undoubtedly assist businesses in their operation and management of groups.

However, this provision must also be considered in the light of the codification provisions on directors' duties. Directors are under a duty to act in such a way as is 'likely to promote the success of the company'. 'Success' is not defined; where a company does not have predominantly commercial objectives or its commercial objectives are insufficiently clear, then there may still be an argument for setting out its purpose in the articles to reduce the risk of challenge by shareholders through derivative actions. This is unlikely to be necessary where sufficient other information is available which makes the position clear and the preferred starting point in the interests of flexibility would be to avoid such provisions. Directors' duties and derivative actions are discussed in further detail in chapter 1.

3.4.3   What are the articles of association?

The relevant provisions of the Companies Act 2006 relating to articles of association are sections 18 to 28.

The Companies Act 2006 stipulates that a company must have articles of association, which set out the internal regulations by which a company governs itself and that these articles must be registered. This is also the position under previous Companies Acts.

Section 18 of the Companies Act 2006 requires the articles to be set out in one single document registered with the Registrar of Companies. These must be kept up to date when changes are made by the shareholders and must be made available for inspection by members of the company at the company's registered office and also to members of the public through Companies House. There is no requirement to register articles where the 2006 model articles apply. This restates the position under previous Companies Acts.

3.4.4   What is 1985 Table A?

All companies are required to adopt articles of association when they incorporate. Tables A to F of the Companies (Tables A to F) Regulations 1985 set out standardised model articles, which companies formed between 1 July 1985 and 1 October 2007 use as the basis for their own articles. 1985 Table A was the most commonly used table; it sets out standardised articles for companies limited by shares, in two versions, one for private and one for public companies. If companies did not register their own articles of association, the 1985 Table A applied by default.

3.4.5   What are 1985 Tables B-F?

The 1985 Tables B to F of the Companies (Tables A to F) Regulations 1985 set out standardised forms of memoranda of association and/or regulations for the adaptation of 1985 Table A to create standardised model articles for the following types of company which were incorporated between 1 July 1985 and 1 October 2007:

(i)   1985 Table B – a private company limited by shares (memorandum of association);

(ii)   1985 Table C – a company limited by guarantee with no share capital (memorandum and articles);

(iii)   1985 Table D – a company limited by guarantee with a share capital (memorandum and articles);

(iv)   1985 Table E – an unlimited company with a share capital (memorandum and articles); and

(v)   1985 Table F – a public company limited by shares (memorandum of association).

3.4.6   How has the Companies Act 2006 impacted on Tables A-F?

The Companies (Tables A to F) (Amendment) Regulations 2007, the Companies (Tables A to F) (Amendment) (No. 2) Regulations 2007 and the Companies (Tables A to F) (Amendment) Regulations 2008 set out the amendments made to each of the 1985 Tables.

Amendments have been made to the 1985 Table A to enable new companies formed on or after 1 October 2007 to take advantage of and to avoid conflict with the provisions of the Companies Act 2006 in force at that date.

Further amendments have been made to 1985 Tables C and E that came into force with effect from 6 April 2008. 1985 Table C has been amended to bring it in line with the new rights for proxies to vote on a show of hands. The effect of the amendments to the 1985 Table E is to provide that all companies must provide at least 14 clear days' notice of a general meeting.

Updated versions of the 1985 Table A, Table C and E can all be found on the Companies House website at *www.companieshouse.gov.uk/*.

3.4.7 Are model articles of association available under the Companies Act 2006?

Yes, new model articles will be introduced for each category of company, i.e. private companies limited by shares, private companies limited by guarantee and public companies, which will apply to all companies incorporated from 1 October 2009. Further sets of model articles for specific types of private companies such as limited by guarantee and unlimited companies will not be issued. At the time of writing the final versions of the 2006 model articles referred to above are not available.

The 2006 model articles for private companies have been designed with the needs of small, owner-managed businesses in mind. The provisions are as simple as possible and do not include a number of provisions which are contained in the 1985 Table A which are not as likely to be used by private companies (for example the ability to appoint alternate directors or to issue partly paid shares).

The 2006 model articles for private companies limited by guarantee are based closely on those for private companies limited by shares, but without the provisions relating to shares.

The 2006 model articles for public companies will have more limited application than those for private companies as public companies are more likely to require tailor-made articles. However, the draft articles cover all the areas dealt with in the 1985 Table A and also include certain provisions which are commonly used by public companies in their articles.

Companies are likely to continue to modify or exclude provisions contained in the model articles in their own adopted articles.

For companies incorporated between 1 October 2007 and 1 October 2009 a Transitional Table A applies which reflects the changes that came into force on 1 October 2007 such as amendments to written resolutions of members, AGMs and notice periods.

For existing companies incorporated under the Companies Act 1985 or earlier the version of the model articles that was incorporated by reference in their articles will continue to apply to that company and they are under no obligation to adopt the 2006 model articles or the Transitional Table A.

3.4.8 How does the 1985 Table A differ from the 2006 model articles?

The table below sets out the differences between 1985 Table A and the 2006 model articles for private companies limited by shares.

1985 Table A regulation	1985 Table A provision	2006 model articles of association provision	Common amendments to model articles
24	Power of directors to refuse to register share transfers.	26(5) – The directors retain the right to refuse to register a transfer of shares. There are no restrictions on the circumstances in which the directors may exercise this right.	None.
32	Power to increase, consolidate, sub-divide or cancel share capital.	The 2006 model articles do not contain any provisions relating to the alteration of the company's share capital. General provisions are set out in Part 17, Chapter 8 of the Companies Act 2006.	None.
37	Directors' power/duty to call a general meeting.	No such provision is included in the 2006 model articles as this power/duty is included in sections 302 and 304 of the Companies Act 2006 respectively.	None.
40	Quorum must be present at a general meeting (two people being a quorum).	39 – The meeting must be quorate. Section 318 of the Companies Act 2006 sets out the quorum requirement.	Companies may amend quorum to a higher number, although the majority of companies appear satisfied to leave quorum at two.
47	Chairman's declaration of vote results.	These provisions are omitted from the 2006 model articles of association as this is addressed by section 320 of the Companies Act 2006.	None.

1985 Table A regulation	1985 Table A provision	2006 model articles of association provision	Common amendments to model articles
49	Procedure for taking a poll, including the appointment of scrutineers.	45 – The procedure for taking a poll has been simplified as it was felt that for most small companies (although some private companies may have a significant number of shareholders) it should be possible to take a poll immediately.	Companies with a significant number of shareholders may wish to include a procedure for taking a poll.
53	Members' written resolutions.	No such provision is included in the 2006 model articles. Written resolutions are now governed by sections 288 to 300 of the Companies Act 2006.	None.
57	Prohibition on voting by members that owe the company money in respect of their shares.	This provision is omitted as it is assumed that most private companies limited by shares will not issue partly paid shares.	Companies that envisage issuing partly paid shares and that adopt the 2006 model articles will need to consider amending the 2006 model articles to include a prohibition on voting by holders of partly paid shares.
64	Minimum number of directors.	The 2006 model articles do not provide for a minimum number of directors and the only restriction will be those set out in section 154 of the Companies Act 2006 (one director for a private company and two for a public company).	Companies sometimes impose a minimum and maximum number of directors that can be appointed in their articles of association.

1985 Table A regulation	1985 Table A provision	2006 model articles of association provision	Common amendments to model articles
65	Directors may appoint alternates.	The authority to appoint alternates is not included in the 2006 model articles as it was felt that most private companies would not want to make use of alternates.	A company adopting the 2006 model articles may want to provide for the appointment of an alternate director.
73	Requirement for directors to retire by rotation.	It was felt that the retirement of directors by rotation was not required by most private companies and as such no provision in this regard is included in the 2006 model articles.	None.
78	Members' right to appoint directors (by ordinary resolution).	17 – members may appoint a director by ordinary resolution.	Commonly, a company will amend its articles of association to enable a majority shareholder to appoint a director by notice.
79	Directors' power to appoint a director subject to re-appointment at the next AGM.	17 – directors may appoint a director without the need for subsequent re-appointment by the shareholders of the company.	None.
92	Acts of persons not properly appointed as directors.	These provisions are now enshrined in section 161 of the Companies Act 2006 and are not therefore included in the 2006 model articles.	None.
94	Conflicted directors may not vote except in certain situations.	14 – A director is still prohibited from voting on a matter in which he is conflicted save for in certain circumstances.	The majority of companies amend their articles to enable a director to vote on an issue on which he is conflicted.

1985 Table A regulation	1985 Table A provision	2006 model articles of association provision	Common amendments to model articles
99	Appointment of secretary.	There is no requirement under the Companies Act 2006 for a private company to appoint a secretary and as such there are no provisions contained in the 2006 model articles in this regard.	None.

3.4.9 Is it possible to entrench provisions in the articles?

Yes, under the Companies Act 1985 it is possible for companies to entrench provisions in their memorandum and not their articles which remain subject to amendment only with the approval of shareholders. Once entrenched no alteration can be made even if required by subsequent demands of the business or shareholders. In practice therefore this provision is not widely used. Unless provisions are entrenched in the memorandum all other provisions of the memorandum or articles of association are capable of amendment.

With effect from 1 October 2009, a company may entrench provisions in its articles in accordance with section 22 of the Companies Act 2006 but only on formation or if all shareholders agree. A company can provide that they are only capable of amendment by a majority which is higher than that required for a special resolution such as unanimity. These provisions are not, therefore, unchangeable, as is the case under the Companies Act 1985. As a result, this should simplify the drafting of share rights or be used to create greater protection for minority shareholders, being a simpler alternative to shareholder agreements.

The Registrar of Companies must be notified if, either on formation or by subsequent amendment to the articles agreed by all the members or by the court, provisions for entrenchment are added or the restrictions are removed or altered.

As with any amendment to the existing memorandum and articles of association, following the alteration of a company's articles an amended copy of the articles, together with a copy of the resolution of the company authorising and evidencing the change, must be sent to the Registrar of Companies within 15 days of the alteration. Failure to comply renders the company and every officer of it in default, rendering the offender liable to summary conviction and a fine.

The Registrar of Companies has the power to compel a company to submit revised articles to him if he has reason to believe the company has failed to supply him with an amended set of articles. Failure to comply within 28 days of receipt of the notice renders the officers of the company potentially liable to criminal proceedings and a fine.

3.4.10 How can a company's articles of association be amended under the Companies Act 2006?

Generally a company may amend its articles of association by special resolution, but certain provisions may be stated as being 'entrenched', either on formation or by subsequent amendment of the company's articles as outlined above in section 3.4.9.

Amendments to a company's articles of association can occur by:

(i)   the passing of an ordinary or special resolution of the members;

(ii)   amendment to legislation which affects the way in which the company is governed; or

(iii)   court order.

The ability to amend articles may also be restricted by contract, commonly shareholder agreements and banking covenants, which should be thoroughly checked in advance of making any alterations. In addition, alterations can require regulatory approval, for example by the Charity Commissioner.

3.4.11 What filings must be made with the Registrar of Companies for a change to the articles of association?

Where the articles are altered by the members, a copy of the resolution must be sent by the directors or officers of the company to the Registrar of Companies within 15 days of it being passed along with a copy of the articles as amended.

Most changes to a company's articles require the passing of a special resolution, but the articles themselves may provide for changes to be made by ordinary resolution, for example to alter the minimum or maximum number of directors required.

A change to a company's articles may be notified to the Registrar of Companies, either electronically or by the documents being physically lodged with the Registrar of Companies. The notice must be accompanied by all relevant documentation, including copies of the resolution or court order evidencing the change. Failure to comply renders the officers of the company liable to summary conviction and a fine.

3.4.12 If a member of a company did not vote in favour of an amendment to the articles is he still bound?

There is no change under the Companies Act 2006. Provided the changes have been validly made, changes are binding upon all shareholders including those voting against them.

3.4.13 Do existing memorandum and articles need to be changed to provide for a single constitution?

No, section 28 of the Companies Act 2006 provides that any statement in an existing memorandum will be treated as forming part of the company's articles. It will not therefore be necessary for amendments to be made, but companies may do so if they wish.

3.4.14 Following the changes introduced on 1 October 2007 is it necessary to amend articles?

The Companies Act 2006 does not require companies incorporated under the provisions of previous legislation to change their articles. However, one of the aims of the Companies Act 2006 is to make it easier to set up and run a company. The new provisions in relation to a company's articles of association are designed to do that.

The announcement of a delay in implementing some of the changes under the Companies Act 2006 to 1 October 2009 has complicated the decision over when changes should be made to a company's articles. However, if companies wish to take advantage of new provisions of the Companies Act 2006 such as to communicate electronically with their shareholders or to dispense with the need for a company secretary (if the article specifically requires one), it will be necessary for amendments to be made to their articles. Some of the changes that companies will need to consider making to their articles are set out in the table below.

Changes under the Companies Act 2006	Impact on articles of association
Directors' Conflicts of Interest From the 1 October 2008 a director will have a statutory duty under section 175 of the Companies Act 2006 to avoid a situation in which he has a conflict of interest, or a possible conflict of interest, with the interests of the company. Such a situation could arise where a director is a major shareholder in the company, where a director owes duties to different entities within a group; or has cross directorships with a supplier or customer of the company. However, this duty will not be infringed if the matter has been authorised by other independent directors.	Private companies incorporated after 1 October 2008 will need to ensure that nothing in their articles invalidates the ability of the board to authorise conflicts of interest. Private companies incorporated before 1 October 2008 will need to either (a) pass an ordinary resolution to permit the directors to authorise conflicts; or (b) pass a special resolution to amend their articles to allow directors to authorise conflicts. Public companies will also need to ensure that a provision is included in their articles to allow directors to authorise conflicts. In all cases, articles should be updated to contain (i) provisions dealing with the use of confidential information received other than as a director of the company; (ii) provisions allowing the director to be absent from meetings and the availability of board papers to protect a director being in breach of duty if a conflict or potential conflict of interest arises; or (iii) provisions allowing the independent directors to impose certain conditions to any authority granted, i.e. relating to the management of confidential information. Governance safeguards will also need to be put in place when directors decide whether to authorise a conflict or potential conflict.

Changes under the Companies Act 2006	Impact on articles of association
Age Discrimination against Directors The 70 year age limit for directors has been removed by the Companies Act 2006. As a result, provisions requiring a director's age to be disclosed could fall foul of the Employment Equality (Age) Regulations 2006.	Ensure that provisions referring to the age of directors are removed.
Company Secretary From 6 April 2008 private companies are no longer required to appoint a company secretary. However, the functions currently undertaken by the company secretary will still need to be performed.	Private companies wishing to remove the position of company secretary will need to check their articles to ensure that no specific requirements for such a role are included.
AGM The Companies Act 2006 abolishes the obligation for private companies to hold annual general meetings unless expressly required to do so by the articles of association. BERR has confirmed that the 1985 Table A does not count as expressly requiring an AGM whereas the 1948 Table A does. However, where the elective regime is in place, companies based on the 1948 Table A continue to be relieved of the need for an AGM.	The articles of association of private companies need to be checked to see whether they require an AGM to be held.
General Meetings The Companies Act 2006 has reduced the notice period applicable for all general meetings, other than AGMs for public companies, from 21 to 14 days. In addition, companies may now hold meetings on short notice with the consent of a majority of 90% of shareholders as opposed to 95% previously.	Private and public companies should check their articles and amend them accordingly to take advantage of the reductions.

Changes under the Companies Act 2006	Impact on articles of association
Form of Resolutions The Companies Act 2006 makes it easier to use written resolutions for decisions by shareholders. Previously, written resolutions required unanimity. Now the Companies Act 2006 refers to two types of resolution: ordinary, which requires a simple majority of those eligible to vote; and special, which requires 75% of those eligible to vote to be in favour. However, the Companies Act 2006 does not override provisions in the articles requiring a higher majority.	Remove references requiring unanimity to pass written resolutions.
Therefore, if the articles refer to written resolutions being passed only by unanimity this requirement will have to be removed before the provisions relating to written resolutions can be fully utilised.	Remove references to the requirement for unanimity in order to pass written resolutions.
Under the Companies Act 2006 public companies can no longer pass written resolutions.	Remove references in public company articles to written resolutions.
The concept of extraordinary resolutions has not been retained under the Companies Act 2006.	Remove references to extraordinary resolutions in the articles and amend accordingly.
Proxies The Companies Act 2006 now allows proxies to speak, demand a poll and vote on a show of hands. In addition, the Companies Act 2006 provides that a company cannot increase the period for the appointment or termination of proxies to more than 48 hours before the meeting. It also provides that non working days shall not be taken into account.	Companies should amend articles that only allow proxies to vote on a poll. References in the articles to time limits for appointing and removing proxies should be removed or amended.

Changes under the Companies Act 2006	Impact on articles of association
Chairman's Casting Vote The Companies Act 2006 abolished the chairman's casting vote on 1 October 2007. However, lobbying by bodies such as the ICSA led to a provision that allows companies incorporated before 1 October 2007 to continue to rely on the relevant article. Any companies who amended their articles removing the casting vote are entitled to reinstate the provision and continue to rely on it. However any companies incorporated on or after 1 October 2007 will not be able to rely on the chairman's casting vote.	Companies incorporated before 1 October 2007 who had previously removed the chairman's entitlement to a casting vote need to amend their articles to reinstate the provision if they wish to continue to rely on it. Companies incorporated after 1 October 2007 will not be able to rely on a chairman's casting vote and will need to consider other mechanisms such as weighted voting rights.
Loans to Directors The Companies Act 2006 allows both private and public companies to make loans to directors provided that the loan has been approved by the members.	Private and public companies should consider removing any prohibition on loans contained in articles.
Electronic Communications The opportunity to communicate with shareholders electronically came into force in January 2007. Many companies will already have taken advantage of the administrative and financial savings available. However, for those companies that have not, a review of their articles allows the opportunity to assess the benefits of adopting an electronic communications regime.	Private and public companies wishing to communicate electronically with their shareholders should review and amend their articles accordingly.

For existing companies formed under previous Companies Acts the version of model articles that was in force at the time the company was incorporated will continue to apply unless they are specifically changed.

It is advisable for companies to review their articles to ensure there are no inconsistencies with the new legislation.

3.4.15   Who has the right to obtain copies of the constitutional documents?

The members are entitled to request copies of any documents that have been filed with the Registrar of Companies (including copies of special resolutions, court orders sanctioning compromise or deeds of arrangement). Members of a company limited by guarantee have a right to obtain a copy of the statement of guarantee.

Failure by the company to comply with such a request renders every officer liable to summary conviction and to a fine.

3.5 Who has the capacity to bind the company?

The relevant sections of the Companies Act 2006 are sections 39 to 52.

3.5.1 If a director breaches a limitation in the constitution is the act still valid?

Yes, under the Companies Act 2006 an action undertaken by a company in breach of a restriction in its constitution, will still be valid. Directors however could be liable for a breach of duty to the company by failing to observe a restriction in the constitution and therefore it remains important to review the constitution before undertaking any action.

Under previous Companies Acts, certain actions could only be undertaken by a company if it had express powers in its articles (such as a purchase by a company of its own shares). In this situation an action undertaken without the express power would not have been valid.

The Companies Act 2006 has generally removed the requirement for express powers in the articles in these situations. This is consistent with the principle that a company should have unrestricted objects.

3.5.2 Who has power to enter into contracts on behalf of the company?

Under a company's constitution the powers of the management of the company are generally delegated to the directors.

As is the case under common law, a person dealing in good faith with the company is entitled to assume the directors have the power to bind the company without limitation and he is not bound to enquire whether the power of the directors is limited. The third party is also presumed to have been acting in good faith in his dealing with the company unless it can be proved otherwise.

Subject to the limitations which may arise through a transaction with directors or their associates and transactions relating to charities, a third party acting in good faith would, therefore, not be prejudiced as a result of a director having exceeded his powers or for not having complied with the articles. This means that a contract entered into by a director in such a situation will still bind both the company and the third party.

3.5.3 Is the position any different if the transaction involves a director?

Yes, where a transaction is entered into by directors of the company in breach of a limitation in its articles with a director of the company or its holding company or connected person (see section 2.3.8) the transaction itself will still be valid but in addition the company can avoid the contract at any time in the future and any party to the transaction and the director who authorised the transaction is liable to account to the company for any gain made or to indemnify the company for any loss, unless he can show that he did not know at the time that the directors were exceeding their powers (section 41 of the Companies Act 2006). Therefore in the context of a transaction involving a director or his connected person it is even more essential that the constitution is reviewed in detail. The Companies Act 2006 does not change the existing law.

3.5.4 How are company documents validly executed?

Under the laws of England and Wales or Northern Ireland a document will be validly executed by a company by:

(i)   affixing the common seal; or

(ii)   signature by two authorised signatories or by a director signing it in the presence of a witness who attests the signature.

For public companies, and private companies who have a secretary, an authorised signatory is any director or secretary (or joint secretary). For a private company without a secretary, an authorised signatory is any director. Any director is deemed to have ostensible authority to execute contracts on behalf of the company.

Private companies that decide to abolish the office of the company secretary should check the provisions of their articles to ensure they do not require documents to be signed by two directors and/or one director and the company secretary.

A company is not obliged to have a common seal, but if it does have one, then the name should be engraved in legible characters on the seal. Companies with a common seal may also have an official seal for sealing share certificates and other securities, which must be a facsimile of the company's common seal.

Specific formalities apply to the execution of documents in Scotland which are discussed further at section 3.5.9.

3.5.5 Why are certain documents required to be executed as a deed?

A deed is generally enforceable despite any lack of consideration. The limitation period for actions brought under a simple contract is six years from the date on which the cause of action accrued whereas the period is generally 12 years in the case of a deed. Where there is a choice, a company may favour the use of deeds as the terms and conditions contained therein survive for 12 years from the date of execution which is particularly important in transactions where, for example, a purchaser of a company may wish to preserve his ability to sue under the warranty provisions for as long a period as possible.

A deed is required for a small number of transactions, for example the granting by a company of a power of attorney, the appointment of trustees, land transfers, most leases or a legal mortgage or charge. All contracts for no consideration must also be executed as a deed to be valid.

A deed is validly executed by a company if it is duly executed by the company in accordance with section 3.5.4 and is stated to be delivered as a deed, which it is presumed to have done unless a contrary intention can be shown.

It should be noted that the concept of execution as a deed does not apply in relation to Scottish registered companies. See section 3.5.9 for further detail relating to the execution of documents by Scottish companies.

3.5.6   Can a company appoint an attorney to execute documents on its behalf?

Yes, in England and Wales and Northern Ireland, a company may also empower a person, either generally or for a specific transaction, to be authorised as the attorney to execute deeds or other documents on its behalf. The original power must also be executed as a deed.

3.5.7   What is the difference between an alternate director and an attorney?

The difference between an attorney and an alternate director is that the attorney has power to act on behalf of the company and he must follow the instructions given to him by the donor of the power of attorney.

By contrast an alternate director assumes the role and responsibilities of being a director and can be held to account by the company and the shareholders for his actions as a fiduciary. Even if an alternate is given specific instructions by the director for whom he is alternate as to how to vote or make decisions, he is still required to act in the manner he considers likely to promote the success of the company in the same way as other directors. This is further discussed in chapter 1.

3.5.8   Can a person sign a contract in the name of the company even if it has not yet been incorporated?

If a contract is signed in the name of a company before the company has been incorporated the contract will not bind the company and the person signing it will be personally responsible for its performance unless the contract is novated by the company following incorporation. The Companies Act 2006 makes no change to the position under the previous Companies Acts.

3.5.9 How are Scottish company contracts validly executed?

The relevant section of the Companies Act 2006 is section 48 which comes into force on 1 October 2009. This section states that any document signed in accordance with the provisions of the Requirements of Writing (Scotland) Act 1995 has effect as if so executed.

A document may be executed by a company where signed by:

(i)   a director of the company;

(ii)   the secretary of the company; or

(iii)   a person authorised to sign on behalf of the company

and where the signature of such person is witnessed (requiring that the full name and address of the witness appears in the document itself or in the testing clause or its equivalent).

Where a document is executed in any of the above mentioned ways there is a presumption (subject to evidence to the contrary) that the document has been executed by the company. However, where the signature by a director, company secretary or person authorised to sign on behalf of the company is not witnessed, it is presumed to have been executed by the company, where signed by:

(i)   two directors of the company;

(ii)   a director and secretary of the company; or

(iii)   two persons authorised to sign on behalf of the company.

Scottish companies need not have a company seal.

3.6   Can a company choose any name?

The relevant sections of the Companies Act 2006 are sections 53 to 74 which come into force on 1 October 2009. The Companies Act 2006 does not make any significant change to the current position under the Companies Act 1985.

Subject to the prohibitions and guidelines set out in the Companies Act 2006, the general rule is that a company may in principle choose any name as long as it is not the same as a name which is already registered or is offensive. However, care should also be taken when choosing a name that trade marks belonging to other companies are not infringed. See section 3.6.1 for further detail in relation to trade marks.

3.6.1 What checks should be undertaken before deciding on a company name?

It is usual to conduct a search against existing registered company names to establish whether a chosen name is available for use and also to ascertain if there is a likelihood of confusion with an existing company name that is registered. The Registrar of Companies will refuse to register a name that is the same as one already registered.

It is also advisable to undertake a search of the UK and European Community Trade Mark Registers to identify any third party marks which are identical or similar to the proposed names. Searches are carried out in relation to specified categories of goods and services, so it is important to consider the different goods and services in relation to which the proposed name may be used. In addition, it is possible to carry out further 'common law' searches to identify whether third parties are using identical or similar names. This would include a search of domain names, business directories and websites (although this is not an exhaustive search of all potential areas where a conflicting name may be in use).

Where an identical or similar name is identified through the searches, an assessment should be made as to whether the use of the proposed company name may infringe third party trade marks or similar rights. It may also be prudent to consider the commercial impact of using a similar name to those registered or used by third parties.

Companies should also consider registering the proposed company name (and any other business names), as a trade mark within the UK (and/or other important markets). Registration as a trade mark will give protection against third parties using identical/similar names in relation to identical/similar goods and services (as registration at Companies House will not afford any protection other than to prevent another person forming a company with an identical or similar name). As with registering the company name, however, there are restrictions on the sorts of marks which can be registered and earlier identical/ similar marks can be used by third parties to prevent registration.

See section 3.6.4 for further details on the procedure for objecting to the use of a company name.

3.6.2 What restrictions are there on the choice of company name?

The Registrar of Companies will reject a choice of name that is the same as a name that is already registered. In determining whether a name is the same as an existing name the Registrar of Companies ignores punctuation, the company's status, and the word 'the' at the start of the name. Words such as 'company' or 'co', and 'and' or '&' are treated as the same. The Registrar of Companies has directed that if two names are phoenetically the same, they may both appear on the index provided they are spelt differently.

A company must not be registered under the Companies Act 2006 by a name, which in the opinion of the Secretary of State, is offensive or whose use would constitute an offence.

Names suggesting connection with government or public authorities will not be permitted, nor will a name that includes certain sensitive words or expressions, e.g. royal. Names including words such as 'holding', 'international' or 'group' are only permitted where a company can demonstrate that it is a holding company or has international connections or is part of a group.

BERR have consulted on the regulations restricting the choice of names under which a company may be registered. At the time of going to print it was proposed to retain the same list of sensitive names under the Companies Act 2006 as under the Companies Act 1985.

A company should indicate in the title its legal form, e.g. a public limited company should state it is a public company either in full or by use of the initials 'plc'. Similarly private limited companies should use 'limited' in full or the abbreviation 'ltd', unless in the case of a company limited by guarantee the relevant exemption has been obtained (see section 3.6.3 for further details). The Welsh equivalent of public limited and private limited may be used instead by companies registered in Wales.

Section 57 of the Companies Act 2006 introduces a new power for the Secretary of State to make regulations to specify what letters and symbols may be used in a company's registered name. The regulations may also specify a standard style or format for a name. At the time of going to print BERR had published draft regulations that cover the choice of characters that may be used and provide that the maximum length of names should be 160 characters.

3.6.3 Is it possible to dispense with the requirement to use 'limited' in a company's name?

It is possible for private companies to apply to the Registrar of Companies for an exemption if certain conditions are met. It must be a private company limited by guarantee and the company's objects must include the promotion of commerce, art, science, education, religion, charity or other profession or anything that is conducive or incidental to such objects. Its articles are also required to satisfy certain conditions, namely that:

(i)   the income of the company is applied in promoting its objectives;

(ii)   the payment of dividends or other distributions is prohibited; and

(iii)   assets on a winding up are transferred to a company having similar objects, or another charity.

Once an exemption is granted it is a criminal offence to change the articles so that the conditions are no longer met. Companies wishing to do so should contact the Registrar of Companies to first withdraw the exemption.

If a private company loses the right to dispense with the requirement to use the word 'limited' in its title, the Secretary of State may require the company to change its name so that it ends with the words 'limited' or a permitted alternative.

Additionally, a company which was a private company limited by shares on 25 February 1982 may also be exempt if it did not include 'limited' in its name because it had a licence under section 19 of the Companies Act 1948 relating to charitable companies and it complies with the requirements set out above.

3.6.4 Who may object to a company's registered name?

Sections 69 to 74 of the Companies Act 2006 are new provisions which set out who may object to a name and the procedures to be followed when an objection is made to a company name.

A person or company is, from 1 October 2008, able to object to a company's registered name on the grounds that it is:

(i)   the same as a name associated with the applicant in which he has goodwill; or

(ii) sufficiently similar that it would be likely to mislead by suggesting a connection between the company and the applicant's company.

A new office of company names adjudicator is created to hear such applications.

The merits of the objection will be reviewed and for the application to fail the respondent must show that:

(i)   the name was registered before the commencement of the activities on which the applicant is relying to show goodwill; or

(ii) the company:

- is operating under the name (or proposed name);

- has incurred substantial start up costs or is proposing to do so; or

- was formerly operating under the name and is now dormant.

(iii) the name was registered in the ordinary course of a company formation and the company was available for sale on the standard terms of that business; or

(iv) that the name was adopted in good faith; or

(v)   that the interests of the applicant are not affected to any significant extent.

In effect the company must have been formed with a genuine commercial intent to run a business.

The decision of the company names adjudicator has to be made public within 90 days of his decision and the respondent company can be ordered to change its name within a certain time period. If the name is not changed by the deadline, the adjudicator may determine a new name for the company.

3.6.5   Is there any power to change a name on the grounds it is misleading?

Yes, the Secretary of State also has residual powers to order a change of name if the information on which the name was chosen turns out to be misleading or if the name with which the company is registered gives a misleading indication of its activities which is likely to cause harm to the public. The Companies Act 2006 does not make any substantive change to existing law.

3.6.6   How does a company change its name?

The relevant sections of the Companies Act 2006 are sections 77 to 81 which are effective from 1 October 2009. The Companies Act 2006 restates the existing provisions under previous Companies Acts which allow a company to change its name by special resolution. The most significant change is that the Companies Act 2006 also allows a company to change its name by whatever means are provided for in the company's articles. The directors can also resolve to change the name if acting under the direction of the Secretary of State or a determination by the company names adjudicator.

The resolution to change the name must be filed with the Registrar of Companies and if the Registrar is satisfied that the new name complies with the regulations and the requirements of the Companies Act 2006, then the Registrar of Companies will issue a certificate of incorporation on change of name showing the new name. The change of name is effective from the date on which the new certificate of incorporation is issued.

The Companies Act 2006 also introduces a requirement to notify the Registrar of Companies of an agreement by special resolution to change the name of the company at some time in the future. This is in addition to the requirement to file the resolution changing the name of the company. This might arise, for example, where a company proposes to change its name at a date in the future following completion of an acquisition by a third party. Where the change of name is conditional, the Registrar of Companies must be notified of those conditions and whether they have occurred and must also be notified once the condition has been satisfied. Companies House will not reserve a company name until they have received all of the required documentation. Therefore, companies that submit a special resolution for a future name change will leave themselves open to losing the name if another party decides to register with that name in the meantime.

3.6.7   When a company changes its name what other changes need to be made?

When any change of name occurs a company is obliged to alter its stationery, website, e-mail footers and other materials (for example cheques and invoices) on which its name appears to reflect its change in name. Any breach by an officer of the company is a summary offence and he is liable to a fine.

A director who signs a contract or payment commitment on behalf of a company in the incorrect name will also be personally liable under that contract or payment commitment.

3.6.8   Is the company obliged to disclose its company name and other information?

Yes, companies are obliged to display the company name in full at the registered office (see section 3.13 for further information relating to the disclosure of business names).

All stationery, printed publicity material, invoices and other communications from a company must contain details of the registered number and registered office as well as the company name. New requirements are effective from 1 January 2007 under the Companies Act 2006 whereby these disclosure obligations have been extended to cover all electronic communications made on behalf of the company and information displayed on company websites.

3.7   What are the rules relating to the requirement for a company to have a registered office?

The relevant sections of the Companies Act 2006 are sections 86 to 88 which are effective from 1 October 2009. There are no substantive changes to the law relating to a company's registered office or the procedure for changing a company's registered office. The only change is in relation to the registered office of Welsh companies.

All companies are required to have a registered office address at all times at which notices and communications may be validly served (section 1139 of the Companies Act 2006). A company may change its registered office by giving notice to the Registrar of Companies and the change will take effect upon receipt of the notice by him, but for a period of 14 days from the date on which notice of the change of registered office was sent to the Registrar of Companies, a person may still validly serve any document on the company at its previous registered address.

Section 88 of the Companies Act 2006 contains new provisions that are applicable to Welsh companies. Under the Companies Act 1985, a company may elect that its registered office is to be situated only in Wales rather than in England and Wales, either on formation of the company or subsequently by special resolution. However, under the Companies Act 1985 it is not possible for a Welsh company subsequently to change such election by changing its registered office address to a place in England and Wales. Section 88(3) of the Companies Act 2006 allows for a Welsh company to cease being a Welsh company by passing a special resolution to change its registered office situation to England and Wales rather than Wales. However, if a company ceases to be a Welsh company using the procedure under section 88 of the Companies Act 2006, it will no longer be able to take advantage of the provisions under the Companies Act 2006 which permit Welsh companies to deliver documents to the Registrar of Companies in Welsh and to end their company name with Welsh versions of the of legal status, for example 'cyfyngedig' in place of 'limited' or 'c.c.c.' in place of 'p.l.c'.

3.8 Can a company change its status by re-registration?

The relevant sections of the Companies Act 2006 are sections 89 to 111 which are effective from 1 October 2009.

As under the Companies Act 1985, companies may continue to change their status by re-registration in the following ways:

(i)   from a private limited company to a public company;

(ii)   from a public company to a private limited company;

(iii)   from a private limited company to an unlimited company; and

(iv)   from an unlimited company to a private limited company.

A public company will be able to re-register directly as an unlimited company. This was not allowed under the Companies Act 1985.

The Companies Act 2006 will also replace the existing requirements for a statutory declaration to be submitted with the application for re-registration, with a statement of compliance. This will reduce the cost and time of getting a statutory declaration sworn.

3.8.1 What does a private limited company need to do to re-register as a public company?

The relevant sections are sections 90 to 96 of the Companies Act 2006. These largely restate the previous Companies Acts provisions and in particular preserve the requirement that a private company cannot register as a public company if it has previously been registered as an unlimited company.

A private company (whether limited or unlimited) may be re-registered as a public company limited by shares if:

(i)   a special resolution is passed;

(ii) an application for re-registration has been delivered to the Registrar of Companies together with the requisite documents and a statement of compliance; and

(iii) the conditions set out below are met.

It should be noted that the relevant forms to be filed with the application for re-registration will be changing following implementation of the relevant sections in the Companies Act 2006.

3.8.2   Do the articles of association need to be changed on re-registration as a public company?

Yes, a company will need to make changes to its name and articles of association to reflect its becoming a public company, for example to reflect the minimum share capital requirements of a public company.

3.8.3   Does the company need to appoint a company secretary on re-registration as a public company?

Yes, the Companies Act 2006 removes the requirements for private companies to have a company secretary. However, the requirement remains for public companies. Private companies without a company secretary will, therefore, need to appoint a company secretary or satisfy themselves that the existing company secretary will meet the required criteria set out in section 3.9.4. The Companies Act 2006 imposes a new requirement for the application to the Registrar of Companies to state that a company secretary has been appointed and must include a consent to act from the company secretary.

3.8.4   Are there any other steps that need to be taken on re-registration?

In addition all stationery and other written or electronic materials used by the company in the course of running its business will need to be amended to reflect its change in status.

3.8.5   What share capital requirements must be met to re-register as a public company?

The following requirements must be met at the time the special resolution is passed:

(i)   the nominal value of the company's allotted share capital must be not less than the authorised minimum of £50,000 or the prescribed Euros equivalent of €65,600;

(ii)   each of the allotted shares must be paid up at least as to one quarter of the nominal value of that share and the whole of any premium must also be paid (note there is an exemption for employee share schemes);

(iii)   if any shares in the company (including any premium) have been paid by an undertaking given by the shareholder that he or another should work or perform services for the company, then that undertaking must have been performed or otherwise discharged; and

(iv)   if shares have been allotted as fully or partly paid up (including any premium), otherwise than in cash and the consideration for the allotment consists of or includes an undertaking by the company, then the undertaking must have been performed or otherwise discharged or there must be a contract between the company under which the contract is to be performed within five years from the date on which the special resolution is passed.

The Registrar of Companies must not re-register a private limited company as a public company if it appears to him that the company has resolved to reduce its share capital and that the effect of the reduction would be to bring the nominal value of the company's allotted share capital to below the authorised minimum limits.

3.8.6   What net asset requirements must be met?

To re-register as a public company, the company must obtain:

(i)   a balance sheet prepared as at a date which is not more than seven months before the date on which the application is delivered to the Registrar of Companies;

(ii)   an unqualified report by the company's auditor on that balance sheet; and

(iii)   a written statement by the company's auditor that in his opinion at the balance sheet date, the amount of the company's net assets was not less than the aggregate of its called-up share capital and undistributable reserves.

In addition, between the date of the balance sheet and the date on which the application for re-registration is delivered to the Registrar of Companies, there must be no change in the company's financial position that results in the amount of its net assets falling to below the aggregate of its called-up share capital and undistributable reserves.

Section 92(3) of the Companies Act 2006 defines an 'unqualified report' as one where the audit report has been properly prepared in accordance with the Companies Act 2006 without material qualifications of the auditor's opinion.

3.8.7 If there has been an allotment of shares for a non-cash consideration since the balance sheet date what additional requirements must be satisfied?

The Companies Act 2006 requires a private company to comply with the requirements of a public company during this period in relation to an allotment of shares for non-cash consideration. The Registrar of Companies will decline to re-register the company unless:

(i)   an independent valuation of non-cash consideration has been obtained which is not more than six months old; or

(ii)   the allotment is in connection with a share exchange; or

(iii)   the allotment is in connection with a proposed merger with another company.

In the case of a share exchange, the Registrar of Companies will consider the application for re-registration where the allotment is in connection with an arrangement under which the whole or part of the consideration for the shares is provided:

(i)   by the transfer to the company allotting the shares of shares of another company; or

(ii)   the cancellation of shares in another company; and

(iii)   the allotment is open to all the holders of the shares of the other company in question.

There is a proposed merger with another company if one of the companies concerned proposes to acquire all the assets and liabilities of the other in exchange for the issue of its shares or other securities to shareholders of the other (whether or not accompanied by a cash payment).

3.8.8 What steps should be taken if the requirements cannot be met?

There may be a situation where the decision to re-register is taken both after the proposed balance sheet date and after the issue of shares for non-cash consideration. If the requirements cannot be met then companies will need to bring forward the balance sheet date to one occurring after the allotment of shares.

3.8.9 What documents must be submitted to the Registrar of Companies?

The application for re-registration as a public company must be accompanied by the relevant documents and contain the following:

(i) a statement of the company's proposed name on re-registration;

(ii) in the case of a private company without a secretary, a statement of the company's proposed secretary, including all the information that is required to be recorded in the company's register of secretaries, including a consent by the proposed named secretary;

(iii) a copy of the special resolution that the company should register as a public company;

(iv) a copy of the company's proposed articles as amended;

(v) a copy of the balance sheet and audited report and written statement;

(vi) if any recent allotment of shares for non-cash consideration is applicable, a statement as to the circumstances together with a copy of the valuation report; and

(vii) a statement confirming that all relevant sections of the Companies Act 2006 have been complied with.

Existing directorships and the company secretary, if any, will continue automatically without the need for any change.

If the company does not already have a secretary, then the proposed secretary is deemed to have been appointed to that office on the date the new certificate of incorporation is issued.

3.8.10 At what date does the re-registration become effective?

The re-registration as a public company will be effective upon the issue of the new certificate of incorporation.

3.8.11 Do I need to apply for a trading certificate once re-registered as a public company?

No, in contrast to the general rule that a public company must have a trading certificate before being able to carry on business or exercise its powers to borrow money, a private company will only be required to obtain a trading certificate on re-registration where it has not previously been trading.

3.8.12 What does a public company need to do to re-register as private limited company?

Many of the deregulatory measures of the Companies Act 2006 apply only to private companies resulting in an increased divergence in the compliance requirements of a private company in comparison with a public company. In addition many relieving provisions (for example, the abolition of financial assistance and the need to obtain court approval on reduction of capital) will only apply to private companies. Groups with wholly-owned public companies may, therefore, wish to consider re-registering those subsidiaries as private companies in due course in order to take full advantage of these deregulatory measures.

The relevant sections of the Companies Act 2006 are sections 97 to 101. The only substantive change to the previous Companies Acts is that the Registrar of Companies can proceed to approve the re-registration during the 28 day period within which dissenting members may apply to the court for an order cancelling the re-registration, providing that he is satisfied that such application cannot be made. The Registrar of Companies will have regard to the number of members who voted in favour of the resolution in making this decision. This change reflects the existing practice of the Registrar of Companies putting it on a statutory footing.

The other main change under the Companies Act 2006 is that there is a new requirement for a statement of compliance to be delivered to the Registrar of Companies.

A public company may re-register as a private company by:

(i)   passing a special resolution of the members;

(ii)   delivering an application to the Registrar of Companies together with the documents listed at (iii) below; and

(iii)   lodging with the Registrar of Companies:

- a copy of the resolution;

- a copy of the proposed amended articles; and

- a statement of compliance.

3.8.13 Does a public company need to change its articles on re-registration as a private limited company?

Yes, as the requirements of the Companies Act 2006 relating to private companies are more flexible than for public companies the articles will need to be changed.

3.8.14   Who can object to re-registration?

The following can apply to the court for the cancellation of the resolution even if the proposed re-registration has already been approved by special resolution. The application must be made within 28 days of the passing of the resolution by:

(i)   the holders of not less than 5% of the nominal value of the company's issued share capital or any class of shares; or

(ii)   5% of the members for a company limited by guarantee; or

(iii)   not less than 50 of the company's members.

A new requirement under the Companies Act 2006 is that an applicant must on making an objection give immediate notice to the Registrar of Companies of the application. This will enable the Registrar of Companies to decide whether the re-registration can still proceed without delay.

If the Registrar of Companies is satisfied the company is entitled to be re-registered and that there are no objections, he will issue a new certificate of incorporation confirming the date of re-registration and the new name. With effect from that date the changes to the company's name and articles of association will take effect.

3.8.15   What other steps should the company take?

Again, following any change of name or status new stationery and other written or electronic materials used by the company in the course of running its business will need to be amended to reflect the new status of the company.

3.8.16   What does a private limited company need to do to register as an unlimited company?

The relevant sections of the Companies Act 2006 are sections 102 to 104 and there are no substantive changes to the position under previous Companies Acts, although there is a change in emphasis in section 102 of the Companies Act 2006 which makes it clear that the assent of all the members of the company to the re-registration is required.

A private limited company may on application be re-registered as unlimited provided that the company files the following documents with the Registrar of Companies:

(i)   a copy of the special resolution evidencing the decision to re-register;

(ii)   a statement made by the directors of the company that the persons by whom, or on whose behalf, the form of consent is made constitutes evidence to confirm the consent of all the members to re-registration; and

(iii)   relevant documents reflecting the proposed changes to the name and amended articles.

Unlike other statements of compliance made under the Companies Act 2006, the statement of compliance made on application for re-registration as an unlimited company must contain a statement made by the directors confirming that:

(i)   the persons by whom, or on whose behalf, the form of assent is authenticated constitute the whole membership of the company; and

(ii)   if any of the members have not authenticated that form themselves, that the directors have taken all reasonable steps to satisfy themselves that each person who authenticated it on behalf of a member was lawfully empowered to do so.

The Registrar of Companies will not grant permission if the company has previously been registered as an unlimited private company and had re-registered as limited. This is also the case under the previous Companies Acts.

If the Registrar of Companies is satisfied that the company is entitled to be re-registered he will issue a new certificate of incorporation confirming the date of re-registration and the new name and from that date the changes to the company's name and articles will take effect.

3.8.17   Why would a private limited company re-register as an unlimited company?

The main advantage of an unlimited company over a private limited company is that it can reduce its share capital in any way that it wishes with a special resolution and it is, therefore, a more flexible vehicle for returning cash or assets to shareholders albeit that it is subject to the same rules on the payment of dividends as a limited company. This is discussed in more detail in chapter 9.

Re-registrations have, therefore, been relatively common where dormant or semi-dormant companies have sought to return assets to shareholders prior to their dissolution. Holding companies without significant creditors have also sometimes re-registered for the same reason.

Members, however, incur unlimited liability for the debts of the company, which will continue for a year after they ceased to be members and therefore any re-registration of a company which has or had a trading activity resulting in actual or contingent liabilities will require very careful consideration.

3.8.18   What does an unlimited company need to do to re-register as a private limited company?

The relevant sections of the Companies Act 2006 are sections 105 to 108.

The Companies Act 2006 contains a new requirement for a private company limited by shares to file a statement of capital in certain circumstances.

An unlimited company must file with the Registrar of Companies:

(i) a copy of the special resolution evidencing the decision to re-register;

(ii) if the company is to be limited by guarantee, a statement setting out the terms of the guarantee and the position of each member if the company is wound up while he is a member (or within one year after ceasing to be a member) regarding the payment of debts and distribution of the assets and adjustment of capital between members;

(iii) relevant documents reflecting the proposed changes to the name and amended articles; and

(iv) a statement of compliance by the directors.

A company which on re-registration already has allotted share capital (i.e. not an unlimited guarantee company), must within 15 days after re-registration, deliver a statement of capital to the Registrar of Companies unless this information has already been supplied or is contained in a recently filed annual return or there has been no change in its share capital since it was first formed.

The statement of capital should include full details of the total number of shares of each class (if there is more than one class of shares), together with the nominal value, amount paid up on each share (including any premium paid) and details of any other rights associated with the issue of such shares.

If the Registrar of Companies is satisfied that the company is entitled to be re-registered he will issue a new certificate of incorporation confirming the date of re-registration and the new name, and from that date the changes to the company's name and articles will take effect.

3.8.19 What does a public company need to do to re-register as an unlimited company?

The relevant sections of the Companies Act 2006 are sections 109 to 111 which are completely new and are effective from 1 October 2009.

Under the Companies Act 1985 a public company first has to re-register as a private limited company before re-registering as an unlimited company. The Companies Act 2006 provisions remove this intermediate step.

A public company limited by shares may apply to the Registrar of Companies to be re-registered as an unlimited company with a share capital provided the company files the following documents:

(i)   a statement confirming all the members of the company have consented to it being so re-registered;

(ii) relevant documents reflecting the proposed changes to the name and amended articles; and

(iii) a statement of compliance by the directors.

The Registrar of Companies will not grant permission if the company has previously been registered either as an unlimited company or as a private limited company.

If the Registrar of Companies is satisfied the company is entitled to be re-registered he will issue a new certificate of incorporation confirming the date of re-registration and the new name.

Revised constitutional documents must be prepared and filed with the Registrar of Companies and new stationery and other materials used by the company in the course of running its business must be changed to reflect the new status of the company.

3.9   What is the role of the company secretary and do companies need to appoint a company secretary?

The relevant sections in the Companies Act 2006 are sections 270 to 280 but much of the company secretary's role and responsibilities have evolved over time and are not purely governed by statute. The most significant change under the Companies Act 2006, with effect from 6 April 2008, is that private companies are no longer required to appoint a company secretary.

As under the Companies Act 1985, the company secretary is not required to be a natural person.

There are significant differences in the role of the company secretary depending on the size and nature of the company and whether or not it is a private or a public company. For further details relating to the role of the company secretary see section 3.9.6.

3.9.1   Is it necessary to appoint a company secretary?

Public companies continue to be required to appoint a secretary, see section 3.9.4 for details of the qualifications required of such a secretary, but with effect from 6 April 2008, a private company no longer needs to have a secretary. The government's rationale behind this change was a desire to be seen to champion a reduction in the regulatory burden on private companies.

3.9.2 What do I need to consider when deciding whether to dispense with the requirement to appoint a company secretary?

For smaller private companies typically run by a sole director, the change will remove the need to appoint a company secretary. However as the role played by the secretary in the preparation and conduct of board meetings, minute taking and other governance duties traditionally assigned to the secretary will still need to be done, private companies may not wish to take advantage of this exemption. Where a company secretary is retained by a private company, he will be able to carry out the function of that office with the full authority that a company secretary has hitherto had under the Companies Act 1985.

3.9.3 What are the relevant considerations if dispensing with a company secretary?

A private company wishing to dispense with the company secretary's role should review its articles before doing so as changes may be needed to remove references to any requirement for a company secretary or acts being performed by the secretary.

The new regime for the execution of documents is discussed under section 3.5.4 above.

Under the Companies Act 1985 if a company had only one director, that sole director could not also be the company secretary. As with effect from 6 April 2008 the Companies Act 2006 does not require a private limited company to have a company secretary; it is now possible for a sole director to also be the company secretary.

3.9.4 What are the qualifications required for the secretary of a public company?

Under section 273 of the Companies Act 2006 the directors of a public company have a duty to take all reasonable steps to ensure that the secretary of the company:

(i)   is a person who appears to them to have the requisite knowledge and experience to discharge the functions of secretary; and

(ii)   has one or more of the following qualifications:

- has held the office of secretary of a public company for at least three of the five years immediately preceding his appointment as secretary; or

- is a member of one of the seven professional bodies (for example the Institute of Chartered Secretaries and Administrators or the Institute of Chartered Accountants in England and Wales); or

- is a qualified barrister or solicitor; or

- is a person who by reason of having held another position or being a member of any other body appears to the directors to be capable of discharging the functions of secretary of the company.

This is largely the position under the previous Companies Acts.

3.9.5 What are the qualification requirements for the secretary of a private company?

The Companies Act 2006 does not contain any qualification requirements for being secretary of a private company and where one is appointed the directors will have responsibility for choosing a suitable person or a corporate secretary. This is the same position as under previous Companies Acts.

3.9.6 What are the key responsibilities of a company secretary?

The company secretary's remit is wide ranging and will vary from company to company, but the secretary has always been seen as playing a key and pivotal role "in ensuring that board procedures are both followed and regularly reviewed"[1].

Although the legal status of the company secretary is not enshrined in statute, it is generally accepted that the secretary is an officer of the company with extensive duties and responsibilities for the day to day running of the company's business. In addition, the secretary has ostensible authority to bind the company as the definition of 'officer' in the Companies Acts is considered by the Court of Appeal to include the secretary. As a result, the secretary may be liable, with the directors, to prosecution for failure to comply with relevant parts of the Companies Acts.

In the case of *Panorama Developments Ltd v Fidelis Furnishing* Ltd [1971] 2 QB 711 (1971) the Court of Appeal held that even where authority is not expressly conferred, the company secretary is nonetheless the company's chief administrative officer and has ostensible authority in day to day administrative matters and therefore the company was bound by the secretary's acts.

The Companies Act 2006, as was the case with the previous Companies Acts, does not provide a definition of the duties assigned to the secretary. However, the company secretary is often seen as the custodian of the corporate conscience and acts as a link between the board and the shareholders and also between the executive and non-executive directors, being responsible for corporate compliance and governance and acting as the board's advisor on legislation and best practice.

---

[1] Report of the Committee on The Financial Aspects of Corporate Governance, 1 December 1992.

In particular the duties may include:

(i)   management of key relationships within the board and company, ensuring that an adequate governance framework is in place, e.g. schedule of matters reserved for the board and delegated authorities;

(ii) organisation and taking the minutes of board and company meetings (including the annual general meeting for public companies);

(iii) assisting the board in the preparation of the annual report and accounts (particularly in the case of listed companies which require governance disclosures);

(iv) compliance with the company's constitution, other relevant regulation and best practice guidance (in the case of the secretary of a listed company with the Listing Rules and investor guidance issued by, for example, the Association of British Insurers);

(v)   management of the annual timetable;

(vi) responsibility for all corporate changes, e.g. share transfers and issues; directors; and new company incorporations and dissolutions;

(vii) maintenance of the statutory registers for all group companies;

(viii) filing of regulatory information (e.g. with the Registrar of Companies and the Financial Services Authority);

(ix) providing training for the board on legislation and best practice; and

(x)   management of share schemes and other employee benefit schemes.

For listed companies and larger private companies, the secretary is usually the conduit for the non-executive directors, shareholders, external advisors, regulators and the press to communicate with the board. The secretary is also usually the secretary to the board as well as board committees, such as the audit, remuneration and nomination committees.

3.9.7   On appointment does the secretary need to file details of his home address with Companies House?

As with other officers of the company, the secretary may from 1 October 2009 choose to use a service address, for example the registered office of the company, as his registered address if he wishes to take advantage of the new rules. However, historic details of his residential address will remain on the public record.

3.9.8   What happens if there is a vacancy?

It is mandatory for a public company to have a company secretary. In the event of a vacancy the Secretary of State has power to issue a direction requiring the company to comply.

In addition, with effect from 6 April 2008, the Companies Act 2006 permits an assistant or deputy secretary to fulfil the role. Alternatively the directors have the power to fill the vacancy with not only an officer of the company (as is the case under the Companies Act 1985) but any other person.

3.9.9   If the company proposes to dispense with the requirement for a company secretary must it notify Companies House?

Yes, if a private company decides it does not wish to replace a retiring company secretary, then it is obliged to notify Companies House of this decision.

3.9.10   Does the company have a duty to keep a register of secretaries?

Section 275 of the Companies Act 2006 specifies that a company with a secretary has a duty to keep a register of its secretaries which contains particulars of, in the case of an individual, the name (former name, if any, including a woman's maiden name), address and date of appointment. In the case of a corporate secretary, details of the legal name and status, registered or principal office and registration number should be shown on the register. This register is open to inspection by shareholders and the public at the company's registered office or such other place as may be specified in the legislation yet to be issued by the Secretary of State.

This information must also be filed with the Registrar of Companies and kept up to date when changes occur.

3.10   What has to be disclosed in the annual return?

The relevant sections are 854 to 859 of the Companies Act 2006, which come into effect on 1 October 2009. There are a number of changes which are brought into force by the Companies Act 2006 which are discussed at section 3.10.1.

The annual return is a snapshot of a company's statutory position at a particular point in time.

Every company has a duty to deliver to the Registrar of Companies successive annual returns each of which must be made up to a date not later than the anniversary of the company's incorporation or, if the company's last return was made up to a different date, the anniversary of that date.

The annual return for all companies (including those without share capital) must state the date to which it is made up and include the following information:

(i)   the address of the company's registered office;

(ii)   the type of company and its principal business activities (see below);

(iii)   particulars of the current directors and secretary (if a private company has elected to have one);

(iv)   address at which the register of members is kept available for inspection; and

(v)   details of any registered debentures and the address at which the register of debentures is kept available for inspection.

Information relating to the company's type and business activities are given by reference to certain prescribed classifications available from the Registrar of Companies. These may subsequently be amended if the nature of the company's business alters.

Companies with share capital and shareholders must also provide the following additional information in the annual return:

(i)   a statement of the share capital including (as at the date of the return):

-   the total number of shares (and if more than one class details of all classes of shares);

-   the aggregate nominal value of the shares;

-   the total number and particulars of the rights attached to each class of shares; and

-   the amount paid up and the amount (if any) unpaid on each share – whether on account of the nominal value or by way of premium).

(ii)   information on every person who is a current member of the company on the date to which the return is made up or who has ceased to be a member since the date of the last annual return (or since incorporation in the case of a first return), including the number of shares in each class held or transferred by the current or former member together with the date of transfer (see below).

A company must provide a full list of members on the first annual return and every third annual return. In other years changes to shareholders during the year are required to be disclosed.

Failure to deliver an annual return within 28 days of the return date is an offence committed by the company and every director (including shadow directors), the secretary (if one is appointed by a private company) and any other officer of the company rendering them liable to summary conviction and a fine. The contravention continues until such time as an annual return made up to the return date is delivered to the Registrar of Companies.

Unlike the position with late filing penalties for the failure to deliver accounts to the Registrar of companies on time, no fines are presently levied for failure to deliver the annual return, but this position is being kept under review and may be subject to change in the future. A company which has failed to deliver its annual return and accounts to the Registrar of Companies on time is at risk that he will deem that the company is defunct and remove it from the register resulting in its dissolution. The consequence of this is that the company's assets become *bona vacantia* (ownerless goods) and the company's officers and shareholders will have to have the company restored to the register to recover them (see chapter 11 for the new procedure under the Companies Act 2006).

3.10.1   Has the annual return changed under the Companies Act 2006?

Yes. The Companies Act 2006 brings in the following changes relating to the information to be disclosed in the annual return:

(i)   only public companies, and private companies who have chosen to retain a company secretary, need give details;

(ii)   annual returns for companies with a share capital must contain a statement of capital (see section 3.10 for further details on statements of capital);

(iii)   where any shares have been admitted to trading on a regulated market since the date of the last annual return this must be stated;

(iv)   companies listed on an EU regulated market need not disclose the addresses of members who hold less than 5% of any class of shares at any time during the year;

(v)   it is necessary to disclose where all registers are kept, not just the register of members and debenture holders;

(vi)   once a company has filed an annual return to a date after 30 September 2007 it will become subject to the new rules relating to access to the register of members which allows a company to apply to court to be relieved from the obligation to provide a copy of the register of members if it is not sought for a proper purpose (see section 3.14 for further details relating to this); and

(vii)   non-traded public companies will be required to disclose the name of every person who is a member of the company at any one time during the return period but the addresses of the members will not need to be disclosed.

3.11 What procedures should be followed when a company creates a charge over the assets and/or property of a company?

The relevant sections are 860 to 877 of the Companies Act 2006 which are effective from 1 October 2009 and largely restate the existing position.

These sections set out the procedures for companies registered in England and Wales or Northern Ireland, separate rules apply to companies registered in Scotland which are set out in sections 878 to 892 of the Companies Act 2006.

3.11.1 What is the position regarding charges created over property which is situated within the UK?

Section 860 provides that a company that creates a charge to which the Companies Act 2006 applies must deliver details of the charge together with a copy of the instrument of charge (if any) to the Registrar of Companies for registration within 21 days of either:

(i)   the charge being created; or

(ii)   the property acquired, where the property is subject to a pre-existing charge which is not being discharged on acquisition and all the rights and obligations created by the charge are transferred to the acquiring company.

The 21 day period begins on the day following the date on which the charge is created or the property is acquired or transferred.

The person in whose favour the charge is created may elect to register the charge instead of the company. In this case the registrant is entitled to recover any fees properly paid by him to the Registrar of Companies on registration.

The following charges created by a company require registration with the Registrar of Companies:

(i)   a charge on land or any interest in land (except a charge for rent);

(ii)   a charge or instrument which, if executed by an individual, would require registration as a bill of sale;

(iii)   a charge securing any type of debenture;

(iv)   a charge on uncalled share capital or a charge on share capital that has been called, but not paid;

(v)   a charge on the book debts of the company;

(vi)   a floating charge on the company's property or undertaking;

(vii)   a charge on a ship, aircraft or any share therein; and

(viii) a charge on goodwill or on any intellectual property.

The Companies Act 1985 provides that the registration provisions extend to charges and mortgages over property in England and Wales that are created by a company incorporated outside England and Wales which has an established place of business or a branch there. This registration requirement applies even if the company has failed to register a place of business or a branch in England and Wales. Registration of charges against overseas companies are recorded by Companies House in what is known as a 'Slavenburg Register'. As the place of business or branch test is a matter of fact and given the difficulty in determining whether an overseas company has made any filings in a Slavenburg Register, the provisions under the Companies Act 1985 were considered by many practitioners to be inadequate.

The Slavenburg registration provisions have been removed from the Companies Act 2006. However, the Secretary of State has been given powers to make regulations requiring overseas companies with a business presence in England and Wales to register specific charges and mortgages over their property in that jurisdiction. These regulations, currently in draft form (the Companies Act 2006 overseas company regulations published 14 July 2008) will still require companies incorporated outside of England and Wales, which have a place of business or branch there, to register at Companies House charges and mortgages over certain assets which are located in that jurisdiction on the date that the security is created. If any such security is not registered, the company and its officers will be liable to a fine and the security will be void against any liquidator, administrator or creditor of the company.

3.11.2   What is the position regarding charges created over property outside the UK?

Section 866 of the Companies Act 2006 provides that where a charge is created outside the UK over property situated outside the UK, the company must deliver to the Registrar of Companies a certified copy of the document by which the statutory charge is created. This should be sent to the Registrar of Companies within 21 days of the date when it would be reasonable to expect a copy of the charge to have been received in the UK if it was sent by the normal postal service.

Where a charge is created in the UK but comprises property outside the UK, the instrument must be sent to the Registrar of Companies for registration, but it may also be necessary for additional steps to be taken to perfect registration in the country in which the property is situated.

3.11.3 What is the position regarding charges created over property which is in another part of the UK?

Under section 867 of the Companies Act 2006 where a charge is created over property situated in a part of the UK, other than the part in which the company itself is registered, then a certified copy of the instrument by which the charge is created together with a certificate indicating in which part of the UK the property is situated should be delivered to the Registrar of Companies.

Additional rules apply to registration of certain charges over land in Northern Ireland, which are contained in section 868 of the Companies Act 2006.

3.11.4 What happens when a charge is satisfied or released?

Section 872 of the Companies Act 2006 provides that where the charge has been wholly or partially paid or satisfied, then a memorandum of satisfaction should be filed with the Registrar of Companies and the register will be amended.

3.11.5 What are the consequences of failure to register charges created by a company?

Under section 874 of the Companies Act 2006, the failure to register a charge within the prescribed time frame renders the security over the company's property or undertaking void against a liquidator, administrator or creditor of the company.

In addition, and without prejudice to any other contract or obligation for repayment of money secured by the charge, when a charge becomes void, then the money secured by it becomes payable in full immediately.

3.11.6 What obligations are imposed on companies to keep a register of charges and copies of the instruments under which charges are created?

Section 876 stipulates that every limited company must keep available for inspection a register of charges which include a summary description of any property charged and all floating charges over the whole or part of the company's property and undertaking.

In addition a company must keep available for inspection a copy of every instrument creating a charge, which must be registered under the Companies Act 2006. Where a series of debentures consists of uniform documents, then a copy of one of them should be kept.

The register and documents should be available for inspection by any member or creditor of the company (without charge) and should be kept at the company's registered office.

See section 3.14 for further information relating to the requirement to make the register of charges available for inspection.

3.11.7 What are the consequences of failure to maintain a register of charges?

An officer of the company who knowingly or wilfully permits or authorises an entry to be omitted commits an offence liable to summary conviction and a fine.

3.11.8 What obligations does the Registrar of Companies have to keep a register of charges?

Section 869 of the Companies Act 2006 requires the Registrar of Companies to keep a register of all charges registered against the company and upon receipt of the completed application form and supporting documentation, the Registrar of Companies will issue a certificate of registration, stating the amount of the charge and other relevant information which will be conclusive evidence that the registration formalities required by the Companies Act 2006 have been completed.

3.11.9 Are there any changes to the rules relating to the registration of Scottish charges?

Yes. Sections 878 to 894 of the Companies Act 2006 deal with the proposed new law relating to the registration of charges in Scotland. At the time of writing draft regulations had not yet been published but it is expected that the regulations will come into force on 1 October 2009.

The main proposal coming out of the consultation was to allow the government to use its new powers under the Companies Act 2006 to treat floating charges registered in the Scottish register of floating charges as having been registered with the Registrar of Companies. The purpose of the proposal is to remove the burden of double registration which will otherwise apply to all floating charges granted under Scottish law, irrespective of whether the grantor company is registered in Scotland, once the provisions of the Bankruptcy and Diligence etc. (Scotland) Act 2007 have been brought into force.

The Bankruptcy and Diligence etc. (Scotland) Act 2007 provides for the establishment in Scotland of a new register to be called the Register of Floating Charges. This register will be set up and maintained by the Keeper of the Registers of Scotland. Once the provisions of this Act have been implemented, registration in the Register of Floating Charges will be essential for the valid creation of a floating charge under Scottish law. This will apply to all companies registering charges in Scotland regardless of whether or not they are a Scottish registered company.

For floating charges created under Scottish law, the deed itself will be registered. The chargee will be required to send the deed to the Keeper, together with an application form. The content of the form which will be prescribed by Scottish Ministers is not yet available. An e-registration option is also likely to be introduced. Provided the application complies with the necessary requirements and is accepted by the Keeper, the floating charge will be created on the date of registration.

There will also be provision for the registration of an advance notice of a floating charge. Provided that the floating charge itself is registered within 21 days of the registration of the advance notice, the date of creation of the charge will be taken to be the date on which the advance notice was registered.

The Bankruptcy and Diligence etc. (Scotland) Act 2007 also provides for Instruments of Alteration to be registered with the Keeper for floating charges created under these provisions. It also provides for the registration with the Keeper of a variety of other deeds, such as assignations to a new creditor.

The Register of Floating Charges will be maintained electronically and will be searchable on-line.

3.11.10   How does the Bankruptcy and Diligence etc. (Scotland) Act 2007 fit with the requirements of the Companies Act 2006?

Under the Companies Act 2006, in the event of a company's insolvency, any charge granted by it will only be valid in the UK against an administrator or liquidator or any creditor of the company if it is registered with the Registrar of Companies within 21 days of it having been created. Under the Bankruptcy and Diligence etc. (Scotland) Act 2007, Scottish law provides that the establishment of a right under a floating charge will take place on its registration in the Register of Floating Charges held by the Keeper. This will apply regardless of the company's place of registration. The combined effect of these provisions is that in the event of the company's insolvency a Scottish floating charge granted by it will not be valid in the UK against an administrator or liquidator or any creditor of the company in the event of the company's insolvency unless it had been registered with the Registrar of Companies within 21 days of its registration with the Keeper. Thus there will be two requirements to register a Scottish floating charge.

In order to avoid the situation where a company has two requirements to register a Scottish floating charge the Companies Act 2006 will contain a new power to make a provision that a charge registered in a special register (such as the Register of Floating Charges) is to be treated as if it were registered with the Registrar of Companies. This power will mean that the requirement to deliver to the Registrar of Companies the prescribed particulars of a Scottish floating charge will be satisfied by registration in the Scottish register.

It is intended that information held by the Keeper in relation to such charges will be fully accessible to anyone searching Companies House records.

In such circumstances the Registrar of Companies will not issue a certificate of registration of that charge, the evidence of registration in the Keeper's register will be conclusive evidence that the requirements to register a charge have been satisfied.

When a Scottish floating charge has been satisfied the company will be subject to Scottish law regarding the required documents of discharge and therefore the required documentation will need to be filed with the Keeper rather than the Registrar of Companies.

3.12 What are the rules relating to the registration and conduct of overseas companies that wish to open a branch in the UK?

The relevant sections of the Companies Act 2006 are sections 1044 to 1059 which come into effect on 1 October 2009.

The current framework for overseas companies that operate their business in Great Britain has two different regimes depending on whether the operation qualifies as a place of business or a branch. Under both regimes, an overseas company must register with the Registrar of Companies and comply with the specific filing obligations relevant to the particular regime applicable to its operation.

The Companies Act 2006 contains little detail of the provisions that apply to overseas companies from 1 October 2009; instead it gives the power to the Secretary of State to make regulations to set out the specific requirements. On 7 December 2007, a draft of the Overseas Companies Regulations was published for consultation until 7 March 2008. The draft regulations create a single regulatory regime for all UK establishments of overseas companies to replace the current place of business and branch regimes.

3.12.1 When does an overseas company have to register as having a branch in the UK?

Section 1044 of the Companies Act 2006 defines an 'overseas company' as a company that is incorporated outside of the UK but there is no definition of a branch.

In relation to overseas companies established under the Companies Act 1985 the courts and BERR have previously provided guidance as to what constitutes a branch or a place of business. At the time of writing no such similar guidance is available for branches established under the Companies Act 2006.

An overseas company must register the relevant particulars and documents set out in section 3.12.2 within one month of establishing a branch in the UK.

3.12.2 What are the registration requirements on establishing a branch?

Every overseas company which has established a branch in the UK is required to deliver the following documents to the Registrar of Companies:

(i)   the prescribed form containing details of the particulars set out below;

(ii)   a certified copy of the company's constitution; and

(ii)   if the overseas company is required to file copies of accounting documents, a copy of the latest accounts required to be prepared in accordance with its parent law before the end of the period allowed for delivery of the form, or if earlier, the date on which the company delivers the form (see 3.12.3 below).

If the company's constitution or accounting documents are not in English they must be accompanied by a certified constitution.

The main particulars to be disclosed are as follows:

(i)   the company's corporate name or an alternative name under which it proposes to carry on business in the UK;

(ii)   the company's legal form;

(iii) the identity of the register in which it is registered and the number with which it is registered;

(iv)   details of its directors and secretary (if applicable) such as in the case of an individual appointed as a director:

- his name;

- any former name;

- his service address;

- his usual residential address;

- his nationality;

- the country or state in which he is usually resident;

- his business occupation (if any);

- his date of birth;

- the extent of his powers to represent the company and whether or not he may act alone or jointly;

and for an individual appointed as secretary:

- his name;

- any former name;

- his service address; and

- his usual residential address.

(v) whether the company is a relevant credit or financial institution;

(vi) the particulars of the branch such as:

- the address;

- the date on which the branch opened;

- the business carried on by the branch;

- the name and service address of every person authorised to accept service of documents on behalf of the company and the extent of their authority; and

- details of every person authorised to represent the company as a permanent representative and the extent of their authority.

If at the time that the overseas company is due to deliver the above documents to the Registrar of Companies the company has another branch registered in the UK and has delivered the required documents to the Registrar of Companies in relation to that branch, the company may instead of delivering the documents again refer in its return to the documents previously delivered to the Registrar of Companies. In such circumstances the return must disclose where the existing branch is registered and give its registered number and also state that the required documents have been delivered in respect of another UK establishment.

3.12.3   What accounts are required to be filed on registration?

For overseas companies that are required to prepare, have audited and disclose accounts in their country of origin, or are incorporated in the EEA and are required to prepare and disclose accounts but are exempted from the requirement to have its accounts audited, a copy of those accounts in relation to the latest financial period must be submitted to the Registrar of Companies along with the registration documents outlined in section 3.12.2. For those companies where no such accounts are required no accounts need to be filed as part of the registration process.

If at the time of registration the overseas company has another establishment in the UK which has delivered copies of the required accounts, such accounts may be relied upon for the new registration. In order to take advantage of the accounts filed by another branch of the overseas company, the company must state that it is relying upon documents delivered by another UK establishment and state where that establishment is registered and provide its registered number.

3.12.4   Are there restrictions on the use of the name?

Circumstances may prevent an overseas company from being able to register its corporate name in the UK, for example where it was too similar or identical to a name that is already registered or the words used are prohibited under UK law. The Registrar of Companies may require the overseas company to choose an alternative name. As referred to in section 3.13, the Companies Act 2006 reinstates the provisions of the Business Names Act 1985 and extends the restrictions under the Companies Act 1985 on the use of business names to cover all overseas companies carrying on business in the UK, not just those with a place of business in the UK. Further detail on the restrictions on the choice of company names can be found in section 3.6 and 3.13.

3.12.5   What information must be disclosed at the address of an overseas company?

An overseas company must continuously display the company's name and country of incorporation in a prominent position so that it may be easily read by any visitor at the service address of every person authorised to accept service of legal notice on behalf of the company and every other location in the UK at which it carries on business.

3.12.6   What happens if there is a change in the registered particulars?

The overseas company must inform the Registrar of Companies of any changes to the information set out in section 3.12.2 or if the overseas company ceases to have a branch in the UK.

3.12.7   What happens if the overseas company changes the location of the branch?

In the event that an overseas company changes the location of its branch from one part of the UK to another such as from England to Scotland it will be necessary for the existing branch to be closed and for another branch to be opened. In such cases it is necessary for the existing establishment to give notice to this effect and for a new branch to be registered in respect of the new establishment. The relocation of a branch within the same part of the UK would not require the existing branch to be de-registered. See section 3.12.2 for further information in relation to the registration of a branch. From the date on which notice is given the overseas company is no longer required to deliver documents to the Registrar of Companies in respect of that establishment.

3.12.8   Is a director of an overseas company or a permanent representative of the company required to make their residential address publicly available?

Yes, but a director of an overseas company or a permanent representative of the company may take advantage of the protection from disclosure regime available to directors and officers of UK registered companies under the provisions of the Companies Act 2006 by the use of a service address instead of their usual residential address.

3.12.9   What happens if the overseas company has multiple branches in the UK?

Where an overseas company has multiple registrations in the UK, the company would be required to deliver all relevant information to the Registrar of Companies for each part of the UK in which the overseas company has a registration. This would apply unless, on initial registration, the particulars registered with the Registrar of Companies state the intention that the filing requirements are to be complied with in respect of another UK establishment and that these have been filed. The particulars should also state where the other UK establishment is registered, its registered number and that the other UK establishment has no outstanding obligation to make returns or file accounts to the Registrar of Companies.

3.12.10   What are the penalties for failure to register?

The person(s) responsible for complying with UK legislation commits an offence if he fails to comply with the registration requirements. A person who is found guilty of such an offence is liable, on summary conviction, to a fine not exceeding level three on the standard scale and for on-going contravention, to a daily default fine not exceeding one tenth of level three on the standard scale. Level 3 of the standard scale is currently £1,000.

3.12.11   What accounts are required to be filed on an annual basis?

Overseas companies that are required to prepare, have audited and disclose accounts in their country of origin, or are incorporated in the EEA and are required to prepare and disclose accounts but are exempted from the requirement to have its accounts audited, must deliver a copy of those accounts to the Registrar of Companies in relation to each financial period.

Overseas companies that are not required to disclose accounts in their country of origin are required to prepare accounts for the company for each of its financial years that are known as individual accounts (subject to the duty to prepare group accounts). The individual accounts may be prepared in accordance with the law in the country of origin, international accounting standards or section 396 of the Companies Act 2006. A company may only prepare individual accounts in accordance with the law in its country of origin if the content of such accounts includes that which is required by section 396 of the Companies Act 2006.

If at the end of the financial year an overseas company is a parent company, the directors must prepare group accounts for the year instead of individual accounts. As for individual accounts the group accounts must be prepared in accordance with the law in the country of origin, international accounting standards or section 404 of the Companies Act 2006. A company may only prepare accounts in accordance with the law in its country of origin if the content of such accounts includes that required by section 404 of the Companies Act 2006.

3.12.12   What must individual accounts for an overseas company comprise?

Overseas companies that are required to prepare individual accounts must comprise a balance sheet as at the last day of the financial year and a profit and loss account. They must also comply with the requirements of Schedule 1 to the Overseas Companies Regulation 2008 as to the content of the balance sheet and profit and loss account and additional information that is to be provided by way of notes to the accounts.

Where the overseas company prepares the individual accounts in accordance with international accounting standards the individual accounts must state the following in the notes:

(i)   that the accounts have been prepared in accordance with international accounting standards;

(ii)   which international accounting standards have been applied; and

(iii)   if they have been audited, whether they have been audited in accordance with Generally Accepted Auditing Standards and, if applicable, which standards have been followed.

Where the overseas company prepares the individual accounts in accordance with the applicable law in the country of origin the individual accounts must state the following in the notes:

(i)   that the accounts have been prepared in accordance with the company's parent law;

(ii)   the name of the legislation under which the accounts have been prepared;

(iii)   whether the accounts have been prepared in accordance with Generally Accepted Accounting Principles, and if so, which principles have been followed;

(iv)   whether the accounts have been audited; and

(v)   if they have been audited, whether they have been audited in accordance with Generally Accepted Auditing Standards and, if applicable, which standards have been followed.

3.12.13   What must group accounts for an overseas company comprise?

Overseas companies that are required to prepare group accounts must include a consolidated balance sheet and a consolidated profit and loss account both of which must include the parent company and subsidiary undertakings.

The group accounts must comply with the provisions of Schedule 2 of the Overseas Companies Regulations 2008 in relation to the content of the consolidated balance sheet, the profit and loss account and additional information to be provided in the notes to the accounts.

As for individual accounts where the overseas company prepares group accounts that have been prepared in accordance with international accounting standards, the group accounts must state the following in the notes:

(i)   that the accounts have been prepared in accordance with international accounting standards;

(ii)   which international accounting standards have been applied; and

(iii) if they have been audited, whether they have been audited in accordance with Generally Accepted Auditing Standards and, if applicable, which standards have been followed.

As for individual accounts where the overseas company prepares group accounts that have been prepared in accordance with the applicable law in the country of origin the group accounts must state the following in the notes:

(i)   that the accounts have been prepared in accordance with the company's parent law;

(ii)   the name of the legislation under which the accounts have been prepared;

(iii) whether the accounts have been prepared in accordance with Generally Accepted Accounting Principles, and if so, which principles have been followed;

(iv)   whether the accounts have been audited; and

(v)   if they have been audited, whether they have been audited in accordance with Generally Accepted Auditing Standards and, if applicable, which standards have been followed.

3.12.14   Are there any additional considerations and requirements for overseas companies listed on a regulated market in the UK?

If an overseas company with a branch is also listed on the Main Market of the London Stock Exchange or on Plus Markets PLUS-listed market, it has to comply with the filing obligations imposed by the Companies Act 2006 and is bound by the requirements of the FSA Listing Rules and the Disclosure Rules and Transparency Rules.

3.13   What is a business name and what restrictions are there on the use of business names?

A business name can be used where a company wishes to carry on business in a name other than that with which it is registered.

The provisions under the Companies Act 2006 relating to 'business names' are set out in sections 1192 to 1208 and are effective from 1 October 2009, this also applies to individuals and partnerships which are outside the scope of this book.

The main change to the Companies Act 1985 relating to companies is that the existing restriction on the use of business names will apply to all overseas companies carrying on business in the UK and not just those with a place of business here in the UK.

As with company names, care should be taken to ensure that use of a business name does not infringe third party trade mark rights. See further details in section 3.6.1.

3.13.1   Are there any sensitive words or expressions that may not be used?

Yes, section 1193 of the Companies Act 2006 provides that names suggesting a connection with government or public authorities may not be used without the express written permission of the Secretary of State or relevant government department and permission may be refused or, if granted, be withdrawn at any time.

Names containing an inappropriate indication of the company type or legal form will be considered misleading and the use of such words in the business name may be prohibited.

In a change to the Companies Act 1985, section 1198 of the Companies Act 2006 also provides that a company may also not carry on business in the UK under a name that gives so misleading an indication of the nature of the activities of the business as is likely to cause harm to the public. See section 3.6 for further details relating to the choice of company name.

3.14 What are the requirements for the inspection and copying of company records?

The relevant sections under the Companies Act 2006 are sections 1134 to 1138 which are effective from 1 October 2009.

3.14.1 What records are companies required to make available for inspection?

Companies are required to keep various statutory books, records and registers and to make them available for inspection by certain people. The rules as to where these records and registers must be kept, who may inspect them and request copies, and whether a charge can be made are set out in the table in section 3.14.4.

3.14.2 Where are these records required to be kept?

The general rule is that company records must be kept at the registered office. However in some cases the Companies Act 2006 allows the record or register to be kept or made available for inspection somewhere else within the company's jurisdiction of incorporation.

3.14.3 Can company records be kept in electronic form?

Yes, the Companies Act 2006 permits records to be kept in hard copy or electronic form, arranged in any manner that the directors think fit provided the information is adequately recorded for future reference and the company is under a duty to make sure that adequate steps are taken to guard against falsification.

3.14.4 What are the inspection and copying rights?

The rules governing inspection and copying of company records are set out in in the table below, some of these rules are still subject to transitional modifications.

Where the Companies Act 2006 specifies that documents should be made available for inspection, then an offence shall be committed by the directors and officers of the company if they fail to comply with a request for inspection and, where permitted under Companies Act 2006, the obtaining of copy documents. Nothing in the Companies Act 2006 prevents a company from giving more extensive access to its records if it so chooses.

Table of information regarding inspection and location of Company Records and Registers

Type of record/ register	Record/register	Place register must be kept/place at which must be made available from inspection*	Inspection rights	Free/fee payable for inspection**
Statutory registers	Register of members.	Registered office or place where register is made up in jurisdiction.	Members	Free
			Any person	Fee
	Register of directors and secretaries.	Registered office.	Members	Free
			Any person	Fee
	Register of investigations into interests in shares (not for private companies).	Registered office or place specified by regulations (until such regulations are made the register may be kept at the same place as the register of members and no notice need be given to the Registrar of Companies as to its location).	Members/ Any person	Free
	Register of mortgages and charges.	Registered office.	Member/ creditor	Free
			Any person	Fee
	Register of debentures.	From 6 April 2008, registered office or place specified by regulations (until such regulation are made the register may be kept at any place where the register is made up within the jurisdiction). New regime enabling companies to deny access to the register if not for a proper purpose.	Debenture holders/ members	Free
			Any person	Fee
Minutes	Minutes of board meetings.	Registered office or place specified in regulations.	N/A	N/A
	Minutes of general meetings.	As determined by directors.	Members	Free

Type of record/register	Record/register	Place register must be kept/place at which must be made available from inspection*	Inspection rights	Free/fee payable for inspection**
Corporate records	Accounting records for financial years beginning on or after 6 April 2008.	Registered office or place where directors determine (if kept outside UK, copies must be kept in UK).	Officers	Free
	Director's service contracts Director's qualifying indemnity provision.	Registered office or place specified in regulations until such regulations are made contracts may be kept at same place as register of members or at the principle place of business if within jurisdiction).	Members	Free
	Contracts for the purchase of own shares.	Registered office.	Members/any person (plc only).	Free

*Generally if the record/register is kept other than at the registered office, notification on the prescribed form must be given to the Registrar of Companies of that address.
**Generally a fee is also payable if copies of records/registers are required.

3.14.5   Are there any changes to the requirements relating to the register of members?

Yes, measures have been introduced under the Companies Act 2006 which modify the right to inspect and be provided with a copy of a company's register of members. Companies will have the right to refer a request to the court if they think that the request may not have been made for a proper purpose.

A person who is seeking to inspect or to be provided with a copy of the register of members must first supply their name and address, the purpose for which the information will be used and, if the information will be disclosed to any other person, the same information relating to them.

It should be noted that the Companies Act 2006 does not define 'proper purpose' for the purpose of this section and guidance from BERR states that it is for the courts to determine whether a particular application is for a proper purpose.

Two new offences have been created by section 119 of the Companies Act 2006 in relation to the register of members as follows:

(i)   it is an offence for a person knowingly or recklessly to make a statement in relation to a request to inspect or be provided with a copy of the register of members that is misleading, false or deceptive in a material particular; and

(ii) it is an offence for a person possessing information obtained from the register of members under these provisions to disclose such information to another person, or to fail to do anything with the result that the information is disclosed to another person, knowing or having reason to suspect that that person may use the information for a purpose that is not a proper purpose.

A person guilty of an offence under this section will be liable to conviction for a term not exceeding two years or a fine (or both).

The Companies Act 2006 also introduces a new requirement for a company where a request is made to inspect or be provided with a copy of the register of members to inform that person whether the information contained in the register of members is up to date and, if not, the date to which it has been made up.

The provision in the Companies Act 1985 that required companies to retain details of former members on the register of members for a period of 20 years has been reduced to 10 years.

3.14.6   Are there any changes to the requirements relating to the register of directors and secretaries?

Yes. A new requirement under the Companies Act 2006 is that in the case of a married woman, the exemption from the requirement to state any former name(s) has been removed. As a result of this, any such former name(s) including a maiden name will need to be included in the register of directors and secretaries. There is also a new requirement for companies to keep a register of the usual residential addresses of directors who are individuals, this is in addition to the details of any service address maintained on the register of directors and secretaries. This register will not be open to public inspection. See the table at 3.14.4 for further details relating to the register of directors and secretaries.

3.14.7   Is there a requirement to maintain a register of substantial interests in shares?

No, the Companies Act 1985 required public companies to maintain a register of substantial interests in shares, but this requirement has been repealed by the Companies Act 2006. There is a new requirement for listed companies to keep a register of information obtained under section 793 of the Companies Act 2006 as a result of an investigation into interests in shares. See the table at

3.14.4 for further details relating to the register of investigations into interests in shares.

3.14.8 Is there a requirement to maintain a register of directors' interests in shares?

No, on 6 April 2007 the requirement for public and private companies to maintain a register of directors' interests in shares was repealed. Listed companies must continue to report to the market changes in the share interests of its directors and other persons discharging managerial responsibilities in accordance with the requirements of the FSA. It must also include directors' share interests in its annual report. In practice therefore it is likely that listed companies will continue to maintain a register.

3.14.9 What are the changes relating to the transfer of debentures and related company books?

The Companies Act 2006 brings together in one part (Part 19) a number of provisions of the Companies Act 1985 relating to debentures. These provisions came into force on 6 April 2008.

Section 738 of the Companies Act 2006 has restated the existing definition of 'debenture' contained in section 744 of the Companies Act 1985.

The main changes in the Companies Act 2006 relating to debentures are as follows:

(i)   there is a new obligation for companies that allot debentures to register an allotment as soon as practicable and in any event within two months of the allotment date;

(ii)   there is a new requirement for a company that refuses to register a transfer of debentures to provide the transferee with reasons for the refusal;

(iii) there is a new requirement for a person making a request to inspect, or be provided with a copy of, the register of debenture holders to provide specified information in his request which must include the purpose for which the information is to be used; and

(iv)   there is a new right which enables a company to apply to court for relief from the obligation to allow the inspection or provision of a copy of the register, where it is felt that the request has not been made for a proper purpose. Such application must be filed with the court within 5 working days of receipt of the request.

At present there are no changes to the method of transferring debentures. However, Chapter 2 of Part 21 of the Companies Act 2006 includes provisions which give the Secretary of State and the Treasury power to make regulations for enabling title to securities to be transferred without a written instrument.

The changes relating to the request to inspect the register of debentures referred to above, namely only where a proper purpose is provided, are similar to those relating to the register of members. The request to inspect or be provided with a copy of the register of debentures must include the following:

(i)   the name and address of the person making the request or, where that person is an organisation, the name and address of the individual within the organisation who is responsible for making the request on behalf of the organisation;

(ii) the purpose for which the information is to be used; and

(iii) whether the information will be disclosed to any other person and, if so, specified details including that person's name and address and the purpose for which the information is to be used by that person.

It should be noted that the Companies Act 2006 does not define 'proper purpose' for the purpose of this section and guidance from BERR states that it is for the courts to determine whether a particular application is for a proper purpose.

Two new offences have been created by section 747 of the Companies Act 2006 which may be committed by a person who is in possession of information from the register of debentures by means of exercising his rights to inspect or obtain a copy of the register of debentures, which are as follows:

(i)   to do anything which would result in the information contained in the register to be disclosed to another person;

(ii) to fail to do anything with the result that the information contained in the register is disclosed to another person; and

knowing, or having reason to suspect, that that person may use the information other than for a proper purpose.

A person found guilty of such an offence will be liable on conviction to imprisonment for a term not exceeding two years or a fine (or both).

There has been an amendment to the provision under the Companies Act 1985 which provided a time limit of 20 years on the liability of a company in relation to entries or deletions in the register of debentures to 10 years from the date of entry or deletion.

3.14.10   What changes are there to the requirement to keep records of meetings and resolutions?

The Companies Act 2006 makes a number of changes relating to the requirements of companies to keep records of meetings, decisions and resolutions as listed below.

(i)   with effect from 1 October 2009 there is to be a new power for the Secretary of State to make regulations (the draft Companies (Companies Records and Fees) Regulations 2007) to keep such records at a place other than at the registered office provided it is in the same part of the UK as the registered office;

(ii)   a company must keep available for inspection at its registered office, or at a single alternative location in the same part of the UK as the company's registered office, records of shareholder meetings and resolutions for a period of 10 years;

(iii) with effect from 1 October 2008 where a company does keep its records other than at the registered office he must notify any person who has requested a copy of a register of that address within five days of receiving a written request;

(iv)   in a change to the Companies Act 1985 there will no longer be a requirement to keep minutes of meetings of managers; and

(v)   with effect from 1 October 2009 there is also a requirement for the location of all books and records kept available for inspection to be stated in the annual return.

3.14.11   When is it necessary to maintain an overseas branch register?

The provisions of the Companies Act 2006 relating to overseas branch registers are contained in sections 129 to 135 and come into force on 1 October 2009 and largely re-state the existing provisions under the Companies Act 1985 other than the new provisions allowing the Secretary of State to make regulations in this area.

If a company having a share capital transacts business in one of the following countries or territories it may be required to keep a branch register of members resident there:

(i)   any part of Her Majesty's dominions outside of the United Kingdom, the Channel Islands and the Isle of Man; or

(ii)   Bangladesh, Cyprus, Dominica, The Gambia, Ghana, Guyana, The Hong Kong Special Administrative Region of the People's Republic of China, India, Ireland, Kenya, Kiribati, Lesotho, Malawi, Malaysia, Malta, Nigeria, Pakistan, Seychelles, Sierra Leone, Singapore, South

Africa, Sri Lanka, Swaziland, Trinidad and Tobago, Uganda and Zimbabwe.

The Secretary of State has power to make provision by regulations as to the circumstances in which a company is to be regarded as keeping a register in a particular country or territory.

3.14.12 What are the requirements relating to the maintenance of a branch register?

Once a company opens a branch register it must notify the Registrar of Companies within 14 days of doing so, the notice must specify the country or territory in which register is kept.

An overseas branch register is regarded as part of a company's register of members. The Secretary of State may however make regulations modifying any of the provisions relating to the register of members as it applies to the overseas branch register.

A company that maintains an overseas branch register must either keep the register or a duplicate copy of the register available for inspection at the place in the United Kingdom where the company's main register of members is kept available for inspection (see section 3.14.5 and the table of information regarding inspection and location of company records and registers in section 3.14.4 for further details relating to the register of members).

Shares that are registered in an overseas branch register must be distinguished from those registered in the main register of members.

3.14.13 What happens if a company is no longer required to maintain an overseas branch register?

If a company discontinues an overseas branch register all entries in the register must be transferred to another overseas branch register kept in the same country or territory, or to the main register of members.

The company must also give notice of the closure of the branch register to the Registrar of Companies within 14 days.

3.15 How can documents be served on a company and when are documents deemed to have been delivered under the Companies Act 2006?

The relevant sections under the Companies Act 2006 are sections 1139 to 1142 which are effective from 1 October 2008.

As is the case under previous company legislation, the Companies Act 2006 provides that a document may be served on a company registered in the UK by leaving it at, or by sending it by post, to the company's registered office.

Service of documents on overseas companies, whose particulars are registered as branches in the UK under the provisions of the Companies Act 2006, may also be made by leaving them at, or posting them to, the registered address of the person who is shown as being resident in the UK and who is authorised to accept service of documents on the company's behalf. If no such person is registered or if they refuse to accept service, then the document may be left or sent to the designated place of business of the company in the UK.

Documents that are served on company directors or other officers for both UK and overseas companies registered in the UK should be also served by leaving them at, or posting them to, the person's registered address as disclosed on the public record.

3.15.1 What happens when there is a change of registered address of a company or a registered address of a director, secretary or other person?

Where a change of address has occurred, the service of a document to any previous registered address is still valid provided service takes place within 14 days of the date on which the change has been notified and the public record amended to show the new address for service.

3.15.2 When does deemed delivery of documents and information occur?

Section 1147 of the Companies Act 2006 provides that where a document is delivered, either by being sent by post or delivered in electronic format, and the company is able to show it was properly addressed and posted or delivered electronically, it is deemed to have been received by the intended recipient 48 hours after it was sent.

Where a document or information is supplied by means of a website it is deemed to have been received by the intended recipient when the material is first made available on the website or if later, when the recipient received (or is deemed to have received) notice of the fact that the material is available on the website.

3.16   What is the role of the Registrar(s) of Companies?

The relevant provisions are contained in sections 1060 to 1120 of the Companies Act 2006 and which, save where indicated, come into effect on 1 October 2009.

One of the most challenging aspects of the implementation of the Companies Act 2006 has been the impact on filing requirements with the Registrar of

Companies and this is one of the main reasons why implementation of certain provisions has been deferred by a further year to 1 October 2009.

For the first time companies' legislation covers the whole of the UK, but it retains the requirement that there shall be a separate Registrar of Companies for each of England and Wales, Scotland, and Northern Ireland.

3.16.1 What are the responsibilities of the Registrar of Companies?

The Registrar of Companies' functions are set out in the Companies Act 2006 and other UK legislation (e.g. the Insolvency Act 1986) and the Secretary of State also has power to direct the Registrar of Companies to perform other functions on his behalf as he sees fit.

The Registrar of Companies has an official seal for the authentication of documents, which he seals in performance of his duties (section 1062 of the Companies Act 2006).

The Registrar of Companies collects fees in respect of the performance of registration services, which are set from time to time by the Secretary of State.

The Registrar of Companies is the channel through which certificates of incorporation for UK companies and branches of overseas companies are issued and information on incorporations or changes of name are published.

The Registrar of Companies is the conduit through which companies must file all information and documents concerning their constitution and changes thereto and the Registrar of Companies is responsible for maintaining a public record of all transactions and documents concerning the companies registered with him.

The Registrar of Companies sets the forms which must be used as standard for the notification of events and registration of information which is required to be filed with him and the manner in which documents should be delivered, the address to which they must be sent and specifies where a hard copy must be used or where the use of electronic filing is permitted.

Companies House is increasing its ability to receive documents electronically and over time it is hoped that the majority, if not all, documents can be delivered to the Registrar of Companies by electronic means.

3.16.2 What are the requirements for the proper form, authentication and manner of delivery of documents to the Registrar of Companies?

The Companies Act 2006 specifies that a document is not properly delivered unless all the requirements are met, including:

(i)   use of the correct Companies House form or document;

(ii) the contents of the document are correct;

(iii) the manner of delivery specified by the Registrar of Companies has been used (e.g. where electronic filing is required that this method of delivery has been adopted);

(iv) unique identifiers have been used (where applicable); and

(v) the appropriate fee has been paid (where required).

The Registrar of Companies has the discretion to accept (and register) documents that do not comply fully with the requirements for proper delivery.

Acceptance of a document by the Registrar of Companies does not affect the Registrar's ability to impose fines for failure to deliver a document on time, but the period after the document is accepted does not count as a period during which there is default in complying with the requirements for proper delivery.

The Companies Act 2006 specifies that a document is not deemed to have been delivered to the Registrar of Companies until it is actually received by him and the provisions for service of notice on companies (namely, deemed receipt within 48 hours of posting) does not apply.

3.16.3 What are the obligations of the Registrar of Companies to keep a register and an index of companies?

The Companies Act 2006 requires the Registrar of Companies to keep records of the certificates of incorporation issued by him and details of all information and documents delivered to him and from 1 January 2007 many of these are kept in electronic form. On incorporation the Registrar of Companies allocates a unique registered number to that company.

The Companies Act 2006 also requires the Registrar of Companies to keep an index of all companies and index of limited or limited liability partnerships registered in the UK as well as societies registered under the Industrial and Provident Societies Act. All of these indexes are required to be available for public inspection.

3.16.4 What are the rules on the allocation and use of unique identifiers?

The Companies Act 2006 contains provisions under which unique identifiers are allocated to identify each person who is a director or officer of a UK registered or overseas company.

Where use is being made of these it will be in the form of a sequence of letters or numbers and the company in question or Registrar of Companies will be required to use the unique identifier when communicating with the Registrar of Companies or for the proper delivery of documents.

3.16.5 What are the Registrar of Companies' obligations for the preservation of original documents for companies currently on the register or for those that have been dissolved?

The Companies Act 2006 obliges the Registrar of Companies to retain original hard copy documents for three years after they are received, after which time they may be destroyed provided the information they contain has been recorded in the register. The Registrar of Companies is under no obligation to keep the originals of documents delivered in electronic form, provided the information contained in them has been recorded in the register (section 1083 of the Companies Act 2006).

Section 1083 of the Companies Act 2006 applies to all documents held by the Registrar of Companies when this section comes into force (1 October 2009) as well as to documents that he subsequently receives.

3.16.6 What rights do the public have to inspect the register and obtain copies of documents filed with the Registrar of Companies?

The law permits any person to inspect the register, including the inspection of originals of any documents held by the Registrar of Companies in hard copy. This request may be satisfied either by the company providing an electronic form or hard copy version of the document if requested to do so within 21 days of the request being received and from 1 January 2007, copies may be obtained in electronic format.

Hard copy documents provided under this right will be certified as true copies, whereas electronic form documents will not be certified as being true copies unless the applicant specifically requests such certification.

3.16.7 Is any material not available for public inspection?

Yes, section 1087 of the Companies Act 2006 sets out the documents which are not available for inspection and these include:

(i) protected information (e.g. directors' residential addresses where a restriction on disclosure is in force and the use of a service address has been agreed);

(ii) documents relating to the giving or withdrawing of consent where the Registrar of Companies has permitted an informal correction to be made;

(iii) documents which are the subject of a rectification of the register order made by the court;

(iv) any material which the court has ordered should not be disclosed; and

(v) any e-mail address, identification code or password deriving from a document delivered to the Registrar of Companies for the purpose of facilitating electronic filing procedures or the providing of such information by telephone.

Where consent has been obtained to withhold details of the residential address of the directors and officers from the register, the Registrar of Companies must nonetheless be provided with the residential address and the company is also required to keep a record of the addresses.

3.16.8 Does the Registrar of Companies have the power to remove material from the register or rectify incorrect information or documents on the register?

Yes, the Companies Act 2006 provides the Registrar of Companies with the power to remove unnecessary material from the register or to permit incorrect information to be rectified in documents held by him either at his own request or that of the company, the Secretary of State, or on the instructions of the court.

This may cover material which is inaccurate or invalid and removal may include a direction that the material is to be kept by the Registrar of Companies but reclassified as not publicly available information (i.e. as would be the case where a residential address for a director or officer of the company was changed to a service address). The Registrar of Companies may arrange for publication in the *Gazette* where he considers the removal or correction of the information requires public notification.

The Registrar of Companies has a wide discretion to accept documents that contain unnecessary material or are defective or incomplete. The Companies Act 2006 sets out detailed provisions on how the Registrar of Companies can accept informal corrections to documents and how he should deal with documents that are delivered in an incomplete or defective state.

3.16.9 What are the language requirements for documents filed with the Registrar of Companies and can the Registrar of Companies require documents to be certified or verified?

The general rule, which is effective from 1 January 2007, is that all documents which are required to be delivered to the Registrar of Companies, must be in English. The only exception to this rule is for companies who have their registered office situated in Wales who may take advantage of the provisions of section 1104 of the Companies Act 2006 which permits them to deliver documents to the Registrar of Companies in Welsh.

With effect from 1 January 2007, under the provisions of section 1105 of the Companies Act 2006, all documents drawn up and delivered to the Registrar of Companies in a language other than English must also be accompanied by a certified English translation when they relate to the company's constitution, its accounts and any instruments of charge.

3.16.10   What is the position where a person makes a false statement to the Registrar of Companies?

An offence is committed by any person who knowingly or recklessly delivers or causes to be delivered to the Registrar of Companies any document that is misleading, false or deceptive in any material manner.

The penalties can include conviction on indictment and imprisonment for up to two years or a fine (or both) or summary conviction including liability to imprisonment for up to 12 months in England and Wales or up to six months imprisonment in Scotland or Northern Ireland.

3.16.11   What powers does the Registrar of Companies have to enforce a company's filing obligations?

The Companies Act 2006 provides the Registrar of Companies or any member or creditor of the company with the power to order a company to deliver documents to the Registrar of Companies or the member or creditor which should be complied with within 14 days of the notice, failing which an application may be made to the court for an order directing the company to make good the default.

3.16.12   Does the Registrar of Companies have the power to insist upon the use of electronic filing of annual returns?

No, but in an effort to encourage companies to use electronic filing the fees payable are generally reduced for the electronic filing of documents.

Companies will still be able to file a paper annual return. However, Companies House is no longer sending out shuttle annual returns (where all the information is completed and the company amends it and returns it to Companies House). Companies can request a company information report free of charge, which contains similar information to an annual return, but may not be up to date. Companies can also request a blank annual return form (or download one) to fill in. If companies choose to web file the annual return then all the information will be on the website for the company to amend (like the previous shuttle 363s).

3.17   What are a company's annual compliance obligations?

The table below sets out a comparison of the annual compliance obligations for private and public companies under the Companies Act 1985 and the Companies Act 2006. The table does not however include the additional filing obligations for listed companies.

| Companies Act 1985 | | Companies Act 2006 | |
Private company	Public company	Private company	Public company
Annual return made up to date on anniversary of incorporation. To be filed within 28 days of made up date.	Annual return made up to date on anniversary of incorporation. To be filed within 28 days of made up date.	Annual return made up to date on anniversary of incorporation. To be filed within 28 days of made up date.	Annual return made up to date on anniversary of incorporation. To be filed within 28 days of made up date.
For first accounting periods exceeding 12 months – annual accounts to be filed 10 months from the first anniversary of incorporation or 3 months from the end of the accounting reference period, whichever expires last.	For first accounting periods exceeding 12 months – annual accounts to be filed 7 months from the first anniversary of incorporation or 3 months from the end of the accounting period, whichever expires last.	For first accounting periods exceeding 12 months – annual accounts to be filed 9 months from the first anniversary of incorporation or 3 months from the end of the accounting reference period, whichever expires last.*	For first accounting periods exceeding 12 months – annual accounts to be filed 6 months from the first anniversary of incorporation or 3 months from the end of the accounting reference period, whichever expires last.*
Subsequent annual accounts to be filed at Companies House within 10 months of the accounting reference date.	Subsequent annual accounts to be filed at Companies House within 7 months of the accounting reference date.	Subsequent annual accounts to be filed at Companies House within 9 months of the accounting reference date.*	Subsequent annual accounts to be filed at Companies House within 6 months of the accounting reference date.*
First AGM to be held within 18 months of the date of incorporation unless relevant elective resolution passed.	First AGM to be held within 18 months of the date of incorporation.	Send copy of accounts to members by the end of the period allowed for filing accounts, or if earlier, the date on which the accounts are delivered to the Registrar of Companies.	Send copy of accounts to shareholders at least 21 days before general meeting.
Subsequent AGMs to be held each calendar year with not more than 15 months elapsing between each AGM subject to the relevant elective resolutions having been passed.	Subsequent AGMs to be held each calendar year with not more than 15 months elapsing between each AGM.	No requirement to hold AGM unless expressly required to do so in accordance with articles of association.	AGM to be held within 6 months beginning with the day following the accounting reference date.*

*For accounting periods beginning on or after 6 April 2008.

3.18 Summary of key changes under the Companies Act 2006

The table below sets out a summary of the key provisions of the Companies Act 1985 and the Companies Act 2006 in respect of setting up and maintaining companies along with any suggested action that may be required.

Issue	Companies Act 1985	Companies Act 2006	Action recommended
Type of company (section 2)	Public Private Unlimited Guarantee.	No change. From 1 October 2009.	No action required but non listed public companies may wish to re-register as a private company to take advantage of various deregulatory provisions for private companies.
Company formations (section 3)	Form 10 Memorandum Articles of association required to be filed. Trading certificate required for public companies.	New forms will be needed. Form of memorandum will change. New statement of capital required. Filing process unaltered and trading certificate required for plcs. From 1 October 2009.	No action required unless new company being formed.
Company constitution (section 4)	Memorandum and articles of association.	Single constitution (the articles) and one-off filing of the memorandum From 1 October 2009.	Companies formed pre-Companies Act 2006 can retain their existing constitutional documents. Decide whether you wish to adopt new articles of association to reflect the new provisions.
Binding the company (section 5)	Documents validly executed by affixing seal, signed by two authorised signatories or director signing in presence of witness.	No change – unless private company no longer has company secretary. From 1 October 2009.	No action required – unless private company with no secretary – ensure articles do not require company secretary to sign any documents.

Issue	Companies Act 1985	Companies Act 2006	Action recommended
Company names (section 6)	Restrictions on registering names which are identical, similar, offensive or suggesting connection with government or public authorities. Change name via special resolution. Company names to be disclosed in all stationery, invoices and other communications including electronic communications and on websites.	No change relating to restrictions. New procedure to object to company name. Change of name may be made as provided for in articles.	Ensure required information disclosed on company correspondence, electronic communications and company websites.
Registered office (section 7)	All companies required to have registered address. Change address by giving notice to the Registrar of Companies.	No change – except if Welsh company. By special resolution may change registered office situation from Wales to England & Wales. From 1 October 2009.	No action required.
Re-registration (section 8)	Private to public Public to private Private to unlimited Unlimited to limited. Statutory declaration.	Private to public Public to private Private to unlimited Unlimited to limited Public to unlimited. Statement of compliance. From 1 October 2009.	No action required.
Role of company secretary (section 9)	All companies required to have company secretary.	Public companies required but private companies optional. From 6 April 2008.	Decide whether to retain company secretary for private companies. Check articles of association do not expressly require a company secretary or require a company secretary to execute specific documents.

Issue	Companies Act 1985	Companies Act 2006	Action recommended
Annual return (section 10)	Required by all companies. Includes information relating to registered office, principal trading activity, type of company, particulars of directors and company secretary, details of share capital, location of register of members and any register of debentures.	Required by all companies. New forms will be required. Includes information relating to registered office, principal trading activity, type of company, particulars of directors and company secretary, statement of share capital, location of all registers. For listed plcs no requirement to disclose members addresses unless hold 5% of more of shares. From 1 October 2009.	No action required until next return due when new forms to be obtained. If listed plc will need to review list of members to remove addresses of shareholder with less than 5% of shares.
Charges (section 11)	Details of charge to be registered with Registrar of Companies within 21 days of charge being created. Requirement to maintain register of charges.	Details of charge to be registered with Registrar of Companies within 21 days of charge being created. Secretary of State has power to make regulation governing the creation of charges by overseas companies over property in the UK. Requirement to maintain register of charges From 1 October 2009.	No action required.
Overseas companies (section 12)	Dual registration regime – branch and place of business.	Branch only, place of business regime disappears. From 1 October 2009.	No action required.
Business names (section 13)	Name used by a company other than the name that the company is registered with.	Name used by a company other than the name that the company is registered with in the UK.	No action required except for companies with branches using business names who will need to comply

Issue	Companies Act 1985	Companies Act 2006	Action recommended
		Applies to all overseas companies carrying on business in the UK, not just those with a place of business in the UK. From 1 October 2009.	with the existing provisions e.g. relating to disclosure of name.
Company records (section 14)	Members. Directors and secretaries. Substantial interests in shares (plcs only). Mortgages and charges. Debentures (if applicable).	Members. Directors and secretaries. Investigations into interests in shares (plcs only). Mortgages and charges. Debentures (if applicable).	Details of maiden names to be added to register of directors and secretaries. Register of usual residential addresses to be created for directors and service address filed with Registrar of Companies. No longer need to maintain register of substantial interests in shares but need to create register of investigations into shares.
Serving of documents (section 15)	Serve at registered office or at address of person authorised to accept service of process for overseas companies with a branch or place of business registered.	Serve at registered office or at address of person authorised to accept service of process for overseas companies with a branch registered.	No action required.
Role of the Registrar of Companies (section 16)	Separate Registrar of Companies for England & Wales and Scotland. Repository for filing of returns and making publicly available.	Separate Registrar of Companies for England & Wales, Scotland and Northern Ireland. Repository for filing of returns and making publicly available. Registrar of Companies has power to remove unnecessary material or to permit incorrect information to be rectified in documents at his own request or that of the company. From 1 October 2009.	Ensure that correct new Companies House forms are used for filings.

Issue	Companies Act 1985	Companies Act 2006	Action recommended
Annual compliance requirements (section 17)	Annual return Accounts AGM.	Annual return Accounts Directors approval of accounts (for private companies) AGM (for public companies).	No action required for public companies. Private companies to check articles of association for provisions requiring AGM.

In light of the changes set out in this chapter companies may find it useful to carry out a gap analysis of their statutory records to highlight changes that may be required to be made in order to be compliant with the Companies Act 2006. A review of the articles of association of existing companies would also be advisable.

Chapter 4

Managing the shareholder relationship

4.1   Introduction 4001
    4.1.1   Scope of the chapter 4001
    4.1.2   What is the background to the changes? 4001
    4.1.3   What are the key changes under the Companies Act
          2006? 4001
4.2   Electronic and website communications 4002
    4.2.1   What is new about electronic and website
          communications? 4002
    4.2.2   Will the provisions apply to all companies? 4002
    4.2.3   What is 'electronic communication'? 4002
    4.2.4   What authority is needed for electronic communication?   4003
    4.2.5   What is 'website communication'? 4004
    4.2.6   What authority is needed for website communication?   4004
    4.2.7   Can a request for deemed website communication be sent
          to individual shareholders before the company has sought
          approval in general meeting? 4005
    4.2.8   What are the disadvantages of the 'deeming' provisions for
          website communications? 4005
    4.2.9   Can a shareholder revoke consent or deemed consent to
          website communication? 4005
    4.2.10   What procedure must be followed to communicate by
          means of a website once consent has been granted? 4005
    4.2.11   Can notice of documents on a website be sent by e-mail?   4006
    4.2.12   For how long must information remain on a website? . . . 4006
    4.2.13   What are the deemed delivery times for electronic and
          website communications? 4006
    4.2.14   Are shareholders entitled to receive hard copy
          documents? 4006
    4.2.15   Do these provisions also apply to nominees appointed by
          the shareholder? 4006
4.3   Indirect investors' rights 4007
    4.3.1   Shareholder rights 4007
          4.3.1.1   What rights do shareholders have to nominate a
                   third party to have voting and other shareholder
                   rights? 4007
          4.3.1.2   Why might this regime be used? 4007
          4.3.1.3   Will a company need to amend its articles? . . . 4007
          4.3.1.4   Do indirect investors count towards the
                   threshold required to trigger a right? 4008

	4.3.1.5	Are there any limitations on shareholder rights?	4008
4.3.2		Information rights	4008
	4.3.2.1	What rights do shareholders have to nominate indirect investors to receive information on the companies in which they have invested?	4008
	4.3.2.2	To what information do the provisions apply?	4008
	4.3.2.3	When will this regime come into force?	4009
	4.3.2.4	When might this regime be used?	4009
	4.3.2.5	Will a company need to amend its articles?	4009
	4.3.2.6	Are there any limitations?	4009
	4.3.2.7	How can a nomination be terminated?	4010
4.3.3		General rules for indirect investors and nominated third parties	4010
	4.3.3.1	What records must be kept of 'shareholder' and 'information rights'?	4010
	4.3.3.2	Do electronic and website communications apply?	4010
	4.3.3.3	Are there any Data Protection considerations?	4010
4.4	General meetings		4010
4.4.1		Does a private company need to hold an annual general meeting?	4011
4.4.2		Does a public company need to hold an annual general meeting?	4011
4.4.3		Are there any exceptions to the date by which the annual general meeting must be held by public companies?	4011
4.4.4		Who has the power to call general meetings of private and public companies?	4011
4.4.5		How can members call general meetings?	4012
4.4.6		What are the notice periods for the holding of general meetings and annual general meetings?	4012
4.4.7		What must the notice contain?	4013
4.4.8		Can the notice be sent electronically?	4014
4.4.9		What notification must a company give when it publishes the notice on its website?	4014
4.4.10		Who is entitled to receive notice of meetings?	4014
4.4.11		Do members have the power to require the company to circulate statements?	4015
4.4.12		What is the quorum requirement at a general meeting?	4015
4.4.13		Who may chair a general meeting?	4016
4.4.14		What are the provisions regarding adjourned meetings and the passing of resolutions?	4016
4.4.15		Does a member need to attend a general meeting in order to vote?	4016
4.4.16		How many proxies can a member appoint?	4016
4.4.17		Who can be appointed as a proxy?	4016
4.4.18		What other powers does a proxy have?	4017

4.4.19   Within what time frame must a proxy appointment be notified to the company? 4017

4.4.20   What happens if the appointment of a proxy is terminated? 4017

4.4.21   How does a corporation attend and vote at a meeting?   4017

4.4.22   By when must a corporation appoint a representative to vote in its place at a general meeting? 4018

4.4.23   How do shareholders vote at general meetings? 4018

4.4.24   Who can demand a poll? 4019

4.4.25   What is the position regarding meetings of a particular class of shareholders? 4019

4.4.26   How may resolutions be passed? 4019

4.4.27   What is the difference between a vote on a show of hands, on a poll and by written resolution? 4020

4.4.28   What is a written resolution? 4020

4.4.29   What are the specific rules relating to written resolutions?   4021

4.4.30   How can a member require the circulation of a written resolution? 4022

4.4.31   What is the position regarding written resolutions and electronic communications with shareholders? 4023

4.4.32   What different types of resolutions exist? 4023

4.4.33   What is the difference between an ordinary resolution and a special resolution? 4023

4.4.34   What is special notice? 4024

4.5   Additional Companies Act 2006 provisions for quoted companies   4024

4.5.1   Is a quoted company required to publish poll results? . . . 4024

4.5.2   Can members challenge the results of a poll? 4025

4.5.2.1   Who should prepare the report and by when must an independent assessor be appointed? . . . 4025

4.5.2.2   What does 'independent' mean? 4025

4.5.2.3   What should the report contain? 4026

4.5.2.4   What rights does the independent assessor have? 4026

4.5.2.5   What notification is the company required to give? 4026

4.6   Power to investigate ownership of shares 4027

4.6.1   Do shareholders need to notify their interest in shares?   4027

4.6.2   Can companies request information about interests in their shares? 4027

4.6.3   Can the notice be sent electronically? 4027

4.6.4   Does the company need to keep a register? 4027

4.7   Political donations and expenditure 4027

4.7.1   What does the Companies Act 2006 cover? 4028

4.7.2   When do the rules come into force? 4028

4.7.3   What is the definition of 'political donations'? 4028

4.7.4   What is the definition of 'political expenditure'? 4029

4.7.5   Is authorisation required for a company to make a political
        donation or expenditure? 4029
4.7.6   Who needs to authorise the donation or expenditure? ... 4029
4.7.7   What information should the resolution contain? 4030
4.8   What statutory rights do minority shareholders have? 4030
4.8.1   What protection does the Companies Act 2006 offer to
        shareholders? 4031
4.8.2   What other statutory powers do minority shareholders
        have? 4032
4.8.3   What are the relevant thresholds for the passing of
        ordinary and special resolutions? 4036
4.8.4   Which matters require approval by an ordinary
        resolution? 4037
4.8.5   Which matters require approval by a special resolution or
        some other threshold? 4038
4.9   Conclusion 4040
4.9.1   List of key changes and actions 4040

Chapter 4

Managing the shareholder relationship

4.1 Introduction

4.1.1 Scope of the chapter

In this chapter we discuss the changes introduced by the Companies Act 2006 in relation to communication with shareholders, rights of shareholders, the holding of general meetings and the types of resolutions that may be passed.

4.1.2 What is the background to the changes?

A major theme of the Companies Act 2006 is to increase shareholder engagement and extend the rights granted to indirect investors.

In addition, a number of deregulatory measures have been introduced which should result in cost savings for businesses.

4.1.3 What are the key changes under the Companies Act 2006?

A summary of the key changes introduced by the Companies Act 2006 is as follows:

(i)   the introduction of default provisions facilitating the use of a company website for shareholder communications;

(ii)   the ability of companies to allow members to nominate third parties to exercise any specified rights of that member;

(iii)   the introduction of new rights to shareholders of traded companies to nominate an indirect investor to enjoy information rights;

(iv)   the abolition of the requirement for private companies to hold annual general meetings;

(v)   the enhancement of rights of proxies to give them the same powers at a general meeting as a member of the company and the right of a member to appoint a proxy for each share that he holds;

(vi)   the abolition of written resolutions for public companies;

(vii)   the ability for members of a quoted company to require an independent report to verify the accuracy of any poll taken; and

(viii) the clarification of the rules on political donations.

4.2 Electronic and website communications

4.2.1 What is new about electronic and website communications?

Electronic communications with shareholders have been possible in limited form since the implementation of the Companies Act 1985 (Electronic Communications) Order 2000. Under this legislation, companies were able to circulate their reports and accounts, summary financial statements, general meeting notices and proxy appointments to a shareholder electronically if that shareholder had positively elected to receive information electronically. As a result, the take-up of electronic communications by shareholders has typically been less than 10%.

The Companies Act 2006 has taken a more radical approach as it changes the default method of communication from hard copy to website communication, with a positive opt-in required for hard copy. This is subject to certain specified procedures being followed, where the shareholder or nominee had not positively elected to receive paper documentation from the company. The Companies Act 2006 has also extended the documents or information that can be sent electronically to any document or information that is required by the Companies Act 2006.

The Companies Act 2006 also grants a shareholder the ability to communicate with the company by electronic means where the company have given an electronic address.

The provisions, which are effective from 20 January 2007 (save for sections 1168 and 1173 which were effective for certain purposes from 1 January 2007), are set out in sections 308–309, 333, 1143–1148, 1168, 1173 in Schedules 4 and 5 of the Companies Act 2006. The procedures to be adopted by companies wishing to take advantage of the new provisions are set out in this chapter.

4.2.2 Will the provisions apply to all companies?

Both public and private companies are subject to the new provisions.

In addition, public companies whose shares are traded on a regulated market (which excludes companies quoted on AIM) are also subject to additional rules regarding communication with their shareholders under the Disclosure and Transparency Rules ('DTR'). The main difference under the DTR Rules is the requirement for shareholders to approve the use of electronic communications at a general meeting.

4.2.3 What is 'electronic communication'?

Electronic communication is the ability of a company to communicate with its shareholders or other third parties by use of electronic data transmission (for example, by e-mail, fax or text message), rather than by the traditional method of printing and posting such information.

Since electronic communication has been possible in limited form since 2000, some companies may already have provisions within their articles permitting the sending of information to shareholders and nominees electronically. Such provisions will remain valid.

However, the Companies Act 2006 has expanded the definition of how a company can communicate electronically to include text messages, compact or data disks, radio transmissions or any other communication that requires electronic equipment to receive the information. Where a company's articles limit the type of documents or information that can be sent electronically, it will be necessary to amend the articles to allow for these forms of communication.

Schedule 4 of the Companies Act 2006 sets out the provisions for sending documents or information electronically to a company and Schedule 5 of the Companies Act 2006 sets out the provisions for electronic communications by a company.

4.2.4 What authority is needed for electronic communication?

Companies are entitled under the Companies Act 2006 to send documents and information in electronic form to any individual shareholder who has agreed (generally or specifically) to receive documents or information in that way. In practice, this could be achieved by a shareholder providing his e-mail address to the company even, for example, on its letterhead.

Strictly speaking, there is no need for a company to have specific provisions in its articles of association for electronic communication. In practice, however, most companies will want to change their articles as section 1143 of the Companies Act 2006 only authorises the sending of any information that is required to be sent or received by the Companies Act 2006. Therefore, most companies will amend their articles to permit the company to send general documents that are outside the scope of the present definition (i.e. those not subject to the Companies Act 2006) electronically as well. Companies may also wish to change the deemed delivery time of an e-mail from the time specified in the Companies Act 2006 of 48 hours (excluding non-working days to deemed delivery on the same day that it is sent).

Where the shareholder is a company, permission to use electronic communications will still need to be obtained.

4.2.5 What is 'website communication'?

Since 2000, companies have been permitted to use a website for the publication of information or documents required or authorised to be sent or supplied under the Companies Act 1985. Therefore, with a shareholder's express agreement, it has been possible for reports and accounts, summary financial statements and notices of general meetings to be published by being posted on the company's website. Companies must send a notification to shareholders when this is done.

Under the Companies Act 2006, a shareholder's consent to the company communicating via its website can be deemed in certain circumstances, as described in 4.2.6 below. This is a new concept and has been introduced to make company legislation more in line with modern communication practices and techniques. It is also seen as an environmentally friendly way for companies to communicate both with their shareholders and the outside world while reducing some of the costs associated with the printing of hard copy communications.

4.2.6 What authority is needed for website communication?

Shareholders must either pass a resolution authorising the company to supply documents or information by publishing them on a website in accordance with the Companies Act 2006, or the company's articles need to contain a provision to that effect.

In addition, the consent of an individual shareholder must be obtained or deemed in accordance with paragraph 10 of Schedule 5 to the Companies Act 2006.

The consent of an individual shareholder can only be deemed to have been given where the following criteria are met:

(i)   the shareholder has been asked individually to consent;

(ii) the company does not receive a response within 28 days beginning with the date on which the company's request was sent;

(iii) the request states clearly the effect of failing to respond; and

(iv) the request has not been sent within 12 months of a previous request.

As companies can only ask shareholders to provide their consent to website communication once in any 12 month period, practical management of the anniversary and a programme for seeking shareholder consent is recommended so that all shareholders can be contacted at the same time.

4.2.7 Can a request for deemed website communication be sent to individual shareholders before the company has sought approval in general meeting?

Although the Companies Act 2006 is silent on this point, a request for consent can be sent to individual shareholders before the company has sought permission of its shareholders in general meeting. However, the request for consent will be conditional upon a resolution being passed at the forthcoming general meeting either authorising the company to use website communication or amending the company's articles of association as appropriate.

4.2.8 What are the disadvantages of the 'deeming' provisions for website communications?

Whilst the potential cost savings for companies with large shareholder registers can be significant, shareholders will always be able to obtain hard copies of documents free of charge if they so wish. Companies therefore need to ensure that they have sufficient hard copies to supply to shareholders on request. As a result, there will be uncertainty for companies when planning print runs of documents such as the annual reports and accounts.

4.2.9 Can a shareholder revoke consent or deemed consent to website communication?

Unless consent has been expressly limited by the individual shareholder, it will apply for an unlimited period. However, a shareholder can revoke consent, whether deemed or actual, at any point in time.

4.2.10 What procedure must be followed to communicate by means of a website once consent has been granted?

The company must send out a notice to its shareholders advising them that the documents are available to be viewed or downloaded on the website.

The notice should state:

(i)   that there is a document on the website;

(ii)   the address of the website;

(iii)   the place on the website where the information can be accessed; and

(iv)   how to access the document or information.

It is not necessary to send notification to shareholders that have previously opted for hard copy communication.

4.2.11 Can notice of documents on a website be sent by e-mail?

The notice can be made by any electronic means such as e-mail provided that the intended recipient has previously agreed to the receipt of information electronically. Where a company has deemed agreement to the use of website communications by a shareholder, it is unlikely to have an e-mail address for that shareholder. Consequently, companies may need to send hard copy communications to many of its shareholders, notifying them that documents are available on its website.

4.2.12 For how long must information remain on a website?

Following notification, the information must remain available on the website for a period of at least 28 days or, if different, for the amount of time stated in the Companies Act 2006 or in the company's articles.

4.2.13 What are the deemed delivery times for electronic and website communications?

The Companies Act 2006 sets out the time periods within which documents are deemed to have been delivered:

Method	Deemed delivery time of the document
Post to an address in the UK	48 hours of the document being posted (excluding non-working days) provided the company is able to show it was properly addressed, prepaid and posted
Electronic communication	48 hours of it being sent (excluding non-working days) provided the company can show the correct address was used
Website communication	When first made available on website, or if later, when recipient is notified (either by post or electronically) of availability on the website.

4.2.14 Are shareholders entitled to receive hard copy documents?

Section 1145 of the Companies Act 2006 grants shareholders and debenture holders the right to request hard copies of any documents which they have received electronically. The company must supply hard copies of such documents within 21 days of the request at no charge.

4.2.15 Do these provisions also apply to nominees appointed by the shareholder?

The rules on electronic and website communication apply to nominees appointed by registered shareholders (see 4.3 below).

4.3   Indirect investors' rights

One of the Government's key aims has been to make it easier for indirect investors to exercise their voting rights and obtain company information. Part 9 of the Companies Act 2006 implements this in a number of ways as described in this chapter.

The relevant provisions are effective from 1 October 2007.

4.3.1   Shareholder rights

4.3.1.1   *What rights do shareholders have to nominate a third party to have voting and other shareholder rights?*

Under section 145 of the Companies Act 2006, a registered shareholder may nominate another person to enjoy or exercise all or any specified rights of the member in relation to the company where provision is made in the company's articles. In particular, this includes the right to:

(i)   be sent proposed written resolutions;

(ii)   require circulation of written resolutions;

(iii)   require directors to call general meetings;

(iv)   receive notice of general meetings;

(v)   require circulation of a statement;

(vi)   appoint a proxy at a meeting;

(vii) require circulation of a resolution at an annual general meeting of a public company; and

(viii) be sent copies of annual reports and accounts.

4.3.1.2   *Why might this regime be used?*

This regime will be useful in situations where the registered shareholder holds shares on trust for a third party and that third party wishes to exercise the same rights as a registered holder. However, the nominated person does not need to hold any beneficial interest in the relevant shares.

4.3.1.3   *Will a company need to amend its articles?*

As mentioned in 4.3.1.1 above, the new provisions in the Companies Act 2006 are subject to authority being granted in the articles.

4.3.1.4 Do indirect investors count towards the threshold required to trigger a right?

Section 153 of the Companies Act 2006 sets out four situations where indirect investors count towards the threshold required to trigger a right. In each circumstance, the threshold is 100 shareholders holding £100 each on average of paid-up share capital. The four situations are:

(i)   the power to require the circulation of a statement (see 4.4.11 for further details);

(ii) the power to require the circulation of a resolution at the annual general meeting of a public company;

(iii) the power to require an independent report on a poll (see 4.5.2 below); and

(iv) the power to require website publication of audit concerns.

If the request is made by an indirect investor, the request must be accompanied by a statement confirming, amongst other matters, the full name and address of the member who holds the shares on that investor's behalf, the number of shares, the total amount paid up on the shares and that the investor has the right to instruct the member how to exercise those rights.

4.3.1.5 Are there any limitations on shareholder rights?

There are a few limitations. Only the registered shareholder will be able to enforce rights against the company or to transfer ownership of the shares. Furthermore, nominations are at the discretion of the shareholders and, therefore, cannot be enforced by an indirect investor.

4.3.2 Information rights

4.3.2.1 What rights do shareholders have to nominate indirect investors to receive information on the companies in which they have invested?

Section 146 of the Companies Act 2006 creates a new regime allowing a registered shareholder who holds shares on behalf of another person to nominate that person to receive information from the company in which he is a shareholder. However, these provisions only apply to public companies trading on a regulated market.

4.3.2.2 To what information do the provisions apply?

Information is defined as all communications that a company sends to shareholders generally or to any class of shareholders. Such general shareholder communications includes all documents or information that are sent to all shareholders. This includes the annual accounts and reports and/or summary financial statements, non-personalised corporate action documents and any other documents sent to registered shareholders that are sent impersonalised. Any documents that are personalised are not required to be sent to nominated individuals, e.g. dividends.

A copy of general communications must be sent to the nominated person in addition to the registered shareholder.

In a takeover situation, shareholders of the target company, in particular, receive various documents specified by the Takeover Code (for example copies of offer related announcements, offer documents, offeree board circulars). These documents are not part of general shareholder communications under the provisions of the Companies Act 2006. There is currently no comparable provision in the Takeover Code for indirect investors to be nominated by registered shareholders and therefore to be sent these documents. However, the Takeover Panel is expected to consider the position of nominated indirect investors in due course and there may, therefore, be amendments to the Takeover Code in this respect in the future.

4.3.2.3 When will this regime come into force?

Although the provisions were enacted from 1 October 2007, companies are only required to comply with them from 1 January 2008.

4.3.2.4 When might this regime be used?

This regime is relevant for investors with indirect holdings in public companies (for example, where a person invests in a company through a nominee or an ISA) but who still wish to receive information on the company which he would not otherwise receive.

4.3.2.5 Will a company need to amend its articles?

The right to nominate a third party to receive information is statutory for public companies on a regulated market and therefore does not require enabling provisions in the articles.

4.3.2.6 Are there any limitations?

Neither a company nor a registered shareholder has the right to limit the type of communications sent to indirect investors. However the number of indirect investors that may be nominated to receive information rights cannot be more than the number of shares that the registered shareholder holds.

4.3.2.7   *How can a nomination be terminated?*

Termination will occur either at the request, death or bankruptcy of either the nominee or the shareholder. If the nominee is a company, termination will occur on winding up of the nominee company.

There is no obligation on either the nominee or the shareholder to advise the company when the nominated person no longer has an interest in the shares. However, the Companies Act 2006 contains powers by which the company can check that the nominee still wishes to receive the information. If no response is forthcoming within 28 days, the company can cease sending information. The company cannot make such an enquiry more than once in any 12 months.

The company can also suspend a nomination at any time when there are more nominated persons than the member has shares.

4.3.3   General rules for indirect investors and nominated third parties

4.3.3.1   *What records must be kept of 'shareholder' and 'information rights'?*

The Companies Act 2006 does not specify that particular records be maintained by companies in respect of the nomination of shareholder rights and/or information rights. However, companies should establish internal policies and systems to manage and record these new rights and, where applicable, agree arrangements with its external share registrar.

4.3.3.2   *Do electronic and website communications apply?*

The same rules regarding electronic and website communications apply for nominees and third parties as for other shareholders. Therefore, a company can request nominees to elect positively to receive hard copy documents and provide a current address. Failure by the nominee to respond entitles the company to use the website default provisions if it so chooses.

4.3.3.3   *Are there any Data Protection considerations?*

The company must remember that the nominee is not a registered member. Therefore, the nomination is not public information and should be kept confidential.

4.4   General meetings

This section covers meetings of shareholders and the rules and regulations concerning their conduct.

The concept of the extraordinary general meeting has disappeared under the Companies Act 2006. All company meetings of shareholders, other than annual general meetings, are now known as general meetings, unless the articles specify otherwise.

4.4.1 Does a private company need to hold an annual general meeting?

Under the Companies Act 1985, a private company was required to hold an annual general meeting unless it had passed an elective resolution to dispense with this requirement. Under the Companies Act 2006, a private company is no longer required to hold an annual general meeting unless its articles of association require otherwise. It should be noted that a company which has incorporated Table A of the Companies Act 1948 will be required to hold annual general meetings unless either (a) it has previously adopted elective resolutions under the Companies Act 1985 or (b) it now amends its articles of association to remove the requirement set out in Table A 1948 to hold an annual general meeting.

Even if a private company does not have a provision in its articles requiring it to hold an annual general meeting, it may hold an annual general meeting on a voluntary basis if it so chooses.

4.4.2 Does a public company need to hold an annual general meeting?

Under the Companies Act 1985, a public company was required to hold an annual general meeting each calendar year with no more than 15 months elapsing since the date of the previous meeting. Under the Companies Act 2006, a public company will continue to be required to hold an annual general meeting but the timing for holding the meeting has changed. For accounting periods beginning on or after 6 April 2008, the annual general meeting must be held within 6 months of the accounting reference date.

4.4.3 Are there any exceptions to the date by which the annual general meeting must be held by public companies?

There will be an exception where a public company has given notice of the alteration of its accounting reference date, and that notice has shortened the current or previous accounting reference period. In these circumstances, the annual general meeting must be held within 3 months of the notice.

4.4.4 Who has the power to call general meetings of private and public companies?

The Companies Act 2006 provides that general meetings may be called either by the directors (section 302) or by members requiring the directors to call a general meeting (section 303).

4.4.5   How can members call general meetings?

Under the provisions of section 303, members of companies with or without share capital and who hold 10% of the paid up capital of the company having the right to vote at general meetings (i.e. excluding any capital held as treasury shares) or the same percentage of the total voting rights of all members entitled to vote at meetings, may require the directors to call a general meeting of the company.

The required percentage falls to 5% for private companies if more than twelve months has elapsed since the last general meeting called by the members.

The request must contain a statement of the general nature of the business to be dealt with at the meeting and include the text of any resolution that is intended to be passed at the meeting (which should not be frivolous, vexatious or defamatory). The request may be delivered in either hard copy or electronic form, identifying the person(s) making the request.

Where the directors have been required by the members to call a general meeting of the company, section 304 of the Companies Act 2006 provides that the direction must:

(i)   call the meeting within 21 days from the date on which they become subject to the requirement; and

(ii)   hold the meeting on a date not more than 28 days after the date of the notice convening the meeting.

The court also has the power under section 306 either on its own motion or following an application by a director or member to order that a meeting be held. In these circumstances the court may set the agenda for the proceedings and make any other directions as to the conduct of the meeting as it sees fit.

4.4.6   What are the notice periods for the holding of general meetings and annual general meetings?

Section 307 of the Companies Act 2006 provides that at least 14 clear days' notice must be given for all general meetings which are not annual general meetings. 21 clear days' notice continues to be required to be given for annual general meetings of public companies. Public companies subject to the best practice guidance contained in the Combined Code will be obliged to follow that guidance which, at the time of going to print provides for a longer notice period to be given.

Private companies which are required by their articles of association to hold annual general meetings should give the length of notice specified in their articles.

The definition of 'clear' days excludes the day of the meeting and the day on which notice is given.

The articles of association may provide for longer periods of notice than those set out in the Companies Act 2006. Furthermore, the articles may provide a longer notice period in relation to a specific type of resolution which would override the notice provisions in the Companies Act 2006. This will typically be the case for companies that have not updated their articles of association following the implementation of the Companies Act 2006.

A general meeting may be called on short notice by agreement of the members of a company with or without a share capital who hold, in the case of:

(i)   a private company, 90% of the nominal value of the shares giving a right to attend or vote at the meeting or, if the company does not have a share capital of 90% of the total eligible voting rights or such higher percentage (not exceeding 95%) as may be specified in the company's articles; or

(ii) a public company, 95% of the nominal value of the shares giving a right to attend or vote at the meeting or, if the company does not have a share capital of 90% of the total eligible voting rights save where the meeting is the annual general meeting, where all the members must agree to the shorter notice period.

4.4.7   What must the notice contain?

All notices of a general meeting of the company must state:

(i)   the date, time and place of the meeting; and

(ii) the general nature of the business to be dealt with at the meeting.

Where the notice relates to an annual general meeting, the notice must state that the meeting is an annual general meeting.

Under section 325 of the Companies Act 2006, the notice must also contain a statement informing every member of his right to appoint a proxy to exercise all or any of his rights to attend, speak and vote at the meeting and, in the case of a company having a share capital, his right to appoint a proxy for each share that he holds.

Failure to comply with section 325 would not affect the validity of the meeting or any business done at it, but if this requirement is not complied with every officer of the company commits an offence rendering them liable to summary conviction and a fine.

4.4.8   Can the notice be sent electronically?

With effect from 20 January 2007, the notice of a general meeting may be given in either hard copy or electronic format (i.e. by e-mail where a shareholder has consented to receiving communications from the company by e-mail and has supplied the company with his details) or by means of a website provided the notification of the availability of the notice on the website is made in accordance with section 309 of the Companies Act 2006.

Where a company has given an electronic address in a notice calling a meeting, it is deemed to have agreed that any document or information relating to the proceedings at the meeting may also be sent by electronic means to that address.

This would include the appointment of proxies in relation to a meeting, the supply of any documents necessary to show the validity or otherwise relating to the appointment of a proxy and the notice of termination of the authority of a proxy.

Further information on the electronic communications regime introduced by the Companies Act 2006 is provided in section 4.2 above.

4.4.9   What notification must a company give when it publishes the notice on its website?

Under section 309 of the Companies Act 2006 a company may give notice of a general meeting on its website so long as it notifies the members of the presence of the notice. The notification must:

(i)   state that it concerns a notice of a company meeting;

(ii)   specify the place, date and time of the meeting; and

(iii)   in the case of a public company, state whether the meeting is an annual general meeting.

The notice must be available on the website throughout the period beginning with the date of that notification and ending with the conclusion of the meeting.

4.4.10   Who is entitled to receive notice of meetings?

Under section 310 of the Companies Act 2006, the notice of a general meeting of the company must be sent to every member and every director of the company. The term 'members' includes any other person who is entitled to a share following the death or bankruptcy of a member so long as the company has been notified of such entitlement.

The accidental failure to give notice to one or more members will not invalidate a general meeting or any resolutions passed at a general meeting.

4.4.11 Do members have the power to require the company to circulate statements?

The provisions of sections 314 to 317 of the Companies Act 2006 replicate previous legislation and entitle members representing:

(i)   5% or more of the total voting rights of all the members, or

(ii)   at least 100 members (including indirect investors) with a right to vote and who hold shares in the company on which an average of at least £100 has been paid up per member,

to require the company to circulate a statement of no more than 1,000 words to all members entitled to receive notice of a general meeting. The statement must be in respect of a proposed resolution or other business which is to be dealt with at the general meeting.

This request may be in either hard copy or, in a change from the previous position, in electronic format. The request must identify the statement to be circulated and must be received by the company at least one week before the meeting to which it relates. Should this occur, the company will be required to circulate a copy of the statement to each member at the same time as the notice of meeting is given, or as soon as reasonably practical thereafter.

The court has the power to grant the company leave not to comply with a request to circulate a member's statement if it considers the rights conferred under section 314 are being abused. The court also may require the member to pay the whole or part of the company's costs.

The members who requested the statement need not pay the expenses of a company in complying with the request if the meeting to which the request relates is the annual general meeting of a public company and the request is received in sufficient time before the end of the financial year preceding the meeting (section 316 of the Companies Act 2006).

4.4.12 What is the quorum requirement at a general meeting?

Subject to the provisions of the company's articles, section 318 of the Companies Act 2006 provides that two persons (present in person, by proxy or by a person authorised to represent a corporate shareholder) form a quorum. Where a private company has only one member, the quorum will be one.

4.4.13   Who may chair a general meeting?

Traditionally, the chairman of a general meeting will be the chairman of the company, or for smaller companies where there is no chairman, a director of a company. The chairman or directors need not hold shares in the company.

Alternatively, subject to any provision of the company's articles which may stipulate or restrict who may or may not be chairman, section 319 of the Companies Act 2006 provides that any member may be elected to be the chairman of a general meeting by resolution of the company passed at the meeting. This includes a proxy (section 328 of the Companies Act 2006).

4.4.14   What are the provisions regarding adjourned meetings and the passing of resolutions?

A chairman can adjourn a meeting to such time and place as he thinks fit, in accordance with the articles.

Section 332 of the Companies Act 2006 provides that where a resolution is passed at an adjourned meeting of the company, the resolution is treated as having been passed on the date on which it is in fact passed rather than the date of the earlier meeting.

4.4.15   Does a member need to attend a general meeting in order to vote?

Under the provisions of section 324 of the Companies Act 2006, a member of a company is entitled to appoint another person as his proxy to exercise all or any of his rights to attend, vote and, for the first time, speak at a meeting of the company. Where the member is a corporation, it may appoint either a proxy or a person to act as its representative to attend, vote and speak at the meeting on its behalf (see 4.4.21 below).

4.4.16   How many proxies can a member appoint?

In the case of a company having a share capital, a member may appoint more than one proxy in relation to any meeting provided that each proxy is appointed to exercise the rights attached to a different share held by him. This has caused considerable concern, particularly for those companies that pass resolutions on a show of hands, as it can be used to swing a vote in favour of a shareholder who appoints a number of proxies (see 4.4.23 below).

4.4.17   Who can be appointed as a proxy?

A shareholder may appoint any person as his proxy and that person need not be a member of the company. Commonly a shareholder will want to appoint the chairman of the meeting as his proxy.

If the company invites members to appoint as proxy a specified person or number of specified persons (e.g. the chairman), the invitation must be issued to all members entitled to vote at the meeting.

4.4.18 What other powers does a proxy have?

Section 328 of the Companies Act 2006 permits a proxy to be elected as chairman of a general meeting by resolution of the company passed at the meeting. A proxy may also exercise the right to demand a poll (see 4.4.24 below for further details).

4.4.19 Within what time frame must a proxy appointment be notified to the company?

Section 327 of the Companies Act 2006 provides that any provision in a company's articles is void if it provides that the appointment of a proxy is to be received by the company more than 48 hours before the time of the meeting. When calculating this period, non-working days are excluded.

As mentioned in 4.4.8 above, a member may send a proxy appointment form to a company electronically if the company agrees or if the company has given an electronic address in the notice of the general meeting.

4.4.20 What happens if the appointment of a proxy is terminated?

Unless the company receives notice of the termination before the commencement of the meeting, the termination of the authority of a person appointed to act as proxy does not affect whether:

(i) his votes count for the purposes of passing resolutions at a meeting;

(ii) he counts towards there being a quorum at a meeting;

(iii) anything he does as chairman is valid; or

(iv) a poll demanded by him is validly called.

Nothing prevents a company's articles from conferring more extensive rights on members or proxies than are conferred under the provisions of the Companies Act 2006.

4.4.21 How does a corporation attend and vote at a meeting?

If a corporation is a member of a company, it may appoint either a proxy or a person or persons to act as its representative at any meeting of the company. Both the proxy or that representative are able to exercise the same powers on behalf of the corporation as the corporation could have exercised if it were an individual member of the company. Prior to the Companies Act 2006, corporations tended to appoint a corporate representative to vote on their behalf as corporate representatives who had the right to speak at the meeting and vote on a show of hands whereas a proxy did not have these rights automatically. As discussed in 4.4.15 above, section 324 of the Companies Act 2006 has introduced these rights for proxies.

Section 323(4) provides that where a corporation appoints more than one representative, if they do not vote in the same way their votes will not be counted. This has caused problems for institutional shareholders who often appoint multiple corporate representatives to vote in different ways according to the wishes of the underlying shareholders. It could also be used by an unscrupulous shareholder who wishes to corrupt the vote of an institution. To get around this problem, the Institute of Chartered Secretaries and Administrators has published guidance recommending the appointment of proxies instead of multiple corporate representatives or, failing that, the appointment of a designated corporate representative who would vote on behalf of all the representatives for the same corporate shareholder following the completion of voting instruction cards by the other representative indicating how they wish to vote.

4.4.22   By when must a corporation appoint a representative to vote in its place at a general meeting?

A corporation may appoint a representative at any time. For this reason, many corporations may continue to appoint representatives rather than proxies as they will have a further 48 hours to appoint a representative (see 4.4.18 above).

4.4.23   How do shareholders vote at general meetings?

Shareholders (including proxies and corporate representatives) can vote on resolutions at general meetings either on a show of hands or on a poll.

On a vote by show of hands, the chairman declares whether the resolution has or has not been passed and whether it has been passed with a particular majority. His decision shall be conclusive evidence of the fact without proof of the number or proportion of the votes recorded in favour or against the resolution (section 320 of the Companies Act 2006).

Under the Companies Act 1985, each shareholder had one vote on a show of hands regardless of the number of shares that he held and a corporation was able to appoint more than one corporate representative where it held more than one share. Under the Companies Act 2006 where a shareholder can appoint more than one proxy so long as each proxy exercises the rights attached to a different share or shares, this will not necessarily be the case. It is possible to envisage a shareholder who holds for example, 100 shares appointing 100 proxies to attend and vote on his behalf at a meeting. As each of the appointed proxies is entitled to vote on a show of hands, they would have considerable power to swing a vote. For this reason, best practice dictates that listed companies in particular should pass resolutions by way of a poll.

On a vote on a resolution at a meeting by way of a poll, every member has the right to exercise a vote in respect of each share that he holds. The vote of a member on a poll overrides any proxy vote submitted in advance of the meeting.

4.4.24 Who can demand a poll?

Section 321 of the Companies Act 2006 provides that a poll may be demanded:

(i)   by five or more members having the right to vote on the resolution; or

(ii) by a member or members representing not less than 10% of the total voting rights (excluding voting rights attached to any shares held by the company as treasury shares); or

(iii) by a member or members holding not less than 10% of the total sum paid up on all shares conferring that right (also excluding treasury shares held by the company).

A member includes a proxy or person authorised to represent a corporation.

Any provision in the company's articles that purports to exclude the right to demand a poll at a general meeting is invalid unless it excludes the right to demand a poll on the election of the chairman of the meeting or the adjournment of the meeting.

On a poll a member entitled to more than one vote need not cast all his votes or cast all the votes he holds in the same manner (but see 4.4.21 above in relation to multiple corporate representation).

4.4.25 What is the position regarding meetings of a particular class of shareholders?

The provisions set out in 4.4.5 to 4.4.24 above apply equally to the meetings of holders of shares in a particular class, both for companies with a share capital and those without one.

4.4.26 How may resolutions be passed?

The relevant provisions are set out in Part 13 (sections 281 to 300) of the Companies Act 2006. These provisions are effective from 1 October 2007.

A resolution of the members (or class of members) of a private company must be passed either at a general meeting of the members or as a written resolution.

By contrast a resolution of the members (or class of members) of a public company may only be passed at a general meeting of the members.

As mentioned in 4.4.23, a resolution proposed at a general meeting may be passed either on a show of hands or on a poll.

4.4.27   What is the difference between a vote on a show of hands, on a poll and by written resolution?

As discussed in 4.4.23, on a show of hands each member who is entitled to vote and who is present in person (or as represented by a proxy or corporate representative) has one vote. If a member has more than one share, he is entitled to appoint a proxy for each share or, if a corporation, a representative for each underlying shareholder. Each proxy or representative would have one vote on a show of hands.

By contrast, on a resolution taken by poll, each member, their proxy or representative has one vote in respect of each share held.

A second important distinction between a vote on a show of hands and on a poll is the acceptance of postal, electronic and, for listed companies, CREST votes on a poll. If a shareholder wishes to exercise his vote on a show of hands, it will be necessary for that shareholder, his proxy or corporate representative to attend the meeting to vote. On a poll, a person may either:

(i)   attend the meeting in person, by proxy or corporate representative and vote by completing and depositing a poll form at the meeting; or

(ii)   appoint a proxy, usually the chairman of the meeting, to vote on the poll on his behalf at the meeting and instruct the proxy how he wishes to vote by sending a proxy voting instruction form to the company by post or, if allowed, electronically or through CREST.

A vote by poll therefore allows a larger proportion of the shareholders to vote, both in terms of the number of shareholders and the percentage of issued share capital carrying the right to vote.

A written resolution is similar to a poll vote in that each member has one vote in respect of each share held. However, to pass a written resolution the requisite majority of the total issued share capital of the company (not just of those who vote) must vote in favour of the resolution. More information on written resolutions is given in 4.4.28 to 4.4.31.

4.4.28   What is a written resolution?

A written resolution is a mechanism for a private company to pass a resolution without the need for a general meeting and it has effect as if passed by the company in general meeting or by the eligible members (or a class of members) of the company who would have been entitled to vote had the resolution been proposed at a meeting.

A written resolution is passed when the requisite majority of shareholders calculated by reference to the total nominal value of the share capital have consented to the written resolution.

Under the Companies Act 1985, a private company could pass written resolutions either in accordance with the Companies Act 1985 or in accordance with the provisions of its articles. Under the Companies Act 2006, a private company can now only pass written resolutions in accordance with that Act. Any provision contained in the articles of a private company is void if it prevents the company from adopting the procedures and use of written resolutions (section 300 of the Companies Act 2006).

Whereas a public company could previously pass a written resolution if allowed by its articles, this option is no longer available following the implementation of Part 13, Chapter 2 of the Companies Act 2006.

4.4.29 What are the specific rules relating to written resolutions?

Certain key changes have been introduced by the Companies Act 2006 in relation to the passing of written resolutions.

Previously written resolutions could only be passed when 100% of those persons entitled to vote had approved the resolution. The Companies Act 2006 has introduced a significant change under which ordinary and special resolutions now only need the normal majority in favour to be passed, i.e. for ordinary resolutions it becomes effective at the moment when a simple majority of those shareholders entitled to vote have signified their approval to the resolution and in the case of a special resolution it becomes effective, when 75% or more of those entitled to vote have approved the resolution (see 4.4.33 below). Those members entitled to vote, known as eligible members, are those members entitled to vote on the circulation date of the resolution.

In addition, the Companies Act 2006 has introduced a new concept under which a proposed written resolution will lapse if it is not passed by the requisite number of shareholders before the end of the specified period, which is either the period contained in the company's articles or, if none is specified, the period of 28 days beginning with the date of circulation of the resolution by the directors to eligible members. Any agreement by a member is ineffective if signified after the expiry of the prescribed period and a written resolution will lapse if the requisite number of votes in favour has not been obtained.

The Companies Act 2006 now also obliges the company to circulate the written resolution with a statement advising a member how he may give his agreement to the resolution, the date by which the resolution must be passed if it is not to lapse and the method by which the member should make the company aware of his decision.

Section 291 of the Companies Act 2006 provides for the company to send or submit a copy of the resolution to every eligible member in hard copy form, in electronic form or by means of its website.

A member signifying his agreement to the company for the passing of a written resolution may do so by identifying the resolution to which his agreement relates and use either hard copy or electronic form. Once signified, his agreement may not be revoked and a written resolution is passed when the required majority of eligible members have signified their agreement.

If a hard copy format is used, the resolution can be validly passed in counterpart without all the eligible members having received and signed the same document, provided that collectively the necessary approval has been obtained.

4.4.30 How can a member require the circulation of a written resolution?

Under section 292 of the Companies Act 2006, the members of a private company holding at least 5% (or such lower percentage as is specified in the company's articles) of the total voting rights of all members entitled to vote on a resolution may require the company to circulate a resolution to be moved as a written resolution. The directors are not required to circulate the resolution if the resolution would breach the company's articles, the law or it is frivolous, vexatious or defamatory.

Where the members require the company to circulate a resolution, they can ask that an explanation of not more than 1,000 words accompany the resolution.

A request may be in hard copy or electronic form, must identify the resolution and the accompanying statement and it must be authenticated by the person making it.

If the company is required to circulate a written resolution then the company must send or submit the request and accompanying statement to every eligible member within 21 days of the request. As before, the company must include guidance on how members may indicate their agreement or otherwise to the resolution and the date by which the resolution must be passed if it is not to lapse.

The company has the right to apply to the court for permission to dispense with the obligation to circulate the member's statement, which may be granted by the court if it is satisfied that the member is abusing his rights under section 292 of the Companies Act 2006.

4.4.31   What is the position regarding written resolutions and electronic communications with shareholders?

Where a company has provided an electronic address on a written resolution, for example a contact e-mail address in the accompanying notes, then the members may signify their agreement to the resolution via that electronic address.

Where a shareholder has consented to receive information via the company's website, then the written resolution and accompanying statement will have been validly submitted to the shareholder provided the information is available on the website throughout the whole period beginning with the circulation date and ending on the date on which the resolution would lapse.

4.4.32   What different types of resolutions exist?

Companies may pass either ordinary or special resolutions and specific rules apply to each. Companies used to be able to pass extraordinary resolutions but this form of resolution no longer appears in the Companies Act 2006. However, if a company's articles require a particular type of resolution to be passed by extraordinary or special resolution, the resolution will be passed if it is passed as either an extraordinary or special resolution.

4.4.33   What is the difference between an ordinary resolution and a special resolution?

Ordinary resolutions

Section 282 of the Companies Act 2006 specifies that an ordinary resolution of the members of a company is one that is passed by simple majority. Where the Companies Act 2006 is silent on the type of resolution that is required to be passed, the resolution will be an ordinary resolution. However, under the Companies Act 2006 anything which may be done by ordinary resolution may also be done by special resolution, but the same is not true in reverse.

An ordinary resolution passed at a meeting on a show of hands is passed if a simple majority in number of the members present in person, by proxy or corporate representative vote in favour.

A resolution passed on a poll taken at a meeting is passed by simple majority if it is passed by members, their proxies or corporate representatives representing a simple majority of the voting rights of those members voting in person or by proxy.

For a written resolution, an ordinary resolution is passed by those members who hold a simple majority of the total voting rights of the members entitled to vote.

Special resolutions

Section 283 of the Companies Act 2006 specifies that a special resolution is a resolution of the members (or class of members) that will only be passed if approved by not less than 75% of the membership voting in favour.

Where a resolution is passed at a meeting, the resolution is not a special resolution unless the notice of the meeting included the text of the resolution and specified the intention to propose the resolution as a special resolution. Similarly, where a resolution is passed by written resolution, it is not passed as a special resolution unless it was stated that it was proposed as a special resolution.

A special resolution may be passed on a show of hands, on a poll or by written resolution.

4.4.34 What is special notice?

Special notice is required to be given of an ordinary resolution to remove a director or an auditor from office.

Where special notice is required of a resolution, the resolution is not effective unless notice of the intention to move it has been given at least 28 days before the meeting at which it is moved.

Where practicable, the company must give its members notice of all resolutions being proposed at the meeting at the same time and in the same manner as it gives notice of the meeting. Where this is not practicable the company may choose another method of giving notice, provided it still gives at least 14 days' notice before the meeting, e.g. by advertisement in the newspaper or by such other method as may be allowed by the company's articles.

Section 312(4) of the Companies Act 2006 provides that notice is deemed properly given if the meeting is called for a date 28 days or less after notice of the intention to move the resolution has been given to the company.

4.5 Additional Companies Act 2006 provisions for quoted companies

4.5.1 Is a quoted company required to publish poll results?

Section 341 of the Companies Act 2006 provides that where a poll is taken at a general meeting of a quoted company, the company must ensure the following information is made available on its website:

(i)   the date of the meeting;

(ii)   the text of the resolution or the description of the subject matter of the poll; and

(iii) the number of votes cast both in favour and against.

The information must be kept available on the website for two years.

4.5.2   Can members challenge the results of a poll?

Section 342 of the Companies Act 2006 introduces a new provision under which members of a quoted company may require the directors to obtain an independent report on any poll taken or to be taken at a general meeting of the company.

To take advantage of this right, the request must be made by:

(i)   any member or members holding not less than 5% of the total voting rights (to exclude the voting rights of any shares held in treasury); or

(ii)   not less than 100 members (including indirect investors) who have the right to vote on the resolution at the general meeting and who hold shares in the company which have been paid up at an average sum per member of not less than £100.

The request can be made in hard copy or electronic form. It must identify the poll or polls to which it relates, be authenticated by the person making it and must be received by the company not later than one week after the date on which the poll is taken (section 342 of the Companies Act 2006).

4.5.2.1   *Who should prepare the report and by when must an independent assessor be appointed?*

Directors who are required to obtain an independent report must appoint, within one week of the request, a person they consider appropriate to be an independent assessor to prepare the report for the company.

Due to this tight timeline, directors may wish to appoint an independent assessor on a standby basis prior to the general meeting, particularly if one or more of the resolutions in the notice of the general meeting is controversial.

4.5.2.2   *What does 'independent' mean?*

Section 344 of Companies Act 2006 provides that to satisfy the 'independence' test, a person so appointed must not be an officer or employee of the company, nor may he be a partner or employee of an associated undertaking of the company. Furthermore, the directors must not appoint a person who has another role in relation to any poll on which he is to report including, but not limited to, a role in connection with collecting or counting votes or with the appointments of proxies. An auditor of the company is not regarded as an officer or employee of the company for these purposes and may, if otherwise 'independent', be appointed as an independent assessor.

4.5.2.3   *What should the report contain?*

Section 347 of the Companies Act 2006 sets out the requirements for the report of the independent assessor which must state, giving reasons, whether in his opinion:

(i)   the procedures adopted in connection with the polls were adequate;

(ii)   the votes cast were fairly and accurately recorded; and

(iii)   the validity of the appointment of proxies was fairly assessed.

If the assessor is unable to form an opinion on any of these matters, then the report must record this fact with the reasons for it.

4.5.2.4   *What rights does the independent assessor have?*

Sections 348 and 349 of the Companies Act 2006 set out the rights of an independent assessor which, if he is appointed prior to the meeting, include the right to attend the meeting and also the right to receive copies of the notice of the meeting and any other communications or documents provided by the company in connection with the matters discussed at the meeting and on which a poll has been taken. In addition he has the right to call upon any officer, employee or member of the company who was present at the meeting to provide him with information to assist him in the preparation of his report.

4.5.2.5   *What notification is the company required to give?*

Section 351 of the Companies Act 2006 provides that where an independent assessor has been appointed to report on a poll, the company must ensure that this fact is made available on its website together with information on the identity of the assessor, the text of the resolution or subject matter of the poll to which his appointment relates and a copy of the report made by him. The website must contain this information for two years.

Failure to comply could render the directors or officers of the company liable to summary conviction or a fine, but will not affect the validity of the poll or resolution or other business to which the poll relates.

Similar provisions apply to polls held in relation to meetings held by the holders of a class of shares in a quoted company in connection with the variation of the rights attached to such shares and include the right to appoint an independent assessor and the requirements to publish the results of the poll and/or independent assessor's report on the company website.

4.6 Power to investigate ownership of shares

There have been a number of significant changes made to the regime for disclosure of interests in shares in public companies. The changes took effect from 20 January 2007 and the majority are set out in DTR 5 of the Disclosure and Transparency Rules. There have been no changes in the power of a public company to investigate the ownership of its own series.

4.6.1 Do shareholders need to notify their interests in shares?

From 20 January 2007, the provisions of sections 198 to 211 of the Companies Act 1985 which set out the requirements for holders of interests in shares in UK public companies to notify those interests to the company were repealed and replaced by DTR 5 of the Disclosure and Transparency Rules. There is no equivalent section in the Companies Act 2006.

Therefore, holdings in UK public companies which are not listed on either a regulated market or prescribed market are no longer required to be disclosed.

4.6.2 Can companies request information about interests in their shares?

Section 793 of the Companies Act 2006 replaced section 212 of the Companies Act 1985 with effect from 20 January 2007. The provisions apply to all public companies whether or not their shares are admitted to trading on a regulated market.

Under the provisions of the Companies Act 2006, a public company can give notice to any person whom the company knows or has reasonable cause to believe to be interested in the company's shares or to have been interested at any period during the previous three years. The company may request a wide range of information such as confirmation of the person's interest, whether the shares were held on behalf of another person and the identity of that person.

4.6.3 Can the notice be sent electronically?

Yes, notices can be sent in electronic form in accordance with the provisions of Schedule 5 to the Companies Act 2006 (see 4.2.3 above for further details).

4.6.4 Does the company need to keep a register?

Section 808 of the Companies Act 2006 requires a company to keep a register of information received by it in pursuance of a notice under section 793. Although the provisions of the Companies Act 2006 are broadly similar to the provisions of the Companies Act 1985, there are several new provisions which make it easier for a company to maintain the register. For example, where the name of the shareholder is not known or there is no shareholder, the information can be entered on the register against the name of the person holding the interest (section 808 of the Companies Act 2006). Section 816 of the Companies Act 2006 allows the company to remove any entry from the register if more than six years has elapsed since the entry was made. The previous requirement for a company to verify third party information supplied in response to a notice before putting in on the register has been removed (section 817 of the Companies Act 2006).

4.7 Political donations and expenditure

The relevant sections of the Companies Act 2006 are contained in Part 14, sections 362 to 379, which are effective from 1 October 2007. Additional rules are also contained in the Parties, Elections and Referendums Act 2000, sections 50 to 53.

The Companies Act 2006 has clarified the rules on political donations and expenditure but, to a large extent, has left the rules unaltered. Many public companies seek shareholder approval at their annual general meetings each year for political donations and expenditure. In most cases, these resolutions are put to shareholders on a precautionary basis because the definitions of political donations and expenditure are so broad that companies do not want to run the risk of inadvertently breaching the requirements. Even following the clarification, we expect that this will continue to be the case under the Companies Act 2006.

4.7.1 What does the Companies Act 2006 cover?

Part 14 of the Companies Act 2006 sets out rules covering:

(i)   donations to political parties or independent election candidates;

(ii)   donations to political organisations other than political parties; and

(iii)   political expenditure.

4.7.2 When do the rules come into force?

The Companies Act 2006 only applies to political donations made after 1 October 2007. The provisions in respect of independent election candidates are effective from 1 October 2008. However, directors' reports for financial years beginning on or after 6 April 2008 will be required to contain details of donations to independent election candidates.

4.7.3 What is the definition of 'political donations'?

The definition is set out in section 364 of the Companies Act 2006 and is wide reaching. Political donations include gifts, sponsorship, subscription or other affiliation fees and moneys spent in paying party expenses together with non-commercial property, services or facilities used by the party.

The definition of donation includes donations to a political party or other political organisation or, for the first time, to any independent election candidate (in the UK or the European Union).

Some donations may fall under the limited exemptions set out in the Companies Act 2006, for example transmitting party political broadcasts free of charge or where the accumulated amount of the donation(s) does not amount to more than £5,000 in any 12 month period.

The Companies Act 2006 has clarified some difficult issues, such as those relating to trade union activity. While a donation to a trade union political fund would count as a political donation, other activities (for example, allowing employees to take paid leave to attend trade union meetings) would not fall within the scope of the regime.

4.7.4 What is the definition of 'political expenditure'?

The definition is set out in section 365 of the Companies Act 2006 as expenditure incurred on preparation of publicity, publication or dissemination of advertising or other promotional or publicity material or activities in general that are capable of being *reasonably* regarded to affect public support for the bodies or individuals they represent.

In relation to the reasonableness requirement, the objective need not be the wish to have an effect on public support as its primary aim, nor does it have to be proven that there has been any effect on public support.

4.7.5 Is authorisation required for a company to make a political donation or expenditure?

Under sections 366 to 368 of the Companies Act 2006, a company cannot make a political donation or incur political expenditure without shareholder approval.

4.7.6 Who needs to authorise the donation or expenditure?

Donations or expenditure must be authorised:

(i)   in the case of a company that is not a subsidiary of another company, by the members of that company; or

(ii) in the case of a company that is a subsidiary of another company, by the members of the company and the members of the holding company.

The relevant holding company is defined by section 366(4) of the Companies Act 2006 as the company's ultimate UK registered parent company and as such, it is not necessary to receive approval from any intermediate holding company nor from an overseas holding company. Furthermore, the provisions under the Companies Act 1985 relating to overseas subsidiaries have not been replicated in the Companies Act 2006 and accordingly, a UK parent company will not need to seek authorisation of political donations or expenditure made by any of its overseas subsidiaries.

No authorisation is required when the aggregate of all political donations or expenditure made by the group does not exceed £5,000.

4.7.7   What information should the resolution contain?

Section 367(5) of the Companies Act 2006 provides that the resolution must be expressed in general terms and must not purport to authorise particular donations or expenditure. Therefore, a resolution to approve a donation of a specified amount to a specified political organisation would not be effective.

The resolution may authorise donations or expenditure under one or more of the following heads:

(i)   donations to political parties or independent election candidates;

(ii)   donations to political organisations other than political parties; and

(iii)   political expenditure.

For each of the above heads, the resolution must specify the amount of the maximum intended donation and the period to which the resolution relates.

Where an ultimate holding company is passing a resolution, it may pass one resolution to cover itself and all of its subsidiaries and may cover all its subsidiaries existing either at the time the resolution is passed or which become subsidiaries at any time during the period to which the resolution relates. Where it wishes to cover specified subsidiaries, separate amounts must be specified for each subsidiary under each head. As a practical point, it may be easier to have one resolution per subsidiary.

The resolution can be for any period up to a maximum of four years. This period will be presumed as the period for which authority is being sought if no period is specified in the resolution.

4.8   What statutory rights do minority shareholders have?

As discussed in Chapter 1, the directors of a company when exercising their statutory duties to promote the success of the company must have regard to the need to act fairly as between the members of the company. Therefore acting in a way which is unfairly prejudicial to one or more shareholders will not only amount to a breach of duty but could also be challenged on application to the court (discussed further below). In addition, minority shareholders have a range of express powers and rights to challenge the actions of boards or to require boards to take certain actions. Minorities can also block the passing of ordinary and special resolutions if their holding of voting rights is sufficiently high. These various rights and powers are summarised in this section with cross references to other chapters (as appropriate) where they are discussed in more detail.

The relevant provisions are contained in Part 30 of the Companies Act 2006 which largely restate sections 459 to 461 of the Companies Act 1985. These provisions are effective from 1 October 2007.

4.8.1 What protection does the Companies Act 2006 offer to shareholders?

Section 994 of the Companies Act 2006 provides that a member of a company may apply to the court by petition for an order that:

(i) the company's affairs are being or have been conducted in a manner that is unfairly prejudicial to the interests of the members generally, some part of its members or the member himself; or

(ii) an actual or proposed act or omission of the company (including an act or omission on its behalf) is or would be prejudicial.

The court can make such order as it thinks fit for giving relief in respect of the petition including but not limited to an order:

(i) regulating the affairs of the company in the future;

(ii) requiring the company to carry out or refrain from carrying out, certain actions;

(iii) authorising civil proceedings to be brought in the name and on behalf of the company against such persons as the court may direct;

(iv) requiring the company to make changes to its articles of association; and/ or

(v) providing for the purchase of the shares of any members of the company by other members or by the company itself.

The ability to bring proceedings in the name of the company with the court's approval has been retained under the Companies Act 2006 notwithstanding the introduction of derivative claims procedures (discussed in Chapter 1). In practice, the majority of applications are made by minority shareholders seeking an order for the purchase of their shares.

4.8.2 What other statutory powers do minority shareholders have?

The statutory powers of minority shareholders are set out below:

For a detailed discussion of these provisions and the extent to which they restate corresponding provisions of the Companies Act 1985 reference should be made to the individual chapters indicated below against each provision. Transitional provisions are also discussed in the relevant chapters.

Power	Threshold	Provision of Companies Act 2006	Date in force
Derivative claims.	Any member.	Section 260 (Chapter 1)	1 October 2007
Application to the court to cancel a resolution approving the purchase by a private company of its own shares out of capital (provided that the member making the application did not vote in favour of the resolution).	Any member.	Section 721 (Chapter 9)	1 October 2009
Application to the court for an order on the ground that the company's affairs are being or have been or are to be conducted in a manner unfairly prejudicial to the interests of the members or some part of its members.	Any member.	Section 994 (see section 4.8.1)	1 October 2007

Power	Minority threshold	Provisions of Companies Act 2006	Date in force
Application to the court to cancel special resolution to re-register a public company as private.	Holders of (a) not less than 5% in aggregate of the nominal value of the company's issued share capital (excluding treasury shares); or (b) not less than 5% of its members (if the company is not limited by shares); or (c) not less than 50 of the company's members. Holders who consented to the resolution do not count for this purpose.	Section 98 (see section 3.8.14)	1 October 2009
Circulation of a written resolution and statement by members of a private company.	Members holding not less than 5% of the total voting rights of all members entitled to vote on the resolution or such lower percentage as may be specified in the articles.	Section 292 (see section 4.4.30)	1 October 2007
Members of a company to require the directors to call a general meeting.	For companies with a share capital the power is exercisable by members holding at least 10% of the paid up share capital carrying voting rights (excluding treasury shares). For companies without a share capital the power is exercisable by members representing at least 10% of the total voting rights of all members. (For private companies the required percentage may be 5% in certain circumstances).	Section 303 (see section 4.4.5)	1 October 2007
Convene a meeting in the event that directors fail to do so pursuant to section 303.	The members who requested the meeting or any of them representing more than 50% of the total voting rights of all of them.	Section 305	1 October 2007
Circulation of a statement prior to a general meeting.	Members representing at least 5% of the total voting rights of all the members (excluding treasury shares) or at least 100 members	Section 314 (see section 4.4.11)	1 October 2007

Power	Minority threshold	Provisions of Companies Act 2006	Date in force
	who have a right to vote and who hold shares paid up as to an average sum of £100 per member.		
Right to demand a poll.	The power is exercisable by: (i) not less than five members; or (ii) by a member or members holding not less than 10% of the voting rights (excluding treasury shares); or (iii) by a member or members holding voting shares being shares which represent at least 10% of the paid up voting share capital (excluding treasury shares).	Section 321 (see section 4.4.24)	1 October 2007
Right to require circulation of resolutions for AGMs of public companies.	The power is exercisable by members: (a) representing at least 5% of the total voting rights of all members having the right to vote at the AGM (excluding treasury shares); or (b) at least 100 members having a right to vote on the resolution at the AGM holding shares which have been paid up as to an average of £100 per member.	Section 338	1 October 2007
Require independent report on a poll undertaken at a general meeting of a quoted company.	The power is exercisable by members: (a) representing not less than 5% of the total voting rights of all members having the right to vote on the matter to which the poll relates (excluding treasury shares); or (b) not less than 100 members having the	Section 342 (see section 4.5.2)	1 October 2007

Power	Minority threshold	Provisions of Companies Act 2006	Date in force
	right to vote on any matter to which the poll relates holding shares which have been paid up as to at least £100 per member.		
Enforce directors' liabilities in the case of unauthorised political donations or expenditure.	The power is exercisable by: (a) holders of not less than 5% of the nominal value of the company's issued share capital; or (b) if the company is not limited by shares, not less than 5% of its members; or (c) not less than 50 of the company's members.	Sections 369 and 370	1 October 2007
Require a company to carry out an audit where it would otherwise be exempt.	Where a company has a share capital, the power is exercisable by members holding not less than 10% of the company's share capital, of any class. Where a company does not have a share capital the power is exercisable by not less than 10% in number of its members.	Section 476	6 April 2008
Prevention by members of the deemed reappointment of the auditors of a private company.	Members holding at least 5% of the total voting rights of all members who would be entitled to vote on the resolution or such lower percentage set out in the articles.	Section 488	1 October 2007
Rights of members of quoted companies to require website publication of audit concerns.	The power is exercisable by (a) members holding at least 5% of the total voting rights of all the members having a right to vote (excluding treasury shares), or (b) at least 100 members holding voting shares and whose shares are paid up as to an average of £100 per member.	Section 527	6 April 2008

Power	Minority threshold	Provisions of Companies Act 2006	Date in force
Rights of members not voting in favour of a resolution varying class rights to apply to the court for an order cancelling the resolution.	Members holding not less than 15% of the issued shares of the relevant class (excluding treasury shares).	Section 633	1 October 2009

4.8.3 What are the relevant thresholds for the passing of ordinary and special resolutions?

These are set out below:

Thresholds for ordinary resolutions	
Ordinary resolution	Simple majority of members voting in person or by proxy.
Written resolution	Members holding a simple majority of the total voting rights of eligible members.
Ordinary resolution on a poll	Members holding a simple majority of the total voting rights, voting in person or by proxy.
Members holding 50% or more of the voting rights of a company therefore can block the passing of an ordinary resolution.	
Thresholds for special resolutions	
Special resolution	Not less than 75% of members voting in person or by proxy.
Written resolution	Members holding not less than 75% of the total voting rights.
Special resolution on a poll	Members holding not less than 75% of the total voting rights voting in person or by proxy.
Members need to hold more than 25% of the voting rights of a company to block the passing of a special resolution.	

4.8.4 Which matters require approval by an ordinary resolution?

Matters requiring an ordinary resolution	Provision of Companies Act 2006	Date in force
A. Powers exercisable by ordinary resolution.		
Remove a director.	Section 168 (Chapter 1)	1 October 2007
Power to remove an auditor.	Section 510 (Chapter 7)	6 April 2008
B. Matters requiring approval.		
Approval of directors' long term service contracts.	Section 188 (Chapter 2)	1 October 2007
Substantial property transactions with directors.	Section 190 (Chapter 2)	1 October 2007
Loans, quasi-loans and credit transactions with directors.	Section 197 (Chapter 2)	1 October 2007
Payments for loss of office.	Section 215 (Chapter 2)	1 October 2007
Payments for loss of office in connection with a transfer of undertaking.	Section 218 (Chapter 2)	1 October 2007
Payment for loss of office in connection with a share transfer resulting from a takeover bid.	Section 219 (Chapter 2)	1 October 2007
Ratification of the acts of a director (director and persons connected with him are not entitled to vote).	Section 239 (Chapter 2)	1 October 2007
Exercise of the power to make provision for employees or former employees of the group on cessation of business in certain circumstances.	Section 247	1 October 2009
Political donations.	Section 364 (see section 4.6)	1 October 2007
Approval of director's remuneration report (quoted companies only).	Section 439	6 April 2008
Appointment of auditors (where required by members).	Section 485	1 October 2007
Approval of audit liability agreements.	Section 536	6 April 2008
Authority to allot shares.	Section 551 (Chapter 9)	1 October 2009

Matters requiring an ordinary resolution	Provision of Companies Act 2006	Date in force
Agreement for the transfer of non-cash assets to a public company in consideration for an issue of shares within two years of the issue of its trading certificate or re-registration as a public company.	Section 601	1 October 2009
Power to subdivide or consolidate shares.	Section 618 (Chapter 9)	1 October 2009
Reconversion of stock into shares.	Section 620 (Chapter 9)	1 October 2009
Redenomination of shares from one currency to another (not involving a reduction of capital).	Section 622 (Chapter 9)	1 October 2009
The grant of power to directors to determine the terms, conditions and manner of redemption of shares.	Section 685	1 October 2009
Authority for market purchase by a company of its own shares.	Section 701	1 October 2009

4.8.5 Which matters require approval by a special resolution or some other threshold?

These are set out below:

Matters requiring a special resolution	Provision of Companies Act 2006	Date in force
Amendment of the articles.	Section 21 (Chapter 3)	1 October 2009
Change of name (unless otherwise provided by the articles).	Section 77 (Chapter 3)	1 October 2009
Re-registration of a private company as a public company.	Section 90 (Chapter 3)	1 October 2009
Re-registration of a public company as a private company.	Section 97 (Chapter 3)	1 October 2009
Re-registration of an unlimited company as a private company.	Section 105 (Chapter 3)	1 October 2009
Disapplication of pre-emption rights on the allotment of shares.	Section 570	1 October 2009
Disapplication of pre-emption rights on a sale of treasury shares.	Section 573	1 October 2009
Reduction of capital following a redenomination of shares.	Section 626	1 October 2009

Matters requiring a special resolution	Provision of Companies Act 2006	Date in force
A variation of class rights where no provision is made in the articles of association.	Sections 630 and 631	1 October 2009
(Note: as an alternative the variation can be approved with the consent in writing of the holders of at least 75% in nominal value of the holders of that class (excluding treasury shares).	Sections 641(a) and 641(2)–(6)	1 October 2008
Reduction of share capital.	Section 641(1)(b)	1 October 2009
Approval and variation of a contract for an off-market purchase by a company of its shares.	Sections 694 and 697	1 October 2009
(Note: the resolution is invalidated if any member holding shares to which the resolution relates votes on the resolution and the resolution would not otherwise have been passed).		
Approval of a release of the company's rights under a contract for an off-market purchase by a company of its own shares.	Section 700	1 October 2009
Approval for the purchase or redemption by a private company of its own shares out of capital.	Section 716	1 October 2009

Matters requiring unanimity	Provision of Companies Act 2006	Date in force
Introduction or amendment of an entrenched provision in the articles.	Section 22 (Chapter 3)	1 October 2009
Re-registration of a private company as unlimited company.	Section 102 (Chapter 3)	1 October 2009
Re-registration of a public company as an unlimited company.	Section 109 (Chapter 3)	1 October 2009
Other Key Thresholds	**Provision of Companies Act 2006**	**Date in force**
Member schemes of arrangement and reconstruction. These in general require the approval of a majority in number representing 75% in value of the members (or class of members) present and voting in person or by proxy.	Parts 26 and 27	6 April 2008

Matters requiring unanimity	Provision of Companies Act 2006	Date in force
Rights of an offeror to buy out a minority shareholder on a takeover offer and corresponding rights of minority shareholders to require an offeror to buy their shares. The offeror must, by virtue of acceptances of the offer, have acquired, or unconditionally contracted to acquire (a) not less than 90% of the value of the shares to which the offer relates and (b) where the shares are voting shares, not less than 90% of the voting rights carried by those shares.	Sections 979 and 983	6 April 2007
Appointment of directors of a public company by a single resolution. This requires approval of the meeting without any vote being cast against it.	Section 160	1 October 2007

4.9   Conclusion

There follows in summary form a list of the key changes introduced by the Companies Act 2006 discussed in this Chapter, together with any corresponding action required:

4.9.1   List of key changes and actions

Issue	Companies Act 1985	Companies Act 2006	Action required
Electronic and website communications (section 4.2)	Limited electronic communications were permitted under the Companies Act 1985 (Electronic Communications) Order 2000, subject to expressly obtaining shareholder consent.	Deemed default for shareholders to receive documents or information via a website subject to certain procedures being followed (section 2.1).	Consider whether changes to the articles are needed to facilitate the application of these provisions and if so, notify shareholders once the articles have been changed.
Indirect investors' rights (section 4.3)	Provision for shareholder to appoint a proxy but that proxy was limited in the scope of its ability to act.	Right of shareholders of private or public companies to nominate a third party to have and exercise all or any specified rights of a member including corporate governance rights and a right to receive certain information.	Indirect investors to consider whether they wish to exercise these rights. Corporates to have systems in place to comply with any requests and to agree these arrangements with their registrars.

Issue	Companies Act 1985	Companies Act 2006	Action required
General meetings (section 4.4)	Extraordinary general meetings.	Abolition of extraordinary general meetings, all meetings are now known as general meetings.	No action required but in due course it is good practice to update the articles to remove references to extraordinary general meetings.
Annual general meeting (section 4.4)	Requirement on all companies to hold an annual general meeting each year unless an elective resolution is in place.	Abolition of annual general meetings for private companies.	Private companies should consider whether it is appropriate to remove any requirement in their articles to continue to hold annual general meetings.
Appointment of proxies (section 4.4)	Right of a member to appoint a proxy to attend at meeting and vote on a member's behalf unless the company's articles provide otherwise. A proxy was not entitled to vote except on a poll. In the case of a private company, a proxy had the same right as the member to speak at the meeting. A member of a private company was not entitled to appoint more than one proxy to attend on the same occasion.	Enhancement of rights of proxies to give them the same powers at a general meeting as a member of the company. On a vote on a resolution by way of a show of hands, every proxy present has one vote. Members of both private and public companies have the right to appoint a proxy to attend, speak and vote at meetings on his behalf. A member is permitted to appoint more than one proxy in relation to a meeting, provided each proxy is appointed to exercise the rights attached to different shares held by him, or to a different £10, or multiple of £10, of stock held by that member.	Proxy cards need to be updated to reflect the fact that proxies can attend and speak at meetings.

Issue	Companies Act 1985	Companies Act 2006	Action required
Written resolution (section 4.4)	Private companies are only able to pass a written resolution, if it is signed by or on behalf of all members of the company	Private companies are able to pass written ordinary resolutions by a simple majority of those eligible to vote and written special resolutions with a 75% majority of those eligible to vote, rather then requiring unanimity.	Written resolution of private companies must contain the additional statements required by the Companies Act 2006.
	No provision for lapse.	Written resolution will lapse after a certain period.	
	Contract requirements.	Additional contract requirements imposed.	
	Both public and private companies can pass written resolutions.	Only private companies can pass written resolutions.	Ensure that members' meetings of public companies are convened for all shareholder resolutions.
Additional provisions for quoted companies (section 4.5)	No provision to require independent report.	Ability of members of a quoted company to require an independent report to verify the accuracy of any poll taken.	Consider whether independent assessor should be available especially at general meetings where contentious matters are being considered.
Power to investigate ownership of shares (section 4.6)	Set out procedure for notification of interests in shares of public companies.	Only holders of interests in listed entities required to disclose interests. Provisions contained in the Disclosure and Transparency Rules rather than the Companies Act 2006.	No action required.
	Required a company to verify third-party information supplied in response to a notice investigating ownership of shares.	This provision has been removed.	No action required.

Issue	Companies Act 1985	Companies Act 2006	Action required
Political donations and expenditure (section 4.7)	There are rules governing political donations and expenditure.	Clarification of the rules on political donations and extension of the regulation of political donations and expenditure to cover independent election candidates.	Identify to what extent additional shareholder approval may be required.

Chapter 5

The preparation of annual accounts and reports

5.1 Introduction 5001
   5.1.1 Scope of this chapter 5001
   5.1.2 What is different and what stays the same? 5002
   5.1.3 What has come into effect prior to 6 April 2008? 5002
   5.1.4 Does an IAS accounts preparer need to be concerned with
       the Accounts regulations? 5003
   5.1.5 Which regulations deal with the form and content of
       Companies Act accounts for banking and insurance
       companies? 5003
   5.1.6 Which regulations deal with the contents of the directors'
       report and directors' remuneration report and information
       about benefits of directors? 5003
5.2 Accounting records 5004
   5.2.1 Is there any change to the duty to keep accounting
       records? 5004
   5.2.2 How does the change in wording in the company's duty
       relate to the auditor's duties in respect of accounting
       records? 5004
5.3 Annual accounts 5005
   5.3.1 Is there still a choice as to which accounting framework
       directors can use to prepare accounts? 5005
   5.3.2 Is there still a 'true and fair' requirement? 5005
   5.3.3 Is the IAS 'present fairly' equal to the Companies Act
       'giving a true and fair view'? 5006
   5.3.4 Does the new overarching requirement correct the
       anomalies in the previous legislation? 5007
   5.3.5 What does 'think small first' mean? 5008
   5.3.6 Are the definitions of small, medium-sized and large
       companies the same as before? 5008
   5.3.7 Are there any changes to the company size definitions for
       companies in the financial services sector? 5009
   5.3.8 Are 'basic size tests' the same as before? 5010
   5.3.9 What about the thresholds for small and medium-sized
       groups? 5010
   5.3.10 Are there any changes to the requirements for small
       companies and groups to prepare accounts? 5011
   5.3.11 Are there any changes to the requirements for medium-
       sized companies and groups to prepare accounts? 5012
   5.3.12 Are there any new disclosure requirements? 5013
   5.3.13 What are the new related party transactions disclosures? 5013

5.3.14   Does a company preparing IAS accounts (an IFRS
         reporter) have more disclosures to make in relation to
         related party transactions? 5014
5.3.15   Does a company preparing Companies Act accounts (a
         UK GAAP reporter) have more disclosures to make about
         related party transactions? 5014
5.3.16   What concerns are there about transactions with directors
         and key management? 5015
5.3.17   Are there any changes to the legality of, and disclosures
         about, directors' loans and other transactions? 5016
5.3.18   What is the main change to the disclosure of directors'
         loans and other transactions, etc.? 5017
5.3.19   What is the effect of the transitional arrangements while
         accounts are still prepared in accordance with the
         provisions of the Companies Act 1985? 5018
5.3.20   Do the new disclosures about off-balance-sheet
         arrangements apply to both IFRS and UK GAAP
         reporters? 5018
5.3.21   Are there any exemptions for small and medium-sized
         companies? 5019
5.3.22   Is there any guidance on how to comply with the new off-
         balance-sheet disclosures? 5019
5.3.23   What should directors do to comply with the new off-
         balance-sheet disclosures? 5020
5.3.24   Are there any changes to the 'Fair value accounting' rules
         in law for Companies Act accounts? 5021
5.3.25   Are there any changes to the concept of 'collective board
         responsibility'? 5022
5.3.26   Are there any changes to the disclosures about employee
         costs and numbers? 5022
5.3.27   Have any other changes been made to the form and
         content of Companies Act group accounts? 5023
5.4   Directors' report 5023
5.4.1   What are the changes to the content of the directors'
         report? 5023
         5.4.1.1   What is the purpose of a business review? 5024
5.4.2   Who is responsible for preparing the business review? ... 5024
5.4.3   What are the disclosure requirements? 5024
5.4.4   Are there any exemptions for small or medium-sized
         companies? 5025
5.4.5   What are the additional requirements for quoted
         companies? 5026
5.4.6   Are there any 'seriously prejudicial' exemptions? 5026
5.4.7   Is there a particular format of the business review? 5027
5.4.8   How does the directors' liability 'safe harbour' apply? ... 5027
5.4.9   How are the requirements applied to different sizes of
         company? 5028

5.4.10   How should the disclosure of principal risks and KPIs (key performance indicators) be made for wholly owned subsidiaries? 5029

5.4.11   What type of information should be included in a business review? 5029

5.4.12   What are the challenging areas: principal risks? 5031

5.4.13   What are the challenging areas: key performance indicators? 5031

    5.4.13.1   What is key? 5032

    5.4.13.2   How many KPIs? 5032

    5.4.13.3   Segmental or group KPIs? 5032

    5.4.13.4   How flexible is the choice of KPIs? 5033

    5.4.13.5   Does reliability matter? 5033

5.4.14   What are the challenging areas: resources available to an entity? 5033

5.4.15   What are the challenging areas: future trends and factors? 5034

    5.4.15.1   Does this mean having to provide potentially competitively sensitive information? 5034

    5.4.15.2   What can be done to ensure the supportability of forward-looking information? 5035

    5.4.15.3   What about profit forecasts? 5035

5.4.16   What are the challenging areas: environmental, employee and social matters? 5036

5.4.17   What are the challenging areas: persons with whom the company has contractual arrangements? 5036

5.4.18   What is the role of the Financial Reporting Review Panel (FRRP) in this area? 5037

5.4.19   What changes are there to the disclosure of directors' interests? 5037

5.4.20   Does the change in the legal disclosure requirements apply to all types of company? 5038

5.4.21   Have the disclosure thresholds for charitable and political donations been increased? 5038

5.5   Directors' remuneration report 5039

    5.5.1   Are there any new disclosures? 5039

5.6   Conclusion 5040

    5.6.1   List of key changes and actions 5040

The preparation of annual accounts and reports

5.1 Introduction

5.1.1 Scope of this chapter

This chapter deals with Part 15 (Accounts and Reports) of the Companies Act 2006 insofar as it introduces changes to the law on the preparation of annual accounts and reports contained in the Companies Act 1985 and its supporting schedules.

Much of the detail supporting the requirements of Part 15 is found in regulations rather than in the body of the Act. In particular, the requirements of the Schedules to the Companies Act 1985 (for example, Schedules 4, 4A, 8, 8A, 9 and 9A to the Companies Act 1985 dealing with the form and content of accounts) are carried forward in such regulations, which for ease are referred to collectively as the 'Accounts regulations'. The main Accounts regulations are:

(i)   the Small Companies and Groups (Accounts and Directors' Report) Regulations 2008 (SI 2008/409);

(ii)   the Large and Medium-sized Companies and Groups (Accounts and Reports) Regulations 2008 (SI 2008/410);

(iii) The Companies Act 2006 (Amendment) (Accounts and Reports) Regulations 2008 (SI 2008/393); and

(iv) the Companies (Revision of Defective Accounts and Reports) Regulations 2008 (SI 2008/373).

Other regulations in the 'Accounts' suite are:

(v)   the Companies (Summary Financial Statement) Regulations 2008 (SI 2008/374); and

(vi) the Companies (Disclosure of Auditor Remuneration and Liability Limitation Agreements) Regulations 2008 (SI 2008/489).

These are discussed in other chapters.

This chapter deals with the changes made by the main 'Accounts regulations'.

To assist companies in applying the legislation the Department for Business Enterprise & Regulatory Reform has issued 'Guidance for UK Companies on

Accounting and Reporting: Requirements under the Companies Act 2006 and the application of the IAS Regulation'.

5.1.2 What is different and what stays the same?

The majority of the legislation simply re-enacts the requirements of the Companies Act 1985, albeit in a different format.

One of the Government's stated objectives in reforming the law was to 'think small first'; that is, to recognise that the vast majority of UK businesses fall into the 'small' category and, accordingly, to draft the law from the perspective of those users. Part 15 therefore sets out the provisions applying to small companies first, with provisions applying to large companies expressed as an addition or amendment to those requirements. Part VII of the Companies Act 1985 is drafted the other way round, with provisions applying to small companies expressed as modifications of those applying to large companies.

Other changes include:

(i)   a new requirement for quoted companies for an enhanced business review in the directors' report; and

(ii)   changes to the requirements which arise from the transposition of the requirements of recent EU legislation that were not part of the modernisation process that culminated in the new Act.

Legislation carried forward to the Companies Act 2006 without amendment includes the following:

(i)   companies continue to be able to choose their accounting framework ('Companies Act accounts' or 'International Accounting Standards (IAS) accounts') as before, under the same conditions and restrictions;

(ii)   the determination of accounting reference dates and the rules applying to changes in accounting reference dates are unchanged;

(iii)   large companies are required to prepare consolidated accounts unless specifically exempted; this requirement and the related exemptions are unchanged (although there is a change for medium-sized companies); and

(iv)   the definitions of parent and subsidiary undertakings are unchanged.

5.1.3 What has come into effect prior to 6 April 2008?

The 'safe harbour provision'[1] ('Liability for false or misleading statements in reports') was implemented on 20 January 2007 and applies to directors' reports and directors' remuneration reports published on or after that date. For

[1]   Section 463, Companies Act 2006.

financial years beginning on or after 1 October 2007, quoted companies have to produce an enhanced business review[2]. From 1 November 2007, the definition of 'connected persons' is expanded for the purposes of capturing loans and other credit facilities extended to directors and their connected persons[3]. The remainder of Part 15 is in force for financial years beginning on or after 6 April 2008.

5.1.4 Does an IAS accounts preparer need to be concerned with the Accounts regulations?

Yes. The Accounts regulations contain a number of matters that are relevant to an IAS[4] accounts preparer, such as the disclosures about related undertakings and the contents of the directors' report and the directors' remuneration report. They also deal with the procedures for correcting defective accounts and the preparation of Summary Financial Statements. However, as previously, IAS accounts preparers are exempt from those parts and schedules that deal with the contents of Companies Act accounts.

5.1.5 Which regulations deal with the form and content of Companies Act accounts for banking and insurance companies?

The equivalents of Schedules 9 (Banking companies) and 9A (Insurance companies) to the Companies Act 1985 are Schedules 2 and 3 respectively of the Large and Medium-sized Companies Accounts regulations[5]. The form and content of Companies Act group accounts are dealt with in Schedule 6 to those regulations, with Parts 2 and 3 providing the necessary modifications for banking and insurance companies respectively. Schedule 4, Part 4 provides additional disclosures for banking companies and groups in respect of their related undertakings.

5.1.6 Which regulations deal with the contents of the directors' report and directors' remuneration report and information about benefits of directors?

For small companies, Schedules 3 and 5 respectively of the Small Companies Accounts regulations[6] deal with the disclosure about directors' remuneration and the matters to be dealt with in the directors' report. See section 5.4 and 5.5.

For all other companies, Schedules 5, 7 and 8 respectively of the Large and Medium-sized Companies Accounts regulations deal with the information about benefits of directors, the matters to be dealt with in the directors' report and quoted companies' directors' remuneration report. See section 5.4 and 5.5.

---

[2] Section 417, Companies Act 2006.
[3] Sections 252 to 255, Companies Act 2006.
[4] International Accounting Standards as adopted by the European Union.
[5] The Large and Medium-sized Companies and Groups (Accounts and Reports) Regulations 2008.
[6] The Small Companies and Groups (Accounts and Directors' Report) Regulations 2008.

5.2 Accounting records

5.2.1 Is there any change to the duty to keep accounting records?

Essentially, no. However, there are some changes to the wording. In particular, the company's duty is now expressed as a requirement to keep 'adequate accounting records'.

Although, the requirements in the Companies Act 1985 and Companies Act 2006 are nearly identical, and the Government did not intend the change in wording to represent a substantive change, it has sparked a degree of controversy and debate. To obtain clarity on this, the Financial Reporting Council (FRC) has adopted a project to assess the implications of the change in wording, which may include instructing company law Counsel to advise. In the meantime, it is considered reasonable for directors to continue to apply the guidance issued in 1992 by the Institute of Chartered Accountants in England and Wales[7] on keeping proper accounting records for the purposes of the previous legislation so as to meet the company's obligation under the new Act[8].

5.2.2 How does the change in wording in the company's duty relate to the auditor's duties in respect of accounting records?

Both Acts require auditors to carry out investigations of a company's accounting records. The Companies Act 1985 requires an auditor to form an opinion as to whether 'proper accounting records' have been kept, but the Companies Act 2006 expresses this as an opinion on whether 'adequate accounting records' have been kept.

The Companies Act 2006 therefore creates an explicit connection between the directors' duty to keep accounting records and the auditor's duty to form an opinion thereon because the duty of both the directors and auditor are expressed in terms of 'adequate accounting records'. There was no such direct connection in the previous legislation, particularly as 'proper accounting records' were not defined and there was no cross reference between the two duties. Nevertheless, a common sense interpretation would almost certainly infer such a connection between the two duties. The functions of the auditor are discussed further in chapter 7.

---

[7] As published in the April 1992 edition of Accountancy. This guidance was settled in consultation with company law counsel at that time.

[8] Section 386, Companies Act 2006.

5.3 Annual accounts

5.3.1 Is there still a choice as to which accounting framework directors can use to prepare accounts?

Yes. Directors still have a choice, subject to some conditions and restrictions[9], as to whether to prepare their companies' individual accounts under UK GAAP ('Companies Act accounts') or IAS ('IAS accounts'). There is one change: as additional reason has been added when the directors may decide that it is appropriate to cease using IAS as the accounting framework and use UK GAAP instead. That reason is that the company ceases to be a subsidiary[10].

The directors of a company admitted to trading on a regulated market in the EU (a 'listed' company) have no choice and must prepare its group accounts in accordance with EU-adopted IFRS. For other companies, the directors still have a choice.

5.3.2 Is there still a 'true and fair' requirement?

Yes, emphatically so. The Government has inserted an explicit 'overarching true and fair requirement' in the Companies Act 2006 that applies irrespective of the accounting framework (UK GAAP or IAS) used by the directors to prepare accounts. This requirement states that:

> 'directors must not approve accounts .... unless they are satisfied that they give a true and fair view of the assets, liabilities, financial positions and profit or loss'[11].

In performing their duties, auditors are required to have regard to the directors' duty not to approve accounts unless those accounts give a true and fair view as stated above.

The insertion of this overarching requirement was partly in response to concerns expressed by some users of IAS accounts to the effect that it might be possible for preparers to comply with the 'letter of IAS' yet still produce accounts that do not give a true and fair view.

This concern has been influenced by recent accounting scandals, particularly in the US (for example, Enron) but also in Europe (for example, Parmalat). There can be a tension between applying accounting rules and applying a broad set of principles, even though accounting standards are themselves based on those principles. This is particularly so where accounting standards become lengthy and more comprehensive in response to the complexity of many transactions

---

[9] Sections 395 and 407, Companies Act 2006.
[10] Section 395(4)(aa), Companies Act 2006.
[11] Section 393(1), Companies Act 2006.

and arrangements. Therefore, it becomes difficult to stand back from the rules and take an 'aerial' view of whether the end result makes sense to the reader of the accounts; a particular weakness perceived with US GAAP.

Although IAS and UK GAAP are still different in volume and approach from US GAAP, and companies are required to override the rules if necessary for the accounts to give a true and fair view[12], the insertion of the 'overarching true and fair requirement' in the Companies Act 2006 places the 'true and fair' principle at the heart of UK directors' reporting of their financial position and performance.

5.3.3 Is the IAS 'present fairly' equal to the Companies Act 'giving a true and fair view'?

Although the concept of 'true and fair' has been part of English law for many decades and is fundamental to the basis of preparation of the financial statements of UK companies, it is not defined in company law. However, it has been the subject of two important Opinions written by Lord Hoffmann and Dame Mary Arden in the 1980s and 1990s.

In a similar vein to the concern about an overly rigid application of detailed accounting rules not resulting in a true and fair view, some have questioned whether these opinions have remained relevant in light of the significant changes in the financial reporting environment, particularly, the introduction of IFRS[13] in 2005 and whether the requirement in IFRS to 'present fairly' is the equal of 'giving a true and fair view'.

To address this concern, the FRC published in May 2008 an opinion from Martin Moore QC (the '2008 Opinion'[14]) on whether the requirements of the Companies Act 2006 or EU legislation (including the application of IFRS to EU listed companies and the subsequent endorsement of international standards and interpretations) require any revisions to the earlier opinions. The 2008 Opinion endorses the analysis in the Opinions of Lord Hoffmann and Dame Mary Arden and confirmed the centrality of the true and fair requirement to the preparation of financial statements in the UK, whether they are prepared in accordance with international or UK accounting standards.

In particular, the 2008 Opinion notes that:

(i) The requirement in IFRS for financial statements to 'present fairly' is not different from the Companies Act requirement to give a true and fair view: it is a different articulation of the same concept.

---

[12] IAS 1(Revised 2007) 'Presentation of Financial Statements'.
[13] International Financial Reporting Standards; the term IFRS is used synonymously with IAS.
[14] Obtainable from the FRC's website at *www.frc.org.uk/about/trueandfair.cfm*.

(ii)   The requirement for financial statements to give a true and fair view (or a fair presentation) is paramount.

(iii)   Like UK GAAP, IFRS permits the departure from an accounting standard, if required, in order to preserve the true and fair view, but only under limited circumstances.

(iv)   Although compliance with accounting standards (either IFRS or UK GAAP) is highly likely to result in a true and fair view (or fair presentation), their application should not be a mechanical process as this outcome cannot be guaranteed.

(v)   The concept of 'true and fair' (or 'fair presentation') comes into play, for example:

- In the way a standard is applied,

- In consideration of whether, in extremely rare circumstances, a standard should be departed from,

- In choices where two or more relevant but incompatible standards could be applied,

- In determining the accounting where no relevant standard exists.

(vi)   The requirement contained in the EU Transparency Obligations Directive for half-yearly reports to give a true and fair view does not change the analysis of what is a true and fair view.

(vii)   The provisions of the Companies Act 2006 have served to underline and reinforce the centrality of the true and fair requirement to the preparation of financial statements. In the 2008 Opinion, Martin Moore QC notes that 'Compliance with accounting standards is not an end in itself, but the means to an end'.

5.3.4 Does the new overarching requirement correct the anomalies in the previous legislation?

Yes. This new overarching requirement fixes two anomalies in the Companies Act 1985, which were:

(i)   For UK GAAP reporters, there was an explicit requirement for directors to prepare accounts that give a true and fair view but no equivalent explicit 'true and fair requirement' for IAS reporters; and

(ii)   The auditor has to give an opinion on the truth and fairness of IAS accounts even though there is no explicit legal requirement for directors to approve only 'true and fair' accounts.

As mentioned earlier, irrespective of the accounting framework, directors now have a duty not to approve accounts that do not give a true and fair view and, in performing their duties, auditors must have regard to the directors' duty.

5.3.5 What does 'think small first' mean?

One of the objectives of the Companies Act 2006 is to 'think small first'; that is, to recognise that the vast majority of UK companies are small enterprises, often with limited accounting and legal expertise, and that, accordingly, the law should be structured and written to make it easy for smaller companies to interpret the law and comply with its provisions. The Companies Act 2006 is expressed, as far as practicable, with the requirements for small companies stated first, with additional requirements set out in further sections applying to larger companies.

Historically, the opposite approach to the requirements for annual reports and accounts had been taken, with the requirements for large companies stated first, with exemptions and modifications then set out for smaller companies. This means that the sections of the Companies Act 1985 applying to smaller companies are set out in a labyrinthine series of provisions and exemptions cross referenced to each other and difficult to analyse.

In addition to the restructuring of the main body of the Companies Act 1985, the regulations setting out the form and content of small company annual accounts and directors' reports are set out in separate regulations, 'The Small Companies and Groups (Accounts and Directors' Reports) Regulations 2008'. These regulations gather together in a single document the requirements of Schedules 5, 6, 7, 8, and 8A to the Companies Act 1985 applicable to small companies. Small companies will therefore only have to look in one place to determine the form and content requirements applying to them.

The form and content requirements for larger companies are dealt with in The Large and Medium-sized Companies and Groups (Accounts and Reports) Regulations 2008.

5.3.6 Are the definitions of small, medium-sized and large companies the same as before?

Not quite. The definitions are as the same as in the Companies Act 1985 except for the changes described below. Consequently, a company still cannot qualify as small if it is a public company or is an authorised insurance company, a banking company, an e-money issuer, a MiFID investment firm (see below) or a UCITS[15] management company, or carries on insurance market activity[16]. A company does not qualify as medium-sized if it is a public company, or is a company that has permission to carry on a regulated activity[17] or carries on insurance market activity[18].

---

[15] Undertaking for Collective Investment in Transferable Securities as defined in the Glossary forming part of the Handbook made by the FSA under the FSMA 2000; obtainable at *http://fsahandbook.info/FSA/html/handbook/Glossary*.
[16] Section 384, Companies Act 2006.
[17] Under Part 4 of the Financial Services and Markets Act 2000.
[18] Section 467, Companies Act 2006.

First, under both the Companies Acts 1985 and 2006, a company is excluded from the small companies regime or does not qualify as medium-sized if it is a member of an ineligible group[19]. Under the Companies Act 1985[20], a group was ineligible, *inter alia*, if any of its members was a public company or a body corporate having the power to issue its shares or debentures to the public. This rule is relaxed in the Companies Act 2006. It no longer focuses on a member of the group having the power to issue securities to the public but instead on whether a member has actually done so. Hence, the group is ineligible if there is within the group either a parent or a subsidiary undertaking that has any of its securities admitted to trading on a regulated market in an European Economic Area (EEA) state. However, the existence within a group of a UK public company, irrespective of whether it has issued securities to the public, still means that the group is ineligible. This relaxation arises from the transposition into UK legislation of the changes made by the EU Accounts Modernisation Directive[21].

Second, for the purpose of the 'basic size test', the 'balance sheet total' is now defined as *'the aggregate of the amounts shown as assets in the company's balance sheet'*[22]. Under the Companies Act 1985 this was the definition for those companies preparing IAS individual accounts but the definition for UK GAAP reporters referred to amounts shown under the formats prescribed by Schedule 4 to the Companies Act 1985. In practice, this amendment will have no impact on the classification of companies as small or otherwise; it is, in substance, a restatement of the existing position.

5.3.7 Are there any changes to the company size definitions for companies in the financial services sector?

Most companies that are subject to the EU Markets in Financial Instruments Directive[23] (MiFiD) cannot qualify as a small or medium-sized company under either the Companies Acts 1985 or 2006[24]. This restriction applies for financial years ending on or after 1 November 2007. The main consequences of not qualifying as a small company are to lose the relaxations in respect of the form and contents of Companies Act individual accounts, the option of not preparing group accounts and the relaxations in respect of the accounts filed with the Registrar of Companies.

More companies in the financial services sector are likely to qualify as a 'MiFID investment firm' than qualified before as an 'ISD investment firm' under the previous EU Investment in Securities Directive. This is because the

---

[19] Sections 384(2) and 467(2) set out the full criteria that can render a group as ineligible for small and medium-sized companies respectively.
[20] Section 247A(2), Companies Act 1985.
[21] EU Directive 2003/51/EC.
[22] Section 382(5), Companies Act 2006.
[23] EU Directive 2004/39/EC.
[24] The Markets in Financial Instrument Directive (Consequential Amendments) Regulations 2007 (SI 2007/2932).

scope of MiFID applies to a wider range of financial services and financial instruments and, for example, some specialist commodity dealers are now subject to the MiFID. There is a transitional provision exempting companies that were previously not ISD companies but are now MiFID companies from the accounting and auditing requirements for their transitional financial years that began before but ended on or after 1 November 2007[25].

Another consequence of not qualifying for the small companies regime is the loss of the audit exemption. However, the definition of a MiFID investment firm[26] has been framed to ensure that those firms benefiting from exemptions from MiFID are excluded and hence are able to benefit from the audit exemption. The definition also allows many independent financial advisers that have opted into the MiFID to continue to be exempt from audit[27].

5.3.8 Are 'basic size tests' the same as before?

Yes, but the size limits are increased for financial years commencing on or after 6 April 2008 in the Amendment regulations[28]. This brings the size limits in line with recent European Union legislation[29] that permits but does not require Member States to adopt the increased limits.

The new size limits are as follows:

	Small	Medium-sized
Annual turnover not exceeding	£6,500,000	£25,900,000
Balance sheet total not exceeding	£3,260,000	£12,900,000
Average number of employees not exceeding	50	250

As previously, a company may qualify as small or medium-sized for a financial year if it satisfies any two of the three conditions under the applicable heading in the table above. In practice, a company qualifies as small or medium-sized if it meets the size tests for two consecutive years or more or it fails the size tests for two consecutive years.

5.3.9 What about the thresholds for small and medium-sized groups?

The size limits for groups are also increased by the Amendment Regulations for financial years commencing on or after 6 April 2008. The new limits are set out in the table below. A 'group' means, in relation to a parent company or a subsidiary undertakings, the entity together with all of its parent, subsidiary and fellow subsidiary undertakings. A group may qualify as small or medium-sized for a financial year (and, therefore, for example be exempted from the

---

25 Regulation 8 of the Markets in Financial Instrument Directive (Consequential Amendments) Regulations 2007 (SI 2007/2932).
26 Section 474, Companies Act 2006.
27 Paragraph 7.7 of the Explanatory memorandum to SI 2007/2932.
28 Companies Act 2006 (Accounts and Reports) (Amendment) Regulations 2008.
29 EU Directive 2006/46/EC.

disclosure of related party transactions) if it satisfies *any two* of the three conditions under the applicable heading in the following table during that year:

	Small	Medium-sized
Aggregate net turnover not exceeding	£6,500,000	£25,900,000
Or		
Aggregate gross turnover not exceeding	£7,800,000	£31,100,000
Aggregate net balance sheet total not exceeding	£3,260,000	£12,900,000
Or		
Aggregate gross balance sheet total not exceeding	£3,900,000	£15,500,000
Average number of employees not exceeding	50	250

For groups, the figures for turnover, balance sheet total and average number of employees are arrived at by adding together the relevant figures for each group company. The net figures refer to the relevant amounts after making consolidation adjustments for set-offs and other matters. As an alternative the gross figures can be applied to the relevant amounts before making such adjustments[30]. A company may satisfy the qualifying criteria on the basis of gross or net figures and in any year it is permissible to mix the use of gross and net figures. Rather than having to eliminate group transactions, the gross size criteria should be checked first, and the net size criteria checked only if required.

5.3.10 Are there any changes to the requirements for small companies and groups to prepare accounts?

Small companies can continue to prepare either IAS individual accounts or full[31] or 'shorter form'[32] Companies Act individual accounts for their members. The form and contents of Companies Act individual accounts are re-enacted from the previous legislation including the option of recognising and measuring financial instruments in the accounts at fair value. This is provided that the relevant accounting standards are complied with and the disclosures required by those standards are given. In practice, this means that small companies may if they wish adopt FRS 26 (IAS 39) 'Financial instruments: Recognition and measurement', and FRS 29 (IFRS 7), 'Financial instruments: Disclosures.'

---

[30] Sections 383(5)(6), 466(5)(6), Companies Act 2006.
[31] Drawn up in accordance with Schedule 1 to the Large and Medium-sized Companies and Groups (Accounts and Reports) Regulations 2008 (SI 2008/410) (previously Schedule 4 to the Companies Act 1985).
[32] Drawn up in accordance with Schedule 1 to the Small Companies and Groups (Accounts and Directors' Report) Regulations 2008 (SI 2008/409) (previously Schedule 8 to the Companies Act 1985).

Irrespective of whether a small company prepares IAS or Companies Act individual accounts they must provide in the notes to the accounts the required disclosures about related undertakings and directors' remuneration[33].

Small companies are, as previously, not required to prepare group accounts. However, if they do so they may prepare IAS group accounts or Companies Act group accounts. The form and content of Companies Act group accounts are re-enacted from the previous legislation as they apply to small companies, with some simplifications to facilitate convergence with international accounting standards.

5.3.11   Are there any changes to the requirements for medium-sized companies and groups to prepare accounts?

Yes. Parent companies of medium-sized groups are required to prepare group accounts for their members for financial years commencing on or after 6 April 2008. Hence, for example, a parent company of a medium-sized group with a 31 May 2009 year end, will have to prepare group accounts for that financial year together with comparative group accounts for the year ended 31 May 2008. The only exemptions from preparing group accounts are where, subject to conditions, the company is an intermediate holding company within either a larger EEA group or a larger non-EEA group or where none of the company's subsidiaries need be included in the consolidation (for example, if the subsidiaries are in aggregate and individually immaterial)[34].

The Government's view is that the increases in the financial thresholds for determining small and medium-sized groups are such that it has become inappropriate for medium-sized groups to continue to have such an exemption, given that they are now quite large in absolute terms, having a turnover of in excess of £6.5 million. Many groups that would previously have been classed as 'medium-sized' are now classified as small and are not required to prepare group accounts. See also chapter 6, sections 6.4.10 and 6.4.12.

Under both the Companies Act 1985 and the Companies Act 2006, the availability of the exemption from the requirement to prepare group accounts is determined by reference to the combined size of the parent and its subsidiaries, not to the size of the group of which the parent is a member. Therefore, where the parent is itself a subsidiary in a large group, this will not be a barrier to obtaining the exemption. This is even though it would not be able to avail of other provisions applying to small groups because it is a member of an ineligible group.

---

[33] Schedules 2 and 3 to the Small Companies and Groups (Accounts and Directors' Report) Regulations 2008 (SI 2008/409) (previously Schedules 5 and 6 to the Companies Act 1985).

[34] Section 399(2), Companies Act 2006.

5.3.12 Are there any new disclosure requirements?

Further to the recent EU Corporate Reporting Directive[35] stemming from the 'Parmalat' accounting scandal, Member States are required to transpose its requirements into national law by 5 September 2008. All of the changes in this Directive impact on Part 15 of the Companies Act 2006 and are dealt with in various[36] regulations, which are in force for financial years beginning on or after 6 April 2008. Two changes impact on the disclosure of related party transactions and the disclosure of off-balance-sheet arrangements.

5.3.13 What are the new related party transactions disclosures?

The disclosure requirement in the regulations is a direct transposition from the EU Corporate Reporting Directive[35], which is stated as:

> "transactions which have been entered into with related parties by the company, including the amount of such transactions, the nature of the related party relationship and other information about the transactions necessary for an understanding of the financial position of the company, if such transactions are material and have not been concluded under normal market conditions. Information about individual transactions may be aggregated according to their nature except where separate information is necessary for an understanding of the effects of related party transactions on the financial position of the company."

'Related parties' are as defined in IAS 24, 'Related party disclosures'.

The regulations take up all the available exemptions from disclosure provided by the Directive:

(i) Small companies are totally exempt;

(ii) Medium-sized companies that are not public companies are totally exempt;

(iii) For medium-sized public companies the disclosures are limited to transactions entered into directly or indirectly between:

- the company and its major shareholders; and

- the company and the members of the administrative, management and supervisory bodies (that is, in effect, its directors and key management); and

---

[35] EU Directive 2006/46/EC.
[36] The Large and Medium-sized Companies and Groups (Accounts and Reports) Regulations 2008 (Related party transactions) and the Companies Act 2006 (Amendment) (Accounts and Reports) Regulations 2008 (Off-balance sheet arrangements).

(iv) Transactions entered into between two or more members of a group are exempt from disclosure, provided that any subsidiary undertakings, which are party to the transaction, are wholly owned by such a member.

5.3.14 Does a company preparing IAS accounts (an IFRS reporter) have more disclosures to make in relation to related party transactions?

No. Although the Directive sets out disclosure requirements that apply to both IFRS reporters and local GAAP reporters, the requirements are only included in the schedules to the regulations that apply to UK GAAP reporters (that is, Companies Act accounts).

This approach is taken on the grounds that EU-adopted IAS 24, 'Related Party disclosures,' already deals adequately with related party disclosure requirements for IFRS reporters, an approach that has the advantage of simplicity for such reporters.

Some uncertainty remains as IAS 24 has no requirement to differentiate related party transactions not concluded under normal market conditions. However, the issue was discussed by the EU's Accounting Regulatory Committee (ARC) at its meeting on 27 November 2007. The European Commission conveyed its view that disclosures made in accordance with EU-adopted IAS 24 complied with the Directive and therefore the lack of differentiation is not a problem[37].

5.3.15 Does a company preparing Companies Act accounts (a UK GAAP reporter) have more disclosures to make about related party transactions?

As indicated above, the new requirements are being implemented in full for large companies and ineligible small or medium-sized companies that prepare Companies Act accounts.

The regulations state[38]:

> 'Particulars may be given of transactions which the company has entered into with related parties, and must be given if such transactions are material and have not been concluded under normal market conditions (see regulation 4(2) for exemption for medium-sized companies).'

There is therefore (as in the Directive) only a requirement to disclose non-arm's length / abnormal market condition transactions. 'Normal market conditions' and thus abnormal ones are not defined in the regulations and separate interpretative guidance has not been provided with the regulations.

---

[37] Notes of the EU ARC meeting of 27 November 2007 are available at *http://ec.europa.eu/ internal_market/accounting/docs/arc/2007-11-02_summary_en.pdf*.

[38] Paragraph 72 of Schedule 1 to the Large and Medium-sized Companies and Groups (Accounts and Reports) Regulations 2008.

However, at the EU ARC meeting on 27 November 2007, the European Commission (EC) expressed its view that the use of EU-adopted IAS 24 on a national level for companies not within the scope of the IAS Regulation would be compliant with the requirements of the Directive.

In this context, the ASB issued an exposure draft[39] that proposes to withdraw FRS 8, 'Related party disclosures,' and to issue a revised Financial Reporting Standard based on IAS 24. This will also include guidance on materiality based on that set out in IAS 1, 'Presentation of financial statements'. There will be one significant difference from IAS 24, in that the new UK standard will provide disclosure exemptions for wholly owned subsidiaries in accordance with the regulations implementing the Directive.

Consequently, in line with the EC's view, compliance with the new UK accounting standard on related party disclosures and the regulations in accounts for financial years beginning on or after 6 April 2008 should achieve compliance, with the requirements of the Directive.

5.3.16 What concerns are there about transactions with directors and key management?

A company's directors are related parties of the company and transactions between the company and its directors must be disclosed. The question then arises: does a company have to disclose dividends paid to directors?

A dividend paid on shares held by a director (or his close family or an entity controlled by him) is a related party transaction. Related party transactions should be disclosed unless exemption is given by the relevant UK or international accounting standard as appropriate.

Both UK and international accounting standards have an exemption from disclosure for providers of finance, but this exemption only applies to transactions undertaken *that are essentially normal dealings with such entities in the course of their business*. Directors are more than mere providers of finance. In the past, although the disclosure has been a requirement for some time, most companies have not disclosed dividends paid to directors separately in the accounts because both the dividend per share and the directors' interests in shares are disclosed within the report and accounts; it was a simple matter for the user of the report and accounts to determine how much dividend was paid to each director, should they wish to do so.

That position has now changed for unlisted companies because directors' interests are no longer required to be disclosed within the directors' report. Therefore, at least for unlisted companies, dividends paid to directors and those connected to them should be disclosed individually.

---

[39] ASB FRED 41, 'Related party disclosures' (IAS 24).

The requirements of the accounting standards apply not just to the company's directors (and to those connected them) but also to its key managers (and to those connected to them). In addition, under both the accounting standards and the Accounts Regulations[40], directors and other key managers of any of the company's parent companies are also related parties.

Interests in shares (including derivatives or other financial instruments related to those shares[41]) of listed companies held by key managers (who are not directors) are not disclosable under the FSA LR. Consequently, listed companies should therefore disclose any dividends (or other returns) paid to such persons in the notes to the accounts.

5.3.17 Are there any changes to the legality of, and disclosures about, directors' loans and other transactions?

Yes. The Government has taken the opportunity to simplify the complex rules regarding the legality of companies making loans, or other forms of credit, available to their directors or for subsidiaries to directors of their holding companies. The changes include abolishing the prohibition on loans, quasi-loans and other credit arrangements and the criminal penalty for breach of the rules. Loans and other credit transactions with directors are discussed further in chapter 2, section 2.4.

The new rules on legality and disclosure are all contained within the body of the new Act and thus apply to all companies irrespective of whether their accounts are prepared using UK GAAP or IFRS. The rules on legality are in force from 1 October 2007; however, the changes to the disclosure rules are, in the main, only in effect for accounts for financial years beginning on or after 6 April 2008. There are some transitional provisions that introduced the new definition of connected persons for purposes of disclosures in accounts drawn up in compliance with the provisions of the Companies Act 1985 from 1 November 2007.

In the case of a private company, which is not part of a group including a public company, the law requires shareholder approval for loans and related guarantees or security made by a company for a director of either the company or its holding company[42].

In the case of a public company, or a private company that is a member of a group containing a public company, the law requires shareholder approval for loans, quasi-loans, credit transactions and related guarantees or security made by the company for a director of either the company or its holding company. In

---

[40] SI 2008/410 The Large and Medium-sized Companies and Groups (Accounts and Reports) Regulations 2008, Schedule 1, paragraph 72.
[41] FSA LR9.8.6 and FSA DTR3.1.2.
[42] Section 197, Companies Act 2006.

addition, approval is also required for the provision of such loans or credit to persons connected to the director or holding company director[43].

Shareholder approval is not required for[44]:

(i) amounts not in excess of £50,000 for each director and any connected person advanced to meet expenditure on company business. The £50,000 is a maximum limit to cover the aggregate of all types of loans and credit;

(ii) money lent to fund a director's defence costs for legal proceedings in connection with any alleged negligence, default, breach of duty or breach of trust, or regulatory action or investigation in connection with such alleged offences;

(iii) amounts not exceeding £10,000 in total for small loans and quasi-loans provided to a director and any connected person;

(iv) amounts up to £15,000 in total for small credit transactions made for a director or any connected person;

(v) credit transactions made in the ordinary course of the company's business;

(vi) intra-group transactions; and

(vii) any loan or quasi-loan made by a moneylending company in the ordinary course of the company's business and on terms no more favourable than to an unconnected person of the same financial standing. Home loans provided by a moneylending company are not subject to the latter restriction if the company makes such loans ordinarily available to its employees. There is no specified monetary limit to any loans or quasi-loans made by a moneylending company.

The Companies Act 2006 specifically provides for retrospective affirmation by the shareholders of any transaction or arrangement entered into by the company in contravention of the new rules[45].

5.3.18 What is the main change to the disclosure of directors' loans and other transactions, etc.?

The main change is the removal of the requirement to disclose transactions between the company and persons connected with the director or between the company and its officers[46]. However, such transactions are mostly caught by the new legal requirement to disclose transactions with related parties, if the transactions are material or by the requirements of the relevant accounting standards. 'Material' is not defined in law but under accounting standards and

---

[43] Sections 197, 198, 200 and 201, Companies Act 2006.
[44] Sections 204 to 209, Companies Act 2006.
[45] Section 214, Companies Act 2006.
[46] Section 413, Companies Act 2006.

principles in UK GAAP and IFRS. It is based on financial amount and the nature of the transaction. In practice all but the most trivial transactions are likely to require disclosure[47].

In the accounts for financial years beginning on or after 6 April 2008, all loans (advances), credits, guarantees, etc. should be disclosed even if they are immaterial to both the company and the director in question.

5.3.19 What is the effect of the transitional arrangements while accounts are still prepared in accordance with the provisions of the Companies Act 1985?

Until accounts for financial years beginning on or after 6 April 2008 are prepared (for a calendar year company that will be its December 2009 accounts), companies must continue to make disclosures in respect of 'connected persons'.

From 1 November 2007, the definition of 'connected persons' for use in respect of the disclosure requirements under the Companies Act 1985 changed to that contained in the Companies Act 2006[48]. The main changes to the definition are the inclusion of a director's parent, life partner and adult children as related parties; this is not necessarily the case under accounting standards. Belatedly, it was recognised by BERR that this imposed a significant amount of extra work on, in particular money-lending, companies to capture the information to be able to make the disclosures for just two years – their December 2007 and 2008 accounts. A transitional amendment has now been made to remove the connected persons' disclosure requirement for accounts for financial years that end on or after 6 April 2008[49].

5.3.20 Do the new disclosures about off-balance-sheet arrangements apply to both IFRS and UK GAAP reporters?

The second 'Parmalat' induced change concerns disclosures of off-balance-sheet arrangements. The Amendment[50] regulations introduce the new disclosure requirement into the body of the Companies Act 2006[51] such that it applies to both IAS accounts and Companies Act accounts for financial years beginning on or after 6 April 2008.

---

[47] For further discussion on materiality and the relevance to disclosures under statutory provisions see ICAEW Technical Release Tech 3/08 Guidance on Materiality in Financial Reporting by UK Entities; obtainable from the ICAEW's website *www.icaew.com/index.cfm?route=154669*.

[48] Sections 252 to 255, Companies Act 2006.

[49] SI 2008/948 The Companies Act 2006 (Consequential Amendments etc.) Order 2008, Schedule 1, paragraph 76.

[50] Companies Act 2006 (Amendment) (Accounts and Reports) Regulations 2008.

[51] Section 410A, Companies Act 2006.

5.3.21   Are there any exemptions for small and medium-sized companies?

The regulations take up the Member State options in the EU Corporate Reporting Directive to exempt small companies entirely from the requirement and medium-sized companies may limit the disclosure to information about the nature and business purpose of such arrangements.

5.3.22   Is there any guidance on how to comply with the new off-balance-sheet disclosures?

The premise underlying the new disclosure requirement is that certain arrangements a company undertakes may have a material impact on the company but may not be included in the company's balance sheet. Consequently, the requirement is phrased such that if a company

> 'is or has been party to arrangements that are not reflected in its balance sheet, and ... the risks or benefits ... are material [there must be given in the notes to the accounts] ... (a) the nature and business purpose of the arrangements and (b) the financial impact of the arrangements on the company ... to the extent necessary for enabling the financial position of the company to be assessed'[52].

When the company belongs to a group, the financial position of the group as a whole may also be affected. Consequently, aggregated disclosures have to be made in the notes to the group accounts, again irrespective of whether those accounts are prepared using IFRS or UK GAAP.

BERR guidance on the application of the requirement draws attention to Recital (9) to the Directive which states:

> "Such off-balance-sheet arrangements could be any transactions or agreements which companies may have with entities, even unincorporated ones, that are not included in the balance sheet. Such off-balance-sheet arrangements may be associated with the creation or use of one or more Special Purpose Entities (SPEs) and offshore activities designed to address, *inter alia*, economic, legal, tax or accounting objectives. Examples of such off-balance-sheet arrangements include risk and benefit-sharing arrangements or obligations arising from a contract such as debt factoring, combined sale and repurchase agreements, consignment stock arrangements, take or pay arrangements, securitisation arranged through separate companies and unincorporated entities, pledged assets, operating leasing arrangements, outsourcing and the like. Appropriate disclosure of the material risks and benefits of such arrangements that are not included

---

[52]   Section 410A(1) to (3), Companies Act 2006.

in the balance sheet should be set out in the notes to the accounts or the consolidated accounts."

However, this may be insufficient. The term 'arrangements' is undefined. Although Recital (9) to the Directive gives some examples of 'arrangements', the first sentence is very broad and could capture all executory contracts. The examples are not an exclusive list. Consequently, there is a danger that some companies may innocently provide unstructured disclosures covering large volumes of extraneous details of arrangements (for example, purchase orders), that are really intended to be outside the scope (if that were made clear) of the legislation. However, it also aids those that may have the intention of obfuscating important information; that is, the reader will not be able to see the wood for the trees. Such a company would nevertheless appear to be compliant.

BERR has said that in providing the guidance it will work with the accounting standard setters to agree what action needs to be taken in respect of UK accounting standards. The issue has been raised with the Urgent Issues Task Force (UITF) but the UITF, although recognising concern regarding the clarity of the disclosure requirement, has stated that it could not issue an Abstract in absence of a definition of 'arrangement'. The UITF stated:

(i)   when a company provides disclosures, it should consider the types of transactions envisaged by the EC (as quoted above) and the aim of the legislation;

(ii)   the disclosure requirement applies only where, at the balance sheet date, the risks or benefits arising from arrangements are material;

(iii)   disclosure need only be given to the extent necessary for enabling the financial position of the company to be assessed; and

(iv)   some accounting standards already require some disclosures that address items not necessarily included in the balance sheet but companies will need to consider whether arrangements outside the scope of those standards will require disclosure.

5.3.23   What should directors do to comply with the new off-balance-sheet disclosures?

It is considered that, in the main, UK GAAP and IFRSs go well beyond the minimum requirements of the law in ensuring that assets and liabilities are not inappropriately excluded from the balance sheet. As noted by the UITF, they also impose disclosure requirements on some types of arrangements, which are not included in the balance sheet, such as operating leases and contingent liabilities. Therefore, in most cases, compliance with accounting standards should be sufficient to ensure compliance with the law. In particular, under UK GAAP, FRS 5 *Reporting the substance of transactions*, requires that:

'disclosure of a transaction in the financial statements, whether or not it has resulted in assets or liabilities being recognised, should be sufficient to enable the user of the financial statements to understand its commercial effect'[53].

As the UITF has indicated, accounting standards do not necessarily provide for all circumstances and, as such, directors should consider making disclosures where, for example, they have had discussions with their auditors about off-balance sheet implications of transactions that their companies undertake or whether entities should be consolidated. In this respect, compliance with the requirements in IAS 1, 'Presentation of financial statements,' to disclose critical accounting estimates and judgments[54] should assist in formulating an appropriate disclosure that meets the legal requirement.

Furthermore, the experience from the 'credit crunch' of 2007 and 2008 and the ensuing problems with liquidity in the markets has highlighted concerns about latent risks and exposures that had not previously been considered an issue. Concerns have focused on, amongst others, unconsolidated Special Purpose Entities, liquidity facilities, loan commitments, guarantees and derivatives. In meeting the new disclosure requirement, directors may need to consider a broader concept of financial impact of its off-balance-sheet arrangements, in terms of liquidity, capital resources, credit risk, etc.

For those companies that are not required to use the financial instruments accounting standards[55], the off-balance-sheet arrangements disclosure overlaps with the existing disclosure requirement about derivatives that a company has not included at fair value on its balance sheet[56]. The requirement is that the extent and nature of the derivatives and their fair value are disclosed. However, as noted above, financial impact is not necessarily just the fair value of the derivatives at the balance sheet date and further information as to the wider financial impact may be needed.

5.3.24 Are there any changes to the 'Fair value accounting' rules in law for Companies Act accounts?

Yes. The Companies Act 2006 permits companies preparing accounts using UK GAAP to use fair value accounting in accordance with the financial instruments accounting standards[56] in both their individual and consolidated accounts.

---

[53] FRS 5, paragraph 30.
[54] IAS 1 (revised 2007), paragraphs 122 and 125.
[55] FRS 26 (IAS 39), 'Financial instruments: Recognition and measurement,' or IAS 39, 'Financial Instruments: Recognition and Measurement'.
[56] Paragraph 56 of Schedule 1 to the Large and Medium-sized Companies and Groups (Accounts and Reports) Regulations 2008 (SI 2008/410).

However, the Amendment regulations[57] update the provisions to reflect the changes that have been made to the financial instruments accounting standards since they were first adopted under the EU Fair Value Directive[58]. These amendments remove the anomalies between the law and the accounting standards. For example, there was a tension between what the law forbade and what the financial instruments accounting standards permit to be fair valued. In particular, the law did not allow the fair valuing of liabilities unless they are derivatives or part of a trading portfolio. The Accounts Regulations[59] now allow fair valuing of assets and liabilities that would be eligible for fair valuing under the financial instruments accounting standards.

This removes the necessity in Companies Act accounts for directors to use the true and fair override over the law to be able to fair value any financial assets and financial liabilities that can be fair valued under FRS 26.

5.3.25 Are there any changes to the concept of 'collective board responsibility'?

The EU Corporate Reporting Directive[60] sets out a requirement for Member States to ensure that board members are collectively responsible, at least towards the company, for drawing up and publishing annual and consolidated accounts and reports and, where produced separately, the corporate governance statement. However, whilst Member States are to refrain from opting for a system of responsibility limited to individual board members this does not preclude the courts or other enforcement bodies from imposing penalties on individual board members.

Under UK law, the board is already collectively responsible for the annual report and accounts and it has, therefore, not been necessary for the Government to create additional legislation in this area.

5.3.26 Are there any changes to the disclosures about employee costs and numbers?

The disclosure requirements[61] about employee costs and numbers are unchanged from the previous legislation, except that individual companies are exempt from making such disclosures if they do not publish the company's individual profit and loss account when publishing their group accounts for the same financial year[62]. This corrects an anomaly in the Companies Act 1985.

---

[57] SI 2008/393.
[58] EU Directive 2001/65/EC.
[59] SIs 2008/409 and 2008/410.
[60] EU Directive 2006/46/EC.
[61] Section 411, Companies Act 2006.
[62] Section 408, Companies Act 2006.

5.3.27   Have any other changes been made to the form and content of Companies Act group accounts?

A number of technical amendments have been made to the provisions on Companies Act group accounts:

(i)   The definitions of 'identifiable assets', 'acquisition costs' and 'adjusted capital and reserves' for the purposes of acquisition accounting have not been restated in the Companies Act 2006.

(ii)   The requirement to explain any significant adjustments in assets or liabilities (and any resulting adjustment to the consolidated reserves) when using the merger method of accounting has not been restated.

(iii)   The requirements on how minority interests are reflected in the balance sheet and profit and loss account formats have been simplified to allow greater flexibility in their presentation. These are in paragraph 17 of Schedule 6 to the Small Companies Accounts regulations (for those small companies that choose to prepare group accounts) and in paragraphs 17, 25 and 36 of Schedule 6 to the Large and Medium-sized Companies regulations.

5.4   Directors' report

5.4.1 What are the changes to the content of the directors' report?

Other than for quoted companies the requirements of the Companies Act 1985 have been restated in the Companies Act 2006 without substantive amendment. These include the disclosures required for companies with listed voting shares that were added by The Takeovers Directive (Interim Implementation) Regulations 2006 (SI 2006/1183) that came into force for financial years commencing on or after 20 May 2006. These requirements are repeated in section 992 of the Companies Act 2006 and are also found in Schedule 7 to The Large and Medium-sized Companies Accounts regulations. For further detail, see Appendix 2, section A2.5.

For quoted companies the major addition is a requirement for an enhanced business review. This requirement applies for directors' reports for financial years beginning on or after 1 October 2007. The other provisions of the Companies Act 2006 for all companies relating to the form and content of the directors' report apply to those reports for financial years beginning on or after 6 April 2008. (See section 5.1.6).

The exemptions contained in the Companies Act 1985, which enable small and medium-sized companies to reduce the information in the directors' report even though they are members of ineligible groups was inadvertently omitted from the Companies Act 2006. However, the exemptions have been reinstated by the Amendment regulations with effect for financial years beginning on or after 6 April 2008. Consequently, the original omission has no practical effect.

As the requirement for a business review is a recent addition to the contents of the directors' report, the following sections of this chapter look at the challenges and experience companies have faced in providing such reviews.

5.4.1.1 What is the purpose of a business review?

The directors are required to include in their report a review of the business of the company and its subsidiaries. Unless the company is subject to the small companies' regime, the directors' report must contain a business review. The purpose of the business review is to:

> 'inform the members of the company and help them assess how the directors have performed their duty to promote the success of the company'.

In particular the review should have regard to:

(i) the likely consequences of any decision in the long term;

(ii) the interests of the company's employees;

(iii) the need to foster the company's business relationships with suppliers, customers and others;

(iv) the impact of the company's operations on the community and the environment;

(v) the desirability for the company maintaining a reputation for high standards of business conduct; and

(vi) the need to act fairly as between the company's members.

5.4.2 Who is responsible for preparing the business review?

Each director individually has responsibility for preparing the business review. The directors have a responsibility to prepare the report even if they were not directors during the period covered by the report. For this purpose every director of the company at the time the accounts are approved is considered to have approved the report, unless the director took all reasonable steps to prevent their approval.

5.4.3 What are the disclosure requirements?

The original requirements for a business review arise from the EU Accounts Modernisation Directive[63] and were introduced into company law in 2005.

---

[63] EU Directive 2003/51/EC.

These requirements have been incorporated into the Companies Act 2006[64] and, from 1 October 2007, further reporting requirements apply for quoted companies.

In summary, management must provide a business review comprising a fair review of the company's business and a description of the principal risks and uncertainties facing the company.

The review requires a balanced and comprehensive analysis of:

(i)   the development and performance of the company's business during the financial year; and

(ii)   the position of the company's business at the end of that year, consistent with the size and complexity of the business.

The review also requires the following, to the extent necessary for an understanding of the development, performance and position of the company:

(i)   an analysis using financial key performance indicators (KPIs); and

(ii)   where appropriate, an analysis using other KPIs, including information relating to environmental matters and employee matters.

The review must also contain, where appropriate, references to, and additional explanation of, amounts included in the financial statements.

Where an entity is a parent company and prepares consolidated financial statements, the business review should be a consolidated review covering the company and its subsidiary undertakings included in the consolidation. There is no requirement for the parent company to prepare a separate review for the company alone.

5.4.4   Are there any exemptions for small or medium-sized companies?

A company that qualifies as small in relation to a financial year, or would do so other than for being a member of an ineligible group, is entitled to an exemption from preparing a business review[65].

Where a company qualifies as a medium-sized company in relation to a financial year, or would do so other than for being a member of an ineligible group, the directors have to prepare a business review but need not provide an analysis of the company's performance by reference to non-financial KPIs[66].

---

[64]   Section 417, Companies Act 2006.
[65]   Section 415A, Companies Act 2006.
[66]   Sections 417(7) and 467(4), Companies Act 2006.

5.4.5 What are the additional requirements for quoted companies?

For quoted companies the content requirements for the business review under the Companies Act 2006 are very similar to those that were required, but withdrawn, for the statutory Operating and Financial Review (OFR) in 2005. The effective reinstatement of the statutory OFR arose as a result of intensive lobbying by various interest groups during the passage of the Companies Bill through Parliament.

Quoted companies can still voluntarily publish an OFR. Such entities should look to the recommendations of the Accounting Standards Board's (ASB) OFR report statement[67] as the most appropriate guidance. Indeed, even if the directors only comply with the minimum legal requirements, use of the guidance in the ASB's OFR statement is helpful. To this effect, the ASB has published a schedule mapping the minimum disclosure requirements to the relevant guidance in the OFR statement[68].

For years beginning on or after 1 October 2007, a quoted company's business review must, to the extent necessary for an understanding of the development, performance or position of the company's business, include:

(i)   The main trends and factors likely to affect the future development, performance and position of the company's business.

(ii)   Information about:

- environmental matters (including the impact of the company's business on the environment);

- the company's employees; and

- social and community issues, including information about any policies of the company in relation to those matters and the effectiveness of those policies.

(iii)   Information about persons with whom the company has contractual or other arrangements which are essential to the business of the company.

If the review does not contain all the information noted above, it must state which elements have been omitted.

5.4.6 Are there any 'seriously prejudicial' exemptions?

Two exemptions have been provided under the Companies Act 2006 such that disclosure will not be required if:

---

[67] ASB Reporting Statement: Operating and Financial Review 2006.
[68] ASB PN 318 Additional narrative reporting guidance for UK Companies, obtainable at *www.frc.org.uk/asb/press/pub1480.html*.

(i)   "Information about impending developments or matters in the course of negotiation if the disclosure would, in the opinion of the directors, be seriously prejudicial to the interests of the company"; and

(ii)   "Information about a person if the disclosure would, in the opinion of the directors, be seriously prejudicial to that person and contrary to the public interest."

The latter exemption was introduced following a lobbying campaign that argued that the disclosure of a company's essential contractual or other arrangements with customers, suppliers and others might be harmful to the company. However, the exemption only applies where the disclosure would be harmful to the other persons concerned and perceived harm to the company is not a consideration. For further discussion see section 5.4.25 below.

5.4.7   Is there a particular format of the business review?

The Companies Act 2006 requires a company to publish its business review within the directors' report. There would be considerable duplication if companies that prepare a voluntary OFR also gave this information in their directors' report.

To avoid such duplication, BERR has confirmed that if a company publishes a voluntary OFR, it is acceptable to cross-refer to it in the business review, provided that the following conditions are met:

(i)   the directors' report and the OFR are published together in such a way that the users can easily refer to both documents; and

(ii)   the cross-reference must clearly indicate which specific sections of the voluntary OFR are relevant, whether by page numbers, paragraph number or headings.

5.4.8   How does the directors' liability 'safe harbour' apply?

A further amendment provided by the Companies Act 2006 is the provision for directors of a 'safe harbour' from civil liability for statements or omissions in the directors' report and the directors' remuneration report (including any summary financial statements derived from those reports).

'Safe harbour' also covers the separate voluntary OFRs or narrative reporting outside the directors' report provided that cross-referencing from the directors' report to the narrative reporting is explicitly provided. Perhaps prompted by this protection, some companies have called the whole narrative section of the annual report a 'Directors' Report'.

Under the Companies Act 2006, directors are liable to the company, not to third parties. They are liable for a loss suffered by the company if statements are untrue or misleading or there is an omission of anything required to be in the reports. They are liable if they knew a statement was made in bad faith or recklessly or an omission was made for deliberate and dishonest concealment of material facts. However, these liability provisions do not affect any liability for a civil penalty or for a criminal offence (section 463).

With an ever increasing litigious environment, directors may need to bolster their internal resources or ensure that they have access to legal advisers to review all aspects of narrative reporting. For further discussion see chapter 6, section 6.6.11.

5.4.9 How are the requirements applied to different sizes of company?

The business review applies to all companies, apart from those that qualify as small, or would do so but for being part of an ineligible group[69]. The ASB's review of narrative reporting by quoted companies[70] provides further guidance on how to interpret various business review requirements. However, guidance to assist directors in preparing a business review is limited for private entities.

The distinctions between companies of various sizes and status can be summarised as follows:

(i)   For owner-managed companies, members already have a good under-
       standing of the development, performance and position of the entity. We
       believe that the minimum information to comply with the legislation is all
       that need be given to present a clear picture to members.

(ii)   The position for wholly owned subsidiaries of a UK parent company is
       similar to that for owner-managed companies – assuming that the UK
       parent company is preparing a business review or voluntary OFR relating
       to its group financial statements. In addition, management and reporting
       of risk and key performance indicators for wholly owed subsidiaries is
       often undertaken at the group level. In such circumstances, it is
       appropriate to refer to further information available in the group annual
       report. The cross-reference should be to a specific paragraph, heading, or
       page in the group annual report.

(iii) For public interest entities (other than quoted companies) and private
       companies, where ownership is distinct from those who manage the entity
       on members' behalf, the amount of information disclosed should reflect
       the explicit requirements implied by the BERR in its pronouncements
       and guidance. The minimum disclosures described for owner-managed
       entities should be supplemented by additional contextual information
       around risk and key performance indicators, as well as a description of
       the entity's strategy and business environment.

---

[69] Section 415A, Companies Act 2006.
[70] ASB: A Review of Narrative Reporting by UK Listed Companies in 2006 (January 2007); obtainable from the FRC's website *www.frc.org.uk/asb/press/pub1228.html.*

(iv) Fuller disclosure is necessary for quoted companies, to assist members in understanding the development, performance and position of the entity. The most appropriate guidance is in the recommendations of the ASB's reporting statement, 'Operating and financial review'.

Given the broad nature of the categories set out above, and particularly public interest entities with dispersed ownership, there needs to be a degree of flexibility in the approach chosen by companies depending on their circumstances[71].

5.4.10 How should the disclosure of principal risks and KPIs (key performance indicators) be made for wholly owned subsidiaries?

One area where specific guidance has been found to be the most pragmatic is with regard to the disclosure of principal risks and KPIs for wholly-owned subsidiaries of a UK parent company, where it is managed on a group basis rather than a statutory basis.

The following is some suggested wording to achieve compliance with the requirements.

Principal risks and uncertainties

From the perspective of the company, the principal risks and uncertainties are integral to the principal risks of the group and are not managed separately. Accordingly, the principal risks and uncertainties of the R Group Limited, which include those of the company, are discussed on page x of the group's annual report which does not form part of this report.

Key performance indicators (KPIs)

The directors of R Group Limited manage the group's operations on a divisional basis. For this reason, the company's directors believe that analysis using key performance indicators for the company is not necessary or appropriate for an understanding of the development, performance or position of the business of R Limited. The development, performance and position of the retail division of R Group Limited, which includes the company, is discussed on page y of the group's annual report which does not form part of this report.

5.4.11 What type of information should be included in a business review?

The table below provides a guide to the type of information that should be included in a business review for private entities with dispersed ownership and public interest entities (other than quoted companies).

---

[71] Illustrative examples may be obtained at *www.corporatereporting.com/practical-guides.html.*

Heading	Suggested type of content
Principal activities	■ Nature of the business, extent of operations. ■ Results in terms of revenues and profits. ■ Net debt position and net cash inflow.
Business environment	■ Description of the market and competitive environment – market factors and dynamics that can affect the business environment, for example, competitors, market outlook. ■ Regulatory environment – legal, agency or other regulatory factors that impose requirements on the conduct of business activities; for example, deregulation, privatisation. ■ Macro environment – factors that could have a material impact on corporate performance; for example, interest rates, demographics, economic outlook.
Strategy	■ Overriding objectives of the group. ■ Group's strategy for achieving these objectives and an explanation of each strategy, as well as how successful implementation of the strategy is measured.
Research and development (R&D)	■ Actions taken in the area of R&D and how these link into the group's strategy.
Future outlook	■ Expected development of the business environment and any planned actions to address these developments.
Principal risks and uncertainties	■ The principal risks and uncertainties that have the focus of the directors' attention – not simply a list of all risk factors that face the group – as well as the approach taken by management to these risks.

Heading	Suggested type of content
Key performance indicators	■ The measures used to assess progress against objectives and strategies – including the quantification of these measures, trend data, definition, method of calculation and any relevant narrative.

5.4.12   What are the challenging areas: principal risks?

As noted previously, the disclosure of principal risks is an explicit requirement of the business review. The ASB found, when assessing narrative reporting in 2006[72], that this was an area companies struggled with as a number of companies simply provided a long list of all potential risks. As the ASB noted:

> "Companies need to assess carefully what are their principal risks and uncertainties, and report on those, together with the approach to managing and mitigating those risks, rather than simply provide a list of all their risks and uncertainties. The number of risks and uncertainties reported in our sample ranged from 4 to 33. We question whether a company can really have 33 principal risks and uncertainties."

Therefore, it is important that companies distinguish principal risks and uncertainties rather than listing all possible risks without highlighting which are the most important in assessing the potential success of the company's strategy.

5.4.13   What are the challenging areas: key performance indicators?

Another area noted for improvement by the ASB relates to KPIs:

> "Many companies are providing a good deal of information on measures and indicators, but improvement could be made in identifying their KPIs, both financial and non-financial. ... Companies can review the implementation guidance accompanying the Reporting Statement, which sets out 23 illustrative KPIs which may assist companies in meeting this recommendation. The Best Practice companies in our sample provided a description of their KPIs and how they link to overall strategy and, in addition, provided details of the results of the KPIs with comparative figures and target figures."[73]

---

[72]   ASB: A Review of Narrative Reporting by UK Listed Companies in 2006 (January 2007); obtainable from the FRC's website *www.frc.org.uk/asb/press/pub1228.html*.

[73]   ASB: A Review of Narrative Reporting by UK Listed Companies in 2006 (January 2007); obtainable from the FRC's website *www.frc.org.uk/asb/press/pub1228.html*.

Key performance indicators are those the directors judge are effective in measuring the entity's development, performance or position. They are quantified measurements that reflect the entity's critical success factors and disclose progress towards achieving a particular objective or objectives.

5.4.13.1   What is key?

The performance indicators that are key to a particular company are those that the directors use to manage the business. Many boards of directors receive financial performance indicators, even though they may be communicating strategies such as maximising customer experience, or attracting and retaining the best and brightest people.

The challenge is whether the KPIs currently presented to the board are those that allow them to assess progress against stated strategies, and when reported externally, allow readers to make a similar assessment. If not, is this because the information is simply not available or because it is not yet escalated to the board but may instead be assessed by management of individual business units?

In addition, the KPIs will to a degree be conditioned by the industry in which a company operates. Comparability will be enhanced if the KPIs are accepted and widely used, either within an industry sector or more generally. However, directors should not feel compelled to create KPIs to match those reported by their peers. The overriding need is for the KPIs to be relevant to that particular company. Directors should explain their choice in the context of the chosen strategies and objectives and provide sufficient detail on measurement methods to allow readers to make comparisons to other companies' choices where they want to.

5.4.13.2   How many KPIs?

Where multiple performance measures are disclosed, directors should explain which are key to managing the business. The choice of which ones are key is unique to each company and its strategy; it is impossible to specify how many KPIs a company should have. However, between four and ten measures are likely to be key for most types of company.

5.4.13.3   Segmental or group KPIs?

Directors should consider how KPIs are collated and reported internally; whether they make sense when aggregated and reported at a group level, or would be more usefully reported at business segment level. In some instances it may be more appropriate to report KPIs for each business segment separately if the process of aggregation renders the output meaningless. For example, it is more informative to report a retail business segment separately rather than combining it with a personal financial services segment.

5.4.13.4   How flexible is the choice of KPIs?

Directors should reflect on whether the KPIs chosen continue to be relevant. Strategies and objectives develop over time, making it inappropriate to continue reporting on the same KPIs as in previous periods. Equally, more information may become available to management, facilitating reporting of new KPIs that provide a deeper understanding of the business, or changing how an existing KPI is calculated.

5.4.13.5   Does reliability matter?

Directors may sometimes be concerned about the reliability of some of the information reported on KPIs, particularly as they are encouraged to move beyond the more traditional financial KPIs that are usually the output of established system and control processes and routine audit. There is no specific narrative reporting requirement for KPIs to be reliable, but the nature of the information should be clear to the users of narrative reports.

In order to address this issue and provide readers with useful information, it is more important that the limitations of the data and any assumptions made in providing it are clearly explained. Readers can then judge the reliability for themselves and make any necessary adjustments in their own analysis. Where data has been specifically assured by independent third parties, identifying this may also assist the reader.

5.4.14   What are the challenging areas: resources available to an entity?

The ASB has interpreted the requirement to 'include references to, and additional explanations of, amounts included in the company's annual accounts' as a requirement to describe the resources available to the business. Again, this is an area the ASB believes could be improved:

> "Companies need to think carefully about the description of the resources available to the entity, in particular on those intangible items not reflected in the balance sheet. ... Companies can refer to paragraph 51 of the Reporting Statement, which sets out examples of resources not included in the balance sheet that may be disclosed. A number of companies have provided information judged as Best Practice, for example, one company in the sample providing details of contractual agreements, reputation, employees and trade marks as examples of resources[74]."

Resources to be disclosed will depend on the nature of the business and the industry in the company operates in.

---

[74]   ASB: A Review of Narrative Reporting by UK Listed Companies in 2006 (January 2007); obtainable from the FRC's website *www.frc.org.uk/asb/press/pub1228.html.*

5.4.15 What are the challenging areas: future trends and factors?

One of the new additional reporting requirements for quoted companies is to provide forward-looking information. With regard to this aspect, the ASB noted:

> "The greatest area of difficulty for companies when producing their narrative reports is the disclosure of forward-looking information. ... To help think about how they can improve their reporting in this area, companies should review paragraphs 8-12 and 48-49 of the Reporting Statement, which outline the principle that the OFR should have a forward looking orientation, and sets out potential areas which may affect the future development and performance of the business. A number of companies have been assessed as providing good disclosures in this area with, for example, one company in the sample providing details of forecast demand and planned capital investment over the next ten years[75]."

5.4.15.1 Does this mean having to provide potentially competitively sensitive information?

For any company, there will be certain information which – were it to be disclosed – would undermine its market position. The business review legislation recognises this and there is, accordingly, no requirement to disclose information about impending developments that would 'in the opinion of the Directors, be seriously prejudicial to the interests of the company'.

However, this should not be used as a convenient smokescreen for avoiding full and frank disclosure. The test here is likely to be high-level, in line with the FSA LR where information can only be withheld if its disclosure would be 'seriously detrimental' (and where the omission of that information would be unlikely to mislead investors).

Directors need to approach the disclosure of forward-looking information with the right mindset. Instead of adopting a compliance based approach and asking 'what are we going to report?', directors need to ask themselves: 'What should we withhold?' For example, pharmaceutical companies disclose details of their products – in terms of pipeline, stage of development, planned launch and potential market size – without prejudicing their competitive position. Specific information on the underlying patent formulations are, however, withheld. With this approach, they provide investors with information which is critical to understanding the sustainability of their performance, without compromising the interests of the company.

---

[75] ASB: A Review of Narrative Reporting by UK Listed Companies in 2006 (January 2007); obtainable from the FRC's website *www.frc.org.uk/asb/press/pub1228.html*.

5.4.15.2 What can be done to ensure the supportability of forward-looking information?

Clearly, forward-looking information cannot, by its nature, be 100 per cent supportable. But companies that attempt to rely on this as a reason for opting out of providing forward-looking information are missing the point. Forward-looking information contained in a narrative report is different from information found in historical financial statements.

Obviously, the fact that information has been disclosed in an Annual Report may raise expectation of reliability in investors. Directors are therefore expected to scrutinise whatever evidence has been used to underpin this information and, where appropriate, to explain its source and the extent to which it is objectively supportable.

The overall intention is for investors to assess this information themselves before deciding whether or not to rely on it. For them to do so effectively, it is important that they should have a clear understanding of how certain (or uncertain) it is.

5.4.15.3 What about profit forecasts?

The requirement that business reviews should incorporate KPIs, alongside the requirement to provide future trends, has led many companies to believe – erroneously – that they will be expected to report profit forecasts. Given the level of concern this has caused amongst UK companies, it should be stressed that profit would not normally be expected to be a KPI. Profit is often the overall objective towards which a company's strategy is geared. KPIs are there to enable a company to monitor progress in implementing its strategies and managing the business towards the achievement of its overall objective.

Forward-looking information, properly presented, can be used to provide investors with a broad-based view of corporate performance – without having to disclose sensitive Prospective Financial Information (PFI). Non-financial drivers of performance can be used as lead indicators of future financial performance. Similarly, market trends and clearly presented strategic priorities will provide investors with valuable insights on which to base their investment decisions. And, of course, targets can also be important aspects of this information, communicating companies' aspirations to the market without straying into the realms of PFI.

Provided directors understand the difference between publishing targets and publishing PFI, they will have limited their exposure. The guidance on PFI issued by the Institute of Chartered Accountants in England & Wales (ICAEW)[76] is helpful on this point:

---

[76] Prospective Financial Information – Guidance for UK Directors (September 2003); obtainable from the ICAEW website, *www.icaew.com/index.cfm?route=118662.*

"It is important to differentiate PFI, which comprises one or more statements about the future, from a target, which is a statement of the company's current intentions or objectives. Targets are aspirational and should not be judged against the principles of PFI set out in this Guidance. It is therefore important that the user should not be led into thinking that a target is PFI, and the issuer should make the status of the information clear."

The distinction between PFI and targets is usually clear cut. For example, if a company says that it is 'aiming for 5% sales growth', this is a target. If, however, it says that 'sales will grow by 5%', the statement becomes a PFI. As noted by the ICAEW in their guidance:

"Once disclosed information crosses the line into PFI, it is vital Directors are aware of the stringent regulations surrounding the publication of profit forecasts. ... Keen to encourage the market's access to forward-looking information (financial and non-financial), regulators recognise that there is often a fine line between what constitutes a profit forecast and what constitutes trend information (a general discussion of the future prospects of the issuer will not normally constitute a forecast). ..."

However, once PFI in prospectuses and similar documents is determined to be a profit forecast, it triggers requirements for directors and third parties, such as auditors, to confirm or determine that the directors have undertaken a process of due and careful enquiry.'

5.4.16 What are the challenging areas: environmental, employee and social matters?

Most companies within the FTSE 350 already provide a Corporate Social Responsibility (CSR) section, which will go some way towards meeting the new reporting requirements for quoted companies. However, such CSR sections are usually separate from the main narrative discussion, which could lead to the impressions that CSR concerns are simply a 'bolt on'. The challenge for companies is to integrate CSR aspects within the discussion of the overall objectives and strategies of the company, and within management processes.

5.4.17 What are the challenging areas: persons with whom the company has contractual arrangements?

This requirement for quoted companies was another example of reporting requirements being lifted from the OFR into the business review for quoted companies. However, this was a very late addition to the Companies Bill and generated much debate. Some in the media suggested that this would require every company to list all their suppliers and the contractual arrangements.

Lord Sainsbury of Turville, in the House of Lords on 2 November 2006 clarified the requirement by stating:

'This is not a requirement on companies to list their suppliers and customers, or to provide details about contracts. The provision is about reporting significant relationships, such as with major suppliers or key customers critical to the business, which are likely to influence directly or indirectly, the performance of the business and its value. It is for the directors to exercise judgment on what is necessary to report. They need only include information to the extent necessary for an understanding of the development, performance or position of the business.[77]'

This is an area where the guidance in the ASB's OFR reporting statement is helpful in determining what can be said in this challenging area[78].

5.4.18 What is the role of the Financial Reporting Review Panel (FRRP) in this area?

When the business review legislation was introduced in 2005, civil enforcement powers were given to the FRRP in respect of directors' reports. This change brought the business review within the FRRP's scope for the first time, and applies to reports for accounting periods commencing on or after 1 April 2006.

There is no change to the FRRP's process for selecting accounts for review – accounts continue to be drawn from the full range of companies within the FRRP's remit with a focus on priority sectors. The role of the FRRP is to examine the directors' report and annual accounts of public and large private companies to see whether they comply with the requirements in the Companies Act, including applicable accounting standards. Where breaches of the Companies Act 2006 are discovered, the FRRP seeks to take corrective action. Such action would normally include voluntary revision to the accounts. If this fails, the FRRP is empowered to make an application to the court. To date no such court applications have been made since the FRRP was formed in 1990.

5.4.19 What changes are there to the disclosure of directors' interests?

Under the Companies Act 1985, there was a requirement to disclose directors' interests in shares or debentures (in respect of any company in the group) in the directors' report. This disclosure requirement was based on the requirement of a director to notify the company of those interests. The company was obliged

---

[77] Lords Hansard 2 November 2006; obtainable at *www.parliament.the-stationery-office.co.uk/pa/ld199697/ldhansrd/pdvn/lds06/text/61102-0008.htm.*
[78] Paragraphs 28(d) and 57 to 59 of ASB reporting Statement: Operating and Financial Review 2006.

to maintain a register of all such notifications and to disclose certain information in that register in the directors' report.

The requirement for directors to notify their interests and for the company to maintain a register of directors' interests was abolished on 6 April 2007. As a consequence, the requirement to disclose directors' interests in directors' reports under company law is abolished for directors' reports approved on or after 6 April 2007. However, for listed companies the disclosure requirement is reinstated through the FSA LR (see below).

5.4.20 Does the change in the legal disclosure requirements apply to all types of company?

The abolition of the disclosure requirement under company law applies to all companies but listed companies still have to make these disclosures under the FSA LR[79]. The source of the information to be disclosed is based on the information notified to the company by the directors under the FSA DTR[80]. This includes:

(i) all changes in the interests of each director that have occurred between the end of the period under review and a date not more than one month prior to the date of the notice of the annual general meeting; or

(ii) if there have been no changes in the period described in paragraph (a), a statement that there have been no changes in the interests of each director.

Interests of each director include the interests of connected persons of which the listed company is, or ought upon reasonable enquiry to become, aware.

5.4.21 Have the disclosure thresholds for charitable and political donations been increased?

The financial threshold for the disclosure of both charitable and political donations is raised, for financial years beginning on or after 6 April 2008, from £200 to £2,000. (For further details on political donations and expenditure see chapter 4, section 4.7.)

---

[79] FSA LR9.8.6.
[80] FSA DTR3.1.2.

5.5   Directors' remuneration report

5.5.1   Are there any new disclosures?

The Accounts regulations for large and medium-sized companies[81] reinstate the previous requirements but create a new disclosure requirement as follows:

> "The directors' remuneration report must contain a statement of how pay and employment conditions of employees of the company and of other undertakings within the same group as the company were taken into account when determining directors' remuneration for the relevant financial year[82]." (See chapter 10, section 10.6.3.2.)

This new disclosure requirement has been included in response to concerns that directors' remuneration needs to be justified to users of the accounts, particularly shareholders and employees, especially in view of criticism from employee representation groups and the press of the pay differentials between directors and others employees of companies. Companies have a year's grace before they have to comply with the requirement as it applies in relation to financial years beginning on or after 6 April 2009[83].

Only quoted companies are required to prepare a directors' remuneration report. Currently, most companies paraphrase the Combined Code 2006 supporting principle in their remuneration reports:

> "[Remuneration Committees] should also be sensitive to pay and employment conditions elsewhere in the group, especially when determining annual salary increases."

Some companies reflect the Combined Code principle by disclosing the overall salary increase for staff (and demonstrating that this was no lower than that for directors).

To date, the Association of British Insurers' Guidelines (guidelines which take the form of disclosures which institutions would expect to see included in the annual report of listed companies) have focused on the tier of management below the board whereas the National Association of Pension Funds have recommended disclosure of the ratio of average director pay to average non-director pay (but this has only been adopted by a few companies).

As can be seen from the quote above, the regulations are not prescriptive as to the level of detail to be provided in the statement. Whilst this means that quoted companies are given flexibility to provide a statement that is most

---

[81]   SI 2008/410 the Large and Medium-sized companies and Groups Accounts and Reports) Regulations 2008, Schedule 8.
[82]   SI 2008/410, Schedule 8, paragraph 4.
[83]   SI 2008/410, Reg 2(3).

appropriate to their circumstances, it also tends to make it possible for companies to make disclosures that comply with the letter of the law but are so vague that they do not shed a great deal of light on the company's pay policy. It is most likely that those companies that are proactive and enthusiastic in their efforts to ensure fair pay across the broad range of their employees are the companies that will give the most meaningful statements in their directors' remuneration reports. Those companies that fulfil the minimum requirements of the law but are less enthusiastic about promoting the interests of their employees are more inclined to include 'boilerplate disclosure' which is of little use to users of the accounts.

5.6 Conclusion

5.6.1 List of key changes and actions

Section	Key change	Action required
5.3.7 to 5.3.9	Increase in financial thresholds for determining small and medium-sized companies and groups, applicable for financial years beginning on or after 6 April 2008.	Determine the classification of the company based on the new limits.
5.3.11	Abolition of exemption from preparing consolidated accounts for medium-sized groups, applicable for financial years beginning on or after 6 April 2008.	Directors should ensure that systems are in place to capture the required information for both the first financial year beginning on or after 6 April 2008, and the comparative period.
5.3.13 to 5.3.16	New disclosure requirements in respect of related party disclosures, applicable for financial years beginning on or after 6 April 2008.	IFRS reporters will have no additional disclosures to make. UK GAAP reporters will be affected by the expected withdrawal of FRS 8, 'Related party disclosures' and its replacement with a standard based on IAS 24. IAS 24 does not give exemption to wholly owned subsidiaries from disclosing transaction with other group members. Companies will therefore need to obtain this information for both the financial year beginning on or after 6 April 2008, and the comparative period.

Section	Key change	Action required
5.3.17 to 5.3.18	Changes to the legality of, and disclosure about, directors' loans and other transactions. The rules on legality apply from 1 October 2007 and those in respect of disclosure apply from accounting periods beginning on or after 6 April 2008.	Consider whether the changes mean additional system requirements to ensure appropriate shareholder approvals are obtained.
5.3.19	Transitional arrangements regarding change of definition of, and disclosures in respect of, 'connected persons'. Change in definition applies from 1 November 2007 and the disclosures are abolished for accounting periods beginning on or after 6 April 2008.	Ensure that the necessary information is captured in respect of the wider pool of persons caught as 'connected persons'. Ensure that appropriate shareholder approvals are obtained. Ensure that appropriate disclosures are made for accounting periods ending on or before 6 April 2008.
5.3.20 to 5.3.23	New disclosure requirement in respect of off-balance-sheet arrangements, applicable for financial years beginning on or after 6 April 2008.	Both IFRS and UK GAAP reporters will be required to disclose off-balance-sheet arrangements for the financial year beginning on or after 6 April 2008, and the comparative period. (Small companies are exempt from the requirement and there are reduced disclosure requirements for medium-sized companies.) Directors will need to review the company's activities to identify those items that fall to be disclosed.
5.4.5	Enhanced business review for quoted companies, applicable to financial years beginning on or after 1 October 2007.	Quoted companies will already be preparing a business review but will need to consider how to meet the additional new disclosure requirements.

Section	Key change	Action required
5.5.1	New disclosure requirement in directors' remuneration report in respect of the impact of employee pay and conditions in the determination of directors' remuneration, applicable for financial years beginning on or after 6 April 2009.	Directors should consider how to meet the additional new disclosure requirements.

Chapter 6

Changes in financial reporting

6.1   Introduction 6001
      6.1.1   Scope of this chapter 6001
      6.1.2   What is different and what stays the same? 6001
      6.1.3   How are the provisions being implemented? 6002
6.2   Approval of accounts 6003
      6.2.1   Are there any changes in the accounts and reports approval
              process? 6003
      6.2.2   Public companies: what is an 'accounts meeting'? 6003
      6.2.3   Private companies: is there an option to lay accounts at a
              general meeting? 6004
      6.2.4   Public companies: what is the new time frame for holding
              Annual General Meetings? 6004
      6.2.5   Quoted companies: can members raise audit concerns at
              the 'accounts meeting'? 6004
6.3   Circulation of accounts 6006
      6.3.1   Who is entitled to receive the accounts and reports? 6006
      6.3.2   When do the accounts have to be circulated? 6006
      6.3.3   Can the accounts and reports be sent to shareholders
              electronically? 6007
      6.3.4   If a company already uses website communications with
              shareholders is a new resolution required to continue doing
              so? 6008
      6.3.5   What does a company need to do to default to using
              website communication? 6008
      6.3.6   Can information also be requested in paper form if it's
              been received electronically? 6008
      6.3.7   Are there additional requirements for companies traded on
              a regulated market? 6009
      6.3.8   Summary financial statement: are there any changes to the
              rules? 6009
      6.3.9   What are the new 'shareholder rights' for indirect
              investors? 6011
      6.3.10 What are the new 'information rights' for indirect
              investors? 6011
      6.3.11 Quoted companies: what is the new requirement to publish
              their accounts on a website? 6012
6.4   Filing accounts and reports with the Registrar of Companies . . . 6012
      6.4.1   Are there any changes to directors' duties to file accounts
              and reports? 6012

6.4.2 How long does a company have to file accounts and reports with the Registrar of Companies? 6012

6.4.3 How is the exact filing deadline calculated? 6013

6.4.4 How is the filing period calculated for a company's first annual accounts and reports? 6013

6.4.5 Are there late filing penalties or other sanctions? 6014

    6.4.5.1 Are there fixed penalty fines? 6014

    6.4.5.2 Can a company be struck off if its accounts and reports are not filed? 6015

    6.4.5.3 Can a company be restored subsequently to the register? 6015

    6.4.5.4 What is *bona vacantia*? 6016

6.4.6 Small and medium-sized companies: do they still have filing exemptions? 6016

6.4.7 Small companies: what are the filing options? 6017

6.4.8 Small companies: what are the filing requirements for ineligible companies? 6017

6.4.9 Medium-sized companies: what are the filing options? ... 6018

6.4.10 Medium-sized companies: are there any changes to the form or content of abbreviated Companies Act accounts? 6018

6.4.11 Medium-sized companies: what are the filing requirements for ineligible companies? 6019

6.4.12 Medium-sized companies: are there any exemptions from, or choices for, filing group accounts? 6019

6.4.13 Large private and all quoted companies: are there any filing options? 6020

6.4.14 Do the copies of the balance sheet and the various reports filed with Registrar of Companies have to be signed? ... 6021

6.4.15 Can documents be filed electronically with the Registrar of Companies? 6021

6.4.16 Are there any changes to rules about publication of statutory accounts? 6022

6.4.17 Are there any changes to the rules about publication of non-statutory accounts? 6023

6.5 Revision of defective annual accounts and reports and half yearly reports 6024

6.5.1 Can directors still revise their company's annual accounts or reports if they believe them to be defective? 6024

6.5.2 Can the Financial Reporting Review Panel (FRRP) or the Secretary of State still request a revision off a company's annual accounts or directors' report? 6024

6.5.3 Listed companies: does the FRRP have powers to review and investigate half yearly reports? 6025

6.5.4 Can a small or medium-sized company's abbreviated Companies Act accounts be revised? 6025

6.5.5 When do the directors have to send out the revised accounts or reports? 6025

6.6   The EU Transparency Obligations Directive 6026
      6.6.1   How does the Directive impact on UK companies? 6026
      6.6.2   What is the period for making public a listed company's
              annual financial report? 6027
      6.6.3   What are the contents of the annual financial report? . . . 6027
      6.6.4   Are directors' responsibility statements mandatory? 6028
      6.6.5   Are preliminary statements of annual results still
              required? 6029
      6.6.6   What are the requirements for half-yearly reports? 6029
      6.6.7   Is there any clarification of the rules on half-yearly interim
              management reports? 6030
      6.6.8   What are the requirements for Interim Management
              Statements? 6031
      6.6.9   What changes have been made in respect of corporate
              governance? 6031
      6.6.10 Are there any changes to the Combined Code (2006)? . . . 6033
      6.6.11 Are there any penalties or liability for compensation for
              breaches of the transparency or corporate governance rules
              or for making false or misleading statements? 6033
6.7   Conclusion 6035
      6.7.1   List of key changes and action points 6035

Chapter 6

Changes in financial reporting

6.1 Introduction

6.1.1 Scope of this chapter

This chapter considers the changes made by the Companies Act 2006 to the requirements of a company to approve and circulate its annual accounts. It also deals with the impact on companies listed on a regulated market from the implementation in the UK of the EU Transparency Obligations Directive[1] and the resulting changes in the FSA's Listing Rules (FSA LR) and Disclosure and Transparency Rules (FSA DTR). The requirements for overseas companies that have a place of business or branch in the UK are dealt with in chapter 3, section 3.12.

6.1.2 What is different and what stays the same?

Much of the Companies Act 2006 re-enacts the requirements of the Companies Act 1985, albeit in a different format designed to make it easier to apply the provisions to small companies. The Companies Act 2006 is intended to simplify and modernise company law, reducing where possible the compliance costs that companies face.

The main changes relevant to the approval and publication of a company's annual accounts include:

(i)   abolition of the statutory AGM for private companies;

(ii)   new provisions regarding electronic and website communication with shareholders;

(iii)   new statutory information rights for investors who hold their shares through an intermediary (indirect investors);

(iv)   the new requirement for quoted companies to publish their accounts on a website; and

(v)   a reduction in the time limit for both public and private companies to file their accounts with the Registrar of Companies and a change in how the filing deadline is calculated.

Legislation carried forward largely without amendment includes the following:

[1]   EU Directive 2004/109/EC.

(i)   the requirement for directors to formally approve and send out copies of the annual accounts;

(ii)   the ability for all companies whose accounts are audited to send out summary financial statements in place of the full accounts in certain circumstances;

(iii)   the option for small companies to file shorter form or abbreviated Companies Act individual accounts with the Registrar of Companies; and

(iv)   the voluntary regime to revise defective accounts and reports.

6.1.3   How are the provisions being implemented?

Implementation of the Companies Act 2006 has been staggered and different parts have different commencement dates, some provisions have been in force since January 2007, others are being implemented in stages over the period until October 2009. The provisions of the Companies Act 1985 and the Northern Ireland Order 1986 are repealed in line with the commencement dates of the Companies Act 2006 but remain effective until then.

In summary, the areas covered by this chapter have the following implementation dates:

(i)   Most of the provisions covering the approval and publication of annual accounts and reports are in force for financial years commencing on or after 6 April 2008.

(ii)   The company communication provisions (including electronic and web site communication provisions) have been in force since 20 January 2007.

(iii)   The provisions on the exercise of member rights (and recognising the rights of indirect investors) are in force from 1 October 2007.

In addition to the changes introduced by the Companies Act 2006, companies that are traded on a UK regulated market are also subject to the amended requirements of the FSA LR and DTR. These changes stem from the EU's Transparency Obligations Directive, Statutory Audit Directive and Corporate Reporting Directive[2]. In the case of the latter two Directives, the changes relate to companies' Corporate Governance Statements and Audit Committee arrangements. The changes to the FSA DTR arising from the Transparency Obligations Directive are effective for all financial reporting periods beginning on or after 20 January 2007. The Corporate Governance Statement and Audit

---

[2]   EU Directives 2004/109/EC, 2006/43/EC and 2006/46/EC respectively.

Committee requirements are in force for financial reporting periods beginning on or after 29 June 2008[3].

6.2 Approval of accounts

6.2.1 Are there any changes in the accounts and reports approval process?

The board of directors has to approve the company's accounts and they must be signed on the board's behalf by a company director signing the company's balance sheet. Every copy of a balance sheet laid before the company in general meeting (the 'accounts meeting' (see section 6.2.2 below)), or otherwise circulated, published or issued, must state the name of the person who signed the balance sheet on behalf of the board. The directors' report and, for quoted companies, the directors' remuneration report must be approved by the board of directors and be signed on the board's behalf by a director or by the company secretary.

In addition to the legal requirements mentioned above, accounting standards[4] require that the accounts should disclose the date on which the accounts were authorised for issue and who gave this authorisation. The date of authorisation will normally be the date on which the board of directors formally approves a set of documents as the accounts. The date of approval for consolidated accounts is the date on which the board of directors of the parent company formally approve them.

6.2.2 Public companies: what is an 'accounts meeting'?

As part of the measures intended to reduce the administrative burden on small companies, the Companies Act 2006 distinguishes between the statutory procedures required in respect of public and private companies.

With effect from 1 October 2007, only the directors of a public company have a duty to present the annual accounts and reports of the company before the shareholders each year at a general meeting of the company. The annual accounts and reports of a public company do not necessarily have to be laid before the shareholders at the annual general meeting (AGM); another general meeting will suffice. The meeting at which the accounts and reports are laid is referred to as an 'accounts meeting'[5]. In practice, however, most public companies do lay their annual accounts and reports before the shareholders at their AGM.

---

[3] FSA Consultation Paper 7/24 (December 2007) proposed removing FSA LR9.8.6(5), and introducing FSA DTR 1B and DTR 7, for financial reporting periods beginning on after 29 June 2008.
[4] IAS 10, 'Events after the balance sheet date', and FRS 21, 'Events after the balance sheet date'.
[5] Section 437(1), Companies Act 2006.

6.2.3 Private companies: is there an option to lay accounts at a general meeting?

Private companies have no statutory obligation to lay accounts and reports in general meetings or hold an annual general meeting (AGM). This change is effective from 1 October 2007 and it automatically makes the previous 'elective regime' the default position for all private companies from this date. This provision does not, however, overturn any requirement in a private company's memorandum or articles to hold an AGM.

Nevertheless, the directors of a private company must formally approve and send the accounts and reports to members.

6.2.4 Public companies: what is the new time frame for holding Annual General Meetings?

The period within which a public company must hold its AGM has been changed. A public company must now hold its AGM within six months of its year end. This is in contrast to the previous regime that simply required an AGM to be held each calendar year and not let more than 15 months elapse between one AGM and the next. Under the transitional provisions of the Companies Act 2006, the timing of the first AGM held by a public company after 30 September 2007 is governed by the old regime's rules. The requirement to hold the AGM within six months of the year end will apply to the following AGM. In most cases, this is the AGM following the completion of the first financial year that commenced after 6 April 2008.

6.2.5 Quoted companies: can members raise audit concerns at the 'accounts meeting'?

Shareholders of quoted companies have a right from April 2008 starting with financial years beginning on or after 6 April 2008 to require the company to publish a statement on its website setting out any matter that the members propose to raise at its next 'accounts meeting' about the audit or a change of auditor. The matters must relate to the company's accounts that are to be laid before the company at that meeting or in respect of the auditor that left office since the last accounts meeting. This new right imposes certain obligations on companies, though no statutory obligation on auditors. A company is required to comply once requests have been received from members holding 5% of the voting rights or 100 members each holding a minimum of £100 of shares.

The Companies Act 2006 sets out the format in which the request should be submitted to the company: it may be in hard copy or electronic form, must identify the statement to which it relates and must be authenticated by the persons(s) making it in accordance with the Act. The request must be submitted so that the company receives it at least one week before the meeting at which the matter is proposed to be raised.

There are some protections built in for the company and any other aggrieved persons. The company is not required to publish a statement if, on an application by the company or another person who claims to be aggrieved, the court is satisfied that the right is being abused (for example, because it is defamatory).

The statement must be made available on the company's website (or one that is maintained on behalf of the company) within three days of the company receiving it. Access to the information on the website or the ability to obtain a hard copy of the information must not be restricted or require payment of a fee. The information must be kept available until after the end of the meeting to which the statement relates. A copy of the statement should be provided to the company's auditor and possibly the former auditor at the same time as the information is published on the website.

Having required a company to publish a statement on its website, it is very likely that the member(s) making the requisition will raise the matter at the meeting. However, there is no obligation for the member(s) to do so. To avoid any argument as to whether any matter contained in a published statement can be dealt with at the meeting, the Companies Act 2006 specifically provides that the business of an accounts meeting includes any statement of audit concerns that the company has published on its website. However, there is no obligation on the company to include the matters from the statement in the agenda for, or notice of, the accounts meeting.

If the matters are raised at the accounts meeting, it is the company that deals with the questions from member(s). The company chairman, or the chairman of the audit committee, usually answer questions on the accounts or related to their audit. However, there is no statutory obligation for them to do so. The Combined Code recommends that the chairmen of the audit, remuneration and nomination committees should attend the AGM to answer questions. Auditors of quoted companies already assist in briefing the audit committee chairman and in developing responses in advance of the meeting for any audit-related matters (such as audit independence).

The introduction of the new obligation for companies to pass through to their auditors the statements of audit concerns in advance of the meeting may make for more interesting and in depth dialogue. However, it is important to note that the new provisions do not provide a mechanism for questions to be asked of, and answered by, the auditor at the accounts meeting. Indeed, there is no obligation on the auditor to attend the accounts meeting or AGM, although the auditor's right to attend and be heard at general meetings of a company is preserved. Should an auditor be invited to respond to a question, or voluntarily decides to do so, they will need to consider their duty of care to the shareholders in body and thus may avail themselves of the protection afforded by the usual disclaimer in the audit report. The auditor will also be mindful of their duty of confidentiality and will need express permission from the company to waive it.

It is unclear the extent to which member(s) may wish to take advantage of their new right to have audit concerns published in advance of an accounts meeting on companies' websites. Quoted companies and audit firms need to establish procedures to deal with the administration that such requests entail. Directors, and the audit committee chairman, need to consider how best to prepare themselves to address any matters proposed to be raised.

6.3 Circulation of accounts

6.3.1 Who is entitled to receive the accounts and reports?

Every member and every debenture holder of the company and every person (including indirect investors[6]) who is entitled to receive notice of general meetings must be sent a copy of the company's annual accounts and reports.

However, a company does not need to send a copy to a person for whom it does not have a current address. A company is deemed to hold a current address if the company has been notified of an address to which documents may be sent and the company has no reason to believe that the documents sent to that address will not reach that person[7].

6.3.2 When do the accounts have to be circulated?

Public companies must send their annual accounts and reports to every person (including indirect investors[8]) entitled to receive them within 21 days of the date of the 'accounts meeting' (see above). Those public companies that have their shares admitted to trading on a regulated market (for example, the 'Main Market' of the LSE or Plus Market 'PLUS-listed' market) must send their annual accounts and reports to any indirect investor nominated by a registered shareholder who is holding shares on behalf of the indirect investors[9].

Private companies have no obligation to lay their accounts and reports before a general meeting[10]. However, they must send their annual accounts and reports to every person entitled (including indirect investors where the company has amended its articles to so[11]) to receive them no later than the earlier of the actual date of delivery to the Registrar of Companies and the filing deadline. (The shortened filing deadlines are discussed in section 6.4.2 below).

---

[6]   See section 6.3.10 below.
[7]   Section 423, Companies Act 2006.
[8]   Section 145, Companies Act 2006, where the company has inserted a provision to this effect in its articles; see section 6.3.9 below.
[9]   Section 146, Companies Act 2006, see section 6.3.10 below.
[10] Section 424, Companies Act 2006.
[11] Section 145, Companies Act 2006.

6.3.3 Can the accounts and reports be sent to shareholders electronically?

Yes. A general principle of the Companies Act 2006 is that companies should, subject to shareholder approval, be able to default to using electronic communications with shareholders (including sending out of accounts and reports). Individuals retain the right to receive information on paper if they wish. The company communications provisions apply to all companies, public and private.

The provisions on company communications in the Companies Act 2006 came into effect on 20 January 2007. The provisions include two significant changes from the previous legislation:

(i)   Firstly, *any* document or information required by the Companies Act to be sent or supplied by or to a company is now allowed to be sent electronically. (This is in contrast to the specific limited electronic communications permitted under the previous legislation).

(ii) Secondly, they allow, subject to certain conditions being met, the default method of communication to change from paper copy communication to website communication, with a positive opt-in required by members to obtain information on paper.

Thus a company may either send out its accounts and reports electronically by:

(i)   using electronic communications to send a copy of the full accounts and reports or summary financial statement to the address notified to the company by a member for that purpose; or

(ii) make a copy of them available to a member on a website provided:

- the company and the member have agreed to their having access to the accounts and reports in question via a website; and

- that member is notified, in the manner agreed with the company of the publication of the accounts and reports on the website, of the address of the website and where and how on the agreed website they may be accessed.

Any information communicated to shareholders via a website must be clearly presented and enable the recipient to retain a copy of the information. The information must be available on the website for 28 days, but the company will not be at fault if the information cannot be displayed for circumstances beyond their control, such as technical difficulties. Electronic and website communication is discussed in chapter 4, section 4.2.

6.3.4 If a company already uses website communications with shareholders is a new resolution required to continue doing so?

If a company already had an individual shareholder's agreement to circulate the annual report and accounts or summary financial statement to the shareholder by website under the terms required by the Companies Act 1985[12], this agreement continues to be valid[13] and no new resolution is required. However, where a company wishes to go further than the terms of the company's articles, for example where the articles only cover certain documents, then a new resolution is required to provide general cover for other documents that the company wishes to communicate by website. See also chapter 4, section 4.2.4.

There is no change to the requirement that the company notifies the shareholder each time that new information is posted on the website[14]. This notification can also be sent electronically via e-mail. However, if an e-mail address has not been provided, companies will have to write to their shareholders to notify them that information has been posted on the company website.

6.3.5 What does a company need to do to default to using website communication?

The concept of deemed agreement to website communication is a new concept in the Companies Act 2006. The company will need both to seek individual agreement of each intended recipient (shareholder or person nominated by a shareholder) and to pass a resolution for the company to use website communications as the default. Where an individual fails to respond within 28 days to say they do not want website communication, the company may consider this as the individual's deemed agreement to website communication. The company's communication that poses this question must be clear about the effect of the failure to respond. Where an individual does not agree to website communications, the company cannot ask again for their agreement within less than 12 months. The comments above regarding notification of information published on a website also apply. See also chapter 4, section 4.2.6.

6.3.6 Can information also be requested in paper form if it's been received electronically?

Shareholders or debenture holders of all companies have the right to require that any document received electronically by that person is sent by the company in paper form within 21 days of the request[15]. Listed companies also

---

[12] Sections 238, 251 and 369, Companies Act 1985.
[13] Paragraph 9 of Schedule 5 to the Companies Act 2006.
[14] Paragraph 13 of Schedule 5 to the Companies Act 2006.
[15] Section 1145, Companies Act 2006.

have to provide documents in paper form, if requested by indirect investors that have been nominated by registered shareholders, on whose behalf they are holding the shares[16]. The company cannot charge for complying with such requests. See also chapter 4, section 4.2.16.

6.3.7 Are there additional requirements for companies traded on a regulated market?

Companies traded on a regulated market in the UK are subject to the FSA DTR, which require that the decision to use electronic means to convey information to shareholders or debenture holders is made in general meeting of shareholders[17]. However, a transitional provision is included in the FSA DTR to ensure that where a company could already lawfully use electronic means for communications to shareholders (or holders of debt securities) under the previous legislation, the company can continue to do so[18].

The FSA has issued some guidance[19] about the approach companies might take when dealing with the introduction of electronic communications. Amongst other things, this guidance covers:

(i)   the letters companies send to their shareholders requesting permission to send future communications electronically; and

(ii)   the content of letters sent notifying shareholders when new communications are available.

However, these communications are subject to the FSA LR requirement that a statement is included asking shareholders to pass on the document to the new holder when the shares have been transferred. In June 2008, the FSA relaxed this requirement where such letters contain shareholder specific details that are of a sensitive and confidential nature[20].

6.3.8 Summary financial statement: are there any changes to the rules?

All companies that have their accounts audited and complying with certain conditions continue to have the option to provide a summary financial statement in place of the full accounts and reports normally required to be sent to members and other entitled persons. There are different form and content requirements depending upon whether the company is quoted or unquoted, is a banking or insurance company and whether it prepares IAS or Companies Act individual or group accounts.

---

[16]   Section 146(2)(b)(ii), Companies Act 2006.
[17]   FSA DTR6.1.8(1).
[18]   FSA DTR TP12 and details of the transitional provisions can found in UKLA's *List!* 14 (revised April 2007); obtainable at *www.fsa.gov.uk/pubs/ukla/list14_apr07.pdf*.
[19]   UKLA *List!* 17 – November 2007, part 12; *www.fsa.gov.uk/pubs/ukla/list_nov07.pdf*.
[20]   UKLA *List!* Update – 6 June 2008; obtainable at *www.fsa.gov.uk/pubs/ukla/ukla_update.pdf*.

Before exercising its option to issue a summary financial statement, a company must have consulted the entitled persons and also established that nothing in the company's constitution, debenture trust deeds or governing instruments requires the full accounts and reports to be sent to the entitled persons. The full details of the method required for consultation and the form and content of the summary financial statement are dealt with in new regulations[21], which are in force from 6 April 2008 and apply in relation to companies' financial years commencing on or after that date.

In addition to the form and content specified for particular types of company in the regulations, all companies must include in a summary financial statement the dividend information and the aggregate directors' emoluments information from the full accounts and reports. For quoted companies, the summary financial statement must contain the whole of, or a summary of, the policy on directors' remuneration and the performance graph from its directors' remuneration report. Companies admitted to the Official List maintained by the FSA must include the earnings per share information from the annual financial report.

Those publicly traded[22] companies that are required to provide information in their directors' report about their capital structure that would be pertinent in the event of a takeover bid must give certain explanatory material about those disclosures in the summary financial statement. Alternatively, it may send the material to the person receiving the summary financial statement separately at the same time as it sends the statement[23]. This may interact with the new requirements on corporate governance statements in the FSA DTR[24].

The various statements and caveats in respect of the information in the summary financial statement required by the previous legislation continue to be required, as does the requirement for the auditor to provide an opinion as to the consistency of the summary financial statement with the annual accounts and reports.

The company communication provisions of the Companies Act 2006 govern the electronic distribution of summary financial information and impose the same rules as apply to the sending out of the full accounts. See section 6.3.3 above.

Where the summary financial statement is accessible on a website to persons other than those entitled to receive the full accounts (entitled persons), the summary financial statement should be treated as non-statutory accounts as it is not the company's statutory accounts and is accessible to a wider audience.

---

[21] SI 2008/374 The Companies (Summary Financial Statement) Regulations 2008.

[22] 'Publicly traded' companies are ones that at the end of a fianancial year had any of their securities carrying voting rights admitted to trading on a regulated market in an EEA Member State. It is therefore a subset of 'quoted' companies.

[23] SI 2008/374 The Companies (Summary Financial Statement) Regulations 2008, Reg 10(1).

[24] FSA DTR7.2.6; see section 6.6.9.

See section 6.4.17. The statement must indicate that it is not the company's statutory accounts for the year (or years) with which it deals and whether the statutory accounts for those years have been or will be delivered to the Registrar of Companies. In addition, the statement must say whether the auditor's report on the company's statutory accounts for the relevant financial years was unqualified, qualified or contained a matter of emphasis or any reservations about accounting records or returns or obtaining necessary information and explanations[25].

6.3.9 What are the new 'shareholder rights' for indirect investors?

For the first time, certain statutory rights have been given to indirect investors. This is in recognition of the fact that increasingly companies' shares are held on behalf of investors by intermediaries either in physical or electronic form. As such, it is the intermediaries that are the registered shareholders with the company. This has led to a situation where thousands of investors have no direct relationship with the company in which they have invested. As a result such investors typically have to rely on contractual arrangements with the intermediaries both to obtain information from their company and also to give any instructions about how voting rights on their shares should be exercised.

All companies can now insert a provision in their articles to extend rights to those holding shares through intermediaries[26]. This provision permits members to nominate another person or persons to receive all or certain specified rights of a member ('shareholder rights'). These rights include voting rights, rights to appoint a proxy, rights to receive general shareholder communications, such as notices of meetings and the annual accounts and reports. Shareholder rights' are discussed further in chapter 4, section 4.3.

6.3.10 What are the new 'information rights' for indirect investors?

In the case of a company whose shares are admitted to trading on a regulated market (for example, the LSE's 'Main Market' and Plus Markets' 'PLUS-listed' market), nominated persons[27] have the right to receive a copy of all general shareholder communications between the company and the registered owner of the shares ('information rights'). Subject to the consent of the nominated person, these communications may be made electronically, with website publication being the default method of communication. The individual with information rights may (prior to the nomination[28]) request that hard copies of the information are provided instead. 'Information rights' are discussed further in chapter 4 section 4.3.

---

[25] Section 435, Companies Act 2006.
[26] Section 145, Companies Act 2006.
[27] Section 146, Companies Act 2006.
[28] Section 147, Companies Act 2006.

These information rights for indirect shareholders are in addition to the existing rights of the registered shareholder (that is, the registered shareholder will continue to receive the company's general shareholder communications).

6.3.11 Quoted companies: what is the new requirement to publish their accounts on a website?

A quoted company must ensure that its annual accounts and reports are available on a website as soon as reasonably practicable and then continuously until the annual accounts and reports for the company's next financial year are available on the website[29]. The website must be the company's own or one that is maintained on its behalf and that clearly identifies the company. Furthermore the access to the accounts and reports, and the ability to obtain a hard copy of the information, must not be restricted or require payment of a fee.

6.4 Filing accounts and reports with the Registrar of Companies

6.4.1 Are there any changes to directors' duties to file accounts and reports?

No. Directors still have a duty for each financial year to file a copy of the company's accounts and reports with the Registrar of Companies. The precise form and content that those filings take is dependent on the size and status of the company concerned[30].

6.4.2 How long does a company have to file accounts and reports with the Registrar of Companies?

The Companies Act 2006 shortens the period allowed for filing accounts and reports with the Registrar of Companies. All accounts and reports for financial years starting on or after 6 April 2008 have reduced filing times. The filing period for a private company's accounts and reports reduces from ten months to nine months and the filing period for a public company's accounts and reports reduces from seven months to six months[31]. The Government's decision to reduce filing periods reflects improvements in technology and the increased rate at which information becomes out of date. The previous filing deadlines had been in force since 1976.

Companies admitted to the Official List maintained by the FSA also have to comply with the even shorter deadline of four months required by the FSA's DTR, as discussed in section 6.6 below.

---

[29] Section 430, Companies Act 2006.
[30] Section 441, Companies Act 2006.
[31] Section 442, Companies Act 2006.

6.4.3   How is the exact filing deadline calculated?

The Companies Act 1985 did not specify how the exact filing deadline was to be calculated. The general rule the Registrar of Companies had used to calculate the period was based on case law[32], which determined that the filing period ended upon the corresponding date in the appropriate month (that is, not necessarily the last day of the month) or, where there is no corresponding date, the last day of that month. Consequently, a private company with an accounting reference date of 28 February would, under the previous legislation, have to file its accounts with the Registrar of Companies by 28 December (not 31 December). This was significant as late filing penalties applied from the date the accounts were due to be filed. Therefore, if the company with a 28 February year end mistakenly filed its accounts on 31 December, it automatically incurred a late filing penalty.

The Companies Act 2006[33] overturns the previous case law and specifies how the exact period for filing is to be calculated. The new method uses full calendar months to calculate the filing period and therefore the deadline will be the last day of the appropriate month (whether or not that is the corresponding date). Under the example above, this would mean the private company with an accounting reference date of 28 February would in theory now have a filing deadline of 31 December. However, if the directors filed its 28 February 2010 accounts on 31 December 2010, it would still incur a late filing penalty. This is because the directors had forgotten that the filing period for financial years beginning on or after 6 April 2008 only have nine months to file the accounts. In this case the accounts should be filed by 30 November 2010.

6.4.4   How is the filing period calculated for a company's first annual accounts and reports?

Where a company's first accounting period from incorporation exceeds 12 months, the time allowed for delivering the annual accounts and reports to the Registrar of Companies is calculated as the later of either:

(i)   nine months (for a private company) or six months (for a public company) from the first anniversary of incorporation of the company: or

(ii)   three months after the end of the accounting reference period[34].

Take, for example, a private company incorporated on 1 April 2009 that has a 13 month first financial year ending on the company's accounting reference date of 30 April 2010. The directors have to deliver its annual accounts and reports for that period to the Registrar of Companies by 1 January 2011 (nine

---

[32]   The House of Lords decision in *Dodds v Walker* [1981] 1 WLR 1441.
[33]   Section 433, Companies Act 2006.
[34]   Section 442, Companies Act 2006.

months after first anniversary of its incorporation) as this is later than 31 July 2010 (three months after the end of its accounting reference period).

6.4.5 Are there late filing penalties or other sanctions?

6.4.5.1 Are there fixed penalty fines?

Yes, significantly increased ones. Where a company's directors do not deliver its annual accounts and reports to the Registrar of Companies within the period allowed, the company is automatically fined even if the company is only just over the filing deadline. Under the Companies Act 2006, new regulations[35] amend the schedule of late filing penalties with effect from 1 February 2009. The notable effects of the amendments are:

(i)   a general increase in the level of penalties to reflect the fact that these have not changed since 1992;

(ii) the introduction of a new 'less than one month late' band and a narrowing of the other bands;

(iii) increases in the level of penalty for the other bands and applying the maximum penalty for more than six months late (previously more than 12 months); and

(iv) a doubling of the penalty for any company that filed late the previous year as well.

The increased penalties apply to all accounts filed late on or after 1 February 2009, regardless of whether they are filed under the requirements of the Companies Act 1985 or the Companies Act 2006. However, the doubling of penalties only applies when two consecutive sets of accounts are filed late under the Companies Act 2006, in other words, filings of accounts for financial years beginning on or after 6 April 2008. For example, the penalties for filing more than six months late are £7,500 and £1,500 respectively for public and private companies. Filing more than six months late the following year would double these amounts to £15,000 and £3,000 respectively. The level of penalty depends upon whether the company was public or private at the end of the financial year in question.

Directors of a company that has a short financial year that is, less than 12 months, which commenced on or after 6 April 2008, must file the accounts for that financial year under the new requirements of the Companies Act 2006. If those accounts are filed late before 1 February 2009, a different scale of penalties applies[36]. The maximum penalties of £2,000 and £500 for public and

---

[35] SI 2008/497 The Companies (Late Filing Penalties) and Limited Liability Partnerships (Filing Periods and Late Filing Penalties) Regulations 2008.

[36] SI 2008/497, Reg 2.

private companies respectively are levied where the filing is more than six months late.

With the shortening of the filing periods and a more aggressive schedule of penalties, directors should plan even more carefully to ensure that their companies' accounts are filed well within the specified period to avoid substantial fines. For a large group of UK companies, late filing penalties could amount to a significant drain on cash resources.

6.4.5.2 *Can a company be struck off if its accounts and reports are not filed?*

As a last resort to encourage directors to meet their duty to file their company's annual accounts and report, the Registrar of Companies may use the power to strike a company's name off the register of companies (section 1000, Companies Act 2006). Not filing accounts and reports may give reasonable cause to believe that the company is not carrying on a business or is in operation. The Registrar of Companies will send the company by post a letter inquiring whether the company is carrying on a business or operation. If no answer is received within a month of the dispatch of the letter, the Registrar of Companies will follow the prescribed procedures to ensure that the company has sufficient notice of the intention to strike the company's name off the register of companies and for it to be dissolved. The elapsed time between the first letter and the striking off is some five and half months.

Private and public companies can apply voluntarily to be struck off the register of companies. In the case of the latter, this is a change from the Companies Act 1985.

6.4.5.3 *Can a company be restored subsequently to the register?*

Should the company's name be struck off the register and/or the company be dissolved, an application can be made by a former director or former member of the company to the Registrar of Companies for an administrative restoration to the register (section 1024, Companies Act 2006) (see chapter 11, section 11.4.7). The conditions for such a restoration (section 1025, Companies act 2006) are:

(i)   the company was carrying on a business or in operation at the time of its striking off;

(ii)   the Crown representative has not objected in writing to the restoration, where any property or right previously vested in or held on trust for company has vested as *bona vacantia* (the applicant has to pay any costs in connection with gaining the consent and in dealing with the property during the company's period of dissolution); and

(iii)   the applicant has delivered all the documents relating to the company as are necessary to update the records kept by the Registrar of Companies (for example, the late accounts and reports) and has paid all the late filing penalties that were outstanding at the date of the striking off (sections 1024 and 1025, Companies Act 2006).

6.4.5.4 *What is bona vacantia?*

When a company is dissolved, all property and rights whether vested in or held in trust for the company immediately before its dissolution (including leasehold property) are deemed to be *bona vacantia* (see chapter 11, section 11.4.11). That is they belong to the Crown or to the Duchy of Lancaster or the Duchy of Cornwall (as the case may be). The Crown's title to the property may be disclaimed by means of a notice signed by the Crown representative within three years (previously 12 months) from the date on which vesting of the property came to the notice of the Crown representative (section 1013, Companies Act 2006).

If an application in writing is made to the Crown representative by a person interested in the property requiring a decision as to whether or not the Crown will disclaim title, any notice of disclaimer must be executed within 12 months (previously three years) after making the application or such further period as may be allowed by the court. A notice of disclaimer must be delivered to and is to be retained and registered by the Registrar of Companies. Copies must be published in the Gazette (as defined in section 1173(1), Companies Act 2006) and sent to any person that has notified the Crown representative of a claim to be interested in the property.

6.4.6 Small and medium-sized companies: do they still have filing exemptions?

The option available to the directors of small and medium-sized companies to file a form of accounts and reports other than those sent to the members has been preserved under the Companies Act 2006. The intention of these provisions is to give small and medium-sized companies some degree of privacy rather than to reduce the burden on them. Where the directors of a small or medium-sized company use the option to file abbreviated Companies Act accounts these are additional to those prepared for the company's members.

Medium-sized companies have lost two of their previous exemptions:

(i)   they must now disclose their turnover on the face of the profit and loss account in their abbreviated Companies Act individual accounts (see section 6.4.10); and

(ii) medium-sized parent companies must, where applicable, prepare and file group accounts (see section 6.4.12).

Both of these requirements must be met when preparing accounts for financial years beginning on or after 6 April 2008.

6.4.7   Small companies: what are the filing options?

The directors of a company subject to the small companies regime that prepare Companies Act individual accounts must file either just a copy of the balance sheet and supporting notes from those accounts[37] (omitting the company's profit and loss account and the directors' report) or abbreviated accounts. Alternatively, they may file a copy of the complete set of accounts and reports sent to the company's members.

In the case where just a copy of the balance sheet and supporting notes are filed there must be a prominent statement on the balance sheet that the company's annual accounts and reports have been *delivered* in accordance with the provisions applicable to companies subject to the small companies regime. The copy balance sheet and notes must be accompanied by a copy of the auditor's report on the accounts sent to the members.

Abbreviated Companies Act individual accounts for a small company consist of a balance sheet and supporting notes prepared in accordance with the form and content requirements specified in the regulations[38] and must be accompanied by special auditor's report on those accounts. In this case, the required prominent statement on the balance sheet must refer to it being *prepared* in accordance with the provisions applicable to companies subject to the small companies regime.

The directors of a small company that prepare IAS individual accounts are not permitted to file abbreviated accounts. They only have a choice between filing the accounts and reports sent to its members or just the balance sheet and notes from those accounts together with auditor's report on the full accounts. In the latter case, the copy of the balance sheet must have the prominent statement about the accounts and reports being *delivered* in accordance with the provisions applicable to companies subject to the small companies regime.

6.4.8   Small companies: what are the filing requirements for ineligible companies?

A small company that is ineligible for the small companies regime only because it is a member of an ineligible group is entitled to the small companies exemption in respect of its directors' report[39]. Where this is the case, the directors must deliver to the Registrar of Companies a copy of the company's annual accounts sent to members[40]. They may, but are not required to, file a copy of the 'reduced disclosure' directors' report[41]. Unless the company is exempt from audit and advantage has been taken of that exemption, the

---

[37]   Sections 444(1)(a) and 472(2), Companies Act 2006.
[38]   SI 2008/409 The Small Companies and Groups (Accounts and Directors' Report) Regulations 2008, Schedule 4.
[39]   Section 415A, Companies Act 2006.
[40]   Section 444A(1)(a), Companies Act 2006.
[41]   Section 444A(1)(b), Companies Act 2006.

directors must also deliver a copy of the auditor's report on those accounts and directors' report[42].

The directors of small companies that are ineligible for the small companies regime and/or not entitled to the small companies exemption must file a copy of the annual accounts and reports sent to their members.

6.4.9 Medium-sized companies: what are the filing options?

The directors of a medium-sized company that prepare Companies Act individual accounts have the option of filing with the Registrar of Companies a complete copy of the annual accounts and reports sent to their members or abbreviated accounts. However, for a medium-sized company that prepares IAS individual accounts there is no choice and its directors must file a copy of the complete IAS annual accounts, the directors' report and the auditor's report as sent to the members[43].

6.4.10 Medium-sized companies: are there any changes to the form or content of abbreviated Companies Act accounts?

A significant change from the previous form of abbreviated accounts for a medium-sized company is the requirement to give the company's turnover (although there is still an exemption from disclosing a segment analysis of turnover). The Government considers that disclosure of turnover provides more transparency and information about the level of a company's trading to users of the accounts (for example, suppliers and customers).

Otherwise, the abbreviated accounts are the company's annual accounts prepared for members from which the segment analysis of turnover is omitted and the profit and loss account format is modified. This modification permits, for those companies adopting format 1 of the profit and loss account formats, the combination into one line item of cost of sales, gross profit (or loss) and other operating income, Those companies adopting format 2 may combine into one line item changes in finished goods and in work in progress, own work capitalised, other operating income, raw materials and consumables and other external charges[44]. From the point of view of the medium-sized company, the previous exemption from disclosing turnover had the advantage that the gross margin could not be determined by competitors from the filed profit and loss account because the gross profit (or loss) was disclosed without the disclosure of the turnover. However, a medium-sized company is now, in any event, required to provide a business review as part of the directors' report, including financial key performance indicators (KPIs) in its directors' report, and turnover might be considered to be a KPI thus requiring disclosure.

---

[42] Section 444A(2), Companies Act 2006.
[43] Section 445, Companies Act 2006.
[44] SI 2008/410 The Large and Medium-sized Companies and Groups (Accounts and Reports) Regulations 2008, Reg 4(3).

The company's Companies Act annual accounts for members, and thus its abbreviated accounts, can omit the disclosures about related party transactions and compliance with accounting standards[45]. These exemptions apply for accounts prepared for accounting periods commencing on or after 6 April 2008. Although medium-sized companies are exempt from certain disclosures relating to off-balance-sheet arrangements, they are required to disclose information about the nature and purpose of such arrangements. See chapter 5, section 5.3.21.

Similarly, the directors' report sent to members, and which has to be filed, can omit from its business review an analysis dealing with the development, performance or position of the business by reference to non-financial KPIs[46]. This exemption also applies to companies that cannot qualify as medium-sized companies only because they are a member of an ineligible group[47].

There is no requirement for a prominent statement on the copy of the balance sheet saying that the abbreviated Companies Act individual accounts have been prepared in accordance with the provisions applicable to medium-sized companies. However, the abbreviated accounts must be accompanied by a copy of the special report of the company's auditor on those abbreviated accounts[48].

6.4.11   Medium-sized companies: what are the filing requirements for ineligible companies?

The directors of a company that is ineligible to qualify as a medium-sized company must file with the Registrar of Companies a complete copy of the annual accounts and reports as sent to its members.

However, a company that does not qualify as medium-sized only because it is a member of an ineligible group can omit from the directors' report that part of the business review dealing with the development, performance or position of the business by reference to non-financial key performance indicators[49].

6.4.12   Medium-sized companies: are there any exemptions from, or choices for, filing group accounts?

No. A medium-sized parent company with subsidiaries must prepare group accounts, unless it qualifies as an intermediate parent company and can take advantage of the exemptions referred to below (see chapter 5, section 5.3.11).

---

[45] SI 2008/410 The Large and Medium-sized Companies and Groups (Accounts and Reports) Regulations 2008, Reg 4(2).
[46] Section 417(7), Companies Act 2006.
[47] Section 467(4), Companies act 2006.
[48] Section s445(4) and 449, Companies Act 2006.
[49] Section 467(4), Companies Act 2006.

Although the Companies Act 2006 has criteria for determining whether a parent company qualifies as medium-sized, such status confers no exemption from the preparation, or filing, of group accounts. It appears that there are no disclosure exemptions or modifications for a medium-sized company's Companies Act group accounts prepared for members or for abbreviated group accounts for delivery to the Registrar of Companies. However, it is held by BERR that the exemptions conferred by regulation 4 of the Large and Medium-sized Companies Accounts regulations for a medium-sized company's Companies Act individual accounts and abbreviated individual accounts (see section 6.4.10) are available for its Companies Act group accounts and abbreviated group accounts. This is through the operation of paragraph 1(1) of Schedule 6 to those regulations. This paragraph states:

"Group accounts must comply so far as practicable with the provisions of Schedule 1 to these Regulations as if the undertakings included in the consolidation ("the group") were a single company."

There are no disclosure exemptions or modifications if the directors prepare IAS group accounts. The full IAS group accounts must be delivered to the Registrar of Companies.

A medium-sized company that is the parent of a group must deliver to the Registrar of Companies a copy of its group accounts (as part of its annual accounts), the directors' report and the auditor's report[50] as sent to its members. Those accounts, however, can omit the company's individual profit and loss account and the notes need not include information on the company's employee numbers and costs provided that the annual accounts disclose that advantage has been taken of the exemption[51]. This publication exemption applies irrespective of whether the group accounts are Companies Act or IAS accounts.

The only exemptions from preparing and thus delivering group accounts are where the company qualifies as an intermediate parent company in either a larger EEA group or a larger non-EEA group or where all of the company's subsidiary undertakings do not need to be included in the consolidation[52].

6.4.13 Large private and all quoted companies: are there any filing options?

The directors of large private and all quoted companies must file with the Registrar of Companies a copy of the complete set of accounts and reports as sent to their members. This provision is unchanged from the Companies Act 1985.

---

[50] Sections 446 and 471, Companies Act 2006.
[51] Section 408, Companies Act 2006.
[52] Section 399(2), Companies Act 2006.

6.4.14 Do the copies of the balance sheet and the various reports filed with Registrar of Companies have to be signed?

For all companies, the copy of the balance sheet filed with the Registrar of Companies must state the name of the person who signed on behalf of the board and must be signed by a director of the company. Similarly, the copy of the directors' report and, where applicable, the directors' remuneration report must state the name of the person who signed it on behalf of the board and must be signed by a director or company secretary.

Any copy of the auditor's report on the company's annual accounts or the auditor's special report on the abbreviated accounts of a small or medium-sized company filed with the Registrar of the Companies must state the name of the auditor and (where the auditor is a firm) the name of the person who signed it as senior statutory auditor. The copy reports must be signed by the auditor or (where the auditor is a firm) in the name of the firm by a person authorised to sign on its behalf.

In circumstances where there are reasonable grounds that the statement of the name of the person who signed the report as senior statutory auditor would create or be likely to create a serious risk of violence or intimidation, the auditor's name can be omitted. However, there must be a statement that the necessary resolution of the company has been passed and notified to the Secretary of State[53].

It is not possible to sign accounts and reports physically that are filed electronically. Where this is the case, the signature is substituted by the company's authentication code (see below).

6.4.15 Can documents be filed electronically with the Registrar of Companies?

The provisions of the Companies Act 2006 dealing with the electronic delivery of documents required to be filed with the Registrar of Companies by the EU First Company Law Directive[54] apply from 1 January 2007[55]. These documents include, amongst other things, companies' annual accounts and reports. The Registrar of Companies cannot require such documents to be delivered in electronic form. However, where they are, the Registrar has the right to reject documents that do not comply with the statutory requirements.

Companies House has established an electronic filing service that enables the electronic submission of statutory documents by e-mail using specialist software. These documents must comply with the structure approved by the

---

[53] Sections 444(7), 444A(5), 445(6), 446(3), 447(4), 449(4) and (4A), Companies Act 2006.
[54] EU Directive 68/151/EEC.
[55] Sections 1068 and 1078, Companies Act 2006.

Registrar of Companies for electronic submission[56]. All documents received via the Electronic Filing Service must be authenticated by (or on behalf of) the company with the company authentication code notified by the company in writing to Companies House together with details of those responsible for presenting them.

Authentication codes are required to replace the signature on paper forms and to comply with the Companies Act. Every document filed electronically must bear the relevant company authentication code or it will be rejected.

Groups of companies can choose to have the same authentication code. However, in order to comply with the Companies Act, the code must initially be delivered to Companies House in writing by the company concerned and signed by a serving officer of the company. This may be done by presenters collating the information from the companies concerned and forwarding to Companies House with the initial application form. In this case, companies must confirm that they have authorised the particular presenter to deliver information on their behalf.

6.4.16   Are there any changes to rules about publication of statutory accounts?

No. The rules under the previous legislation have been carried forward. Essentially, these are:

(i)   whenever a company's statutory accounts are published they must be accompanied by the auditor's report on those accounts (unless the company is exempt from audit and the directors have taken advantage of that exemption); and

(ii)   a company is not allowed to publish its individual statutory accounts without publishing with them its statutory group accounts, where relevant.

Statutory accounts are the company's accounts that are required to be delivered to the Registrar of Companies, which can vary depending on a company's size or status. Therefore, they can be the annual accounts as prepared for members, which comprise a company's individual accounts and any group accounts, or other permitted forms such as abbreviated Companies Act individual accounts.

All companies' balance sheets and directors' reports and, quoted companies' directors' remuneration reports that are published by or on behalf of the company must state the name of the person who signed them on behalf of the board. If a copy of a balance sheet or a report is published without stating the

---

[56] As documented in the Software Filing Technical Interface Specification available through Companies House website *www.companies-house.gov.uk*.

signatory's name, the company and every officer of the company who is in default has committed an offence and they are liable to fines if convicted.

A company is regarded as publishing a document if it publishes, issues or circulates it or otherwise makes it available for public inspection in a manner calculated to invite members of the public generally or any class of members of the public to read it.

6.4.17 Are there any changes to the rules about publication of non-statutory accounts?

The rules are essentially the same as in the previous legislation. Any document that purports to deal with a company's, or its group's, balance sheet or profit and loss account for a financial year of the company, otherwise than as part of its statutory accounts, must state that they are not statutory accounts. The statement must also say whether statutory accounts dealing with any financial year that are covered by the non-statutory accounts have been delivered to the Registrar of Companies. In addition, the statement must say whether the auditors have reported on the statutory accounts and, if so, whether their report was qualified or unqualified, or contained a matter of emphasis, or any reservations about accounting records or returns or obtaining necessary information.

Where published non-statutory accounts deal with more than one year, the document may contain two (or more) sets of non-statutory accounts (for example, preliminary statements of the annual results of listed companies have two years that must be covered – the current year and the comparative previous year). Where this applies, the wording of the statement should be adapted so that it confirms that the statutory accounts for any previous year had been delivered to the Registrar of Companies and those for the current year will be delivered.

A company's summary financial statement that is available to the public, for example, through the company's website, is a form of non-statutory accounts, which must comply with the publication rules.

Half yearly reports issued by listed companies in compliance with the FSA DTR contain a set of non-statutory accounts – the comparative information for the last full financial year is presented in accordance with IAS 34[57].

Published non-statutory accounts must not include the auditors' report on the company's annual accounts. A company and any of its officers that do not comply with all the requirements for publishing non-statutory accounts commit an offence and they are liable to fines if convicted.

---

[57] IAS 34 'Interim financial reporting'.

6.5 Revision of defective annual accounts and reports and half yearly reports

6.5.1 Can directors still revise their company's annual accounts or reports if they believe them to be defective?

Yes. New regulations[58] under the Companies Act 2006[59] set out how the provisions of the Companies Act 2006 are applied where directors voluntarily revise the annual accounts, the directors' report, summary financial statement or, for quoted companies, the directors' remuneration report because the originals do not comply with the statutory requirements. The new regulations have replaced the previous ones with effect for accounts or reports for financial years commencing on or after 6 April 2008.

6.5.2 Can the Financial Reporting Review Panel (FRRP) or the Secretary of State still request a revision of a company's annual accounts or directors' report?

Yes. The Secretary of State is so empowered and can either request a revision or ask the directors to explain an apparent non-compliance with the law[60]. The FRRP may also request a revision but it also has the authority to apply for a court order requiring the directors to revise the annual accounts or directors' report[61].

The Defective Accounts Regulations[62] set out how the provisions of the Companies Act 2006 are applied in the circumstances of a request to revise being made by either the Secretary of State or the FRRP.

For the purposes of facilitating the FRRP in discovering whether there are any grounds for, or deciding to make an application to the courts, the Commissioners of HMRC are authorised to disclose pertinent information to the FRRP. This authority overrides any other statutory or other restrictions on disclosure of information, other than personal data that is protected from disclosure by the Data Protection Act 1998. Where a case concerns accounts subject to the FSA DTR, the FRRP, as the supervising body for issuers of listed securities, may report its findings to the FSA for action by that regulator.

Where it appears to the FRRP that there might be a question as to whether a company's annual accounts or directors' report is defective, it has powers to require any documents, information and explanations that are reasonable and relevant. Such documents, information or explanations can be obtained from

---

[58] SI 2008/373 The Companies (Revision of Defective Accounts and Reports) Regulations 2008.
[59] Section 454, Companies Act 2006.
[60] Section 455, Companies Act 2006.
[61] Section 456, Companies Act 2006 and SI 2008/623 The Companies (Defective Accounts and Directors' Reports) (Authorised Person) and Supervision of Accounts and Reports (Prescribed Body) Order 2008.
[62] SI 2008/373 The Companies (Defective Accounts and Reports) Regulations 2008.

the company, any officer, employee or auditor of the company or previous officers, employees or auditors. The FRRP can apply to the courts, if necessary, to force such persons to produce the documents or provide the information or explanations. Any statement made by a person to the FRRP under these powers cannot be used in evidence in criminal proceedings. Furthermore documents or information that are subject to legal professional privilege (or equivalent in Scotland) cannot be compelled to be disclosed.

6.5.3 Listed companies: Does the FRRP have powers to review and investigate half yearly reports?

Yes. The FRRP's powers to review and investigate for compliance with reporting requirements extend to the half yearly reports of listed companies that are subject to the FSA DTR[63]. In this capacity, the FRRP has to report any findings on those companies that it has investigated to the FSA for action by the FSA against the offending company.

6.5.4 Can a small or medium-sized company's abbreviated Companies Act accounts be revised?

The Defective Accounts Regulations provide for the revision of a company's abbreviated Companies Act accounts, where these are affected by the revision of the company's accounts prepared for members that either means that the company would not have qualified as a small or (as the case may be) medium-sized company or because the accounts have been revised in a manner which affects the content of the abbreviated accounts[64].

Even if the revision of the accounts prepared for members has no consequential effect on the abbreviated accounts, the directors must deliver to the Registrar of Companies a note stating that the annual accounts have been revised in a respect that has no bearing on the abbreviated accounts together with a copy of any auditor's report on the revised annual accounts[65].

A small or medium-sized company's abbreviated accounts may be revised if they do not comply with the requirements of the Companies Act 2006[66]. We note that the regulation uses the word 'shall' but we understand that this does not override the voluntary nature of the regime described in section 6.5.1. Accordingly, we have used the word 'may'.

6.5.5 When do the directors have to send out the revised accounts or reports?

If the original accounts or reports have already been sent to members and others entitled to receive copies (including indirect investors), the directors

---

[63] Section 14, Companies (Audit, Investigations and Community Enterprise) Act 2004.
[64] SI 2008/373, Reg 15(2).
[65] SI 2008/373, Reg 15(3).
[66] SI 2008/373, Reg 16.

must send them within 28 days of the revisions being approved copies of the revised accounts and/or reports.

In the case where accounts or reports were laid before members, the revised accounts or reports also have to be so laid at the next 'accounts meeting' or at an earlier general meeting of members.

Where the original accounts (including abbreviated accounts, where applicable) or reports have been delivered to the Registrar of Companies, the replacements (or in the case of a note stating that a company's abbreviated accounts are unaffected by the revision of the accounts prepared for members) must be filed with the Registrar within 28 days of the revision.

6.6   The EU Transparency Obligations Directive[67]

6.6.1   How does the Directive impact UK companies?

The EU Transparency Obligations Directive seeks to improve the quality, quantity and timeliness of periodic financial information produced by regulated market issuers and used by investors. It sets out requirements on the content and timing of annual and half-yearly financial reports and introduces the concept of interim management statements (IMS) for issuers of shares that do not produce quarterly reports.

The provisions of the Directive have been transposed into UK law through Part 43 of the Companies Act 2006, which in the main amends the FSMA 2000. The amendments to that Act provided the FSA (the 'competent authority') with the powers to make the disclosure and transparency rules (the FSA DTR).

The FSA DTR require:

(i)   holders of votes attached to shares in issuers to make disclosure about their holdings at certain thresholds;

(ii)   issuers to make public their annual accounts and reports, prepared in accordance with the EU-adopted IAS, and, where appropriate, half-yearly and interim management statements about their business (see section 6.6.2 to 6.6.8);

(iii)   issuers to make notification about voting rights held by themselves in respect of their own voting shares;

(iv)   issuers to notify the FSA and the market of any proposed change to their constitution; and

---

[67]   EU Directive 2004/109/EC.

(v)   issuers to disclose whether they have an Audit Committee and to include a Corporate Governance Statement as a specific section of the directors' report (see section 6.6.9 to 6.6.10).

Following the implementation of the EU Transparency Obligations Directive in the UK on 20 January 2007, the FSA LR were amended and the FSA DTR were added to the FSA Handbook. These rules are applicable to companies admitted to the Official List maintained by the FSA for all accounting periods beginning on or after 20 January 2007.

The FSA DTR requirements are very similar to, but often extend beyond, those previously contained in the FSA LR. For example, the FSA DTR set more prescriptive content requirements in certain areas, shorter deadlines for production of information and cover additional types of periodic reporting.

6.6.2   What is the period for making public a listed company's annual financial report?

A significant change is the shortening to four months from six months of the period after the year end in which a listed company must make public its annual financial report[68]. The FSA has issued a reminder that companies with financial years ending after 20 January 2008 must publish their annual report and accounts within the new four-month deadline. It has also noted that publishing a preliminary statement of annual results does not meet the requirements. The FSA has the power to suspend listing or take enforcement action where the required financial information is not published within the required deadlines and the FSA stresses that it may employ this sanction where necessary in future[69].

A listed company has to ensure that its annual financial report remains available for at least five years[70].

6.6.3   What are the contents of the annual financial report?

A listed company's annual financial report comprises:

(i)   the audited financial statements;

(ii)   a management report; and

(iii) responsibility statements.

The financial statements for a UK incorporated company are its annual accounts as drawn up to meet the requirements of the Companies Act 2006 for quoted companies. There are a few additional disclosures in the FSA LR. The

---

[68]   FSA DTR4.1.3.
[69]   UKLA *List!* Update – 6 June 2008; obtainable at *www.fsa.gov.uk/pubs/ukla/ukla_update.pdf.*
[70]   FSA DTR4.1.4.

content of the management report is nearly identical to the requirements for the directors' report under the Companies Act 2006. The FSA LR form the basis of the corporate governance requirements discussed below. The responsibility statements are addressed below.

6.6.4 Are directors' responsibility statements mandatory?

The requirement for a mandatory directors' responsibility statement is new. The practice of providing a directors' responsibility statement originated from an auditing standard's requirement that the auditor should include in their report the responsibilities of the directors for preparing the annual accounts and reports, if a statement of such responsibilities is not available elsewhere in the annual accounts or reports. This is now codified as a requirement for the auditor to include in their report a reference to a description of the relevant responsibilities of those charged with governance[71].

The Combined Code[72] provides that the directors of listed companies should explain in the annual financial report their responsibilities for preparing the accounts and that there should be a statement by the auditor about their reporting responsibilities.

For annual financial reports for financial years commencing on or after 20 January 2007, the FSA DTR[73] has added a mandatory requirement for a directors' responsibility statement. The directors must set out in the statement that to the best of their knowledge:

(i)   the financial statements, prepared in accordance with the applicable set of accounting standards, give a true and fair view of the assets, liabilities, financial position and profit or loss of the issuer and the undertakings included in the consolidation taken as a whole; and

(ii)   the management report includes a fair review of the development and performance of the business and the position of the issuer and the undertakings included in the consolidation taken as a whole, together with a description of the principal risks and uncertainties that they face.

The name and function of every director making a responsibility statement must be clearly indicated in the responsibility statement. The FSA has indicated that it does not expect this information to be cross-referenced to other documents.

As the contents of the FSA DTR directors' responsibility statement is not inclusive of all the director's responsibilities in connection with a company's annual accounts and reports, the new required statement may be combined

---

[71]   International Standard on Auditing (UK & Ireland) 700, The auditor's report on financial statements.
[72]   Combined Code (2006), provision C.1.1.
[73]   FSA DTR4.1.12.

with that made previously under the Combined Code and/or that provided for the purposes of the auditing standard.

6.6.5 Are preliminary statements of annual results still required?

For accounting periods commencing on or after 20 January 2007, preliminary statements of annual results are voluntary following the shortening to four months of the period after the year end in which a listed company must make public its annual accounts and reports. Preliminary announcements are expected to continue to be produced as they are generally considered to play a key part in the annual financial reporting cycle as they are the first public communication of companies' results for the whole year.

Where, a listed company issues a voluntary preliminary announcement it must comply with the content requirements as set out in the FSA LR[74] and be published as soon as possible after it has been approved by the board. The specified contents are unchanged from the previous requirement[75], when preliminary announcements were mandatory. The FSA has clarified that it is not the intent of the LR or DTR to require a voluntary preliminary announcement to be prepared, or for its contents to be, in accordance with IAS 34[76].

6.6.6 What are the requirements for half-yearly reports?

For accounting periods commencing on or after 20 January 2007, FSA LR[77] on half-yearly reports was withdrawn and replaced by the provisions of the FSA DTR[78]. Issuers of any shares and debt (denominated in units of less than 50,000 euro) admitted to trading on a regulated market must now publish half-yearly reports within two months of the period end[79]. A half-yearly report prepared in accordance with the DTR must include, as a minimum, a condensed set of financial statements[80], an interim management report and responsibility statements[81]. These should be prepared on a group basis where relevant[82].

If the half-yearly financial report has been audited or reviewed by auditors[83] the audit report or review report must be reproduced in full. Alternatively, if no

---

[74] FSA LR9.7A.1.
[75] FSA old LR9.7.
[76] UKLA *List!* 18 March 2008, paragraph 6.2; obtainable at *www.fsa.gov.uk/pubs/ukla/ list_mar08.pdf.*
[77] FSA LR9.9.
[78] FSA DTR4.2.
[79] FSA DTR4.2.2.
[80] Prepared in accordance with IAS 34 or if prepared using UK GAAP in accordance with the ASB Statement: Half yearly financial reports – July 2007.
[81] FSA DTR4.2.3.
[82] FSA DTR4.2.4, 4.2.7 and 4.2.10.
[83] Pursuant to the Auditing Practices Board ISRE 2410on Review of interim financial information performed by the Independent auditor of the entity.

such audit or review has been carried out there must be a statement to this effect in the half-yearly report[84].

For accounting periods beginning on or after 20 January 2007, companies are not required to send half-yearly reports by post to holders of their listed securities, or insert those reports as paid advertisements in at least one national newspaper. However, the information must still be made public within two months of the period end and disseminated to the market by a Regulatory Information Service (RIS). Every half-yearly report must be available to the public for at least five years. The FSA has clarified that the FSA DTR do not make a distinction between the information transmitted via an RIS and the information presented on the company's website and that all the required items must be included in the RIS announcement[85].

6.6.7 Is there any clarification of the rules on half-yearly interim management reports?

Yes. The FSA has clarified that the directors can meet the requirement for the interim management report to contain a "description of the principal risks and uncertainties for the remaining six months of the financial year" by:

(i)   stating that the principal risks and uncertainties have not changed from those reported in the annual report;

(ii)   providing a summary of those principal risks and uncertainties; and

(iii)   including a cross-reference to where a detailed explanation of the principal risks and uncertainties can be found in the annual report.

If the risks and uncertainties have changed since the annual report, the company should describe the new principal risks and uncertainties in the interim management report. In deciding whether to include additional description, consideration should be given to the effect of the current economic environment at the time the interim management report is prepared[86].

The FSA DTR require a "responsibility statement to be made by the persons responsible within the issuer" and also "the name and function of any person who makes a responsibility statement must be clearly indicated in the responsibility statement." While 'person' is not defined in the FSA DTR, the FSA has said that there must be an explicit statement of the names and functions of all those responsible in the responsibility statement. The FSA does not expect this information to be cross-referenced to other documents[87].

---

[84]   FSA DTR4.2.9.
[85]   UKLA *List!* 18 – March 2008, paragraph 6.1.3; obtainable at *www.fsa.gov.uk/pubs/ukla/list_mar08.pdf.*
[86]   UKLA *List!* 18 – March 2008, paragraph 6.1.1.
[87]   UKLA *List!* 18 – March 2008, paragraph 6.1.2.

6.6.8   What are the requirements for Interim Management Statements?

For accounting periods commencing on or after 20 January 2007, companies with listed ordinary shares that do not report quarterly are required to prepare and publish interim management statements (IMS)[88]. However, an IMS need not necessarily be made at the end of the first and third quarters. The FSA DTR requires that the IMS is made in a period between ten weeks after the beginning, and six weeks before the end, of the relevant six-month period[89]. For example, a company with a calendar year ending 31 December 2008 must issue its first quarter IMS between 11 March and 19 May 2008. The third quarter IMS must be issued between 8 September and 19 November 2008. The requirements do not apply to companies that only have listed preference shares or listed retail debt.

The IMS must contain information that covers the period between the beginning of the relevant six-month period and the date of publication of the statement. Therefore, although any financial data will cover the period prior to the publication of the statement, any material events or transactions up to the date of publication must be covered in the narrative.

The IMS must provide:

(i)   an explanation of material events and transactions that have taken place during the relevant period and their impact on the financial position of the issuer and its group; and

(ii)   a general description of the financial position and performance of the issuer and its group during the relevant period.

The content requirements are not extensive and the FSA has left the market to develop its own preferences; accordingly, no detailed rules on prescriptive content have been set.

There is no specific requirement for numerical data and the requirements might be met by narrative explanation alone. In practice, companies are providing selected key operating statistics. What is not required is the inclusion of a condensed quarterly profit and loss account.

6.6.9   What changes have been made in respect of corporate governance?

Part 43 of the Companies Act 2006 also gave the FSA the power to make rules implementing, or enabling the implementation of or dealing with matters arising out of EU obligations on corporate governance of issuers on regulated markets. The power given to the FSA allows it to make corporate governance

[88]   FSA DTR4.3.2.
[89]   FSA DTR4.3.3.

rules to cover issuers for whom the UK is the home Member State, and whose securities are traded on a regulated market in the UK or elsewhere in the EEA.

Following the implementation of the EU Statutory Audit Directive and the EU Company Reporting Directive[90] in 2008, the FSA DTR are amended to include further DTR on Corporate Governance[91]. These requirements apply to a UK incorporated company that has any of its transferable securities admitted to trading on any regulated market in the UK or other EEA Member States. The requirements are:

(i)   a statement that must be available to the public that the company has an Audit Committee (or equivalent body), the names of its members and how it meets the independence and competence in accounting require-ments. The latter may be met by the same or different members of the committee. In the FSA's view, compliance with the relevant provisions of the Combined Code will result in compliance with these requirements[92]; and

(ii) a Corporate Governance Statement that must be included as a specific section of the directors' report, or in a separate report published together with and in the same manner as its annual accounts and reports, or by means of a reference in its directors' report as to where such document is publicly available on the company's website[93].

The Corporate Governance Statement must contain the following[94]:

(i)   a reference to the corporate governance code to which the company is subject or which it has decided to apply voluntarily or provide all relevant information about the corporate governance practices applied beyond the requirements of national law. If the company does not use a corporate governance code, it must explain its reasons for deciding not to apply a corporate governance code, must make those practices publicly available and state in the directors' report where they can be found;

(ii) a statement as to where the relevant corporate governance code is publicly available and, to the extent that the company departs from that code, explain which parts of the code it departs from and the reasons for doing so. In the FSA's view, a company that follows the 'comply or explain' rule[95] in relation to the Combined Code will satisfy the requirements where a code is followed;

[90] EU Directives 2006/43/EC and 2006/46/EC respectively.
[91] FSA Consultation Paper 7/24 (December 2007) proposed that DTRs 1B and 7 should come into force for financial reporting periods beginning on or after 29 June 2008.
[92] FSA DTR7.1.7.
[93] FSA DTR7.2.1 and 7.2.9.
[94] FSA DTR7.2.2 to 7.2.10.
[95] FSA LR9.8.6(6).

(iii) a description of the main features of the company's and, where applicable, its group's internal control and risk management systems in relation to the financial reporting process (including those in relation to preparing consolidated accounts);

(iv) information about share capital required under the Takeover Directive's disclosures that must be given in the directors' report[96] (where the company is subject to those disclosure requirements); and

(v) a description of the composition and operation of the company's administrative, management and supervisory bodies and their committees. In the FSA's view, the information specified in the relevant provisions of the Combined Code will satisfy this requirement.

6.6.10   Are there any changes to the Combined Code (2006)?

The Combined Code (2006) has been updated to:

(i) remove the restriction on an individual chairing more than one FTSE 100 company; and

(ii) allow the chairman of a listed company below the FTSE 350 to be a member of, but not chair, the audit committee provided they were considered independent on appointment.

The revised code applies for accounting periods beginning on or after 29 June 2008. In practice, this means most companies will apply it in 2009, and will report against the revised provisions for the first time in 2010.

6.6.11   Are there any penalties or liability for compensation for breaches of the transparency or corporate governance rules or for making false or misleading statements?

Yes. The Companies Act 2006 amended the FSMA 2000 to provide the FSA with the power to levy penalties or issue censure statements generally on any issuer that the FSA believes has contravened a provision of the transparency or corporate governance rules. If the FSA considers that a director of the issuer at the time of the contravention was knowingly concerned in the contravention it may impose upon them a penalty (or censure statement) of such amount as it considers appropriate[97].

Although, no issuer has previously been found liable to damages under English law in respect of statements in narrative reports or financial statements, the law relating to financial markets and to obligations of issuers to investors on those markets has been developing, in light of increased regulation of both domestic

---

[96] SI 2008/410 the Large and Medium-sized Companies and Groups (Accounts and Reports) Regulations 2008, Schedule 7, paragraph 13.
[97] Section 91(1B), FSMA 2000

and European origin. There has been an increased level of uncertainty as to whether any actionable duty is owed by an issuer and its directors to investors. To provide clarity in this uncertain area of the law, the FSMA 2000 is amended to provide a regime of civil liability to third parties by issuers admitted to trading on a regulated market in respect of disclosures made public under the FSA DTR.

The Government's intention is to ensure that the potential scope of liability is reasonable, in relation both to expectations and the state of the law after implementation of the Transparency Objective Directive. The Government was anxious not to extend unnecessarily the scope of any duties that might be owed to investors or wider classes of third parties, in order to protect the interests of company members, employees and creditors[98].

The new civil liability regime provides that a UK incorporated company, which has any of its securities traded on a regulated market, is liable to pay compensation to any person that has acquired any of its securities and has suffered a loss on them. The acquirer has to demonstrate that they suffered the loss as a result of relying on a false or misleading statement, or the omission of a material matter required to be made, in the issuer's periodic financial information published in accordance with the FSA LR and DTR. The periodic financial information concerned is a company's:

(i)   annual report;

(ii)   half yearly report;

(iii)   interim management statements; and

(iv)   any mandatory or voluntary preliminary statement of results[99].

As noted in Chapter 5, Section 5.4.8, the Companies Act 2006[100] provides directors with a 'safe harbour' from civil liability for statements or omissions in the directors' report and the directors' remuneration report (including any summary financial statement derived from those reports) or any narrative reporting that is expressly cross-referenced into the directors' report. Directors are liable to the company not to third parties. However, the 'safe harbour' provision does not affect any liability for a civil penalty or for a criminal offence.

With an ever increasing litigious environment, company secretaries may need to bolster their internal resources or ensure that they have access to legal advisers to review all aspects of narrative reporting.

---

[98]   Explanatory Notes to the Companies Act 2006, paragraphs 1636 to 1643.
[99]   Section 90A(1), FSMA 2000.
[100] Section 463, Companies Act 2006

6.7 Conclusion

6.7.1 List of key changes and actions

Section	Key change	Action required
6.2.3	Abolition of the statutory AGM for private companies, effective 1 October 2007.	Review the company's articles to determine if AGM is required. If not, consider whether AGM should be held on a voluntary basis.
6.2.4	For public companies, AGMs must be held within six months of the end of the financial year, effective 1 October 2007. (Previously, AGM would be required in each calendar year with no more than 15 months between AGMs).	Consider timing of AGMs.
6.2.5	For quoted companies, statement of shareholders' audit concerns to be published on the companies' websites.	Company secretaries need to ensure that procedures are in place to deal with the administration of such requests. Directors, the audit committee chairman and the auditors need to prepare responses to the questions raised and identify who is best to answer them.
6.3.3 to 6.3.7	New provisions regarding electronic and website communication with shareholders, applicable from 20 January 2007.	Determine which, of the company's communications with shareholders should be electronic or by website. To the extent not already authorised by shareholders, put a resolution to members to obtain authorisation for electronic/ website communication. Obtain individual authorisation for electronic or website communication from shareholders. Develop systems for maintaining e mail addresses of shareholders, if appropriate.

Changes in financial reporting

Section	Key change	Action required
6.3.9 to 6.3.10	New statutory 'shareholder and information rights' for indirect investors, effective 1 October 2007.	Develop systems to allow shareholders to nominate another party to 'receive shareholder rights' or 'information rights'. Liaise with Registrars. Amend company's articles to permit exercise of shareholders' rights for indirect investors. (Amendment of articles will not be required in respect of 'information rights').
6.3.11	New requirement for quoted companies to publish accounts on a website, applicable for financial years beginning on or after 6 April 2008.	Determine whether the accounts are to be published on the company's own website and, if not, determine on which website maintained on the company's behalf, the accounts will be published.
6.4.2 and 6.6.2	Reduction in periods allowed for filing accounts (ten months to nine months for private companies, seven months to six months for public companies, six months to four months for listed companies).	Ensure that internal reporting deadlines are advanced to enable the new time limits to be observed.
6.4.5	Increased fines for late filing of accounts and reports.	Ensure that internal reporting deadlines are observed and allow sufficient time for completion of the audit process (where required).
6.4.6	For medium-sized parent companies loss of the exemption from preparing and filing group accounts. Group accounts with comparatives need to be prepared for financial years beginning on or after 6 April 2008 (for example, December 2009 for calendar year companies).	Ensure that reporting timetable is expanded to allow for capture of necessary information and for the preparation and audit of the group accounts. Consider when and how to capture information and prepare comparative group accounts.

Section	Key change	Action required
6.6.2, 6.6.6 and 6.6.8	For listed companies, changes to the timing of the content and publication of annual reports and half yearly reports and the introduction of interim management statements for quarters one and three.	Ensure that directors, company secretaries and finance personnel are familiar with the requirements of the FSA DTR.
6.6.9 to 6.6.10	For listed companies, Corporate Governance Statement is a statutory requirement for financial periods commencing on or after 29 June 2008. Some changes to the content and position of disclosures from that recommended by the Combine Code.	Company secretaries should familiarise themselves with the new requirements and look to see how best to reformat the Corporate Governance Statement and the directors' report.
6.6.11	Imposition of fines or public censure for breaches of the transparency and corporate governance rules and a new civil liability regime for making false or misleading statements in narrative reporting.	Company secretaries may need to review their resources and access to legal advisers to review all aspects of narrative reporting.

Chapter 7

Working with the auditors

7.1   Introduction 7001
     7.1.1   Scope of this chapter 7001
     7.1.2   What is different and what stays the same? 7002
     7.1.3   When does the new legislation come into force? 7003
7.2   Requirement for audited accounts 7004
     7.2.1   Are there changes to the requirement for an audit? 7004
     7.2.2   Small companies: are there any exemptions from audit? 7005
     7.2.3   Small companies in the financial services sector: are there
             any changes to the audit exemption? 7006
     7.2.4   Dormant companies: are they still exempt from audit? . . 7006
     7.2.5   Dormant companies in the financial services sector: can
             they claim an exemption from audit? 7006
     7.2.6   Audits of small charitable companies: what are the
             changes? 7007
     7.2.7   Audits of public sector companies: what are the changes? 7007
     7.2.8   Medium-sized companies: is there an audit exemption? . . 7007
     7.2.9   Small and medium-sized companies abbreviated
             Companies Act accounts: is there a special form of audit
             report? 7007
7.3   Appointment of auditors 7008
     7.3.1   What's new and what's not? 7008
     7.3.2   Private companies: what are the changes? 7008
     7.3.3   Public companies: are there any changes? 7010
     7.3.4   Terms of all audit appointments: what has to be
             disclosed? 7011
     7.3.5   Disclosure of auditor remuneration: are there any
             changes? 7012
7.4   Functions of auditors 7013
     7.4.1   Are there any changes to auditors' access to a company's
             and its group's accounting records and personnel 7013
     7.4.2   Are directors required to make voluntary disclosures to the
             auditor? 7013
     7.4.3   How and when should relevant audit information be
             communicated to the auditor? 7014
     7.4.4   What are the implications of auditors' communications
             with directors? 7015
     7.4.5   The auditor's report: are there any changes or differences
             between private and public companies? 7015
     7.4.6   What are the changes related to signing the auditor's
             report? 7017

7.4.7 Does the 'senior statutory auditor' have to sign the copy audit reports that are filed with the Registrar of Companies? 7017

7.4.8 Who is the 'senior statutory auditor'? 7017

7.4.9 What happens if the senior audit partner changes during the reporting period or is unable to be present to sign the audit report? 7018

7.4.10 What happens when there are joint auditors? 7018

7.4.11 What if the senior statutory auditor is at risk from violence or intimidation? 7018

7.4.12 In what circumstances does an auditor commit a criminal offence in connection with auditor's report? 7019

7.4.13 What behaviour is caught by the new offence? 7020

7.5 Removal and resignation of auditors 7020

7.5.1 What's new and what's not? 7020

7.5.2 Is there a change to reporting auditor resignations and removals? 7020

7.5.3 Are there any differences between an auditor's cessation statement for unquoted and quoted companies? 7021

7.5.4 When must the auditor deposit their cessation statement with the company? 7022

7.5.5 What are a company's duties in relation to the auditor's cessation statement? 7022

7.5.6 When does an auditor's cessation require notification to regulators? 7023

7.5.7 What is a 'major audit'? 7023

7.5.8 Which audit authority must the auditor notify? 7024

7.5.9 Who must the company notify? 7025

7.5.10 Who must notify the accounting authorities on a change of auditors? 7025

7.6 Auditors' liability 7026

7.6.1 What's new and what's not? 7026

7.6.2 What is a 'liability limitation agreement'? 7026

7.6.3 What authority must the company have to enter into such an agreement? 7026

7.6.4 What is fair and reasonable? 7027

7.6.5 What guidance is there on preparing liability limitation agreements? 7027

7.6.6 What are the main issues? 7028

7.6.6.1 The nature of the arrangements 7028

7.6.6.2 Directors' responsibilities 7028

7.6.6.3 The reaction of the SEC 7028

7.6.6.4 The meaning of 'fair and reasonable' as applied to limitation of liability arrangements 7028

7.7 Statutory auditors 7029

7.7.1 What's new and what's not? 7029

7.7.2　What change has been made to the 'statutory auditor'
　　　　category? 7029
7.7.3　Does this affect the regulation of auditors of building
　　　　societies, industrial and provident societies and friendly
　　　　societies? 7029
7.7.4　Are there any requirements imposed on auditors of
　　　　companies incorporated outside the EU – Registered third
　　　　country auditors? 7029
7.8　Conclusion 7031
7.8.1　List of key changes and actions 7031

Chapter 7

Working with the auditors

7.1 Introduction

7.1.1 Scope of this chapter

This chapter deals with Part 16 (Audit) and Part 42 (Statutory Auditors) of the Companies Act 2006. Part 16 covers matters relating to the appointment and functions of auditors, and their removal and resignation. Part 42 covers other provisions relating to auditors, covering matters such as eligibility for appointment as auditors and supervision of auditors.

Parts 16 and 42 bring together various provisions on the audit of companies from the Companies Act 1985, the Companies (Audit, Investigations and Community Enterprise) Act 2004 and the Companies Act 1989. They also introduce a number of significant changes to the law on auditing. Much of the law in this area reflects EU Company Law Directives, including parts of the Fourth, Seventh and Eighth Company Law Directives, and of the new Statutory Audit Directive[1], which replaces the Eighth Directive.

The new EU Statutory Audit Directive seeks to enhance confidence in financial reporting by strengthening the EU framework of standards and public oversight for the audit profession. This is achieved by substantially revising the previous framework with regards to audits, including introducing key provisions in areas such as auditing standards, public oversight, auditor independence, third country auditors (auditors from non-EU countries) and a definition of an auditor's network and ownership.

However, the UK framework for statutory audits is well established, through a combination of provisions, including the Companies Act 1989, the delegation of some powers to parts of the Financial Reporting Council (FRC), such as the Professional Oversight Board (POB), the standards set by the Auditing Practices Board (APB) and the Audit Regulations of the Recognised Supervisory Bodies (the accountancy institutes). Therefore many of the provisions of the new Statutory Audit Directive are already in place in the UK and thus the changes are fewer than perhaps faced by other EU Member States.

Two of the principal changes to be found in Part 16 of the Companies Act 2006 are the requirement for the senior statutory auditor to sign audit reports and provisions that allow for liability limitation agreements for auditors.

---

[1] EU Directives 78/660/EEC, 83/349/EEC, 84/253/EEC and 2006/43/EC respectively.

In line with harmonising EU regulation, the European Commission also has the aim of boosting the EU economy and, in particular, reducing the administrative burden on small or medium-sized companies. Although accounting and auditing directives have significantly raised the quality of financial reporting and auditing in the EU, the existing requirements under these directives can be unnecessarily burdensome for small and medium-sized entities[2].

The European Commission is currently considering this issue in the midst of others as part of a simplification project for such entities.

7.1.2   What is different and what stays the same?

The majority of the legislation simply re-enacts the requirements of the Companies Act 1985, albeit in a different format. The provisions of Part VII of the Companies Act 1985 relating to audit are replaced by provisions in Part 16 of the Companies Act 2006. As with Part 15 (Accounts and Reports), the legislation is written from the private company perspective first with provisions applying to public companies shown as a modification of those requirements.

Significant changes from previous legislation contained in Part 16 are derived mainly from the new EU Statutory Audit Directive and are found in the following areas and in the case of items (i) to (viii) below[3]:

(i)   audit exemptions for certain public sector clients;

(ii)   removal of special rules for charities;

(iii)   term of office and appointment procedures for auditors of private companies;

(iv)   disclosure on terms of engagement;

(v)   modifications of the auditor's report;

(vi)   signature on audit report;

(vii)   new criminal sanctions for the inclusion of false or deceptive material matters in an audit report;

(viii) transparency around auditor resignations and removals;

(ix)   rights of quoted company shareholders to raise audit concerns at Annual General Meetings ('AGM') (see chapter 6, section 6.2.5); and

(x)   limitation of auditor liability.

---

[2]   Draft EU legislation: Communication from the commission on a simplified business environment for companies in the areas of company law, accounting and auditing (24 July 2007).

[3]   Based on explanatory notes to the Companies Act 2006.

In terms of Part 42[4], most of the legislation is re-enacted from the Companies Act 1989, with changes stemming from the new EU Statutory Audit Directive. These changes include the following:

(i)   to extend the category of auditors that are subject to regulation; and

(ii)   introduce new provisions relating to Third Country Auditors.

Legislation re-enacted from the Companies Act 1985 in Part 16 includes:

(i)   the requirement for company accounts to be audited and the existing exemptions (except for the special provisions about charities);

(ii)   the way in which shareholders appoint a company's auditors for public companies;

(iii)   rules on auditors' remuneration and the disclosure required of services provided by them;

(iv)   the auditor's responsibility in relation to the directors' report and the directors' remuneration report; and

(v)   duties and rights of auditors.

Whilst legislation re-enacted from the Companies Act 1989 in Part 42 includes:

(i)   provisions relating to the eligibility for appointment as statutory auditors;

(ii)   the effect of appointment of a partnership as statutory auditors;

(iii)   eligibility/independence regime in respect of auditors appointed (there are minor changes);

(iv)   provisions relating to supervisory bodies and their exemptions from liability for damages;

(v)   the requirement for appropriate qualifications and the definition of qualifying bodies that provide this qualification;

(vi)   approval of overseas qualification; and

(vii)   requirements around the register of auditors.

7.1.3 When does the new legislation come into force?

The majority of Part 16 (Audit) is in force from 6 April 2008, but only applicable to audits for financial years commencing on or after that date. However, the provisions[5] relating to appointment of auditors of private

---

[4]   Based on explanatory notes to the Companies Act 2006.
[5]   Sections 485 to 488, Companies Act 2006.

companies apply to the audits of accounts for financial years beginning on or after 1 October 2007.

New provisions that apply to audits for financial years commencing on or after 6 April 2008 include:

■   The requirement that an audit report be signed by an individual (the senior statutory auditor); and the new criminal sanctions relating to audit reports[6].

New provisions that came into effect immediately on 6 April 2008 include:

(i)   the statements that auditors have to make when ceasing to hold office[7] apply to all departures on or after that date; and

(ii)   the new rules allowing auditors and companies to agree limitations of the auditor's liability.

All of the provisions relating to Part 42 will be applied to the audits of accounts for financial years beginning on or after 6 April 2008.

7.2   Requirement for audited accounts

7.2.1   Are there changes to the requirement for an audit?

The general requirement for accounts of companies to be audited and the relevant exemptions from audit (for companies subject to the small companies regime) have been re-enacted from the Companies Act 1985. However, this obligation[8] is now expressed as a duty on the company to have its accounts audited. Previously it was expressed as a duty on the auditors to audit the accounts. This change is to reinforce that it is the responsibility of the directors to ensure the company's accounts are audited while auditors have a responsibility to audit those accounts once they are appointed as the company's auditors.

There are two changes from the existing law in this area. One is to remove the special rules for the audit of the accounts of small charitable companies and to put such companies out of the scope of the audit provisions of the Act. The second removes certain companies that are audited by public sector auditors from the scope of the audit provisions of the Act.

---

6   Section 507, Companies Act 2006.
7   Sections 519 to 525, Companies Act 2006.
8   Section 475, Companies Act 2006.

7.2.2 Small companies: are there any exemptions from audit?

Yes. Consistent with the previous legislation, companies that are not part of a group, are subject to the small companies regime and meet certain conditions are exempt from audit. The criteria for being within the small companies regime are set out in chapter 5.

Besides meeting the qualifying criteria to be within the small companies regime, the company must not have received a notice of a requirement to obtain an audit from members holding in total 10% or more of the nominal value of its issued share capital or 10% or more of a particular class of share. If the company does not have share capital, the notice must be given by 10% or more of the members. The notice must be given after the start of the financial year to which it relates but no later than one month before the end of that year.

Furthermore, a company is not entitled to the exemption unless, as required by sections 475(2), (3) and (4) of the Companies Act 2006, its balance sheet contains a statement above the name and signature required by section 414 of that Act to the effect that:

(i)   the company is entitled to the exemption under section 477 (small companies) of the Companies Act 2006;

(ii)   the members have not required the company to obtain an audit of its accounts for the year in question; and

(iii)   the directors acknowledge their responsibilities for complying with the requirements of the Act with respect to accounting records and the preparation of accounts.

A small company that is a parent company or a subsidiary undertaking cannot claim the exemption, unless the whole group qualifies as a small and is not an 'ineligible group'[9]. However, as noted in chapter 5, the definition in the Companies Act 2006 of an 'ineligible group' has been modified and some small group companies previously excluded may be able to claim the exemption for their accounts for financial years commencing on or after 6 April 2008.

Previously, a group was an 'ineligible group' if any of its members (a parent or subsidiary undertaking or fellow subsidiary undertaking) was a body corporate (essentially any entity equivalent to and including a UK company) having the power to issue its shares or debentures to the public. This rule is relaxed in the Companies Act 2006 such that a group is only ineligible if the securities of the body corporate (other than a UK company) are admitted to trading on a regulated market in an European Economic Area (EEA) state. However, the existence within a group of a UK public company will still make the group ineligible.

---

[9]   Sections 384(2) and (3), Companies Act 2006.

A company that is a parent company or a subsidiary undertaking for any part of a financial year can be entitled to the exemption from audit if it was both a subsidiary undertaking and dormant throughout the whole of the period or periods during the financial year when it was a subsidiary undertaking.

7.2.3 Small companies in the financial services sector: are there any changes to the audit exemption?

As discussed in chapter 5, there are changes caused by the transposition of the EU Markets in Financial Instruments Directive (MiFID)[10] that replaced the previous EU Investments in Securities Directive (ISD). These changes apply to the accounts and audit of MiFID companies for financial years ending on or after 1 November 2007.

Generally, small companies that were ISD companies and are now MiFID companies cannot claim the audit exemption. However, small companies that were not ISD companies but are MiFID companies are exempt from the accounting and auditing requirements of the Companies Acts 1985 and 2006 for their accounts for financial years that began before 1 November 2007 but ended on or after that date.

7.2.4 Dormant companies: are they still exempt from audit?

Yes. The law has been re-enacted and companies that have been dormant since their formation or have been dormant since the end of the previous financial year, subject to certain conditions, are exempt from audit. The conditions are that the company is subject to the small companies regime and is not required to prepare group accounts.

A public company or a member of an ineligible group can still claim the audit exemption if they would have qualified for the small companies regime but for being such a company or member of such a group. Again they should not be required to prepare group accounts.

7.2.5 Dormant companies in the financial services sector: can they claim an exemption from audit?

A dormant company that is an authorised insurance company, a banking company, an e-money issuer, a MiFiD firm, a UCITS[11] management company or one that carries on insurance market activity cannot claim the audit exemption.

---

[10] EU Directive 2004/39/EC.
[11] Undertaking for Collective Investment in Transferable Securities as defined in the Glossary forming part of the Handbook made by the FSA under the FSMA 2000; obtainable at *http://fsahandbook.info/FSA/html/handbook/Glossary.*

7.2.6 Audits of small charitable companies: what are the changes?

Small companies that are charities were under the previous legislation subject to audit, or to an accountant's report. Such requirements are removed[12] for charitable companies that would fall within the small companies regime with effect for financial years beginning on or after 1 April 2008 and are replaced by the charity law accounts scrutiny provisions. These provisions are in force from 1 April 2008 under the Charities Act 2006 (Charitable Companies Audit and Group Accounts Provisions) Order 2008 (SI 2008/527).

7.2.7 Audits of public sector companies: what are the changes?

A new provision[13] exempts certain public sector bodies from audit[14]. This clarifies for certain non-commercial, public sector bodies constituted as companies that are audited by a public sector auditor that they are not subject to the audit requirements of the Companies Act 2006. Such companies will be audited by the National Audit Office on behalf of the UK Comptroller and Auditor General. This recognises that although the directors of these companies are held accountable, their accountability is for a different purpose than would apply to a private sector company.

7.2.8 Medium-sized companies: is there an audit exemption?

No. All companies that qualify as medium-sized must have an audit.

7.2.9 Small and medium-sized companies abbreviated Companies Act accounts: is there a special form of audit report?

Yes. The auditor's special report must state whether in their opinion the company is entitled to deliver abbreviated accounts and those accounts to be delivered are properly prepared in accordance with Regulation 3 of The Small Companies Accounts regulations or Regulation 4 of The Large and Medium-sized Companies Accounts regulations, as appropriate[15]. If the auditors' report on the company's annual accounts is qualified, the special report must set out that report in full together with any further material necessary to understand the qualification. Similarly, any statement included in the auditor's report on the annual acounts about inadequate accounts, records or returns or accounts not agreeing with the records and returns, or about a failure to obtain necessary information or explanations must be reproduced in full in the special report[16].

---

[12] Section 1175 of and Schedule 9 to the Companies Act 2006.
[13] The Government's response to Lord Sharman's report 'Holding to Account' *www.hm-treasury.gov.uk/media/7/8/dao0702a.pdf*.
[14] Section 482, Companies Act 2006.
[15] SI 2008/409, SI 2008/410 and s449(2) of the Companies Act 2006.
[16] Section 449(3), Companies Act 2006.

7.3 Appointment of auditors

7.3.1 What's new and what's not?

The Companies Act 2006 broadly re-enacts the existing law on the way in which shareholders appoint a company's auditors. As explained below, there are some changes for private companies relating to the auditor's term of office and the reappointment of auditors that apply for financial years beginning on after 1 October 2007.

The provisions have been reorganised to deal with private and public companies separately.

New regulations dealing with disclosure of auditors' remuneration and liability limitation agreements[17] are in force for financial years commencing on or after 6 April 2008. These regulations are virtually identical to the requirements in the previous regulations issued in 2005, with the exception of introducing an exemption from disclosure of fees for services paid to a 'distant associate' of an auditor and introducing new disclosures about auditors' liability limitation agreements.

In addition, the Companies Act 2006 introduces a new power for the Secretary of State to require disclosure of the terms of audit appointments[18]. At the time of writing, although the disclosure applies for auditors appointed for financial years commencing on or after 6 April 2008, the necessary regulations have not been published.

7.3.2 Private companies: what are the changes?

The Companies Act 2006 re-enacts the general requirement for auditors to be appointed annually each year by shareholders by ordinary resolution, unless a company is taking advantage of an exemption from audit. However, this requirement is tempered by the two changes referred to below dealing with the term of appointment and the automatic reappointment of incumbent auditors. These provisions of the Act are in force for appointments for financial years beginning on or after 1 October 2007[19]. In essence, the detail about the appointment of auditors is only relevant for the appointment of a company's first auditors or for new auditors.

For appointments for financial years beginning before 1 October 2007, the provisions of the Companies Act 1985 continue to apply. In addition, the transitional provisions make clear that where a private company has elected to

---

[17] The Companies' (Disclosure of Auditor Remuneration and Liability Limitation Agreements) Regulations 2008 (SI 2008/489).

[18] Section 493, Companies Act 2006.

[19] SI 2007/2194 The Companies Act 2006 (Commencement No.3, Consequential Amendments, Transitional Provisions and Savings) Order 2007, Schedule 3, paragraph 44.

dispense with the annual appointment of auditors, and the election is in force immediately before 1 October 2007, this does not mean that the incumbent auditors cannot be deemed to be automatically re-appointed because they had been, in effect, appointed by the directors[19]. Automatic reappointment under the Companies Act 2006 is not permitted where the auditors were appointed by the directors (see below).

The general requirement for any financial year after the first is that the audit appointment must be made before the end of the period of 28 days from the end of the time allowed for circulation to a company's shareholders of its accounts for the previous year. The time allowed for accounts to be sent to shareholders is linked to the permitted time period for filing those accounts with the Registrar of Companies. This is the maximum period allowed for appointing an auditor. Nothing prevents a company appointing its auditor earlier, other than the new auditor cannot take office until any previous auditor has ceased to hold office.

This 28-day period effectively commences from the earlier of the date on which the accounts for the previous year are filed, or the end of the period allowed for filing those accounts, with the Registrar of Companies. For example, a private company with a 31 December 2008 year end has to file its accounts for that year by 30 September 2009. If the company waits until that day to file its accounts with the Registrar of Companies, its 28-day period to appoint auditors for the financial year ending 31 December 2009 ends on 28 October 2008. If the company files its December 2008 accounts on 31 July 2009, the 28-day period to appoint auditors for 2009 expires on 28 August 2009.

In the first year of a company's existence (or for the first year after a period of audit exemption), the directors can appoint the company's first auditors[20]. The directors also have the right to fill a casual vacancy.

If a company fails to appoint its auditors within the allotted period, it must inform the Secretary of State within one week of the end of that period. Failure to do so will result in a fine. In these circumstances, the Secretary of State has the power to appoint an auditor[21].

The two important changes from the existing legislation[22] that simplifies most private companies' administration relating to the audit appointment are:

(i) Auditors are now deemed to be reappointed (subject to certain exceptions (see below) unless the company decides otherwise. Previously the auditors had to be appointed annually unless the company had elected (by elective resolution under the previous elective regime) to dispense with the obligation to appoint auditors annually.

---

[20] Section 485, Companies Act 2006.
[21] Section 486, Companies Act 2006.
[22] Sections 485(2) and 487, Companies Act 2006.

(ii)   If new auditors are to be appointed, the existing auditor's term of office is deemed to run from the end of the 28-day period allowed for the appointment of auditors (see above) until the end of the corresponding period the following year, unless the auditor is reappointed. This will apply even if the auditors are appointed at a meeting where the company's accounts are laid. (Private companies are not required to lay accounts in general meetings under the Companies Act 2006 but some may decide to do so voluntarily). The change made in the Companies Act 2006 is connected to the removal of the obligation for private companies to hold an Annual General Meeting.

The exceptions to the deemed reappointment arise in the following circumstances:

(i)   the auditors were appointed by the directors, or

(ii)   the company's articles require actual reappointment, or

(iii)   the deemed reappointment is prevented by the members[23] or

(iv)   the members have resolved that auditors should not be reappointed, or

(v)   the directors have resolved that no auditors should be appointed for the financial year in question.

In these cases the auditors will need to be appointed again[24].

When there is a change of auditors, the term of office of the incoming auditors does not begin before the end of the previous auditors' term. This means that a new auditor's term will typically begin immediately after the end of the 28-day period for appointing auditors referred to above.

Members with at least 5% of the voting rights in a private company can prevent an auditor being automatically reappointed by giving notice to the company. The company's articles can enable members to do this with less than 5% of the voting rights, but cannot increase the required percentage. The notice may be in hard copy or electronic form but must be authenticated by the person giving it, and must be received by the company before the end of the financial year for the accounts that the current auditor is auditing[25].

7.3.3   Public companies: are there any changes?

There are no changes in the procedure for appointment of auditors for public companies. The re-enacted provisions apply to appointments for financial

---

[23]   Section 488, Companies Act 2006.
[24]   Section 487, Companies Act 2006.
[25]   Section 488(3), Companies Act 2006.

years beginning on or after 6 April 2008[26]. As previously, auditors of a public company hold office until the end of the meeting at which the accounts are laid, unless reappointed. Where there is a change of auditors, the term of office of the incoming auditors does not begin before the end of the previous auditor's term. This means that a new auditor's term will typically begin immediately after the end of the meeting where accounts are laid[27]. This is different to private companies as explained above.

The auditors of a public company must be appointed for each financial year of the company, unless the directors reasonably resolve otherwise on the ground that audited accounts are unlikely to be required. They do not have 'deemed re-appointment' as a choice, which is the case for private companies.

The directors also have the right to fill a casual vacancy[28].

In a situation where the company's shareholders fail to appoint the auditors, the Secretary of State has the same powers as for a private company and can appoint the auditors (see above). The same regulations in terms of reporting to the Secretary of State and fines in cases of failure to report also apply.

7.3.4 Terms of all audit appointments: what has to be disclosed?

The key change here is that the Secretary of State has been given the power to create regulations (subject to the Parliamentary affirmative resolution procedure) that would require companies to disclose information about the terms on which they engage their auditors[29]. Although the Secretary of State has this power from 6 April 2008 the necessary regulations have not been published at the time of writing. The requirements could apply to both private and public companies.

Auditors set out the terms of their appointment in engagement letters which are agreed with the client. The regulations may require disclosure of a copy of an auditor's engagement letter and, if necessary, a written memorandum of any terms that are not in writing. The regulations can require disclosure of changes in terms as well as the terms at the time of appointment.

The power allows the Secretary of State to decide when the terms should be disclosed and a number of choices as to the place and means of disclosure. The place of disclosure could be in the notes to the accounts, or the directors' report or the auditor's report.

---

[26] SI 2007/3495 The Companies Act 2006 (Commencement No.5, Transitional Provisions and Savings) Order 2007, Schedule 4, paragraph 10.
[27] Section 491, Companies Act 2006.
[28] Section 489(3), Companies Act 2006.
[29] Section 493, Companies Act 2006.

As indicated earlier, no regulations (even in draft) have yet been released and thus the disclosure requirements have not yet come into force. Indications are that there is a lack of enthusiasm within BERR for taking this forward.

If and when this disclosure requirement comes into effect, the clause in an audit engagement letter likely to be of most public interest is any limitation of liability agreed between the auditor and client. However, disclosure of the existence of such an agreement in a note to the company's annual accounts[30] is already in force for financial years commencing on or after 6 April 2008.

7.3.5 Disclosure of auditor remuneration: are there any changes?

For all companies that have auditors, the provision regarding the fixing of auditor's remuneration is in force for financial years beginning on or after 6 April 2008. It reinstates the existing requirement for the remuneration to be fixed by ordinary resolution or in such a manner as the members may by ordinary resolution determine. Remuneration includes sums paid in respect of expenses and any benefits in kind[31].

The disclosure of auditor remuneration, in their capacity as auditors, and also in respect of services other than audit, remains largely unchanged. The new regulations[32] apply to accounts for financial years beginning on or after 6 April 2008. The previous exemptions from disclosure for small and medium-sized companies are carried forward in the new regulations.

There is one small relief introduced by the new regulations from disclosure of amounts paid for the supply of services to a 'distant associate' (as defined[33]) of a company's auditor. The disclosure is not required if the amount receivable by the 'distant associate' is less than £10,000 or 1% of the total audit remuneration received by the company's auditor in the auditor's relevant financial year[34].

Frequently asked questions on auditors' remuneration are found in the Institute of Chartered Accountants in England and Wales (ICAEW) Technical release Tech 6/06 (revised in July 2007)[35]. The new regulations apply to all companies incorporated in Great Britain and in Northern Ireland.

---

[30] SI 2008/489 The Companies (Disclosure of Auditor Remuneration and Limitation of Liability Agreements) Regulations 2008, Reg 8.

[31] Section 492, Companies Act 2006.

[32] Section 494, Companies Act 2006 and SI 2008/489The Companies (Disclosure of Auditor Remuneration and Limitation of Liability Agreements) Regulations 2008.

[33] SI 2008/489 The Companies (Disclosure of Auditor Remuneration and Limitation of Liability Agreements) Regulations 2008, Schedule 1, paragraph 4.

[34] SI 2008/489 The Companies (Disclosure of Auditor Remuneration and Limitation of Liability Agreements) Regulations 2008, Reg 5(6).

[35] Obtainable from the ICAEW's website at *http://www.icaew.com/index.cfm?route=143686*.

7.4 Functions of auditors

7.4.1 Are there any changes to auditors' access to a company's and its group's accounting records and personnel?

The rules about auditors' access to accounting records and personnel were tightened up in the Companies (Audit, Investigations and Community Enterprise) Act 2004. Consequently, they have been re-enacted without amendment in the Companies Act 2006. The statutory rights of auditors cannot be restricted in any way.

The rules provide that auditors have a statutory right of access, at all times, to the company's accounting records and to require from its officers and employees such information as the auditors think necessary for the performance of their duties[36]. Directors must therefore ensure that the auditors have all the information they need. However, directors are not required to disclose to auditors any information in respect of which a claim to legal professional privilege could be maintained in legal proceedings[36] although this might lead to a qualified audit report if the auditor fails to obtain such information and explanations as they think necessary for the performance of their duties.

Further, the auditor of a parent company may require information and explanations from UK subsidiary undertakings and their auditors. In relation to overseas subsidiary undertakings, the auditor can require the company to seek from that undertaking or its officers, employees or auditors, such information as the auditor considers necessary[37].

A person who knowingly or recklessly makes a statement to the auditor in the course of their audit that is misleading, false or deceptive in a material particular is guilty of a criminal offence, as is any person who delays in complying with a request for information[38].

7.4.2 Are directors required to make voluntary disclosures to the auditor?

In effect, yes. Directors are required to include a disclosure in the directors' report to the effect that:

> 'so far as each director is aware there is no information, needed by the auditor ('relevant audit information'), of which the auditor is unaware; and that each director has taken all the steps, as required by the duty to exercise reasonable care, skill and diligence, to make themselves

---

[36] Section 499, Companies Act 2006.
[37] Section 500, Companies Act 2006.
[38] Sections 499 to 501, Companies Act 2006.

aware of such information and to establish that the auditor is aware of it[39].'

If this disclosure contains a statement that is false, a director is guilty of a criminal offence if he knows of or was reckless as to the falsehood and failed to take all reasonable steps to prevent the directors' report from being approved.

The legislation specifies that the steps the director ought to have taken, which include (but are not limited to) making enquiries of his fellow directors and of the auditor. This requirement, in effect to ensure that information is obtained and passed on, is closely related to the requirement upon the directors to prepare accounts that give a true and fair view and comply with the Companies Act 2006.

The information required for the accounts, and the processes and oversight of its production, usually form the basis of relevant audit information. The additional challenges for directors are in relation to the measure of individual responsibility of each director and to the communication of the information to the auditor.

In the usual way, under the duty to exercise reasonable care, skill and diligence, more is expected of a director with an executive function and, similarly, more is also be expected of a director having specifically relevant knowledge, skills and experience. However, as the Explanatory Notes to the predecessor legislation make clear, this is not a requirement that each director should ensure that they and every other director have each disclosed all relevant audit information. Rather, the requirement might be characterised as one relating to the information that the individual has or ought reasonably to have and requiring the directors to communicate with each other so far as necessary to capture all relevant audit information and communicate it to the auditor.

7.4.3 How and when should relevant audit information be communicated to the auditor?

To meet the legislative requirement it is not sufficient for the directors to ask the auditor whether they have all the information that they require; more pointedly the auditor will not answer such a question. Communication with the auditor should be made at relatively frequent intervals and involves more than just the final audit meeting. There should, for example, be consideration of the auditor's plan for the audit and whether there are risks hitherto unknown to the auditor that they have not planned for. It is, however, difficult to generalise on this topic. The arrangements for the identification and communication of relevant audit information will vary according to the size and complexity of any particular company's circumstances.

---

[39] Sections 418(2) and (3), Companies Act 2006.

Directors may be asked by the company's auditors to make written representations to confirm information on which the auditors have placed reliance in forming an opinion on the annual accounts. Such confirmations are sought as part of the auditors' duty to obtain audit evidence, and, in accordance with auditing standards, when the matter is material to the accounts and other sufficient appropriate audit evidence cannot reasonably be expected to exist. To comply with auditing standards, directors are asked to include in written representations an acknowledgement of their responsibility for internal controls and a statement that the directors believe that the effect of uncorrected accounts misstatements, identified by the auditor, are immaterial.

7.4.4 What are the implications of auditors' communications with directors?

It is a requirement of auditing standards that an auditor reports to the directors after an audit, drawing attention to any weakness in internal controls identified during the audit, although this is not a comprehensive list of all weaknesses that may exist. While there are no specific legal requirements relating to such reports, directors should consider them with care. The auditors may request a reply to the points raised in the management report and, in certain cases, may request that the directors' discussion of the report be recorded in the board minutes. Such a report may contain information that should put the directors on enquiry as to the existence of inadequacies in their company's systems or personnel. This is particularly relevant to companies on the Official List; for such companies the FSA LR require the company to state in its annual report that it complies with the Combined Code[40]. This provides that the board, in particular its audit committee, should conduct an annual review of effectiveness of internal controls and report that fact to shareholders[41].

7.4.5 The auditor's report: are there any changes or differences between private and public companies?

The Companies Act 2006[42] re-enacts, with modifications, the provisions of the Companies Act 1985 as to what should be included in an auditor's report on a company's accounts.

There is no real difference between private companies and public companies. In both cases, the audit report has to be included in the annual accounts and reports for shareholders. For a private company, it has to send out those accounts and reports to its members before the expiry of the time period for filing them with the Registrar of Companies. A public company has to lay its annual accounts and reports before its members at an accounts meeting (normally the AGM) and it has to send its members a copy of those accounts and reports at least 21 days before the date of that meeting.

---

[40] FSA LR9.8.6(6).
[41] Combined Code 2006, paragraphs C.2.1 and C.3.2, which is obtainable from the FRC's website *www.frc.org.uk/corporate/combinedcode.cfm*.
[42] Sections 495 to 497, Companies Act 2006.

The basic duty to produce an audit report and the requirement that it should set out the way the auditor has approached the audit remain unchanged. The audit report wording is structurally different but the content is virtually identical to current reports in that it provides opinions on whether the accounts:

(i) give a true and fair view;

(ii) have been properly prepared in accordance with the relevant financial reporting framework (that is, IFRSs as adopted by the European Union or UK GAAP); and

(iii) have been prepared in accordance with the requirements of the Companies Act 2006 (and, where applicable, Article 4 of the IAS Regulation[43]).

and, in respect of the directors' report and (for quoted companies) the directors' remuneration report whether:

(i) the information given in the directors' report is consistent with the accounts[44]; and

(ii) the auditable part of the directors' remuneration report has been properly prepared in accordance with the Companies Act 2006[45].

The audit report is required to be either qualified or unqualified, though it is open to the auditor to draw attention to aspects of the audit without qualifying the report.

Consistent with the Companies Act 1985, the auditor is required to report certain matters by exception, for example, if the auditor is of the opinion that adequate accounting records have not been kept.

The new structure to the audit report applies to financial years commencing on or after 6 April 2008. This new structure addresses perceptions that the opinion in relation to the 'true and fair view' had been diluted by the manner in which references to the accounting framework (EU-adopted IFRS or UK GAAP) were made. The APB will during 2008 issue revised guidance on the audit report wording, incorporating the above.

Additionally, the APB is currently considering how the audit report might be changed in the light of International Standard on Auditing 700 (revised), which has not yet been adopted in the UK, and recommendations from the ICAEW's Audit Quality Forum on how to make the audit report more helpful to users. These recommendations address areas such as improving readability of audit reports through use of different fonts, or removal of some wording to an

---

[43] EC Regulation No 1606/2002 of the European Parliament and the Council of 19 July 2002.
[44] Section 496, Companies Act 2006.
[45] Section 497, Companies Act 2006.

appendix. More fundamentally, it has been suggested that positive statements should be made on the adequacy of the accounting records and the fact that there are no matters of emphasis that auditors wish to draw attention to. Consequently, the revised guidance may include other potentially significant changes to the audit report.

7.4.6 What are the changes related to signing the auditor's report?

Previously, where the auditors are a firm, the audit engagement partner signed the audit report in the name of the firm. However, the Companies Act 2006[46] makes a change from this practice as a result of the EU Statutory Audit Directive. This requires that, where the auditor is a firm, the audit report is signed by the 'senior statutory auditor' (defined below) in their own name, for and on behalf of the audit firm. The signature must be dated.

Where the auditor is an individual, the audit report should be signed in their name. Again, the signature must be dated.

This change applies for audit reports in respect of accounts for financial years beginning on or after 6 April 2008.

7.4.7 Does the 'senior statutory auditor' have to sign the copy audit reports that are filed with the Registrar of Companies?

No. Copy audit reports for filing with the Registrar of Companies must state the name of the individual auditor or the senior statutory auditor, as appropriate. It has to be signed by the individual auditor or (where the auditor is a firm) in the name of the firm by a person authorised to sign on its behalf[47]. This person need not be the senior statutory auditor.

7.4.8 Who is the 'senior statutory auditor'?

The APB was appointed by the Secretary of State to issue guidance on the meaning of the term 'senior statutory auditor', in the absence of European standards on this topic[48]. The APB has determined that the term 'senior statutory auditor' equates to the term 'engagement partner' when used in International Standards on Auditing (ISAs) (UK and Ireland)[49].

Accordingly, in most cases, the person signing the audit report is the same person that has previously signed a company's audit report albeit just in the name of the firm.

---

[46] Section 503, Companies Act 2006.
[47] Section 444(7) as amended by paragraph 6 of the Companies Act 2006 (Commencement No.5, Transitional Provisions and Savings) order 2008 (SI 2007/3495).
[48] Section 504, Companies Act 2006 and Article 11 of the Statutory Auditors (Delegation of Functions etc) Order 2008 (SI 2008/496).
[49] Paragraph 5 of the APB Bulletin 2008/6 The 'Senior Statutory Auditor' under the United Kingdom Companies Act 2006.

For a person to be a senior statutory auditor, they must also be eligible for appointment as auditor of the company in question (discussed in Part 42 of the Companies Act 2006). Part 42 also ensures that for an individual to be nominated as senior statutory auditor will not affect their exposure to liability in any way.

7.4.9 What happens if the senior audit partner changes during the reporting period or is unable to be present to sign the audit report?

In the case of a change of the senior statutory auditor (that is, the engagement partner) it is the new senior statutory auditor that takes responsibility for signing.

In circumstances where the senior statutory auditor is unable to continue to take responsibility for the direction, supervision and performance of the audit, the audit firm appoints a replacement and it is treated as change of senior statutory auditor as described above.

In situations where the senior statutory auditor is absent but is still able to, and does, control the direction, supervision and performance of the audit, the senior statutory auditor may sign the audit report using electronic means (for example, e-mail or fax).

In other situations, it would be expected that audit firms would have a contingency plan in place to cover situations where the audit is at an advanced stage but the senior statutory auditor is unable to sign the audit report. *In extremis*, it might be possible for the engagement quality control reviewer to be appointed as a replacement senior statutory auditor. This, however, would mean appointing a new engagement quality control reviewer[50].

7.4.10 What happens when there are joint auditors?

Each of the auditing firms appointed as joint auditors appoints a senior statutory auditor and all of these persons are required to sign the audit report. The names of both firms will also be stated.

7.4.11 What if the senior statutory auditor is at risk from violence or intimidation?

Every copy of the auditor's report published by or on behalf of the company, must state the name of the auditor and (where the auditor is a firm) the name of the person who signed it as senior statutory auditor. The only time the company is exempt from providing this information is if it meets the following conditions:

---

[50] APB Bulletin 2008/6 'The Senior Statutory Auditor under the United Kingdom Companies Act 2006'.

(i)   the company resolves on reasonable grounds that the statement of the auditor's name would create or be likely to create a serious risk that the auditor or senior statutory auditor, or any other person, would be subject to violence or intimidation, and

(ii)   the company has given notice of the resolution to the Secretary of State, stating:

- the name and registered number of the company,

- the financial year of the company to which the report relates, and

- the name of the auditor and (where the auditor is a firm) the name of the person who signed the report as senior statutory auditor.

This particular change applies to audit reports relating to accounts with financial years beginning or after 6 April 2008 as discussed above.

7.4.12   In what circumstances does an auditor commit a criminal offence in connection with auditor's report?

The Companies Act 2006[51] contains a new provision that makes it a criminal offence for an auditor, punishable by a fine, if they knowingly or recklessly allow an audit report on the annual accounts to include any matter that is misleading, false or deceptive.

This provision applies to financial years commencing on or after 6 April 2008. The offence is also committed if the auditor knowingly or recklessly causes the incorrect omission in an audit report of:

(i)   a statement that company's accounts do not agree with accounting records and returns;

(ii)   a statement that necessary information and explanations have not been obtained; or

(iii)   a statement that directors wrongly took advantage of exemption from obligation to prepare group accounts.

The above three matters are those that auditors are required to report by way of exception. Although, the auditors have other matters that are reportable, these were considered to involve too much subjective judgement to include in a criminal penalty regime if the auditor fails to report them[52]. The test of recklessness does not include a test of dishonesty, which is covered separately under the Fraud Act 2006.

---

[51] Section 507, Companies Act 2006.
[52] Section 498, Companies Act 2006 contains a full list.

7.4.13 What behaviour is caught by the new offence?

The new requirement stemmed from the Government's original concept of a criminal offence for auditors who exhibit a criminal character in giving their audit reports, that is, those who behave dishonestly or fraudulently. BERR is of the view that the words 'knowingly and recklessly' is a standard construct in English law and that 'reckless' behaviour requires a high degree of criminal intent. However, there is a concern in the auditing profession that the use of these words, together with others aspects of these sections, will result in criminal charges where there has been an honest mistake or the behaviour was at worst negligent.

It is noted that the Explanatory Notes to the Companies Act 2006 state that in respect of liability for false or misleading statements in reports (section 4.6.3) auditors remain liable only to the company for negligence in preparing their report.

7.5 Removal and resignation of auditors

7.5.1 What's new and what's not?

The Companies 2006 Act restates the law concerning auditors ceasing to hold office[53]. The basic rules governing the rights of a company to remove its auditor, and the ability of an auditor to resign from office, remain unchanged. However the significant change is the introduction of a new reporting regime when auditors leave office. There are also some modifications resulting from the changes elsewhere in the Companies Act 2006 relating to written resolutions of private companies.

The change to the reporting regime discussed below is part of a series of regulatory and statutory changes designed to strengthen shareholders' and creditors' access to information, as well as to provide better information to regulators in relation to audits. Whilst inevitably increasing the number of auditors' cessation statements, which can make for rather uninteresting reading, the requirements also increase the chances of shareholders and creditors receiving information of additional value.

The new reporting regime applies from 6 April 2008 and, therefore, catches any change of auditor on or after that date.

7.5.2 Is there a change to reporting auditor resignations and removals?

The Companies Act 2006 increases the transparency around auditor resignation and removals. The new approach builds on the existing law by

---

[53] Section 388 and sections 391 to 391A, Companies Act 1985 are restated as sections 510 to 518, Companies Act 2006.

adding new reporting obligations on auditors regarding resignation, particularly in relation to the statutory audits of quoted companies and other statutory audits of major public interest. Importantly, and for the first time, companies themselves will, in many circumstances, also have a duty to report directly to the appropriate audit authorities the reason why the auditors are standing down before the end of their term, and they should be mindful of their new obligations when they change auditors.

The provisions of the Companies Act 2006 address the EU Statutory Audit Directive's requirement that Member States must ensure that statutory auditors are 'dismissed only where there are proper grounds' and that the public oversight bodies are given 'adequate explanation of the reasons' for any resignation or dismissal[54].

As noted above, the purpose of the change in legislation is to ensure that shareholders, creditors and regulators receive all the information they require in relation to changes in auditors. Failure to comply with these new requirements is a criminal offence for the auditors. This regime also mirrors elements of regimes established in other countries. For example, in the USA, the Securities Exchange Commission (SEC) rules require an issuer to make a public disclosure (a 'Form 8-K statement') if there is an occurrence of any material event or change that would be important to investors/security holders and the information has not been previously disclosed.

7.5.3 Are there any differences between an auditor's cessation statement for unquoted and quoted companies?

The Companies Act 2006[55] differentiates between quoted and unquoted companies in relation to the auditor's written statements of circumstances on removal or resignation.

The rules on the contents remain the same as before in relation to unquoted companies[55]. The written statement should include any matters connected with their ceasing to hold office that the auditor considers should be brought to the attention of the members or creditors of the company. If there are no such matters, the auditor must give a statement to that effect. The auditor is the sole judge of whether any particular matter requires reporting.

However, for quoted companies, the auditor must always describe the circumstances connected with their ceasing to hold office. The auditor has no discretion about whether or not the circumstances connected with their ceasing to hold office are of a sufficient level of interest and relevance that members or creditors should be notified.

---

[54] Article 38 of the Statutory Audit Directive (2006/43/EC).
[55] Section 519, Companies Act 2006.

7.5.4   When must the auditor deposit their cessation statement with the company?

Irrespective of whether the company is unquoted or quoted, the Companies Act 2006 sets out deadlines by when the auditor must deposit their statement at the company's registered office, namely:

(i)   if the auditor is resigning, the statement should accompany the resignation letter;

(ii)   if the auditor is not seeking reappointment, the statement should be deposited at least 14 days before the end of the time allowed for appointing the next auditor; or

(iii)   in any other case, no more than 14 days after the date on which they stop being the auditor.

Should the company wish to challenge any written statement made by the auditors, there are rules in terms of the application to court.

7.5.5   What are a company's duties in relation to the auditor's cessation statement?

Unless the departing auditor's statement says that there are no circumstances to be brought to the attention of shareholders and creditors (unquoted companies only), the company is required to circulate the statement to all persons entitled to receive its annual accounts. The company must do this within 14 days of receiving the auditor's statement.

Alternatively, within the same time period, if the directors consider the contents of the statement to be defamatory they can apply to the court for an order not to circulate the statement. The company must notify the auditor of the court application. If after 21 days from depositing their statement with the company, the auditor has received no notification from the company that it has made a court application, the auditor must file their cessation statement with the Registrar of Companies within a further seven days, that is, within a total of 28 days from depositing the statement at the company's registered office. The time limits and required actions are critical and companies that wish to make applications to the court should take care to ensure that they are observed. Otherwise, the statement will be filed with the Registrar of Companies and hence will be a matter of public record.

The court can direct that the auditor's cessation statement should not be circulated if it is satisfied that the auditor is using their statement to secure needless publicity for a defamatory matter. In particular, case law has held that the company needs to establish a motive on the part of the auditor bordering on the dishonest. If an application to the court is successful, the company must send within 14 days of the court's decision a statement setting out the effect of the order to all those entitled to receive its annual accounts. If the application fails or is discontinued, the company must within 14 days of the court's decision send the auditor's cessation statement to those entitled to receive the annual accounts and notify the auditor. Within seven days of receiving this notification, the auditors must send a copy of their cessation statement to the Registrar of Companies[56].

Where the auditor's cessation statement is made by an auditor of a quoted company and it contains price sensitive information then, as under the Companies Act 1985, the directors should be alert to the risk that any challenge by the company to the release of the auditor's statement may be seen by the FSA as an attempt to delay timely disclosure.

7.5.6 When does an auditor's cessation require notification to regulators?

There are new requirements for auditors and some companies[57] respectively to report to regulators. These requirements have to be considered carefully because they apply in different ways depending on whether:

(i)   the audit constitutes a 'major audit' under the Companies Act 2006; or

(ii) in the case of an audit that is not a major audit, the auditor ceases to hold office before the end of their term of office.

7.5.7 What is a 'major audit'?

A major audit is defined[58] as a statutory audit conducted in respect of:

(i)   a UK incorporated company with equity and/or debt securities admitted to the Official List maintained by the FSA on the date on which the auditor ceases to hold office. Where the listed equity or listed debt has been issued by a separate entity within a group structure, the audit of the any group accounts including the entity should be considered as a major audit. This includes Plus Markets PLUS-listed companies[59]; or

(ii) any other person in whose financial condition there is a major public interest.

The POB[59], has published statutory guidance[59] on those audits that fall within category (ii) above and are thus also classified as 'major audits'. These follow, where possible, the scope of inspections by the POB's Audit Inspection Unit (AIU) in relation to companies, though there are some important differences.

---

[56] Section 521, Companies Act 2006.
[57] Sections 522 and 523, Companies Act 2006.
[58] Section 525, Companies Act 2006.
[59] Guidance on Notification of Change of Auditor issued by the Professional Oversight Board is obtainable from *www.frc.org.uk/pob/regulation/auditfirms.cfm*.

(i)   All UK incorporated companies traded on the LSE's AIM or Plus Markets 'PLUS-quoted' market on the date on which the auditor ceases to hold office. (The AIU scope is restricted to companies with a market capitalisation in excess of £100million.)

(ii) Unquoted companies, which have either:

   ■   Group turnover in excess of £500million; or

   ■   Group long term debt in excess of £250million and turnover in excess of £100million.

   This category is intended to include companies or groups of companies that are privately owned, whether directly or through another UK or overseas investment vehicle, or trust. It is also intended to include those companies owned by private equity funds or other institutions. It is not intended to include subsidiaries of any other category in this list. This matches the AIU scope. The requirement to notify POB applies in respect of companies who meet one of the above criteria, as shown in the last set of audited accounts.

(iii) Unquoted companies or groups which are subsidiaries of foreign parent companies where the turnover of the UK group or company is in excess of £1,000 million.

   This category is intended to cover major subsidiaries of overseas groups. If there are a number of separate subsidiaries trading in the UK and no UK group consolidated accounts are produced, this measure should be applied on an individual company basis. This matches the AIU scope. The requirement to notify POB applies in respect of companies who meet above criterion, as shown in the last set of audited accounts.

(iv) Charitable companies with income exceeding £100million. This matches the AIU scope. The requirement to notify POB applies in respect of companies who meet the above criterion, as shown in the last set of audited accounts.

(v)   Subsidiary companies of any of the above. These may be treated as a 'major audit'. This avoids the need in the case of groups to notify different audit authorities in respect of different companies in the group.

7.5.8   Which audit authority must the auditor notify?

Where an auditor ceases to hold office before the end of their term for a statutory audit that does not qualify as a 'major audit', the auditor must notify their Recognised Supervisory Body (which is the accountancy institute with which they are registered and which is responsible for the direct regulation of the auditor).

In the case of a 'major audit', the auditor must notify the POB when they cease to hold office for any reason.

This notice must inform the appropriate audit authority that the auditor has left office and be accompanied by a copy of the auditor's cessation statement discussed above. Where that statement says that there are no matters that need to be brought to the attention of members or creditors, the auditor, nevertheless, must give the regulator a statement of the reasons for their ceasing to hold office.

In case of a 'major audit', the copy of the auditor's cessation statement must be deposited with the POB at the same time as it is with the company. In case of any other statutory audit, the appropriate audit authority specifies the deadline. However, it cannot be earlier than that required for a 'major audit'.

7.5.9 Who must the company notify?

Where an auditor ceases to hold office before the end of their term of office for any statutory audit, the company also has to notify either the POB if it is a 'major audit' or, in all other cases, the auditor's Recognised Supervisory Body, as the appropriate audit authority. The company must give this notice within 14 days after the date on which the auditor deposited their cessation statement at the company's registered office.

This notice must also be accompanied by either a:

(i)   a statement by the company of the reasons for the auditor ceasing to hold office, or

(ii)   a copy of the auditor's cessation statement, where that contains details of the circumstances relating to the auditor's departure.

The POB's website[60] provides two useful pages with flowcharts and notes to assist companies and auditors to identify the appropriate audit authorities that must be informed when an auditor ceases to hold office.

7.5.10 Who must notify the accounting authorities on a change of auditors?

The reports to regulators do not stop there. The appropriate audit authorities must refer the notices of auditors ceasing to hold office to the accounting authorities that have the authority to take companies to court for having defective accounts. These are the FRRP for public and large private companies and BERR for medium-sized companies and those small companies that require an audit or have not taken advantage of any audit exemption. This means that a company whose auditor ceases to hold office early, or, for any major audit, ceases to hold office for any reason may, as a result, find its accounts under scrutiny.

---

[60] Obtainable from the FRC's website at *www.frc.org.uk/pob/regulation/auditfirms.cfm*.

7.6 Auditors' liability

7.6.1 What's new and what's not?

Changes that permit auditors to enter into agreements with audit clients to limit their liability are in effect from 6 April 2008, as part of the introduction of the Companies Act 2006. The law now permits such agreements, but does not require them. Previously, such agreements had been rendered null and void under the Companies Act 1985[61].

7.6.2 What is a 'liability limitation agreement'?

A 'liability limitation agreement' is defined by the Companies Act 2006[62] as:

> 'an agreement that purports to limit the amount of a liability owed to a company by its auditor in respect of any negligence, default, breach of duty or breach of trust, occurring in the course of the audit of financial statements, of which the auditor may be guilty in relation to the company.'

Such agreements are only valid for one financial year at a time. The Secretary of State has the power to specify which provisions can and cannot be included in such agreements but the Government has indicated that this power will only be used if problems arise in practice.

7.6.3 What authority must the company have to enter into such an agreement?

When companies and their auditors enter a liability limitation agreement (LLA), the board has to secure shareholder authorisation for the agreement to take effect. The authorisation for such an agreement depends on whether the company is public or private. For public companies, approval must be obtained at a General Meeting. The members of a private company can pass a resolution waiving the need for approval. As an LLA cannot cover more than one financial year, it has to be renewed every year.

Members of a private or a public company can pass a resolution before an agreement is signed approving its principal terms, or can approve the agreement after it is signed. The resolution may be an ordinary resolution, unless a higher threshold is set in the company's articles.

The Companies Act 2006 does not specify how the limitation of liability should be arranged but states that any arrangements to limit liability are not effective except to the extent they are 'fair and reasonable'. Even where an LLA has

[61] Section 310, Companies Act 1985.
[62] Section 534, Companies Act 2006.

been authorised by members, a court can override those with liability limits that it considers to be unfair or unreasonable and can substitute its own limit.

Since limitation of liability must be approved by shareholders in public companies at a General Meeting, in practical terms this means that for quoted companies with a calendar year end, AGMs in Spring 2009 are the earliest opportunity to obtain such approval. However, chairmen may receive questions from the floor at AGMs in 2008.

7.6.4 What is fair and reasonable?

In determining what is fair and reasonable, the court cannot take into account matters arising after the loss or damage was incurred or matters (whenever arising) affecting the possibility of recovering compensation from other persons liable in respect of the same loss or damage. This is intended to prevent the court from making auditors liable for more than their 'fair share' of the loss or damage simply because they are the 'last one standing'[63].

The Companies Act 2006 permits liability to be limited either by a cap on the total amount which can be claimed or by a limit on the proportion of the loss or damage that can be claimed or both, subject to the agreement being deemed to be fair and reasonable. Concerns have been expressed that the 'cap' approach will give the large audit firms an unfair competitive advantage as smaller firms will not be able to match them; on the other hand, a 'proportionate' approach can lead to the auditor being responsible for loss or damage that is life-threatening to the audit firm and excessive when compared with the audit fee. BERR intends to keep such agreements under review and to bring in regulations to address undesirable practice should the need arise.

7.6.5 What guidance is there on preparing liability limitation agreements?

The FRC has issued[64] guidance and practical assistance for directors, auditors and shareholders considering how to apply the new legislation. This guidance was written by a working group comprising members from business, investors and auditors. The FRC's guidance:

(i)   explains what is and is not allowed under the Companies Act 2006;

(ii)   sets out some of the factors that will be relevant when assessing the case for an agreement;

(iii)   explains what matters should be covered in an agreement, and provides specimen clauses for inclusion in agreements; and

---

[63] Section 537, Companies Act 2006.
[64] Obtainable at the FRC's website at *www.frc.org.uk/publications/pubs.cfm*.

(iv)   explains the process to be followed for obtaining shareholder approval, and provides specimen wording for inclusion in resolutions and the notice of the general meeting.

7.6.6   What are the main issues?

7.6.6.1 The nature of the arrangements

Limitation of liability is a term which covers several possible types of arrangement. The FRC has provided specimen terms and clauses which address arrangements for (1) proportionality, (2) a 'fair and reasonable' test and (3) a fixed cap.

7.6.6.2 Directors' responsibilities

To agree to a limitation of liability clause, it is expected that directors will wish to have clarity on how such an agreement accords with their other responsibilities, including their fiduciary duties. It is unlikely that directors or shareholders would surrender lightly the current legal rights connected with 'joint and several' responsibility. It is expected that they will look for guidance that explains how any agreement fits with their responsibilities.

7.6.6.3 The reaction of the SEC

This has a direct bearing for UK companies that are registered with the SEC as Foreign Private Issuers, ('FPIs'). Currently the SEC does not permit any limitation of liability arrangements in connection with audit reports filed with them and accordingly for UK FPIs, the SEC's reaction is important. Although the SEC has indicated that it will reconsider the position in light of the FRC guidance, there can be no presumption that limitation of liability will ever be possible for FPIs or indeed the timescale upon which is might be possible. This directly affects approximately 30% of the FTSE 100. It is expected that multi-national companies that are not registered with the SEC will be interested to note the position that applies to their SEC-registered peers.

7.6.6.4 The meaning of the term 'fair and reasonable' as applied to limitation of liability arrangements

Here it is simply too early to predict the position with certainty. It is expected that the FRC's guidance will help steer a court in their consideration of the issues in a particular case. However, it is case law itself that will ultimately determine this.

7.7   Statutory auditors

7.7.1   What's new and what's not?

Part 42 generally restates regulatory requirements surrounding auditors from the Companies Act 1989 as to who can and cannot be appointed. The modifications and new provisions which have been introduced in, and through regulations[65] made under, the Companies Act 2006 relate primarily to an extension of the 'statutory auditor' category and requirements in respect of 'third country' auditors.

7.7.2   What change has been made to the 'statutory auditor' category?

The main purpose of Part 42 is:

(i)   to secure that only persons who are properly supervised and appropriately qualified are appointed as statutory auditors; and

(ii)   to secure that audit by persons so appointed are carried out properly, with integrity and with a proper degree of independence.

7.7.3   Does this affect the regulation of auditors of building societies, industrial and provident societies and friendly societies?

Yes. To achieve more consistency of regulation of auditors, from 6 April 2008 the existing regulatory regime for 'company auditors' appointed under Part 16 is extended to cover auditors of building societies and auditors of those industrial and provident societies or friendly societies that are banks or insurance undertakings. All existing auditors will have to register as 'statutory auditors'. These provisions apply to the appointment of auditors for financial years beginning on or after 6 April 2008[66].

7.7.4   Are there any requirements imposed on auditors of companies incorporated outside the EU – Registered third country auditors?

The Companies Act 2006 introduces requirements applicable to the auditors of companies incorporated outside the EU whose transferable equity securities are admitted for trading on a regulated market in the UK, such as the London Stock Exchange 'Main Market' or Plus Market's 'PLUS-listed market'.

This requirement stems from the EU Statutory Audit Directive and the basic premise is that all auditors should be subject to an equivalent minimum level of regulation, regardless of whether the issuer is incorporated within or outside the EU. These provisions are important because for the first time non-EU

---

[65]   SI 2007/3494 Statutory Auditors and Third Country Auditors Regulations 2007.
[66]   Section 1210, Companies Act 2006 and Statutory Instrument 2007/3495, 'The Companies Act 2006 (Commencement No 5,Transitional Provisions and Savings) Order 2007.

companies with a listing in the UK will be required to engage auditors who meet EU regulatory requirements. They are also important because of the large and growing numbers of non-EU listings in the UK.

The Companies Act 2006 sets out the definition of a third country auditor and a registered third country auditor as above and the various provisions these auditors have to follow[67]. The requirements relating to their duties, their qualification, appointments and matters that must be notified to the Secretary of State are identical to those for auditors in the UK. Third country auditors must also participate in the UK's independent monitoring and investigation arrangements of auditors[68].

The definition of a third country auditor and the provisions dealing with powers of Secretary of State are in force from 6 April 2008. The provisions dealing with the duties of these auditors and the requirements for notification of information to the Secretary of State apply from 29 June 2008[69].

---

[67] Sections 1241 to 1247, Companies Act 2006.
[68] Schedule 12 to the Companies Act 2006.
[69] Statutory Instrument 2007/3495, The Companies Act 2006 (Commencement No 5, Transitional Provisions and Savings) Order 2007.

7.8 Conclusion

7.8.1 List of key changes and actions

Section	Key change	Action required
7.1.2 and 6.2.5	For quoted companies, statement of shareholders' audit concerns to be published on the companies' websites.	Company secretaries need to ensure that procedures are in place to deal with the administration of such requests. Directors, the audit committee chairman and the auditors need to prepare responses to the questions raised and identify who is best to answer them.
7.3.2	Deemed automatic re-appointment of auditors of private companies for financial years beginning on or after 1 October 2007.	Ensure that none of the circumstances listed prevent the automatic reappointment of incumbent auditors.
7.5.1, 7.5.5, 7.5.6, 7.5.7 and 7.5.9	New reporting regime for companies on the resignation and removal of their auditors for all cessations from 6 April 2008.	Ensure that the duties on the company are met within the relevant time periods to notify the appropriate 'audit authorities' (where appropriate).
7.5.5	Short time period if a company wishes to challenge in the court a matter in the auditor's cessation statement.	Ensure that the auditor's cessation statement is dealt with promptly as it becomes a matter public record within 28 days of being deposited with the company.
7.6	Auditors' liability: limitation of liability agreements, applicable to audits of accounts for financial years beginning on or after 6 April 2008.	Company secretaries and directors to familiarise themselves with the FRC guidance. Discuss with auditors. Plan to obtain necessary approval from shareholders.

Chapter 8

Share capital and transactions involving shares

8.1	Introduction	8001
	8.1.1 Scope of this chapter	8001
	8.1.2 What are the most common types of shares?	8002
	8.1.3 What rights are inherent in a share?	8004
	8.1.4 What steps are taken on incorporation relating to share capital?	8004
	8.1.5 What is the difference between a 'member' and a 'shareholder'?	8005
	8.1.6 What is the 'nominal value' of a share?	8006
	8.1.7 Why is the nominal value of a share important?	8006
	8.1.8 Can a company issue shares of no par value?	8007
	8.1.9 What changes are being made to issues of redeemable shares?	8007
8.2	What legal considerations arise when increasing the issued share capital of a company?	8008
	8.2.1 What company law issues arise?	8008
	8.2.2 What are the main regulatory issues?	8009
	8.2.3 What is the difference between an 'allotment' and an 'issue' of shares?	8010
8.3	Is a company still required to have an authorised share capital?	8011
	8.3.1 What changes are introduced by the Companies Act 2006?	8011
	8.3.2 Is any action required before 1 October 2009?	8011
8.4	Do directors still need shareholder authority to allot shares in a company?	8011
	8.4.1 What must the authorisation include prior to 1 October 2009?	8012
	8.4.2 What about offers or agreements made before the authorisation expires but under which 'relevant securities' are allotted after expiry?	8012
	8.4.3 How can a company renew, revoke or vary the authorisation?	8013
	8.4.4 What are the filing requirements?	8013
	8.4.5 What changes are introduced by the Companies Act 2006?	8013
	8.4.6 Summary of the position before and after implementation of the Companies Act 2006	8014
	8.4.7 Is any action required before 1 October 2009?	8015
8.5	What statutory pre-emption rights do shareholders have?	8016
	8.5.1 What is a right of pre-emption?	8016

	8.5.2	To whom must the pre-emption offer be made?	8017
	8.5.3	On what terms must the pre-emption offer be made? . . .	8017
	8.5.4	How is notice of the offer given?	8018
	8.5.5	Can a company exclude or disapply the pre-emption requirements?	8018
		8.5.5.1 What is the position before 1 October 2009? . .	8018
		8.5.5.2 What is the position from 1 October 2009? . . .	8019
	8.5.6	What are the sanctions for non-compliance with these provisions?	8019
	8.5.7	Is any action required before 1 October 2009?	8020
	8.5.8	Summary of the position before and after implementation of the Companies Act 2006	8020
8.6	What steps must be taken after allotment?		8022
	8.6.1	What changes are introduced by the Companies Act 2006?	8022
	8.6.2	What post-allotment steps must be taken under the Companies Act 1985?	8022
		8.6.2.1 Filings	8022
		8.6.2.2 Issue of share certificates	8023
		8.6.2.3 Update the statutory registers	8023
	8.6.3	What post-allotment steps need to be taken on or after 1 October 2009?	8023
		8.6.3.1 Filings at Companies House	8023
		8.6.3.2 Issue of share certificates	8024
		8.6.3.3 Register the allotment and update the statutory registers	8024
	8.6.4	How do these requirements apply to unlimited companies?	8025
	8.6.5	What are the penalties if a company does not comply with the requirements?	8025
	8.6.6	Summary of the position before and after the implementation of the Companies Act 2006	8025
8.7	What restrictions are there on the amount and nature of the consideration payable on a subscription for shares?		8026
	8.7.1	Are there any restrictions on the price payable on a subscription for shares or how it is satisfied?	8026
	8.7.2	What are 'nil' or 'part paid' shares?	8027
	8.7.3	Can shares be allotted with different payment terms? . . .	8027
	8.7.4	What are the consequences if a subscriber fails to pay an outstanding instalment on his shares?	8027
	8.7.5	What are the rules for determining what constitutes payment in cash for subscription?	8028
	8.7.6	What are bonus issues of shares and scrip dividends? . . .	8029
8.8	How is an issue of shares accounted for?		8029
	8.8.1	What changes are introduced by the Companies Act 2006?	8030

8.8.2   What changes are introduced by the Companies Act 2006
        to the uses of share premium? 8030
8.8.3   What is group reconstruction relief? 8031
8.8.4   How is the relief reflected in the company's balance
        sheet? 8032
8.8.5   When is merger relief available? 8033
8.8.6   Summary of the position before and after implementation
        of the Companies Act 2006 8035
8.9   What are the restrictions on making a public offer of securities?   8036
8.9.1   What is an 'offer to the public'? 8036
8.9.2   To which securities does the prohibition apply? 8037
8.9.3   Can a private company allot or agree to allot securities to a
        third person with a view to their being offered to the
        public? 8038
8.9.4   What changes have been made by the Companies Act
        2006? 8038
        8.9.4.1   Offers in contemplation of re-registration as a
                  public company 8038
        8.9.4.2   Injunctive action 8038
        8.9.4.3   De-criminalisation 8038
        8.9.4.4   Remedial orders 8039
        8.9.4.5   Is the validity of the allotment affected? 8039
8.10 What additional restrictions apply to payment for shares allotted by
      a public company? 8039
8.10.1   What are the restrictions? 8039
8.10.2   What are the sanctions for not complying with the
         requirements? 8040
8.10.3   When is a public company required to obtain a valuation
         for an allotment of its shares? 8040
8.10.4   Are there any exemptions from the requirement to obtain a
         valuation? 8041
8.10.5   Are there special requirements where the company has
         been incorporated or re-registered recently? 8041
8.10.6   What implications are there for the interposition of a new
         plc holding company? 8042
8.10.7   What happens if there is a contravention of the
         restrictions? 8042
         8.10.7.1   Liability of the officers of the company 8042
         8.10.7.2   Liability of the allottee 8042
         8.10.7.3   Other consequences 8043
8.10.8   Are there additional requirements when allotting shares in
         a public company? 8043
8.11 What are the implications for subsequent acquirers of shares from a
      person in breach of the Companies Act? 8044
8.11.1   When can liability arise? 8044
8.11.2   Power of the court to grant relief 8045

8.12 Can a company pay commissions, discounts and allowances on an allotment of shares? 8045

    8.12.1 What is the current position? 8045

    8.12.2 Are any changes introduced by the Companies Act 2006? 8046

8.13 Consolidation and subdivision of shares 8046

    8.13.1 Why does a company sub-divide or consolidate its shares? 8046

    8.13.2 What is the position from 1 October 2009? 8046

    8.13.3 What changes are introduced by the Companies Act 2006? 8047

    8.13.4 Can a company restrict its ability to consolidate or sub-divide its shares? 8047

    8.13.5 Will the filing requirements at Companies House change? 8047

8.14 What is the procedure for a redenomination of share capital? ... 8047

    8.14.1 Why does a company redenominate its shares? 8047

    8.14.2 What is the procedure before 1 October 2009? 8047

    8.14.3 What changes are introduced by the Companies Act 2006? 8048

    8.14.4 How are fractions arising following a conversion dealt with? 8048

        8.14.4.1 Special resolution 8049

        8.14.4.2 Maximum limit 8049

        8.14.4.3 Time limit 8049

        8.14.4.4 Filing requirements 8049

        8.14.4.5 Redenomination reserve 8049

    8.14.5 What if a company has not followed the requirements under the Companies Act 2006? 8049

    8.14.6 What action should a company take in advance of 1 October 2009? 8050

8.15 How are class rights varied? 8050

    8.15.1 What are the main changes introduced by the Companies Act 2006? 8050

    8.15.2 What is the procedure before 1 October 2009? 8051

    8.15.3 What is the position from 1 October 2009? 8053

    8.15.4 Can shareholders of a class object to the variation? 8053

    8.15.5 Are there any filing requirements? 8054

    8.15.6 Is there any action required before 1 October 2009? 8054

8.16 Cross holdings 8054

    8.16.1 What are cross holdings? 8054

    8.16.2 What is the position under the Companies Act 2006? ... 8054

    8.16.3 Can a company be a member of its holding company? .. 8055

    8.16.4 Can a UK company acquire shares in a company which holds shares in its parent? 8055

    8.16.5 Are there any exemptions? 8056

    8.16.6 What are the consequences where a crossholding arises? 8056

8.17 Transfer of shares 8056

	8.17.1	What changes are introduced by the Companies Act 2006?	8056
	8.17.2	What are the two main procedures for transferring shares in a company?	8057
	8.17.3	What is the process for transferring certificated shares?	8057
	8.17.4	What is the process for transferring uncertificated shares?	8058
8.18	Share warrants		8059
	8.18.1	What is a share warrant?	8059
	8.18.2	What rights do share warrants carry?	8059
	8.18.3	How are share warrants issued prior to 1 October 2009 under the Companies Act 1985?	8059
	8.18.4	How are share warrants issued after 1 October 2009 under the Companies Act 2006?	8060
8.19	What are treasury shares?		8060
	8.19.1	Which shares can be held as treasury shares?	8060
	8.19.2	Is there a limit on the holding of treasury shares?	8061
	8.19.3	Where shares are held by a company as treasury shares are there any restrictions on the exercise of shareholder rights?	8061
	8.19.4	What restrictions are there on dealings by a company in treasury shares?	8061
	8.19.5	Can treasury shares be cancelled?	8062
	8.19.6	How are the proceeds of sale accounted for?	8062
8.20	Summary of key changes and actions		8063
8.A.1	Appendix 1		8065
	8.A.1.1	Summary of the situations in which a statement of capital is required to be filed	8065
8.A.2	Appendix 2		8067
	8.A.2.1	Checklist for an allotment of shares by a private limited company under the Companies Act 2006	8067
8.A.3	Appendix 3		8069
	8.A.3.1	Checklist for an allotment of shares by a public company under the Companies Act 2006	8069

Chapter 8

Share capital and transactions involving shares

8.1 Introduction

8.1.1 Scope of this chapter

A share is the basic structural unit of a modern company. Although there are types of company that do not have share capital, the overwhelmingly majority of UK companies are those which are 'limited by shares' and most unlimited companies also have a share capital.

Shares underpin the mechanisms for the injection of funds into a company, for the transfer of ownership of a company, for the distribution of a company's profits and capital, and for the management and control of a company's activities. They are fundamental to our way of doing business, to the operation of our investment exchanges, to the remuneration of senior employees, to our investments in pension schemes and other funds – in fact to our whole economy.

But for all their importance, there is little magic to what a share actually is. In law, a share is nothing more or less than a bundle of rights: the right to vote on a company's affairs; the right to receive a part of the company's earnings; and the right to receive a part of the company's capital value when they are distributed or the company is wound up.

Of course, the law has evolved over almost two centuries to regulate, protect and prioritise these rights, culminating in the Companies Act 2006, which dedicates two whole parts to the regulation of the issue and transfer of shares and introduces a number of deregulatory measures in this area. In addition, the rights of shareholders are governed by the company's articles of association, which in law forms a contract between the company and the shareholders, and which may modify and prioritise the rights attaching to different classes of shares, amending the position that would otherwise be implied by law[1].

The areas covered by this chapter are:

(a) Types of shares;

(b) The allotment;

(c) Payment for shares;

---

[1] *Hickman v Kent or Romney Marsh Sheep Breeders Association* [1915] 1 Ch 881.

(d) The accounting treatment of an issue of shares;

(e) Consolidations, subdivisions, redetermination of shares;

(f) Variation of class rights;

(g) Cross holdings;

(h) Transfers of shares; and

(i) Issue of share warrants.

8.1.2 What are the most common types of shares?

There are very few limits on the rights and restrictions that can be granted on the issue of a share. The table below describes some of the most common categories of shares, but it should be noted that this list is far from exhaustive, and that the names given to the categories of shares are not legal terms, but simply commonly understood terms of usage. Shares can be given any name, and any rights, and it is of course the rights of the shares as set out in the company's articles, rather than the name they are given, which is important to their owner.

Ordinary shares	Overwhelmingly the most common type of share, the ordinary share confers the right to vote in shareholders' meetings, the right to a proportionate share of any dividends which might be declared, and the right to a proportionate share of any distributions out of capital.
	Most companies have only ordinary shares in their capital, so that all shares rank equally in all rights. However, where a company has other classes of shares, these may rank ahead of or behind the ordinary shares, effectively altering the rights of the ordinary shares themselves.
	A company may have different classes of ordinary shares, differentiated by name, e.g. 'A' Ordinary and 'B' Ordinary shares. These would typically enjoy identical financial rights, but would be held by different shareholders and might have different rights or restrictions in relation to voting, control or transfer.
Preference shares	Preference shares confer enhanced financial rights on their holders, but very often carry no right to vote in a shareholders' meeting except on certain specified matters.
	They may entitle their holder to a fixed annual dividend in priority to any payment of dividend to the holders of other classes of shares; or to receive

	a fixed sum on a capital distribution, again in priority to other classes.
	Preference shares therefore provide their owners with something resembling a debt instrument, in the sense that they will usually receive a fixed percentage preference dividend in a similar way to a lender receiving interest, and their capital investment will usually be repaid at the end of the life of the company. However, it should always be remembered that these shares rank behind the genuine creditors of the company, even though they usually rank ahead of the ordinary shares.
Redeemable shares	A redeemable share is one which may be repaid by the company to the holder upon the occurrence of a future event or date. Either the amount initially paid up on the share, or a higher or lower amount, may be repaid, but there are restrictions in particular on the payment of higher amounts. There are also detailed company law requirements for the funding of redemption of shares which are discussed in chapter 9.
	The circumstances in which shares can be redeemed will be specified in the articles and such shares can be redeemed at the option of either the shareholder and/or the company.
	It is common for redeemable shares also to have preferred economic rights, making them redeemable preference shares.
Deferred shares	The rights attached to a deferred share are subordinate to the rights attached to other classes of share in the company. Deferred shares usually carry no right to vote, and may be entitled to a dividend or a capital payment only after all other classes of shares have received dividends or capital payments above a defined threshold.
	In many cases, the threshold which other classes must achieve is set so high as to render the rights attached to the deferred share almost valueless, since it is so unlikely that any financial return will ever be received. This is appropriate where, in order to vary the relative economic holdings of different shareholders, valuable classes of shares convert on certain events to deferred shares, thus boosting the relative economic value of the other classes of shares in the company.

Convertible shares	A convertible share will convert into a share of a different class upon the occurrence of certain events specified in the articles of the company. Conversion rights are useful where different shareholders wish to vary their relative economic positions, usually in response to strong economic performance of the company's business. For example, a manager might hold deferred shares which, upon attainment of performance targets, automatically convert to ordinary shares. The manager then gains increased economic rights in the company without acquiring any new shares.

8.1.3   What rights are inherent in a share?

As described above, a share is, in law, a bundle of rights, and these rights are the right to vote on the company's affairs, the right to receive a share of the earnings of the company, and the right to receive a share of the capital assets of the company on its winding up or other capital distribution.

These rights may be limited by the terms of the articles of association and are also subject to a range of creditor and minority shareholder protections, as discussed in chapters 3 and 9.

The rights of shareholders always rank after the rights of the creditors of a company in the event of insolvency. In the case of a limited company the shareholders cannot be required to pay any more towards those creditors than they have already paid or committed to pay on their shares. This is the meaning of 'limited liability' which refers to the liability of the shareholders and not of the company itself.

8.1.4   What steps are taken on incorporation relating to share capital?

Both the memorandum and the articles of association of a company, which are filed at incorporation, contain provisions relating to the company's share capital.

Subscribers: By signing the company's memorandum of association, the subscribers agree to take, and pay for, a number of shares. In most cases the subscribers will take only one share each, but they may take any number, limited only until 1 October 2009 to the level of the company's authorised share capital.

Memorandum: The memorandum of association filed at incorporation will, until 1 October 2009, state the authorised share capital of the company and the classes and numbers of shares into which it is divided. This is not determined forever but can be altered by taking the appropriate procedural steps. From 1

October 2009, as explained in section 8.3, the requirement to have an authorised share capital will no longer apply.

Articles: The articles of association set out the rights attaching to the company's shares and the way in which these rights may be exercised. For example, the articles usually include provisions relating to the conduct of shareholders' meetings, and may also include provisions relating to the payment of dividends. Where the company's share capital is divided into classes of shares, there will be detailed provisions relating to the rights of each class.

Statement of capital: After 1 October 2009, an application to the Registrar of Companies for the incorporation of a company must include a statement of capital in the statutory form. This will state the names and other details of the company's subscribers and will show the numbers of shares to be taken by each of them.

8.1.5 What is the difference between a 'member' and a 'shareholder'?

These two phrases are used interchangeably much of the time but there are differences. A 'member' of a company is a person who has consented to be entered in the register of members of that company and has in fact been entered in the register of members. The Companies Act 2006[2] also provides that the subscribers to the memorandum become members on registration of the company even if the company fails to enter their names in the register of members. Currently the entry of the names of the subscribers in the register of members is commonly overlooked and this can cause considerable difficulties at a later date. This provision, which is effective from 1 October 2009, is intended to address that situation and to remove the possibility of a company having no members in the period between incorporation and the completion of the register of members. It nevertheless remains a requirement that the names of all members, including subscribers, should be entered in the register of members.

The Companies Acts predominantly refer to the term 'member' rather than 'shareholder' for provisions that apply not only to companies with a share capital but also companies that do not, such as companies limited by guarantee.

The timely completion of the register of members will therefore determine the precise point at which a person who has acquired shares becomes entitled to rights conferred on 'members' by the Companies Acts.

A person is capable of being the beneficial owner of shares without being entered in the register of members.

---

[2]   Section 112, Companies Act 2006.

In general the Companies Acts are only concerned with the rights of the registered owners of shares. However, as discussed in chapter 4, the rights of beneficial owners have been increased in a number of respects by the Companies Act 2006.

8.1.6 What is the 'nominal value' of a share?

Share capital is required to be divided into shares, each of which has a fixed nominal value.

Under the Companies Act 1985[3], on incorporation, a company is required to state the amount of its initial authorised share capital and the way in which that share capital is divided into shares of a fixed amount. For example, a company may have authorised share capital of £1,000 divided into 1,000 ordinary shares of £1 each.

From 1 October 2009, there will no longer be any requirement for a company to have an authorised share capital. However, shares in a limited company with a share capital will still be required to have a fixed nominal value[4]. This implements the requirement under the Second EC Directive (Dir 77/91/EEC) for a public company to have a fixed nominal value for all of its shares, but the Companies Act 2006 requirement applies to all companies with a share capital.

This nominal value may be expressed in any currency[5] (although in the case of a public company its statutory minimum share capital must on incorporation be denominated in either Sterling or Euros). Furthermore, the nominal value of a share may be a fraction of an individual unit of currency even if that fraction is not legal tender.

8.1.7 Why is the nominal value of a share important?

The nominal value of a share usually bears no relation to its actual value. However, it remains of considerable importance for a number of legal reasons:

(i)   the issue of a share 'at a discount', meaning the issue of the share for consideration lower than its nominal value, is prohibited;

(ii)   the issue of a share for consideration in excess of its nominal value will lead to the excess of the consideration over the nominal value being required to be transferred to the company's share premium account rather than its share capital account (unless it qualifies for relief, see section 8.8); and

(iii)   a company can only reduce or alter the nominal value of its shares or share premium in specific ways which are regulated by the Companies Acts.

---

[3]   Section 2(5)(a), Companies Act 1985.
[4]   Section 542(1), Companies Act 2006.
[5]   Section 542(3), Companies Act 2006.

These issues are discussed further in this chapter and in chapter 9.

8.1.8 Can a company issue shares of no par value?

No. For the reasons given in section 8.1.6 a company limited by shares cannot issue shares with no nominal or par value[6]. However, this restriction does not apply to unlimited companies.

8.1.9 What changes are being made to issues of redeemable shares?

Under the Companies Act 1985[7] a company can only issue redeemable shares if:

(i)   it is authorised under the articles of association to do so;

(ii)   there are other non-redeemable shares in issue;

(iii)   the redemption dates are specified in the articles of association or if permitted by the articles of association, fixed by the directors, and in the latter case fixed before the shares are issued; and

(iv)   all other terms of redemption, including the redemption amount and circumstances of redemption, must be specified in the articles of association and in particular, the terms of redemption must provide for payment on redemption.

The Companies Act 2006[8] introduces a number of deregulatory changes from 1 October 2009. These are as follows:

(i)   it is no longer a requirement for a company to have authority in the articles of association before issuing redeemable shares;

(ii)   the articles of association, or the shareholders, may confer power on the directors to determine the term, condition and manner of redemption of redeemable shares; and

(iii)   the requirement for payment on redemption is removed, which will mean that payment may be deferred.

---

[6]   Section 542(1), Companies Act 2006.
[7]   Sections 159–159A, Companies Act 1985.
[8]   Sections 684–685, Companies Act 2006.

8.2   What legal considerations arise when increasing the issued share capital of a company?

8.2.1   What company law issues arise?

The allotment and issue of shares are regulated by the Companies Acts in a number of respects. The key issues are set out below and discussed in further detail in this chapter:

(i)   (Until 1 October 2009), does the company have sufficient authorised but unissued share capital?

(ii)   (Until 1 October 2009), is a valid authority in place giving the directors authority to allot the shares?

(iii)   Have statutory pre-emption rights been disapplied?

(iv)   What is the subscription price for the share?

(v)   How will the subscription price be paid?

(vi)   Will the shares be issued fully or partly paid?

(vii)   Are the shares to be issued for non-cash consideration?

(viii) How will the subscription price be accounted for?

(ix)   Will the proposed issue of shares constitute an offer to the public?

(x)   Will the proposed issue of shares constitute a variation of class rights?

(xi)   Are there any restrictions in the memorandum and articles of association?

(xii)   Are there any contractual restrictions which restrict the ability of the company to issue further shares; for example, the terms of a joint venture or a shareholder agreement may require shareholder or third party consents to be obtained?

(xiii) What steps need to be carried out to effect the issue of further shares?

In addition to the above the following legal issues may also arise which are discussed in Chapters 1, 4 and 9:

(i)   Are there any financial assistance issues?

(ii)   Will the agreed amount and method of payment also constitute a proper discharge of the directors' duties?

(iii)   Will the further issue of shares unfairly dilute minorities?

8.2.2   What are the main regulatory issues?

The issue of shares is not only regulated in the UK by the Companies Acts, but is also subject to a body of other law and regulation which assists in protecting investors, and which also impacts on the marketing of share issues. These requirements can apply to both private companies and public ones.

The requirements are principally found in the Financial Services and Markets Act 2000 (as amended) ('FSMA') and its subsidiary legislation, the FSA Handbook of rules and guidance, the EU Prospectus Regulation and the LSE's AIM rules.

Breaches of many of these requirements are criminal offences, and other possible sanctions for contraventions include financial penalties and public censures. In addition, for example, investors may be entitled to compensation for losses suffered as a result of breaches, and agreements entered into with investors may not be enforceable against them.

This area should therefore be looked at an early stage, with a view to identifying any applicable exclusions. It is also important to bear in mind that many other jurisdictions have equivalent rules and restrictions on share promotions. As such, further legal issues will almost inevitably arise where a contemplated share offer is also to be made to investors outside the UK.

Key regulatory issues in the context of share issues and promotions include those outlined below.

Regulated activities: FSMA provides that no person may carry on a regulated activity in the UK, or purport to do so, unless that person is authorised by the FSA or exempt. While an offer of shares is potentially the FSMA regulated activity of 'dealing in investments as principal', there is an exclusion under the Financial Services and Markets Act (Regulated Activities) Order 2001, as amended, that allows a company to issue its own shares or share warrants without being authorised by the FSA. However, an issuer could inadvertently engage in other regulated activities such as that of 'advising on investments'. Third parties involved in the marketing of the shares could also carry on this FSMA regulated activity, as well as other regulated activities such as that of 'arranging deals in investments'.

Financial promotions: FSMA provides that no person in the course of business may communicate an 'invitation or inducement' to engage in investment activity unless the person making the communication is authorised by the FSA, the content of the communication is approved by an FSA authorised firm, or an exemption is available to the person making the communication under the Financial Services and Markets Act 2000 (Financial Promotion) Order 2005, as amended ('the FPO'). This requirement is known under FSMA as the 'financial promotion restriction'. A share offer made in the UK potentially falls within the scope of the financial promotion restriction (though there is an exemption for statements contained in an approved prospectus). It follows that unless an issuer is a FSA authorised person, it will need to be able to rely on an exemption under the FPO. The financial promotion restriction is also potentially relevant to third parties involved in the marketing of shares.

Prospectus requirements: Under FSMA, in the absence of an exemption, it is unlawful for transferrable securities to be offered to the public unless a prospectus approved by the FSA has been made available to the public before the offer is made. FSMA sets out various exemptions where a prospectus is not required. The high level obligation regarding the content of a prospectus is set out in section 87A of FSMA which states that a prospectus must contain the necessary information to enable investors to make an informed assessment of the assets and liabilities, financial position, profits and losses and prospects of the issuer and of any guarantor and of the rights attached to transferrable securities. The FSA's Prospectus Rules and the EU Prospectus Regulation set out the detailed content requirements for prospectuses.

For quoted companies a further issue of shares will be governed by the Listing Rules or AIM Rules, which will prescribe detailed procedural and regulatory requirements relating to the issue.

8.2.3   What is the difference between an 'allotment' and an 'issue' of shares?

An 'allotment' of shares has occurred when a person becomes unconditionally entitled to be entered in the register of members as the holder of those shares[9]. This will be the case when the company's directors have resolved to allot and issue the shares to that person, when he has agreed to subscribe for the shares, has consented to be entered in the register of members, and when he has (if the shares are to be paid up) complied with the agreed terms as to payment up of those shares.

An 'issue' of shares has occurred only when that person's name has been entered in the register of members in respect of those shares. Usually but not always, this will be accompanied by an issue of a share certificate to the shareholder for the shares concerned.

The distinction can be important. For the purpose of calculating the period of ownership, which may be relevant for tax purposes, it may not be sufficient that the shares have been allotted if they have not been issued. Further, distributions and dividends are usually made to the registered owners of shares and if one is therefore made between allotment and issue, the allottee may not be entitled to receive his respective share of that distribution.

---

[9]   Section 558, Companies Act 2006.

8.3 Is a company still required to have an authorised share capital?

On incorporation, until 1 October 2009, a company is required to state its initial authorised share capital in its memorandum. The authorised share capital may be increased from time to time with shareholder approval[10]. A company may not allot shares in excess of its authorised share capital (even if its directors have an otherwise valid authority to allot shares).

For convenience, therefore, companies frequently increase their authorised share capital to a level significantly in excess of their issued share capital. The term 'headroom' is often used to describe the excess of the authorised share capital over the issued share capital.

8.3.1 What changes are introduced by the Companies Act 2006?

From 1 October 2009, companies will no longer be required to have an authorised share capital. Instead, a company will be able to issue as many shares as it requires unless otherwise restricted by its articles of association.

8.3.2 Is any action required before 1 October 2009?

If the memorandum and articles of association of the company contain a limit on the share capital of the company, the company will continue to be restricted unless the articles of association are amended. Therefore, any existing restriction needs to be identified and consideration given to whether an amendment is needed. For companies formed on or after 1 October 2009, shareholders will need to consider whether it would be appropriate in the company's particular circumstances to introduce a restriction on the number of shares that may be issued.

8.4 Do directors still need shareholder authority to allot shares in a company?

Under the Companies Act 1985 directors require shareholder authority to allot shares in a company (or to grant rights to subscribe for, or to create securities convertible in to shares). The shares and all rights to subscribe for shares are referred to in the Companies Act 1985 as 'relevant securities'[11]. There is an exemption for employee share schemes[12]. This authority may either be contained in the articles of association or conferred by ordinary resolution.

---

[10] Section 121(2)(a), Companies Act 1985.
[11] Section 80, Companies Act 1985.
[12] See Chapter 10 section 10.2.2.5.

8.4.1 What must the authorisation include prior to 1 October 2009?

The authority can be given for a particular allotment and issue of shares, or for the allotment and issue of shares generally. It can be conditional or unconditional. It must, however, specify the maximum aggregate nominal value of the securities that may be allotted, and the date on which the authority will expire (which cannot exceed five years from the date of the resolution), or if the authority is contained in the articles on incorporation, the date of incorporation (or adoption of those articles, if later)[13].

In practice, most companies grant authority to the directors to allot and issue shares up to the level of the then authorised but unissued share capital, and most companies grant the authority for the full five year maximum period. Quoted companies are additionally subject to the recommended limits of the Investor Protection Committees (such as the Association of British Insurers (ABI) and the National Association of Pension Funds). These bodies issue guidelines relating to, amongst other things, the allotment of shares and appropriate levels of approval, which, in the case of ABI, is currently the lesser of the unissued share capital of the company and one third of the issued ordinary share capital. It is worth noting that although companies are not legally obliged to adhere to the recommended limits they are usually followed to as otherwise the company could face public criticism for breaching the guidelines and the resolution itself may not be passed.

Prior to 1 October 2007, a private company could pass an elective resolution granting its directors authority to allot shares for a fixed period exceeding five years, or for an indefinite period[14]. In the latter case this would mean that a private company could dispense with the requirement to obtain authorisation altogether. The ability to pass elective resolutions was abolished on 1 October 2007, although elective resolutions already in place on that date will remain valid[15].

8.4.2 What about offers or agreements made before the authorisation expires but under which 'relevant securities' are allotted after expiry?

Where the company has made an offer or has agreed to allot 'relevant securities' prior to the expiry of the authorisation, any allotment made pursuant to such an offer or agreement will be valid provided that the original authorisation expressly authorised it[16].

---

[13] Section 80(4), Companies Act 1985.
[14] Section 80(A), Companies Act 1985.
[15] Companies Act 2006 (Commencement No 3, Consequential Amendments, Transitional Provisions and Savings) order 2007.
[16] Section 80(7), Companies Act 1985.

8.4.3   How can a company renew, revoke or vary the authorisation?

The authorisation can be renewed at any time. There are no limits on the number of times that the authorisation can be renewed. The renewal must comply with the same requirements specified above in relation to maximum amount and maximum period.

The authorisation can be revoked or varied by an ordinary resolution of the shareholders at any time.

8.4.4   What are the filing requirements?

The resolution granting the directors authority to allot shares (or revoking, varying or renewing such authority) must be filed with Companies House within 15 days of its passing[17].

8.4.5   What changes are introduced by the Companies Act 2006?

As the principle of authorised share capital will no longer apply after 1 October 2009, it follows that there should be no limit on the power of the directors of a company to allot shares, unless to do so could alter the relative holdings of shareholders, or the relative weight attaching to different classes of shares. Accordingly, from 1 October 2009, private companies with a single class of shares will not be required to obtain shareholder authority for the allotment of shares unless their articles require it. The new provisions are contained in sections 549 to 551 of the Companies Act 2006.

A company has one class of shares if the rights attached to its shares are in all respects uniform[18]. Directors of such companies will therefore have unrestricted authority to:

(i)   allot shares; or

(ii)   grant rights to subscribe for shares; or

(iii)   convert any security into shares;

unless restricted from doing so by the articles of association.

Directors of a private company with more than one class of shares and directors of a public company will need prior authorisation from shareholders to allot shares. The requirements for obtaining, and the restrictions applicable to, the authority are largely re-stated in the Companies Act 2006. This authorisation can be given by ordinary resolution of the company or in the company's articles of association, whether adopted on incorporation or subsequently amended.

---

[17]   Section 80(8), Companies Act 1985.
[18]   Section 629, Companies Act 2006.

As the elective regime has been abolished, private companies that need shareholder authority to allot shares (by virtue of having more than one class of shares or by virtue of there being restrictions in the articles of association) are no longer able to grant directors indefinite authority to allot shares.

8.4.6 Summary of the position before and after implementation of the Companies Act 2006

Issue	The position under the Companies Act 1985	The position under the Companies Act 2006 with effect from 1 October 2009
Will the allotment of shares or right to acquire shares require shareholder approval?	The Companies Act 1985 applies to 'relevant securities', i.e.: (i) shares in the company other than subscriber shares or shares allotted pursuant to an employee share scheme; and (ii) rights to subscribe for or convert any security into shares in the company (including options, warrants, convertible loan stock and other convertible securities).	The defined term 'relevant securities' is no longer used but the types of shares and types of transaction for which shareholder approval is required remain unaltered. Authority is not required for private companies with one class of shares (unless otherwise required under the articles of association).
By what method must the authorisation be given?	(i) ordinary resolution; or (ii) the articles of association of the company adopted on the incorporation of the company or as amended subsequently.	No change.
Scope of authorisation	Can be for a particular allotment or be general; may be subject to conditions or unconditional.	No change.
Duration of authorisation	Must be specified in the authorisation and may not exceed five years, subject to election by private companies for a fixed period exceeding five years or an indefinite period of authority (in relation to the then authorised but unissued share capital) by passing an elective resolution.	Must be specified in the authorisation and may not exceed five years. Elective resolutions were abolished on 1 October 2007.

Issue	The position under the Companies Act 1985	The position under the Companies Act 2006 with effect from 1 October 2009
Amount of shares subject to authorisation	Maximum number of shares or maximum aggregate share capital amount must be specified.	No change.
Renewal	Permissible, by ordinary resolution.	No change.
Revocation	Revocable and variable, by ordinary resolution.	No change.
Saving provisions	Authorisation continues to be valid (even if expired) if shares are allotted or rights to subscribe for or to convert any security into shares are granted pursuant to an offer or agreement made by the company before the authorisation expired, provided that this is expressly authorised in the authorisation.	No change.
Filing with Companies House	Yes – the ordinary resolution giving the authorisation must be filed within 15 days.	No change.

8.4.7 Is any action required before 1 October 2009?

Existing authorities will continue to have effect, and will need no amendment before 1 October 2009 and remain subject to the management of the Companies Act 1985. On expiry of any current authority on or after 1 October 2009, companies will need to consider whether they fall within the category of company that no longer requires authority to be granted by shareholders (i.e. whether the company is a private one and if so whether it only has one class of shares) or whether a new authority will be required for future issues of shares.

For companies with elective resolutions in place, transitional provisions are expected to be published in due course but were not available at the time of writing. It is, however, expected that an authority granted by elective resolution[19] that was in force immediately before 1 October 2009 will continue to have effect on and after that date.

---

[19] Section 80A, Companies Act 1985.

Companies whose shareholders wish to restrict the power of directors to allot new shares, but who have hitherto relied on the requirement for shareholders to give express authority for such allotments, should consider introducing a restriction on allotment in the company's articles of association.

8.5 What statutory pre-emption rights do shareholders have?

8.5.1 What is a right of pre-emption?

Pre-emption rights entitle an existing shareholder to preserve a proportionate interest in a company's capital by giving him a right of first refusal where a future allotment of shares is to take place[20].

The Companies Act 1985[21] requires a company that is proposing to allot equity securities first to offer them to existing shareholders in proportion to the nominal value of their existing shareholdings. The Companies Act 2006 preserves this basic principle and the relevant provisions are contained in sections 560 to 577 which come into force on 1 October 2009.

The statutory right of pre-emption may be supplemented or substituted by pre-emption rights in the company's articles of association, or by contract, for example, within the provisions of a shareholder's agreement or a contract for sale or purchase.

The rules in both the Companies Act 1985 and the Companies Act 2006 apply only to allotments of 'equity securities'[22], though this phrase is slightly differently defined in each Act. In the Companies Act 1985 'equity securities' do not include:

(i)   shares which, as respects dividends and capital, carry a right to participate only up to a specified amount in a distribution (such as preference shares); or

(ii)   shares acquired or to be acquired, in pursuance of an employees' share scheme[23]; or

(iii) shares taken by the subscribers to the memorandum of the company on its formation; or

(iv)   bonus shares.

In the Companies Act 2006, the definition of 'equity securities' is drafted in a different way but in essence remains the same.

---

[20]   A right of pre-emption is widely applied in relation to share transfers, usually in articles of a company or in a relevant shareholders' agreement. There is no statutory right of pre-emption on share transfer.

[21]   Section 89, Companies Act 1985; Section 561(1), Companies Act 2006.

[22]   Section 94, Companies Act 1985; Section 560(1), Companies Act 2006.

[23]   See Chapter 10, section 10.2.2.6.

Both Companies Acts exclude from the provisions allotments that are to be paid up wholly or partly for non-cash consideration[24].

In addition, statutory pre-emption rights apply to a right to subscribe for, or to convert securities into, shares that would otherwise be subject to the pre-emption rights. However, the pre-emption rights do not apply to the allotment of shares pursuant to the grant of a right to subscribe for such shares[25]. Statutory pre-emption rights also apply to the sale of shares that are held by the company as treasury shares[26], unless the shares are being transferred to an employees share scheme.

8.5.2 To whom must the pre-emption offer be made?

Under the Companies Act 1985, the right of 'first refusal' must be made to any pre-existing member holding 'relevant shares'[27] or 'relevant employee shares'. Under the Companies Act 2006, an offer must be made to any person who holds 'ordinary shares' in the company. However, in practice the position is the same under both Companies Acts – pre-exemption rights benefit the holders of shares other than shares which, as respects dividends and capital, carry a right to participate only up to a specified amount in a distribution (for example preference shares).

The offer does not need to be made to the company if it is holding shares in treasury.

8.5.3 On what terms must the pre-emption offer be made?

Under both of the Companies Acts, the offer must be:

(i)   in proportion to the shareholdings of relevant shares of the pre-existing shareholders;

(ii) on terms that are the same as or more favourable than those that would be or are offered to a third party; and

(iii) available for acceptance for a period of not less than 21 days during which time the offer may not be withdrawn[28].

After 1 October 2009, the Secretary of State has the power to reduce the 21 day period to 14 days. It is not known at the time of writing whether the Secretary of State will exercise this power.

---

[24]   Section 89(4), Companies Act 1985; Section 565, Companies Act 2006.
[25]   Section 89(3), Companies Act 1985; Section 561(3), Companies Act 2006.
[26]   Section 94(3A), Companies Act 1985; Section 573, Companies Act 2006.
[27]   Section 89(1), Companies Act 1985; Section 561(1)(a), Companies Act 2006.
[28]   Section 90(6), Companies Act 1985; Section 562(4)–(5), Companies Act 2006.

8.5.4 How is notice of the offer given?

Until 1 October 2009, individual notice need only be given to shareholders who have given a service address in the UK; otherwise notice can be given by publication in the *London, Belfast* or *Edinburgh Gazettes*[29].

From 1 October 2009 the provision is extended so as to require individual notices to be given to shareholders who have given a service address anywhere in the EEA and the notices may be given in hard copy or electronic form[30].

8.5.5 Can a company exclude or disapply the pre-emption requirements?

8.5.5.1 What is the position before 1 October 2009?

A private company can exclude statutory pre-emption rights by an appropriate provision in its articles of association[31] and all companies can, if they wish, provide for specific pre-emption provisions in their articles, to have effect in place of the statutory pre-emption provisions[32].

In the case of both private and public companies, where directors have been given general or specific authority to allot shares by the company, the statutory pre-emption rights may also be disapplied. The disapplication may be made either by (a) specific provision of the memorandum or the articles of association; or (b) by a special resolution to that effect[33]. However, the disapplication will be subject to the same limitations as to length of time and amount as the general or specific allotment authority to allot shares[34].

Where the special resolution to disapply is in relation to a specific allotment of shares it must have been recommended by the directors and the notice of the meeting at which the resolution is proposed must be accompanied by a written statement by the directors setting out:

(i)   their reasons for making the recommendation;

(ii) the amount to be paid to the company in relation to the shares to be allotted; and

(iii) the directors' justification of that amount[35].

---

[29] Section 90(5), Companies Act 1985.
[30] Section 562(3), Companies Act 2006.
[31] Section 91, Companies Act 1985; section 567, Companies Act 2006.
[32] Section 89(3), Companies Act 1985; section 568 (1) and (2), Companies Act 2006.
[33] Section 95(1), Companies Act 1985; section 570(1), (2); Section 571(2), (3), (5), Companies Act 2006.
[34] Section 95(3), Companies Act 1985; section 570(3), section 571(3), Companies Act 2006.
[35] Section 95(5), Companies Act 1985.

8.5.5.2   *What is the position from 1 October 2009?*

The Companies Act 2006 will still permit a private company to exclude the statutory pre-emption rights by way of express provision in the articles of association[36] and for all companies to include alternative, equivalent pre-emption provisions in their articles[37].

Pre-emption rights can also be disapplied or modified either generally or in relation to a specified allotment by:

(i)   private companies with only one class of shares by either (a) specific provision in the articles of association or (b) a special resolution[38]; or

(ii)   public or private companies where the directors have been given authority to allot shares by either (a) specific provision in the articles of association or (b) a special resolution, in each case in line with any restrictions (as to number of nominal value of shares, or as to duration) which have been imposed on the directors' power of allotment[39].

In relation to a special resolution to disapply the preemption rights in respect of a specific allotment of shares there is no change to the requirements for the notice of meeting to be accompanied by a recommendation from the directors and details in relation to the price to be paid to the company[40].

Any disapplication contained in the memorandum or articles of association of a company may, after 1 October 2009, only be contained in the articles of association and not the memorandum (as this document is a one-off filing made on the incorporation of the company (see chapter 3).

8.5.6   What are the sanctions for non-compliance with these provisions?

The company and every officer who knowingly authorised or permitted the breach are jointly and severally liable to compensate any person to whom an offer should have been made for any loss, damage, costs or expenses that the person has sustained or incurred as a result[41]. This liability is subject to a limitation period of two years from the date of the delivery of the return of the allotment to Companies House. In the case of a grant of a right to subscribe for or convert into ordinary shares, the two year period runs from the date of the grant.

---

[36]   Section 567, Companies Act 2006.
[37]   Section 568, Companies Act 2006.
[38]   Section 569, Companies Act 2006.
[39]   Section 570 and 571, Companies Act 2006.
[40]   Section 571(5), (6), Companies Act 2006.
[41]   Section 92, Companies Act 1985; Section 563, Companies Act 2006.

8.5.7 Is any action required before 1 October 2009?

There is no immediate requirement to take any action in relation to existing authorities. However, regard should be had to the new provisions when entering into new shareholder arrangements or seeking shareholder authorities that are likely to extend beyond 1 October 2009. In addition the text of shareholder resolutions may require amendment once the Companies Act 2006 provisions come into force as the expression 'relevant securities' is no longer retained.

8.5.8 Summary of the position before and after implementation of the Companies Act 2006

Issue	The position under the Companies Act 1985	The position under the Companies Act 2006 with effect from 1 October 2009
When do pre-emption rights apply?	The allotment of shares (other than shares with limited rights to participate in dividends and capital) for cash consideration (subject to certain exemptions). This includes treasury shares save where they are to be transferred to an employee share scheme.	The term 'relevant shares' is no longer used but there is no overall substantive change.
To whom must the offer be made?	Holders of shares with unlimited rights to participate in dividends and capital (other than to the company in respect of treasury shares).	No change.
How must the pre-emption offer be made?	In writing, and individuals that have submitted a UK address must be individually served.	In writing (in hard copy or electronic form), and individuals that have submitted an address in the EEA must be individually served.
	The offer must be open for 21 days (without revocation) or more.	The offer period must not be less than 21 days but the Secretary of State has power to reduce or increase this period (subject to a minimum of 14 days).

Issue	The position under the Companies Act 1985	The position under the Companies Act 2006 with effect from 1 October 2009
When can the company allot shares?	When the offer period has expired and the company has received notice of acceptance or refusal (including by default) of every offer.	No change.
Is it possible to exclude the application of statutory pre-emption rights?	Permissible for private companies by virtue of their memorandum or articles of association.	Permissible for private companies by virtue of their articles of association.
Is a general disapplication permissible?	Yes, for any company by provision in the articles or by special resolution if directors have been given general authority to allot shares. The disapplication will be subject to the restrictions contained in the authority to allot shares.	Yes, with specific requirements: (i) a private company with only one class of shares can disapply by provision in its articles or by special resolution. (ii) any company by provision in its articles or by special resolution if the directors have been given general authority to allot shares. The disapplication will be subject to the restrictions contained in the authority to allot shares.
Is a specific disapplication permissible?	Yes, for any company by special resolution where directors have been given general or specific authority to allot shares (such resolution must be recommended by the directors, supported by a written statement, and a notice of the meeting at which the resolution is proposed, together with the directors' written statement, must be circulated to shareholders).	No change.
Filing with Companies House	The disapplication resolution should be filed within 15 days.	No change.

8.6 What steps must be taken after allotment?

8.6.1 What changes are introduced by the Companies Act 2006?

The main provisions are contained in sections 554 to 557 of the Companies Act 2006. These sections come into force on 1 October 2009 and amend and replace sections 88 and 123 of the Companies Act 1985.

The main changes are as follows:

(i)   there is a new requirement for the directors to register an allotment in the statutory registers of the company within two months (unless a share warrant has been issued in respect of the shares (see section 8.18 below))[42];

(ii)   a return of allotments must still be filed with Companies House but it must also be accompanied by a statement of capital (which will provide details of the issued share capital of the company including rights attaching to the shares); and

(iii)   where shares are allotted for non-cash consideration it will no longer be a requirement to file a copy of the underlying contract or a memorandum of the terms with Companies House. This change was made to address concerns that the Companies Act 1985 could require commercially sensitive information to be disclosed. The return of allotments will, however, still have to contain details of the consideration paid for the shares.

8.6.2 What post-allotment steps must be taken under the Companies Act 1985?

8.6.2.1 Filings

All shareholder resolutions relating to the allotment must be filed at Companies House within 15 days of being passed.

A return of allotments in the prescribed form (Form 88(2)) must be filed with Companies House within one month from the date of the allotment[43]. It must state the number and nominal amount of the shares allotted, names and addresses of the allottees and the amount (if any) paid or due on each share, whether on account of the nominal value or by way of the premium.

Where the allotment is made, in whole or in part, for a consideration other than cash, the contract in writing (if any) constituting the right of the allottee to the allotment must also be filed together with a return (Form 88(3)) stating:

---

[42]   Section 554, Companies Act 2006.
[43]   Section 88, Companies Act 1985.

(i)   the number and nominal amount of the shares allotted;

(ii)   the extent to which the shares are to be treated as paid up; and

(iii)   the consideration for which they have been allotted.

In each case the contract must have been duly stamped.

The requirement to file a return of allotment with Companies House applies only to limited companies having a share capital (including companies limited by guarantee and having a share capital). It does not apply to unlimited companies.

8.6.2.2   Issue of share certificates

A company has a duty to issue a certificate within two months of an allotment of shares unless:

(i)   the terms of issue provide otherwise; or

(ii)   the allotment is to a financial institution[44].

A share certificate is *prime facie* evidence of title to the shares[45].

8.6.2.3   Update the statutory registers

The register of members must be updated but no time limit is specified[46] for its completion. As discussed in section 8.1, it is only once registered that a person acquires the rights of a member of the company.

8.6.3   What post-allotment steps need to be taken on or after 1 October 2009?

8.6.3.1   Filings at Companies House

As at present, all shareholder resolutions relating to the allotment must be filed at Companies House within 15 days of being passed. A return of allotments must also be filed at Companies House within one month of an allotment.

There is a new requirement for the return to be accompanied by a statement of capital[47] (which implements a requirement of the Second Company Law Directive 77/91/EEC). Whilst this directive applies only to public companies, the Companies Act 2006 requirement applies to all companies with a share capital and is intended to ensure that the public register will contain up to date information on a company's share capital.

---

[44]   Section 185(4) and (4A), Companies Act 1985.
[45]   Section 186, Companies Act 1985.
[46]   Section 352, Companies Act 1985.
[47]   Section 555, Companies Act 2006.

Share capital and transactions involving shares

The statement of capital must state, with respect to the company's share capital at the date to which the return is made up, the following information:

(i)   the total number of shares of the company;

(ii)   the aggregate nominal value of those shares;

(iii) for each class of shares, (a) prescribed particulars of the rights attached to the shares (b) the total number of shares of that class and (c) the aggregate nominal value of shares of that class; and

(iv)   the amount paid up and the amount unpaid (if any) on each share (whether on account of the nominal value or by way of a premium)[48].

The 'prescribed particulars' of the rights attaching to the shares include:

(i)   any rights to vote at general meetings of the company;

(ii)   any rights as respects dividends to participate in a distribution;

(iii) any rights as respects capital to participate in a distribution (including a winding up); and

(iv)   whether the shares are to be redeemed or liable to be redeemed by the company or the shareholder (and any terms and conditions relating to such redemption).

A summary of the situations (including allotments) in which a statement of capital is required to be filed is contained in appendix 1 to this chapter.

Under the Companies Act 2006 there is no longer a requirement to register a contract or prescribed details when shares are allotted for a consideration other than cash, but the return of allotments is required to state the consideration paid for the shares.

8.6.3.2   Issue of share certificates

The position is unchanged.

8.6.3.3   Register the allotment and update the statutory registers

Section 554 of the Companies Act 2006 is a new provision which requires the directors to register an allotment of shares in the statutory registers of the company as soon as practicable (and in any case no later than two months from the date of the allotment). However, this does not apply if the company has issued a share warrant in respect of the shares.

---

[48]   Section 555, Companies Act 2006.

8.6.4 How do these requirements apply to unlimited companies?

In general, unlimited companies are not required to file returns of allotments. However the Companies Act 2006 introduces a new requirement for unlimited companies to file a return of allotments where the shares allotted are not in all respects the same as shares previously allotted. For this purpose shares are not to be treated as different from shares previously allotted by reason only that the new shares do not carry the same rights to dividends as the latter during the 12 months following the former's allotment[49]. This provision is effective from 1 October 2009.

8.6.5 What are the penalties if a company does not comply with the requirements?

It is a criminal offence for the company and any officer in default to fail to comply with the filing requirements or to complete the statutory registers.

8.6.6 Summary of the position before and after the implementation of the Companies Act 2006

Issue	The position under the Companies Act 1985	The position under the Companies Act 2006 with effect from 1 October 2009
Which companies are required to file a return of allotments?	Companies limited by shares and companies limited by guarantee with a share capital. No requirement for unlimited companies to file a return of allotments.	Companies limited by shares and companies limited by guarantee with a share capital. Unlimited companies are required to file a return of allotments in certain circumstances.
What form does the return of allotments take?	Form 88(2) or 88(3).	No prescribed form available as at the date of writing.
What information must the return include?	(i) number and nominal amount of the shares allotted; (ii) names and addresses of the allottees; and (iii) the amount (if any) paid or due and payable on each share, whether on account of the nominal value or by way of the premium.	No change to the requirements.

---

[49] Section 556, Companies Act 2006.

Issue	The position under the Companies Act 1985	The position under the Companies Act 2006 with effect from 1 October 2009
What other documents must be filed where shares are allotted for a cash consideration?	No other documents are required.	A statement of capital with additional prescribed information must also be filed.
What specific information should be included for a return of allotments where shares are allotted for non-cash consideration (in whole or in part)?	The contract(s) (or the written particulars of such contract(s) if the contract(s) are not in writing) in respect of such allotment must be filed with Companies House.	No longer required.
When must the return be filed?	Within one month of the allotment.	No change.
Registers of allotments and members	They must be completed but no time limit is specified.	Two month time limit imposed.

8.7 What restrictions are there on the amount and nature of the consideration payable on a subscription for shares?

8.7.1 Are there any restrictions on the price payable on a subscription for shares or how it is satisfied?

Shares may not be allotted at a discount to their nominal value which means that the value of the consideration payable to the company on allotment must be at least equal to the nominal value of the shares allotted.

If shares are allotted at a discount the allotment is still valid but the allottee is obliged to pay up the amount of the discount plus interest at the appropriate rate[50]. Subject to this, shares may be paid up (in relation to their nominal value and any premium) in consideration of an undertaking to pay at a future date and in money or money's worth (including goodwill and know-how).

The Companies Act 2006 makes no change to the Companies Act 1985 or the principles set out above. Section 580 of the Companies Act 2006 restates section 100 of the Companies Act 1985 in relation to the prohibition on the issue of shares at a discount and is effective from 1 October 2009.

---

[50] Section 100, Companies Act 1985.

There are additional rules applicable to payment for shares allotted by a public company. The majority of these rules have been restated in the Companies Act 2006 and are discussed further in section 8.10.

Directors in the proper performance of their duties to the company will need to consider the appropriate consideration to be charged on the issue of new shares.

8.7.2 What are 'nil' or 'part paid' shares?

Shares can also be issued 'nil paid' or 'part paid' which means that the subscribers will have either not paid the subscription price or that only a proportion has been paid. The shares are not issued at a discount in this situation as long as the subscription price paid is not less than the amount by which the shares are paid up. The nominal value can be paid up in instalments as and when the further subscription monies are paid. The provisions relating to payment of the balance will either be set out in a subscription agreement or in the articles of association of the company. In an insolvent liquidation the subscriber will be obliged to pay the unpaid balance of the subscription price.

8.7.3 Can shares be allotted with different payment terms?

A company, if authorised by its articles[51], may:

(i)   arrange (at the time of the issue) for a difference between the shareholders in the amounts and times of payment of calls on their shares; and

(ii)   accept any payment due on any share even if the amount has not been called up.

8.7.4 What are the consequences if a subscriber fails to pay an outstanding instalment on his shares?

This situation is usually governed by the articles of the company, general principles of contract law and the Insolvency Act 1986.

In essence, if the shares are issued fully paid in consideration of an undertaking to pay at a future specified date, then the company will have a contractual right to sue the subscriber for the price. The shares will, however, remain in the ownership of the subscriber as fully paid shares in the absence of any agreement to the contrary. Directors might be held personally liable to the company for the loss if it can be established that acceptance of the undertaking was a breach of duty.

Where the shares are issued nil or part paid, there is no debt due from the shareholder to the company until the company calls for payment to be made by

---

[51] Section 119, Companies Act 1985; Section 581, Companies Act 2006.

the shareholder, known as a 'call'. If, when the company has made a call on the shares, the shareholder fails to pay the due amount to the company, the articles usually provide for the company to have power to forfeit the shares. In this situation, the shares are not automatically cancelled but continue to be held by the company (in an exception to the prohibition on a company holding its own shares) until such time as they are cancelled by way of a reduction of capital as permitted under the Companies Acts.

Public companies have a statutory obligation to cancel shares that have been forfeited within three years and to reduce the amount of share capital by the nominal value of the shares cancelled[52].

Forfeiture will not relieve the subscriber of his obligation to pay the company where a call has been made, and on a liquidation of a company the holder of the shares at the time will become liable to pay the unpaid amount.

A variation of the terms of an undertaking to pay up shares or a call once made can have a number of other company law implications: for example, it might constitute unlawful financial assistance and, if the subscriber is a director, may require shareholder approval under the provisions governing loans and credit transactions (see chapters 2 and 9).

8.7.5 What are the rules for determining what constitutes payment in cash for subscription?

It is important to establish whether the price paid for the issue of shares is cash (because, for example, an issue of shares by a public company for a non-cash consideration will require a valuation of that consideration first to be obtained) and because it will determine whether statutory pre-emption rights will apply.

The Companies Act 1985 specifies the circumstances in which the shares will be treated as allotted for cash[53]. These are where the consideration received by the company falls within one of the following categories:

(i)   cash;

(ii)   a cheque received in good faith which the directors have no reason for suspecting will not be paid;

(iii) a release of a liability of the company for a liquidated sum;

(iv)   an undertaking to pay cash at a future date; or

(v)   payment by any other means giving rise to a present or future entitlement to a payment, or credit equivalent to payment, in cash.

---

[52] Section 146, Companies Act 1985; Section 662, Companies Act 2006.
[53] Section 738(2), Companies Act 1985; Section 583, Companies Act 2006.

These provisions are restated in the Companies Act 2006, the relevant provisions of which are effective from 1 October 2009. However, the Secretary of State is granted power to add to the list in the future so that other forms of payment or settlement systems can be clarified.

8.7.6 What are bonus issues of shares and scrip dividends?

A bonus issue is an issue of new shares to existing shareholders in the same proportions as their existing holdings for which the shareholders make no payment, but where the shares are paid up out of other reserves, such as the share premium account or the profit and loss reserve. In the case of a 'scrip dividend' a shareholder opts to waive his entitlement to receive a dividend in exchange for an issue of new shares paid up by the amount of the dividend.

Usually, the company's total value will be unaffected by either transaction as they bring in no new money, but the total number of shares in issue will be increased. The value of each share in the company will therefore fall as a result of a bonus issue. In the case of a 'scrip dividend' value is retained in the company which would otherwise have been distributed, so that the issue of the scrip shares may not result in a reduction in value of each share.

8.8 How is an issue of shares accounted for?

In general, where the subscription price exceeds the aggregate nominal value of the shares issued, the amount of the excess is known as share premium and must be transferred to a share premium account to which various restrictions as to its use apply. There are two reliefs from this requirement, group reconstruction relief and merger relief.

The accounting for, and presentation in a company's financial statements of, share capital and transactions in shares is also subject to the requirements of accounting standards. The accounting standards' definition of equity differs from the Companies Act 2006 definition of equity shares. This can result in some shares and their related premium being presented as financial liabilities in financial statements. Accounting standards can also limit or restrict choices available in legislation, for example, in relation to group reconstruction and merger reliefs. Furthermore, the interaction between the accounting rules and the statutory and common law rules on capital maintenance and distributions applicable to shares can be complex. The detail on the application of accounting standards to share capital and transactions involving shares is beyond the scope of this book. For such detail, reference should be made to chapter 23 of PricewaterhouseCoopers' Manual of Accounting – IFRS for the UK or Manual of Accounting – UK GAAP and the ICAEW's Technical Release Tech 1/08.

8.8.1 What changes are introduced by the Companies Act 2006?

The Companies Act 2006 largely restates the provisions of the Companies Act 1985 in relation to accounting for share premium, although there is less flexibility as to how share premium can be used.

The provisions are contained in Chapter 7 of Part 17 of the Companies Act 2006 which govern:

(i)   when share premium should be recorded and the reliefs available; and

(ii)   what it can be used for.

These provisions are effective from 1 October 2009.

8.8.2 What changes are introduced by the Companies Act 2006 to the uses of share premium?

Section 130 of the Companies Act 1985 and section 610 of the Companies Act 2006 provides that where shares are issued at a premium, whether for cash or otherwise, the excess of the amount over the nominal value of the shares allotted must be transferred to a share premium account, unless one of the exemptions below apply.

The Companies Act 1985 provides that the share premium may only be applied by the company in certain ways, namely:

(i)   in paying up unissued shares to be allotted as bonus shares;

(ii)   in writing off the company's preliminary expenses; or the expenses of or commission paid or discount allowed on, any issue of shares or debentures of the company; or

(iii) in providing for the premium payable on redemption of debentures of the company.

Subject to this, all of the provisions of the Companies Act 1985 relating to the reduction of share capital (discussed further in chapter 9) apply as if the share premium account were paid-up share capital of the company.

The Companies Act 2006 further reduces the applications of the share premium account from 1 October 2009 by providing that it may only be used:

(i)   to write off the expenses or the commission on the issue of the shares which gave rise to the share premium (it will therefore no longer be possible to apply share premium for this purpose to the issue of any shares or debentures); or

(ii)   in paying up unissued shares to be allotted as bonus shares (this restates the Companies Act 1985).

It will also no longer be possible to apply share premium to the premium payable on the redemption of debentures.

The Companies Act 2006 is therefore more restrictive than the Companies Act 1985. However, as the Companies Act 2006 also introduces a simplified procedure for reductions of share capital (discussed further in chapter 9) that will also apply to the share premium account, the practical impact may not be as significant as might first appear.

8.8.3   What is group reconstruction relief?

Section 611 of the Companies Act 2006 restates the provisions of section 132 of the Companies Act 1985 and permits a wholly-owned company that issues shares (the 'issuing company') to either the holding company or to another wholly-owned subsidiary (either of which can be the 'transferor company'), in exchange for a non-cash asset (for example shares, a building, trade and assets) to record an amount not in excess of minimum premium value in its share premium account.

Minimum premium value is defined as the amount by which the base value of the consideration (being the amount by which the cost of those assets to the transferor company, or if less, the amount at which those assets were recorded in the books of the transferor company immediately prior to transfer exceeds the value of any liabilities assumed by the issuing company) exceeds the aggregate nominal value of the shares issued.

This relief is optional, but to the extent it is not applied, share premium must be recorded in accordance with usual principles[54].

The table below summarises the share premium which would be recorded in a number of situations depending on whether section 611 is applied:

---

[54]   Section 610(1), Companies Act 2006.

	A Base Value of Consideration	B Aggregate value of consideration received (i.e. fair value of asset)	C Aggregate nominal value of shares issued	D Share premium if s611 applied (minimum premium value) D = A − C (unless negative and then nil)	E Share premium if s611 not applied (i.e. s610(1) value) E = B − C
Situation 1	100	200	60	40	140
Situation 2	100	200	120	nil	80
Situation 3	100	200	200	nil	nil

8.8.4 How is the relief reflected in the company's balance sheet?

Section 615 allows a company that is applying section 611 (or section 613[55] – discussed below) to disregard premiums (or part of premiums) in the carrying value of assets to the related extent share premium is disregarded as a result of sections 611 and 613. As such the carrying value of the asset transferred to the issuer will be equal to the aggregate share capital and premium (if applicable) recorded.

The effect of this in relation to section 611 is that the historic carrying value of assets can be preserved as they are transferred around a group. For example, if Situation 1 is considered from the table above, the carrying value of the asset transferred in the issuer's records is 100 (i.e. equal to the base value of the consideration, being the historic carrying value of the asset). However, a company that applies EU-adopted IFRS in its individual accounts usually recognises the acquired asset in its balance sheet at its fair value at the point of acquisition. This can be accommodated by section 615, which permits the asset to be recorded at either the aggregate of the nominal value of the shares issued and any minimum premium amount or its fair value.

Where the acquired asset is an investment in a subsidiary IAS 27 'Consolidated and Separate Financial Statements' applies. The interaction of the accounting and legal rules can be complicated. This has become more complex following the recent amendment to IAS 27 (and IFRS 1 'First-time adoption of International Financial Reporting Standards') where a parent company reorganises the structure of its group by establishing a new entity as its parent. For further detail on the interaction between the accounting rules and

[55] See 8.8.5.

group reconstruction and merger reliefs, reference should be made to chapters 23 and 24 of PricewaterhouseCoopers' Manual of Accounting – IFRS for the UK.

8.8.5   When is merger relief available?

Section 612[56] merger repeals rejects the provisions of section 131 of the Companies Act 1985 and is applicable (when section 611 is not applicable) where the issuing company secures a holding of at least 90% of the equity in another company, the consideration for which is the issue of equity shares in the issuing company.

This 90% stake can be achieved by way of the issue / transfer to the issuing company of equity shares in the other company or by way of the cancellation of shares not held by the issuing company. In assessing whether a 90% equity stake has been secured:

(i)   shares held by the issuing company, by its subsidiaries and by a nominee on its behalf are considered;

(ii)   shares held by the issuing company (its subsidiaries or nominees) whether acquired at an earlier date or at the same time but for consideration other than the issue of equity shares are taken into account;

(iii)   treasury shares held by the company whose shares are being acquired are not taken into account in calculating the 90%; and

(iv)   to the extent there is more than one class of equity shares, each class is considered (i.e. the issuing company needs to hold at least 90% of each class of equity share).

To the extent that the issuing company secures at least a 90% equity holding in the other company, no share premium is recorded in respect of that share issue. This relief is mandatory and cannot be disapplied (as with section 611)[57].

Applying section 615[58] (as discussed above) to a scenario where section 611 is applicable results in the carrying value of the investment being equal to the aggregate share capital issued (since no share premium is recorded).

However, a company can record a merger reserve (being an unrealised reserve, similar in nature to a revaluation reserve) equal to the value of share premium which would have been recorded had the provisions of this section not been applicable.

---

[56]   Section 612, Companies Act 2006.
[57]   Section 611, Companies Act 2006.
[58]   Section 615, Companies Act 2006.

This occurs, for example, where a company applies EU-adopted IFRS in its individual accounts and has to apply IAS 27. As referred to in section 8.8.4, satisfying the accounting and legal requirements can be complicated and further detail on the interaction with merger relief can be found in chapters 23 and 24 of PricewaterhouseCoopers' Manual of Accounting – IFRS for the UK.

To the extent a merger reserve is recorded, this is treated as a 'premium' for the purposes of section 615 of the Companies Act 2006 and as such the carrying value of the investment would be equal to fair value.

Example

Company A already owns 40% of the equity shares in Company B (which it carries at 120 in its books). It acquires the remaining 60% of the equity shares in Company B in consideration for the payment of 70 in cash and the issue of shares with an aggregate nominal value of 100. The market value of Company B is 700, from which it can be determined that 10% of the acquired shares are acquired for cash and the remaining 50% are acquired for shares.

In accordance with sections 613 and 615 of the Companies Act 2006, Company A would make the following entries:

DR	Cost of investment	170
CR	Cash	70
CR	Share capital	100

i.e. the carrying value of Company A's investment in Company B would be 290 (120 (existing) + 70 (cash consideration) + 100 (shares issued applying section 612).

As noted above, it may also record a merger reserve of 250 (being the difference between the market value of the shares acquired for shares in this transaction (700 x 50%) less the aggregate nominal value of the share capital issued (100)). If it opted to do this, the following additional accounting entries would be made

DR	Cost of investment	250
CR	Merger Reserve	250

i.e. the carrying value of Company A's investment in Company B would be 540 (120 (existing) + 70 (cash consideration) + 100 (shares issued applying section 612) + 250 (merger reserve)).

As noted above this merger reserve is unrealised. It is available to absorb impairments of the investment in Company B or make a bonus issue from it and will become realised as and when Company B is sold for qualifying consideration (as defined by Tech 1/08).

8.8.6 Summary of the position before and after implementation of the Companies Act 2006

Issue	The position under the Companies Act 1985	The position under the Companies Act 2006 with effect from 1 October 2009
What is share premium?	Share premium is recorded (subject to the exceptions detailed below) when a company issues shares for a subscription price that exceeds the aggregate nominal value of the shares issued, and is the amount of the excess of the subscription price over nominal value. It is irrelevant whether the shares are issued for cash or otherwise. Share premium must be transferred to an account called a 'share premium account'.	Sub-section 610(1) restates the Companies Act 1985.
What can share premium be used for?	Share premium may be applied for: (i) issuing and paying up bonus shares; (ii) writing off a company's preliminary expenses (i.e. expenses on formation); (iii) writing off expenses in relation to the commission paid / discount allowed on any issue of shares or debentures; (iv) providing for a payable on redemption of debentures.	The permitted uses of share premium are restricted further by the Companies Act 2006. Sub-sections 610(2) and (3) permit share premium to be applied only to: (i) issuing and paying up bonus shares to members; (ii) writing off expenses in relation to *that issue* of shares; (iii) writing off commission paid on *that issue* of shares.

Issue	The position under the Companies Act 1985	The position under the Companies Act 2006 with effect from 1 October 2009
Group reconstruction relief	Where a wholly-owned company issues shares to either its holding company or another wholly-owned company in exchange for a non-cash asset, it is only required to record share premium equal to the minimum premium value.	Section 611 restates the Companies Act 1985.
Merger relief	Where a company issues equity shares (and does not fall within the provisions of group reconstruction relief) to acquire at least 90% of the equity shares in another entity, no share premium is recorded. The application of merger relief is considered compulsory.	Sections 612 and 613 restate the Companies Act 1985.
Provisions supplementing group reconstruction relief and merger relief	To the extent share premium is disregarded (in part or in full) due to the application of group reconstruction or merger relief, no premium will be included in the carrying value of the related asset.	Section 615 restates the Companies Act 1985.

8.9 What are the restrictions on making a public offer of securities?

In any proposed new issue of shares by a company, consideration must be given at an early stage as to whether the issue will constitute an 'offer to the public'.

8.9.1 What is an 'offer to the public'?

Private companies are prohibited from making public offers of their shares or debentures or from allotting or agreeing to allot shares and debentures with a view to their being offered to the public and may therefore need to re-register as a public company first.

The relevant provisions of the Companies Act 2006 (sections 755 to 757) are effective from 6 April 2008.

The term 'public' is not defined but the Companies Act 2006 provides that the expression 'public' does not just include the public in general, (for example on an IPO) but it can include 'an offer to any section of the public, however selected'[59]. Therefore the term is capable of a wide meaning. The Companies Act 2006 also provides that an offer will not be an offer to the public if:

(i)   it is not calculated to result directly in securities of the company becoming available to anyone other than those receiving the offer; or

(ii)   the offer is otherwise a private concern of the person receiving it and the person making it.

An offer is a private concern if:

(i)   it is made to a person already connected with the company and, where it is made on terms allowing that person to renounce his rights, the rights may only be renounced in favour of another person already connected with the company; or

(ii)   it is an offer to subscribe for securities to be held under an employees' share scheme and, where it is made on terms allowing that person to renounce his rights, the rights may only be renounced in favour of another person entitled to hold securities under the scheme, or a person already connected with the company.

A person is 'already connected with the company' if they are[60]:

(i)   an existing member or employee of the company; or

(ii)   a member of the family of a person who is or was a member or employee of the company; or

(iii)   the widow or widower, or surviving civil partner of a person who was a member or employee of the company; or

(iv)   an existing debenture holder of the company; or

(v)   a trustee of a trust of which the principal beneficiary is any of the above.

8.9.2   To which securities does the prohibition apply?

The prohibition applies to offers of shares and debentures and it is usual practice to treat convertible securities, warrants and options as within the scope of the prohibition.

---

[59]   Section 756, Companies Act 2006.
[60]   Section 756(5), Companies Act 2006.

8.9.3 Can a private company allot or agree to allot securities to a third person with a view to their being offered to the public?

This is also prohibited. There is a presumption that a company makes such an allotment where an offer to the public is made[61]:

(i)   within six months after the allotment or agreement to allot; or

(ii) before the acceptance by the company of the whole of the consideration to be received by it in respect of the securities.

This presumption can however be rebutted by evidence to the contrary.

8.9.4 What changes have been made by the Companies Act 2006?

The Companies Act 2006 largely restates the Companies Act 1985. However, the following changes have been made:

8.9.4.1 *Offers in contemplation of re-registration as a public company*

The Companies Act 2006 introduces a new exemption where a company[62]:

(i)   acts in good faith in pursuance of arrangements under which it is to re-register as a public company before the securities are allotted; or

(ii) as part of the terms of the offer, undertakes to, and does re-register as a public company within a specified period.

8.9.4.2 *Injunctive action*

The Companies Act 2006 introduces a new power for members and creditors to apply to the court to restrain a private company from making an 'offer to the public' in breach of the provisions[63].

8.9.4.3 *De-criminalisation*

It is no longer a criminal offence if the provisions are contravened. Instead new powers are introduced under which the members or the creditors, or the Secretary of State, can apply to the court for an order requiring the company to re-register as a public company or to be wound up[64].

---

[61] Section 755(2), Companies Act 2006.
[62] Section 755(3), Companies Act 2006.
[63] Section 757, Companies Act 2006.
[64] Section 757(3), Companies Act 2006.

8.9.4.4 Remedial orders

The court also has a new power in the event of a contravention to require any person to put a person affected by the breach into the position he would have been in had the breach not occurred. Such an order could require any person (not just the company) knowingly concerned in the contravention to purchase any of those securities at such price and on such other terms as the court thinks fit[65].

8.9.4.5 Is the validity of the allotment affected?

No. The Companies Act 2006[66] confirms that neither the validity of the allotment nor any sale or agreement or offer to sell or allot securities is affected.

8.10 What additional restrictions apply to payment for shares allotted by a public company?

There are a range of additional restrictions in the Companies Act 1985 that apply to the nature of the consideration payable for an allotment of shares by a public company. The relevant provisions are restated in sections 540 to 657 of the Companies Act 2006 which are effective from 1 October 2009.

8.10.1 What are the restrictions?

The following restrictions apply to the payment for shares to be allotted by a public company:

(i)   Shares taken by a subscriber to the memorandum (and any premium) must be paid up in cash[67];

(ii)   Payment for services: A public company must not accept in payment for its shares an undertaking given by any person that he (or another) should do work or perform services for the company (or any other person)[68]. Special care is therefore needed when structuring payments for the services of directors and employees where shares are to be issued;

(iii)   Shares to be paid up as to at least one-quarter: a public company must not allot a share except as paid up at least as to one-quarter of its nominal value (and the whole of any premium). There is an exemption for employee share schemes (where the issue of nil paid shares is common)[69];

---

[65] Section 759, Companies Act 2006.
[66] Section 760, Companies Act 2006.
[67] Section 106, Companies Act 1985; Section 584, Companies Act 2006.
[68] Section 99, Companies Act 1985; Section 585, Companies Act 2006.
[69] Section 101, Companies Act 1985; Section 586, Companies Act 2006.

(iv) Long term undertaking: a public company must not allot shares as fully or partly paid up otherwise than in cash if the consideration for the allotment is (or includes) an undertaking to be performed more than five years after the date of the allotment[70].

8.10.2 What are the sanctions for not complying with the requirements?

The consequences are:

(i) payment by services and by long term undertaking: the holder will be liable to pay the company such amount treated as paid up for the shares allotted, with appropriate interest[71];

(ii) payment as to at least one-quarter of the nominal value: the holder will be liable to pay the company the minimum amount which should have been received for the shares allotted (less the amount actually received), with appropriate interest[72].

The court has the power to exempt a person from liability if it is fair to do so[73].

8.10.3 When is a public company required to obtain a valuation for an allotment of its shares?

Where a public company proposes to allot shares as fully or partly paid for a non cash consideration it must first ensure that:

(i) the consideration for the allotment has been independently valued in accordance with the Companies Acts[74];

(ii) the valuer's report has been issued to the company during the six months immediately preceding the allotment[75]; and

(iii) a copy of the report has been sent to the proposed allottee[76].

A copy of the valuation report must also be filed with Companies House at the same time as the filing of the return of allotment[77].

The provisions are contained in sections 103 and 104 of the Companies Act 1985 which are restated in sections 593, 594 and 595 to 603 of the Companies Act 2006 which are effective from 1 October 2009.

---

[70] Section 102, Companies Act 1985; Section 587, Companies Act 2006.
[71] Section 101, Companies Act 1985; Section 586(2)(a), Companies Act 2006.
[72] Section 101, Companies Act 1985; Section 586, Companies Act 2006.
[73] Section 113, Companies Act 1985; Section 589, Companies Act 2006.
[74] Section 103(5), Companies Act 1985; Section 593(1)(a), Companies Act 2006.
[75] Section 103(5), Companies Act 1985; Section 593(1)(b), Companies Act 2006.
[76] Section 103(5), Companies Act 1985; Section 593(1)(c), Companies Act 2006.
[77] Section 111, Companies Act 1985; Section 597(1), Companies Act 2006.

8.10.4   Are there any exemptions from the requirement to obtain a valuation?

There is an exemption where the shares are issued either:

(i)   as consideration for the acquisition or cancellation of the whole or some of the shares of a company or of a particular class of another company as long as the arrangement has been made available to all of the holders of shares which are to be acquired or cancelled; or

(ii)   as consideration upon a merger with another company under which securities are issued in exchange for the acquisition of all of the assets and liabilities of another company.

In both cases detailed additional conditions apply to the exemptions[78].

In addition there is an exemption to the extent that a company's reserve account or the profit and loss account are applied in paying up shares (or any premium) on any shares allotted to members of the company[79].

8.10.5   Are there special requirements where the company has been incorporated or re-registered recently?

Under both the Companies Act 1985 and the Companies Act 2006, special rules apply to a public company that was formed as such and has obtained a trading certificate, or a company which has re-registered as a public company in each case less than two years before the proposed issue of shares[80]. In this situation where:

(i)   the transaction is with a subscriber to the memorandum[81] (or a member[82], in the case of re-registration);

(ii)   the agreement is for the transfer to the company of non-cash assets; and

(iii)   the consideration represents more than one-tenth of the company's issued share capital issued at that time[83];

the company must, before entering into the agreement to effect the transaction, obtain shareholder approval by way of an ordinary resolution as well as a valuation and the valuation must be circulated to all shareholders. In addition, the valuer's report must have been made to the company during the six months preceding the date of the agreement and sent to the other party to the agreement together with the text of the proposed resolution. The exemptions

---

[78]   Section 595, Companies Act 2006.
[79]   Section 103(2), Companies Act 1985; section 593, Companies Act 2006.
[80]   Section 104(1), (3), Companies Act 1985; section 603, Companies Act 1985.
[81]   Section 104(1)(a), Companies Act 1985; section 598(1)(a), Companies Act 2006.
[82]   Section 104(3)(a), Companies Act 1985; section 603, Companies Act 2006.
[83]   Section 104(1)(b), Companies Act 1985; section 598(1)(c), Companies Act 2006.

set out in paragraph 8.10.4 (share for share exchanges and mergers) do not apply.

However the restrictions do not apply to agreements where:

(i)   the arrangement is entered into as part of the company's ordinary business to enquire or arrange for other persons to acquire assets of a certain description; and

(ii)   an agreement entered into under the supervision of the court for the transfer of an asset by or to the company[84].

8.10.6   What implications are there for the interposition of a new plc holding company?

It is common to interpose a new holding company between shareholders and an existing company by way of share-for-share exchange particularly where an IPO is proposed. In this situation the public company is likely to be newly incorporated and directors and shareholders of the existing company may well be subscribers to the memorandum (particularly as this will facilitate obtaining stamp duty relief on the share-for-share exchange).

In this case, the procedures described in 8.10.5 may nevertheless be required even if all parties are in agreement to the transaction occurring.

8.10.7   What happens if there is a contravention of the restrictions?

There are a range of serious consequences:

8.10.7.1   *Liability of the officers of the company*

It is a criminal offence to fail to file the valuation report with the Registrar of Companies at the same time as the return of allotments[85].

8.10.7.2   *Liability of the allottee*

Where there has been a breach of the requirements set out in section 8.10.3 because the allottee does not receive the valuer's report or there has been some other contravention which he knew or ought to have known about then he is liable to pay an amount equal to the aggregate nominal value of the shares acquired together with any premium and interest. The allotment however remains valid[86].

---

[84]   Section 104(6), Companies Act 1985; section 598(4), (5), Companies Act 2006.
[85]   Section 111(1) and 111(2), Companies Act 1985; sections 597 and 602, Companies Act 2006.
[86]   Section 103(6), Companies Act 1985; section 593(3), Companies Act 2006.

8.10.7.3 *Other consequences*

Where a public company which has been newly incorporated or re-registered (see section 8.10.5) enters into an agreement in contravention of the requirements and either the other party to the agreement has not received the valuer's report or there has been some other contravention which the other party knew or ought to have known amounted to a contravention then:

(i)   the agreement for the acquisition of the non-cash asset so far as not carried out is void (this would mean, for example, that warranties or provisions for deferred payment would be invalidated);

(ii)   the company can recover any consideration paid by it under the agreement or an amount equal to its value.

Where the agreement is for the allotment of shares and to the extent that the allottee is also liable to pay the company an amount equal to the nominal value of the shares and any premium (together with interest)[87].

8.10.8   Are there additional requirements when allotting shares in a public company?

A public company must not allot shares following an offer for subscription unless the offer is subscribed for in full[88] or it is made on the express terms that the shares will be allotted in any event[89] or where other specific conditions have been met[90]. If the conditions for the allotment are not satisfied, the consideration received by the company must be returned to the applicants for shares immediately on expiry of 40 days from the date of the first making of the offer[91].

Interest becomes payable after the 48th day at a rate of interest to be determined under the Judgments Act 1838 (currently 8%) as opposed to 5% under the Companies Act 1985[92].

The additional provisions are contained in sections 578 to 579 of the Companies Act 2006. They largely restate the Companies Act 1985 and come into force on 1 October 2009.

There are criminal penalties for any director who knowingly contravenes or permits a contravention of these requirements and he is liable to compensate the company and the allottee for any loss, damages, costs or expenses that the

---

[87] Section 105, Companies Act 1985; section 604, Companies Act 2006.
[88] Section 84(1), Companies Act 1985; Section 578(1)(a), Companies Act 2006.
[89] Section 84(1), Companies Act 1985; Section 578(1)(b)(i), Companies Act 2006.
[90] Section 84(1), Companies Act 1985; Section 578(1)(b)(ii), Companies Act 2006.
[91] Section 84(2), Companies Act 1985; Section 578(2), Companies Act 2006.
[92] Section 84(3), Companies Act 1985; Section 578(3), Companies Act 2006.

company or allottee may have sustained or incurred (subject to a limitation period of two years from the date of allotment)[93].

In addition any allotment is voidable at the instance of the applicant within one month after the date of the allotment.

8.11   What are the implications for subsequent acquirers of shares from a person in breach of the Companies Act?

8.11.1   When can liability arise?

In certain situations liability can extend to subsequent acquirers of shares from a person who has themselves acquired shares in breach of the allotment rules. The rules are complex and case law is relatively undeveloped in this area.

The situations where a subsequent acquirer can incur liability are where the original allottee is liable as a result of a contravention of the rules relating to:

(i)   the prohibition on public companies from accepting as payment up of the shares (or any premium), an undertaking to perform services for the company or any other person (see section 8.10.1);

(ii)   the prohibition on the allotment of shares at a discount (which applies to both public and private companies (see section 8.7.1);

(iii)   the prohibition on private companies allotting shares paid up as to less than one quarter of their nominal value, or the whole or any premium (see section 8.10.1); and

(iv)   the requirement for a public company to obtain a valuation and comply with the other requirements disclosed in sections 8.10.3 and 8.10.5[94].

In these cases the acquirer will become jointly and severally liable with the allottee unless:

(i)   he acquired the shares for value and did not know of the breach; or

(ii)   the purchaser acquired the shares from a person who became a holder, but who was not himself under a liability for the breach.

---

[93]   Section 85 Companies Act 1985; section 579, Companies Act 2006.
[94]   Section 112, Companies Act 1985; sections 588 and 605, Companies Act.

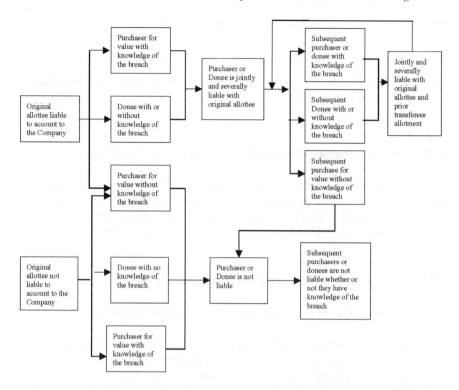

When acquiring shares, particularly those that are not traded, it is therefore essential that thorough due diligence is undertaken beforehand to ensure that the Companies Acts requirements have been satisfied.

8.11.2   Power of the court to grant relief

The court has power on application to grant relief from liability if it is just and equitable to do so but this should be regarded as a last resort[95].

8.12   Can a company pay commissions, discounts and allowances on an allotment of shares?

8.12.1   What is the current position?

A company is generally prohibited from applying its shares or capital money in the payment of any commission, discount or allowance to any person whether directly or indirectly in consideration of his subscribing (or agreeing to subscribe) for any shares in the company, or procuring (or agreeing to procure) subscriptions for any shares in the company[96].

---

95   Section 113, Companies Act 1985; sections 589 and 605, Companies Act.
96   Sections 97 and 98, Companies Act 1985.

However, payment of such a commission is permitted if:

(i)   it is authorised by the company's articles of association; and

(ii)   it does not exceed 10% of the price at which the shares are issued or the amount or rate provided for in the articles of association whichever is less.

8.12.2   Are any changes introduced by the Companies Act 2006?

No. The new provisions relating to the prohibition of commissions, discounts and allowances payable in relation to an allotment of shares are contained in sections 552 and 553 of the Companies Act 2006 is effective from 1 October 2009 and restate sections 97 and 98 of the Companies Act 1985.

8.13   Consolidation and subdivision of shares

8.13.1   Why does a company sub-divide or consolidate its shares?

A company may wish to consolidate or sub-divide shares to eliminate unusual nominal values which have arisen as a result of prior variations of share capital or to create a greater number of smaller shares available to potential subscribers (such as in connection with an employee share scheme). Share subdivisions can also be used as a means of adjusting voting rights as between shareholders.

8.13.2   What is the position from 1 October 2009?

Section 121 of the Companies Act 1985 provides that where the articles of a company allow it to do so, the company by passing an ordinary resolution in a general meeting can:

(i)   consolidate and divide all or any of its share capital into shares of a larger amount than its existing shares; and

(ii)   sub-divide its shares into shares of a smaller amount than is fixed by the memorandum.

In the case of a sub-division, the proportion between the amount paid and the amount unpaid on a share must remain the same as it was prior to the sub-division[97].

---

[97] Section 121(3), Companies Act 1985.

8.13.3   What changes are introduced by the Companies Act 2006?

A company will still be required to obtain an ordinary resolution in order to sub-divide or consolidate its share capital but it will no longer require authority in its articles[98].

The requirement to maintain the proportion of paid-up to unpaid share capital is extended to cover shares which are consolidated as well as shares which are sub-divided.

8.13.4   Can a company restrict its ability to consolidate or sub-divide its shares?

Yes, both the resolution to sub-divide or consolidate and the articles may restrict the exercise of more than one power (i.e. to sub-divide and consolidate) at a time or under certain circumstances.

8.13.5   Will the filing requirements at Companies House change?

Yes. Under the Companies Act 2006, companies will continue to be required to file a notice of alteration of share capital on a subdivision or consolidation with Companies House within one month of exercising the power. The number of the required form will change. In addition, the Companies Act 2006 will also require a statement of capital to be filed[99].

8.14   What is the procedure for a redenomination of share capital?

8.14.1   Why does a company redenominate its shares?

Redenomination is the process of converting the nominal value of shares from one currency to another. A company may wish to redenominate its share capital to facilitate/mitigate exchange rate risks and to align its share capital with the currency most frequently used in the operation of its business. Redenomination can also be the alteration of the monetary unit of the nominal value of shares arising in the context of a consolidation or subdivision.

8.14.2   What is the procedure before 1 October 2009?

There is no specific redenomination procedure under the existing Companies Act 1985. As such, where a company wishes to change the currency of the nominal value of the shares, it is compelled to cancel the existing shares which it wishes to redenominate and then issue new shares in the required currency. Usually this is effected by way of a share buyback financed from the proceeds of a fresh issue of shares made for the purpose or by way of a court approved

---

[98] Section 618(3), Companies Act 2006.
[99] Section 619(1) and Section 619(2), Companies Act 2006.

reduction of capital. The procedure is, however, a cumbersome process (see chapter 9) particularly as it should have minimal impact on creditors.

8.14.3 What changes are introduced by the Companies Act 2006?

The Companies Act 2006 sections 622 to 628 are effective from 1 October 2009 and introduce a simplified procedure to facilitate the redenomination of share capital. A company will be able to redenominate its share capital by simply passing an ordinary resolution.

The resolution approving the redenomination must set out an appropriate spot rate of exchange by which the conversion has been calculated[100]. The resolution may take effect on the day it is passed or may require certain conditions to be fulfilled before the conversion can take effect, although the authority conferred by the resolution will expire 28 days after it is passed[101].

The Companies Act 2006 confirms[102] that the process of redenomination does not affect the rights or obligations of the shareholders of those redenominated shares.

Where the nominal allocated share capital of a public company falls below the limits set by the regulations and by statute the company must within one year of the passing of the resolution authorising the redenomination apply for the re-registration of the company as a private company[103].

The Companies Act 2006 also enables a public limited company, once it has satisfied the minimum share capital requirements (£50,000 or €65,6000) to obtain a trading certificate, to redenominate the whole of its share capital in a currency of its choosing.

Details of the redenomination and a statement of capital must be filed with the Registrar of Companies.

8.14.4 How are fractions arising following a conversion dealt with?

The process of redenomination may give rise to a remainder which is a fraction of a nominal value due to conversion rates and rounding issues.

The Companies Act 2006 provides for a limited reduction of capital to allow a company to provide a suitable fixed nominal value for the redenominated shares. The process involves the following requirements:

---

[100] Section 622(2), Companies Act 2006.
[101] Section 622(3), Companies Act 2006.
[102] Section 624, Companies Act 2006.
[103] Regulations 5 to 8 Companies (Shares, Share Capital and Authorised Minimum) Regulations 2007.

8.14.4.1   Special resolution

A company may by special resolution reduce its share capital to cancel any outstanding shares and to facilitate the redenomination without the need for either a solvency statement or court approval[104].

8.14.4.2   Maximum limit

The reduction of capital arising from the redenomination must not be in excess of 10% of the company's allotted share capital, calculated after the reduction has become effective.

8.14.4.3   Time limit

The reduction must take place within three months of the special resolution authorising it.

8.14.4.4   Filing requirements

The reduction will only become valid when notice of the reduction[105] is filed, together with a statement of capital, at Companies House.

As well as the filing of the notice of the reduction with the statement of capital, a company which takes advantage of the ability to reduce its share capital as a result of a redenomination must also file a statement with the Registrar of Companies confirming that the reduction does not exceed the 10% maximum reduction[106].

8.14.4.5   Redenomination reserve

A company that reduces its share capital as a result of redenomination must transfer an amount equal to the reduction to a non-distributable reserve called the 'redenomination reserve'[107]. This reserve can only be applied by the company in paying up shares to be allotted to members as fully paid bonus shares. The redenomination reserve is treated in much the same way as a capital redemption reserve.

8.14.5   What if a company has not followed the requirements under the Companies Act 2006?

If a company does not follow the procedures set out in the Companies Act 2006 then every officer in default and the company itself may be subject to criminal

---

[104] Section 627, Companies Act 2006.
[105] Section 627(5), Companies Act 2006.
[106] Section 627(6), Companies Act 2006.
[107] Section 628, Companies Act 2006.

penalties. A person guilty of an offence under this section is liable on summary conviction to a fine, and for continued contravention a daily default fine [108].

8.14.6 What action should a company take in advance of 1 October 2009?

Companies should review their articles of association to ensure that they do not contain any restrictions that would prevent the company from taking advantage of these simplified procedures. If a redenomination is proposed consideration could also be given to deferring the process until on or after 1 October 2009 when the simplified procedures will be available.

8.15 How are class rights varied?

Class rights are the specific rights attached to a group or class of shares. They are commonly set out in the articles of association but may also be found in the memorandum or in an agreement for the subscription for the shares. Typically classes of shares will differ from one another by virtue of differing voting rights, rights to dividends or the rights to capital, or any combination of these.

The Companies Acts provide that shares are of the same class when their rights are uniform in all respects (save that differences in the amount of dividend paid in the 12 months from the date of issue are permitted)[109]. The definition of a class right or a variation of rights is covered by common law.

A variation of class rights arises where the rights pertaining to a particular class of shares in the articles are altered. A variation of the rights of one class may, as a matter of law, also constitute a variation of the rights of the holders of another class or classes of shares, as, for example, increasing the voting rights of one class may in effect reduce the voting rights of another.

A variation of class rights, which are set out in the articles of association, is effected by amending the articles, or by adopting new articles altogether which contain the varied class rights subject to the further procedures expanded below. The procedures described below do not apply when a company has only a single class of shares in issue, as in that situation there are no class rights, only shareholder rights.

8.15.1 What are the main changes introduced by the Companies Act 2006?

The Companies Act 2006 sets out the procedure to be followed in order to vary class rights[110]. These provisions are effective from 1 October 2009 when sections 125 to 129 of the Companies Act 1985 will be repealed.

---

[108] Sections 619, 621 and 625, Companies Act 2006.
[109] Section 128(2), Companies Act 1985; section 629, Companies Act 2006.
[110] Sections 629 to 640, Companies Act 2006.

The Companies Act 2006 makes a number of changes which are designed to simplify and clarify the process of varying class rights. Some of the main changes are as follows:

(i) variations of class rights may be effected by special, rather than extraordinary, resolution (as extraordinary resolutions have been abolished);

(ii) new provisions are introduced setting out the process for variation of class rights for companies without a share capital (such as companies limited by guarantee);

(iii) companies will be required to file details of the variation (including the change of name of a class) at Companies House regardless of how the variation is effected. Prior to this change, there was no obligation to file an additional notice of variation if the rights were varied by way of amendment to the memorandum or articles, special resolution or agreements as these were required to be filed under section 380 of the Companies Act 1985 anyway.

8.15.2   What is the procedure before 1 October 2009?

The Companies Act 1985 sets out different procedures to be followed in order to vary class rights, depending on how the rights have been attached to the shares and whether a procedure for a variation of those rights is contained in the articles. The purpose of these provisions is to protect holders of a class of shares with minority, or no, voting rights, from having their rights amended without their consent. The chart below shows the way in which this protection is given.

Summary of the procedure for a variation of class rights under the Companies Act 1985

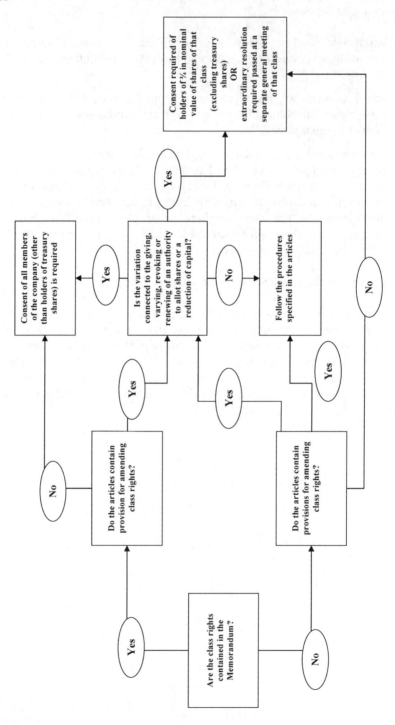

8.15.3   What is the position from 1 October 2009[111]?

The Companies Act 2006 simplifies the procedure for the variation of class rights by providing that class rights can be varied (a) in accordance with the provisions set out in the articles of association of the company; or (b) where the articles do not contain provisions in respect of variation, with the consent of the holders of shares of that class. Consent must be in writing by either:

(i)   the holders of at least three quarters in nominal value of the issued shares of that class[112]; or

(ii)   a special resolution passed at a separate general meeting of the holders of that class sanctioning the variation.

The provisions of the Companies Act 2006 allow a company to incorporate higher or lower thresholds of consent in the articles if it chooses to do so.

The Companies Act 2006 also extends the same procedure for variation of class rights to companies having no share capital, e.g. companies limited by guarantee having different classes of members[113].

It can therefore be seen that the new provisions greatly simplify the Companies Act 1985 requirements:

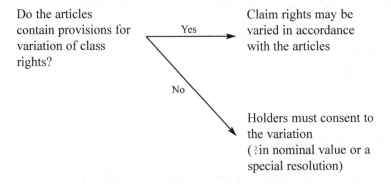

Do the articles contain provisions for variation of class rights?

Yes → Claim rights may be varied in accordance with the articles

No → Holders must consent to the variation ($\frac{3}{4}$ in nominal value or a special resolution)

8.15.4   Can shareholders of a class object to the variation?

Where holders of at least 15% of the issued shares in the class object to the variation they may apply to court to have the variation cancelled[114]. Such an application must be made within 21 days of the date of consent or of the passing of the resolution. Once an application is made the variation of class rights is postponed until such time as the court approves the variation[115]. The

[111] Sections 630–640, Companies Act 2006.
[112] Excluding any shares held as treasury shares.
[113] Section 631, Companies Act 2006.
[114] Section 127, Companies Act 1985; sections 633 and 634, Companies Act 2006.
[115] Section 127(2), Companies Act 1985; section 633(3), Companies Act 2006.

court will examine the effect of the variation, and if it believes that the variation will unfairly prejudice the rights of the shareholders of that class it has power to disallow the variation. These provisions are restated in the Companies Act 2006 and the rights to object extended in relation to companies without a share capital.

8.15.5 Are there any filing requirements?

Where the memorandum or articles has been amended, a copy of the special resolution[116] together with a copy of the revised memorandum or articles must be filed with the Registrar of Companies within 15 days of the passing of the resolution.

Where a company allots shares or varies share rights that are not stated in the memorandum or articles, a statement in the prescribed form containing particulars of those rights must be filed within one month of the allotment or variation[117]. Such provisions also apply to a company that does not have a share capital, which creates a class of members or varies the rights of such a class of members[118]. These provisions are restated in the Companies Act 2006[119]. However, a statement of capital is not required as there will be no change in the aggregate amount of the company's subscribed capital.

8.15.6 Is there any action required before 1 October 2009?

No particular action is required. The Companies Act 1985 will apply to the variation of all class rights until 1 October 2009 and the Companies Act 2006 will apply thereafter.

8.16 Cross holdings

8.16.1 What are cross holdings?

Cross holdings exist where a company holds shares in another company in the same group.

8.16.2 What is the position under the Companies Act 2006?

The relevant provisions are sections 136 to 144 which are in force from 1 October 2009. They make no change to the position under the Companies Act 1985[120].

---

[116] Section 18, Companies Act 1985; section 30(1), Companies Act 2006.
[117] Section 128, Companies Act 1985.
[118] Section 129, Companies Act 1985.
[119] Section 640, Companies Act 2006.
[120] Section 23, Companies Act 1985.

8.16.3   Can a company be a member of its holding company?

Neither a UK incorporated subsidiary, nor an overseas incorporated subsidiary can hold shares in its parent, if the parent is incorporated in the UK. This is due to the general prohibition on a body corporate (which can include non-UK incorporated companies) from holding any shares in any 'company', which is its holding company. 'Company' for this purpose means a company formed and registered under the Companies Acts (which includes predecessor legislation)[121]. A 'parent company' is an undertaking in relation to another that:

(i)   holds a majority of the voting rights in the undertaking;

(ii)   is a member of the undertaking and has the right to appoint or remove a majority of its board of directors;

(iii)   has the right to exercise a dominant influence over the undertaking; or

(iv)   is a member, and pursuant to an agreement with the other members, controls alone the majority of the voting rights[122].

There is no prohibition on a UK incorporated company holding shares in its non-UK incorporated parent (although there might be restrictions under the applicable law of that parent). In addition, there are no restrictions on a UK company having a cross holding in one of its corporate members as long as that corporate member is not its parent.

There are equivalent prohibitions for companies, which do not have a share capital, such as companies limited by guarantee[123].

8.16.4   Can a UK company acquire shares in a company which holds shares in its parent?

In principle, according to case law, this should be a permissible transaction as long as the purpose was not to circumvent the general prohibition on a subsidiary holding shares in its parent.

However, the voting rights attaching to the shares of the parent will cease to be exercisable.

---

[121] Section 735(1) Companies Act 2006; section 1, Companies Act 2006.
[122] Section 736, Companies Act 1985; section 1159, Companies Act 2006.
[123] Section 23(8), Companies Act 1985.

8.16.5   Are there any exemptions?

Yes, there are certain exemptions where:

(i)   the subsidiary is acting as personal representative or trustee provided that neither the holding company nor any of the subsidiaries is beneficially interested under the trust (with certain interests under an employee share scheme or pension scheme being disregarded for this purpose)[124]; and

(ii)   where the subsidiary is acting as an authorised dealer in securities in the ordinary course of the business (certain businesses such as insurance are excluded for this purpose)[125].

These are complex rules defining the scope of these exemptions which are set out in the Companies Acts.

8.16.6   What are the consequences where a crossholding arises?

Any allotment or transfer of shares in breach of the Companies Acts 2006 is void[126]. There can be situations where a corporate shareholder (A) of a company (B) is then acquired by that company giving rise to a crossholding by A, in its resultant parent, B. In this case the acquisition of A is not prohibited but the shares A holds in B are disenfranchised for as long as the crossholding exists[127]. Dividends can continue to be paid and A can participate in any further bonus issue of shares, but again the shares are disenfranchised for the duration of the crossholding.

8.17   Transfer of shares

8.17.1   What changes are introduced by the Companies Act 2006?

Sections 768 to 778 of the Companies Act 2006 came into force on 6 April 2008, and restates the existing provisions of the Companies Act 1985 with the addition of a new requirement that directors must state their reasons if they refuse to register a transfer of shares.

---

[124] Section 23(2), Companies Act 1985; section 138(1), (2), Companies Act 2006.
[125] Section 23(3), Companies Act 1985; section 141(1), (2), Companies Act 2006.
[126] Section 23(1), Companies Act 1985; section 136(1), Companies Act 2006.
[127] Section 23(5), Companies Act 1985; section 137, Companies Act 2006.

8.17.2 What are the two main procedures for transferring shares in a company?

There are two primary methods.

(i) Transfers of certificated shares:

This is the procedure which is used when transferring shares in public and private companies and which requires a stock transfer form and the original share certificate.

(ii) Transfers of uncertificated shares:

This is the process by which shares are transferred electronically through the CREST transfer system, and which applies to listed companies.

8.17.3 What is the process for transferring certificated shares?

(i) Identify applicable instructions on share transfers.

Most commonly these will be found in the articles of association of the company and can include pre-emption rights or other restrictions on transfers. Restrictions can also be imposed by contract, with employment contracts and joint venture agreements being common examples.

(ii) Formalities for the transfer of shares.

The Companies Act 2006[128] provides that a company is prohibited from registering a transfer of shares unless a 'proper instrument of transfer' is used. This means that a transfer must be in writing and than an oral transfer of shares is not permissible (unless it is by operation of law such as to personal representatives in the event of the death of the holder).

Where the transfer is of fully paid shares the Stock Transfer Act 1963 will generally apply. The Stock Transfer Act 1963 Act contains the form of stock transfer that may be used and which constitutes a 'proper instrument of transfer' for this purpose.

The stock transfer must be executed by the transferor and satisfy certain content requirements, but need not be signed by the transferee or witnessed.

The Stock Transfer Act 1963 does not apply to unlimited companies, or to companies limited by guarantee or to part paid shares. In this situation the procedure for transferring shares should be set out in the company's articles of association and will usually require the transfer to be executed by the transferee as well as the transferor.

(iii) The transferor must deliver the transfer and share certificate duly stamped to the transferee:

---

[128] Section 770(1), Companies Act 2006.

If all the shares on the share certificate are being transferred, the certificate can simply be handed to the transferee. However, if only a proportion of the shares are being transferred, the transferor must send the certificate to the company with details of the amount of shares being sold. The company can then mark the share certificate so that two new certificates in the relevant proportions are issued on the conclusion of the transfer process.

(iv) The transferee must then deliver the documents to the company for registration:

Once the company receives the stamped transfer form and the certificate, it can then register the transfer of the shares. The company is now required, within two months, either to register the transfer or to give notice to the transferee that the request has been refused, together with reasons for the refusal.

This refusal will not affect the transferee's beneficial interest in the shares but he will not be able to exercise all the rights attaching to those shares. For example, he may not vote at meetings until such time as the transfer is approved and he is entered on the register of members. There is, however, no statutory power to compel directors to register a transfer of shares.

(v) The company enters details on to register of members and sends out share certificates:

The details of the new shareholder must then be entered onto the register of members and a new share certificate must be issued within two months. The issue of the share certificate will not be necessary where (a) the terms of the issue of the shares provide otherwise, (b) the transfer is to a financial institutions, or (c) the transfer and allotment is followed by the issue of a share warrant in respect of those shares[129].

8.17.4 What is the process for transferring uncertificated shares?

Since July 1996 companies listed on the London Stock Exchange or AIM must have the option of having their securities traded electronically. These are transferred through CREST. The uncertificated securities regulations provide for the treasury to approve persons applying to act as operator of an uncertificated transfer system although only CREST has so far done so. Even if an issuer has joined the CREST system, investors retain the right to have hard copy certificates sent to them. The Companies Act 2006 enables the Secretary of State to make regulations requiring a company to permit the paperless transfer and holding of its securities. Whether or not such regulation will be made is still under consideration.

---

[129] Section 776(2), Companies Act 2006.

8.18 Share warrants

8.18.1 What is a share warrant?

A share warrant entitles the bearer to the shares specified in the warrant and significantly, it allows the specified shares to be transferred by delivery of the warrant[130]. The warrant need not follow the transfer formalities mentioned in section 8.17 above, as they can simply be transferred by deliverance of the warrant to the transferee.

Share warrants can only be issued on fully paid-up shares.

8.18.2 What rights do share warrants carry?

The rights of holders of share warrants are contained in a company's articles of association. Table A of the Companies Act 1985 is silent as to share warrants. However, the Companies (Model Articles) Regulations (relevant to companies incorporated on or after 1 October 2009) do contain provisions on share warrants. The Model Articles state the rights of holders and directors in regards to share warrants. The articles provide that the holders of share warrants have the same rights as shareholders who have their names entered into the register of members[131], but this can be varied by special resolution.

8.18.3 How are share warrants issued prior to 1 October 2009 under the Companies Act 1985?

The following steps are needed:

(i)   check that the company has permission in its articles of association to issue share warrants – there is no provision in Table A of the Companies Act 1985 for the rights of the holders of share warrants or for the issue of them;

(ii)   the company issues registered shares (see sections 8.3 to 8.12); and

(iii)   the company converts fully paid registered shares into share warrants.

By this process the share certificate would be recalled and a share warrant would be issued. The register of members must then be updated to remove the shareholder's name against the specified shares and in their place the register must state that a share warrant has been issued, the identification numbers of the shares and the date of the warrant[132].

---

[130] Section 779, Companies Act 2006.
[131] Regulation 51(6), Companies (Model Articles) Regulations 2008.
[132] Section 355, Companies Act 1985.

8.18.4   How are share warrants issued after 1 October 2009 under the Companies Act 2006?

The Companies Act 2006 simplifies the process. Registered shares no longer have to be issued first[133]; the share warrant can be issued at the outset and the warrant entered directly onto the register. The articles of association must still authorise the issue of share warrants and the same information must be entered onto the register of members as under the Companies Act 1985.

Under the Companies Act 2006 there is a new requirement to issue a share certificate within two months of the holder of a warrant wishing to surrender it for cancellation[134].

8.19   What are treasury shares?

Section 162A to 162G of the Companies Act 1985 set out the rules relating to treasury shares. These provisions are largely restated by sections 724 to 732 of the Companies Act 2006 which are effective from 1 October 2009.

Where a limited company purchases its own shares out of distributable profits[135] it can, provided that the shares are 'qualifying shares', elect to hold the shares as treasury shares or dispose of them provided certain conditions are met. This means that the shares once purchased are not cancelled but remain in existence and that some of the process that would otherwise be involved in a purchase of own shares followed by a reissue is reduced.

8.19.1   Which shares can be held as treasury shares?

The shares have to be 'qualifying shares'[136] which are shares that are:

(i)   officially listed on the London Stock Exchange;

(ii)   traded on AIM;

(iii)   officially listed in an EEA State; or

(iv)   traded on a regulated market.

Private companies which do not have traded shares cannot therefore take advantage of these provisions.

Once the shares have been purchased the company may hold all or any of them or deal with them. If the company holds the shares it must be entered in the register of members as the holder of the shares.

---

[133] Section 122(1)(b), Companies Act 2006.
[134] Section 122 (4), Companies Act 2006.
[135] See Chapter 9 for the detailed value.
[136] Section 724, Companies Act 2006.

8.19.2   Is there a limit on the holdings of treasury shares?

Yes. There is a limit on the number of shares that can be held in treasury. Where the company has only one class of shares the aggregate nominal value that can be held in treasury is 10% of the aggregate nominal value of the shares in issue[137].

Where the company has more than one class of shares and holds shares of a particular class in treasury then the limit is 10% of the aggregate nominal value of the issued shares of that class[138].

If the limit is breached, the company must either dispose of or cancel the excess shares within twelve months[139].

8.19.3   Where shares are held by a company as treasury shares are there any restrictions on the exercise of shareholder rights?

Yes. A company is not entitled to exercise any shareholder rights in respect of treasury shares (in particular the right to attend or note at meetings[140]). In addition no distributions may be made by a company in respect of treasury shares[141] although they do qualify for bonus issues of fully paid shares and they can be redeemed[142].

8.19.4   What restrictions are there on dealings by a company in treasury shares?

A company may at any time sell treasury shares for a cash consideration or transfer them into an employees' share scheme[143] (see Chapter 10, section 10.4.1.3).

'Cash' for this purpose means:

(i)   cash received by the company;

(ii)   a cheque received by the company in good faith that the directors have no reason to believe will not be paid;

(iii)   a release of a liability of the company to pay a liquidated sum;

(iv)   an undertaking to pay cash to the company no later than 90 days after the company agree to sell the shares; or

---

[137] Section 725(1), Companies Act 2006.
[138] Section 725(2), Companies Act 2006.
[139] Section 725(3), Companies Act 2006.
[140] Section 726(2), Companies Act 2006.
[141] Section 726(3), Companies Act 2006.
[142] Section 726(4), Companies Act 2006.
[143] Section 727, Companies Act 2006.

(v)   payment by any other means giving a present of future entitlement (of the company or a person acting on the company's behalf) to a payment, or credit equivalent to payment, in cash.

Cash also includes foreign currency[144].

The company must file details of the disposal with the Registrar of Companies within 28 days[145].

8.19.5   Can treasury shares be cancelled?

The company can at any time cancel treasury shares and must do so if they cease to be 'qualifying shares'[146]. In this situation the company does not need to comply with the rules relating to reductions of capital (see Chapter 9) and the company's share capital is reduced by the nominal amount of the shares cancelled[147].

Details must be filed with the Registrar of Companies within 28 days of the cancellation together with a statement of capital[148].

8.19.6   How are the proceeds of sale accounted for?

If the proceeds of sale are equal to or less than the purchase price paid by the company for the shares then the proceeds are treated as a realised profit of the company[149]. If they exceed the purchase price paid by the company then an amount equal to the purchase price is still treated as a realised profit but the excess must be transferred to the share premium account.

The weighted average price method must be used to determine the purchase price paid by the company and if shares were allotted to the company as fully paid bonus shares the purchase price for them is treated as nil[150].

---

[144] Section 727, Companies Act 2006.
[145] Section 728, Companies Act 2006.
[146] Section 729(1), (2), Companies Act 2006.
[147] Section 730(3), (4), Companies Act 2006.
[148] Section 730(1), (5), Companies Act 2006.
[149] Section 731(2), Companies Act 2006.
[150] Section 731(4), Companies Act 2006.

8.20   Summary of key changes and actions

There follows a summary of the key changes, implementation dates and key actions:

	Key change	Implementation date	Action required
1. Requirement for authorised share capital **(section 8.3)**	There is no longer a requirement to have an authorised share capital.	1 October 2009	Restrictions on the share capital of a company contained in the constitution require review and amendment.
2. Authority to allot shares **(section 8.4)**	This is no longer required for private companies with a single class of share.	1 October 2009	As above.
3. Statutory pre-emption rights **(section 8.5)**	Where the statutory pre-emption procedures apply there are changes to the individual notices required to be served.	1 October 2009	Due to definitional changes in the Companies Act 2006 the wording of the standard pre-emption disapplication resolution will require amendment.
4. Post allotment steps **(section 8.6)**	Allotment must be registered within two months. Where shares are issued for a non-cash consideration the underlying contract need not be filed. A statement of capital is required. Unlimited companies are required to file a return of allotment in certain cases.	1 October 2009	No action required.
5. Payment for shares **(section 8.7)**	No change.	1 October 2009	No action required.
6. Accounting for an allotment of shares **(section 8.8)**	The uses of share premium are more restricted.	1 October 2009	No action required.

	Key change	Implementation date	Action required
7. Offers to the public (section 8.9)	Offers of securities to the public may be made by a private company in contemplation of their re-registration as public companies.	6 April 2008	No action required.
8. Allotment of shares by a public company (sections 8.10 & 8.11)	No change.	1 October 2009	No action required.
9. Payment of commissions (section 8.12)	No change.	1 October 2009	No action required.
10. Consideration and subdivision of share capital (section 8.13)	Authority is no longer required in a company's articles of association.	1 October 2009	No action required.
11. Redenomination of share capital (section 8.14)	Simplified procedure introduced.	1 October 2009	Consider deferring redenomination until simplified procedures are introduced.
12. Variation of class rights (section 8.15)	Simplified procedure by ordinary resolution.	1 October 2009	Review articles and consider deferring any proposed redenomination to after 1 October 2009.
14. Cross holdings (section 8.16)	No change.	1 October 2009	No action required.
15. Transfers of shares (section 8.17)	Directors must now give reasons for refusal of transfer.	6 April 2008	No action required.
16. Share warrants (section 8.18)	Companies no longer have to issue and register shares before issuing share warrants.	1 October 2009	No action required.
17. Treasury shares (section 8.19)	No significant change.	1 October 2009	No action required.

8.A.1   Appendix 1

8.A.1.1   Summary of the situations in which a statement of capital is required to be filed

A statement of capital must contain the following information:

(i)   the total number of shares allotted;

(ii)   the aggregate nominal value of those shares;

(iii)   for each class of share:

- the prescribed particulars of the rights attached to the shares;

- the total number of shares of that class;

- the aggregate nominal value of shares of that class; and

(iv)   the amount paid and (if any) unpaid on each share.

No statement of capital is required where there is a variation of the rights attaching to the shares provided there is no change in the number or nominal value of those shares.

The following situations require a statement of capital to be filed with Companies House (section references are to the Companies Act 2006):

(i)   Incorporation and allotment of new shares (sections 9 and 555);

(ii)   Re-registration of a company which already has share capital (section 108);

(iii)   Subdivision or consolidation of shares (section 619);

(iv)   Reconversion of stock into shares (section 621);

(v)   Redenomination of shares (section 625);

(vi)   Reduction of capital in connection with redenomination (section 627);

(vii)   Court-confirmed and solvency statement capital reductions (section 649)*;

(viii) Cancellation of shares (section 663);

(ix)   Redemption of shares (section 689);

(x)   Cancellation of shares in connection with share buybacks (section 708);

(xi)   Cancellation of treasury shares (section 730); and

(xii)   Within an annual return (section 856).

*note that until 1 October 2009, when this section is in force, a memorandum complying with section 622(2) is required in place of a statement of capital[151].

---

[151] Companies Act 2006 (Commencement No. 7 and Transitional Provisions) Order 2008.

8.A.2   Appendix 2

8.A.2.1   Checklist for an allotment of shares by a private limited company under the Companies Act 2006

	Action	Comment
1.	**Before making the allotment** Confirm whether the allotment is to be made for cash consideration only.	If yes, the pre-emption provisions will be relevant.
	Check articles of association: (i) to confirm if pre-emption provisions have been excluded or disapplied (if not, consider disapplying them by special resolution or follow the procedure for pre-emption offers); and (ii) for any prohibition or restriction on the directors' power to allot shares.	If pre-emption provisions have not been excluded or disapplied, consider disapplying them by a special resolution (otherwise you will need to follow the pre-emption offers procedure). If there are prohibitions or restrictions on allotment, you will need to prepare new authorisation by ordinary resolution.
	If applicable, prepare pre-emption offers to existing shareholders.	
	Check whether authority to allot is required.	A company with only one class of shares does not require authority to allot further shares of the same class. If the company has more than one class of shares, prepare new authorisation by ordinary resolution (unless an existing authority has yet to expire or you can rely on existing authorisation in the articles of association).
	Prepare ordinary resolution authorising directors to allot shares (if required).	Not required if the company has only one class of shares and there are no prohibitions or restrictions on allotment in the articles of association.
	Prepare special resolution disapplying pre-emption provisions (if required).	This should be combined with the ordinary resolution above.
	Prepare application to subscribe for shares (if applicable).	
	Prepare resolution of the board of directors to accept the application (if applicable) and to allot shares.	
2.	**Within one month from the date of allotment** File a return of allotment, together with a statement of capital, with Companies House.	
3	**Within two months from the date of allotment** Register the allotment in the statutory registers of the company.	The allotment must be registered in the statutory registers as soon as practicable and in any event within two months of the date of allotment.

Share capital and transactions involving shares

	Action	Comment
	Account for the allotment in the books of the company.	Not required to credit share premium to share premium account if group reconstruction relief or merger relief is available.
	Issue a share certificate to the allottee.	
	Credit any share premium to the share premium account.	

8.A.3   Appendix 3

8.A.3.1   Checklist for an allotment of shares by a public company under the Companies Act 2006

	Action	Comment
1.	**Before making the allotment** Confirm whether the allotment is to be made for cash consideration only.	If yes, the pre-emption provisions will be relevant. In addition, the further restrictions on issue of shares by a public company must be considered.
	Check articles of association: (i) to confirm if pre-emption provisions have been disapplied (if not, consider disapplying them by special resolution or follow the procedure for pre-emption offers); and (ii) any prohibition or restriction on the directors' power to allot shares.	If pre-emption provisions have not been disapplied, consider disapplying them by a special resolution (otherwise the company must need to follow the pre-emption offers procedure).
	If applicable, prepare pre-emption offers to existing shareholders	
	Check whether authority to allot is required.	A new authority will not be required if an existing authority (either as contained in the articles or passed by ordinary resolution) has yet to explore.
	Prepare special resolution disapplying pre-emption provisions (if required).	This should be combined with the ordinary resolution above.
	Prepare application to subscribe for shares (if applicable).	
	Prepare resolution of the board of directors to accept the application (if applicable) and allot shares.	
	Where shares are issued for non-cash consideration, obtain an independent made up to a date during the six months immediately preceeding the allotment valuation report of such consideration and send a copy to the proposed allottee.	
2.	**Within one month from the date of allotment** File a return of allotment, together with a statement of capital and a copy of the valuation report (where relevant), with Companies House.	

	Action	Comment
3.	**Within two months from the date of allotment** Register the allotment in the statutory registers of the company.	The allotment must be registered in the statutory registers as soon as practicable and in any event within two months from the date of allotment.
	Account for the allotment in the books of the company.	Not required to credit share premium to share premium account if group reconstruction relief or merger relief is available.
	Issue a share certificate to the allottee.	
	Credit any share premium to the share premium account.	

Chapter 9

Returning cash or other assets to shareholders and group reorganisations

9.1	Introduction	9001
9.2	Dividends	9002
	9.2.1 What changes have been introduced by the Companies Act 2006?	9003
	9.2.2 What are the key requirements?	9003
	9.2.3 What can be paid out to shareholders?	9006
	9.2.4 What are 'distributable reserves'?	9007
	9.2.5 Does the company have to prepare accounts specially?	9008
	9.2.6 What if further distributions have been made after the date of the relevant accounts?	9010
	9.2.7 What shareholder procedures are required to pay a dividend?	9010
	9.2.7.1 Final dividend	9011
	9.2.7.2 Interim dividend	9011
	9.2.7.3 Non-cash dividend	9011
	9.2.8 Can a different dividend be paid to the holders of the same class of shares?	9011
	9.2.9 How is a distribution accounted for?	9011
	9.2.10 Are there any other legal issues?	9012
	9.2.11 What are the consequences of a breach of the statutory requirements?	9012
9.3	Reduction of share capital	9013
	9.3.1 Under what circumstances will a company consider a reduction of share capital?	9013
	9.3.2 What changes have been introduced by the Companies Act 2006?	9014
	9.3.3 What are the key requirements?	9014
	9.3.4 What can be reduced?	9018
	9.3.5 Which general issues need to be considered before a capital reduction?	9018
	9.3.5.1 Review the articles of association of the company	9019
	9.3.5.2 Is the company subject to any restriction or prohibition on capital reduction under its agreements with third parties?	9019
	9.3.5.3 Will the capital reduction result in a variation of the class rights of the other shareholders?	9019
	9.3.5.4 What is the creditor position of the company?	9019
	9.3.5.5 Directors' duties	9020

9.3.6 What is the procedure for a court approved reduction of
       capital under the Companies Act 2006 from 1 October
       2009? 9020
       9.3.6.1 What is the procedure? 9020
       9.3.6.2 What are the key documents? 9021
       9.3.6.3 How are creditors protected? 9021
       9.3.6.4 What are the filing requirements? 9023
       9.3.6.5 When will the reduction take effect? 9023
9.3.7 What does the solvency statement procedure for private
       companies involve? 9023
       9.3.7.1 What is the procedure? 9023
       9.3.7.2 What form must the solvency statement take? 9024
       9.3.7.3 What are the filing requirements? 9024
       9.3.7.4 When will the reduction take effect? 9025
9.3.8 Why might a private company still wish to apply to the
       court? 9025
9.3.9 In what circumstances might a public company be required
       to re-register as a private company? 9026
9.3.10 What is the accounting treatment of the capital reduction
       under both options? 9026
9.3.11 What are the penalties for a breach of the statutory
       requirements? 9027
9.3.12 Sample timetable for a reduction of capital supported by
       solvency statement under the Companies Act 2006 9028
9.3.13 Sample timetable for a court approved reduction of capital
       under the Companies Act 2006 9028
9.4 Purchase or buyback of own shares 9029
9.4.1 Under what circumstances will a company consider
       purchasing or buying back its own shares? 9029
9.4.2 What types of share repurchases are permitted and what
       shareholders' approvals are required under the Companies
       Act 1985? 9030
       9.4.2.1 Market purchase 9030
       9.4.2.2 Off-market purchase 9030
9.4.3 What changes have been introduced by the Companies Act
       2006? 9031
9.4.4 What are the key requirements? 9032
9.4.5 What preliminary issues should a company consider when
       planning a purchase of its own shares? 9035
       9.4.5.1 Listed and AIM companies 9035
       9.4.5.2 Listed convertible securities 9036
       9.4.5.3 Public companies – the City Code on Takeovers
                and Mergers (the 'Takeover Code') 9036
       9.4.5.4 Will the share repurchase result in a variation of
                the class rights of the other shareholders? 9037
       9.4.5.5 Are any of the shares listed or traded overseas? 9038

9.4.5.6   Is the company subject to any pre-emption rights or other restrictions on share repurchase under its agreements with third parties? 9038

9.4.5.7   Are any directors of the company selling any of their shares? 9038

9.4.5.8   Are creditors likely to object? 9038

9.4.5.9   Will other shareholders be disadvantaged? 9039

9.4.5.10   Is the company a single member company? ... 9039

9.4.5.11   What is the price for the purchase? 9039

9.4.5.12   How is the purchase financed? 9039

9.4.5.13   Are the shares fully paid? 9040

9.4.5.14   What is the stamp duty position? 9040

9.4.5.15   Must the company have at least one shareholder holding shares other than redeemable shares? .. 9040

9.4.5.16   Have the articles of association been reviewed?   9040

9.4.5.17   Is there any need to cancel the shares on repurchase? 9040

9.4.6   What factors should a company consider in deciding whether to purchase its own shares or carry out a reduction of capital? 9041

9.4.7   Are there restrictions on how the purchase can be financed? 9041

9.4.7.1   Share purchase out of distributable reserves ... 9041

9.4.7.2   Share purchase out of capital by a private company 9041

9.4.8   How is capital maintained? 9044

9.4.9   Sample balance sheets of a company before and after the share repurchase 9044

9.4.9.1   Public and private company – purchase out of distributable reserves 9044

9.4.9.2   Public and private company – purchase at a premium 9045

9.4.9.3   Private company – purchase out of capital 9047

9.4.10   Sample timetable for a purchase of own shares by a private company out of capital under the Companies Act 1985 and the Companies Act 2006 9048

9.4.11   What are the penalties for a breach of the statutory requirements? 9051

9.4.12   What special rules apply to a purchase of treasury shares?   9051

9.5   Redemption of redeemable shares 9052

9.5.1   What are the differences between a purchase of own shares and a redemption of redeemable shares? 9052

9.5.2   What are the key requirements? 9053

9.6   Intra-group reorganisations 9055

9.6.1   Under what circumstances will a company carry out an intra-group reorganisation? 9055

9.6.2   What issues arise if an asset is transferred intra-group for less than market value? 9056

9.6.3   What changes have been introduced by the Companies Act 2006? 9057

9.6.4   Summary of the rules relating to the value at which assets can be transferred intra-group 9058

9.6.5   To which intra-group transactions do these principles apply? 9058

    9.6.5.1   Transfers between sister companies 9058

    9.6.5.2   Transfers to a parent company 9059

9.6.6   How does a company value the asset to be transferred?   9059

9.6.7   What other general legal issues may arise from an undervalue transaction? 9060

    9.6.7.1   Financial assistance 9060

    9.6.7.2   Insolvency Act 1986 – undervalue transactions   9061

    9.6.7.3   Directors' duties 9061

    9.6.7.4   Other general issues 9061

9.6.8   Do businesses need to change existing procedures? 9062

9.7   Demergers 9062

9.7.1   What are the reasons for carrying out a demerger? 9062

9.7.2   What are the main ways of effecting a demerger? 9062

    9.7.2.1   Distribution in kind 9063

    9.7.2.2   Three-cornered or indirect demerger 9064

    9.7.2.3   'Section 110 Scheme' 9064

    9.7.2.4   Scheme of arrangement 9066

9.8   Schemes of arrangement 9067

9.8.1   Under what circumstances will a company consider a scheme of arrangement? 9067

9.8.2   What changes have been introduced by the Companies Act 2006? 9069

9.8.3   What are the advantages of a scheme of arrangement (in the context of a Topco scheme or a Takeover scheme) in comparison with other methods? 9069

9.8.4   What are the main statutory requirements under the Companies Act 2006? 9069

    9.8.4.1   Court meeting 9069

    9.8.4.2   Explanatory statement 9070

    9.8.4.3   General meeting of shareholders 9070

    9.8.4.4   Court approval 9070

9.8.5   Sample timetable of a Topco scheme under the Companies Act 2006 9071

9.9   Financing the acquisition of shares 9073

9.9.1   What changes have been introduced by the Companies Act 2006? 9073

9.9.2   What should a company consider before providing financial assistance? 9073

    9.9.2.1   Directors' duties 9073

	9.9.2.2	Transactions at an undervalue	9074
	9.9.2.3	Contractual restrictions	9074
9.9.3	What is the new position under the Companies Act 2006?		9074
	9.9.3.1	In what circumstances may financial assistance arise?	9074
	9.9.3.2	What is financial assistance?	9076
9.9.4	Will directors of a private company be comfortable with giving financial assistance going forward?		9079
	9.9.4.1	What is the 'whitewash' procedure under the Companies Act 1985?	9079
	9.9.4.2	'Whitewash' procedure checklist under the Companies Act 1985	9079
	9.9.4.3	The common law position	9081
9.9.5	What transactions are permitted?		9081
	9.9.5.1	Purpose exemptions[1]	9081
	9.9.5.2	Lawful exceptions[2]	9082
9.9.6	What are the consequences of a breach of the statutory requirements?		9083
9.9.7	Summary flowchart: financial assistance under the Companies Act 1985		9084
9.9.8	Summary flowchart: financial assistance under the Companies Act 2006		9085
9.10	Unlimited companies		9085
9.10.1	Why are unlimited companies used for reorganisations?		9085
9.10.2	What changes have been introduced by the Companies Act 2006?		9086
9.10.3	Table of comparison of the procedures for returning cash/ assets to shareholders by unlimited companies under the Companies Act 1985 and the Companies Act 2006		9086
9.10.4	What are the risks associated with unlimited companies?		9088
9.10.5	How does an unlimited company make a distribution? . .		9089
9.10.6	How does an unlimited company reduce its share capital?		9089
	9.10.6.1	What is the procedure under the Companies Act 2006?	9089
	9.10.6.2	What can be reduced?	9089
	9.10.6.3	What issues does the unlimited company need to consider before carrying out a capital reduction?	9090
	9.10.6.4	Are the reserves created from the reduction distributable?	9090
	9.10.6.5	What are the filing requirements?	9090
	9.10.6.6	When will the reduction take effect?	9090
9.10.7	How does an unlimited company purchase its own shares?		9091

---

[1]   Sections 678(2) and (4) Companies Act 2006.
[2]   Section 681 and 682, Companies Act 2006.

9.10.7.1 What is the procedure under Companies Act 2006? 9091

9.10.7.2 What issues should a company consider before repurchasing its shares? 9091

9.10.8 Do the financial assistance rules apply? 9091

9.11 Summary and conclusion on returning cash/assets to shareholders 9092

Returning cash or other assets to shareholders and group reorganisations

9.1 Introduction

This chapter discusses in a practical context several key provisions of the Companies Act 2006 which are designed to ensure that creditors of a company are protected in situations where the interests of shareholders and creditors potentially conflict. These provisions are typically of relevance in the following situations, each of which involves or can involve the passing of value from a company to its shareholders:

(i)   payment of a dividend;

(ii) reduction of share capital;

(iii) redemption or purchase of own shares (including redeemable shares);

(iv) intra-group reorganisations;

(v)   demergers;

(vi) schemes of arrangement; and

(vii) where a company provides financial assistance for the subscription or transfer of its own shares or shares in its holding company or companies.

Each of these situations is considered in turn. It is not an exhaustive list and any given transaction may involve some of the above. This chapter is predominantly concerned with return of value where the company or the trading activities are to continue. The procedure for a return of assets on the liquidation of a company is discussed in chapter 11.

In general, the Companies Act 2006 does not increase the existing levels of creditor protection in any of the above situations; in fact, there are several areas in which the Companies Act 2006 potentially reduces creditor protection by simplifying procedures (as in court approved reductions of capital) or by removing existing prohibitions (such as the prohibition on private companies from giving financial assistance for the acquisition of their own shares or shares in their private holding companies). These are intended to relieve administrative burdens on private companies, whilst making no change to the requirements for public companies.

Compliance with these provisions does not absolve directors of their general duties which have been discussed in detail in chapter 1. As has already been seen, where a company is solvent, a director's primary duty is to act in a way that he considers will best promote the success of the company for the benefit of its shareholders, having regard to the interests of a wide range of stakeholders. In cases of actual or prospective insolvency, this duty is supplanted by a duty to act in the best interests of its creditors[1].

Several of the areas examined in this chapter are regulated by other statutes and regulations, for example the Listing Rules, the Disclosure and Transparency Rules, the City Code on Takeovers and Mergers, the Financial Services and Markets Act 2000 and investor guidelines and recommendations. An analysis of these regulations is outside the scope of this book and a full review of their application to any particular set of circumstances should be undertaken before implementation of any of the transactions discussed below.

In many situations, a company will have a choice of which method to adopt in order to return value to its shareholders, the choice of which is usually driven by tax and cost considerations.

In addition, where a company has a defined benefit pension scheme which is in deficit, early consideration must be given to whether advance clearance should be sought from the Pensions Regulator. Under the Pensions Act 2004, the Pensions Regulator has extensive powers to issue contribution notices and financial support notices to persons connected and associated with the scheme's employer, to ensure that a particular transaction will not have an adverse impact on a company's funding obligation. Whilst applying for consent remains a voluntary matter, the Government has announced that from 14 April 2008, the Pensions Regulator will be able to issue contribution notices to companies or individuals when an act has a material effect on the ability of the pension scheme to meet current and future liabilities. As the Pensions Regulator has the ability to examine acts up to six years in the past, clearance applications are likely to increase.

Finally, the balance sheets contained in this chapter are simplified accounts that are intended only to illustrate the general application of legal principles. Accounting advice should be taken in respect of each transaction as accounting treatments and accounting standards can be different, or change, depending on the company involved.

9.2   Dividends

A company can distribute its assets in a number of ways to its shareholders, but the most common form is a distribution of profits by way of a dividend. The rules that follow apply equally to the payment of dividends between a subsidiary and its parent company as they do to dividends paid by a parent company to its shareholders.

---

[1]   Section 172, Companies Act 2006.

9.2.1 What changes have been introduced by the Companies Act 2006?

The Companies Act 2006 largely restates the provisions of the Companies Act 1985 relating to distributions by way of a dividend and, therefore, no changes are needed to existing procedures provided they comply with the current provisions of the Companies Act 1985.

The relevant provisions are contained in sections 829 to 853 in part 23 of the Companies Act 2006. The provisions are effective from 6 April 2008.

9.2.2 What are the key requirements?

This table sets out a comparison of the key requirements to be satisfied under the Companies Act 1985 and the Companies Act 2006 before any dividend can be paid:

Key requirement	Position under the Companies Act 1985	Position under the Companies Act 2006 from 6 April 2008
What can be paid out to shareholders?	A distribution can only be made by a company out of 'profits available for the purpose'[2] which means its 'accumulated, realised profits, so far as not previously utilised by distribution or capitalisation, less its accumulated, realised losses, so far as not previously written off in a reduction or reorganisation of capital duly made'[3].	Section 830 restates the Companies Act 1985.
How is the amount of distribution to be determined?	By reference to the following items as stated in the company's accounts: – profits, losses, assets and liabilities; – in the case of Companies Act accounts, provisions of any kind mentioned in paragraphs 88 and 89 of schedule 4 to the Companies Act 1985 (depreciation, diminution	Section 836 largely restates the Companies Act 1985.

---

[2] Section 263(1), Companies Act 1985.
[3] Section 263(3), Companies Act 1985.

Key requirement	Position under the Companies Act 1985	Position under the Companies Act 2006 from 6 April 2008
	in value of assets, retentions to meet liabilities, etc) and in the case of IAS accounts, provisions of any kind; and − share capital and reserves (including undistributable reserves)[4].	
Must the distribution be made by reference to specific accounts?	Distributions must be determined by reference to 'relevant accounts' which are the company's last annual accounts or where these indicate that there are insufficient distributable reserves, accounts which are drawn up to enable a reasonable judgment as to the items set out above[5] ('interim accounts' or in the case of a newly incorporated company, 'initial accounts')[6].	Section 836 largely restates the Companies Act 1985. Sections 837 to 839 provide the specific requirements for each form of accounts.
What are the additional requirements for a public company?	A public company can only make a distribution at a time when: − the amount of its net assets is not less than the aggregate of its called-up share capital and undistributable reserves; and − the distribution does not reduce the amount of the net assets to less than the aggregate of its called-up share capital and undistributable reserves[7].	Section 831(1) restates the Companies Act 1985.

---

[4]   Section 270(2), Companies Act 1985.
[5]   Sections 270-273, Companies Act 1985.
[6]   Sections 270-273, Companies Act 1985.
[7]   Section 264(1), Companies Act 1985.

Key requirement	Position under the Companies Act 1985	Position under the Companies Act 2006 from 6 April 2008
What are 'undistributable reserves'?	– share premium account; – capital redemption reserve; – the amount by which the accumulated, unrealised profits (so far as not previously utilised by capitalisation) exceeds the accumulated, unrealised losses (so far as not previously written off in a reduction or reorganisation); or – any other reserve stated as not being capable of distribution (e.g. merger reserve and revaluation reserve)[8].	Section 831(4) restates the Companies Act 1985.
How is a final dividend declared?	If 1985 Table A articles are adopted then the company may declare a final dividend recommended by the directors by passing an ordinary resolution[9].	The 2006 model articles largely restate the existing provisions under the 1985 Table A articles.
How is an interim dividend approved?	If 1985 Table A articles are adopted, directors have the power to pay an interim dividend if it appears to them that they are justified by the profits of the company available for distribution[10].	The 2006 model articles largely restate the existing provisions under the 1985 Table A articles
Who has a right to receive a dividend?	The articles will usually set out the rights of shareholders to a dividend. In the absence of such a provision, then all shareholders will receive a dividend in proportion to the amounts paid up on the shares for which the dividend is paid[11].	The 2006 model articles provide that dividends shall be paid by reference to each shareholder's holding of shares on the date of the resolution (subject to the terms of the relevant resolution or the articles).

---

[8] Section 264(3), Companies Act 1985.
[9] Regulation 102, Companies (Tables A to F) Regulations 1985 (as amended).
[10] Regulation 103, Companies (Tables A to F) Regulations 1985 (as amended).
[11] Regulation 104, Companies (Tables A to F) Regulations 1985 (as amended).

Key requirement	Position under the Companies Act 1985	Position under the Companies Act 2006 from 6 April 2008
Must a company also have sufficient distributable reserves at the time of payment of the dividend?	Yes, this is a common law requirement which is expressly preserved by the Companies Act 1985[12].	Section 851 restates the Companies Act 1985.
What are the filing requirements?	Public companies using interim or initial accounts are required to file a copy of the accounts used for the purposes of determining the dividend (together with, in the case of initial accounts, the auditors' report) with Companies House before the dividend is paid[13]. There are no filing requirements for private companies before or after a dividend is paid.	Section 838(6) and section 839(7) restate the Companies Act 1985.
What are the consequences of an unlawful distribution?	If a dividend is paid in breach of the statutory requirements and the shareholder has knowledge or reasonable grounds for belief of this fact it is liable to repay the dividend to the company[14]. The directors could also be in breach of their duties under common law.	Section 847 restates the Companies Act 1985. The directors could be in breach of their duties as set out in sections 171 to 177 of the Companies Act 2006.

Some of the above issues are discussed in more detail below.

9.2.3 What can be paid out to shareholders?

As noted in the table above, a company may only make a distribution out of profits available for the purpose ('distributable reserves', which in practice are also commonly referred to as 'distributable profits' or 'available profits'). Additional guidance on distributable reserves is provided in Tech 01/08, which was published by the Institute of Chartered Accountants of England and Wales and the Institute of Chartered Accountants of Scotland. This is discussed in more detail below. There are additional provisions relating to investment and

---

[12] Section 28, Companies Act 1985.
[13] Sections 272(4) and 273(6), Companies Act 1985.
[14] Section 277, Companies Act 1985.

insurance companies which are beyond the scope of this book. The text of Tech 01/08 can be found on the Institutes' websites.

In addition, a public company is only able to pay a dividend provided that both before and after the distribution, the net assets of the company are not less than the aggregate of its share capital and undistributable reserves (including, but not limited to, share premium, capital redemption reserve and revaluation reserve)[15]. In effect, this means that whilst a private company can ignore unrealised losses in assessing its ability to pay a dividend, a public company needs to have realised profits sufficient to cover such losses before it is able to pay a dividend.

9.2.4 What are 'distributable reserves'?

Before a dividend is paid, directors must determine whether the company has sufficient distributable reserves from which to pay the dividend. It is therefore not sufficient merely to rely on the reserves in the 'P/L reserves' section of the company's accounts as a dividend can only be paid out of 'distributable' reserves.

The Companies Act 2006 provides that a company's distributable reserves shall be its 'accumulated, realised profits, so far as not previously utilised by distribution or capitalisation, less its accumulated, realised losses, so far as not previously written off in a reduction or reorganisation of capital'[16]. However, the definitions of 'realised profits' and 'realised losses' refer to such profits and losses as shall be treated as realised with principles generally accepted at the time when the relevant accounts are prepared[17]. In practice, this means the determination of 'realised losses' and 'realised profits' is not merely a legal question, but an accounting one, too.

As noted above, Tech 01/08 provides guidance as to whether profits are realised and therefore whether they are available for distribution. To ascertain whether profits are realised, there must be a clear understanding of the specific transactions that gave rise to the profits and any related transactions. In many cases, realised profits will represent trading profits in cash terms or the sale of an asset for a monetary amount in excess of its book value. The position is, however, less clear where the consideration for the sale of an asset is deferred or is not a monetary amount (for example, a non-cash asset).

Therefore, when assessing, for example, whether an intra-group transaction gives rise to a realised profit, consideration needs to be given as to whether the company that recorded the profit received 'qualifying consideration' – only then can it treat the profit as realised.

---

[15] Section 831, Companies Act 2006.
[16] Section 830, Companies Act 2006.
[17] Section 853, Companies Act 2006.

Tech 01/08 explains the concept of 'qualifying consideration' in determining when consideration does constitute a realised profit. It has a number of forms, which includes (but is not limited to):

(i) cash or cash equivalent;

(ii) a debt which is expected to be settled in a reasonable period of time and in relation to which there is reasonable certainty that the debtor is capable of settling; and

(iii) the release from a liability for which qualifying consideration was received.

However, it is not sufficient to consider the transaction or arrangement in isolation. Tech 01/08 requires a series of transactions and arrangements to be considered in their entirety[18]. This can be illustrated, in its simplest form, in a situation where a parent company is to make a loan to its subsidiary and the subsidiary uses this cash to fund a dividend out of distributable reserves it already had. In such a case, the parent company should not treat the dividend received as realised profit. If the dividend from the subsidiary was considered in isolation, the parent company would be seen to be receiving cash (which would meet Tech 01/08's criteria of 'qualifying consideration') such that this profit might be treated as realised. However, if the two transactions (the loan and the dividend) are considered together, it is clear that the cash position of the parent company has not increased as a result of these transactions. In practice, however, the application of the rules is much more complex than this.

Where a company has insufficient distributable reserves, it may be possible to create them by carrying out an intra-group reorganisation, but this will need careful structuring.

To the extent that the dividend is to distribute a non-cash asset, there are also statutory provisions[19] that allow the company making the distribution to treat any amount that the asset to be distributed is stated in the relevant accounts as realised profits for the purpose of calculating the distributable reserves of the company in making that distribution. This typically allows reserves such as a revaluation reserve, provided it relates to the asset to be distributed, to be treated as realised for the purpose of that distribution. Further issues on a non-cash distribution are discussed in section 9.2.7.3 and section 9.6.

9.2.5 Does the company have to prepare accounts specially?

There are mandatory provisions in relation to the accounts to be used to determine whether a dividend may be payable. A dividend will only be lawful if made in accordance with these provisions. It is therefore important that the statutory requirements are fully observed, since a procedural breach will render

---

[18] Section 3.5, Tech 01/08.
[19] Section 846, Companies Act.

the dividend unlawful even if the company has sufficient distributable reserves at the time of payment.

A company must determine whether it has sufficient distributable reserves by reference to its own 'relevant accounts'[20], which are the individual accounts of the relevant entity and not any consolidated accounts of the group. This is an important point that is sometimes not initially appreciated. Such accounts are generally (with the exception of a newly formed company) the company's most recent audited statutory accounts which have been circulated to its shareholders and which contain an unqualified auditors' report. If the accounts are qualified, the auditors must state whether the qualification is material and that statement must have been circulated to shareholders (if a private company) or laid before the company in general meeting (if a public company). However, in cases where:

(i)   the last set of statutory accounts shows that there are insufficient distributable reserves to support the level of the distribution proposed; or

(ii)   the directors are aware (or should be aware) that events have occurred since the date of such accounts which means they should no longer be relied upon for the purposes of justifying a dividend (for example, the profits reflected in these accounts no longer exist by virtue of a change in accounting policy which is to be applied in the next set of statutory accounts or the company having incurred trading or other losses since the date of the accounts); or

(iii)   there are no previous statutory accounts as it is a newly incorporated company,

then the directors will be required to prepare interim accounts (or in the case of a new company, initial accounts) to justify the dividend.

Private companies can use management accounts as interim accounts or initial accounts but they must be sufficient to enable a reasonable assessment to be made of the profits, losses, assets and liabilities, share capital and reserves (including undistributable reserves) of the business and include all provisions required by the Companies Act 2006[21]. If they are insufficient for this purpose, the dividend will be unlawful even if the company has, as a matter of fact, sufficient distributable reserves to enable a dividend to be paid. If management accounts are prepared for a different purpose, then the directors will need to take additional steps to ensure that the statutory test is satisfied.

However, in the case of a public company, interim accounts and initial accounts must be properly prepared[22] and as such must include a balance sheet, profit and loss account and related notes. The balance sheet must be approved

---

[20]   Section 836, Companies Act 2006.
[21]   Please refer to the table in section 9.2.2 for details of the provisions.
[22]   Sections 838 and 839, Companies Act 2006.

by the directors and signed on behalf of the board by a directors[23]. These accounts must also be filed with Companies House before any dividend is paid. In the case of interim accounts, there is no requirement for an auditors' report, but in the case of initial accounts, an auditors' report must be included. Where the report is qualified, the auditors must also issue a statement confirming whether the qualification is material and this must have been laid before the company in general meeting. The auditors' report and/or statement must also have been filed at Companies House before any dividend is paid.

In relation to both public and private companies, where the last set of audited accounts do show sufficient distributable reserves, but considerable time has passed, the directors should also have regard to the latest management accounts before declaring a dividend. This will be evidence that the directors exercised due care in determining the amount and will also satisfy the common law requirement for the company to have sufficient distributable reserves as at the date of the dividend, which is expressly preserved by both the Companies Act 1985 and the Companies Act 2006. Directors should also consider obtaining comfort from their auditors on the level of 'realised profits' and 'realised losses' even where a report is not specifically required.

9.2.6 What if further distributions have been made after the date of the relevant accounts?

For the purposes of establishing whether there are sufficient distributable reserves at least equal to the amount of the dividend, the dividend that a company proposes to pay should be increased by the amount of any distribution that has been made since the date of the relevant accounts (for example, a dividend or a distribution of a non-cash asset) or where certain other payments have been made by the company which have the effect of reducing its distributable reserves since that date (for example, as a result of a purchase of its own shares (see section 9.4) or the giving of lawful financial assistance (see section 9.9)[24].

9.2.7 What shareholder procedures are required to pay a dividend?

Neither the Companies Act 1985 nor the Companies Act 2006 sets out the procedure for paying a dividend but a company must be authorised in its articles of association to do so and the procedure should also be set out in the articles. The procedure as set out in the 2006 model articles (which are discussed in more detail in chapter 3) for each form of dividend is summarised below.

---

[23] As a transitional measure expected to apply until 1 October 2009, the balance sheet should also state the name of the person signing it on behalf of the board. See paragraph 35, schedule 4 of the Companies Act 2006 (Commencement No 5, Transitional Provisions and Savings) Order 2007.

[24] Section 840, Companies Act 2006.

9.2.7.1   Final dividend

A final dividend is based on the annual audited accounts of a company and is formally recommended by the directors of the company to its shareholders. The amount declared must not exceed the amount recommended by the directors. Traditionally, the final dividend is declared by way of an ordinary resolution of the shareholders at an annual general meeting, although given that a private company is no longer required to hold an annual general meeting it is likely that final dividends, in the case of a private company, will in the future be approved at a general meeting or by way of a written resolution. It is at this point in time that the distribution becomes a liability and is recognised for accounting purposes.

A final dividend once declared cannot be revoked without shareholder approval and as such constitutes a debt owing from the company to its shareholder(s).

9.2.7.2   Interim dividend

An interim dividend is a dividend declared by the directors of the company if authorised by the company's articles. An interim dividend can be revoked by directors at any time up until payment and will not give rise to any debt owing from the company to its shareholder(s). Consequently, it is not recognised for accounting purposes until it is paid.

9.2.7.3   Non-cash dividend

On the recommendation of directors, a company can declare a non-cash dividend by way of an ordinary resolution. Further issues in relation to distributions of non-cash assets arising from intra-group transactions will be discussed in section 9.6.

9.2.8   Can a different dividend be paid to the holders of the same class of shares?

If authorised by the articles of association, a company may pay a dividend in proportion to the amount paid up on each share where a larger amount is paid up on some shares than on others[25].

9.2.9   How is a distribution accounted for?

When a distribution becomes a legal liability it is recognised for accounting purposes and has the effect of reducing the net assets of the company making the distribution. The company should record an equivalent reduction in its distributable reserves.

---

[25] Section 581, Companies Act 2006.

9.2.10 Are there any other legal issues?

The directors of the company must also be satisfied that recommending or approving the payment of a dividend of the amount proposed complies with their duties as directors (see chapter 1).

It is worth noting that the Companies Act 2006 carves out the following from the requirements discussed above on a dividend distribution:

(i)   an issue of shares as fully or partly paid bonus shares;

(ii)   the redemption or purchase of the company's own shares in accordance with the provisions of the Companies Act 2006;

(iii)   the reduction of share capital by extinguishing or reducing shareholder's liability or any of the issued share capital of the company or by repaying paid up share capital; and

(iv)   a distribution of assets to shareholders of a company on its winding up.

9.2.11 What are the consequences of a breach of the statutory requirements?

The procedures described above for the payment of dividends are mandatory. Since they are for the protection of a company's creditors, dividends made in breach of these procedures are not capable of variation or ratification by shareholders. If these procedures are not followed, then the dividend will be unlawful even if the company has sufficient distributable reserves to pay the dividend.

Examples of failures to follow the correct procedure might include:

(i)   omission of a material provision in interim accounts;

(ii)   the amount of a dividend being determined by reference to consolidated, rather than entity accounts;

(iii)   (in the case of a public company) failure to file relevant accounts at Companies House before a dividend is paid; and

(iv)   failure to take account of an impairment resulting from an upstream payment of a dividend by a subsidiary.

If a shareholder of a company receives a dividend, all or part of which he knows or has reasonable grounds for believing is in breach of the requirements under the Companies Act 2006, he is liable to repay the cash amount received or the equivalent value of a non-cash asset received which was unlawful[26].

---

[26] Section 847, Companies Act 2006.

In addition, a director who has authorised an unlawful distribution may have breached his statutory duties and will be personally liable to the company for the amount distributed.

A common remedial course of action is for the dividend to be repaid and then declared again by the company. This can be achieved by the recipient agreeing to repay and the company satisfying its obligation to pay the dividend by waiving its rights against the recipient to call for repayment of the earlier dividend. Shareholders can also agree to release directors from any liability for breach of duty (see chapter 1).

9.3   Reduction of share capital

9.3.1   Under what circumstances will a company consider a reduction of share capital?

A company may wish to reduce its share capital for a variety of reasons, the most common ones being:

(i)   where the company has surplus capital in excess of its needs which it proposes to return to shareholders; this could be as part of its trading operations or as part of a corporate simplification programme (which is further discussed in chapter 11);

(ii)   where the company has a dividend block (i.e. it is unable to pay a dividend or make other distributions because it has negative or insufficient distributable reserves);

(iii)   where the company needs to create distributable reserves to finance a redemption or purchase of its own shares or a dividend;

(iv)   where the company wishes to render a non-distributable reserve distributable (for example, share premium or capital redemption reserve);

(v)   where a company wishes to release a liability to pay up capital. For example, it may have issued partly paid shares and wishes to cancel the unpaid amount; or

(vi)   where a company is undertaking a major reconstruction such as a scheme of arrangement of which a court approved reduction forms part.

However, the circumstances listed above are not exhaustive. The reduction will usually be *pro rata* to all shareholders rather than in favour of just an individual shareholder (although this is permissible subject to protection of minority's rights which is discussed in chapter 4). The reduction can be effected at parent company level as a means of returning cash or assets to its shareholders directly or it can be undertaken at subsidiary level within a group. All of these methods are appropriate where the continuance of the company is desired but the same result can be achieved by a dissolution if the purpose of the company has come to an end (this is discussed further in chapter 11).

9.3.2 What changes have been introduced by the Companies Act 2006?

The majority of provisions dealing with the court approval procedure have been restated in the Companies Act 2006 (with minor amendments). The key changes under the Companies Act 2006 are therefore as follows:

(i)   private companies will have the option of reducing their share capital either by applying to the court for approval or by issuing a solvency statement[27]; and

(ii)   it will no longer be necessary for a company to have express authority in its articles of association to reduce share capital (unless there is a specific prohibition or restriction in the articles). This is, however, anticipated to be subject to the transitional provisions which require public companies incorporated under the Companies Act 1985 and transitional companies incorporated under the transitional provisions of the Companies Act 2006 to have authority either (a) in its articles of association or (b) granted by way of a special resolution before it can carry out a court approved reduction of share capital. It is not clear, as at 30 June 2008, whether or when these anticipated transitional provisions will be terminated.

Public companies will, however, still require court approval for a reduction of capital.

The new provisions in relation to a court approved reduction of share capital are contained in section 641(1)(b) and section 645 to section 650 of the Companies Act 2006 and are effective from 1 October 2009. However, the provisions in relation to reduction of share capital by a private company using the solvency statement procedure, which are contained in section 641(1)(a), sections 641(2) to (6) and sections 642 to 644 of the Companies Act 2006 and the provision in relation to treatment of reserve arising from a capital reduction is effective earlier, on 1 October 2008.

9.3.3 What are the key requirements?

This table sets out a comparison of the key requirements for a capital reduction under the Companies Act 1985 and the Companies Act 2006:

---

[27]   Section 642, Companies Act 2006.

Key requirement	Position under the Companies Act 1985	Position under the Companies Act 2006 from 1 October 2009 (except otherwise indicated)
Is court approval required?	Yes[28]	Court approval still required for public companies. Court approval optional for private companies[29]. New solvency statement procedure for private companies available from 1 October 2008.
Is authority in articles required?	Yes	No longer required (unless there are specific prohibitions or restrictions) but please refer to section 9.3.2, point (ii).
Is a special resolution required?	Yes[30]	Yes[31]
What is the time frame?	Court approval – normally takes six to eight weeks to complete.	Court approval – similar time frame. Solvency statement procedure (available from 1 October 2008) – it is anticipated this will take about four weeks to complete (depending on complexity of individual circumstances).

---

[28] Section 135(1), Companies Act 1985.
[29] Section 641(1), Companies Act 2006.
[30] Section 135, Companies Act 1985.
[31] Section 641, Companies Act 2006.

Key requirement	Position under the Companies Act 1985	Position under the Companies Act 2006 from 1 October 2009 (except otherwise indicated)
What key documents are required?	Court approval: – Special resolution; – Claim form; – Director's witness statement or affidavit.	Court approval: – No change in documentation. Solvency statement procedure (available from 1 October 2008): – Special resolution; – Directors' solvency statement (to be made by <u>all</u> of the directors of the company); – Directors' statement confirming that the solvency statement was properly made. – statement of capital[32].
What powers do creditors have to object?	Court approval[33]: – Creditors' right to object if the reduction involves either a reduction of liability of unpaid share capital or payment to a shareholder of paid-up share capital; – need to settle a list of creditors with the court unless dispensation obtained by providing other creditor protection measures; – the court can make provision for creditor protection; and – onus of proof on creditors to show prejudice.	Court approval[34]: – no change to creditor protection procedures (however, provisions relating to onus to proof yet to be finalised as of 30 June 2008). Solvency statement procedure (available from 1 October 2008): – satisfied by virtue of the making of the directors' solvency statement but no other specific measures are required for creditors' protection and creditors do not have a statutory right to object.

---

[32] As a transitional measure and for the period from 1 October 2008 to 1 October 2009, a memorandum giving particulars of the company's capital will be filed instead of a statement of capital.

[33] Section 136, Companies Act 1985.

[34] Sections 645 and 646, Companies Act 2006.

Key requirement	Position under the Companies Act 1985	Position under the Companies Act 2006 from 1 October 2009 (except otherwise indicated)
Can the share capital be reduced to zero?	Yes, with court approval.	Yes, with court approval. Solvency statement procedure (available from 1 October 2008): there must be one shareholder remaining after the reduction holding at least one share, which must not be a redeemable share[35].
Filing with Companies House?	Yes. Court approval: – special resolution; – court order; and – minute of capital reduction approved by the court[36].	Yes. Court approval: – special resolution; – court order; and – statement of capital. Solvency statement procedure (available from 1 October 2008): – special resolution; – directors' solvency statement; – statement of capital[37]; and – directors' statement confirming solvency statement was properly made[38].

[35] Section 641(2), Companies Act 2006.
[36] Section 138, Companies Act 1985.
[37] As a transitional measure and for the period from 1 October 2008 to 1 October 2009, a memorandum giving particulars of the company's capital will be filed instead of a statement of capital.
[38] Section 644, Companies Act 2006.

Key requirement	Position under the Companies Act 1985	Position under the Companies Act 2006 from 1 October 2009 (except otherwise indicated)
When does the reduction take effect?	On registration of the court order and the minute at Companies House[39].	Court approval – on registration of the court order and the statement of capital at Companies House[40]. Solvency statement procedure (available from 1 October 2008) – on registration of the directors' solvency statement and the statement of capital[41] at Companies House[42].

9.3.4   What can be reduced?

A company may reduce its share capital under the Companies Act 2006 as follows:

(i)   by extinguishing or reducing the liability on any unpaid share capital;

(ii)   by cancelling any paid-up share capital which is lost or not represented by available assets; or

(iii)   by repaying any surplus paid-up share capital[43].

A company can therefore reduce its issued share capital, share premium account and capital redemption reserve as share premium and capital redemption reserves constitute share capital for the purpose of a reduction. However, other types of reserves such as a revaluation reserve cannot be reduced by way of a capital reduction and will need to be capitalised into shares prior to the reduction.

9.3.5   Which general issues need to be considered before a capital reduction?

Before commencing a capital reduction procedure, there are a number of preliminary issues to be considered:

---

[39]   Section 138(2), Companies Act 1985.
[40]   Section 649(3), Companies Act 2006.
[41]   As a transitional measure and for the period from 1 October 2008 to 1 October 2009, a memorandum giving particulars of the company's capital will be filed instead of a statement of capital.
[42]   Section 644, Companies Act 2006.
[43]   Section 641(4), Companies Act 2006.

9.3.5.1   Review the articles of association of the company

While the Companies Act 2006 has removed the requirement under the Companies Act 1985 for specific authority to reduce share capital to be included in the articles of association, the articles should still be reviewed to ensure there are no specific prohibitions or restrictions. Please also refer to section 9.3.2 point (ii) for details of the transitional provisions.

9.3.5.2   Is the company subject to any restriction or prohibition on capital reduction under its agreements with third parties?

It is not unusual for agreements with third parties such as shareholders' agreements, loan agreements or debentures to contain restrictions on a company reducing its share capital. It will therefore be necessary to review the major agreements of the company to ascertain if there are any such restrictions and seek consents from third parties where necessary.

9.3.5.3   Will the capital reduction result in a variation of the class rights of the other shareholders?

If the capital reduction will result in a variation of the class rights of the other shareholders of the company, it will be necessary to seek class consent from these shareholders prior to the reduction (unless the articles provide for an alternative mechanism).

For example, if the capital reduced is to be repaid to the ordinary shareholders where there are preference shares in issue (the holders of which have preferential right to a return of capital), the repayment will be a deemed variation of the class rights of the preference shares. As such, the consent of the preference shareholders will be required for the capital reduction.

9.3.5.4   What is the creditor position of the company?

The company can only carry out the capital reduction procedure if it is solvent (irrespective of whether it applies the court approval procedure or the solvency statement procedure). In both procedures, the company will need to consider whether it has sufficient assets to discharge its liabilities (including prospective and contingent liabilities). The nature and composition of the creditors of the company is of particular relevance in a court approval procedure, as it will affect the type of creditor protection measures required (if any). These will be discussed in further detail in section 9.3.6.3 below. Notwithstanding these measures, a creditor has a statutory right to object in certain situations and therefore an assessment of this likelihood is sensible. If, for example, there is litigation, actual or threatened, an objection might be used tactically by the claimant to secure early settlement of a claim.

9.3.5.5   *Directors' duties*

The directors of the company need to consider all of the above issues as well as whether the reduction of capital will promote the success of the company, and whether the reduction of capital is the best use of the company's capital. These duties are discussed in more detail in chapter 1.

9.3.6   What is the procedure for a court approved reduction of capital under the Companies Act 2006 from 1 October 2009?

The court approval procedure to reduce share capital will continue to be available to both public and private companies under the Companies Act 2006 with effect from 1 October 2009.

9.3.6.1   *What is the procedure?*

The procedural requirements for a court approved capital reduction is as follows (this largely restates the current position):

(i)   the company passes a special resolution approving the capital reduction;

(ii)   a timetable is agreed with an officer of the court (typically this will be over a four to six week period depending on how busy the court schedule is) – this assumes the relevant due diligence has been done to identify all creditors;

(iii)   a claim form is filed at the court for approval of the reduction and a director of the company will need to sign a witness statement or an affidavit in support of the claim form;

(iv)   a directions hearing is held at which the court will confirm whether the special resolution has been duly passed and all requisite consents obtained. It will also consider creditors' protection. Usually, the court will dispense with the requirement to draw up a list of creditors either because their interests are fully protected (please refer to section 9.3.6.3 below for details) or because their express consent has been obtained. The court will then direct that (i) the date of the final hearing of the claim be fixed and (ii) that the claim form be advertised in a national broadsheet daily newspaper;

(v)   the reduction is advertised as directed and will provide that any shareholders or creditors who object to the reduction may appear at the final hearing if they wish; and

(vi)   at the final hearing (which usually takes place in open court), the court will be asked to confirm the capital reduction and the reduction becomes effective once the order is registered by Companies House together with a statement of capital (approved by the court).

9.3.6.2   What are the key documents?

The key documents required for the court approved procedure are as follows:

(i)   special resolution: to be passed prior to the application to the court;

(ii)   claim form: containing particulars of the incorporation and capital history of the company and setting out the special resolution for reducing share capital, together with the grounds upon which approval is sought; and

(iii) director's witness statement or affidavit: supporting the claim form which must confirm that all of the information stated in the claim form is correct and will need to exhibit the relevant documentation (for example, the memorandum and/or articles of association of the company, the special resolution authorising the capital reduction and the company's accounts). The witness statement or affidavit should also give details of the company's creditors and set out how they are to be protected in view of the proposed reduction. A thorough due diligence exercise should be completed prior to any application to court to identify all actual and contingent liabilities and the amounts actually or potentially owing to these creditors. The witness statement or affidavit is a court document and therefore subject to the rules on perjury.

9.3.6.3   How are creditors protected?

The court will only confirm a capital reduction if it is satisfied that the interests of the creditors of the company are properly protected.

Where the reduction involves a reduction of liability in respect of unpaid share capital or a payment of any paid-up capital, creditors (including contingent and prospective creditors) have a statutory right to object to the reduction. In such an instance, the court is required to settle a list of creditors (with particulars of their names and the nature and extent of their debts or claims) with the company. The definition of 'creditor' for this purpose is very wide and includes actual, contingent or prospective creditors.

In other situations, such as where the reduction is to eliminate an accumulated loss, the court has a discretion as to whether to allow creditors to object.

If an objection is made, the current provisions of the Companies Act 2006 place the onus on the company to show to the court that the proposed reduction will not adversely affect the interests of its creditors. However, it is anticipated these Companies Act 2006 provisions will be changed following the recent amendment to the Companies Act 1985 by virtue of the Companies (Reduction of Capital) (Creditor Protection) Regulations 2008[44] which shifted

---

[44] Effective from 6 April 2008.

the onus to the creditors to show that there is a real likelihood that their liability will not be duly discharged as a result of the reduction in order to raise any objection. However, as at 30 June 2008, regulations to amend these provisions of the Companies Act 2006 have yet to be published by the Government.

In practice and in most cases, the court will dispense with the settlement of a creditors' list if sufficient measures are taken by the company to protect the interests of the creditors. These measures vary, depending on the number and nature of creditors and the type of reduction, but briefly they include:

(i)   obtaining consent from all of the creditors of the company;

(ii)   if the company can demonstrate that it has sufficient 'liquid assets' to cover (a) the amount of capital proposed to be repaid, and (b) the amount of the creditors, together with a minimum 10% margin. 'Liquid assets' for this purpose includes cash and certain specified securities (the market value of which will depend on the nature of the assets);

(iii)   setting aside the money owed to the non-consenting creditors in a blocked bank account, which will only be used to repay the debts of those creditors;

(iv)   procuring a bank guarantee guaranteeing the repayment by the company of the amount to be repaid under the proposed capital reduction or the amount owed to the non-consenting creditors, whichever is less; or

(v)   undertaking not to make any repayment until all creditors have been repaid or consented to the reduction or that it will transfer all distributable reserves created as a result of the capital reduction to a separate reserve which will not be distributed until such time as all creditors have been repaid or consented.

Before commencing the capital reduction procedure, it is therefore important for the company to carry out a detailed analysis of their creditors to consider what sort of protection measures are appropriate.

If, however, the court declines to dispense with the requirement for the creditors' list, the process can become a time consuming one. In such instances, the company will need to prepare a detailed list of creditors, which will be supported by a witness statement (or affidavit). This is then advertised and creditors are invited to come forward if their names are not on the list or to contest the amount shown. The court will then determine the list of names and amounts shown and issue a certificate, after which the hearing can proceed. Once the list is settled, the court will require the company to set aside such amount as will ensure that any creditor who has not consented is paid in full.

9.3.6.4 *What are the filing requirements?*

The special resolution should be filed at Companies House within 15 days from the date of its passing[45].

In addition, once the court order approving the reduction has been confirmed, it will need to be filed at Companies House, together with a statement of capital, which is a new requirement.

On registration of the court order and the statement of capital at Companies House, it will issue a certificate which is conclusive evidence that all the requirements of the Companies Act 2006 in relation to the capital reduction have been complied with and that the company's share capital is as stated in the statement of capital.

9.3.6.5 *When will the reduction take effect?*

The reduction will only take effect once the court order and the statement of capital are registered with Companies House.

9.3.7 What does the solvency statement procedure for private companies involve?

A private company limited by shares will be able to reduce its share capital using the new solvency statement procedure under the Companies Act 2006 from 1 October 2008, although it retains the right to apply to the court.

9.3.7.1 *What is the procedure?*

The procedural requirements for a capital reduction by using the solvency statement procedure are as follows:

(i) all of the directors of the company must make a 'solvency statement' in prescribed form. If any directors are unable or unwilling to make this statement, the company will not be able to use the solvency statement procedure unless the dissenting directors resign;

(ii) a copy of the directors' solvency statement is circulated to all of the shareholders (where a written resolution is being proposed) or made available at the shareholders' meeting (where a shareholders' meeting is being convened to pass the special resolution referred to below); and

---

[45] Section 29 and Section 30, Companies Act 2006.

(iii)   within 15 days of the making of the solvency statement by the directors, the company passes a special resolution to reduce its share capital[46].

9.3.7.2   What form must the solvency statement take?

The solvency statement must be in prescribed form[47], stating the following:

(i)   the date on which it is made;

(ii)   the name of each director (there is no requirement that the directors must all be in the same location for the purpose of making this statement); and

(iii)   that the directors are of the opinion that:

- as regards the situation of the company at the date of the statement, there is no ground on which the company could then be found to be unable to pay or discharge its debts; and

- if it is intended to commence the winding-up of the company within 12 months of that date, that the company will be able to pay or discharge its debts in full within 12 months of the commencement of the winding-up, or, in any other cases, the company will be able to pay or discharge its debts as they fall due during the year immediately following that date.

In forming their opinions, the directors must take into account all of the company's liabilities, including contingent and prospective liabilities[48]. However, there is no requirement for the directors to prepare any statutory accounts for this purpose or to obtain an auditors' report.

Directors could face claims for breach of duty if a solvency statement was found to be incorrect and criminal penalties apply under the Companies Act 2006 if a statement is made without having reasonable grounds to do so[49]. Therefore, directors should seriously consider whether they need advice when carrying out their creditor review, particularly where the company has had a lengthy history or is an active trading company.

9.3.7.3   What are the filing requirements?

Within 15 days of the passing of the special resolution, the following documents should be filed at Companies House[50]:

---

[46] Section 642, Companies Act 2006. In addition and as a transitional requirement, the special resolution should make any necessary alterations to the company's memorandum by reducing the amount of its share capital and of its shares. See paragraph 3 of the Companies Act (Commencement No 7, Transitional Provisions and Savings) Order 2007.
[47] Section 643, Companies Act 2006.
[48] Section 643(2), Companies Act 2006.
[49] Section 643(4), Companies Act 2006.
[50] Section 644, Companies Act 2006.

(i)   a copy of the directors' solvency statement;

(ii) a statement of capital[51];

(iii) a copy of the special resolution; and

(iv) a statement by the directors confirming that the solvency statement was:

- made no more than 15 days before the passing of the special resolution; and

- a copy has been provided to or made available to shareholders of the company.

9.3.7.4   When will the reduction take effect?

The reduction will only take effect once the directors' solvency statement and the statement of capital[52] are registered at Companies House[53].

9.3.8   Why might a private company still wish to apply to the court?

Under the new regime, it is anticipated that a large number of private companies wishing to reduce their share capital will opt for the solvency statement procedure rather than applying to the court for the following reasons:

(i)   the process will take less time to complete;

(ii) it is likely to cost less as counsel will not be needed to represent the company at court; and

(iii) the company will have more flexibility as to the levels of creditor protection it wishes to put in place and it is likely that these will be less costly than those imposed by the court.

However, there might be certain situations where a court approved procedure will be necessary or advisable because:

(i)   with the approval of the court it is possible to reduce a company's share capital to zero. In practice this is done as part of a scheme of arrangement (which is discussed later in this chapter) where shares are immediately issued in replacement. Under the solvency statement procedure, a company must have at least one shareholder remaining after the proposed reduction holding at least one non-redeemable share;

---

[51] As a transitional measure and for the period from 1 October 2008 to 1 October 2009, a memorandum giving particulars of the company's capital will be filed instead of a statement of capital.

[52] As a transitional measure and for the period from 1 October 2008 to 1 October 2009, a memorandum giving particulars of the company's capital will be filed instead of a statement of capital.

[53] Section 644(4), Companies Act 2006.

(ii) the court determines the appropriate level of creditor protection rather than the board. In complex creditor situations or where creditors are unknown, this will provide a greater level of protection for directors from actions for breach of duty;

(iii) it may not be possible for all directors to sign the solvency statement or there may be directors who refuse to do so; and

(iv) pursuant to the provisions of the Companies Act 1985, a court approved reduction will always create realised profits while it will be necessary to have qualifying consideration for the capital reduced by a company by other means (which, typically, involve a reduction of capital by an unlimited company by passing a special resolution[54]). However, as discussed in section 9.3.10 below, the Government has published regulations pursuant to the Companies Act 2006, which provide that a court approved reduction and a reduction by way of the solvency statement procedure will equally create realised profits with effect from 1 October 2008. The advantage of a court approved procedure (over the other procedures) to reduce capital by creating distributable reserves from the capital reduction will therefore no longer apply.

9.3.9   In what circumstances might a public company be required to re-register as a private company?

Where the court approval of a capital reduction of a public company results in the company having a share capital below the authorised minimum (please refer to chapter 8 for details of this requirement), the company must re-register as a private company (unless the court directs otherwise). There is an expedited procedure available under the Companies Act 2006 for the company to do so.[55]

9.3.10   What is the accounting treatment of the capital reduction under both options?

Under the Companies Act 1985 and prior to 1 October 2008, the question as to whether a reserve arising from the reduction of a company's share capital may be treated as a realised profit for the purpose of computing whether a company has sufficient distributable reserves to make a distribution is the subject of Tech 01/08 (which is discussed earlier in this chapter – see section 9.2.4). The guidance provides that a profit is realised if it arises from 'a reduction or cancellation of capital (i.e. share capital, share premium account or capital redemption reserve) which results in a credit to reserves where the reduction or cancellation is approved by the court, except to the extent that, and for as long as, the company has undertaken that it will not treat the reserve arising as a

---

[54] See guidance in Tech 01/08.
[55] Section 651, Companies Act 2006.

realised profit, or where the court has directed that it shall not be treated as a realised profit'[56].

The Companies Act 2006 provides that the reserve arising from such a reduction (whether by the court approved procedure or the solvency statement procedure) is not distributable save to the extent provided by secondary legislation[57]. This provision is effective from 1 October 2008. In July 2008, the Government published the Companies (Reduction of Share Capital) Order 2008. This order provides that realised profits will be created for the purpose of a distribution under the Companies Act 2006 with effect from 1 October 2008 in the case of:

(i)   a court approved reduction (except where restrictions are imposed by the court);

(ii) a reduction by way of the solvency statement procedure; and

(iii) a reduction of capital by unlimited companies.

As such, reserves created by any of these mechanisms will be treated as distributable from the effective date of the order.

It is important to note that if a distribution is contemplated after a reduction of capital, interim accounts of the company are likely to be required showing the financial position of the company after the reduction (see section 9.2 above dealing with dividends).

9.3.11   What are the penalties for a breach of the statutory requirements?

As noted above, if a director makes a solvency statement without having reasonable grounds for the opinions expressed in it, and that statement is subsequently delivered to Companies House, the director commits a criminal offence and will be liable, on conviction, to imprisonment and/or a fine as specified in the Companies Act 2006[58].

In addition, if the company fails to provide a copy of the directors' solvency statement to its shareholders as required or fails to deliver the documents required for registration to Companies House, every officer of the company who is in default commits an offence and will be liable to a statutory fine[59].

---

[56] Section 3.9(g), Tech 01/08.
[57] Section 654, Companies Act 2006.
[58] Section 643(5), Companies Act 2006.
[59] Section 644(7) and section 644(8), Companies Act 2006.

9.3.12 Sample timetable for a reduction of capital supported by solvency statement under the Companies Act 2006[60]

Actions	Timetable
Due diligence.	Before day 0.
Board meeting to approve the capital reduction and authorise all of the directors to make the solvency statement.	Day 0.
All of the directors to make the solvency statement.	Day 0.
Circulate a copy of the directors' solvency statement to entitled shareholders.	Before the passing of the special resolution.
Special resolution to approve the reduction of capital. Class consent (if required).	By day 15.
File directors' solvency statement, statement of capital[61], directors' statement confirming the solvency statement was properly made and special resolution with Companies House.	By day 30.

9.3.13 Sample timetable for a court approved reduction of capital under the Companies Act 2006[62]

Actions	Timetable
Due diligence and preparation of evidence.	Before day 0.
Agree timetable with court.	Before day 0.
Board meeting to approve the capital reduction, circulate special resolution (to be passed by way of a written resolution), approve documents and authorise a director to sign the witness statement or affidavit.	Day 0.
Special resolution to approve the reduction of capital[63]. Class consent (if required).	Day 0.

---

[60] Assuming shareholder approval is obtained by way of a written resolution.

[61] As a transitional measure and for the period from 1 October 2008 to 1 October 2009, a memorandum giving particulars of the company's capital will be filed instead of a statement of capital.

[62] Assuming the creditors' list has been dispensed with and that shareholder approval is obtained by written resolution.

[63] If a shareholder meeting is required, a further 14 days should be added to the timetable.

Actions	Timetable
Claim form to be filed with the court, together with the director's witness statement or affidavit.	Day 0.
Court reviews evidence.	By day 14.
Directions hearing.	Day 14.
Filing of special resolution with Companies House.	Day 15.
Advertise the final hearing (at least 7 clear days before such hearing) in a broadsheet national daily newspaper.	Day 17.
Final hearing of claim form at court.	Day 26.
Order of court issued confirming the reduction and approving a statement of capital. Register court order and statement of capital with Companies House upon which the reduction becomes effective.	Day 28.
Certificate of reduction received by company.	Day 32.
Advertising of registration of order and statement of capital.	By day 53.

9.4 Purchase or buyback of own shares

9.4.1 Under what circumstances will a company consider purchasing or buying back its own shares?

A company may wish to repurchase its own shares for a variety of reasons, and these will differ between listed and unlisted companies (both public and private ones). The most common ones for listed companies are:

(i) to return surplus cash to shareholders (as an alternative to a reduction of capital);

(ii) to improve liquidity; or

(iii) to improve earnings or net assets per share by having fewer shares in circulation (which payment of a dividend alone would not achieve).

For unlisted companies, in addition to returning surplus cash, the most common reasons are:

(i) to acquire the shares of an existing shareholder (a typical situation might be where a shareholder ceases to be an employee of the company, where the company wishes to create a market in its shares or where the company wishes ownership of its shares to be kept to a limited pool of investors);

(ii) where it wishes to convert its existing share capital from one currency to another (please refer to chapter 8 on this issue, from 1 October 2009, this conversion can be achieved without a purchase of the company's own shares or a reduction of capital); or

(iii) to assist in a redistribution of shares pursuant to an employee incentive plan.

9.4.2 What types of share repurchases are permitted and what shareholders' approvals are required under the Companies Act 1985?

The Companies Act 1985 permits two methods of purchase:

(i) market purchases made on a 'recognised investment exchange', which includes the Official List of the London Stock Exchange; and

(ii) off-market purchases, which are purchases which are either not made on a recognised investment exchange or which are, for example, the acquisition of shares in a private company pursuant to a direct contract with specific vendor shareholders.

9.4.2.1 *Market purchase*

The Companies Act 1985 requires a market purchase to be authorised by an ordinary resolution (but most companies will require a special resolution in order to comply with ABI guidelines). The authority may be unconditional or subject to conditions and may give general or specific authority. The resolution must specify the maximum number of shares which may be purchased, the maximum and minimum prices which may be paid and the date on which the authority will expire (not more than 18 months after the resolution is passed)[64].

9.4.2.2 *Off-market purchase*

An off-market purchase can only be made pursuant to a contract and must be approved in advance by a special resolution[65]. Purchases of own shares can also be made pursuant to conditional contracts which do not themselves constitute a contract to purchase the shares (called 'contingent purchase contracts' under the Companies Act 1985[66]) but these too must be approved in advance by special resolution before they are entered into. Examples might include put and call options over shares.

---

[64] Section 166(1) and section 166(2), Companies Act 1985.
[65] Section 164, Companies Act 1985.
[66] Section 165, Companies act 1985.

For listed companies the requirement to obtain shareholder approval before the contract is entered into can pose timing problems, as it means that shareholders have to be approached before a binding commitment is entered into. In practice, this issue can be addressed if the seller is prepared to enter into a unilateral commitment to sell before the circular is posted but the arrangements need to be carefully structured so that a 'contingent purchase contract' does not come into existence until after shareholder approval has been obtained.

A vendor shareholder should not vote on the special resolution approving an off-market purchase if the resolution would not be passed were he not to vote in favour of it[67]. In the case of a written resolution, such a shareholder should not sign the resolution.

A copy of the contract must be made available for inspection for at least 15 days before and at the shareholders' meeting[68] (or, in the case of a written resolution, the contract be sent to every eligible shareholder before or at the time the proposed resolution is submitted). The resolution will not be effective if these requirements are not met.

9.4.3 What changes have been introduced by the Companies Act 2006?

The new provisions in relation to the purchase of the company's own shares are contained in sections 690 to 723 of the Companies Act 2006 are effective from 1 October 2009.

The key changes are as follows:

(i)   it is not necessary for the company to have express authority in its articles of association to purchase its own shares (unless there is a specific prohibition or restriction in the articles). This is, however, anticipated to be subject to the transitional provisions which require companies incorporated under the Companies Act 1985 and transitional companies incorporated under the transitional provisions of the Companies Act 2006 to have authority either (a) in its articles of association or (b) granted by way of a special resolution before it can carry out a purchase of own shares. It is not clear, as at 30 June 2008, whether or when these anticipated transitional provisions will be terminated;

(ii)   in the case of an off-market purchase it will be permissible to enter into a contract which is conditional upon obtaining shareholder approval as long as it provides that no purchase will be made until the approval is obtained (this will address the timing issue discussed above);

(iii) it is not necessary for a private company to have express authority in its articles of association to purchase its own shares out of capital (unless

---

[67] Section 164(5), Companies Act 1985.
[68] Section 164(6), Companies Act 1985.

there is a specific prohibition or restriction in the articles). This is, however, anticipated to be subject to the transitional provisions which require companies incorporated under the Companies Act 1985 and transitional companies incorporated under the transitional provisions of the Companies Act 2006 to have authority either (a) in its articles of association or (b) granted by way of a special resolution before it can carry out a purchase of own shares out of capital. It is not clear, as at 30 June 2008, whether or when these anticipated transitional provisions will be terminated;

(iv)   the directors' statutory declaration to be made in a purchase financed out of capital by a private company is replaced by a requirement for a solvency statement (which should make the procedure simpler);

(v)   the range of liabilities that directors must take into account when making a solvency statement are potentially wider than those for a statutory declaration; and

(vi)   the notification of cancellation of shares purchased to be registered with Companies House must be accompanied by a statement of capital.

9.4.4   What are the key requirements?

The following table sets out a comparison of the key procedural issues under the Companies Act 1985 and the Companies Act 2006 for a share repurchase.

Key requirement	Position under the 1985 Companies Act	Position under the Companies Act 2006 from 1 October 2009
Authority to purchase in articles required?	Yes[69]	No longer required (unless there are prohibitions or restrictions in the articles). Please refer to section 9.4.3, point (iii) for details of transitional provisions.

---

[69]   Section 162, Companies Act 1985.

Key requirement	Position under the 1985 Companies Act	Position under the Companies Act 2006 from 1 October 2009
Off-market purchase and contingent purchase agreements	The contract for off-market purchase (including a 'contingent purchase contract') must be approved in advance by special resolution[70].	The contract for an off-market purchase must be approved in advance by a special resolution. The contract may also be entered into conditional upon shareholder approval, provided that the terms of contract provide that no repurchase be made until the contract has been so approved[71].
	In the case of a public company, the resolution must specify a period (not exceeding 18 months) after which the resolution will expire if the purchase is not completed.	No change[72].
	The purchase may be approved by written resolution (which will require the approval of all shareholders other than the shareholder whose shares are being acquired).	The changes to written resolutions mean that a special resolution (to be passed by way of a written resolution) can be passed by 75% of those shareholders entitled to vote (these changes came into force on 1 October 2007).
Market purchase – shareholder approval	The purchase must be authorised by an ordinary resolution specifying[73]: — maximum number of shares to be repurchased; — set maximum and minimum prices; and — expiry date (not exceeding 18 months for both public and private companies).	No change[74].

[70] Section 164 and section 165, Companies Act 1985.
[71] Section 694, Companies Act 2006.
[72] Section 694(5), Companies Act 2006.
[73] Section 166, Companies Act 1985.
[74] Section 701, Companies Act 2006.

Key requirement	Position under the 1985 Companies Act	Position under the Companies Act 2006 from 1 October 2009
Financing of the repurchase	Out of distributable reserves and/or proceeds of a fresh issue[75] made for the purpose of financing the repurchase. Any premium payable should be paid out of distributable reserves; but it can also be financed by the proceeds of a fresh issue to the extent that the shares to be repurchased were issued at a premium. This is subject to a maximum amount equal to the actual premiums received or the current share premium account (whichever is less).	No change
	Out of capital (private companies only). A statutory declaration of solvency is required to be sworn by directors[76].	No change to payment out of capital[77] but a solvency statement of directors is required instead of a statutory declaration which takes into account a broader range of liabilities than under the Companies Act 1985.
Timing of payment	Payment must be made on purchase. Deferred payment terms not permitted[78].	No change[79].
Filing with Companies House?	A return in prescribed form (Form 169) must be filed within 28 days from the date of the repurchase.	(i) A return of purchase of own shares and (ii) a notice of cancellation of shares (where the shares repurchased are cancelled), together with a statement of capital must be filed[80].

---

[75] Section 160, Companies Act 1985.
[76] Section 171, Companies Act 1985.
[77] Section 709, Companies Act 2006.
[78] Section 159(3), Companies Act 1985.
[79] Section 691(2), Companies Act 2006.
[80] Section 708, Companies Act 2006.

Key requirement	Position under the 1985 Companies Act	Position under the Companies Act 2006 from 1 October 2009
Effect of repurchase	Shares repurchased treated as cancelled unless the shares are to be held in treasury[81] (applicable to public companies whose shares are listed – please refer to section 9.4.12 below).	No change[82].
	Issued share capital diminished by the nominal value of shares repurchased.	No change[83].
	Authorised share capital remains unchanged.	There is no longer the concept of 'authorised share capital'.
Capital redemption reserve	If shares are purchased wholly out of distributable reserves, the amount by which the issued share capital is diminished shall be transferred to the capital redemption reserve[84].	No change[85].
	If financing is wholly or partly out of proceeds of fresh issue, any excess of the nominal value of shares repurchased over the proceeds shall be transferred to the capital redemption reserve.	No change.

9.4.5 What preliminary issues should a company consider when planning a purchase of its own shares?

9.4.5.1 Listed and AIM companies

Listed companies (namely those whose securities are admitted to the Official List) must comply with the Listing Rules and the Disclosure and Transparency Rules which contain detailed requirements relating to the timing of share buybacks, announcements, and the number of shares which may be acquired.

---

[81] Section 160(4) and section 162A, Companies Act 1985.
[82] Section 706, Companies Act 2006.
[83] Section 706(b), Companies Act 2006.
[84] Section 170, Companies Act 1985.
[85] Section 733, Companies Act 2006.

A tender offer must be made if the shares to be acquired represent 15% or more of the equity shares of any class.

In addition, the Financial Services and Markets Act 2000 and the Code of Market Conduct contain a number of provisions regulating own share purchases and provide a 'safe harbour' from conduct amounting to market abuse provided certain conditions are met.

There are also a number of other requirements set out in the Listing Rules and ABI guidelines which impact on listed companies making market purchases of their own shares. These relate to the following areas:

(i)   the price offered for the shares;

(ii)   the number of shares remaining in public ownership after the purchase;

(iii)   whether additional shareholder approval is required because of the size of the transaction or because it is with a related party;

(iv)   the frequency of obtaining shareholder authority;

(v)   the circumstances in which the authority will be exercised;

(vi)   the public notification that needs to be made to the Regulatory Information Service; and

(vii)   the content requirements of shareholder circulars.

AIM companies need to consider the requirements of the AIM Rules and the Disclosure and Transparency Rules which also contain disclosure obligations.

9.4.5.2   Listed convertible securities

If a listed company has in issue any securities which confer rights to subscribe for, or which are convertible into or exchangeable for shares which are of the same class as those to be purchased, the Listing Rules require the prior consent by way of a special resolution of the holders of those securities to be obtained, unless the share rights or the trust deed constituting the securities contain express provision permitting own share purchases[86].

9.4.5.3   Public companies – the City Code on Takeovers and Mergers (the 'Takeover Code')

The Takeover Code applies to all public companies whether or not their shares are listed or publicly traded. It contains a number of provisions which are directly relevant to purchases by public companies of their own shares. In summary, these are as follows:

[86]   LR 12.4.7, the Listing Rules.

Mandatory Offers

Where any person (including those acting in concert with him) acquires shares with voting rights representing 30% or more of the total voting rights of a company, he is required to make a mandatory cash offer for the remaining shares (there are detailed rules specifying which shares are required to be subject to the offer). These provisions apply even where the person concerned has taken no active steps to increase his percentage interest, and so apply where a percentage interest has increased as a result of a purchase of the company's own shares. The Panel on Takeovers and Mergers (the 'Panel') can waive the requirement if the acquisition is approved by an ordinary resolution of the independent shareholders and the board obtains independent advice on the implications of the offer. The mandatory offer provisions also apply where a person already holds 30% or more of the voting rights but not more than 50% and increases his percentage holding.

In general, the Panel will not waive the obligation to make a mandatory offer where shares have been acquired by a director (or person acting in concert with him) in the knowledge that the company is likely to be approaching its shareholders for approval of a purchase of the company's own shares.

Takeover offers

No purchases of a company's own shares may take place without shareholder approval where a takeover offer is imminent or current.

A purchase of its own shares by a target company during an offer period must be publicly disclosed and share buybacks in the 12 months proceeding an offer disclosed in the target company's circular to the shareholders. The bidder may also be required to make disclosure of any purchases of its own shares in certain situations.

9.4.5.4 *Will the share repurchase result in a variation of the class rights of the other shareholders?*

If the share repurchase will result in a variation of the rights attached to any class of shares in the company, it will be necessary to seek class consent from those shareholders prior to the repurchase. For example, if the shares to be repurchased are ordinary shares where there are preference shares in issue (the holders of which have a preferential right to a return of capital), the repurchase will be a deemed variation of the class rights of the preference shares and the consent of the preference shareholders will be required for the repurchase (unless the articles provide for an alternative mechanism).

ABI guidelines also provide that a special resolution of preference shareholders should be sought where a share buyback is proposed, and that the board should consider the impact of the share buyback on the company's ability to continue to pay dividends on the preference shares or to meet the payment obligation on redemption.

9.4.5.5 *Are any of the shares listed or traded overseas?*

The relevant securities laws of those countries might impose additional restrictions or requirements.

9.4.5.6 *Is the company subject to any pre-emption rights or other restrictions on share repurchase under its agreements with third parties?*

It is not unusual for agreements with third parties such as shareholders' agreements, loan agreements or debentures to contain restrictions (in particular pre-emption rights in the case of a shareholders' agreement) on a company purchasing its own shares. It is therefore necessary to review the major agreements of the company to ascertain if there are any such restrictions and seek consents from third parties where necessary.

9.4.5.7 *Are any directors of the company selling any of their shares?*

If any of the sellers under the share repurchase is also a director of the company, and the shares to be purchased from such a director have a value exceeding 10% of the company's asset value and are more than £5,000, or, have a value exceeding £100,000, the transaction might constitute a substantial property transaction requiring shareholder approval (see chapter 2)[87]. However, there is a new exemption introduced on 1 October 2007 by the Companies Act 2006 which applies where the transaction is entered into with a person in his character as a shareholder and may therefore apply in this instance[88]. There is also an exemption where the transaction takes place on a recognised investment exchange[89].

9.4.5.8 *Are creditors likely to object?*

The interests of creditors are generally protected by the restrictions (discussed further in section 9.4.7) on how an own share purchase is financed. Nevertheless, the directors should, in the proper discharge of their duties, consider whether and if so, to what extent, a purchase of the company's own shares affects the company's ability to pay its creditors.

In addition, where a private company proposes to finance the purchase out of capital, creditors of the company will have the right to object to the court on application. Therefore, it would be prudent to assess the likelihood of any such challenge at the outset.

---

[87] Section 190, Companies Act 2006
[88] Section 192, Companies Act 2006.
[89] Section 194, Companies Act 2006.

9.4.5.9 *Will other shareholders be disadvantaged?*

Similarly, the interests of shareholders are generally protected by the restrictions on how a share repurchase is financed and by the need to obtain shareholder approval (under which the shareholder whose shares are being acquired is not entitled to vote). Nonetheless, a purchase of the company's own shares can result in the passing of value to some shareholders to the exclusion of others and directors should therefore be satisfied that the purchase will promote the success of the company and, in this situation, should have regard in particular to the need to act fairly as between shareholders (see chapter 1).

Even where the requisite shareholder approval is obtained, minority shareholders have certain general rights to challenge the transaction (see, for example, derivative claims in chapter 1). A dissenting shareholder has a statutory right to object to the court where a purchase of own share out of capital is proposed. It is therefore prudent to assess the impact on and likely reaction of the minority shareholders at the outset.

9.4.5.10 *Is the company a single member company?*

A single shareholder company cannot pass a written resolution to approve a share repurchase from itself, as the single shareholder is not entitled to vote on such a resolution. As such, it is common practice for the single shareholder to appoint a nominee holder prior to the repurchase for the purpose of the passing of a written resolution[90].

9.4.5.11 *What is the price for the purchase?*

Shares may be purchased at a price which is at, or less or more than the nominal value of the shares. The directors need to consider the purchase price with regard to their duties as directors (see chapter 1).

9.4.5.12 *How is the purchase financed?*

The purchase price must be made in cash (not payment in kind) on the purchase. It has been suggested in a court case (*BDG Roof Bond Limited* v *Douglas* [2000] I BCLC 401) that payment can be made in kind but this view has not been widely followed. Furthermore, the price must be paid on purchase and cannot be left outstanding.

If a company proposes to borrow the money to fund its purchase or to lend money to its parent to enable it to fund a purchase of its own shares, careful consideration should be given to the rules regarding unlawful financial assistance (see section 9.9 below).

---

[90] Section 695(2), Companies Act 2006.

9.4.5.13   Are the shares fully paid?

Partly paid shares cannot be the subject of a share repurchase[91]. The shares have to be fully paid up first. Either a call can be made on shareholders or reserves can be capitalised to pay up the shares (if permitted by the articles).

9.4.5.14   What is the stamp duty position?

A purchase of the company's own shares in principle attracts stamp duty unless intra-group relief is available.

9.4.5.15   Must the company have at least one shareholder holding shares other than redeemable shares?

Yes. It is a requirement after a purchase of the company's own shares that there must be at least one shareholder holding shares other than redeemable shares[92].

9.4.5.16   Have the articles of association been reviewed?

Until 1 October 2009, it remains a requirement that a company can only purchase its own shares if it has express authority in its articles; where the purchase is to be made out of capital the articles must also make express provision. As the financing of the purchase can constitute financial assistance in connection with the acquisition by a company of its own shares, it is also usual to remove any such restrictions in the constitution prior to a repurchase (these are typically found in older sets of articles).

These requirements are essential as, if not met, they will invalidate the purchase even if the shareholder resolution is properly obtained.

After 1 October 2009, there is no longer a requirement for express authority in the articles, but articles must still be reviewed to identify any relevant restriction which may need to be removed. Please, however, refer to sections 9.4.3, points (i) and (iii) for details of transitional provisions.

9.4.5.17   Is there any need to cancel the shares on repurchase?

No, the shares are automatically cancelled on completion of the purchase unless the shares are to be held in treasury (please refer to section 9.4.12 for details on treasury shares). Issued share capital will be reduced by the nominal amount of the shares cancelled; authorised share capital will remain the same.

---

[91]   Section 159(3), Companies Act 1985 and section 691(1), Companies Act 2006.
[92]   Section 162(3), Companies act 1985 and section 690(2), Companies Act 2006.

9.4.6 What factors should a company consider in deciding whether to purchase its own shares or carry out a reduction of capital?

There may be situations where a company cannot satisfy the requirements for an own share purchase and therefore a reduction of capital (either by court approval or the solvency statement procedure, subject to the applicable requirements) is more appropriate. For example:

(i)   if it is a public company, it may not have sufficient realised profits to fund the purchase and it will not qualify for the private company exception to purchase shares out of capital;

(ii)   if the shares are not fully paid;

(iii)   if the company wishes to cancel the entirety of its share capital;

(iv)   where a court approved reduction is part of a larger transaction such as a scheme of arrangement which requires court approval in any event and it is therefore convenient to include the capital reduction as part of the court process; and

(v)   where the consideration for the purchase is a non-cash asset or is to be deferred.

9.4.7 Are there restrictions on how the purchase can be financed?

9.4.7.1 Share purchase out of distributable reserves

The purchase monies must be paid out of distributable reserves or from the proceeds of a fresh issue of shares. However, the fresh issue of shares must be made for the purpose of financing the repurchase.

Distributable reserves for this purpose are calculated in the same way as for dividends (see section 9.2 above) and the requirement for 'relevant accounts' also applies.

Any premium over the nominal value of the shares to be purchased must be paid out of distributable reserves save where the shares were originally issued at a premium. In this case, any premium on the purchase may be paid out of a fresh issue of shares up to the aggregate of the original premiums received on the shares to be purchased or the current amount of the company's share premium account (after the new share issue has taken place), whichever is less.

9.4.7.2 Share purchase out of capital by a private company

A private company may, if it has insufficient distributable reserves, purchase its own shares out of capital provided it has power in the articles to do so. 1985 Table A articles do contain such a power but companies incorporated prior to 1 July 1985 and which have not updated their articles do not. After 1 October

2009, it is no longer a requirement for private companies to have express authority in their articles to purchase shares out of capital (subject to any express restrictions or prohibitions). Please refer to section 9.4.3 (iii) for details of the transitional provisions. However, the company must first use any available distributable reserves and any proceeds of a fresh issue of shares made for the purpose of the purchase to finance the purchase[93]. This requirement is to ensure that any distributable reserves and proceeds of fresh issue are used to the maximum extent to fund the repurchase before the company can resort to its capital – such a payment is referred to as the 'permissible capital payment'. A private company cannot therefore elect to finance a purchase of its shares out of capital instead of its distributable reserves.

There are special provisions for computing distributable reserves for this purpose under both the Companies Act 1985 and the Companies Act 2006 (the provisions for computing distributable reserves for a general dividend or distribution as discussed in section 9.2 do not apply)[94].

The distributable reserves are determined by reference to the following items as stated in the 'relevant accounts':

(i)   profits, losses, assets and liabilities;

(ii)   certain specified provisions; and

(iii)   share capital and reserves (including undistributable reserve),

from which are deducted, (a) any distributions lawfully made by the company and (b) any other relevant payment out of distributable profits made by the company, in both cases since the date of the 'relevant accounts'[95].

'Relevant accounts' cannot be more than three months old (from the date of the directors' statement as referred to below) and need not be audited[96]. However, directors may wish to seek comfort from their auditors that the figures are correct and can have the amounts audited if they wish to do so.

Under the Companies Act 2006 and with effect from 1 October 2009, the payment out of capital must be carried out as follows (which largely restates the Companies Act 1985 provisions except as otherwise indicated)[97]:

(i)   all the directors of the company must make a statement (a) confirming the permissible capital payment and (b) stating that they have made full enquiry into the affairs and prospects of the company and that they have formed the opinion that, upon the payment out of capital, the company

---

[93] Section 171(3), Companies Act 1985 and section 710, Companies Act 2006.
[94] Section 172, Companies Act 1985 and section 712, Companies Act 2006.
[95] Section 172(3), Companies Act 1985 and section 712(3), Companies Act 2006.
[96] Section 172(6), Companies Act 1985 and section 712(6), Companies Act 2006.
[97] Section 714, Companies Act 2006.

will be able to pay its debts and will continue as a going concern for at least one year after the repurchase. This statement supersedes the statutory declaration of solvency required of the directors under the Companies Act 1985;

(ii)   in forming their opinion, the directors must consider all of the company's liabilities, including any contingent or prospective liabilities. This potentially expands the requirement under the Companies Act 1985 for directors to consider liabilities only relevant to the solvency of the company;

(iii)   the directors' statement must be confirmed by a report from the company's auditors, and sufficient time therefore needs to be built into any transaction for this report;

(iv)   within the week immediately following the directors' statement, the purchase contract and the capital payment must be approved by a special resolution[98];

(v)   a vendor shareholder should not vote on the special resolution approving the payment out of capital if the resolution would not be passed were he not to vote in favour of it (such a shareholder will not be considered as an eligible shareholder in the case of a written resolution)[99];

(vi)   the directors' statement, the auditors' report and the special resolution must be filed with Companies House;

(vii)   within the week after the passing of the special resolution and after completing the filing at Companies House, a notice should be published in the *London Gazette* giving details of the payment out of capital; a similar notice must also be published in a national newspaper (unless a specific notice is given to each and every creditor of the company[100]);

(viii)   a copy of the directors' statement and the auditors' report must be made available for inspection at the relevant shareholders' meeting (or, in the case of a written resolution, be sent to every eligible shareholder before or at the time the proposed resolution is submitted) and throughout the period from the date of publication of the above notices and five weeks after the passing of the special resolution;

(ix)   any dissenting shareholder or any creditor of the company may apply to the court within five weeks from the date of the resolution for it to be cancelled. The court may make such order as it thinks fit. The payment out of capital must be made no earlier than five, nor more than seven weeks, after the date of the resolution to allow time for objection[101]. In practice, this is a rare occurrence as most companies will have reached a

---

[98] Section 716, Companies Act 2006.
[99] Section 717(3), Companies Act 2006.
[100] Section 719, Companies Act 2006.
[101] Section 723, Companies Act 2006.

consensus between shareholders and creditors before embarking on the process; and

(x) a return of repurchase and, with effect from 1 October 2009, a notice of cancellation (together with a statement of capital) must be filed with Companies House within 28 days after the completion of the purchase.

9.4.8 How is capital maintained?

If the financing for the purchase is wholly out of distributable reserves, the amount by which the issued share capital is diminished must be transferred to a capital redemption reserve[102].

If the financing for the purchase is wholly or partly out of proceeds of a fresh issue of shares, only the excess of the nominal value of shares purchased over the proceeds is transferred to the capital redemption reserve.

Such a reserve can be used to pay up new shares to be allotted by the company to its shareholders as fully paid bonus shares (if permitted by its articles). Subject to that, the reserve is treated as part of the company's share capital and is subject to the same restrictions on reduction of capital.

To the extent the purchase is out of permissible capital payment, the capital is not maintained. However, the creditor protection is provided by, under the Companies Act 1985, the statutory declaration of solvency process undertaken by the company and auditors or, under the Companies Act 2006, the solvency statement process undertaken by the company and auditors (as described in section 9.4.7.2 above).

9.4.9 Sample balance sheets of a company before and after the share repurchase

9.4.9.1 *Public or private company – purchase out of distributable reserves*

Company X proposes to purchase 100,000 shares of £1 each out of its 1,000,000 shares (all of which were originally subscribed for at par), at a price of £2.20 per share (i.e. a premium of £1.20 per share). It has distributable reserves of £500,000. The double entries and the summary balance sheets are set out below:

Purchase of shares

DR[103]	Share capital	£100,000
DR	P&L reserves	£120,000
CR[104]	Cash	£220,000

---

[102] Section 170, Companies Act 1985 and section 733, Companies Act 2006.
[103] DR = Debit
[104] CR = Credit

Maintenance of capital

As the shares are to be purchased out of distributable reserves, it is necessary to maintain the capital and therefore transfer a balance from distributable reserves to the capital redemption reserve of an amount equal to the nominal value of the shares purchased (in this case, £100,000):

DR	P&L reserves	£100,000
CR	Capital redemption reserve	£100,000

Overall impact

The overall impact of these transactions is:

DR	Share capital	£100,000
DR	P&L reserves	£220,000
CR	Capital redemption reserve	£100,000
CR	Cash	£220,000

	Opening position (k)	Purchase of shares (k)	Maintenance of capital (k)	Closing position (k)
Cash	400	(220)	–	180
Other Net Assets	1,100	–	–	1,100
Net Assets	**1,500**	**(220)**		**1,280**
Share capital	1,000	(100)	–	900
Capital redemption reserve	–	–	100	100
Capital	**1,000**	**(100)**	**100**	**1,000**
P&L reserves	500	(120)	(100)	280
Shareholders' funds	**1,500**	**(220)**	**–**	**1,280**

9.4.9.2 Public and private company – purchase at a premium

Company Y proposes to purchase 200,000 preference shares of £1 each (which were originally issued at a premium of 10 pence per share) at a price of £1.50 per share (i.e. a premium of 50 pence per share). At the same time, it is issuing 50,000 ordinary shares of £1 each at a price of £2 (i.e. at a premium of £1 each). It has distributable reserves of £500,000. The double entries and the summary balance sheets are set out below:

Issue of shares

DR	Cash	£100,000
CR	Share capital	£50,000
CR	Share premium	£50,000

Purchase of shares

DR	Share capital	£200,000
DR	Share premium*	£20,000
DR	P&L reserves	£80,000
CR	Cash	£300,000

* As discussed in section 9.4.7.1 above, where shares are to be repurchased at a premium, the amount which can be debited to share premium account is restricted to the lower of the amount of premium recorded on the original issue of the shares to be purchased (£20,000 in this case) and the amount of the company's share premium account after taking into account any premium recorded on the new issue made to fund the repurchase (£70,000 in this case).

Maintenance of capital

As previously, since a proportion of the shares are repurchased out of P&L reserves, it is necessary to make a transfer to the capital redemption reserve to ensure the capital of the company is maintained. The amount to be transferred to the capital redemption reserve is equal to the difference between (a) proceeds of the fresh issue (£100,000) and (b) the aggregate of (i) the amount debited to the share premium account (£20,000) and (ii) the nominal value of the shares to be purchased (£200,000). As such, the aggregate value of the share capital, share premium and capital redemption reserve is equal before and after these transactions (please refer to illustrative balance sheet below).

DR	P&L reserves	£120,000
CR	Capital redemption reserve	£120,000

Overall impact

The overall impact of these transactions is:

DR	Share capital	£150,000
DR	P&L reserves	£200,000
CR	Share premium	£30,000
CR	Capital redemption reserve	£120,000
CR	Cash	£200,000

	Opening position (k)	Issue of shares (k)	Purchase of shares (k)	Maintenance of capital (k)	Closing position (k)
Cash	400	100	(300)	–	200
Other Net Assets	1,100	–	–	–	1,100
Net Assets	**1,500**	**100**	**(300)**	**–**	**1,300**
Share capital	1,000	50	(200)	–	850
Share premium	20	50	(20)	–	50
Capital redemption reserve	–	–	–	120	120
Capital	**1,020**	**100**	**(220)**	**–**	**1,020**
P&L reserves	[480]	–	(80)	(120)	280
Shareholders' funds	**1,500**	**100**	**(300)**	**–**	**1,300**

9.4.9.3 Private company – purchase out of capital

Company Z proposes to purchase 100,000 ordinary shares of £1 each at a price of £1.50 each (i.e. a premium of 50 pence per share). It has distributable reserves of £20,000 and is issuing 50,000 ordinary shares of £1 each at a price of £2 per share (i.e. a premium of £1 per share). The double entries and the summary balance sheets are set out below:

The permissible capital payment (as discussed in section 9.4.7.2 above) is calculated as:

Price of shares being purchased	£150,000
Less profits available for distribution	(£20,000)
Less proceeds of a fresh issue	(£100,000)
Permissible capital payment	**£30,000**

Issue of shares

DR	Cash	£100,000
CR	Share capital	£50,000
CR	Share premium	£50,000

Purchase of shares

DR	Share capital	£100,000
DR	Share premium	£30,000
DR	P&L reserves	£20,000
CR	Cash	£150,000

Overall impact

The overall impact of these transactions is:

DR	Share capital	£50,000
CR	Share premium	£20,000
DR	P&L reserves	£20,000
CR	Cash	£50,000

	Opening position (k)	Issue of shares (k)	Purchase of shares (k)	Closing position (k)
Cash	400	100	(150)	350
Other Net Assets	1,120	–	–	1,120
Net Assets	**1,520**	**100**	**(150)**	**1,470**
Share capital	1,000	50	(100)	950
Share premium	500	50	(30)	520
Capital	**1,500**	**100**	**(130)**	**1,470***
P&L reserves	20		(20)	–
Shareholders' funds	**1,520**	**100**	**(150)**	**1,470**

* There is an overall reduction in the amount of capital of £30,000 – being the amount of the permissible capital payment.

9.4.10 Sample timetable for a purchase of own shares by a private company out of capital under the Companies Act 1985 and the Companies Act 2006[105]

Actions	Deadline
Check articles of association and statutory books of the company to ensure (i) (a) before 1 October 2009, there is express authority to purchase shares out of capital and (b) after 1 October 2009, there are no restrictions on the company purchasing its own shares out of capital (please refer to section 9.4.3, point (iii) for details of transitional provisions, (ii) shares are fully paid, (iii) non-redeemable shares will be left in issue after the repurchase, and (iv) no class consents are required.	Before day 0.
Transfer at least one share to a nominee if the company is a single shareholder company.	Before day 0.

[105] Assuming shareholder approval is obtained by way of a written resolution.

Actions	Deadline
Accounts of the company prepared to ascertain distributable reserves.	Prepared as at a date not more than three months before the directors' statutory declaration (or the directors' statement from 1 October 2009). Need to take account of subsequent reductions in distributable profits.
Determine the amount of the permissible capital payment.	Before day 0.
Prepare directors' statutory declaration or (with effect from 1 October 2009) a directors' statement specifying the amount of the permissible capital payment and stating the company will be able to carry on business as a going concern (and pay its debts as they fall due) for 12 months.	Before day 0.
Confirm auditors' report to support directors' opinion in their statutory declaration or (with effect from 1 October 2009) a directors' statement can be issued.	Before day 0.
Prepare purchase contract between the company and the vendor shareholder(s).	Before day 0.
Prepare all board minutes, shareholders' written resolution and related documents.	Before day 0.
Confirm availability of all directors of the company to make the statutory declaration or (with effect from 1 October 2009) the directors' statement.	Before day 0.
Arrange date of publication of advertisements with the *Gazette* and a national newspaper.	Before day 0.
Hold company board meeting to: (i) approve purchase contract (ii) (authorise all directors to make the statutory declaration or (with effect from 1 October 2009) the directors' statement relating to the payment out of capital; (iii) approve relevant accounts and receive auditors' report; and (iv) approve shareholders' written resolution.	Day 0.

Actions	Deadline
Shareholders' written resolution to approve (i) the purchase, (ii) the purchase contract and (iii) the purchase out of capital to be signed in writing by the non-vendor shareholder (i.e. the nominee), and to have available with it a copy of the purchase contract, the directors' statutory declaration or (with effect from 1 October 2009) the directors' statement made and the signed auditors' report.	Day 0. Passed on same day as directors' statutory declaration or directors' statement is made or within one week after.
File copy directors' statutory declaration or (with effect from 1 October 2009) directors' statement, auditors' report and shareholders' written resolution with Companies House.	Day 0 (before advertisements are published).
Advertisements to appear in the *Gazette* and a national newspaper.	Day 1. Within one week after the passing of the shareholders' resolution.
Original directors' statutory declaration or (with effect from 1 October 2009) directors' statement, auditors' report and purchase contract deposited at the company's registered office.	Day 0 – Day 35. Directors' statutory declaration or (with effect from 1 October 2009) directors' statement and auditors' report to be available for inspection from the date advertisements are published until five weeks after the date of the shareholders' resolution. Purchase contract to be available for inspection for ten years.
Board meeting of the company to approve signing of purchase contract.	Day 35.
Completion of purchase contract: (i) surrender of share certificate(s) for shares purchased; (ii) payment of purchase price; and (iii) cancellation of shares purchased.	Day 35. Between five and seven weeks after the date of the shareholders' resolution.
File return of repurchase and, with effect from 1 October 2009, a notice of cancellation of shares together with a statement of capital, with Companies House.	Within 28 days after completion of purchase.
Write up the company's statutory books.	As soon as possible after completion of purchase.

9.4.11 What are the penalties for a breach of the statutory requirements?

If a company purchases its own shares in breach of the requirements under either the Companies Act 1985 or the Companies Act 2006, the consequences are as follows:

(i)   the share purchase will be void with the result that a shareholder can apply for rectification of the register;

(ii) the company and every officer in default commit an offence and will be liable, on conviction, to imprisonment and/or a fine as specified under the relevant Act;

(iii) directors will be in breach of their general duties;

(iv) if the company fails to file the required documents with Companies House after a repurchase of shares, every officer of the company in default commits an offence and will be liable on conviction to a fine; and

(v)   if, notwithstanding all of the above, the company is wound up within one year, the vendor shareholders and any director who made the statutory declaration or the solvency statement will be liable to repay to the liquidator the amount paid by the company insofar as it was a payment out of capital to the extent necessary to discharge the liabilities of the company. However, directors will not be liable if they can show that they had reasonable grounds for forming their opinion.

9.4.12 What special rules apply to a purchase of treasury shares?

As mentioned above, as a general rule, where shares are repurchased by a company they are automatically cancelled on purchase and the amount of the company's issued share capital is reduced accordingly. In 2003, new rules were introduced under which, in certain cases, public companies whose shares were included on the Official List of the London Stock Exchange (or traded on AIM or elsewhere in the EEA) can buy and hold up to 10% of those shares in treasury without the shares being cancelled. The shares held in treasury (the treasury shares) can then be redistributed at a later date. There are, however, a number of requirements:

(i)   the shares can only be purchased out of distributable reserves;

(ii) the company must not exercise any rights attaching to the shares whilst they are held in treasury;

(iii) no distributions can be made by the company in respect of shares held in treasury although redemption payments for redeemable shares and bonus issues are permitted;

(iv)   the company can only deal with the shares by (a) selling them for cash (b) transferring them to or for the purposes of an employees' share scheme or (c) cancelling them; and

(v)   if the shares cease to meet the requirements then they must be cancelled immediately.

The existing provisions of the Companies Act 1985 (sections 162A to 162G) relating to treasury shares summarised above are largely restated in the Companies Act 2006 in sections 724 to 732 which are effective from 1 October 2009.

9.5   Redemption of redeemable shares

9.5.1   What are the differences between a purchase of own shares and a redemption of redeemable shares?

A company may issue shares on terms that they are liable to be redeemed at a future date. The Companies Act 1985 and Companies Act 2006 provisions described above relating to the financing of a purchase of own shares will apply equally to a redemption of redeemable shares save that as from 1 October 2009, payment on the redemption of redeemable shares may be left outstanding[106]. With a purchase of own shares, payment has to be made on purchase and no deferral is permitted[107].

A redemption of redeemable shares is less cumbersome than a purchase of own shares as:

(i)   the redemption terms are set out in the share rights which are approved by shareholders on issue and there is no further requirement to obtain shareholder approval on redemption; and

(ii)   a redemption of shares does not constitute an acquisition of shares and therefore financial assistance considerations do not apply (albeit this will be less of an issue when the prohibition on financial assistance by private companies is abolished from 1 October 2008).

The accounting for the redemption of redeemable shares, however, is more complex than a purchase of own shares.

---

[106] Section 686(2), Companies Act 2006.
[107] Section 159(3), Companies Act 1985 and section 691(2), Companies Act 2006.

9.5.2 What are the key requirements?

	Position under the Companies Act 1985	Position under the Companies Act 2006 from 1 October 2009
Issue of redeemable shares	Permissible for a limited company if authorised to do so by its articles[108].	Authority no longer required in its articles for a private company (unless there are express prohibitions or restrictions). This is, however, subject to the transitional provisions which require private companies incorporated under the Companies Act 1985 and companies incorporated under the transitional provisions of the Companies Act 2006 to have authority either (i) in its articles of association or (ii) granted by way of a special resolution before it can issue redeemable shares. Permissible for a public company if authorised to do so by its articles[109].
Are there any restrictions on the issue of redeemable shares?	There must be other issued shares which are not redeemable[110].	No change[111].

---

[108] Section 159(1), Companies Act 1985.
[109] Section 684, Companies Act 2006.
[110] Section 159(2), Companies Act 1985.
[111] Section 684(4), Companies Act 2006.

	Position under the Companies Act 1985	Position under the Companies Act 2006 from 1 October 2009
Terms and manner of redemption	The date of redemption may be specified in the articles or fixed by the directors if authorised by the articles. All other terms of redemption must be specified in the articles[112].	Directors can determine the terms and conditions of redemption if they are authorised by the articles or an ordinary resolution to do so (this must be done prior to the allotment)[113].
Payment	Terms of redemption must provide for payment on redemption[114].	Payment must be made on redemption unless the terms of redemption provide that the amount payable may be paid on a date later than the redemption date (by agreement between the company and the relevant shareholder)[115].
Filing with Companies House	If redeemable shares are being redeemed, a return in prescribed form to be filed within one month of redemption[116].	If redeemable shares are being redeemed, a notice, together with a statement of capital, must be filed with Companies House within one month of redemption[117].

If the company fails to give notice to Companies House of a redemption of redeemable shares, the company and every officer of the company in default commit an offence and will be liable on conviction to a fine.

---

[112] Section 159(A), Companies Act 1985.
[113] Section 685, Companies Act 2006.
[114] Section 159(3), Companies Act 1985.
[115] Section 686(2), Companies Act 2006.
[116] Section 122, Companies Act 1985.
[117] Section 689, Companies Act 2006.

9.6 Intra-group reorganisations

9.6.1 Under what circumstances will a company carry out an intra-group reorganisation?

There are a number of situations where groups will wish to reorganise their corporate structures by combining businesses or restructuring holdings in subsidiaries, for example:

(i)   to reorganise assets with a view to sell;

(ii)   to integrate companies post acquisition;

(iii)   to achieve cost savings and improved corporate governance by reducing the numbers of active trading companies and replacing some with branches;

(iv)   to align their corporate and operational structures;

(v)   to refinance subsidiaries; and

(vi)   to achieve tax efficiencies.

Intra-group reorganisations are effected through a series of steps carried out between each of the companies concerned and which can typically include all or some of the following:

(i)   issues and transfers of shares;

(ii)   transfers of business or individual assets;

(iii)   intra-group loans;

(iv)   capitalisation of subsidiaries or of loans;

(v)   novation or waiver of liabilities;

(vi)   payments of dividends (in cash or in kind); and

(vii)   purchases of own shares and reductions of capital.

Each of these will raise a series of legal questions which will require analysis; (i), (vi) and (vii) in the paragraph above are already covered elsewhere in this chapter and in chapter 8. However, companies legislation does not specifically regulate intra-group reorganisations or set out a statutory procedure for carrying them out. This often means that a wide range of legal issues should be considered prior to such a reorganisation, of which the most common are set out in this section.

9.6.2   What issues arise if an asset is transferred intra-group for less than market value?

One of the most difficult questions that arises in the context of intra-group reorganisations is the value at which assets can be transferred intra-group.

The directors of each company involved in an intra-group reorganisation owe their duties to that company alone and not to the group as a whole. Therefore, their starting point should be to ensure that value is retained within their company for the benefit of the company's shareholders. In principle, therefore, the sale of an asset intra-group for less than its market value is potentially a breach of the fiduciary duties of those directors. In practice, however, it is frequently more convenient to transfer assets at their historic book values. Case law has held that directors will not be in breach of their duties when they carry out such a transaction provided that (i) they are satisfied that it will be of benefit to the group, and (ii) by benefiting the group, their particular company will also benefit.

Where this is doubtful, directors can protect themselves by obtaining prior shareholder approval or by having the transaction ratified as long as the company is solvent and will remain so once the transaction has taken place.

The second question is whether an intra-group transaction at an undervalue will constitute a distribution by a company and, if so, to what extent should a company have sufficient distributable reserves.

We have discussed already in section 9.2 that both statutory procedures and common law requirements must be met before a dividend can be paid. In relation to undervalued transfers (which can involve the passing of value to shareholders), the application of the common law value on distributions was discussed in the case of *Aveling Barford Ltd v Perion Ltd* [1989] BCLC 626.

The facts were as follows:

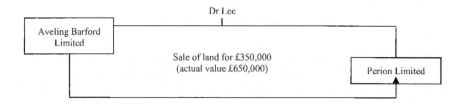

Key facts:

1.   Aveling Barford Limited had negative reserves and was solvent.

2.   Perion sold the land to a third party for £1.5 million.

As the transfer was held by the court to be void on the ground that it was an unauthorised return of capital, beneficial ownership in the asset did not pass to Perion Limited, which was held liable to account for the whole of the sale proceeds to Aveling Barford Limited as a constructive trustee.

The case also raised a number of technical issues regarding the value at which companies could transfer assets intra-group, and importantly whether a transfer at an undervalue could amount to a 'distribution' under section 263 of the Companies Act 1985 and, if so, how the amount of the distribution was calculated.

The principles apply not only to a sale of assets intra-group at an undervalue but also to a sale of assets intra-group at an overvalue.

A breach of the *Aveling Barford* principles cannot be ratified by shareholders as they are for the benefit of the protection of creditors' interests. This is the position even if both companies remain solvent after the transaction.

In the context of intra-group reorganisations, structuring transfers in compliance with the *Aveling Barford* principles is, therefore, of critical importance as title issues will directly impact on tax filings and financial reporting. In the context of third party acquisitions, any predisposal reorganisation will necessitate detailed due diligence to ensure that the beneficial ownership of assets is as contemplated.

9.6.3 What changes have been introduced by the Companies Act 2006?

Section 845 of the Companies Act 2006 (which is effective from 6 April 2008) clarifies the issues arising from the *Aveling Barford* principles and confirms that a transaction at book value will amount to a distribution of the company's assets. It provides that where a company has profits available for distribution of at least £1 then it can lawfully transfer an asset at book value and the amount of the distribution will then be taken to be:

(i)   zero, where the consideration for the asset is not less than book value; and

(ii) in all other cases, the amount by which the book value exceeds the consideration.

The Companies Act 2006 also states that where the consideration exceeds the book value of its assets, the company's profits available for distribution will be increased by the amount by which the consideration exceeds the book value. However, this merely refers to consideration and does not state that this needs to be qualifying consideration (as defined by Tech 01/08). The market position on this interpretation has yet to be settled.

9.6.4 Summary of the rules relating to the value at which assets can be transferred intra-group

---

When can a company transfer assets at market value?

A company can always transfer an asset at market value. Where the market value is less than book value, the company will need to account for a loss on the sale (but this will not amount to a distribution). In effect, the asset was impaired prior to transfer and this loss represents an impairment which should be recorded prior to the transfer such that the market value would not be less than book value at the time of the transfer.

When can a company transfer assets at book value?

Where a company has distributable reserves of at least £1, it can transfer an asset at book value.

When can a company transfer assets at less than book value?

Where a company has distributable reserves at least equal to the difference between the book value and the consideration to be received in return for the asset.

9.6.5 To which intra-group transactions do these principles apply?

These principles will apply to:

9.6.5.1 *Transfers between sister companies*

<u>Example</u>

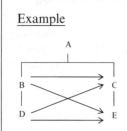

Transfers from B to C or E or from D to C or E.

9.6.5.2 *Transfers to a parent company*

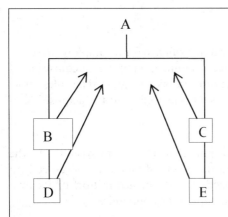

- Transfers from D to A, B to A, C to A or E to A.
- Note that a D to A or E to A transfer might also constitute a distribution by B to A or C to A, respectively.

However, it will not apply to downstream transfers.

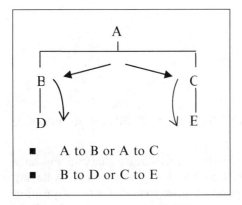

- A to B or A to C
- B to D or C to E

9.6.6 How does a company value the asset to be transferred?

Generally, a formal valuation is not a legal requirement but is certainly best practice. If the directors of the company reasonably consider themselves competent to assess value then they may do this. Other incidental benefits (for example, tax) may also be considered when assessing value.

When considering value, it is important that directors consider whether the purchase price is to be paid in cash or left outstanding as an inter-company loan. If a loan, the repayment terms and interest rate will affect value along with the credit risk. This may be taken into account when calculating the true value of the receivable.

9.6.7   What other general legal issues may arise from an undervalue transaction?

9.6.7.1   *Financial assistance*

Under the Companies Act 1985, it is a criminal offence for a company or any of its subsidiaries to give financial assistance in connection with an acquisition of its shares whether before or after the acquisition takes place[118]. The rules apply equally to transfers and subscriptions of shares as well as to the acquisition of securities convertible into shares.

However, from 1 October 2008 and pursuant to the provisions of the Companies Act 2006, the prohibition on the giving of financial assistance by a private company is abolished in connection with an acquisition of its own shares or shares of its private holding company or companies.

Particular care is therefore needed in the context of post-deal integration and pre-deal reorganisations as a wide range of potential transactions are caught by this prohibition, for example:

- In contemplation of the sale of T by B to A, T sells certain non-core assets at an undervalue to C.

- The undervalue transaction by T reduces its overall value and will have the effect of transferring value in T to B and its group without A having to account for such value in the purchase price payable for the acquisition of T. This amounts to the giving of financial assistance by T in connection with the purchase of T's shares by A. The directors of T will have committed an offence and the contract between T and C will be unenforceable. However, this would not be an issue if the sale by T was at market value.

The financial assistance prohibition, together with the available exemptions, are discussed in section 9.9.

---

[118] Section 151, Companies Act 1985.

9.6.7.2 *Insolvency Act 1986 – undervalue transactions*

If a company becomes insolvent, its liquidator or administrator can apply to the court to set aside any transactions made at an undervalue, provided they have been entered into by the company in the two years prior to the date of insolvency[119].

A company's liquidator or administrator has a similar power in respect of transactions entered into by the company in the two years prior to insolvency which are deemed to be preferences, i.e. where the company intentionally put a creditor or guarantor in a better position to other creditors[120].

Whether or not the company is insolvent at the time or following a transaction, creditors, shareholders, an administrator, a liquidator or a supervisor of a voluntary arrangement can make an application to court to set aside any transaction at an undervalue[121]. This will succeed where they can establish to the satisfaction of the court that the aim of that transaction was to place assets of the company beyond the reach of creditors (i.e. to defraud creditors). A challenge can be made in respect of any past transaction, regardless of passage of time.

This means that in practical terms when carrying out a pre-sale reorganisation, the safest course will be to carry out all transactions between the subsidiaries to be sold and the remainder of the seller's group at market value.

9.6.7.3 *Directors' duties*

Directors must have regard to their statutory and common law duties (as referred to in chapter 1) in approving any undervalue or overvalue transactions.

9.6.7.4 *Other general issues*

There are a number of general legal issues that the directors of a company should consider before carrying out an intra-group transfer of an asset or a business (this is by no means an exhaustive list but rather an indicative list of matters that should be considered):

(i)   identity of the seller and the buyer – this is relevant in understanding the relationship of the parties;

(ii)   identification of the assets to be transferred;

(iii)   identification of licences or consents required to transfer the asset or business;

---

[119] Section 238, Insolvency Act 1986.
[120] Section 239, Insolvency Act 1986.
[121] Section 423 and section 424, Insolvency Act 1986.

(iv) understanding the employment law implications in the context of a transfer of a business as a going concern;

(v) identifying any pensions issues; and

(vi) identifying any data protection issues.

In structuring such transfers, it is also important to bear in mind a subsidiary (whether incorporated in the UK or overseas) cannot hold shares in its UK-incorporated parent company[122].

9.6.8 Do businesses need to change existing procedures?

The Companies Act 2006 has largely codified the existing common law of distributions insofar as it applies to intra-group transactions. As such, businesses do not need to change existing procedures if they comply with current practice.

However, the procedures for effecting intra-group business transfers, particularly cross border ones, may well change over time with the implementation of the Cross Border Mergers Directive (2005/56/EC) which will enable companies to merge cross border by way of absorption and avoid the need for a business contract and individual customer and creditor novations. This, however, is outside the scope of this book.

9.7 Demergers

9.7.1 What are the reasons for carrying out a demerger?

Demergers are often carried out for the following reasons:

(i) where greater value can be realised by separating individual businesses than by continuing to run them together;

(ii) as a means of facilitating the sale of part of a business; or

(iii) as a means of splitting the assets of a company following a shareholder dispute (typically in family owned businesses).

9.7.2 What are the main ways of effecting a demerger?

There are a number of ways in which demergers are typically undertaken. The selection of the appropriate method in any given circumstance will be highly dependent on a combination of tax, company law and commercial considerations. In most cases and to avoid resulting tax at company and shareholder level, it is critical to fall within the specific tax reliefs for demergers or to qualify as a scheme of reconstruction.

[122] Section 23, Companies Act 1985 and Section 136, Companies Act 2006.

9.7.2.1 Distribution in kind

A company will declare a dividend which is satisfied by the distribution of a particular asset. This is the simplest method.

A distribution in kind is a dividend (final or interim) which is satisfied by the transfer to shareholders of a non-cash asset. As in the case of a final dividend, a distribution in kind should be recommended by the directors of the company and will invariably require shareholder approval[123].

The rules on distributions as discussed in section 9.2 above will apply equally to a dividend in kind. However, it is worth noting the following issues:

Issue	Position under the Companies Act 1985	Position under the Companies Act 2006 from 6 April 2008
How is an asset valued for the purpose of determining the amount of the distribution?	The Companies Act 1985 was not altogether clear on this point but it was accepted practice to calculate the amount of the distribution by reference to the book value of the asset to be distributed.	Section 845 which came into force on 6 April 2008 confirms the position and specifies that the amount of the distribution of a non-cash asset is determined by reference to its book value.
Are any reliefs available?	Yes. Section 276 allows an unrealised reserve to be treated as realised for the purpose of distributing the asset to which the reserve relates.	Section 846 restates this provision.

---

[123] Assuming 1985 Table A articles have been adopted.

Example of the application of section 846 of the Companies Act 2006

A fixed asset is carried in the accounts at £100, of which £40 represents historic cost and £60 by a revaluation reserve (ordinarily treated as unrealised). If the company has at least £40 of realised reserves, it is able to distribute the total fixed asset by utilising £40 of its realised reserves and treating £60 of the revaluation reserve as distributable (for the purposes of the distribution):

DR	Revaluation reserve	60
CR	P&L reserves – realised	60
DR	P&L reserves – realised	100
CR	Fixed assets	100

However, the revaluation reserve can only be used if it relates to the asset to be distributed.

9.7.2.2 Three-cornered or indirect demerger

Instead of Company A making the distribution direct to shareholders, it will transfer the asset to be distributed to a new company which will then issue shares to Company A's shareholders. This is a common method where a business is to be demerged.

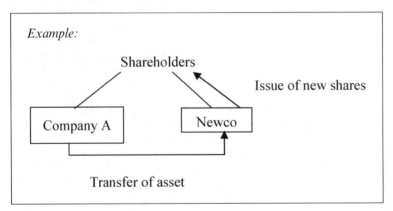

9.7.2.3 'Section 110 Scheme'

This is a scheme under section 110 of the Insolvency Act 1986 which involves the solvent liquidation of the parent company (Company A in the example below) holding the assets to be demerged and the transfer of these assets by the liquidator to newly formed companies (Newco 1 and Newco 2 in the example below), in consideration for the issue of shares by these newly formed companies to the shareholders of the parent company, at the liquidator's direction. It has a number of variations but a typical structure is as follows:

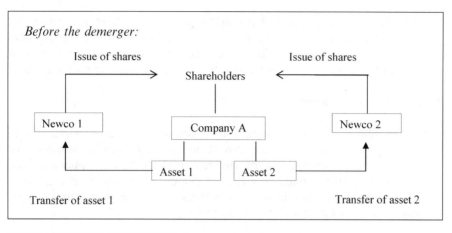

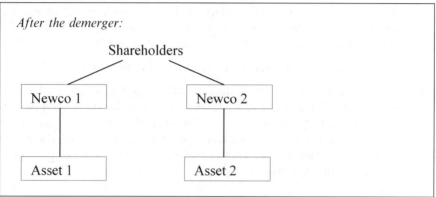

Where the parent is a trading company, or it only wishes to demerge part of its business, it is common to transfer the assets to be demerged into a new holding company first as this will facilitate the liquidation process.

There are provisions under section 111 of the Insolvency Act 1986 to allow those who have not voted for the scheme to require to be paid out in cash. This is a crucial hurdle for section 110 schemes for companies with a large shareholder base and, in these cases, a scheme of arrangement (referred to below) is often preferred instead. The section 110 procedure is, as a result, typically structured so that there is first a shareholder's meeting to obtain the sanction for the section 110 scheme transfers, followed by a second meeting to place the company in liquidation seven days later (i.e. the period to raise objection[124]). The second meeting would, however, be aborted if too many entitled persons raise objections and the company would not therefore be placed in liquidation. This approach is likely to be impracticable for a listed company.

---

[124] Section 111, Insolvency Act 1986.

Section 110 schemes are also widely used to 'partition' companies, whereby the company to be liquidated is first reorganised into two or more share classes with rights to specified assets. Those assets are then transferred to separate new companies whose shares are issued just to shareholders of the relevant class.

9.7.2.4 Scheme of arrangement

Under the new provisions pursuant to the Companies Act 2006, effective from 6 April 2008, a court has the power to sanction any compromise or arrangement with a company's shareholders or creditors on application (and can therefore approve almost any kind of demerger). A scheme is a complex process and is often contemplated in situations where one of the other options discussed above is not available, for example:

(i)   the company does not have sufficient distributable reserves to make a distribution (although in such circumstances the demerger can also be combined with a court approved reduction of capital);

(ii)   the company does not wish to use a liquidation procedure; or

(iii)   the demerger is part of a broader restructuring for which a scheme is appropriate. Under the scheme process, the court has very wide powers to make ancillary orders relating, for example, to the disposition of assets, the novation of contracts, the transfer of liabilities and the cessation of litigation which might be necessary steps as part of a particular demerger process.

Example: a typical structure might be:

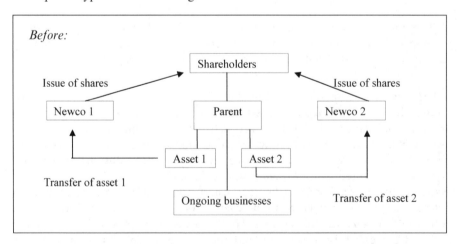

- The Parent remains in existence.

- Newco 1 and Newco 2 issue shares to the shareholders of the Parent.

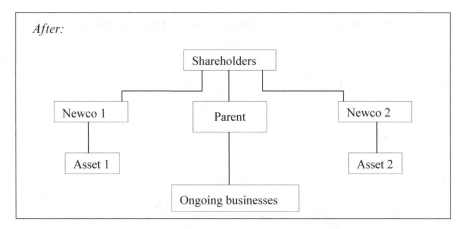

Schemes of arrangement are further discussed in section 9.8 below.

9.8 Schemes of arrangement

As noted in section 9.7.2.4 above, a scheme of arrangement is a statutory procedure under which a company can make a compromise or arrangement with its shareholders and/or creditors with the approval of the court. Schemes of arrangement can be used for a wide variety of transactions and can be specifically tailored to a particular company's requirements. There are extensive requirements and a company will require a range of professional advisers at an early stage in order to implement a scheme. In this section, therefore, only an overview of the key features of a scheme is provided.

9.8.1 Under what circumstances will a company consider a scheme of arrangement?

The court exercises a wide discretion in relation to schemes of arrangement which, as a consequence, take many forms and concern a wide variety of transactions. However, their most common uses are:

(i)   demergers (as discussed in section 9.7 above);

(ii) interposition of a new holding company which is commonly undertaken prior to an initial public offering (or a relisting); and

(iii) takeovers: schemes have become an increasingly common method of implementing a recommended takeover bid.

Schemes of arrangement can also be made between a company and its creditors with the approval of the court. These arise more commonly in insolvent situations but can be applicable to solvent reconstructions, for example, where the interposition of a new holding company requires the novation of liabilities of the current holding company to its bondholders with the new holding company.

Example: interposition of a new holding company ('Topco scheme')

Before:

Existing shareholders

After:

1. Topco buys shares in PLC.
2. As consideration, Topco issues shares to existing PLC shareholders.

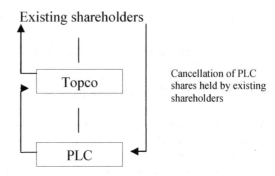

Cancellation of PLC shares held by existing shareholders

Such a scheme could also be combined with a court approved reduction of capital in Topco to create distributable reserves. This is a common pre-IPO structure[125].

Example: Takeover bid ('Takeover scheme')

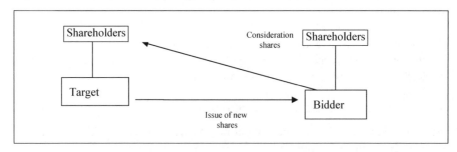

■ Shares in Target are cancelled and the reserve arising on cancellation is capitalised and applied in paying up new shares to Bidder, in exchange for issue of new shares by Bidder to the shareholders of Target.

■ As an alternative, a court could instead order the transfer of shares in Target to Bidder (a 'transfer scheme').

---

[125] Re: Ratner Group plc [1988] BCLC 685, 687.

9.8.2 What changes have been introduced by the Companies Act 2006?

Parts 26 and 27 of the Companies Act 2006 which are effective from 6 April 2008 largely restate the provisions of section 425 to 427A and schedule 15B of the Companies Act 1985, with some minor amendments to the process for obtaining a court order and filing requirements with Companies House.

Part 27 contains additional requirements for schemes involving a merger or a division in relation to a public company which restates the implementation of the Third Council Directive 78/855/EEC and the Sixth Council Directive 82/891/EEC. New independence requirements have been introduced for experts and valuers which correspond with those introduced for statutory auditors[126].

9.8.3 What are the advantages of a scheme of arrangement (in the context of a Topco scheme or a Takeover scheme) in comparison with other methods?

A scheme has a number of advantages, of which the most common ones are:

(i)   stamp duty savings can be achieved on takeovers where shares in the target are cancelled and then reissued to the bidder of the target or the new holding company as stamp duty is only payable in respect of transfers of shares; and

(ii)   the scheme requires approval by the shareholders (please refer to section 9.8.4.1 below for details). Once approved, the scheme will be binding on all shareholders. In a conventional share for share offer (such as may be used for a Takeover or a Topco scheme), the relevant threshold is 90%, after which the remaining shares could only be acquired using the 'squeeze-out' procedure (a note summarising these procedures and the changes made by the Companies Act 2006 to implement the Takeovers Directive is set out in Appendix 2). This will be an important consideration where the acquisition of 100% of the issued share capital of the target is required. If this is not essential, then the advantages of a scheme are less clear, as, in principle, voting control can be acquired once shareholders holding shares representing more than 50% of the voting rights have accepted the offer. It may also be possible to acquire 50% in a shorter period of time than under a court approved scheme.

9.8.4 What are the main statutory requirements under the Companies Act 2006?

These are the key elements:

9.8.4.1   Court meeting

A scheme requires the approval of the shareholders of the company (or each class of the shareholders) at a special meeting convened at the direction of the

---

[126] Sections 936 and 1214, Companies Act 2006.

court[127]. The court has the power to determine what constitutes a 'class' for this purpose and it might determine that different classes exist amongst the shareholders holding shares with the same rights. There are equivalent requirements for creditors' schemes. Determining what constitutes a 'class' for this purpose is one of the most difficult issues when implementing a scheme as the membership of a particular class is determined on the basis of whether they have similar rights which make it possible for them to consult together with a view to a common interest. It is quite possible, for example, that holders of a single legal class of shareholders or bondholders may constitute separate classes for the purposes of a scheme.

There is a dual test requiring approval by a majority in number of those present at the meeting who represent 75% in value of the shareholders voting, whether in person or by proxy[128]. Therefore, the vote must always be taken on a poll.

9.8.4.2   Explanatory statement

A detailed explanatory statement must be sent to the shareholders which will set out the reasons for the scheme and comply with a range of detailed content requirements set out in the Companies Act 2006[129], as well as where applicable the Takeover Code, the Listing Rules and the Prospectus Rules.

In particular, the statement must clearly explain the effect of the scheme and give all relevant information sufficient to enable the shareholders to determine how to attend the meeting and/or how to vote[130].

9.8.4.3   General meeting of shareholders

The court meeting is usually followed immediately by a general meeting of the shareholders (to be convened and held in accordance with the articles of association of the company), the purpose of which is to approve the various resolutions required to implement the scheme.

9.8.4.4   Court approval

Once shareholders' approval has been obtained, the court will proceed to consider and, if appropriate, sanction the scheme. The court has a discretion as to whether to sanction the scheme and in exercising this discretion the court has a number of duties[131].

---

[127] Section 896, Companies Act 2006.
[128] Section 899, Companies Act 2006.
[129] Section 897, Companies Act 2006.
[130] Tiessen v Henderson [1899] 1 Ch 681.
[131] *Re Anglo – Continental Supply Co Ltd* [1922] 2 Ch 723 and *Re National Bank Limited* [1966] 1 WLR 819.

These duties are as follows:

(i)   that the approval of the overall scheme is reasonable. The test is whether the scheme 'is such that an intelligent and honest man, a member of the class concerned acting in respect of his interests might reasonably approve' (*Re Dorman Long & Co. Ltd* [1934] 1 Ch 635); in other words, whether a shareholder could reasonably approve it. The court does not itself judge the commercial element of the scheme; only whether the scheme itself is fair and equitable. Where there are dissenting shareholders or creditors, it can impose conditions to the approval or decline to sanction the scheme;

(ii) to ensure that each class is fairly represented by those attending the meeting, that they have sufficient information and that the statutory majority are not acting in bad faith and are not covering the minority to promote interests of the class they are purporting to represent; and

(iii) to ensure that statutory provisions have been complied with, including not only adherence to the procedures required for the scheme itself but also the legality of any individual legal steps to be undertaken, for example, if a reduction of capital forms part of the scheme.

A court is unlikely to sanction the scheme if it is effected purely for tax purposes, although as long as there is an underlying commercial transaction then using a scheme on the grounds of tax efficiency is permissible.

The court order is effective once filed at Companies House and will then be binding on all shareholders (and, if applicable, creditors) whether they voted in favour of it or not.

9.8.5   Sample timetable of a Topco scheme under the Companies Act 2006

DAY	STEP
Day 0	a) Announcement of scheme. b) Issue of claim form for leave to convene court meeting(s) (and all matters relating to the scheme if settled). c) Sign and file witness statement in support of application exhibiting draft scheme documents.
Day 7	a) 1st directions hearing of application to commence court meeting(s) before Companies Court Registrar and submission of draft order, notice of, and proxy for, court meeting(s). b) Registrar of Companies approves scheme with or without modification and makes order to convene meeting(s), send out notice(s), appoint chairman of meeting and if necessary advertise notice of meeting(s) in press c) Settle court order, adverts, notices and proxy.

DAY	STEP
Day 10 Court meeting and general meeting at least 23 days after posting of scheme document.	Post scheme document and forms of proxy to shareholders and advertise notice of court meeting(s) in newspapers if directed by court. This period should be the minimum practicable notice period for general meetings under the articles.
Day 34	Court meeting(s) and general meeting(s) held
Day 36 Cannot sign witness statement until result of poll at court meeting(s) is known.	a) Witness statement signed to confirm outcome of court meeting(s), to approve the scheme and provide a copy of the chairman's report on the court meeting(s). b) Seek leave to amend claim form (unless full claim form submitted on Day 0) by application to the court prior to the hearing or at the second directions hearing itself. c) File at court witness statement and witness statements of service of notice convening court meeting(s) (1 week before directions hearing for capital reduction). d) File at court special resolution approving reduction of capital (if any) and the scheme passed at the general meeting.
Day 46 Court usually requires 7 working days from issue to hearing to consider evidence.	Hearing of application for directions (only if reduction of capital).
No later than **Day 47** Advertise at least 5 clear working days before hearing.	Advertise final hearing (only if reduction of capital).
Day 48	Deliver court bundle and skeleton argument for final hearing (1 week before final hearing).
Day 55	Final hearing before Companies Court Judge to sanction the scheme. Order confirming scheme sealed by court.
Day 56 (or the day following the adjourned hearing date).	Deliver court order and statement of capital at Companies House for filing and registration.
Day 57	a) Order filed and registered with Companies House. b) Effective date of scheme and reduction
Within 21 days of registration	Second advertisement appears in designated newspaper.

9.9 Financing the acquisition of shares

Under the Companies Act 1985, a company is prohibited from giving direct or indirect financial assistance for an acquisition of shares in itself or its holding company. The prohibition finds its roots in the principle of maintenance of capital; if a company is assisting a purchaser to acquire shares in itself, it is not generating any new capital but instead it is diminishing its existing capital base.

The prohibition commonly arises in pre and post-acquisition financing as well as intra-group reorganisations, and carries with it criminal sanctions as well as rendering a transaction unenforceable. It is widely acknowledged that the prohibition as currently drafted under the Companies Act 1985 is overly complex and ambiguous and captures a number of transactions which it is believed the legislature did not intend to prohibit. The need to obtain advice on the extent of the prohibition impacts on both the overall costs and timing of transactions.

9.9.1 What changes have been introduced by the Companies Act 2006?

From 1 October 2008, the prohibition on the provision of financial assistance by private companies for the acquisition of their own shares or shares of their private holding companies is abolished in a deregulatory measure. This should greatly facilitate the mergers and acquisition process for private companies as well as pre and post-deal reorganisations. The existing prohibition on (a) public companies giving financial assistance in connection with the acquisition of their own shares or shares of their private holding companies and (b) private companies giving financial assistance in connection with the acquisition of shares of their public holding companies remains unaltered under the Companies Act 1985 and will remain in place until the new Companies Act provisions come into effect.

Chapter 2 of Part 18 of the Companies Act 2006 (sections 677 to 683) contains the new provisions relating to financial assistance and is effective from 1 October 2009.

9.9.2 What should a company consider before providing financial assistance?

Certain types of financial assistance are permitted under the Companies Act 2006 (please refer to section 9.9.5 below). Nevertheless, there are certain matters the directors of a company should consider before providing financial assistance even where they are legally permitted to do so.

9.9.2.1 Directors' duties

Where a company proposes to give direct or indirect financial assistance for the acquisition of shares in the company (or its holding company), the directors should carefully consider whether the company is authorised by its constitution to give financial assistance. In addition, directors should have careful regard to their duties as directors. The directors must carefully consider the benefit to the company of assisting a purchaser (directly or indirectly) to buy shares in the company and, in cases of doubt, seek prior shareholder approval (these issues are discussed further in chapter 1).

9.9.2.2 Transactions at an undervalue

Directors will also need to consider whether the provision of financial assistance may constitute a transaction at an undervalue.

They should consider the solvency of the company at the time of the giving of the assistance, having particular regard to the provisions of the Insolvency Act 1986 in relation to preferences and transactions at an undervalue (see section 9.6).

9.9.2.3 Contractual restrictions

All material contracts such as loan agreements and joint venture and shareholder agreements and the terms of issue of other securities need to be checked, as it is common for these to have restrictions on the type of transactions which can constitute financial assistance. Third party consents may be required or variations or waivers negotiated.

9.9.3 What is the new position under the Companies Act 2006?

The most significant change made pursuant to the new Companies Act 2006 is the removal of the prohibition on a private company providing financial assistance for the acquisition of its own shares or shares of its private holding companies and as a result, the repeal of the 'whitewash' procedure (to be discussed below).

From 1 October 2008, the prohibition only applies to public limited companies which provide financial assistance for an acquisition of their own shares or shares in a parent which is either a public or private company[132]. A private company subsidiary also remains prohibited from providing financial assistance for the acquisition of shares in a public parent company. The financial assistance provisions under the Companies Act 1985 are, subject to this, largely restated in the Companies Act 2006.

9.9.3.1 In what circumstances may financial assistance arise?

The Companies Act 2006 restates the prohibition on financial assistance in respect of public companies giving financial assistance before or at the same

---

[132] Sections 678 and 679, Companies Act 2006.

time as the acquisition, and financial assistance where a person has acquired shares and incurred a liability as follows[133]:

(i)   where a person is acquiring or proposing to acquire shares in a public company, it is not lawful for that company, or a company that is a subsidiary of that company, to give financial assistance directly or indirectly for the purpose of the acquisition before or at the same time as the acquisition takes place; and

(ii)   where (i) a person has acquired shares in a company; and (ii) a liability has been incurred (by that or another person) for the purposes of that acquisition, it is not lawful for that company or a company that is a subsidiary of that company to give financial assistance directly or indirectly for the purpose of reducing or discharging the liability if, at the time the assistance is given, the company in which the shares were acquired is a public company.

The prohibition on financial assistance contains a number of key phrases. These are summarised below:

Acquire: Financial assistance only arises where shares have been or are about to be acquired. A subscription for shares as well as a share for share exchange will constitute an acquisition for this purpose.

Shares: A share is a share in the share capital of a company[134], and also includes securities which are convertible into shares and other rights to acquire shares.

Company: A company means a company incorporated under the Companies Act 2006, or previous companies legislation and includes unlimited companies. The prohibition does not therefore apply to companies incorporated outside the United Kingdom, meaning that a foreign subsidiary is free to provide financial assistance for the purchase of shares in its UK parent; and that a company incorporated in the United Kingdom can give financial assistance for the acquisition of shares in its foreign parent. However, the laws applicable to the foreign entities will need to be considered.

Subsidiaries: A company is the subsidiary of another if that other company holds the majority of the voting rights in the company, or has the right to appoint or remove a majority of the board of directors, or by agreement with other shareholders holds the majority of the voting rights in the company[135].

Directly or indirectly: Financial assistance does not need to be given by the target company directly to the purchaser. Financial assistance can be given indirectly as a result of a series of steps, and it is for this reason that financial

---

[133] Sections 678(1) and (3), Companies Act 2006.
[134] Section 540, Companies Act 2006.
[135] Section 1159, Companies Act 2006.

assistance can be difficult to identify, especially in circumstances where a number of complex transactions are being entered into.

A liability has been incurred: When assessing whether there is post-acquisition financial assistance it is important to analyse the past history of the companies concerned, to identify whether there have been any previous acquisitions of shares which would bring a present transaction within the scope of the financial assistance provision. There is no time limit on the application of the post-acquisition financial assistance rules, although it is more likely that with the passage of time intervening activities of the companies will break the link. There is, however, no hard and fast rule.

These key phrases are broadly the same as under the Companies Act 1985. In particular, references to a person reducing or discharging a liability incurred continue to include circumstances where a purchaser changes its financial position which is later fully or partially restored[136].

However, where the financial assistance is given for the purpose of reducing or discharging a liability incurred, there is a new provision under the Companies Act 2006 providing that the assistance will only be unlawful if at the time of providing the assistance the company continues to be a public company. Where a company has re-registered as a private company after the share acquisition but before or at the time the financial assistance is given, the prohibition will no longer apply to that company.

9.9.3.2 *What is financial assistance?*

'Financial assistance' remains undefined in the Companies Act 2006 and there are no significant changes to the summary of forms of financial assistance[137] as follows:

(i)   gift;

(ii)   guarantee, security or indemnity or by way of release or waiver;

(iii) loan or other agreement under which any of the obligations of the person giving the assistance are to be fulfilled, at a time when in accordance with the agreement any obligation of another party to the agreement remains unfulfilled, or by way of novation of, or assignment of rights arising under a loan or such other agreement; or

(iv) any other financial assistance given by a company whereby the net assets of the company are reduced to a material extent by the giving of assistance, or the company has no net assets. 'Net assets' being the aggregate amount of the assets of the company less the aggregate amount of the liabilities.

---

[136] Section 683(2), Companies Act 2006.
[137] Section 677(1), Companies Act 2006.

Set out below are some illustrative examples of financial assistance but these examples should not be considered as exhaustive.

Illustrative examples of financial assistance under Companies Act 2006

Loan or other deferred agreement

Buyer wishes to purchase shares in Target plc but does not have sufficient funds. A private company subsidiary of Target plc makes a loan to the Buyer to enable it to purchase the shares. Even though the assistance is given by a private company, this transaction would still contravene the prohibition on financial assistance as the assistance is given for the purchase of shares in a public limited company.

Buyer acquires Target plc for cash. Target plc has a profitable business and after the acquisition transfers the business to the Buyer at market value for a consideration left outstanding. As a result the Buyer's financial position is restored as it has the benefit of a business which is cash generative. The sale by the Target plc for a deferred consideration is prohibited as a form of credit transaction. If, however, Target plc had sold the business at market value for a cash consideration and then returned cash to the parent by way of a reduction of capital or lawful dividend, then the transaction would have been permitted.

Guarantee or security

Buyer obtains a loan to acquire Target plc, a private company with several subsidiaries including one public limited company. Following the acquisition, the Buyer proposes to refinance the borrowing arrangements of the group and all subsidiaries of Target plc are required to provide cross guarantees to the bank. The public company subsidiary would be unable to provide the cross guarantee as it would constitute post-acquisition financial assistance insofar as the Buyer's loan obtained to acquire Target plc remains undischarged. It would be permitted to do so if it is first re-registered as a private company.

A public company proposes to buy back its shares. It borrows from the bank in order to finance the repurchase and provide security to the bank. A purchase by a company of its own shares constitutes 'an acquisition' of shares and the provision of security for the loan will constitute unlawful financial assistance.

Gift

This is generally a transaction for no consideration. By way of example, following an acquisition, a public company subsidiary transfers an asset to its new private holding company and leaves the consideration outstanding. In due course, the public company subsidiary waives the right to receive payment. The waiver would constitute a gift and would be unlawful financial assistance if it reduces or discharges the holding company's liability incurred for the purpose of acquiring that subsidiary.

Novation

Buyer takes out a loan in order to acquire shares in Target plc. Following the acquisition, Buyer and Target enter into an agreement to novate the loan agreement to Target plc under which Target plc assumes the liability for repayment of the loan in place of Buyer. The novation of the loan agreement would constitute post acquisition financial assistance.

Sale of an asset at an undervalue – reduction of net assets

Buyer takes out a loan to purchase shares in Target plc. Shortly after the acquisition, Target plc sells assets to the Buyer at their book value which is less than market value. This is an example of post-acquisition financial assistance as the element of undervalue in the sale constitutes a benefit to the Buyer which can then be used to reduce or discharge the liability incurred for the purposes of the acquisition. If the assets were sold to the Buyer at market value for cash payment on completion then Target plc could realise a profit and pay a dividend to the Buyer. This latter transaction will not give rise to unlawful financial assistance.

Repayment of existing debt

Buyer proposes to purchase shares in Target plc. Target plc has an outstanding interest free term loan from the Buyer which is due for repayment in three years time and chooses to repay the loan early. Buyer uses the funds repaid by Target plc to purchase the shares. The repayment of the loan early represents financial assistance because Target plc has lost the benefit of the interest free loan (which could constitute a reduction in its net assets if it has to refinance and this is done to enable Buyer to purchase its shares). The position might well have been different if the loan had been on normal commercial terms and repayable on demand.

Reduction of net assets

Buyer acquires Target plc. Target plc, a trading company bears a proportion of the professional costs incurred by the Buyer. This can constitute a reduction in the net assets of Target plc and, if material, will be prohibited. There is no definition of materiality but the general view is 1% of the net assets of a company and the definition of 'net assets' is very widely drafted to include all assets and liabilities of the company and not only those recorded in its books. Where a company is insolvent (i.e. it has no net assets), this catch-all provision is very widely interpreted.

As will be seen from the examples set out above, the restrictions on financial assistance are capable of very wide application and it is possible for transactions with similar financial outcomes to be permitted or prohibited dependent on how they are structured. Had private companies been involved in these examples above instead of a public limited company in *all* instances (both as buyer and target), these transactions would not be prohibited by the financial assistance rules under the Companies Act 2006.

9.9.4 Will directors of a private company be comfortable with giving financial assistance going forward?

9.9.4.1 What is the 'whitewash' procedure under the Companies Act 1985?

Under the Companies Act 1985, private companies could apply a procedure to 'whitewash' a transaction which would otherwise constitute unlawful financial assistance and thereby be prohibited. While the prohibition for giving financial assistance by a private company for the acquisition of its own shares or shares of its private holding company, as well as the 'whitewash' procedure, have been abolished under the Companies Act 2006 from 1 October 2008, it is likely that in practice directors of private companies will, in approving the giving of financial assistance, continue to seek comfort by applying a procedure which will be similar to the 'whitewash' procedure. Banking practice may well dictate this to be a standard requirement for private companies giving financial assistance that would otherwise be lawful under the Companies Act 2006. The 'whitewash' procedure is therefore summarised below.

Under the Companies Act 1985, a statutory procedure can be used by a private company for an acquisition of shares in itself or in its private holding company[138]. In order to take advantage of this relaxation, the company giving the financial assistance must have net assets which are not reduced by the giving of such financial assistance, or to the extent that they are reduced, the assistance is provided out of distributable reserves.

In practice, the 'whitewash' procedure brings with it its own problems. All of the directors of the company need to swear a statutory declaration on the solvency of the company. Leaving aside the practicality of arranging for all the directors to be available, it is often the case that directors of a target company on a disposal will be reluctant to provide such a statement, whilst the directors who will be appointed post-completion will not have sufficient knowledge to give the declaration. In addition, sufficient time needs to be built into a timetable to allow the directors and auditors to make due enquiry into the affairs of the company (in the case of the latter so that they can prepare their report to support the directors' statutory declaration).

9.9.4.2 'Whitewash' procedure checklist under the Companies Act 1985

	Action	Confirm
1	Check that the memorandum and/or articles of association of the company providing the assistance give authority for the company to give financial assistance. (*n.b. if the memorandum and/or articles do not provide such authority, the articles can be amended by way of a special resolution.*)	☐

---

[138] Section 155, Companies Act 1985.

	Action	Confirm
2	Where the company giving the financial assistance is a subsidiary of the company whose shares are being acquired, check that there is not an intermediate holding company which is a public company between the subsidiary and the company whose shares are being acquired (not permitted to apply the 'whitewash' procedure in such instances).	☐
3	Confirm that if the net assets of the company providing the assistance will be reduced by the giving of assistance, the company has sufficient distributable reserves to cover any such reduction.	☐
4	If the company giving the assistance is not a wholly owned subsidiary then the financial assistance must be approved by a special resolution of that company. *(n.b. the special resolution must be passed on the date of or within a week following the directors' statutory declaration[139].)*	☐
5	If the financial assistance is to be given by a company in respect of shares in its holding company, then the holding company and any intermediate holding companies must also approve the financial assistance by way of a special resolution (except in circumstances where the company giving the assistance is a wholly owned subsidiary). *(n.b. as above, the special resolution must be passed on the date of or within the week following the directors' statutory declaration.)*	☐
6	A statutory declaration must be sworn by all the directors of the company that in their reasonable opinion the company will remain solvent and that it will be able to pay its debts as they fall due within the 12 months following the giving of the assistance. *(n.b. a director who makes a statutory declaration without having reasonable grounds for the opinion expressed is liable to imprisonment or a fine or both[140].)*	☐
7	If the assistance is being given by a subsidiary to its holding company, the directors of such holding company and of all of the intermediate holding companies must also swear a statutory declaration in respect of the company for which they are a director.	☐
8	An auditors' report confirming that the auditors have enquired into the state of affairs of the company and are not aware of anything to indicate that the opinion expressed by the directors in the statutory declaration is unreasonable in all the circumstances.	☐
9	If the special resolution is passed unanimously, the financial assistance may be provided immediately.	☐

[139] Section 157, Companies Act 1985.
[140] Section 156(7), Companies Act 1985.

	Action	Confirm
10	If the special resolution is not passed unanimously, the financial assistance cannot be given before the expiry of four weeks but no longer than eight weeks from the date of the last special resolution having been passed.	☐

9.9.4.3 The common law position

The Companies Act 2006 (Commencement No. 5, Transitional Provisions and Savings) Order 2007 confirms that the common law rule in relation to the giving of financial assistance by private companies for the acquisition of their own shares or shares of their private holding companies (as currently prohibited under the Companies Act 1985) will no longer be applicable. This is to prevent any common law rule being applied to transactions that will otherwise be lawful under the Companies Act 2006. However, this saving provision is limited in scope and does not disapply any other common law rules which may still be relevant to a transaction that would previously have been prohibited by the Companies Act 1985. For example, where a company has no or insufficient distributable reserves and it makes a gift of money to a shareholder with which to purchase further shares in the company, this transaction will still be prohibited, notwithstanding the repeal of the relevant provisions in the Companies Act 1985, because it will result in an unlawful reduction of capital by the company. As such and going forward, irrespective of the abolition of the financial assistance prohibition in relation to private companies as noted above, any transactions involving the giving of financial assistance by private companies will still need to be reviewed to ensure they do not give rise to any unlawful reduction of capital issues.

9.9.5 What transactions are permitted?

The Companies Act 2006 restates a number of the exceptions to financial assistance prohibition contained in the Companies Act 1985, with some minor changes:

9.9.5.1 Purpose exemptions[141]

The purpose exemptions continue to render lawful a transaction which would otherwise be unlawful where the principal purpose of the transaction is not to give financial assistance for either the acquisition of shares or to reduce or discharge a liability incurred, or where the giving of the financial assistance is only an incidental part of some larger transaction and the assistance is given, in good faith, in the interests of the company. It is anticipated that this exemption will continue to be of limited application, as it is at present.

---

[141] Sections 678(2) and (4), Companies Act 2006.

In order to rely on this exemption, the directors must be satisfied that the giving of the financial assistance is not the principal purpose of the transaction and that the transaction is genuinely in the best interests of the company. However, in practice, it is difficult to establish that financial assistance falls within this exemption, particularly as the purpose exemptions have been interpreted very narrowly by the court. As a result, there can be significant risks in proceeding on the basis of these exemptions[142].

9.9.5.2 *Lawful exceptions*[143]

The new Act splits the lawful exceptions to the prohibition on financial assistance into two forms of exceptions: unconditional and conditional exceptions:

Unconditional exceptions:

(i)   a distribution of the company's assets by way of (a) a dividend lawfully made or (b) distribution on a company's winding-up;

(i)   allotment of bonus shares;

(iii)   a reduction of capital (both court approved and under the solvency statement procedure for private companies);

(iv)   a redemption or purchase of own shares;

(v)   anything done in pursuance of a court order under Part 26 of the Companies Act 2006 (i.e. a scheme of arrangement);

(vi)   anything done in connection with section 110 of the Insolvency Act 1986; or

(vii)   anything done under an arrangement made between a company and its creditors which is binding on its creditors pursuant to the Insolvency Act 1986.

Conditional exceptions:

If the company giving the assistance is a private company; or if the company giving the assistance is a public company and its net assets[144] are not reduced by the giving of the assistance or, to the extent that those assets are reduced, the assistance is provided out of distributable reserves then the following exceptions are available:

(i)   where lending money is part of the ordinary course of business of that company;

---

[142] See *Brady v Brady* [1989] A.C. 755.
[143] Section 681 and 682, Companies Act 2006.
[144] Sections 682(3) and (4), Companies Act 2006.

(ii)   transactions in connection with an employee's share scheme; or

(iii)   loans to employees.

9.9.6   What are the consequences of a breach of the statutory requirements?

If a company contravenes the prohibition on financial assistance under the Companies Act 2006, an offence is committed by the company and every officer of the company who is in default. A person found guilty of an offence is liable to imprisonment or a fine[145].

In addition, a director who has approved the entry into such a transaction may also be liable for a breach of directors' duty and personally liable for any loss arising from the transaction, and the contract giving rise to the transaction will be unenforceable[146].

---

[145] Section 680, Companies Act 2006.
[146] See *Brady v Brady* and *Neilson v Stuart* 1991 SC (HL) 22.

9.9.7 Summary flowchart: financial assistance under the Companies Act 1985

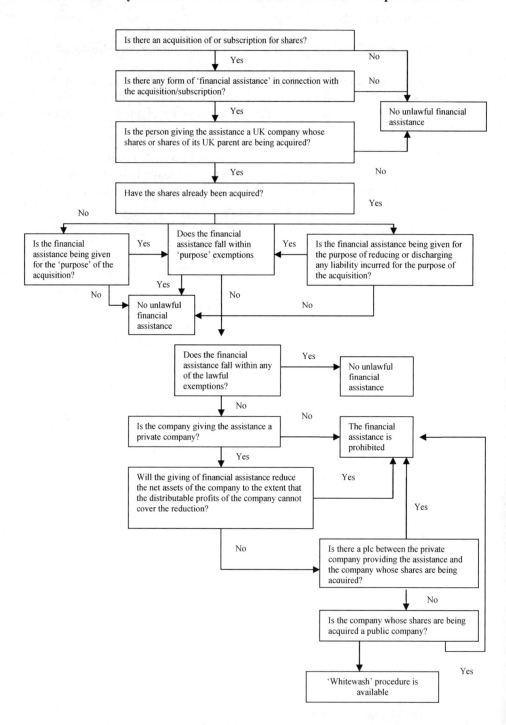

9.9.8 Summary flowchart: financial assistance under the Companies Act 2006

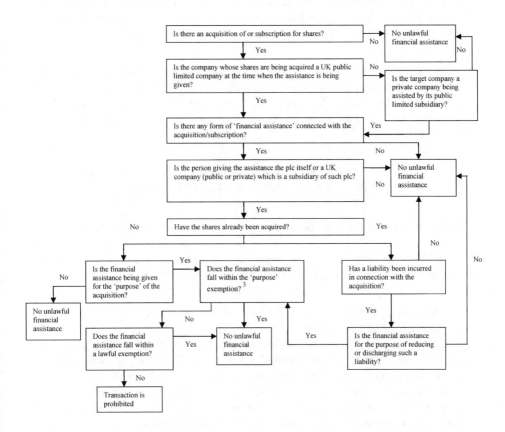

9.10 Unlimited companies

9.10.1 Why are unlimited companies used for reorganisations?

Unlimited liability companies are not widely used but where they are present it is often for the reason that they can reduce their share capital without having to apply to the court. In the context of intra-group reorganisations, the practice has been to re-register limited companies as unlimited as an intermediate step before a reduction of capital in order to avoid the need to apply to the court. It remains to be seen whether unlimited companies will continue to be used for this purpose once the solvency statement procedure for private companies is introduced on 1 October 2008.

An unlimited company can only distribute cash or assets to its shareholders by way of a dividend distribution where it has sufficient distributable reserves to do so. The rules governing distributions apply equally to limited and unlimited companies.

Unlimited companies are able to purchase their own shares pursuant to the terms of their articles of association but the purchase must be financed out of distributable reserves as a repurchase out of capital only applies to private limited companies (see section 9.4 above).

The prohibition on financial assistance applies to unlimited companies. However, the exemption for reduction of capital from the financial assistance prohibition only applies to a court approved reduction and does not apply to a reduction of capital by an unlimited company by special resolution.

The procedures to distribute assets, reduce share capital and purchase own shares are set out in sections 9.2, 9.3 and 9.4 of this chapter.

9.10.2   What changes have been introduced by the Companies Act 2006?

From 1 October 2009 public companies can re-register as unlimited companies without first having to register as a private company[147].

As mentioned above, the prohibition on financial assistance by private companies for the acquisition of their own shares and shares of their private holding companies is abolished with effect from 1 October 2008. This applies to unlimited as well as private limited companies. However, as with private limited companies, unlimited companies will remain subject to the financial assistance prohibition if the acquisition is of shares in a parent which is a public company. The financial assistance exemptions for purchases of own shares and reduction of capital will not apply to unlimited companies.

9.10.3   Table of comparison of the procedures for returning cash/assets to shareholders by unlimited companies under the Companies Act 1985 and the Companies Act 2006

	Companies Act 1985	Companies Act 2006
Distributions	The provisions in the Companies Act 1985 regarding distributions apply equally to limited and unlimited companies.	A limited or unlimited company will continue to be restricted from making distributions except out of profits available for the purpose.

---

[147] Section 109, Companies Act 2006.

	Companies Act 1985	**Companies Act 2006**
Reduction of capital	Unlimited companies may reduce their share capital in any way permitted by its articles of association without the approval of the court. Table E articles (applicable to unlimited companies)[148] provide that an unlimited company may reduce its share capital and share premium account in any way by special resolution.	The provisions of the Companies Act 2006 dealing with a reduction of capital by solvency statement do not apply to unlimited companies and therefore unlimited companies may continue to reduce share capital in accordance with the authority contained in their articles of association.
Purchase of own shares	The general prohibition on a company purchasing its own shares[149] does not apply to unlimited companies. An unlimited company may purchase any of its own shares, if its articles of association authorise it to do so, even though the shares are only partly paid and the company uses its own assets to do so[150]. However, the company can only do so out of distributable reserves[151] and it is not able to make a permissible capital payment for that purpose.	No change[152]

[148] Companies (Tables A to F) Regulations 1985 (as amended).
[149] Section 143, Companies Act 1985.
[150] *Re Borough Commercial and Building Society* [1893] 2 Ch 242.
[151] Section 168, Companies Act 1985.
[152] Section 658, Companies Act 2008.

	Companies Act 1985	Companies Act 2006
Financial assistance	The prohibition on financial assistance applies to limited and unlimited companies[153]. An unlimited company does not benefit from the lawful exceptions to the prohibition in respect of court approved reduction of capital and purchase of own shares[154].	From 1 October 2008 the prohibition on financial assistance given by private companies (including unlimited companies) for the acquisition of their own shares or shares of their private holding companies will be abolished. An unlimited company will not benefit from the exceptions to the prohibition in respect of a reduction of capital (both court approved and by solvency statement) and a purchase of own shares.
Directors' duties	Common law principles apply equally to limited and unlimited companies (see chapter 1).	Directors' duties are codified and apply to limited and unlimited companies (see chapter 1).

9.10.4 What are the risks associated with unlimited companies?

The shareholders of an unlimited company can be made liable without limit for the debts and obligations of the company in the event of its being wound up. However, while the company is a going concern, its shareholders can only be called upon to contribute any capital unpaid on their shares to the company (if any).

Therefore, any decision to re-register a private limited company as unlimited or to incorporate an unlimited company requires careful consideration, particularly by boards in the case of corporate shareholders. In the context of a group, the removal of the protection of limited liability may have little practical impact if cross guarantees are already in place; nevertheless, any changes to the risk profile of the group or individual subsidiaries must be identified and analysed. A measure of additional protection for the shareholder(s) can be obtained by interposing a limited liability company as a 'buffer' between the unlimited company and the current shareholders. In most cases, unlimited companies are used only as intra-group financing vehicles where creditors tend to be intra-group and it is very rare for unlimited companies to be used for third party trading operations.

[153] Section 151(1), Companies Act 1985.
[154] Sections 153(3)(c) and (d), Companies Act 1985.

The laws on directors' duties apply equally to limited and unlimited companies. In addition, the directors of an unlimited company may be held liable for its debts in the event of an insolvency if it is shown that there had been a breach of duty or wrongful trading.

Under the Companies Act 1985, a sole shareholder of an unlimited company which carries on business for more than six months, and who knows that it is carrying on business with a sole shareholder after the six month period, is liable (jointly and severally with the company) for the payment of the company's debts contracted during the period following such six month periods[155]. However, this provision is abolished under the Companies Act 2006 with effect from 1 October 2009 as it is no longer required to have two shareholders to set up and maintain an unlimited company.

9.10.5 How does an unlimited company make a distribution?

The rules and restrictions applicable to a limited company (discussed in section 9.2 of this chapter) will apply equally to an unlimited company.

9.10.6 How does an unlimited company reduce its share capital?

9.10.6.1 What is the procedure under the Companies Act 2006?

The procedure to reduce share capital of an unlimited company remains unchanged under the Companies Act 2006. An unlimited company can, provided it is authorised by its articles to do so, reduce its issued share capital and/or its share premium account. Regulation 4(e) of Table E contains such a provision.

9.10.6.2 What can be reduced?

An unlimited company can, provided it is authorised by its articles to do so, reduce its issued share capital and return the excess to shareholders. This can be achieved either by a reduction in share capital and cancellation of issued shares or by a reduction in the nominal value of issued shares without reducing the total number of shares in issue. The share premium account of the company may be reduced or cancelled in the same way as the issued share capital. Other reserves such as the revaluation reserves can be capitalised by way of a bonus issue of shares to the shareholders prior to the capital reduction (which will then form part of the share capital being reduced).

The reduction in share capital or share premium may be used (i) to fund a repayment to the company's shareholders or (ii) to credit an amount to reserves. In the case of (i), there is no requirement for the company to have distributable reserves equal to the amount of the repayment. In the case of (ii),

---

[155] Section 24, Companies Act 1985.

the company must have distributable reserves equal to the amount of any dividend to be distributed to its shareholders.

9.10.6.3   What issues does the unlimited company need to consider before carrying out a capital reduction?

The considerations which are referred to in section 9.3 above are also relevant to an unlimited company. Special consideration should also be given to the company's liabilities to ensure that the reduction of capital will not result in the company not being able to meet its liabilities on a winding-up and the shareholders having to settle such liabilities from their own resources.

Whilst there is no mandatory procedure for the protection of creditors in a reduction of capital of an unlimited company, the directors must nevertheless consider their duties as directors carefully. Directors should seek advice from their professional advisors where in doubt.

9.10.6.4   Are the reserves created from the reduction distributable?

Under the Companies Act 1985 and prior to 1 October 2008, whether or not the reserves created by an unlimited company which undertakes a capital reduction are distributable was dictated by the guidance in Tech 01/08. Under the guidance, the reserves would only have been distributable if the consideration received for the capital to be reduced had been (initially or subsequently) settled in 'qualifying consideration' (please refer to section 9.2). However, under the regulations discussed in section 9.3.10 of this chapter, the reserves created by an unlimited company which undertakes a capital reduction will be distributable (regardless of the nature of the consideration received for the capital). Alternatively, the unlimited company can pay out the capital reduced by way of a capital payment which is not required to be supported by distributable reserves.

9.10.6.5   What are the filing requirements?

The special resolution should be filed with Companies House within 15 days of the passing of the special resolution[156].

9.10.6.6   When will the reduction take effect?

The reduction takes effect immediately on the passing of the special resolution.

---

[156] Sections 29 and 30, Companies Act 2006.

9.10.7 How does an unlimited company purchase its own shares?

9.10.7.1 What is the procedure under the Companies Act 2006?

The procedure for repurchasing shares in an unlimited company remains unchanged under the Companies Act 2006. If authorised by its articles of association, an unlimited company may purchase any of its own shares, even though the shares are only partly paid. The company can also use its own assets to fund the purchase and is not reacquired to satisfy the purchase price in cash or to make payment on completion of the purchase (unlike a limited company).

9.10.7.2 What issues should a company consider before repurchasing its shares?

Whilst the formal procedural requirements relating to the purchase by a company of its own shares do not apply to unlimited companies, consideration should be given to the factors set out in section 9.4, in relation to the repurchase of shares by limited companies.

The articles of association must provide authority for the purchase by a company of its own shares, and should also contain the procedure to be followed. The date on which the purchase will take effect should also be contained in the articles of association.

9.10.8 Do the financial assistance rules apply?

From 1 October 2008, the prohibition on financial assistance given by private companies (including unlimited companies) for the purchase of their own shares or shares of their private holding companies will be abolished.

The only circumstances in which an unlimited company could be prohibited from giving financial assistance is where the unlimited company is giving assistance to its public holding company for the purpose of an acquisition of shares in the holding company.

An unlimited company will not benefit from the exceptions to the prohibition in respect of a reduction of capital (both court approved and by solvency statement) and a purchase of own shares in compliance with the statutory requirements.

9.11 Summary and conclusion on returning cash/assets to shareholders

Issue	Companies Act 1985	Companies Act 2006	Action required
Payment of dividends (section 9.2)	Distributable reserves. Relevant accounts.	Restates Companies Act 1985. From 6 April 2008.	No changes to pre-Companies Act 2006 procedures required (provided they comply with current practice).
Reduction of capital (section 9.3)	Court approval.	– Court approval required for public companies. – Court approval optional for private companies from 1 October 2008. – New solvency statement procedure for private companies from 1 October 2008.	Private companies have the option of applying to court for approval or using the solvency statement procedure. Review and update articles of public companies incorporated under the Companies Act 1985 and the transitional provisions of the Companies Act 2006, if no express authority is contained in current articles (this will be the case until the anticipated transitional provisions requiring authority to be contained in the articles or granted by special resolution are revoked).

Issue	Companies Act 1985	Companies Act 2006	Action required
Purchase of own shares (section 9.4)	– Contract must be approved by shareholders in advance of the purchase. – To be financed out of distributable reserves or proceeds of a fresh issue made for the purpose of repurchase. – Purchase out of capital by private companies supported by directors' statutory declaration and auditors' report.	– Permissible to have a purchase contract conditional on obtaining shareholders' approval. – To be financed out of distributable reserves or proceeds of a fresh issue made for the purpose of repurchase – Purchase out of capital by private companies supported by director's solvency statement and auditors' report. – From 1 October 2009.	Review and update articles of companies incorporated under the Companies Act 1985 and the transitional provisions of the Companies Act 2006, if no express authority contained in current articles (this will be the case until the anticipated transitional provisions requiring authority to be contained in the articles or granted by special resolution are revoked).
Redemption of redeemable shares (section 9.5)	Cash payment on redemption.	– Deferred payment permissible on redemption (if part of the agreed redemption terms). – From 1 October 2009.	No changes required.

Issue	Companies Act 1985	Companies Act 2006	Action required
Intra-group reorganisations (section 9.6)	– Transfer at book value intra-group requires at least £1 positive distributable reserves in transferor company. – Transfer at below book value requires distributable reserves at least equal to the difference between book value and the consideration received by the transferor company.	– Restates the common law position. – From 6 April 2008.	No changes required.
Demergers and schemes of arrangement (sections 9.7 and 9.8)	Demerger by way of: – Distribution in kind. – 'Three-cornered' or indirect merger. – Section 110 scheme. – Section 425 scheme.	Restates current position.	No changes required.

Issue	Companies Act 1985	Companies Act 2006	Action required
Financing the acquisition of shares (section 9.9)	– Financial assistance prohibition applies to both public and private companies. – 'Whitewash' procedure available for private companies for the purchase of their own shares or shares of their private holding companies.	– Financial assistance prohibition abolished for private companies for the purchase of their own shares or shares of their private holding companies from 1 October 2008. – 'Whitewash' procedure abolished from 1 October 2008. – Prohibition on public companies providing or receiving financial assistance remains. – Other new provisions to come into force from 1 October 2009.	Financing structures by private companies involving share issues should be facilitated.
Unlimited companies (section 9.10)	Return share capital without court approval if authorised by its articles.	No changes.	No changes required.

Chapter 10

Employee incentive share plans

10.1 Introduction 10001
    10.1.1   What are the main company law considerations that
           arise? 10002
10.2 What are the main company law considerations that arise when
    setting up and offering employee incentive share plans? 10005
    10.2.1   What documents are needed to set up the plan? 10006
           10.2.1.1 Plan rules 10006
           10.2.1.2 Option grant certificate 10007
           10.2.1.3 Exercise notice 10007
    10.2.2   Which company law issues are common to all employee
           share plans and how do they change under the Companies
           Act 2006? 10007
           10.2.2.1 Corporate capacity 10008
           10.2.2.2 Why is it important whether the plan is an
                    employees' share scheme? 10008
           10.2.2.3 Will shareholder approval be required to allot
                    shares for the purposes of the plan? 10010
           10.2.2.4 Authorised share capital 10011
           10.2.2.5 Authority to allot 10012
           10.2.2.6 Statutory pre-emption rights 10013
           10.2.2.7 Are there any financial assistance issues? 10013
    10.2.3   Conclusion 10016
10.3 What are the common types of employee share plan? 10017
    10.3.1   Share options 10017
    10.3.2   Free shares 10017
    10.3.3   Restricted shares 10018
    10.3.4   Phantom share options 10018
    10.3.5   Tax-favoured plans 10018
    10.3.6   Enterprise Management Incentives (EMI) 10018
           10.3.6.1 The independence requirement 10019
           10.3.6.2 The qualifying subsidiaries requirement 10019
           10.3.6.3 The gross assets requirement 10019
           10.3.6.4 The trading activities requirement 10019
           10.3.6.5 The working time requirement 10021
           10.3.6.6 Material interest 10021
           10.3.6.7 The number of employees requirement 10021
    10.3.7   Approved company share option plan 10021
    10.3.8   Approved save as you earn option scheme 10021
    10.3.9   Approved share incentive plan 10022
10.4 What additional company law issues may be relevant? 10022

10.4.1 How can shares be sourced? 10023
    10.4.1.1 Issuing new shares 10023
    10.4.1.2 Existing shares 10023
    10.4.1.3 Treasury shares 10023
10.4.2 What company law issues arise when establishing an employee benefit trust (EBT) 10024
    10.4.2.1 Formation 10024
    10.4.2.2 Who should act as trustee? 10024
    10.4.2.3 Beneficiaries 10025
    10.4.2.4 Directors' meetings 10025
    10.4.2.5 Funding the EBT 10025
10.4.3 When were the restrictions on making tax free payments to directors and on dealings by directors in share options repealed? 10026
10.4.4 What additional issues arise where the arrangements compromise partly paid shares? 10026
    10.4.4.1 What constitutes partly paid shares? 10027
    10.4.4.2 Could the issue of partly paid shares be unlawful financial assistance? 10028
10.4.5 Can a company provide finance to a director or employee to help meet the cost of acquiring shares? 10029
10.5 What other technical issues arise when setting up or operating employee share plans? 10030
10.5.1 How do securities laws apply? 10030
10.5.2 Are the arrangements subject to pay as you earn and national insurance contributions liabilities? 10031
10.5.3 What are the tax reporting obligations? 10032
10.5.4 Are there any other issues to consider? 10032
10.6 What disclosures are required in respect of employee share plan awards? 10033
10.6.1 What disclosures are required of directors' emoluments? 10033
    10.6.1.1 Schedule 5 to the Large and Medium-sized Accounts Regulations (Schedule 5) – aggregate emoluments 10033
10.6.2 What disclosures are required of director's shares emoluments? 10035
    10.6.2.1 Schedule 7 to the Large and Medium-sized Accounts Regulations (Schedule 7) – directors' interests 10035
10.6.3 What is the remuneration report required to contain? . . 10035
    10.6.3.1 Schedule 8 to the Large and Medium-sized Accounts Regulations (Schedule 8) – content of remuneration report 10035
    10.6.3.2 Statement of remuneration policy (not auditable) 10035
    10.6.3.3 Disclosure of share options and long-term incentives (auditable) 10036

10.6.3.4   Share options 10036
10.6.3.5   Long-term incentive awards 10037
10.6.4   What do the Listing Rules require? 10039
10.6.5   What do accounting standards require? 10039
10.6.6   What disclosures are required under the Disclosure and
Transparency Rules? 10039
10.6.7   Glossary 10039
10.7   What issues arise when a company with an existing share plan is to
be acquired? 10040
10.7.1   How can the share plan impact on the transaction? 10041
10.7.2   Which provisions of a share plan are particularly
relevant? 10043
10.7.2.1   Those provisions dealing with the vesting or
exercise of rights in the ordinary course 10043
10.7.2.2   Any provision which will trigger an early vesting
or right to exercise on a takeover – the impact of
performance conditions 10044
10.7.2.3   If there is a provision which permits option
exercise or award vesting in the course of the
takeover, at what point will the right to exercise
or vesting arise? 10044
10.7.2.4   Provisions dealing with the payment of an
exercise price or other payment as a condition of
exercise or vesting 10045
10.7.2.5   Provisions which allow the employer company
(or the employer's parent company) to recover
PAYE and NIC from the employee 10046
10.7.2.6   Provisions requiring that the employee meet any
employer's NIC 10047
10.7.2.7   Provisions which specify when the award or
option will lapse 10047
10.7.3   Will the issue of additional shares impact on the overall
acquisition cost? 10048
10.7.4   Is there any alternative to award vesting or option exercise
– rollovers and cash cancellation? 10048
10.7.5   What is the entitlement of 'lay' employees? 10049
10.7.6   What process should be adopted for securing the support
of employee award and option holders? 10050
10.7.7   What issues arise where the transaction is a sale and
purchase of a business as a going concern rather than a
share purchase? 10050

Chapter 10

Employee incentive share plans

When a company introduces an employee share incentive plan, consideration must be given to a range of technical and practical matters, including company law. This chapter sets out the changes introduced by the Companies Act 2006 in the context of those other matters. It concludes that, in practical terms, the process of introducing and running employee share incentive plans is not significantly changed by the new law.

10.1 Introduction

This chapter addresses the company law implications of designing, implementing and operating employee incentive arrangements. While such plans can be either cash or share-based, the focus is on the latter, as company law is much more relevant to share plans. The primary company considerations are set out, and differences between the Companies Act 1985 and the Companies Act 2006 are highlighted. The Companies Act 2006 also has implications for other elements of employee remuneration, which are touched on below. It is important that the wider context in which share plans are implemented is appreciated. The following are among the factors outside company law that will impact on a company's decisions relating to its share plans:

(i)   income tax position of the employee participants;

(ii)   withholding and national insurance contributions liabilities;

(iii)   corporate tax position of the company;

(iv)   accounting implications;

(v)   securities and financial services law considerations; and

(vi)   regulatory requirements.

Company law is only one of a number of influences in this area. This chapter addresses the key company law issues, as well as setting them in context by describing common employee incentive arrangements and the requirements that typically shape them. The accounting implications of employee share schemes can be complex and are beyond the scope of this book. However, they are considered in detail in Chapter 12 of the *PricewaterhouseCoopers Manual of Accounting – IFRS for the UK* and *Manual of Accounting – UK GAAP*.

Tax is probably the single most significant influence over design. The taxation of employee incentives is an area that has seen unprecedented change over the last few years, with major changes to the legislation applying to shares acquired by employees. Directors need to appreciate the complex interaction of tax with company law and the other factors listed above, in order to operate an arrangement that is both compliant with the necessary laws and regulations, as well as optimising the tax and accounting position.

This chapter is structured to provide a practical guide to the issues to consider. It starts with an example company, Widget Limited, which wishes to implement a relatively straightforward employee incentive plan. This introduces the company law issues that arise in putting a plan in place. Secondly, the operating and funding of share plans is considered. This describes the various types of share plans that are typically used by companies, and why. It highlights particular issues that can arise when less common structures are implemented, and also briefly describes the disclosure requirements relevant to share awards, as well as some of the non-company law issues a company will need to deal with. Lastly, the effect of transactions on incentive arrangements, and the decisions that need to be made in such situations, is addressed.

10.1.1 What are the main company law considerations that arise?

The table below summarises the main company law issues to consider when implementing and operating employee share plans, along with other sections that affect the manner in which companies remunerate their employees. It sets out both the Companies Act 1985 and the Companies Act 2006 provisions. All these issues are addressed in this chapter in the context of employee share plans. For further information on the changes generally, reference is made in some instances to other chapters of this book.

Issue to address	Relevant Companies Act 1985 provision	Relevant Companies Act 2006 provision	Date new provisions come into effect
Definition of employees' share scheme. Relevant when applying various exemptions.	Section 743	Section 1166. Definition not substantively changed.	1 October 2009
Power to introduce share plan under memorandum.	Section 2. Objects of company must be stated in memorandum.	Sections 8, 28 and 31 (parts 2 and 3). Memorandum has very restricted use. Company has unrestricted authority unless articles contain restrictions.	1 October 2009

Issue to address	Relevant Companies Act 1985 provision	Relevant Companies Act 2006 provision	Date new provisions come into effect
Shareholder approval – authorised share capital. Relevant when issuing new shares for purposes of a share plan.	Section 2 Share capital of company on incorporation must be stated in memorandum.	Concept of authorised share capital is being removed. Instead a company must file a statement of capital each time it allots shares (s555 part 17).	1 October 2009
Shareholder approval – allotment of shares. Relevant when issuing new shares for purposes of a share plan.	Section 80 Company cannot issue new shares without prior approval of shareholders or authority in the articles. Exemption for employees' share schemes in s80(2)(a).	Sections 549 to 551 (part 17) Position remains the same, except that private companies with only one class of shares can allot shares without shareholder authority.	1 October 2009
Statutory pre-emption rights. Relevant when issuing new shares for the purposes of a share plan.	Section 89 A company issuing shares must first offer them *pro rata* to existing shareholders, unless disapplied by the articles or special resolution of shareholders (section 95). Exemption for employees' share schemes in section 89(5).	Section 561 (part 17) Position remains the same. Employees' share scheme exemption at section 566.	1 October 2009
Prohibition on allotting shares at a discount to their nominal value.	Section 100 Shares must not be allotted at a discount.	Section 580 (part 17) Position remains the same.	1 October 2009

Employee incentive share plans

Issue to address	Relevant Companies Act 1985 provision	Relevant Companies Act 2006 provision	Date new provisions come into effect
Private companies – prohibition of public offers.	Section 81 A private limited company commits an offence if it offers shares to the public.	Section 755 (part 20) Position remains the same.	6 April 2008
Prohibition on company giving financial assistance for the purchase of its own shares.	Sections 151 to 158 Employees' share scheme exemption in section 153(4).	Sections 677 to 683 (part 18) Private companies – broadly the statutory prohibition is abolished. Public companies – prohibition retained. Employees' share scheme exemption contained in section 682.	1 October 2009
Treasury shares.	Sections 162A to 162G Provides that treasury shares may be transferred for the purposes of or pursuant to an employees' share scheme.	Sections 724 to 732 (part 18) Position remains the same.	1 October 2009
Prohibition on a subsidiary being a member of its holding company. This is an issue because sometimes the trustee of an EBT will be a subsidiary within the sponsoring company's group.	Section 23(2) Contains exemption that trustee company relies upon.	Section 138 (part 8) Provides that the general prohibition (in section 136) on a subsidiary being a member of its holding company does not apply where the subsidiary is concerned only as a trustee.	1 October 2009

Issue to address	Relevant Companies Act 1985 provision	Relevant Companies Act 2006 provision	Date new provisions come into effect
Schemes of arrangement. Typically referred to in employee share plan rules.	Section 425	Sections 895 to 901 (part 26)	6 April 2008
Squeeze-out provisions. Typically referred to in employee share plan rules.	Section 429 and The Takeovers Directive (Interim Implementation) Regulations 2007	Sections 979 to 982 (part 28) Apply to all companies and replace the regulations, which applied to listed companies only.	6 April 2007
Prohibition on loans to directors.	Section 330	Sections 197 to 214 (part 10) No longer an absolute prohibition; instead it is possible if it has been authorised by shareholders.	1 October 2007
Tax-free payments to directors.	Section 311	Repealed by section 1177	6 April 2007
Directors dealings in share options.	Section 323	Repealed by section 1177	6 April 2007
Disclosure of directors dealings in shares. Directors had to disclose when an EBT of which they were a beneficiary bought or sold shares.	Sections 324 to 329	Repealed under section 1177 Listed companies will remain subject to the Listing Rule disclosure requirements.	6 April 2007
Directors' remuneration report. Requirement for quoted companies to prepare a report in accordance with Schedule 7A Companies Act 1985 (chapter 10).	Section 234B	Sections 420 and 421 Section 421 provides that the contents requirements of the remuneration report will be set out in regulations.	6 April 2008 (for accounting periods starting on or after 6 April 2008).

10.2   What are the main company law considerations that arise when setting up and offering employee incentive share plans?

The example below summarises the structure of a typical employee share plan. It is common for such a plan to be structured so as to be eligible for certain tax advantages (see later in the chapter).

An example – Widget Limited

Background

Widget Limited is a company recently listed on the Alternative Investment Market (AIM). It was founded 10 years ago and is now 30% owned by its founders, A and B. It has a large number of other shareholders, including shares held by employees who subscribed for shares at the time of listing. The company has no subsidiaries. The company is growing rapidly and A and B, the chief executive officer and chief financial officer respectively, wish to introduce an employee share plan in order to assist with recruitment, as well as incentivise, retain and motivate the company's employees. It has been decided to adopt a share option plan that will operate as follows:

- Selected employees will be granted options to acquire shares in Widget;

- Option holders will have the right (but not the obligation) to exercise their options and acquire shares in Widget between three and ten years after the date of option grant;

- The options will be capable of being exercised in whole or in part, so may be exercised in as many tranches within that period as the option holder wishes;

- The price payable upon exercise of the option (the exercise price) will be equal to the market value of the underlying shares on the day of grant (in other words, the price at which Widget shares are trading on AIM on that day); and

- New shares will be issued to satisfy the exercise of options. Once shares are acquired the shareholder will be free to either retain or sell their shares.

10.2.1   What documents are needed to set up the plan?

10.2.1.1   *Plan rules*

This legal document will set out the terms of the options that are to be granted under the plan. The company can include such terms as it considers suitable. If the plan is designed to take advantage of certain tax reliefs available to plans approved by HM Revenue & Customs, there are certain requirements as to the contents of the plan rules that will have to be met (see further below). The plan rules are effectively a contract between the company and the option holders under which the employees will be eligible to exercise the options if they fulfil certain conditions. These will typically include continued employment until the option is exercised, plus corporate performance conditions imposed in relation to each grant of options if the company is listed. There will be special provisions that apply if the option holder ceases employment before exercise of the option; these are generally more generous to those who leave as so-called good leavers, for example, due to ill health or disability. Such option holders may retain the ability to exercise their options for a certain period. This is in contrast to the position of someone who resigns, whose options are likely to lapse immediately. In addition, a range of other matters will be addressed in the plan rules, including the applicable legal jurisdiction, the procedure and requirements for amending rules and the effect of a corporate transaction on plan participants.

10.2.1.2   *Option grant certificate*

This will be personal to each option recipient and will typically set out the number of shares over which an option has been granted, the exercise price, the period during which the option can ordinarily be exercised, and other key terms. It is common for the option certificate to have attached a notice of renunciation, enabling the employee to refuse the option within a set period if they do not wish to accept it.

10.2.1.3   *Exercise notice*

When the employee becomes able to exercise the option (after three years under the fictional Widget plan), an exercise notice will usually need to be submitted. This notifies the company of the wish to exercise the option and acquire the underlying shares.

At the same time as drafting these documents, Widget can expect to receive advice in relation to the areas set out below.

10.2.2   Which company law issues are common to all employee share plans and how do they change under the Companies Act 2006?

A and B will need to address the following company law and other questions in setting up the new plan:

(i)   Does the company have corporate capacity (i.e. the power to set up the plan)?

(ii)   Is the plan an 'employees' share scheme' for the purposes of company law?

(iii)   Will shareholder approval be required to allot shares for the purposes of the plan?

(iv)   Are there any financial assistance issues?

(v)   What other issues need to be considered?

10.2.2.1   *Corporate capacity*

Under the Companies Act 1985 and preceding company legislation, for a company to be able to set up an employee share plan, it must have the power to do so under its memorandum and articles of association. The memorandum of a company sets out the objects (i.e. the powers) that the company has; it is not permissible for a company to do anything outside these powers. It has been customary for a company to have a power to establish and operate an employees' share scheme as one of its objectives. Companies that do not have this power will have to amend their objects by shareholder resolution to include such a provision in their memorandum before they can set up a share plan.

The position changes when the provisions of Companies Act 2006 parts 2 and 3 come into effect on 1 October 2009. Under section 31 of the Companies Act 2006, the objects of a company incorporated from that date are unrestricted unless the company specifically restricts the objects. If a company wishes to do this, the restriction is placed in the articles of the company. For companies incorporated from 1 October 2009, there is therefore no longer a need to ensure there is a specific power to set up an employee share plan.

For companies incorporated prior to this date, it is still necessary to check the objects clause of the memorandum for the powers of the company, unless that company has amended its articles after 1 October 2009 to include a provision saying that its objects are unrestricted. Being a pre-1 October 2009 incorporated company, Widget will need to check its memorandum in relation to this.

10.2.2.2   *Why is it important whether the plan is an employees' share scheme?*

This is an important question for Widget to consider in the drafting and introduction of the new plan because it will affect the manner in which a range of company law requirements impact on the plan. If a share plan falls within the definition of an employees' share scheme there are a number of consequences, including the following:

(i)   the provisions of section 80 of the Companies Act 1985, which require shareholder authority to enable directors to allot shares, do not apply;

(ii)   the provisions of sections 89 to 95 of the Companies Act 1985, which require any newly issued shares to be first offered *pro rata* to existing shareholders (pre-emption rights), do not apply; and

(iii) the rules that prohibit a company from giving financial assistance for the purchase of its own shares may not apply.

These requirements are dealt with in detail below.

The definition of an employees' share scheme under the Companies Act 1985 is as follows:

> "....a scheme for encouraging or facilitating the holding of shares or debentures in a company by or for the benefit of:
>
> (a)   the bona fide employees or former employees of the company, the company's subsidiary or holding company or a subsidiary of the company's holding company, or
>
> (b)   the spouses, civil partners, surviving spouses, surviving civil partners, or children or stepchildren under the age of 18 of such employees or former employees."

There are a number of elements of this definition that warrant closer consideration.

> '...a scheme...'

This is not further defined in the legislation, but the fact that the word 'scheme' is used, rather than 'scheme or arrangement', implies that the terms of the share plan should apply to more than one person. For this reason it is usual practice for a company to prepare a set of rules containing the terms of the share options, or other awards that can be made under it, which can apply to any number of potential participants. This can be contrasted with a situation where an employee is granted an option in terms set out in that individual's employment contract. The latter is unlikely to be viewed as a scheme, whilst the former is more likely to be viewed as one, even if in the event, only one person participates in the arrangement.

> '...encouraging or facilitating the holding of shares...'

This requires the purpose of the scheme to be to encourage or facilitate the holding of shares. This test may not be met if a scheme was structured so that its purpose was not that employees acquired interests in, or benefited from, the holding of shares.

> '...by or for the benefit of...'

Employee incentive share plans

It may be that an employee share plan does not provide for, or involve, the acquisition by employees of the legal interest in shares. This would not prevent it being an employees' share scheme provided shares are nevertheless held for their benefit. Companies often set up employee benefit trusts (EBTs) which act as a warehouse, holding shares for use in relation to share plans. Under the terms of such trusts, the shares are generally held for the benefit of a class of beneficiaries that reflects the drafting of section 743 of the Companies Act 1985, and would therefore qualify as an employees' share scheme.

'...*bona fide* employees...'

For a person to be an employee, the individual needs to have a contract of employment as opposed to a contract for services; the latter is indicative of a self-employed consultant or contractor. Therefore, a non-executive director will not be an employee for these purposes, and it is common practice for non-executive directors to be excluded from participation in employee share plans.

In preparing the terms of the share plan that Widget wishes to introduce, it must consider whether it is happy for the plan to be structured to meet the requirements of an employees' share scheme. If correctly carried out, the drafting of the plan documentation, and the way that the plan is operated in practice, will ensure that the plan remains an employees' share scheme, with the administrative and legal advantages that this provides.

Under the Companies Act 2006, section 1166 provides an updated definition of employees' share scheme. It does not contain any substantive changes to the Companies Act 1985. Draft regulations propose (at the time of writing) that this will take effect from 1 October 2009.

10.2.2.3 Will shareholder approval be required to allot shares for the purposes of the plan?

There is no provision in either the Companies Act 1985 or the Companies Act 2006 that requires specific shareholder approval for an employee share plan. In relation to listed companies, the Listing Rules section of the Listing, Prospectus, Disclosure and Transparency Rules requires shareholder approval for certain types of incentive plans. Companies listed on AIM are not subject to such a requirement, although shareholder approval may be required for company law reasons set out below.

Depending on the circumstances of the company in relation to its share capital, it may be necessary to gain shareholder approval to facilitate the operation of the share plan. When option holders under the plan exercise their options, it may be necessary to allot new shares to satisfy those options. We will assume this is necessary in the case of Widget. As alternatives to newly allotted shares, companies can also meet the exercise of options by using shares bought on the market and currently held in an EBT, or transfer shares that have been held in treasury (or a mixture of these methods). More of this is covered later.

There are three questions for Widget to consider in relation to its share capital:

(i)   Does it have sufficient authorised share capital?

(ii) Are the directors authorised to allot shares for the purposes of the share plan?

(iii) If the directors wish to allot the shares for the purposes of the plan, are they subject to statutory pre-emption rights?

10.2.2.4   *Authorised share capital*

The first question for Widget to consider under the terms of the Companies Act 1985 is whether it has sufficient authorised share capital. Before the directors of a company can consider issuing new shares, they first need to check whether the company has, either by shareholder resolution, or provision in the articles, authorised sufficient share capital. It is not possible to issue shares out of capital that has not been authorised. If there is insufficient authorised, but unallotted share capital, it will be necessary to increase the authorised share capital by resolution of the company in general meeting. Section 2 of the Companies Act 1985 provides that a company's authorised share capital must be stated in its memorandum, and sections 121 to 123 of the Companies Act 1985 set out the mechanism for this share capital to be increased or adjusted, including the requirement to notify the Registrar of Companies of any such change.

The concept of authorised share capital is being removed by the introduction of the Companies Act 2006 with effect from 1 October 2009. It will no longer be necessary to create authorised share capital as a separate step to the issue and allotment of shares, which are addressed below. Instead, there will simply be a requirement for the company to file a statement of capital whenever it allots shares in accordance with section 555(3) and (4) of the Companies Act 2006. This change will simplify the procedures a company has to follow for issuing shares under a share plan or for any other reason.

While historically companies had to include their initial share capital in the memorandum, for companies incorporated after parts 2 and 3 of Companies Act 2006 take effect from 1 October 2009, this will no longer be the case. Instead the application for registration of a company will need to include a statement of initial share capital (section 9 of the Companies Act 2006).

Until these changes are introduced, Widget will need to ensure that it has sufficient share capital to issue new shares to satisfy the exercise of options by the time they occur. Best practice would be to ensure that there is sufficient authorised share capital to be able to satisfy all outstanding options at any time, even though the terms of those options may mean that they are not yet capable of being exercised by the employees.

There is a further provision for private companies to take into account. Private companies are currently prohibited from offering shares to the public, which is why private companies need to re-register as public prior to listing their shares on AIM or the London Stock Exchange. Widget will have undergone such a re-registration prior to listing on AIM. Although the definition of public for these purposes is quite broad, neither an offer of shares to an existing employee, nor an offer to subscribe for shares to be held under an employees' share scheme, is considered to be an offer to the public for the purposes of this specific prohibition. From 6 April 2008, there will be a specific exemption providing that offers to subscribe for shares to be held under an employees' share scheme will be regarded as a private concern and therefore not considered to be an offer to the public.

There is other legislation that also needs to be considered when offers are made under share plans, in particular the requirements of the European Union Prospectus Directive needs to taken into account. This is addressed in the second section of this chapter.

10.2.2.5 *Authority to allot*

The Companies Act 1985 does not allow directors of a company to allot shares without the prior authority of shareholders. This may be provided in the articles of the company or by resolution in a general meeting of shareholders. However, this restriction does not apply if the shares are allotted under the terms of an employees' share scheme (including by way of exercise of an option granted under an employees' share scheme).

If the share plan does not fall within the definition of an employees' share scheme (for example, because the terms of the plan allow the grant of options to non-executive directors), then it will be necessary to ensure that shareholder authority is secured. This authority must state the maximum nominal amount of shares which may be allotted (or options to subscribe may be granted) under it, and must be for a maximum period of five years. The authority can be given for a specific purpose or generally for any purpose. It is customary for companies to renew the authority each year on a rolling five-year basis. If the requirement for authority is breached, the allotment of shares remains valid, but any director who knowingly and wilfully allowed the breach is liable to a fine.

The new regime is contained in sections 549 to 551 of the Companies Act 2006 and it is proposed that this will apply from 1 October 2009. Although the detailed drafting differs, the essence of the exemption for employees' share schemes remains. The Companies Act 2006 has a further relaxation for private companies with only one class of shares; if this is the case, then under section

550 the Companies Act 2006, the directors may exercise the power to allot shares of that class without the need for shareholder approval (provided they are not prohibited from doing so under the company's articles). This means that the directors of a company with only one class of shares will not have to secure approval for the grant of options over, or the allotment of shares made under, the terms of a share plan that does not satisfy the conditions to be an employees' share scheme.

Under both the current and future regimes, it will therefore be possible for the directors of Widget to both grant options, and allot shares in satisfaction of the exercise of those options, without securing prior shareholder approval, provided the Widget's plan falls within the employees' share scheme definition.

10.2.2.6 Statutory pre-emption rights

When a company allots new shares, then by section 89 of the Companies Act 1985, the company is currently required to offer shareholders a number of new shares proportionate to their existing holdings. If section 89 is not complied with, the company and any officer of the company who allowed this to occur, can be held liable to compensate those shareholders to whom an offer should have been made for any losses incurred as a result of the contravention (see section 8.5).

This requirement can be disapplied by the articles of the company or a special resolution of shareholders. It is common for this to be put in place at the same time as directors are authorised to allot shares, so that, to the extent directors are authorised to allot those shares, they are not subject to the statutory pre-emption rights.

However, by section 89(5) of the Companies Act the statutory pre-emption rights do not apply to the allotment of shares to be held under or in pursuance of an employees' share scheme. Therefore, provided a share plan complies with the Companies Act 1985 employees' share schemes definition, shares can be allotted to employees under that plan without the need to first offer shares *pro rata* to existing shareholders.

Under Companies Act 2006, from 1 October 2009, section 561 replaces the Companies Act 1985 provisions, but contains no substantive changes to the previous law. The employees' share scheme exemption is at section 566 of the Companies Act 2006.

Widget will therefore be able to operate its new share plan free from the statutory pre-emption provisions under both the current and future laws, provided its plan is an employees' share scheme. It should however, be noted that private companies often include detailed pre-emption procedures in their articles that replace the statutory provisions, and such procedures will need to be separately disapplied or varied as necessary.

10.2.2.7 Are there any financial assistance issues?

What is financial assistance?

The current general rule under section 151 of the Companies Act 1985, is that it is unlawful for a company or any of its subsidiaries to give financial assistance to a third party for the acquisition of its own shares, or for the purposes of reducing or discharging any liability that has been incurred by a third party in acquiring shares in the company. This applies to the acquisition of newly issued shares and the transfer of existing shares.

Financial assistance is defined in the legislation as including gifts, loans, guarantees, security, waivers or indemnities, and also includes any other financial assistance which materially reduces the net assets of the company giving the assistance (or is given by a company which has no net assets). Directors of a company can be held criminally liable for unlawful financial assistance, so compliance with the rules is very important.

Are there any exceptions?

There are a number of exceptions to the rule. There are two provisions under the Companies Act 1985 that are most applicable to share plans. The first of these (section 153(4)(b) of the Companies Act 1985) permits:

> "...the provision by a company, in good faith in the interests of the company, of financial assistance for the purposes of an employees' share scheme..."

To fall within this exemption, the assistance must be given for the purposes of a share plan that falls within the employees' share schemes definition. This may be a share option plan or another type of employee share plan under which employees acquire shares. The exemption will generally also apply to an EBT, which will qualify as an employees' share scheme in its own right if its class of beneficiaries is limited to those listed in the Companies Act 1985. It is common for a company or its subsidiary to make loans or contributions to an EBT to finance the purchase of shares in the company, or guarantee a loan made by a third party, and this will be within the exemption, provided the EBT in question complies with the previous legislation.

Care must be taken to ensure that any financial assistance given is 'in good faith in the interests of the company'. The directors will need to be able to satisfy themselves that the assistance being given is indeed in the interests of the company; this will generally be the case as share plans are commonly perceived to be an important part of the remuneration of employees, and employees are usually key to the success of a business. But there are occasionally circumstances where it will not necessarily be the case that the interests of the company are being put first.

The second exemption that may apply to share plans is that contained in section 153(4)(bb) of the Companies Act 1985. This applies to:

"...the provision of financial assistance by a company or any of its subsidiaries for the purposes of or in connection with anything done by the company (or a company in the same group) for the purpose of enabling or facilitating transactions in shares in the first-mentioned company between, and involving the acquisition of beneficial ownership of those shares by [the class of individuals set out in s743 Companies Act 1985]..."

The application of this exemption is generally limited to arrangements that a company may put in place to create a market for shares that employees hold, such as a mechanism to match sales and purchases of shares by employees. It does not itself permit financial assistance for the purchase of those shares in the first place (for which the section 153(4)(b) of the Companies Act 1985 exemption must be relied upon).

The whitewash procedure

For private companies, the Companies Act 1985 provides a mechanism for financial assistance to be permitted by a special resolution of shareholders under sections 155 to 158 of the Companies Act 1985, provided certain conditions are also fulfilled and procedures followed in accordance with a statutory timetable. A statutory declaration of the directors and accompanying auditor's report must be made in relation to the solvency of the company, and the financial assistance can only be given if the net assets of the company are not reduced, or, if they are, the assistance is out of distributable profits. This is commonly known as the whitewash procedure. It may be followed by a private company if the exemption is not available (for example because the share plan in question includes non-executive directors, so the class of potential recipients does not comply with section 743 of the Companies Act 1985).

Companies with a foreign parent

Companies are generally accustomed to dealing with the financial assistance rules, and by ensuring that the class of potential recipients of share awards/ options (and beneficiaries in the case of an EBT) is no wider than that defined in section 743 of the Companies Act 1985, fall within the exemption in section 153(4)(b) of the Companies Act 1985, referred to above. One quirk of the legislation is that when 'company' and 'subsidiaries' are referred to in section 151 of the Companies Act 1985, these are only companies incorporated under the Companies Act 1985. This means that it is not unlawful under Companies Act 1985 for a UK incorporated and registered subsidiary to give financial assistance for the purposes of employees purchasing shares in its non-UK parent. The rules of employee share plans applying to a United States parent and its subsidiaries, including one in the UK, will often contain a class of potential recipients that is wider than section 743 of the Companies Act 1985 – for example, including self-employed consultants – and this will not fall foul of the UK financial assistance rules. However, the laws applicable to the parent company will also have to be considered as many jurisdictions also have prohibitions equivalent to the UK financial assistance rules.

The charges introduced by Companies Act 2006

Substantial changes are introduced to the financial assistance provisions from 1 October 2009. The new provisions are contained in sections 677 to 683 of the Companies Act 2006. For private companies, the current prohibition on giving financial assistance in connection with the acquisition of its own shares (or the shares of its private company parent) is abolished with effect from 1 October 2008. As a consequence of this, the whitewash procedure will become redundant and is being repealed also with effect from 1 October 2008.

For public companies, the prohibition on the giving of financial assistance in connection with the acquisition of its own shares is retained; this also applies to a private company subsidiary giving financial assistance for the acquisition of shares in its public company parent.

There remains in the new legislation an exemption for employees' share schemes, which is contained in section 682 of the Companies Act 2006. This is substantively the same as the exemption in Companies Act 1985. As currently proposed, from 1 October 2009, private companies no longer need to consider the implications of financial assistance in relation to their share plans, but public companies will still need to ensure they are within the terms of the employees' share schemes exemption.

For Widget, as its new share plan will be introduced prior to the relevant provisions of the Companies Act 2006 coming into force, it will need to ensure that its arrangements fall within the employees' share scheme exemption to avoid having to address any financial assistance issues.

It should not be assumed that because financial assistance is being abolished for private companies that the subject is no longer relevant. If there has been any unlawful financial assistance prior to abolition there is still a criminal offence. Identification of past unlawful financial assistance by a prospective share purchaser is likely to generate significant issues requiring resolution before the share purchase can proceed to completion.

10.2.3 Conclusion

From a company law point of view, the questions that A and B must consider with their advisers in relation to the set-up of the Widget share option plan are as follows:

(i)   Is there sufficient authorised share capital?

(ii)   Do directors have authority to allot shares for the purposes of the plan, or does this fall within the employees' share scheme exemption?

(iii) Do statutory pre-emption rights need to be disapplied (if the employees' share scheme exemption does not apply) and do any pre-emption provision in the articles need to be varied to enable the plan to operate?

(iv) Is the company satisfied that there are no financial assistance issues?

10.3   What are the common types of employee share plan?

10.3.1 Share options

A share option is a right to acquire shares in future at a price (the exercise price or strike price) set when the option is granted. The exercise price will typically be at least equal to the company's share price on the date of grant. The option holder becomes a shareholder when he exercises the option.

Options are often described as being a 'one way bet' for employees because if the company's share price increases, the employee will make a gain if he exercises his option. If, however, the company's share price performs badly, so that it is less than the exercise price (often referred to as an underwater option), the employee will choose not to exercise the option.

Options may be granted under schemes which have been approved by HM Revenue & Customs and carry certain tax benefits, or under unapproved arrangements. In tax terms, the main difference between the two types of arrangement is that the exercise of options granted under one of the HM Revenue & Customs approved schemes can be free from income tax and national insurance contributions, whereas the exercise of options granted under an unapproved arrangement will be subject to income tax and generally national insurance contributions.

10.3.2 Free shares

Free share arrangements are often referred to as long-term incentive plans or performance share plans. Under these arrangements, employees are entitled to the entire value of a share (rather than the just the growth in value of the share between grant and exercise, which an option would deliver), generally subject to the achievement of a performance target linked to the company's performance, such as an earnings per share or total shareholder return measure.

Awards of free shares would typically be structured as either a nil cost option or a contingent right to acquire shares. The difference between the two types of award is that with the latter, once the holder becomes unconditionally entitled to the shares, these are transferred to the holder, whereas the holder of an option is able to control the timing of acquisition of their shares as they will need to take action to exercise his option.

10.3.3   Restricted shares

An increasing number of companies, particularly unlisted companies have introduced restricted shares arrangements. Unlike an option or free shares arrangement, the employee becomes the legal and beneficial owner of shares at the outset. The shares may be issued on terms requiring the employee to sell the shares if his employment ceases, and/or other conditions.

These arrangements are popular with companies which may not qualify to introduce the Enterprise Management Incentive share option arrangement and which expect substantial growth in value of their shares, relative to the value at the time of acquisition.

10.3.4   Phantom share options

Phantom share options are cash bonus arrangements under which the cash bonus paid to participants is calculated by reference to the growth in the company's share price over a defined period of time.

Phantom share option arrangements can be suitable for companies where the shares are potentially problematic e.g. in a private company where there is no ready market for the shares.

10.3.5   Tax-favoured plans

There are a variety of share plans which potentially have beneficial tax treatment for UK taxpayers. The shares used in HM Revenue & Customs-approved share arrangements must satisfy a number of criteria, and there are other conditions that must be fulfilled in order to benefit from this treatment. Professional advice should be sought by companies considering implementing any of these arrangements, but an outline of each of these arrangements, together with an indication of the associated tax benefits, is set out below.

10.3.6   Enterprise Management Incentives (EMI)

An EMI is a discretionary share option plan, which means that a company can select the employees it grants options to. Options may be granted over a maximum of £120,000 of shares to each participant (subject to certain limits including an overall aggregate limit of £3 million). There are no restrictions on the exercise price – it may be equal to the company's share price on the date of grant, or set at a premium or discount to this price.

This type of option plan is regarded as the most tax efficient share option plan available in the UK. Where options are EMI qualifying options, capital gains tax applies from the date of grant of the option, rather than the date of exercise of the option, which is the case for all other option arrangements.

EMI plans are particularly popular with private and smaller listed companies, due to the tax benefits they offer. They are not used by larger companies however, due to the limit on the size of company that is permitted to grant options, which is limited to those with gross assets not exceeding £30 million.

Given the complexity of the legislation and potential uncertainties in relation to whether companies qualify to grant EMI qualifying options, companies can apply to HM Revenue & Customs (Small Company Enterprise Centre in Cardiff) for advance assurance that they meet the legislative requirements.

The legislative requirements for EMI option arrangements are as follows.

10.3.6.1   *The independence requirement*

The company over whose shares EMI options are to be granted must not be a subsidiary or under the control of another company (or another company or anyone connected with the other company), and must not be a 51% subsidiary of another company (a company is a 51% subsidiary if another company has more than 50% of the ordinary share capital). Additionally, there must be no arrangements in place by virtue of which the company could become a subsidiary or controlled.

10.3.6.2   *The qualifying subsidiaries requirement*

If the company over whose shares EMI options are to be granted has subsidiary companies, these must be at least 51% subsidiaries, no other company must have control of the subsidiaries and no arrangements must exist by virtue of which these requirements would cease to be satisfied.

If the subsidiary is a 'property managing subsidiary' (i.e. the subsidiary's business consists of the holding or managing of land or any property deriving its value from land), this must be a 90% subsidiary, directly owned by the company whose shares are to be subject to option.

10.3.6.3   *The gross assets requirement*

In the case of a single company, the value of its gross assets must not exceed £30 million.

10.3.6.4   *The trading activities requirement*

In the case of a single company, this must exist wholly for the purpose of carrying on a qualifying trade and be carrying on that qualifying trade (or preparing to do so).

Employee incentive share plans

A trade is a qualifying trade if it is:

(i)   carried on wholly or mainly in the UK;

(ii) conducted on a commercial basis and with a view to the realisation of profits; and

(iii) does not consist (either wholly or as to a substantial part) in the carrying on of excluded activities.

The following are excluded activities:

(i)   dealing in land, commodities or in futures or in shares, securities or other financial instruments;

(ii)   dealing in goods otherwise than in the course of an ordinary trade of wholesale or retail distribution;

(iii) banking, insurance, moneylending, debt factoring, hire purchase financing or other financial activities;

(iv)   leasing, including letting ships on charter or other assets on hire;

(v)   receiving royalties or licence fees;

(vi)   providing legal or accountancy services;

(vii) property development;

(viii) farming or market gardening;

(ix)   holding, managing or occupying woodlands, any forestry activities or timber production;

(x)   shipbuilding;

(xi)   producing coal;

(xii) producing steel;

(xiii) operating or managing hotels or comparable establishments, or managing property used as a hotel or comparable establishment;

(xiv) operating or managing nursing homes or residential care homes, or managing property used as a nursing home or residential care home; and

(xv)   providing services or facilities for a business carried on by another person.

In addition to the company satisfying these requirements, the employees who will be granted EMI options must meet the working time requirement and not have a material interest in order to be eligible to receive EMI options. These are summarised below.

10.3.6.5   *The working time requirement*

The time which the employee is required to spend on the business of the relevant company (where the company is a single company) must be at least:

(i)   25 hours a week, or

(ii)   if less, 75% of the employee's working time (working time refers to time spent on remunerative work as an employee or self-employed person).

10.3.6.6   *Material interest*

An employee must not have a material interest in the company. A material interest for this purpose means beneficial ownership of, or the ability to control (directly or indirectly), more than 30% of the ordinary share capital of the company.

10.3.6.7   *The number of employees requirement*

The number of employees (in case of a single company) must be less than the equivalent of 250 full-time employees.

10.3.7   Approved company share option plan

The company share option plan (CSOP) is a discretionary share option plan. Options may be granted over a maximum of £30,000 of shares to each participant. The exercise price must be at least equal to the market value of the company's shares on the date of grant.

Provided that the option holder exercises their option at least three years after the date of grant of the option, the exercise of the option should be free from income tax and national insurance contributions. Capital gains tax is likely to arise on the disposal of the shares on the difference between the market value of the shares on the date of disposal and the exercise price paid for the shares.

10.3.8   Approved save as you earn option scheme

The save as you earn (SAYE) scheme is an all employee option arrangement, which means that all employees of a company must be offered the opportunity to participate in it on similar terms. Options granted under a SAYE Scheme are linked to a three or five year savings contract under which the employee makes savings from their net pay at weekly or monthly intervals in order to fund the option exercise price. The maximum monthly saving is £250. The exercise price can be set at a discount of up to 20% to the market value of the company's shares on the date of grant.

Exercise of the option more than three years after grant will generally be free from income tax. Capital gains tax is likely to arise on disposal of the shares on the difference between the market value of the shares on the date of disposal and the exercise price paid for the shares.

10.3.9 Approved share incentive plan

The share incentive plans (SIP) is an all employee share acquisition (not option) arrangement. Employees may acquire shares in up to four ways:

(i) via the purchase of up to £1,500 shares per annum from their gross pay (partnership shares);

(ii) via the company matching the purchased shares with free shares at a maximum of two free shares for each purchased share i.e. a maximum of £3,000 (matching shares);

(iii) via the company awarding up to £3,000 of shares per annum for no payment (free shares); and

(iv) via investing dividends received on his partnership, matching and free shares to a maximum of £1,500 per annum (dividend shares).

Shares acquired under a SIP must all initially be held in a form of UK resident employee benefit trust established specifically to operate in conjunction with the SIP. Once the shares have been held in the SIP for at least five years they can be sold free from income tax, national insurance contributions and capital gains tax.

10.4 What additional company law issues may be relevant?

The Widget option plan is a common and relatively straightforward plan structure, and the company law implications are therefore likely to be limited to those addressed above. Companies sometimes adopt more complex structures, which can give rise to other company law implications, and these are also addressed in the next section.

This section addresses some specific company law issues that can arise depending on how the plan is structured as follows:

(i) How do companies typically source shares for the purposes of employee share plans?

(ii) What company law issues arise when establishing an employee benefit trust (EBT)?

(iii) What additional issues arise when shares are issued partly paid in share plans? Sourcing shares for an employee share plan.

10.4.1   How can shares be sourced?

Share awards or options can be satisfied by a company either by issuing new shares or by using existing shares. Both are considered below.

10.4.1.1   *Issuing new shares*

Where new shares are issued to satisfy awards, this dilutes the holdings of existing shareholders. Many companies, in particular listed companies, therefore agree a limit with their investors on the number of new shares which may be issued to satisfy employee share awards.

As discussed later in this chapter, companies are prohibited from issuing shares for less than their nominal value.

10.4.1.2   *Existing shares*

Until December 2003, companies were unable to purchase and hold their own shares and therefore companies which wished to hold their own shares in order to satisfy employee share awards had to establish an EBT to act as the holding vehicle.

Since 1 December 2003, listed companies have been able to purchase their own shares and hold them as treasury shares (subject to the limitations below). Private companies continue to need an EBT to hold their shares, and many listed companies continue to have EBTs for this historic reason.

10.4.1.3   *Treasury shares*

Since 1 December 2003, UK incorporated companies whose shares are included in the Official List or traded on AIM (or a European Economic Area stock exchange) have been permitted to purchase their own shares and hold these as treasury shares in accordance with sections 162A to 162G of the Companies Act 1985.

A maximum of 10% of the issued share capital can be held in treasury (section 162B of the Companies Act 1985) and the shares must be purchased out of distributable profits (section 162A of the Companies Act 1985). While held in treasury the shares have no voting or dividend rights (section 162C of the Companies Act 1985).

When shares are held in treasury, a company may use the shares to satisfy awards made to employees under an employees' share scheme, or sell or cancel the shares (section 162D of the Companies Act 1985).

Approval from shareholders by way of ordinary resolution is required for the purchase of shares to be held as treasury shares. The resolution must specify the maximum number of shares which may be purchased and the authority can be given for a maximum of 18 months.

It is proposed that the provisions on treasury shares will be replaced from 1 October 2009, but no significant changes will be made to the position outlined above.

10.4.2 What company law issues arise when establishing an employee benefit trust (EBT)?

EBT is a term commonly used to describe a discretionary trust for the benefit of employees, former employees and possibly also their spouses and dependents.

The trust is created by vesting trust property in the trustees and the execution of a trust deed which sets out the powers and duties of the trustee. The trust fund is normally created by an initial payment to the trustees of a lump sum, often £100.

There are various aspects of company law which need to be considered both prior to establishing an EBT and in relation to the ongoing operation of the EBT, as follows:

(i)   formation;

(ii)   who should act as trustee?

(iii)   defining the class of beneficiaries;

(iv)   directors' meetings; and

(v)   funding the EBT.

10.4.2.1 Formation

An EBT is formed by the execution of a trust deed between the company establishing the EBT (typically referred to as the sponsoring company) and the trustee. The trust deed sets out the trustees' powers, duties and the relationship between the trustee and the company.

The first point to check is whether the sponsoring company has the power to establish the EBT under its memorandum and articles of association, and the comments made in relation to the issue of corporate capacity in 10.2.2.1 apply equally here.

10.4.2.2 Who should act as trustee?

The trustee will generally be a corporate entity which is either a subsidiary company of the sponsoring company or an independent trust company. Where the EBT is intended to be non-UK tax resident, the trustee will typically be an independent trust company incorporated outside the UK, the directors of which will be resident outside the UK.

If the trustee is a subsidiary company of the sponsoring company, section 23 of the Companies Act 1985 is potentially relevant. This provides that a company cannot be a member of a company which is its holding company, and any allotment or transfer of shares in a company to its subsidiary is void. However, there is an exemption where the subsidiary is only holding shares in its capacity as trustee and is not a beneficiary of the trust. These provisions are retained in section 138 of the Companies Act 2006.

10.4.2.3 Beneficiaries

The beneficiaries of an EBT will generally be employees, former employees, their spouses, civil partners, children and step children under the age of 18. This is to ensure that the EBT is an employees' share scheme for company law purposes and that the exemptions from certain requirements of company law referred to throughout this chapter are available to it.

This means that a non-executive director would not be within this class of beneficiaries, since non-executive directors would generally be office holders, rather than employees.

10.4.2.4 Directors' meetings

A director who is interested in a contract with the company is under a duty to declare their interest at the board meeting at which the contract is discussed under section 317 of the Companies Act 1985. Each executive director is likely to be interested in the establishment of an EBT as each executive director would potentially be within the class of beneficiaries. Each executive director should therefore declare their interest to the board meeting.

The articles of association should also be checked to confirm whether directors are able to vote on matters in which they have an interest. If not, unless non-executives outnumber the executive directors, the board meeting which considers the establishment of the EBT may not have sufficient directors in attendance to take place. New provisions on the regulation of directors' conflicts of duties and interests are introduced by the Companies Act 2006 and are discussed in more detail in chapter 2.

10.4.2.5 Funding the EBT

The EBT needs to be funded by the sponsoring company (or a third party) in order to acquire shares. Typically, funds are provided by the sponsoring company in the form of a contribution (an outright gift) or a loan. The EBT then either subscribes for shares or purchases shares in the market, or does a combination of these.

The company must have power to fund the EBT, and the comments made in this chapter on corporate capacity in section 10.2.2 will apply equally here.

The sponsoring company must ensure that the funding of the EBT does not amount to illegal financial assistance and the relevant comments made in section 10.2.2.7 will need to be carefully considered.

If the EBT is subscribing for shares, the comments made above in section 10.2.2 in relation to authorised share capital and authority to allocate shares will also need to be considered.

10.4.3 When were the restrictions on making tax free payments to directors and on dealings by directors in share options repealed?

The Companies Act 2006 has already repealed two provisions that were relevant to the remuneration of directors. This took effect on 6 April 2007 as a result of section 1177 of the Companies Act 2006. The first of these, the prohibition on tax-free payments to directors contained in section 311 of the Companies Act 1985, also restricted the ability of companies to be able to calculate payments to directors by reference to the amount of income tax payable by that individual. The intention of the provision was originally to prevent directors taking advantage of their position by arranging for their companies to enter into open-ended and potentially unquantifiable liabilities to meet whatever tax might be due on a particular benefit. However, potentially, it had application in circumstances where there was no aggressive tax planning involved. An example was internationally mobile directors who were tax-equalised. This involves remunerating executives by reference to the tax rates of the country from which they are on assignment, so they are in the same after-tax position as they were prior to the international secondment. The change makes such structuring easy to do.

The second repealed provision is that the prohibition on directors dealing in share options under sections 323 to 327 of the Companies Act 1985. This prevented directors from, for example, buying options over shares in their companies. Given that most options granted under share option plans are non-transferable, this relaxation is unlikely to have much practical effect in the short term. However, it may be relevant for companies considering tradeable option plans.

10.4.4 What additional issues arise where the arrangements compromise partly paid shares?

Senior employees and directors of companies are sometimes subject to a minimum shareholding requirement, particularly those of listed companies.

This is part of the strategy used by companies to align the interests of those individuals with the shareholders of the company. The cost of acquiring these shares at their full market value may be prohibitive for those individuals, and this is one reason that partly paid shares may be issued. Alternatively, consideration may be given to making a loan (see below). The following questions are addressed here in connection with the issue of partly paid shares:

(i)   What constitutes partly paid shares?

(ii)   Could the issue of partly paid shares be unlawful financial assistance?

10.4.4.1   *What constitutes partly paid shares?*

Under section 100 of the Companies Act 1985, shares cannot be allotted at a discount to their nominal value. So, for example, a company with shares which have a nominal value of £1 cannot accept less than £1 as a subscription for a share. However, it is possible for shares to be partly paid, which means that the shareholder is liable to pay the full nominal value of the shares, but does not actually do so until the company requires the unpaid capital. When a call is made, the capital has to be paid by the relevant shareholders. The articles of a company generally provide for the ability to issue partly paid shares and the procedure that applies in calling for unpaid capital. This can contain an ultimate sanction of forfeit of the relevant shares if the call is not met within the stipulated period.

In addition, when the shares are issued, companies can require that not only the nominal value of the shares, but also a premium, is payable. If that is the case, the same principles of calling for full payment, set out in the previous paragraph, apply to unpaid premium as it does to unpaid nominal.

There is an additional restriction that applies to public companies; section 101(1) of the Companies Act 1985 specifies that:

> "a public company shall not allot a share except as paid-up at least fully as to one-quarter its nominal value and the whole of any premium on it."

This means that, generally, public companies may not leave the premium on any allotted share capital unpaid. However, if shares are allotted in pursuance of an employees' share scheme with the definition of section 743 of the Companies Act 1985, then there is an exemption to this under section 101(2) Companies Act 1985 (see section 10.2.2.2). Companies should exercise caution in this area as partly paid shares allotted to an individual may not constitute a scheme for this purpose.

Whether or not a share is paid-up can depend on the detailed structuring of the arrangement. For example, if an individual is issued shares and does not pay the full nominal value of those shares, but at the same time promises to pay the outstanding amount in the future, the shares would be deemed to be fully paid under section 738(2) of the Companies Act 1985, which states that:

> "...a share in a company is deemed fully paid-up...if the consideration for the allotment...is an undertaking to pay cash to the company at a future date."

It is very important to note that the issue of partly paid shares to individuals as a result of their being an officer or employee of a company, has potential tax implications for both the individuals and the company, and these should be taken into account when deciding whether to issue partly paid shares.

From 1 October 2009 the provisions mentioned above are replaced with the following:

(i)   Section 100 of the Companies Act 1985 with section 580 Companies Act 2006;

(ii) Section 101 of the Companies Act 1985 with section 586 Companies Act 2006; and

(iii) The definition of 'paid-up' in section 738(2) of the Companies Act 1985 with that in section 583 of the Companies Act 2006.

10.4.4.2   *Could the issue of partly paid shares be unlawful financial assistance?*

As stated in section 10.2.2, there is a general rule that a company may not provide financial assistance to buy its own shares. The question here is whether the fact that employees or directors do not need to pay full nominal value for the shares until called at a later date is itself financial assistance. The definition of financial assistance includes at section 152(1)(a)(iii) and (iv) of the Companies Act 1985:

> "financial assistance given by way of a loan or any other agreement under which any of the obligations of the person giving the assistance are to be fulfilled at a time when in accordance with the agreement any obligation of another party to the agreement remains unfulfilled, or

> ...any other financial assistance given by a company the net assets of which are thereby reduced to a material extent or which has no assets..."

The language used implies that the assisting needs to be a separate action from the acquisition. However, when shares are allotted partly paid, this is one and the same action, to which the company and the director or employee are both party. That the shares are issued partly paid is merely a term of the allotment of the shares. Furthermore, in issuing partly paid shares, a company does not reduce its net assets. It therefore seems a reasonable conclusion that issuing shares partly paid to directors or employees is not financial assistance. In the case of share plan arrangements that fall within the Companies Act 1985 definition of employees' share scheme, an exemption will be available, but if this not the case, care should be taken.

It is proposed that the financial assistance provisions at section 152 of the Companies Act 1985 will be replaced from 1 October 2009 by section 677 of the Companies Act 2006, which contains no significant changes from its predecessor (insofar as they apply to public companies). For private companies, the statutory prohibition is abolished.

10.4.5 Can a company provide finance to a director or employee to help meet the cost of acquiring shares?

As mentioned above, as an alternative to issuing partly paid shares to enable an employee or director to meet the cost of acquiring shares, a company may consider making a loan to that individual. Whilst there have not been any company law barriers to this in relation to employees, loans to directors were restricted under the Companies Act 1985.

This is an area that has already been subject to change by the Companies Act 2006. Under sections 330 to 342 of the Companies Act 1985, there was a general prohibition on loans and related dealings between a company and its directors. There were a number of exceptions, including where the loan was for an aggregate amount not exceeding £5,000.

These changes were introduced by sections 197 to 214 of the Companies Act 2006 with effect from 1 October 2007 and include:

(i) the removal of the current general prohibition on loans to directors;

(ii) replacement of this with a requirement (for all companies) to secure shareholder approval; and

(iii) an increase in the ceiling of the exception for small loans from £5,000 to £10,000.

For public companies (and private companies associated with them) there are provisions also requiring shareholder approval for quasi-loans and credit transactions in relation to directors, and loans to connected persons. A range of other detailed changes was also made and those are discussed in chapter 2.

As a result of these changes loans to directors are now permitted in principle. However, companies should ensure that they follow the necessary formalities. In particular, care should be taken when structuring employee incentive and remuneration arrangements so that loans to directors are not made without first securing shareholder approval.

10.5 What other technical issues arise when setting up or operating employee share plans?

10.5.1 How do securities laws apply?

Major changes to both the legislation and regulation of financial services and investment activity in the UK were introduced from 1 December 2001. Broadly, the Financial Services and Markets Act 2000 provides that:

(i)   a person may not carry on a regulated activity in the UK unless they are authorised to do so, or are exempt from regulation; and

(ii)   a person must not, in the course of business, communicate an invitation or inducement to engage in an investment activity unless that person is authorised, or the content of the communication is approved by an authorised person.

Given that share-based incentive plans include an investment element, i.e. that employees are becoming owners of shares, and so taking on the risks inherent in being a shareholder, the Financial Services and Markets Act 2000 needs to be considered when implementing and operating incentive plans.

Regulations issued under the Financial Services and Markets Act contain various exceptions to the Financial Services and Markets Act 2000 prohibitions, including a number that may be relevant to the operation of employee share plans. However, not all activities carried out in connection with employee share plans will be within these exceptions. The detailed structure, manner of operation and form of communications issued in relation to an arrangement will need to be checked for Financial Services and Markets Act 2000 implications. In some circumstances, certain share plan activities will need to be carried out by an authorised person, or approved by one. There are criminal penalties for breach of some provisions of the Financial Services and Markets Act 2000.

Where international share plan arrangements are in operation, the equivalent legislation in the other countries where share plan participants are based will need to be considered too.

Another securities law issue to be considered is the European Union Prospectus Directive (EUPD), which was implemented in the UK from 1 July 2005. Broadly, this governs public offers of securities made in the UK and the rest of the European Economic Area (EEA), and in the UK replaced the previous regulation in this area, the Public Offers of Securities Regulations 1995. The purpose of introducing the EUPD was to provide a harmonised set of disclosure rules, seeking to ensure that adequate and equivalent disclosure standards are in place in all EU member states in relation to the issue of certain securities, which includes shares in a company.

An offer of securities caught by the EUPD requires the issue of a prospectus. In relation to this prospectus, the EU PD provides for a 'single passport', aimed at reducing the administration and cost for companies of issuing new shares. Once approved by the regulatory authority in one member state, a prospectus has to be accepted everywhere else in the EU.

The EUPD can potentially apply to employee share plans. It contains a number of exclusions and exemptions, including one that applies to shares offered to current or former employees of a company that has already listed on a regulated market within the EU securities regulated by the EUPD. To qualify for this exemption, a company must make available to employees a document containing information on the number and nature of securities involved, other details of the offer, and the reasons for it.

However, there is no blanket exemption for employee share plans, as there are different implications for different types of plan, and it is possible that some plans could require a prospectus. The EUPD therefore needs to be carefully considered by companies offering shares to employees in the UK or elsewhere in the EEA.

10.5.2 Are the arrangements subject to pay as you earn and national insurance contributions liabilities?

When employees or directors receive benefits through employee share plans, these are generally subject to income tax, although there are certain exceptions to this, such as the HM Revenue & Customs-approved plans outlined above. The timing and amount of benefit, and the associated income tax, will depend on a number of factors including the tax residence status and personal circumstances of the employees and the structure of the arrangement. The UK tax legislation that applies to share and share-related benefits acquired by employees and directors is complex, and companies should ensure they are aware of the treatment of their particular plans and arrangements.

The income tax liabilities that arise may be subject to withholding through the pay as you earn (PAYE) system. Where it exists, this obligation generally falls on the employing company and there are penalties for both employee and employer if it is not operated within the requisite timescale. Companies should ensure they have the contractual right under the rules of the relevant plans to withhold income tax from their employees for the purposes of PAYE. There are circumstances where PAYE does not apply, and some private companies may not need to operate it in relation to their share plans.

Where PAYE applies, the benefits under share plans are also generally subject to national insurance contributions (NICs), although again this will depend on a number of factors relating to both company and employee. The timing of the NICs charge usually (but not always) mirrors the timing of the income tax charge. Where it applies, the company will be liable to pay employer's NICs at the prevailing rate and also to withhold employee's NICs.

It is not uncommon for UK companies to overlook their PAYE and NICs obligations, particularly where they are the subsidiaries of overseas parent companies that are making grants under the relevant share plan. HM Revenue & Customs is paying increasingly close attention to this area, so companies are advised to seek appropriate professional advice and implement processes to ensure their statutory obligations are met.

10.5.3   What are the tax reporting obligations?

There are tax reporting obligations for both employer and employee in relation to share-based incentive plans.

Employees and directors are subject to an obligation to enter details of all taxable income and gains on their annual self-assessment tax returns. This will include the income tax liabilities that arise in connection with share plans, as well as capital gains tax to which they might be subject to on the sale of shares acquired through these plans. There are limited circumstances in which an employee is not currently required to report, for example the exercise of a HM Revenue & Customs-approved share option in circumstances which qualify for income tax relief. Companies often invest time and resources in educating their employees about the tax consequences and reporting obligations attaching to their share-related benefits, which can help enhance the value put on those benefits by the employee population.

The employer company also has a range of reporting obligations. There are different HM Revenue & Customs forms that must be prepared and submitted after the end of each tax year for different types of plans. It is important that companies have robust systems in place to collect the quite detailed information that needs to be included in these forms, and penalties can be imposed for late submission of the forms, or for incorrect or omitted information. In addition to these forms, there are various PAYE and NIC-related forms that share benefits need to be included on.

10.5.4   Are there any other issues to consider?

In addition, there are a range of other issues that companies should address, which are outlined below.

Data protection legislation regulates the collection, manipulation and sharing of information relating to employees, among other things. Data often needs to be collected in relation to employee share plans. The way that this is done, and the manner of transmission of information should be checked to ensure it falls within the relevant legislation, particularly in the context of an international group.

There are employment law implications of share plans that should be considered. For example, companies should be careful not to inadvertently give employees a contractual right to receive options or share awards each time it makes a grant. The rights given to employees by legislation such as the Transfer of Undertakings (Protection of Employment) Regulations SI 1981/1794 and the Age Discrimination Regulations 2006, need to be taken into account in structuring share plan arrangements and drafting of plan rules.

Corporate tax issues need to be considered. Companies will generally want to be able to claim a tax deduction in relation to their share plans, but again the structure of the plan and other factors will influence this. There could also be transfer pricing and value added tax issues to check, particularly if there is an international group.

The manner in which the arrangements are structured will also influence the accounting for the share plan. Under International Accounting Standards, most share plans will result in a charge to the profit and loss account, but the exact structure will influence the amount and timing of that charge. It is therefore important to look at the likely accounting implications for share incentive arrangement at the design stage.

10.6 What disclosures are required in respect of employee share plan awards?

Provision is made for the disclosure of directors' salary and share interests in sections 412, 420 and 416 (respectively) of the Companies Act 2006. These apply from 6 April 2008 in relation to accounting periods commencing on or after that date. The requirements previously found in schedules 6, 7, and 7A to the Companies Act 1985 are now found largely unaltered under the new legislation Schedules 5, 7 and 8 of the Large and Medium-sized Companies Accounts Regulations. The restated requirements are described below.

10.6.1 What disclosures are required of directors' emoluments?

10.6.1.1 *Schedule 5 to the Large and Medium-sized Accounts Regulations (Schedule 5) – aggregate emoluments*

Schedule 5 requires more detailed disclosure of directors' emoluments for quoted companies than unquoted companies. For these purposes, companies listed on AIM are not regarded as quoted companies. 'Emoluments' is defined widely to include salary, fees, bonuses and certain other benefits.

Employee incentive share plans

Quoted companies

The information required to be disclosed in a company's annual report and accounts in respect of share incentives held by directors of quoted companies is set out below:

(i)   the aggregate of the gains made by directors on the exercise of share options;

(ii) the aggregate of the amount of money paid to or receivable by directors under long-term incentive schemes in respect of qualifying services; and

(iii) the net value of assets (other than money and share options) received or receivable by directors under such schemes in respect of qualifying services.

Definitions of long-term incentive schemes and qualifying services are set out in the glossary.

For the purposes of Schedule 5, any of the above information, other than the aggregate gain on the exercise of share options, is treated as disclosed if it can be ascertained from other disclosed information. As quoted companies are required to provide more detailed information than that required by Schedule 5 under Schedule 8 (see below), the only additional disclosure to be shown is the aggregate gain on the exercise of share options.

Salary or share options granted to directors should be treated as received for services as a director.

Unquoted companies

Unquoted companies are not required to disclose the aggregate gains on share options nor the net value of any shares received under long-term incentive schemes. However, they must disclose the number of directors exercising options and receiving shares under long-term incentive schemes in respect of qualifying services.

Where the total of the aggregate emoluments of directors, together with the aggregate amount of money paid to or receivable by directors for the year exceeds £200,000, an unquoted company must disclose:

(i)   the aggregate amount paid or receivable under long-term incentive plans that is attributable to the highest-paid director; and

(ii) the amount of net assets received or receivable under long-term incentive schemes by the highest-paid director.

Disclosures by unquoted companies under Schedule 6 will normally be shown in the notes to the accounts.

10034

10.6.2 What disclosures are required of director's shares emoluments?

10.6.2.1 Schedule 7 to the Large and Medium-sized Accounts Regulations (Schedule 7) – directors' interests

Schedule 7 provides for disclosure in the notes to the accounts of directors' shareholdings in accordance with the register of directors' interests. As there is no requirement under the Companies Act 2006 for companies to maintain a register of directors' interests, this disclosure is no longer relevant for unquoted companies from 6 April 2008.

However, the Listing Rules require companies listed on the London Stock Exchange to disclose in their annual report beneficial and non-beneficial interests in shares of any individual who has been a director during the year, and any changes between the end of the financial year and a date no more than one month or less before the AGM. In addition, companies must include a statement showing all disclosures made to the company in accordance with section 793 of the Companies Act 2006 (notice requiring information about interests in shares).

10.6.3 What is the remuneration report required to contain?

10.6.3.1 Schedule 8 to the Large and Medium-sized Accounts Regulations (Schedule 8) – content of remuneration report

It is important to note that the requirement to prepare a remuneration report under section 420 of the Companies Act 2006 is limited to quoted companies. Companies listed on AIM and unlisted companies therefore do not need to prepare a remuneration report or make the disclosures prescribed by Schedule 8.

Schedule 8 requires companies to disclose the following information in respect of directors' share incentive arrangements (part of which is not auditable and part of which is auditable).

10.6.3.2 Statement of remuneration policy (not auditable)

In the statement of remuneration policy, the company must give a detailed summary of the performance conditions to which any outstanding option or share award, held by directors between the end of the financial year and the AGM, are subject.

This disclosure is generally interpreted as applying to options or awards outstanding at the end of the financial year under review. Any performance conditions that have been met need not be included in this disclosure. Similarly, any awards that are held by an individual who was a director during the year under review, but who is not a director in the period from the end of the year to the AGM, do not need to be included.

The policy statement must also:

(i)   explain why the performance conditions were chosen;

(ii)   summarise the methodology for assessing whether they have been met;

(iii) explain why those methods have been selected;

(iv)   summarise any factors used for external comparison;

(v)   provide the identity of other companies with which any such comparison will be made;

(vi)   describe any significant amendments proposed to the terms of any outstanding options or awards; and

(vii) explain why any option or award is not subject to performance conditions.

In addition, the policy statement must explain the relative importance of the fixed and variable elements of each director's remuneration package. This disclosure will generally involve the assessment of expected values or outcomes in different performance scenarios for long-term share incentives.

For financial years beginning on or after 6 April 2009, Schedule 8 introduces a new requirement for a statement in the remuneration report of how pay and employment conditions or the company and its group's employees were taken into account when determining director's remuneration (see Chapter 5, section 5.5.1.).

10.6.3.3   *Disclosure of share options and long-term incentives (auditable)*

Schedule 8 requires the detailed disclosure of share options and long-term incentive awards held by an individual who is a director of the company at any time during the financial year (in tabular format). The requirements differ slightly between those for options and those for long-term incentive awards and it is generally better to detail both types of award in separate tables. Information that is required to be disclosed in the auditable part of the report may not be imported by cross-reference to the non-auditable part.

10.6.3.4   *Share options*

The following information must be disclosed in respect of share options that were granted to a director for qualifying services (see glossary at end of this section):

(i)   the number of shares the subject of a share option:

- at the beginning of the year or, if later, at the date of appointment; and

- at the end of the year or, if earlier, on the cessation of appointment.

(ii) differentiating between options having different terms and conditions;

(iii) identification of options granted, exercised, expired and unexercised in the year and those the terms and conditions of which have been varied; and

(iv) for each option that is unexpired at any time during the year,

- the price paid for its award;

- the exercise price;

- the date from which it may be exercised; and

- the date on which it expires.

The information must be set out in a table. In addition, there must be:

(i) a description of any variation made in the terms and conditions of an option in the year; and

(ii) a summary of any performance conditions to which the option is subject (including any variations thereto in the year).

If an option is exercised in the year, the remuneration report must state the market value of the underlying share at the date of exercise. Disclosure must also be made of the share price at the end of the year, and the highest and lowest prices during the year for all shares which are the subject of options.

In order to avoid excessively long disclosures, companies may adopt the concise method of disclosure so that all share options held by a director are aggregated and a weighted average exercise price and range of dates for exercise are disclosed. However, options that are granted or exercised (or have had their terms varied) during the year may not be aggregated. Options that are 'in the money' and options that are 'out of the money' must be separately aggregated.

10.6.3.5 Long-term incentive awards

The following information must be disclosed in a table for 'scheme interests' under long-term incentive plans:

(i) details of scheme interests held by the director at the beginning of the year or, if later, at the date of appointment;

(ii) the following details of scheme interests awarded to the director during the year:

- number of shares;
- share price at award date; and
- details of performance conditions.

(iii) details of the scheme interests held at the end of the year or, if earlier, at the date of appointment;

(iv) for each of the above:

- the end of the performance or vesting period; and
- a description of any variation in the terms and conditions of the scheme interest during the year.

(v) for scheme interests that have vested in the year:

- the number of shares;
- award date;
- share price of the shares at award date;
- share price at the date of vesting;
- details of performance conditions;
- the amount of any money; and
- the value of any other assets.

If long-term incentive awards are structured as nil or nominal value options, they should be disclosed in the options table described above. However, best practice suggests that the market value of the underlying shares at the grant date should also be disclosed in these circumstances.

The main differences between the disclosure requirements for options and those for long-term incentive awards are:

(i) there is generally only a requirement to disclose performance conditions in respect of long-term incentive awards for the years in which they are awarded;

(ii) it is only necessary to disclose options that are granted by reference to qualifying services, but any long-term incentive awards that have performance or vesting periods spanning a director's period of office should be disclosed;

(iii) it is not a requirement to disclose the year end and range of share prices for long-term incentive awards; and

(iv) there is no concise method of disclosure for long-term incentive awards.

10.6.4 What do the Listing Rules require?

The FSA LR require companies admitted to the Official List to include in their annual reports a statement of their policy on the granting of options and long-term incentive awards, explaining and justifying any departure from that policy in the year under review and any change in policy from the previous year.

10.6.5 What do accounting standards require?

International Accounting Standard 24 requires companies to disclose in a note to the accounts the aggregate cost of providing share-based payment to key management personnel in the financial year. (See glossary in section 10.6.7).

10.6.6 What disclosures are required under the Disclosure and Transparency Rules?

It is a requirement of the FSA DTR, which apply to companies admitted to the Official List, that notification must be made to the company by Persons Discharging Managerial Responsibilities (PDMRs) (and anyone connected to them) of any transactions conducted on their own account in the company's shares or derivatives of the company's shares. Notification must be made within four business days of the transaction.

A company receiving notification of a transaction by a PDMR (or his connected person) or under section 793 of the Companies Act 2006 must notify a regulated information service by the end of the following business day.

10.6.7 Glossary

'Key Management Personnel' means those persons having authority and responsibility for planning, directing and controlling the activities of the entity, directly or indirectly, including any director (whether executive or otherwise) of that entity.

'Long term incentive scheme' means any agreement or arrangement under which money or other assets may become receivable by a director and which includes one or more qualifying conditions with respect to service or performance which cannot be fulfilled within a single financial year; and for this purpose the following shall be disregarded, namely:

(i)   bonuses, the amount of which fails to be determined by reference to service or performance within a single financial year;

(ii)   compensation for loss of office, payments for breach of contract and other termination payments; and

(iii)   retirement benefits.

'Persons discharging managerial responsibilities' means a director of the company (assuming a UK company) or a senior executive of the company who has regular access to inside information relating directly or indirectly to the issuer and has power to make managerial decisions affecting the future development and business prospects of the company.

'Qualifying services' means a person's services as a director of the company and his services at any time while he is a director of the company:

(i)   as a director of an undertaking that is a subsidiary undertaking of the company at that time;

(ii)   as a director of any other undertaking of which he is a director by virtue of the company's nomination (direct or indirect); or

(iii)   otherwise in connection with the management of the affairs of the company or any such subsidiary undertaking or any such other undertaking.

'Scheme interests' means an interest in a long-term incentive scheme that is an interest in respect of which assets may become receivable under the scheme in respect of qualifying services dealing with share plans on a transaction.

10.7   What issues arise when a company with an existing share plan is to be acquired?

Employee share plan issues form an increasingly important area for investigation, consideration and review by both vendor and purchaser in any corporate transaction. This section addresses these issues by looking at the implications of the purchase of a parent company.

In the context of a transaction, for the purchaser employee shares and rights to shares can represent a cost in the short term. For example, if the transaction should cause options to be exercisable then:

(i)   more shares may have to be issued to satisfy these options and the purchaser may be compelled to buy those additional shares; and

(ii)   this may trigger substantial employer national insurance charges.

It is also important that the purchaser identifies the various obligations and liabilities that may arise in relation to the employee shares. When target company employees acquire shares in the course of a transaction, it is likely that this will generate pay-as-you-earn obligations. Failure to meet these obligations or secure recovery of employee tax charges within statutory time limits can lead to additional charges and costs for the employer.

For the purchaser, employee equity can represent a cost in a much longer-term sense. Target company employees may expect that, post-acquisition, they will be awarded shares or options equivalent in value to those enjoyed pre-acquisition. That may create a new cost for the expanded group:

(i)   in the demand on limited share capital;

(ii)   in funding employee share acquisitions, for example the cost of purchasing shares on the market to satisfy options; and

(iii)   in the resulting accounting charges that could arise.

But there may be some countervailing benefit. If conditions for statutory corporation tax relief are satisfied when options are exercised or share awards vest, substantial relief may be available. It is not unknown for this relief to be equal to almost half of the total purchase price paid by the purchaser in a takeover. However, securing that relief can sometimes require detailed planning and consideration.

For this reason purchasers and vendors must be alert to the potential risks and benefits of employee equity in the course of the transaction; purchasers must seek detailed information on employee equity in the target, and carefully consider the material provided. Vendors should take great care in the information they provide.

This section looks at the processes and issues that can arise in the course of a transaction in relation to employee share plans.

10.7.1   How can the share plan impact on the transaction?

Before the impact of a transaction on employee shares, options and awards can be assessed, it is important to understand the nature of the transaction and the means by which it will be effected.

Most acquisitions generally involve:

(i)   the acquisition of the whole of the issued share capital of a company that is a stand-alone entity or the parent company of a group;

(ii)   the acquisition of the whole of the issued share capital of a subsidiary company;

(iii)   the acquisition of something less than a controlling interest in the target company; or

(iv)   the acquisition of a business, i.e. plant, equipment and other assets, as a going concern, as distinct from, say, the shares in the company that owns that business.

Note that understanding what is 'control' or a 'controlling interest' can be important for corporate law and tax reasons. For most purposes, a party can be taken to have 'control' when they hold a majority of the voting share capital or if they have a right to appoint a majority to the board of directors or a person who will hold majority voting rights on the board.

Most share plans contemplate that certain transactions will impact on subsisting awards or options made under the plan, generally either by causing rights to crystallise or lapse. Commercially, a takeover is something of a watershed and the general rationale in designing share plans is that a transaction of this kind should allow employees to realise their gains and the new owners to develop new share plans without restriction by what has been done in the past.

The way in which a transaction takes place is important. For example, the acquisition of the whole of the issued share capital of a target company could be by:

(i)   A private agreement – that is, one contract signed by the purchaser and vendor shareholders. This is usually found where the target is an unlisted entity with a relatively small number of shareholders.

(ii)   A general offer – that is, literally, an offer to each shareholder capable of acceptance and by acceptance constituting a contract to purchase subject to certain conditions. This is usually found where the target is a listed company with a large number of shareholders.

(iii)   A scheme of arrangement – a complex procedure administered by the court under Companies legislation and, generally, involving an arrangement which has been approved by a majority of shareholders (and, perhaps, creditors) binding all shareholders (and creditors). These are also usually found where the target is a listed company (see sections 895 to 901 of the Companies Act 2006, which replaces sections 425 to 427A of the Companies Act 1985 from 6 April 2008).

(iv)   A 'squeeze-out' – UK companies legislation enables a shareholder with at least 90% of the company to compulsorily acquire minority shareholder interests in certain circumstances. The market refers to this situation as a 'squeeze out' (sections 974 to 990 of the Companies Act 2006, which came into effect from 6 April 2007). This is discussed in more detail in Chapter 9.

The difficulty is that some plans will provide for the crystallisation or lapse of rights where a transaction is effected by a 'general offer' but not a 'scheme of arrangement'. So a change of control as a result of a 'general offer' might trigger a right to exercise an option, but not where the change of control arises as a result of a scheme of arrangement. That said, many corporate transactions are so complex that one may be able to identify some 'general offer' within a 'scheme of arrangement'.

10.7.2 Which provisions of a share plan are particularly relevant?

The next step is to review the rules, terms and or conditions of the plan or scheme or other arrangement. It is important not to just consider the more formalised arrangements. Both purchaser and vendor must consider any situation where officers, employees, former officers or employees or any spouse may hold shares, or a right to shares, and review any document which may relate to that arrangement.

It is difficult to provide a comprehensive guide on what should be looked for and why, as this will depend on the particular circumstances. However, as a general rule, the focus should be on establishing how many shares may be acquired by employees in the course of the transaction and what will be the cost of the employee share plans in the form of:

(i)   the additional cash cost of purchasing shares acquired by employees;

(ii)   national insurance charges; and

(iii)   any corporation tax relief, indemnities or exercise price payments which can be offset against this cost.

10.7.2.1   *Those provisions dealing with the vesting or exercise of rights in the ordinary course*

Share award or option plans will set out the circumstances in which shares will 'vest' in the employee (i.e. when a share is transferred into the employee's ownership or ceases to be forfeitable), and when an option will become exercisable.

It is quite common that vesting or exercise will not arise until after the expiry of a given period; and the satisfaction of some other precondition.

This other precondition might be an exit, such as the takeover or flotation of the parent company or the sale of the parent company's business, or a performance related target, e.g. profitability or share value.

The questions to be asked in this situation include the following: has the precondition been satisfied and any time period expired at the time of the transaction? Where the precondition is an exit does this include the forthcoming transaction? However, what if it is a performance related target? And what if, notwithstanding the precondition, the relevant time period has not expired?

10.7.2.2 *Any provision which will trigger an early vesting or right to exercise on a takeover – the impact of performance conditions*

Most well drafted plans, schemes and other arrangements will allow for the possibility that there is a takeover at some point prior to the expiry of the relevant time period or the satisfaction of the other precondition. It is common to find that this takeover will to some extent trigger an early vesting or right to exercise, even if neither the precondition nor the time period has been satisfied.

Practice in this area has altered over recent years. Older plans tend to provide that a takeover will trigger 100% vesting or a right of exercise in respect of all the shares subject to the award or option, regardless of whether or not time periods or other preconditions have been satisfied. However, later investor guidelines have discouraged terms which waived the requirement to satisfy the performance target on a takeover. So with more recent arrangements it is common to find either that:

(i)   on a takeover, early exercise or vesting will still be subject to the expiry of the relevant period of time and satisfaction of performance target, i.e. so unless the target is satisfied in full and the correct period has expired the award will not vest and the option will not be exercisable notwithstanding the takeover; or

(ii)   on takeover, early exercise or vesting will be subject to an adjusted time period and performance target, i.e. the performance target will be measured over a shorter period (usually the time elapsed since the award was made or option granted) and if this adjusted target is satisfied, an equivalent proportion of the award or option will be exercisable or will vest.

Frequently, there is a further discretionary power in the plan rules which allows the board of directors to permit an award to be exercisable or vest on some different basis where there is a takeover. This power tends to be utilised in one-off circumstances for particular individuals rather than for all employee participants in the plan.

10.7.2.3 *If there is a provision which permits option exercise or award vesting in the course of the takeover, at what point will the right to exercise or vesting arise?*

Historically, when most share plans provide for early exercise or vesting, the trigger point will usually be a change of control arising as a result of a private agreement, general offer, scheme of arrangement, or squeeze-out.

In other words, the right to exercise, or vesting, does not arise until control has passed to the purchaser. At that point, the target company will be a subsidiary and the option will then be exercisable or the award will vest. However, more recent plans tend to include a provision which allows exercise or vesting immediately prior to a change of control (usually at the discretion of the board). This is for the purposes of being able to secure statutory corporate tax relief for the vesting or exercise (Schedule 23 of the Finance Act 2003), for which certain conditions must be met. These include that the shares acquired must either be of a class listed on a recognised stock exchange or they must be shares in a company that is not under the control of another company (unless that company is listed on a recognised stock exchange).

For example, if an unlisted company is the subject of a takeover by another unlisted company and options are exercised or awards vest, on a change of control, then the employee has acquired shares in a company that is now a subsidiary. In this event, the condition will not be satisfied and there will be no corporation tax relief.

10.7.2.4 *Provisions dealing with the payment of an exercise price or other payment as a condition of exercise or vesting*

Most option plans provide for the payment of an exercise price as a condition of exercise of the option. Clearly this payment is an important part of the exercise process. But it also has other significance:

(i)   any cash paid to the target company needs to be factored into assessing the net cost of the employee share plan to the purchaser, the purchaser will, after all, be acquiring a company which holds this cash; and

(ii)   where the exercise price exceeds the likely sum to be paid per share, then the employee is unlikely to enforce his right to a share. The award or option in question may then be factored out of any calculations assessing the overall cost of the acquisition.

However, it is also important to identify the party to whom any such payment is to be made.

Usually the payment is made to the party which granted the award or option. However this is not always the company. Sometimes an employee benefit trust will be established and this trust will grant the award or the option and any exercise price is paid to it. The problem is that if the cash is paid to the trust then, broadly, that trust can only apply the cash for the benefit of beneficiaries (generally employees, former employees and certain members of their respective families), and in meeting costs and expenses.

In other words the cash is then locked into the trust, so its use is confined to certain narrow purposes, i.e. to benefit the beneficiaries of the trust. The cash could be applied for post acquisition incentive arrangements (though not to relieve the company of any existing obligations or liabilities, as the trust would then be acting be acting in breach of its terms), but the amounts involved can sometimes exceed immediate and planned needs. That cash may then be trapped in the trust.

10.7.2.5 Provisions which allow the employer company (or the employer's parent company) to recover PAYE and NIC from the employee

When an option is exercised or an award vests in the course of a takeover so that there is (broadly) a gain subject to income tax, then this will be subject to PAYE. In general, this requires the employer to account for the income tax to HMRC and recover the income tax from the employee. This must be done within certain time limits, failing which there may be additional income tax, interest and penalties.

The problem for the employer company is that, in both a practical and legal sense, it will be primarily responsible for payment of the income tax charge to the tax authorities, even though this is the employee's liability. Unfortunately the law does not give the employer a general right to recover this tax from the employee. For this reason most well drafted plans will include some provision by which:

(i)   the employee agrees to indemnify his employer against any obligation to pay income tax under PAYE in relation to his award or option; and

(ii)   the employer may withhold any income tax subject to PAYE from the proceeds of sale of any shares or may sell certain of the employee's shares sufficient to meet that income tax charge.

In most cases:

(i)   where the employment continues; or

(ii)   where the employer company will control distribution of the proceeds of sale of the employee's shares (sold in the course of the takeover),

the presence or absence of these provisions will not be an issue. If the company controls any distribution, then any PAYE is deducted and the employee paid the balance. An existing employee is unlikely to dispute this, as they will not in practice have suffered a loss.

Generally, however, it is only where the proceeds of sale are paid directly to the employee, or where a PAYE liability was not properly identified, that the point will prove important.

Whenever any income charge arises, subject to PAYE, then there will also be a NIC charge for both employer and employee. Further the employer will be responsible for accounting to HMRC for both charges. For this reason it is also important to identify the existence of a provision in the plan documentation which will entitle the employer to recover any employee NIC from the employee.

10.7.2.6 *Provisions requiring that the employee meet any employer's NIC*

Legislation allows the employer to pass to the employee award or option holder the cost of any employer NIC arising on exercise or vesting of an award or option. But this must be with the agreement of the employee award or option holder. One way to do this is to ensure that an obligation to meet the employer NIC cost is incorporated in the terms and conditions of the award or option. It is therefore important to establish whether any provision has been included in this arrangement and, if so, whether it has been correctly and effectively structured. The existence of such an arrangement could influence the amount of employer's NIC arising as a result of exercises and vestings in consequence of a change of control, and this should be factored into the total acquisition cost.

10.7.2.7 *Provisions which specify when the award or option will lapse*

When considering an award or option it is necessary to determine whether, and when, the award or option will lapse. This is important for two reasons:

The lapse date sets out the time period in which the exercise or vesting process in the course of the takeover must be completed by. Where there are a large number of participants in the plan, it may take time to ensure that all relevant documentation is completed and payments made. The lapse date is the end date by which this process must be finalised and allows appropriate planning. Failure to complete the exercise or vesting process prior to the lapse date may mean the employee has no entitlement to shares. The employees' loss may have consequences for the employer both in terms of employee motivation and incentivisation and liability for that loss.

The purchaser will want to ensure that after the acquisition is completed it does not find an individual is entitled to acquire shares in the target company. If, say, an option was to be exercised some months after the target had become a 100% subsidiary of the purchaser, this could involve some administrative inconvenience and cost. In a worst case scenario, the issue of these shares would prejudice the target's status as a 100% subsidiary with other unforeseen consequences.

This problem can be dealt with by making an amendment to the articles of association of the target company so as to require any shares acquired on exercise of an option to be immediately transferred to the parent.

10.7.3 Will the issue of additional shares impact on the overall acquisition cost?

Once the plans and particulars of employees holding shares, or some right to shares identified, the parties may be in a good position to estimate how many shares are likely to be acquired by employees. The next step is to establish where these shares are going to come from.

Practically, in most cases, the shares will be issued from the company's authorised but unissued share capital. This raises two questions.

Does the company have sufficient unissued share capital to meet this requirement? This question will only apply until the concept of authorised share capital is removed by Companies Act 2006 from 1 October 2008.

If all these additional shares are issued how will this impact the cost of the acquisition?

Where the acquisition involves an offer being made per share, then the issue of additional shares will increase the cost of the acquisition to the purchaser. This will generally be the case where the target company is listed. However, where the target is unlisted and the acquisition is by a private agreement, the purchase price tends to a fixed total offer with the vendors being left to divide these proceeds of sale between themselves.

Sometimes the company will set up a 'warehouse' of issued shares to satisfy options or other awards. This could be by means of either an employee benefit trust or shares held in treasury.

The consequences for the purchaser though will be very different. If the shares are held by an employee benefit trust, then the purchaser will probably buy those shares as part of the acquisition. If the employee benefit trust holds more shares than are necessary to satisfy these awards and options, this can lead to cash being locked into the trust.

But where the shares are held as treasury shares and these shares are transferred to the employee, this can increase the cost for the purchaser. Arguably, when the purchaser acquires the company they acquire the treasury shares held by that company. But if the treasury shares are transferred to the employee, the purchaser must then acquire those shares and this increases the cost of the acquisition if the acquisition is by an offer of a given sum per share.

10.7.4 Is there any alternative to award vesting or option exercise – rollovers and cash cancellation?

There may be alternatives to simply allowing the employee to exercise his right to a share and to sell that share in the course of the transaction. Further, these alternatives may offer certain tax and or other cost efficiencies. For example, where the employee has a right to a share in the target company, the employee may be invited to waive that existing right in return for an equivalent right over shares in the purchaser.

Under UK law this rollover will not generally involve any other immediate tax or cash cost. However, this may not be acceptable to the purchaser. For example, where the purchaser is a private equity fund, the purchaser is unlikely to be interested in offering employees any entitlement to an interest in the fund. In addition, it may not be attractive to the employee, who may consider that they have worked for their own gain and are now entitled to some benefit. To accept a new award or option defers this benefit and entails some risk that this award or option may never be realised.

Whether or not a rollover is acceptable will usually be a matter for the employee. Some plans include a provision to the effect that where a rollover is offered to the employee, the employee must accept or face the loss of his original award or option. When most plans are prepared, the parties tend to take the view that a takeover involves some turning point in the affairs of the company and the careers of individual participants, who should be given some opportunity to realise a gain.

A cash cancellation can also offer efficiencies. This is broadly where an employee is paid a cash sum in return for surrendering a right to shares. For example, say the employee had an option to acquire shares worth £1,000. But to exercise the option the employee must pay 99p per share, i.e. a total of £990. The employee makes a gain of £10 on exercise, subject to PAYE and NIC and acquires his shares. Those shares are sold to the purchaser for £1,000. The purchaser is paying £1,000 for those shares and is acquiring a company with an employer national insurance charge on the £10 gain.

It may be simpler and more cost effective for the purchaser to offer the employee £10 in return for the employee waiving his right to the shares. The £10 payment will still be subject to PAYE and NIC but the purchaser avoids having to purchase the employee's share for £1,000.

Of course, the employee is not bound to accept this offer so if this route is to be pursued it requires effective communication between purchaser and employee.

10.7.5 What is the entitlement of 'lay' employees?

For the purchaser and vendor it may be necessary to consider the position of the more important individuals holding shares or rights to shares, that is, the people who might be key to the organisation's success post-acquisition. Clearly, some employees may have extremely valuable shares or share options and the realisation of their gain in the course of a transaction might leave them with a substantial cash sum.

It is common to find that a substantial cash gain, and a takeover with all the change and other dislocation that can follow, is enough to make some individuals reconsider their career or lifestyle. Identifying these people beforehand as those likely to leave the organisation offers the chance of action being taken to reduce that risk by, for example:

(i)   post-acquisition incentives; or

(ii) a restriction on the ability to realise cash in the course of the takeover, e.g. some deferred payment terms, so payment of the gain is spread over a period of time.

This matter is relevant to both vendor and purchaser. The vendor's consideration may be linked to post-acquisition performance and the loss of key employees may prove detrimental. On the other hand, the purchaser does not want to find the value in the acquired company disappearing after completion as key staff resign.

10.7.6   What process should be adopted for securing the support of employee award and option holders?

Once the various rights and alternatives have been considered, a decision will be reached on the way forward. Communication with those holding awards or options is likely to be needed.

Communication with participants is usually carried out in the form of a letter which typically covers matters such as:

(i)   the execution of documents necessary to exercise or vest awards;

(ii) authority to sell shares and remit proceeds of sale less any amounts due in respect of PAYE or NIC; or

(iii) if relevant, the offering and acceptance of some alternate offer to vesting or exercise, such as rollover and/or cash cancellation.

However, it is important for the parties to consider whether this letter is enough to secure an appropriate response from employees. A more sophisticated communication process may be more successful in this respect.

10.7.7   What issues arise where the transaction is a sale and purchase of a business as a going concern rather than a share purchase?

Most transactions will involve the sale and purchase of shares as a company passes from the control of one party to another. Occasionally, however, the transaction will involve the sale and purchase of certain assets of that company which taken together constitute a business, i.e. there is no dealing in the company's shares.

This sale and purchase of a business creates different issues from the sale and purchase of a company's shares. Generally, by statute (Transfer of

Undertakings (Protection of Employment) Regulations SI 1981/1794) those individuals employed in the business cease to be employees of the vendor company and become employees of the purchaser. Although much depends on the terms and conditions of the given plan, scheme or other share arrangement, this tends to have the following result.

With an option plan or a plan where shares vest in the employee, there will usually be certain provisions which detail the individual's entitlement when they cease to be employed by the company or a member of the company's group – this sale of business means the individual will cease to be such an employee. It should be checked how the plan rules will treat the individuals entitlement in this instance.

A large number of plans tend to treat an individual who ceases to be an employee on a sale of business as a good leaver who will, to some extent, retain their existing entitlement. If they are treated as a bad leaver under the plan rules, their right or entitlement will usually lapse and that is an end of the matter.

If the employee's right or entitlement survives, the ensuing problems tend to focus on ensuring the collection and recovery of PAYE and NIC (where relevant).

Chapter 11

Corporate simplification

11.1 Introduction 11001
11.2 What is a dormant company? 11002
    11.2.1 What is the difference between legal and commercial
          dormancy? 11003
    11.2.2 Why are so many dormant companies retained? 11003
    11.2.3 What risks are associated with retaining dormant
          companies? 10004
    11.2.4 Why do latent issues remain? 11004
          11.2.4.1 Internal transfer of trades 11005
          11.2.4.2 Leasehold properties 11006
    11.2.5 How long do 'long-tail' liabilities last? 11008
11.3 What are the methods of removing dormant companies? 11008
11.4 Striking-off 11009
    11.4.1 Which legislation governs applications for a striking-
          off? 11009
    11.4.2 What preconditions for striking-off must be met? 11009
    11.4.3 What preliminary actions should a company take before
          making a striking-off application? 11010
          11.4.3.1 Preliminary notification of intention to strike-
                  off 11010
          11.4.3.2 Simplification of the company's balance sheet 11011
    11.4.4 What is the procedure for making a formal striking-off
          application? 11011
          11.4.4.1 Submission of Form 652A 11012
          11.4.4.2 Registration of the application for a striking-
                  off 11012
          11.4.4.3 Statutory notification of application to
                  strike-off 11012
    11.4.5 Who has the power to object to the strike-off
          application? 11013
    11.4.6 When is a company formally dissolved? 11014
    11.4.7 Can a company be restored to the register after its
          dissolution? 11014
    11.4.8 What liabilities can directors incur? 11014
    11.4.9 What changes are made by the Companies Act 2006? . . 11015
    11.4.10 Are there situations where a striking-off would not be
          suitable? 11015
          11.4.10.1 Relationship with creditors 11015
          11.4.10.2 Distribution of assets to members 11016
          11.4.11 What is *bona vacantia?* 11017

         11.4.11.1 Extra-statutory concession C16 11018
11.5 Members' Voluntary Liquidation 11019
    11.5.1   When can a company be put into Members' Voluntary
           Liquidation? 11019
    11.5.2   What are the key elements of the liquidation process? . . 11020
           11.5.2.1 Final board meeting 11021
           11.5.2.2 Declaration of Solvency 11021
           11.5.2.3 General meeting of members 11024
    11.5.3   When is the liquidator appointed? 11024
    11.5.4   How will the liquidation be publicised? 11025
    11.5.5   What is the effect of the liquidation on corporate status
           and ongoing maintenance requirements? 11025
           11.5.5.1 Statutory filing and compliance 11025
           11.5.5.2 Tax affairs 11026
           11.5.5.3 Shareholdings in the company 11027
    11.5.6   What is the role of a liquidator when conducting the
           liquidation? 11027
           11.5.6.1 What powers does a liquidator have? 11028
           11.5.6.2 What are the statutory duties of a liquidator? 11028
           11.5.6.3 What happens if creditor claims take more than
                   a year to resolve? 11030
    11.5.7   When can distributions be made? 11030
    11.5.8   How is the liquidation concluded? 11031
    11.5.9   When is the company finally dissolved? 11032
11.6 Comparison between striking-off and Members' Voluntary
    Liquidation 11032
11.7 Conclusion 11033

Corporate simplification

11.1 Introduction

Research on the FTSE100 shows that more than 50% of their subsidiaries are dormant confirming that most groups have dealt with their dormant companies by simply leaving them alone. There are two principal reasons for this. First, it is not as easy to eliminate dormant companies as you might imagine – for the reasons discussed further below. Second, there is rarely a compelling commercial reason for doing so and other issues can too easily push 'good housekeeping' off the agenda in favour of more urgent matters. The following benefits can be realised, however:

(i)   reduction of ongoing maintenance costs;

(ii) release of locked in capital – of particular relevance to regulated entities; and

(iii) unwinding of intra-group balances which may be required to be interest bearing under the transfer pricing tax regime.

In addition, there is a growing trend to simplify and standardise business operations and then to seek to align legal entity structures more closely to the streamlined supply chain. Such simplification projects range from truly transformational projects such as seeking to transfer all activities out of separate legal entities into branches of a European Company (S.E) to the relatively mundane and familiar intra-group mergers of duplicative business activity. What these approaches have in common is that they do not in themselves result in the elimination of legal entities; they simply change the status of those entities from active to dormant. There is an inherent absurdity in having a lean and clean operational structure represent itself to the external world through a tangled web of inactive companies and in practice there is a tipping point where dealing with dormant companies becomes a business issue. This chapter will steer you through it. It discusses the two most common methods in which dormant companies can be dissolved (namely by application for striking-off or by liquidation) and the respective merits of each option.

In summary, this chapter will address the following topics:

(i)   why so many dormant companies are retained and associated issues;

(ii) an examination of internal transfers of trades and leasehold properties as examples of issues that can prevent a commercially dormant company being considered legally dormant; and

(iii) methods of removal: striking-off and Members' Voluntary Liquidation.

Corporate Simplification Funnel

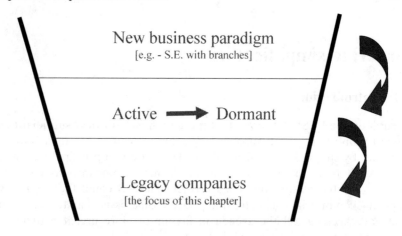

The Companies Act 2006 makes minor changes to these methods, in particular:

(i) the changes to resolutions and shareholder meetings generally introduced on 1 October and discussed in chapter 3 will apply;

(ii) from 1 October 2009 a public company will be capable of being struck off (at present striking-off only applies to private companies); and

(iii) from 1 October 2009 an application can be made to restore a company which has been dissolved (either by striking-off or pursuant to a liquidation) within six years of the dissolution. At present, applications may be made within 20 years of a dissolution by way of strike-off and two years of a dissolution following a liquidation.

11.2   What is a dormant company?

When applied to a company, the term dormant means there have been 'no significant accounting transactions' during the last financial year.

The Registrar of Companies has confirmed that the following do not count as significant transactions:

(i) payment for subscriber shares on the incorporation of the company;

(ii) payments made to the Registrar of Companies for standard compliance activities, such as change of name or filing annual returns; and

(iii) payments made to the Registrar of Companies in relation to accounts filing penalties.

If the company complies with the requirements for dormancy it may file an abbreviated set of accounts without the need for these to be subjected to an audit. Professional accountants do not therefore need to be involved with the preparation or submission of the dormant accounts.

11.2.1 What is the difference between legal and commercial dormancy?

The rules for dormant companies are very restrictive and refer only to the financial status of corporate entities. However, what happens when a company has no accounting entries, but still guarantees property leases or contracts from their former trading activities?

These organisations are commercially dormant as they have no accounting entries, but as they retain legal obligations which may crystallise at some stage in the future they would not be considered to be legally dormant.

In general, when a company ceases to trade it becomes dormant in a commercial sense, but it will not be legally dormant if it has outstanding debtors, creditors and bank accounts.

To be legally dormant, a company must fully wind down its affairs – realise debtors, pay creditors, close bank accounts, deregister for VAT, finalise tax affairs and so on. With regard to contractual obligations, these must either be transferred or end through the passage of time.

The company should also no longer have any contingent or existing legal liabilities associated with its former trade. Only when this is the case the company can safely be eliminated.

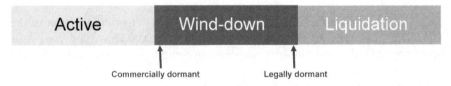

11.2.2 Why are so many dormant companies retained?

There are many reasons why groups retain dormant companies. These include the desire to prevent competitors using the company name or because the entity is (or was) part of a group tax planning structure.

Unfortunately, many others entities are retained because the existing management has no knowledge of what the dormant entity did and are therefore unwilling to disturb the *status quo*.

This lack of knowledge often arises because the dormant entities were historic acquisitions often as part of larger commercial transactions. In these circumstances the due diligence process will invariably have concentrated on the key trading company being acquired rather than any associated dormant companies.

It is common for any knowledge to be in the heads of individuals rather than on files and, therefore, is at risk if those individuals leave the organisation.

These knowledge problems are not restricted to entities which have been acquired. There are often institutional reasons why dormant entities are retained. In general, companies rarely review the status of their group structure or the individual components within it unless there is a compelling reason. As a result, group structures can become increasing complex over time and dormant entities, initially retained for a commercial reason, are not reviewed and dealt with when their original purpose has expired.

The net effect of the above factors is that groups are left not knowing what they may find if they seek to eliminate the companies and have appetite to either waken sleeping dogs or to spend the time and effort in regaining the knowledge that has been lost. This results in increasing large and complicated group structures and creates an impression of undue complexity.

11.2.3   What risks are associated with retaining dormant companies?

Following the catastrophic failure of the US energy giant Enron and the subsequent demise of the WorldCom communications group, many large companies have faced questions about the integrity of their existing structures.

There has been increasing pressure from corporate analysts, shareholders and in many cases management boards themselves for simple, straightforward corporate structures where every entity has a place and a purpose.

This US-led reappraisal of corporate structures is also gaining traction in the UK, with management teams not wanting to divert key resources from their operating activities to administer non-trading companies. There is also growing recognition that latent issues, which would traditionally have been ignored in dormant companies, are possible sources of actions for individuals using no win/no fee legal arrangements.

11.2.4   Why do latent issues remain?

Issues which prevent a commercially dormant company being considered legally dormant relate primarily to the common law concept of privity of contract. This legal doctrine, provides that, as a general rule, the burden of contract terms (i.e. the obligation to perform) cannot be transferred to another party without the consent of the original contract parties. The benefit (namely the right to receive payment or to sue for performance) can generally be transferred unless there is an express restriction in the contract.

This means that where an active trading company has become commercially dormant it may still retain contractual liabilities which might crystallise at a future date.

For example:

A company ('A') was formerly a manufacturing business which entered into a number of long-term supply contracts under which it provided various warranties as to the quality of the goods. It has since largely ceased to trade and wishes to transfer the residual business to an affiliate ('B') as a preliminary to dissolution. It is still owed some money by its customers.

Under the business transfer agreement A will be able to assign its debtors to B but it will not be able to assign the potential liability under the warranties unless the customer to whom they were given expressly agrees and, ideally, agrees to substitute B for A (this is a novation).

In many cases obtaining individual novations is impractical and therefore most business transfer agreements will provide for B to discharge A's liabilities and to indemnify A for any warranty claims. Notwithstanding this practical solution, A will remain primarily liable to the customers under the trading agreement.

This is particularly relevant in the following circumstances:

(i)   internal transfer of trade between group companies; and

(ii)   where entities have previously owned leasehold properties.

11.2.4.1   *Internal transfer of trades*

Transfers of trade between group companies are common where the group has:

(i)   acquired subsidiaries from third parties and subsequently amalgamated the business with their existing trades; or

(ii)   rendered subsidiaries dormant before eliminating them.

In both these scenarios, privity of contract is an important consideration. Generally the documentation prepared for the sale of the business will transfer not only the benefit of existing key commercial contacts to the transferee, but as consideration for the transfer will also make the transferee responsible for settling outstanding trade creditors.

In general, this type of internal transfer is commercially expedient and it is rare for creditors to complain as long as their debts are ultimately settled. This informal transfer of benefits and burdens only tends to occur when the group seeks to formally eliminate the transferor company before those debts are settled.

Until this stage, external creditors are likely to be unaware of the purported transfer of their debts and will often assume they are continuing to trade in the normal way. In an extreme situation, this belief only shifts when the creditor's finance team note that their debtor is shown as in liquidation and take action to try and mitigate their position. It should be noted that where such transfers have occurred, the transferor company will still have primary responsibility for the payment of the creditor obligations associated with the former business. As a result, the directors of the transferor would not be able to sign the declaration confirming that the company has no assets or liabilities but rather would have to notify all of the trade creditors of their intention to remove the entity and hope that no objections were received.

11.2.4.2   Leasehold properties

The impact of privity on leasehold properties contracts is even more pronounced and now has statutory weight through the operation of the Landlord and Tenant (Covenants) Act 1995 (LTCA) which came into force on 1 January 1996.

The position of leases before and after this date differs significantly, with the effect on leases prior to the introduction of LTCA (old leases) being far more wide reaching.

Old leases

The general position for old leases is that the original tenant remains liable for the covenants in the lease (including payment of rent and dilapidations) throughout the full term of the lease. This applies irrespective of how many times the lease has been assigned or transferred since the group company was the main tenant.

The practical impact of this rule is that, notwithstanding the fact that the lease may have been transferred by the company, if the existing tenant defaults on payment of rent or other clauses, the landlord may look to the company in its capacity as signatory to the head lease for settlement. The company is then required to seek redress from the defaulting tenant.

In order to avoid this continuing chain of liability, a company must seek a formal novation of their agreement with the landlord. If granted, this has the effect of extinguishing the liabilities under the original contract. The new tenant will enter a new contract under which they will become liable as if they were the original tenant.

However, obtaining a release from the contract usually requires a commercial compromise to be reached with the landlord and invariably requires some payment to be made. The ultimate amount of any such payment will be affected by factors such as the covenant of the entity to which the company wishes to transfer its lease, the commercial awareness of the landlord, and ultimately the state of the property market at the time of the transaction.

New leases

The introduction of the Landlord and Tenant (Covenants) Act 1995 (LTCA) brought about what was initially thought to be a softening of the old leases situation. Under the new legislation, when a tenant assigns its lease, its liability under the contract ceases and, in effect, they achieve the same outcome as a formal novation of the contract under the old legislation.

However, in order to provide landlords with some protection, the LTCA also introduced the concept of the Authorised Guarantee Agreement (AGA). This is an agreement between the landlord and the departing tenant in which the departing tenant guarantees that the new tenant will continue to meet the obligations of the lease and, if the new tenant fails to do so, the departing tenant will meet the obligations directly.

The practical effect of the landlord requesting an AGA as condition of agreeing to the transfer of the lease, is that it puts the company in a similar position to the old legislation with a continuing contingent liability to the landlord. The only difference is that the AGA is not a continuing obligation, and in the event that the new tenant subsequently seeks to transfer the lease again, it would then provide a new AGA for that transfer which would supersede the original one provided by the company.

Example

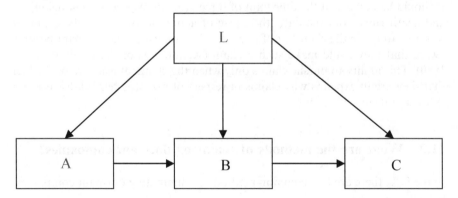

(1)   *A assigns lease to B*

If A provides an AGA to L then it would be liable to L if B defaults under the lease

(2)   *B assigns the lease to C*

If B provides an AGA to L then A's liability to L will cease. If it does not then A's liability will remain.

11.2.5 How long do 'long-tail' liabilities last?

One of the key issues to be considered when looking at the contingent liabilities of companies due to be wound down, is whether the potential claims are subject to any particular time bar specified in either the Limitation Act 1980 or any other legislation.

The Limitation Act 1980 sets out a plethora of time limits including those relating to commercial contracts. The most common commercial time limits are set out below:

Section 19	Normal commercial contracts	6 years
Section 8	Speciality contracts (e.g. under seal)	12 years
Section 24	Enforcement of judgments	6 years
Section 11	Personal injury and death	3 years
Section 2	Tort (other than above)	6 years
Section 19	Arrears of rent	6 years

In addition to the above, there are specific timescales contained in other legislation which may also impact on companies being wound up, for example, a 10-year longstop applied by section 4 of the Consumer Protection Act 1987.

It should be noted that the time limit of three years in respect of personal injury and death runs from the date 'the cause of action accrued' (i.e. the claimant was able to make the claim) or, if later, the date on which the claimant became aware that they could make such a claim (section 4(1) of the Limitation Act 1980). This ability to pursue claims only when the claimant is aware of the fact that they are ill explains why claims in respect of asbestos related diseases are still being dealt with today.

11.3 What are the methods of removing dormant companies?

In the UK, there are two common methods of eliminating dormant companies, namely:

(i) voluntary dissolution (section 652A of the Companies Act 1985) (striking-off); and

(ii) members' voluntary liquidation (MVL) in accordance sections 89 – 94 of the Insolvency Act 1986 and the associated insolvency rules.

Both options result in the elimination of the corporate entity but, otherwise, they are very different processes in terms of both their risk profiles and their costs.

11.4   Striking-off

Applications for voluntary striking-off are the most common way of removing unwanted UK companies. The Registrar of Companies received over 3.5 million applications in the last three years, compared with less than 10,000 solvent liquidations for the same period.

Whilst the process for voluntary striking-off is subject to minor alteration in the Companies Act 2006, the basic provisions remain the same as in the Companies Act 1985. The existing provisions are considered below, and the amendments in the new Act are set out at the conclusion of the summary.

11.4.1   Which legislation governs applications for a striking-off?

The ability for companies to voluntarily apply to the Registrar of Companies to be struck off was introduced into the Companies Act, as section 652A, by the Deregulation and Contracting Out Act 1994. Prior to this, entities were only removed from the register if they failed to file accounts, comply with other administrative procedures or were the subject of a formal insolvency process.

The introduction of section 652A provided companies with a more proactive method of managing their group structures without the need for formal insolvency procedures. It was not, however, designed to replace insolvency procedures where there were creditors or outstanding issues relevant to the company and the legislation put in place a number of restrictions designed to ensure the striking-off provisions were not used in a way which would otherwise avoid the need to deal with these issues prior to the company being removed.

11.4.2   What preconditions for striking-off must be met?

To protect creditors, the following preconditions must be met before an application for striking-off can be submitted to the Registrar of Companies:

(i)   the company must be a private company (although see changes in the 2006 Act at the conclusion of this section);

(ii)   In the previous three months before an application is made, the company must not have:

- traded or carried on any business;

- changed its name;

- obtained value for goods which it would otherwise have sold in business;

- engaged in any other activity except one necessary or expedient for making:

- the striking-off application;
- settling the company's affairs; or
- meeting a statutory requirement such as advice on the application process.

The company cannot apply to be struck off if it is the subject of, or likely to be the subject of:

(i)   any insolvency proceedings; or

(ii)   a compromise or voluntary arrangement with its creditors (under the terms of section 425 of the Companies Act 1985 which will become section 895 *et seq* of the Companies Act 2006).

11.4.3   What preliminary actions should a company take before making a striking-off application?

If a company meets these preconditions it can make an application to strike off. However, before doing this, it should undertake the following preliminary actions.

11.4.3.1   *Preliminary notification of intention to strike-off*

Where the company has recently ceased trading and, as a result, is likely to still have creditors, it is advisable to warn them of the company's intention to strike off so that any issues they have with the proposed elimination of the company can be addressed amicably. Failure to do this could result in the creditors lodging a formal objection to the dissolution after they become aware of the application. This could delay matters for some months.

In addition to the general commercial creditors, it is critical that HM Revenue & Customs (HMRC) are advised separately of the proposed striking-off. In most cases, if the company meets the preconditions set out above, there are unlikely to be any tax issues which would cause concerns. However, where there has been active trading in the last year, HMRC will require a tax computation to be submitted to ensure the tax affairs of the company are up to date prior to the application for dissolution.

Failure to discuss the proposed strike-off application with HMRC, even when the company has been dormant for a significant period of time, may result in an objection being raised. If this occurs, the time period for the dissolution is likely to be significantly extended until either HMRC confirms to the Registrar that it is willing to allow the application to proceed, or the objection period elapses.

General notifications should also be given to any other parties the directors believe may have an interest. This can include bodies such as local authorities and trustees of any pension scheme to which the company belonged.

In addition to the notifications mentioned above, it is advisable that appropriate advice is sought from professionals before any striking-off applications are made because the formal dissolution of a company:

(i)   may crystallise tax charges which may have otherwise have been avoided;

(ii)   may cause an event of default or crystallise an acceleration provision in extant commercial contracts;

(iii)   may crystallise underfunding liabilities in legacy-defined benefit pension schemes.

Note: These issues apply equally to planning for a MVL.

11.4.3.2   *Simplification of the company's balance sheet*

After the decision has been made to eliminate the company, it is key that the balance sheet is simplified as much as possible and that all residual assets are either transferred to the shareholders as dividends or sold and the cash paid as a dividend. Particular care should be taken at this stage to ensure that actions taken to simplify the balance sheet comply with appropriate accounting provisions (such as the need for distributable reserves to declare a dividend) and are tax efficient.

Even though these steps are preparatory to a striking-off, all of the company law considerations discussed in chapter 10 will continue to apply (payment of dividends, reduction of capital, undervalue transactions etc.).

If the above action is not undertaken, or not completed prior to the application for dissolution being submitted, any residual assets held by the company will transfer to the Crown as *bona vacantia,* or ownerless goods. Any credit balances remaining in bank accounts will be frozen and the residual value paid directly to HM Treasury Solicitor. The Treasury Solicitor may also call in debts, including inter-company debts, due to the dissolved company. This is discussed further in section 11.4.10 below.

11.4.4   What is the procedure for making a formal striking-off application?

In general, the process of applying for a voluntary striking-off should consist of the following fundamental steps:

(i)   meeting of the board of directors to consider and recommend the striking-off process to the members of the company;

(ii)   general meeting of the members of the company to approve the directors making the striking-off application;

(iii) filing of the statutory form 652A together with the applicable filing fee; and

(iv)   post-filing notification procedures.

It is common for companies reading striking-off advice from the Registrar of Companies to forget that this advice concentrates heavily on the legislative provisions relevant to section 652A of the Companies Act 1985. It is therefore common for companies to overlook the need to hold both board and members meetings to consider the merits, or otherwise, of the application. This is particularly important for members whose rights in relation to the company will ultimately be extinguished following the application.

11.4.4.1   *Submission of Form 652A*

When the directors and members are content that the striking-off application is the most appropriate way to proceed, statutory Form 652A should be completed, signed and dated by:

(i)   the sole director, if there is only one;

(ii)   by both, if there are two; or

(iii) by the majority, if there are more than two.

This form confirms that the company has complied with the preconditions necessary for the application to proceed, in particular that the company has not traded or changed its name within the last three months and is not the subject to any insolvency proceedings or other compromise with its creditors.

Once completed, the form should be sent directly to the Registrar of Companies with a cheque for the filing fee.

11.4.4.2   *Registration of the application for a striking-off*

On receipt of the completed form, the Registrar of Companies will place a copy on the company's public file and an acknowledgement will be sent to the presenter's address shown on the form plus the company's registered office address. The Registrar will advertise the proposed striking-off in the *London Gazette* and invite objections to be submitted if any party feels aggrieved by the proposal.

11.4.4.3   *Statutory notification of application to strike off*

Within seven days of filing the complete Form 652A with the Registrar of Companies, the company should provide a copy of the form to the following interested parties:

(i)   members of the company (irrespective of the fact that they will be aware of the application from the general meeting);

(ii)   creditors of the company – including contingent and prospective creditors;

(iii)   employees;

(iv)   managers or trustees of any employee pension fund of which the company was participant of; and

(v)   any directors who did not sign the original Form 652A.

The notifications should be delivered to the relevant parties:

(i)   if they are an individual, to their last known address; or

(ii)   if they are a company or partnership, to their main place of business or registered office address.

Copies of the Form 652A should also be issued to anyone who becomes a member of any of the above classes after the original notification period. This should be undertaken within seven days of the person becoming a member of the class.

11.4.5   Who has the power to object to the strike-off application?

If the application proceeds without appropriate consultation or notification, any interested party may submit an objection to the Registrar of Companies. The objections must be made in writing and clearly set out the basis of the objection, together with any supporting documentation.

Objections tend to be for the following reasons:

(i)   the company has failed to comply with the preconditions necessary for the application;

(ii)   the directors have not informed the required interested parties;

(iii)   the declarations made by the directors on the statutory form are incorrect;

(iv)   there is a pre-existing or impending action being taken against the company for recovery of money; or

(v)   other legal action is being pursued against the company.

If, at any time, the directors become aware that they have, or are likely to, breach any of the critical conditions, they should withdraw their application for strike-off by filing a statutory form, 653(C).

11.4.6   When is a company formally dissolved?

If no objections are received and the Registrar of Companies is unaware of any reason to prevent the dissolution, he will publish a further notice in the *London Gazette* advising of the formal dissolution of the company. The formal date of dissolution will be not less than three months after his initial notice of intention to dissolve the company.

11.4.7   Can a company be restored to the register after its dissolution?

When a company has been formally dissolved following a voluntary striking-off application, any parties who should have been notified of the application can apply to the High Court for the company to be restored to the register. This previously had to be within 20 years but, as from 1 October 2009 the period is reduced to a period of six years from the date of dissolution (sections 1024 – 1025 of the Companies Act 2006).

The court has jurisdiction in hearing any restoration application and may order a restoration if it is satisfied that:

(i)   the claimant was not given appropriate notice of the striking-off;

(ii)   the striking-off application was in breach of the preconditions; or

(iii) the court feels it is just and equitable to order the restoration.

In the event that the company is restored to the register, the company will be treated as though it had continued in existence and never been struck off. The officers of the company at the date of the dissolution will be recalled to office and required to deal with the affairs of the company again. Any outstanding statutory filings, i.e. statutory accounts, annual returns and other documentation will be required to be updated. Penalties for late filing of accounts do not cover the period during which the company was dissolved. Late filing penalties will only accrue in respect of documents which were already late at the date of the dissolution.

11.4.8   What liabilities can directors incur?

There are a variety of penalties which may apply in striking-off situations. In particular, it is an offence for directors to:

(i)   apply for striking-off when the company fails to meet the preconditions and is therefore ineligible;

(ii)   provide false or misleading information in relation to an application for striking-off;

(iii) fail to provide copies of the application to all interested parties within seven days of the submissions of the application to the Registrar of Companies; or

(iv) fail to withdraw the application if the company becomes ineligible.

If found guilty of any of these offences the directors face a fine of up to £5,000 on summary conviction, or an unlimited fine if convicted on indictment. In addition, if the directors are deemed to have deliberately concealed an application for striking-off from interested parties they may be liable to up to seven years imprisonment, in addition to a fine.

Furthermore, if a director is ultimately found guilty of any of these offences, they may also be disqualified from acting as a director for up to 15 years.

11.4.9 What changes are made by the Companies Act 2006?

Sections 1003 to 1110 of the Companies Act 2006, do not fundamentally change the historic provisions surrounding striking-off applications. There are, however, a small number of amendments, the most important being the relaxation of the rules to allow for the dissolution of public limited companies. Section 652A previously restricted applications to private limited companies.

The Companies Act 2006 has not made any material amendments to the rules relating to *bona vacantia* or, ownerless goods other than those mentioned below. It is unlikely that public limited companies, which are required to have minimum share capital levels of £50,000 paid up by at least one quarter, will be suitable for striking-off without some form of capital reduction exercise.

The other key amendment introduced in the Companies Act 2006 relates to the dates within which the Crown must disclaim property which would otherwise belong to it as *bona vacantia*. This period is now three years from the date of dissolution.

11.4.10 Are there situations where a striking-off might not be suitable?

Although the process of applying for a striking-off is relatively straightforward and the costs and formalities associated with it are less than those required in a more formal insolvency proceeding, it is not a universally applicable way of eliminating companies. There are a number of commercial concerns that relate to both the company's relationship with creditors and the company's ability to distribute assets to shareholders.

11.4.10.1 *Relationship with creditors*

Although the statutory striking-off procedure is designed to ensure creditors are advised of the process, the only way in which creditors become aware of it is if the directors notify them or they see the Registrar of Companies' notice in the *London Gazette*.

In reality therefore, if the directors fail to recognise that a creditor exists, it is highly unlikely that anyone will pick up the striking-off application in time to make an objection. The company will then be faced with the risk of a restoration application. There are no other mechanisms for directors to draw the proposed application to the attention of the world at large.

The risk associated with this notification procedure is placed solely on the directors of the company and any breach, no matter how inadvertent, may render the directors open to a potential fine. This contrasts significantly with a liquidation where one of the key procedural steps is the statutory notification of the liquidation in both the *London Gazette* and other appropriate newspapers with the sole intention of bringing the process to the attention of those who may have had previous dealings with the company.

11.4.10.2   *Distribution of assets to members*

To avoid *bona vacantia* issues, one of the pragmatic steps which directors should consider undertaking prior to striking-off is the simplification of the balance sheet. This means the distribution of surplus assets to the members as far as possible. The simplest way of returning funds to shareholders is by way of a cash distribution.

When considering preliminary actions before making distributions directors must consider section 829 of the Companies Act 2006, which states that a company shall not make a distribution other than from profits available for this purpose. This means that the company must have sufficient distributable reserves to meet the dividend. The detailed requirements are discussed in chapter 10.

There are four exceptions to this general rule:

(i)   distribution by way of an issue of fully or partly paid bonus shares;

(ii)   the purchase of the company's shares out of capital;

(iii)   an approved reduction of a company's share capital; and

(iv)   a distribution of assets to the members of a company on its winding-up.

These exceptions have a common trait in that they protect the position of the creditors either by statutory procedures and notifications or the appointment of liquidators whose duty it is to protect and settle creditor claims before making a distribution to members. In all other cases, including striking-off, the company's share capital should remain intact and distributions only paid out of appropriate reserves. In contrast no reserves are needed where a distribution is made by a liquidator on the winding-up of a company.

If there are insufficient reserves to effect a cash distribution, then prior to an application for striking-off intermediate steps will have to be taken to return capital by some of the other methods discussed in chapter 10.

The effect of unlawful dividends

As mentioned above, distributions should only be made from distributable reserves. Section 277(1) of the Companies Act 1985 states that if a member receives an unlawful dividend, which they know, or ought to know is unlawful, they are liable to repay it.

If a member receives a dividend knowing there are no profits they will be required to repay it. Even if this is not the case, and the member was unaware of the profits position, section 277(2) of the Companies Act 1985 means they will be obliged to repay the dividend.

If a company distributes dividends which subsequently transpires to be unlawful, the company will not be able to divest itself of the cash or property it is seeking to put beyond the reach of the Crown. The company, and subsequently the Crown, will remain the beneficial owners of the property, with the recipient holding the assets in a constructive trust and liable to repay them.

11.4.11   What is *bona vacantia*?

In English law, property must belong to someone, either an identifiable person or a body. If legal ownership of assets cannot be established, it falls to the Crown to deal with them as an owner of last resort. Such property is known as *bona vacantia* and is generally dealt with by the Crown following the dissolution of companies or the death of intestate individuals.

In relation to company assets, section 654 of the Companies Act 1985 provides that where a company is dissolved, all property and rights vested in the company immediately before the dissolution are deemed to be and the Crown, via the Treasury Solicitor, either collects or disposes of the goods. The concept of *bona vacantia* is retained in the Companies Act 2006.

In addition to the Treasury Solicitor, *bona vacantia* can also be held by the Duchy or Lancaster and the Duchy of Cornwall if the registered office address of the company being dissolved is located in either of these two counties.

The Crown has traditionally taken a passive attitude to the collection of corporate *bona vacantia* goods and there has been little evidence to date of an active pursuit of such assets. However, in March 2007 the Treasury Solicitor's department issued an updated guidance note Form BVC17, 'Important notes on the Guidelines about Distribution of a Company's Share Capital' in which it clarified the department's stance on the collection of *bona vacantia* confirming:

"It has been recognised that it would be unreasonable for the Treasury Solicitor to expect that a company is put into formal liquidation when that would be uneconomic, especially bearing in mind that HM Revenue & Customs Extra Statutory Concession permits a distribution for tax purposes without the company having to incur the costs of a formal liquidation. It is therefore agreed with HM Treasury that if:

- a company has been struck off under either section 652A of the Companies Act 1985; and

- the shareholders have taken advantage of the extra statutory concessions C16; and

- the amount of the distribution is less than £4,000, then as a concession the Treasury solicitor will waive the Crown's right to any funds which were distributed to the former members prior to dissolution."

It appears the Treasury has set this level as it believes it represents the likely commercial costs of a straightforward liquidation process. Whilst it is helpful that the Treasury Solicitor has clarified the position regarding the minimum level at which it will ignore its rights to claim assets, the fact that it has placed a limit on this amount increases the likelihood that it will start to actively claim assets above this level.

For example, if a company targeted for elimination through striking-off has a balance sheet which has little or no ability to pay dividends to reduce the net asset position to below £4,000, there is a significant chance that these assets will be locked in the company or become *bona vacantia* on dissolution.

11.4.11.1   *Extra-statutory concession C16*

HMRC Extra Statutory Concession (ESC) C16 states that where a company is removed from the register, other than as part of a formal winding-up under the provisions of the Insolvency Act 1986, a distribution to members is treated for tax purposes as though it had been made in a winding-up and be treated as a return of capital rather than an income dividend.

In order to obtain this concession, the company must provide a number of assurances to HMRC that it will:

(i)   collect any outstanding debts;

(ii)   settle any outstanding creditors; and

(iii)   distribute any surplus funds remaining after the above to the members of the company.

In such circumstances, HMRC will treat the final payment to members as a capital distribution under section 122 of the Taxes and Capital Gains Act 1992, and not as an income distribution which would normally be disadvantageous for shareholder individuals.

Notwithstanding the above concession, and the dovetailing of the Treasury's position regarding *bona vacantia* assets of less than £4,000, there remains concern on the scope of the concession from a corporate law perspective.

The necessary pre-requisite for ESC C16 to be operative is that there is a return of capital to members other than via a winding-up. As discussed, distributions to members are generally only available to be paid from *profits available for the purpose*. Any distribution of assets worth more than £4,000, whilst effective for tax purposes, would fall into the remit of an unlawful dividend and potentially be liable to be claimed by the Crown.

Where the potential distribution to members is in excess of £4,000, there may be three solutions:

(i)   ignore ESC C16 and appoint liquidators to undertake a formal winding-up;

(ii) apply ESC 16 and ensure that the level of any unlawful distribution is minimised to the £4,000 cap, or if greater, accept that the excess over this amount is potentially at risk; or

(iii) consider using ESC C16 alongside a possible legal return of capital to members such as an authorised reduction in share capital or a purchase of own shares out of capital (See chapter 10 for further details).

11.5   Members' Voluntary Liquidation

A common alternative to striking-off dormant companies is to appoint liquidators to wind up the company under the provisions of the Insolvency Act 1986.

The process of liquidation is more protracted than striking-off and the process is controlled by an independent licensed practitioner, rather than the directors themselves. As a result, the costs of liquidation are invariably higher.

However, this additional expense may be justified when the company would benefit from the greater degree of flexibility available to a liquidator to make returns of capital without the need for appropriate accounting reserves.

11.5.1   When can a company be put into Members' Voluntary Liquidation?

The following analysis sets out some of the key features applicable to solvent liquidations in England and Wales. The procedure is similar in Scotland and

Northern Ireland, but references to the Insolvency Rules applicable in these territories are sufficiently different to fall outside the scope of this chapter.

Section 84 of the Insolvency Act 1986 confirms that there are three grounds under which a company may apply for a voluntary liquidation. These are:

(i) when the period fixed for the duration of the company by the articles expires, or an event occurs of which the articles provide for the company to be dissolved, and the company has passed a resolution requiring it to be wound up voluntarily;

(ii) if the company resolves by special resolution that it be wound up voluntarily; or

(iii) if the company resolves by extraordinary resolution that it cannot continue its business due to its liabilities and it is advisable to wind up.

When it is decided to bring solvent companies to an end, the appropriate liquidation process is that of an MVL. Unlike striking-off, MVL is a process rather than an event and can take anywhere between three and 12 months from commencement to conclusion.

MVL Timeline

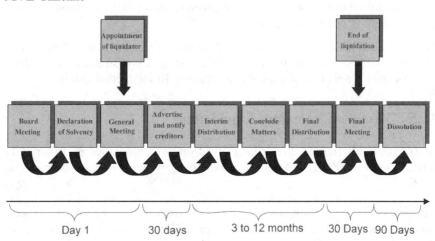

11.5.2 What are the key elements of the liquidation process?

There are two key steps involved in placing a company into liquidation:

(i) a final meeting of the board of directors is held to swear the statutory declaration of solvency and convene the final general meeting of members; and

(ii)   the final general meeting of members is held to approve the appointment of the liquidators and place the company into liquidation.

11.5.2.1 Final board meeting

A final meeting of the board of directors is generally held to begin the liquidation process. At this meeting, the directors consider the financial status and future of the company and confirm they will recommend to the members that the company be placed into MVL.

As a prerequisite of entering MVL, the directors will also consider and approve a Declaration of Solvency confirming that the company is solvent and will authorise the directors, or a majority of their number, to proceed to swear such a declaration. Finally, the directors will resolve to convene a general meeting at which amongst other things, a special resolution to liquidate the company will be proposed to the members.

11.5.2.2 Declaration of Solvency

The Declaration of Solvency required by section 89 of the Insolvency Act 1986, is the key document because without this the company cannot be placed into MVL. Even if the company is solvent at the time of its liquidation, if no Declaration of Solvency is made and filed with the Registrar of Companies, the liquidation would be considered to be a creditors' voluntary liquidation. Section 90 of the Insolvency Act 1986 states that:

> "a winding-up in the case of which a directors' statutory declaration under section 89 has been made is a 'members' voluntary winding up'; and a winding up in the case of which such declaration has not been made is a creditors' voluntary winding-up."

The format of the Declaration of Solvency is contained in statutory form 4.70 and confirms that the relevant directors have made a full enquiry into the affairs of the company and believe the company will be able to pay its debts in full (together with statutory interest) within 12 months.

The declaration must also embody a statement of the company's assets and liabilities drawn up to the latest practicable date prior to the liquidation.

This statement of assets and liabilities need not be audited for the purposes of the declaration and it is usual, where the company has not been required to file statutory accounts immediately prior to the liquidation date, for the figures from the most up to date management accounts balance sheet to be used. Whilst there is no requirement for closing accounts to be audited, they should be sufficiently detailed to allow the company to produce appropriate tax computations for the period up to liquidation.

All, or a majority, of the directors must swear the Declaration of Solvency before a solicitor or commissioner for oaths within five weeks immediately preceding the passing of the special resolution to wind up the company (i.e. the date of the members' meeting). If the general meeting does not take place within five weeks, a fresh declaration must be sworn.

Section 89(5) of the Insolvency Act 1986 provides a safeguard for creditors of companies which have begun a solvent liquidation but which subsequently fail to pay their debts in full. In these circumstances there is a rebuttable presumption that the directors of the company did not have reasonable grounds for swearing the declaration and, if this is found to be the case, the directors may face two years imprisonment or a fine, or both. This factor will significantly influence how any subsequent liquidators of an insolvent liquidation will complete their statutory reporting obligations to BERR regarding the directors' conduct.

Whilst the rebuttable presumption mentioned above is only directly applicable to a solvent liquidation which subsequently becomes insolvent, the reporting requirements mentioned in relation to directors' conduct would be equally applicable to a company which had be struck off and was subsequently restored to the register by a creditor to allow them to pursue an insolvent liquidation.

Fig 1 – Extract from Declaration of Solvency

The Insolvency Act 1986   **Form 4.70 cont'd**
Members' Voluntary Winding Up
Declaration of Solvency
Embodying a Statement of
Assets and Liabilities

Company Number: 0012345

Name of Company: Sample Company Name Limited

Presented by: PricewaterhouseCoopers LLP
                    12 Plumtree Court
                    London, EC4A 4HT

Declaration of Solvency

We:

(a) Insert names
and addresses

Mr A Director of 1 Acacia Avenue, Random Town, SW22 8ZA

Mrs B Director of 2 Frimlington Gardens, Random Town, SW22 9PB

(b) Delete as   being (b) all the directors of (c) Sample Company Name Limited do solemnly
applicable   and sincerely declare that we have made a full inquiry into the affairs of this
(c) Insert name   Company, and that, having done so, we have formed the opinion that this
of company   Company will be able to pay its debts in full together with interest at the
(d) Insert a period of   official rate within a period of 12 months, from the commencement of the
months not exceeding 12 winding-up.

(e) Insert date   We append a statement of the Company's assets and liabilities as at (e) 20
                     April 2008, being the latest practicable date before the making of this
                     declaration.

                     We make this solemn declaration, conscientiously believing it to be true, and
                     by virtue of the provisions of the Statutory Declarations Act 1835.

_____   _____
Mr A Director   Mrs B Director

Declared at _____

        this 25th day of April 2008

Before me,

                                          Mr A Solicitor
                              Solicitor or Commissioner of Oaths

11.5.2.3 General meeting of members

A general meeting of the members is held to pass the special resolution (requiring a 75% majority) to wind up the company.

On 1 October 2007, the Companies Act 2006 reduced the notice period for the passing of these and the other associated resolutions from 21 to 14 days. Previously, 21 days notice was required for liquidation meetings due to the common use of extraordinary resolutions to provide the liquidators with powers in schedule 4 of the Insolvency Act 1986. The Companies Act 2006 dispenses with the need for such extraordinary resolutions and reduces them to special resolutions with a standard 14-day notice period to members.

Where the company is part of a wholly owned group, or where a majority of members hold at least 90% of the voting shares, this period may be reduced by consent (section 307 of the Companies Act 2006) and is usually shortened to such an extent that the notice period is effectively waived. This allows the general meeting to be held immediately after the board meeting.

Other business normally conducted at the general meeting would include the appointment of the liquidators of the company by way of ordinary resolution and setting the basis for the liquidators' remuneration and powers. If these resolutions are passed, a 75% majority of members voting is required, but if undertaken by a written resolution there was until 1 October 2007 a requirement for 100% consent of members. This was changed with the introduction of the Companies Act 2006 where such written resolutions are now effective if passed by a 75% majority, as for meetings at present (sections 282 and 283 of the Companies Act 2006).

To validate the appointment of liquidators, the chairman of the meeting must certify the appointment. This happens after the chairman has received a written statement from the liquidators confirming they are qualified to act and they have consented to act as liquidators for the company.

11.5.3 When is the liquidator appointed?

The appointment of the liquidators takes immediate effect after the members have passed the appropriate resolutions. From this time, the directors and other officers of the company are divested of their powers in relation to the company and these pass to the appointed liquidator, unless either the liquidators or the company sanctions their continuance.

Whilst the directors are divested of their powers, they retain their obligations in respect of their previous corporate actions. They are obliged to assist the liquidators in the winding-up of the company, including providing information about the affairs of the company. They also retain their responsibilities and to look after and hand over the company's assets and statutory books and records.

11.5.4   How will the liquidation be publicised?

Following the passing of a resolution to wind up the company, the liquidators must attend to a number of statutory formalities to advise creditors and the world at large of the change in the company's corporate status. These requirements include the following.

(i)   Publishing a notice of the passing of the resolution to wind up and appointment of the liquidators in the *London Gazette*. This advertisement must be placed within 14 days of the resolution being passed;

(ii)   The liquidators must file both the original resolution to wind up and the Declaration of Solvency with the Registrar of Companies in Cardiff within 15 days of being appointed; and

(iii)   The liquidators must give written notice to all creditors they are aware of within 28 days of their appointment. It is also the common practice of many liquidators to place a further advertisement in a national newspaper to seek out claims from any creditors they are unaware of.

11.5.5   What is the effect of the liquidation on corporate status and ongoing maintenance requirements?

Following the commencement of the liquidation, the status of the company changes in a number of ways. Section 87(1) of the Insolvency Act 1986 confirms that:

> "in the case of a winding-up, the company shall from the commencement of the winding-up cease to carry on its business, except in so far as may be required for its beneficial winding-up."

However, "the corporate state of the company and the corporate powers of the company continue until the company is dissolved" (section 87(2) of the Insolvency Act 1986).

11.5.5.1   Statutory filing and compliance

One of the most obvious changes to the company's status is the impact on its statutory filing position and the associated administrative burden. This is felt particularly in relation to the normal requirement to file both statutory accounts and an annual return.

The first filing change, and probably most important one after the commencement of the liquidation, is the fact that from this date the company is no longer required to prepare and file statutory accounts with the Registrar of Companies. This is the case even if the company has been placed into liquidation in the period between the end of the company's financial year and the time for filing the audited accounts with the Registrar of Companies. A similar situation applies in relation to applications for striking-off, but in the event that an objection is received, or the application is withdrawn, then the company would be liable to file any accounts which should have been filed during the period in which the application was being considered.

The basis for this change in obligations in relation to a company being placed in to liquidation is twofold. Firstly, the directors of the company will have been divested of their powers from the appointment of the liquidators and have no power to sign the statutory directors' report or other documents. Secondly, the liquidators have a statutory duty to maintain accounts relating to the conduct of the liquidation and must file these with the Registrar of Companies on the first anniversary of the liquidation and, if the liquidation continues beyond this date, every six months thereafter.

Secondly there is no longer any need to file an annual return as any change in either the company's officers or the members is very rare in the post-appointment period and, even where a change is required, it cannot happen without the sanction of the liquidators.

11.5.5.2   Tax affairs

A company which is resident in the UK for tax purposes, continues to be subject to corporation tax on profits arising in its winding up (section 8(2) of the Income Taxes Act 1988 (ICTA)).

The commencement of the liquidation brings a tax accounting period to an end and starts a new one. The winding-up is taken to have started on the passing of the resolution to wind up and the tax accounting period ends on the anniversary of the appointment, or on the completion of the winding-up. (section 12(7) Income Taxes Act 1988).

From the date on which the liquidators are appointed, they become the proper officer for taxation purposes. This means that any tax calculations, correspondence or other formal obligations to HM Revenue & Customs should be executed and dealt with by the liquidators rather than the former directors of the company. This is the case even where the returns submitted relate to periods which pre-date the commencement of the liquidation.

A further, critical, change to the tax affairs of the company occurs following the appointment of the liquidators and relates to the standard Corporate Tax Self-Assessment (CTSA) regime. In normal circumstances, the CTSA regime requires companies to self-assess and report tax to HMRC on a yearly basis. Following receipt of the tax returns, HMRC has two years to decide whether it wishes to enquire into the affairs of the company. If it does not, the self-assessed return is deemed to have been accepted and considered closed. If an enquiry is raised the matter is dealt with in the normal way and the period kept open until formal confirmation is received from the relevant inspector to close the enquiry.

Where companies are placed into liquidation, HMRC accepts that implementing the normal enquiry window would protract the timescale for the completion of the liquidation. HMRC will generally not rely on the enquiry window and, when requested by liquidators, will confirm whether they intend to enquire into specific tax accounting periods. In the event that they do not, they will also normally provide a formal clearance to liquidators confirming they are content for the liquidation to conclude.

11.5.5.3   *Shareholdings in the company*

After the resolution to wind up the company has been passed the membership of the company is frozen. This ensures there is a clear understanding of who is entitled to any distribution of surplus assets following settlement of any creditor claims and avoids reducing the covenant on unpaid shares.

After this point, there can be no transfer of shares in the company without the sanction of the liquidators. Any transfer undertaken without sanction is deemed to be void.

In reality, the provisions regarding the freeze on the membership structure are only of importance in the liquidation of a large public limited company. In smaller private companies, consent to transfer shares, normally requested between group companies, will invariably be granted by the liquidators.

11.5.6   What is the role of the liquidator when conducting the liquidation?

Following the completion of the statutory advertising in the press and notification procedures, the liquidators are responsible for ensuring that the key stages in the liquidation are followed.

The liquidators are essentially appointed to wind up the company's affairs by realising the company's assets. This must be done by satisfying the company's liabilities and then distributed to the members in accordance with their statutory rights.

In summary, the general duties result in the liquidators being responsible for:

(i)   realising the assets;

(ii)   seeking out and settling creditor claims; and

(iii)   distributing the surplus (of the assets less the claims) to the shareholders.

11.5.6.1 *What powers does a liquidator have?*

To ensure that the liquidators are capable of fulfilling their statutory duties, the Insolvency Act 1986 has set out a number of statutory powers which liquidators can draw upon. The powers are found in schedule 4 to the Insolvency Act 1986 which has three general classes of powers exercisable by liquidators. These are:

(i)   Part I – powers exercisable with sanction of the members;

(ii) Part II – powers exercisable without sanction in a voluntary winding-up; and

(iii) Part III – powers exercisable without sanction in any winding-up.

In general the powers available to the liquidator include the following:

- power to pay any class of creditors in full;

- power to make any compromise or arrangement with creditors or persons claiming to be creditors or alleging to have a claim against the company;

- power to bring or defend any action or other legal proceeding in the name and on behalf of the company;

- power to carry on the business of the company so far as may be necessary for its beneficial winding up;

- power to sell any of the company's property;

- power to act and execute, in the name and on behalf of the company, all deeds, receipts and other documents and to use the company's seal for these purposes;

- power to prove, rank and claim in the bankruptcy, insolvency or sequestration of any contributory for any balance against the estate and receive dividends from the balance;

- power to raise any money required against the security of the assets;

- power to appoint an agent to do any business which the liquidators are unable to do themselves; and

- power to do all such things as may be necessary for winding up the company's affairs and distributing its assets.

11.5.6.2 *What are the statutory duties of a liquidator?*

(a) Realising assets

The first duty of the liquidators is to identify and collect or secure the assets of the company over which they have been appointed.

This will involve the control of bank accounts in the name of the company, realisation of debtor monies (potentially including inter-company positions), notification of insurable interests in fixed assets and other property.

(b) Seeking out creditor claims

Once the assets are known and protected, the liquidators should identify all of the company's creditors and settle them in priority to the members. To do so, the liquidators will be guided by the statutory advertising and notification provisions contained in the Insolvency Act and Rules.

To eliminate the company by way of solvent liquidation, Rule 4.139(4) of the Insolvency Rules 1986 requires the liquidators to write to every known creditor within 28 days of their appointment seeking details of their claims against the company.

Most liquidators also place a general 'notice for creditors to claim' in a newspaper such as *The Times,* or another publication which may be relevant to the former business of the company. This general advertisement will usually allow between 21 and 30 days for creditors to come forward with any claims against the company.

In the event that creditors fail to claim, the liquidators will rely on the inclusion of wording pursuant to Rule 4.812.A. This rule confirms that, if claims are not received by the requisite date, the liquidators are entitled to pay a distribution to other creditors and members without reference to a late claim. Should a creditor prove a claim after this date, they will not be entitled to disturb any previous distribution and may only claim from any surplus which remains or otherwise at the liquidator's discretion.

(c) Dealing with creditor claims

It is the creditor rather than the liquidators who bears the burden of proving a claim. The creditor must provide information that the liquidators reasonably require in order to validate the claim. In the event that the creditor fails to prove their claim to the satisfaction of the liquidators, the liquidators have a number of options. They can:

(i)   admit the claim in its entirety;

(ii) partially admit the claim and reject a certain element; or

(iii) reject the total claim.

If a claim is proved, the liquidators must ensure it is settled in full and must also account for statutory interest on the principal from the date of the appointment.

11029

If, on the other hand, the liquidators reject a claim, they must provide the creditor with a written statement explaining why the claim is being rejected and advise the creditor that they have 21 days from the rejection notice to refer the matter to the court.

Consideration of the position of the Crown agencies is a further key creditor concern for liquidators. The Crown agencies comprise the various different elements of HMRC, particularly the inspectors dealing with corporation tax, VAT and PAYE/NIC. Despite the fact all these departments fall under the remit of the Crown agency, it is sensible to treat each separately for the purposes of obtaining clearances. No final distribution to members should be made until appropriate statements confirming that there are no outstanding issues have been obtained in writing from each.

11.5.6.3 What happens if creditor claims takes more than a year to resolve?

If the settlement of creditor claims is protracted, which is often the case when either the amounts in question are significant to either party or there are complex issues to resolve, it is possible that the liquidation may be held open for more than 12 months.

In such circumstances, section 93 of the Insolvency Act 1986 requires that the liquidators convene a general meeting of the company at the anniversary of the appointment or within three months following this anniversary. The purpose of the meeting is for the liquidators to present an account of the progress of the liquidation, together with a summary of the acts and dealings of the liquidators. Such a meeting must be convened each year thereafter until the conclusion of the liquidation.

11.5.7　When can distributions be made?

Once all creditors have been settled and the Crown clearances have been obtained, it is possible for the liquidators to make distributions from the surplus to the members.

There is significant case law on the issue of distributions in solvent liquidations and the key rule is that no dividend should be paid until either creditors have been settled in full or suitable reserves have been made to cover them. If the liquidators pay distributions to members before creditors, they will be held personally liable for the value of any subsequent proven creditor claim (up to a maximum value of the assets which came into their hands on appointment). Furthermore, they may also be sued for negligence in the conduct of the liquidation.

In practice, it is possible that earlier interim distributions may be required to enable clients to meet tax or other financial deadlines. Where this is necessary, such distributions will generally be made against a suitable indemnity provided by the shareholders which will provide the liquidator with protection against any unknown creditor claims arising after payment of the interim distribution.

Assuming the liquidators are confident all creditors have been settled, the starting point for the calculation of the distribution should be the members shown on the register of members at the commencement of the liquidation. Each member will receive a distribution based on the rights set out in the articles of association.

If a member requests a dividend be paid to someone other than themselves, this should be confirmed in writing.

It is common for distributions in group reorganisations to be undertaken by way of *specie distribution* rather than in cash. This form of distribution, if sanctioned at the EGM, allows the liquidators to distribute assets in their existing form, rather than converting them to their cash value. It is particularly useful for the transfer of inter-company debt balances, which if realised in cash would require a circular flow of funds. (See also chapter 10 on Distributions *in specie*)

11.5.8   How is the liquidation concluded?

Following completion of the statutory duties and receipt of appropriate statutory clearances from the Crown agencies, including HM Revenue & Customs, the liquidators will conclude the liquidation process by convening a final meeting of members.

This final meeting is prescribed by section 94 of the Insolvency Act 1986 and requires that, as soon as the affairs of the company have been fully wound up, the liquidators must:

(i)   prepare an account of the winding-up showing how the liquidation has been conducted, and the company's property has been disposed of; and

(ii)   convene a general meeting to lay the above account before the members and to explain it to them.

This final meeting of members must be convened by statutory advertisement placed in the *London Gazette* one month before the due date of the meeting. This timescale, unlike the company meetings at the commencement of the liquidation, cannot be shortened by consent of the members.

At the meeting, the liquidators (or their nominated representative) will take the chair and explain the conduct of the liquidation to the members. Within one week of this meeting, the liquidators must send a final return to the Registrar of Companies enclosing a copy of the final account and confirm that the date on which the final meeting of members was held.

Normally, this final meeting is treated as a statutory formality by the members as they will have previously received their final distribution of assets and generally will have very little interest in the liquidation unless there is a requirement to agree any final fees due to be paid to the liquidators at the meeting. In these circumstances, it is not uncommon for no members to attend or even submit proxies. Section 94(5) of the Insolvency Act 1986 states:

"if a quorum is not present at the meeting, the liquidators shall, in lieu of the return mentioned above, make a return that the meeting was duly summoned and that no quorum was present; and upon such a return being made, the provisions..... as to the making of the return are deemed to have been complied with."

11.5.9   When is the company finally dissolved?

On registration of the final return by the Registrar of Companies, the liquidators are formally released from office and the liquidation concluded (section 171(6) of the Insolvency Act 1986).

At this stage the company still remains in existence and the Registrar of Companies will place a further advertisement in the *London Gazette* notifying creditors of the intention to dissolve the company from the register. If no objections are received in response to this advertisement, the company is deemed to have been dissolved three months after registration of the final liquidation return.

Following dissolution of the company, there is now a contingency period of six years (previously two years) within which an interested party may seek a court order for the restoration of the company. This limitation period does not apply in relation to personal injury matters.

11.6   Comparison between striking-off and Members' Voluntary Liquidation

As can be seen both the key procedures result in the elimination of unwanted corporate entities, but the individual processes are very different.

A summary comparison of both has been set out below:

	Striking off	MVL
PLCs	• Now possible under Companies Act 2006	• Possible
Asset Distribution	• Requires compliance with detailed accounting and corporate legislation	• Totality of assets can be distributed – timing can be managed to optimise tax planning
Timelines	• Timing of dissolution in the hands of the Registrar of Companies	• Date of liquidation and subsequent steps including dissolution are under the control of shareholders and the liquidator when appointed
Creditor Claims	• Inappropriate when there are creditors	• The liquidation process is specifically designed to seek out and finalise the claims of creditors so surplus assets can be returned to shareholders
Unidentified Assets	• Pass to the Crown unless company restored – involves application to court and legal costs	• Liquidation distributions permit return of all assets to shareholders
Directors Responsibility	• Directors responsible for the application	• From the date of liquidation only the liquidator can act on behalf of the company – directors' powers/responsibilities transfer to him
If the Company is restored to the register	• Previous directors' responsibilities continue	• Responsibilities rest with the liquidator not the directors

11.7   Conclusion

It will be apparent that the Companies Act 2006 has not radically altered the ways of dealing with dormant companies but the alternatives of striking-off and liquidation are now more closely aligned in that both now provide a six year restoration window (previously two years for liquidation and 20 years for striking-off). Where striking-off is preferred, the ability to reduce capital without court approval will reduce the *bona vacantia* risk identified at [11.4.11] above.

The following table summarises the key features which would normally influence the choice of process:

Consideration	Strike-off	MVL
Share capital/reserves < £4,000	✓	✗
Large distributions to members > £4,000	✗	✓
Good knowledge of corporate transactions	✓	✗
Company acquired/management changed	✗	✓
Active external trading in the last 6 years	✗	✓
Only activity internal to the group	✓	✗
Risk of contingent external creditors	✗	✓
Previous employees/pension schemes	✗	✓
Previous leasehold property ownership	✗	✓

11.7.1 What does the future hold?

In any revision of this chapter it is likely that we will report the growing influence of European legislation in these matters. There is significant interest at the time of writing in employing the Cross-Border Merger Regulations to eliminate companies by means of mergers that result in the dissolution without liquidation of the transferor. However, court approval is required and the attitude of the UK Courts has yet to be tested.

Chapter 12

The process of managing regulatory change

12.1 Introduction 12001
12.2 Management control 12002
12.3 Consequences of incomplete implementation 12004
12.4 Benefits of an integrated approach 12006
12.5 Conclusion 12006

The process of managing regulatory change

12.1   Introduction

The Companies Act 2006, probably more than many others, is striking not only for the scale but for the range of people who need to have knowledge and awareness to varying degrees of its provisions.

It will now be apparent that effective transition will require active steps to be taken by individuals with a wide range of responsibilities both at board and senior management level including the company secretary, in-house legal counsel and senior management (including financial reporting, human resources, corporate social responsibility, treasury and tax). The Companies Act 2006 also impacts on a wide range of external relationships including shareholders, employers, suppliers, auditors and registrars.

In turn this leads to consideration not only of the practical implications of the new legislation but also the means by which organisations can address regulatory change effectively through their internal management and processes.

This chapter therefore concludes this book with a more general consideration of how companies deal with the wide range of legislation they are required to implement, placing the Companies Act 2006 into a broader context.

In summary, this chapter will address the following topics:

(i)   the three typical forms of managements control;

(ii)   the importance of a full and proper implementation; and

(iii) achieving implementation through an integrated approach.

Most organisations are on a journey with their governance, with the intended direction of travel being towards more efficient and effective management of business opportunities and performance. The same levers which are used to drive high performance and successfully deliver strategic initiatives are also used to manage business risk and ensure regulatory compliance.

Lack of attention to these can impact on corporate and personal reputations, lead to fines and destroy value. The impetus for change in the quality of risk management is often a high profile incident of non-compliance, or evolving legal requirements (e.g. US Federal Sentencing Guidelines, Foreign Corrupt Practices Act and Sarbanes-Oxley Act). However, the response needs to go beyond legal compliance and take account of the need to win hearts and minds and achieve the wider performance benefits which have been shown to be correlated to good governance. The Companies Act 2006 differs from other types of legislation in that it is predominantly deregulatory. Nevertheless there are certain areas where the risk has increased (particularly for directors) or where risk has been maintained at Companies Act 1985 levels (for example financial reporting) where the operation of effective governance systems will be of critical importance.

12.2 Management control

The management of leading businesses typically exercises control in three ways:

(i)   culture and values – which establish principles to guide an individual's sense of appropriate personal behaviour, set by the "tone at the top" and supported by a code of conduct;

(ii)   management systems – providing instructions and guidance on how particular types of task should be undertaken, and the processes and technologies necessary to achieve them; and

(iii)   oversight – ensuring the right people are asked to do the right tasks, that they have sufficient resource to support them, and are properly supervised and monitored.

Each of these three mechanisms informs the day to day decisions made by the leaders within an organisation. The emphasis of the mix varies widely between organisations, and also within different business units within individual organisations. In practice, most organisations use all three mechanisms, though the degree of formality around them varies. In areas of high risk, leading organisations use all three elements of the governance mix in combination to ensure risks are appropriately mitigated.

In practice though, many organisations are still managing Governance, Regulation and Compliance in organisational silos on a piecemeal, bottom up basis. The challenge is to ensure a single robust framework is in place for an organisation to manage all these elements effectively and consistently, as shown in Figure 1.

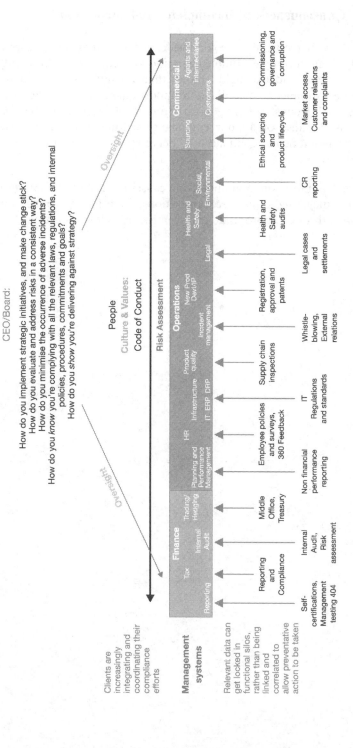

Figure 1: How organisations manage Governance, Regulation and Compliance

12.3   Consequences of incomplete implementation

An analysis of recent high profile incidents shows that root causes are often related to an incomplete implementation of requirements for culture and values, systems and oversight   rather than an unforeseeable change in the external environment.   The diagram opposite (see figure 2) shows that most failures result from staff failing to carry out defined responsibilities on a day to day basis, because of a poor compliance culture, insufficient resources to achieve commitments, complacency, perverse incentives, and low employee morale.

The next two most common underlying causes are failure to monitor activities properly, including outsourced operations, and failure to act on known exceptions through appropriate enforcement or follow-up action.

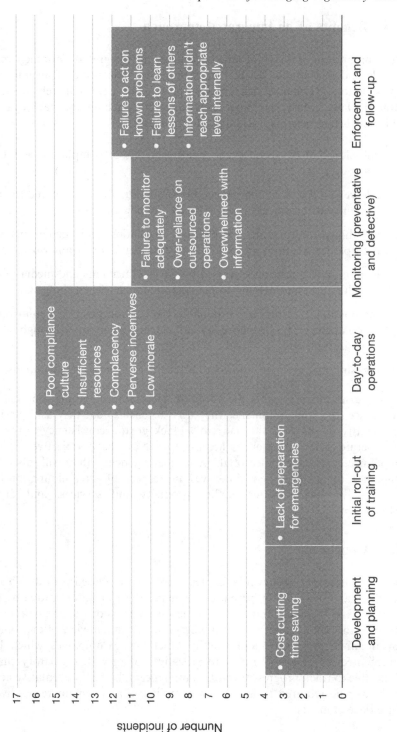

Figure 2: Contributing factors to recent high profile incidents

12.4   Benefits of an integrated approach

Those organisations that are able to achieve an integrated approach realise tangible and measurable benefits from doing so. The value of an integrated approach to governance, risk and compliance far exceed merely operating within the law. In fact, our experience shows that such an approach can yield significant broad benefits, including the following:

(i)   cohesion and consistency across all elements of compliance within the company;

(ii)   a lower total cost of compliance by eliminating duplication and the need to 'reinvent the wheel' in response to any new initiative;

(iii) an ability to integrate quickly new legislation and regulations from multiple jurisdictions and into an existing regulatory framework;

(iv)   helping to avoid being surprised by adverse incidents and media reports and litigation and helping to manage the impact when things go wrong;

(v)   the possibility of driving sustainable growth and positively contributing to competitive performance by influencing behaviour throughout the organisation; and

(vi)   focusing management information on the right non-financial areas.

As businesses move towards the adoption of a more integrated approach to governance, risk and compliance they need to ensure that they ask questions that identify the barriers that currently block greater consistency in the way they operate today. As well as helping to achieve basic objectives of legal compliance, risk avoidance and issue management, this will also help companies to achieve their objectives in respect of streamlining business processes, producing better quality products and services, and driving performance.

12.5   Conclusion

The Companies Act 2006 will be implemented over a phased period. This has the advantage of enabling businesses to make the transition gradually, take account of the benefits, and make the necessary revisions to their processes. However, this phased approach also presents challenges in view of the complex transitional arrangements and lengthy timetable. Companies which have implemented a framework for systematically dealing with regulatory change will be able to track progress towards compliance, take any preventative action which may be required to avoid non-compliance, and remain responsive to future developments.

Appendix 1

Overview of key changes introduced by the Companies Act 2006

A1.1   Introduction A1001
A1.2   Provisions implemented in January 2007 .... A1001
A1.3   Provisions implemented in April 2007 .... A1002
A1.4   Provisions implemented in October 2007 .... A1003
A1.5   Provisions implemented in April 2008 .... A1009
A1.6   Provisions implemented in October 2008 .... A1012
A1.7   Provisions implemented in October 2009 .... A1014

A1 ii

Overview of key changes introduced by the Companies Act 2006

A1.1 Introduction

The tables below set out key aspects of the Companies Act 2006, highlighting the differences (if any) of the application of those key provisions to public and private companies.

A1.2 Provisions implemented in January 2007

Provision and implementation date	Former position under Companies Act 1985	Private company (limited by shares)	Public company (traded and non-traded)	Action
Content requirement for e-mails and websites From 20 January 2007	Did not require the details of a company to be included on the website or other forms of electronic correspondence such as e-mails.	All e-mails and websites must now contain the following information: (i) the company's name; (ii) the company's place of registration and registration number; (iii) the address of the company's registered office; (iv) if applicable, that the company is an investment company; (v) if the company is exempt from having the word 'limited' in its name the fact that it is a limited company; and (vi) if there is a reference to share capital the reference must be to paid-up share capital.		Ensure that all the necessary information appears on all e-mails and websites.

Provision and implementation date	Former position under Companies Act 1985	Private company (limited by shares)	Public company (traded and non-traded)	Action
Electronic communications with shareholders (both by e-mail and via website) From 20 January 2007	Companies were able to send only certain documents electronically. Positive consent was required by individual shareholders.	All companies will be able to communicate with their shareholders via e-mail provided the shareholder has consented to receive such communication. All companies can publish information via their website provided the shareholders have either passed a resolution authorising such publication or the articles of the company permit such publication. In addition, each shareholder has consented to receive information in this manner. It should be noted that if a shareholder fails to respond to a request to consent within 28 days then the shareholder is deemed to have consented.		If this form of communication is desirable, if necessary, propose a resolution or amend the articles as appropriate to give authority and write to each shareholder to seek consent.

A1.3   Provisions to be implemented in April 2007

Provision and implementation date	Former position under Companies Act 1985	Private company (limited by shares)	Public company (traded and non-traded)	Action
Details for company records (section 1134 – 1138) From 6 April 2007	Required to maintain register of: members; directors and secretaries; mortgages and charges; debentures (if applicable) and directors' interests and substantial interests (where applicable).	Required to maintain register of: members; directors and secretaries; mortgages and charges; debentures; directors' maiden name; directors' residential address.	Required to maintain register of: members; directors and secretaries; mortgages and charges; debentures; directors' maiden name; directors' residential address; investigations into share interests; substantial share interests.	Details of maiden names to be added to register of directors and secretaries and residential addresses. Create register of investigations into shares.

A1.4   Provisions implemented in October 2007

Provision and implementation date	Former position under Companies Act 1985	Private company (limited by shares)	Public company (traded and non-traded)	Action
Nomination of a third party to enjoy shareholder rights (section 145) From 1 October 2007	A shareholder did not have the right to nominate a third party to have and exercise shareholder rights.	Right of shareholders of private or public companies to nominate a third party to have and exercise all or any specified rights of a member including corporate governance rights and a right to receive certain information.		A company will need systems in place to comply with any requests and to agree these arrangements with their Registrars.
Nomination of the beneficial owner of shares to enjoy 'information rights' (section 146) From 1 October 2007 (Grace period until 01 January 2008 for companies to act on a nomination)	Nomination of the beneficial owner to enjoy information rights was not possible.	Not applicable	The registered shareholder of a traded company can nominate that the beneficial owner of these shares receives 'information rights', i.e. the right to receive copies of all information sent by the company to its shareholders. A partial nomination of information rights is not permitted.	No immediate action required.
Minimum number of directors (section 154) From 1 October 2007	One for private companies, two for public companies	One	Two	No immediate action required.

Overview of key changes introduced by the Companies Act 2006

Provision and implementation date	Former position under Companies Act 1985	Private company (limited by shares)	Public company (traded and non-traded)	Action
Directors' duties (sections 171 to 174 and section 180). From 1 October 2007 (sections 175 to 177 are effective from 1 October 2008).	Directors' duties were primarily derived from common law principles.	Directors duties are codified and apply to all directors (executive and non-executive) of all companies. Four out of seven directors' duties come into effect on 1 October 2007. These are the duty to act within the powers of the company, to promote the success of the company, to exercise independent judgment and to exercise reasonable care, skill and diligence.		Review existing directors' and officers' insurance, corporate hospitality policies and terms of reference for the board.
Directors' long-term service contracts: requirement of members' approval (section 188) From 1 October 2007	Shareholder approval was required for service agreements with a guaranteed term in excess of five years.	Shareholder approval is required for service agreements with a guaranteed term in excess of two years.		Review and update where necessary policies relating to the approval of directors' service agreements.
Substantial property transactions (section 190) From 1 October 2007	Shareholder approval was required prior to the transaction being entered into.	A company may enter into a substantial property transaction that is conditional upon shareholder approval.		No immediate action required.
Loans to directors (section 197) From 1 October 2007	Generally prohibited save for a few minor exceptions.	Loans to directors will now be permitted if the loan has been approved in advance by shareholders and provided full disclosure has been made to shareholders as to the amount and purpose of the loan and any liability of the company thereunder. Neither the director nor any person connected with the director will be entitled to vote to approve the loan.		No immediate action required.
Directors' liabilities (sections 232 – 238) 1 October 2007	No provision for companies to provide indemnities for pension fund trustees.	New third party indemnity for pension fund trustees.		Consider whether to provide indemnities in favour of trustees of occupational pension schemes.

Overview of key changes introduced by the Companies Act 2006

Provision and implementation date	Former position under Companies Act 1985	Private company (limited by shares)	Public company (traded and non-traded)	Action
Ratification of directors' conduct (section 239) From 1 October 2007	Permitted under common law.	The common law position that a director's breach of duty may be ratified by ordinary resolution is put on a statutory footing.		Ensure that independent shareholders ratify directors' acts (unless the resolution is passed unanimously).
Derivative claims (sections 260 – 264) From 1 October 2007	No express provisions governed by common law.	The circumstances in which a derivative claim may be brought has been widened to include negligence and breach of duty/trust.		Companies should consider whether they have exposure to possible derivative claims.
Written Resolutions (sections 281 and 288-300) From 1 October 2007	A written resolution was only effective if it had been signed by all members of the company. Both public and private companies could pass written resolutions.	Written resolutions may now be passed by the members of a private company by a simple majority in the case of an ordinary resolution and by 75% of the members entitled to vote in the case of a special resolution. The written resolution must be passed within 28 days of it being circulated (unless a different period is specified in the articles) or it will lapse.	Written resolutions of a public company are not effective.	Written resolution of private companies must contain the additional statements required by Chapter 2 of Part 13 of the Companies Act 2006. Ensure that members' meetings of public companies are convened for all shareholder resolutions.

Overview of key changes introduced by the Companies Act 2006

Provision and implementation date	Former position under Companies Act 1985	Private company (limited by shares)	Public company (traded and non-traded)	Action
General Meetings (section 301) From October 2007	All shareholder meetings other than the annual general meeting were extraordinary general meetings.	Abolition of extraordinary general meetings. All meetings, other than the annual general meeting of a public company, are now known as general meetings.		No immediate action required but in due course it is good practice to update the articles to remove references to extraordinary general meetings.
Proxies (sections 324-331) From 1 October 2007	Right of a member to appoint a proxy to attend a meeting and vote on a member's behalf. No statutory right to speak or vote in a poll but this was possible if permitted by the company's articles.	Enhancement of rights of proxies to give them the same powers at a general meeting as a member of the company. On a vote on a resolution by way of a show of hands, every proxy present has one vote. Members of both private and public companies have the right to appoint a proxy to attend, speak and vote at meetings on his behalf. A member is permitted to appoint more than one proxy in relation to a meeting, provided each proxy is appointed to exercise the rights attached to different shares held by him.		Proxy cards need to be updated to reflect the fact that proxies can attend and speak at meetings. Notice of meetings should be updated to contain a statement of the rights of proxies.
Requirement to hold an AGM (section 336) From 1 October 2007	Both public and private companies were required to hold an AGM every year.* *Private companies could elect not to hold AGMs.	A private company will no longer be required to hold an AGM unless the articles so require.	A public company must continue to hold AGMs.	Private companies should consider whether it is appropriate to remove any requirement in their articles to continue to hold annual general meetings.

Overview of key changes introduced by the Companies Act 2006

Provision and implementation date	Former position under Companies Act 1985	Private company (limited by shares)	Public company (traded and non-traded)	Action
Poll results to be made available on a website (section 341) From 1 October 2007	Companies were not required to place poll results on a website.	Not applicable.	Where a poll is taken at a general meeting of a quoted company (main market not AIM) it must make available on its website: (i) the date of the meeting; (ii) the text of the resolution; and (iii) the number of votes cast in favour / against.	No immediate action required.
Independent report on poll (sections 342-354) From 1 October 2007	No power for members to require an independent report on a poll to confirm the accuracy of the poll results.	Not applicable.	Members of a quoted company (main market not AIM) who hold not less than 5% of the total voting rights of all members or number not less than 100 (and also hold an average of at least £100 of paid up share capital) may insist that the company obtains an independent report on a poll taken, or to be taken, at a general meeting of the company.	Consider whether independent assessor should be appointed on a stand-by basis, especially for general meetings where contentious matters are being considered.
Control of political donations and expenditure (sections 362-379) From 1 October 2007	Rules were complex and difficult to interpret.	Clarification of the rules on political donations and extension of the regulation of political donations and expenditure to cover independent election candidates.		Identify to what extent additional shareholder approval may be required.

Overview of key changes introduced by the Companies Act 2006

Provision and implementation date	Former position under Companies Act 1985	Private company (limited by shares)	Public company (traded and non-traded)	Action
Deemed re-appointment of auditors (sections 487-488) From 1 October 2007	Shareholders were required to appoint auditors annually at each AGM, where accounts were being laid.	Auditors who were appointed by the shareholders, or who were not required to be re-appointed following the passing of an elective resolution, are deemed re-appointed. Otherwise, the auditors must be appointed by the directors each financial year. Members holding at least 5% of the total voting rights of the company are entitled to object to a deemed re-appointment.	Shareholders are required to appoint auditors annually at each AGM, were accounts are being laid.	No immediate action required.

A1.5   Provisions implemented in April 2008

Provision and implementation date	Former position under Companies Act 1985	Private company (limited by shares)	Public company (traded and non-traded)	Action
Execution of documents (section 44) From 6 April 2008	Documents validly executed by affixing company seal or if signed by two directors or director and secretary. Documents may also be executed by one director who signs in the presence of a witness.	As before. The sole director of a private company with no company secretary must execute a deed in the presence of a witness.	No change for public companies.	No action required.
Requirement to appoint a company secretary (sections 270-80) From 6 April 2008	All companies were required to appoint a secretary.	A private company may appoint a secretary if it so wishes. If a company dispenses with the role of company secretary the functions of the company secretary will still need to be performed.	A public company (trading or otherwise) will still need to appoint a company secretary.	No immediate action required.
Reduction in time limit for filing accounts (section 442) From 6 April 2008	Ten months from the end of the financial year for a private company, seven months for a public company.	Nine months from the end of the financial year.	Six months from the end of the financial year.	No immediate action required.

Provision and implementation date	Former position under Companies Act 1985	Private company (limited by shares)	Public company (traded and non-traded)	Action
Requirement for auditors to deposit a statement upon termination of their appointment setting out the circumstances of the auditors' termination. (section 519) From 6 April 2008	The auditor must deposit a statement setting out the reasons for the termination of the auditor's appointment save when the auditor does not consider there to be any matter that should be brought to the attention of the members or creditors of the company in which case the auditor may deposit a statement to that effect.	No change.	Where the company is quoted (main market not AIM) the auditor must deposit a statement setting out the reasons for the termination of the auditor's appointment. If the company is not quoted, the auditor may follow the same rules as those for private companies.	No immediate action required.
Right of members of quoted companies to raise audit concerns (sections 527-531) From 6 April 2008	No such right existed.	Not applicable.	Members of a quoted company (main market not AIM) holding not less than 5% of the total voting rights of the company (or who are at least 100 members that hold a charge of £100 of paid up share capital) may raise audit concerns at the next accounts meeting of the company and may require that the company places those concerns on its website.	No immediate action required.

Provision and implementation date	Former position under Companies Act 1985	Private company (limited by shares)	Public company (traded and non-traded)	Action
Liability limitation agreements with auditors (section 532) From 6 April 2008	Companies were only able to indemnify the auditor against successfully defending proceedings brought against the auditor.	Companies may enter into liability limitation agreements with their auditors that limit the liability of their auditors to an amount that is fair and reasonable. The agreement can only relate to one financial year and therefore must be renewed each year and must be approved by an ordinary resolution of the company's members.		No immediate action required.

A1.6   Provisions implemented in October 2008

Provision and implementation date	Former position under Companies Act 1985	Private company (limited by shares)	Public company (traded and non-traded)	Action
Companies required to have at least one director who is a natural person (section 155) From 1 October 2008 (Grace period until October 2010 for companies without a natural director)	A company could have a sole corporate director.	All companies must have at least one natural director.		Identify boards consisting solely of corporate directors and appoint at least one natural person.
Minimum age for directors (sections 157-159) 1 October 2008	No minimum age requirement.	16	16	Review board composition and appoint additional overage directors prior to 1 October 2008 if necessary.
Directors' duties (sections 175 to 177 and 182 to 187). From 1 October 2008.	Directors' duties were primarily derived from common law principles.	Remaining three directors' duties are codified: duty to avoid conflicts of interest, not to accept benefits from third parties and to declare interest in proposed or existing transactions or arrangement.		Review arrangements for disclosing and tracking conflicts. Review articles of association and amend if necessary to allow independent directors to authorise conflicts.

Overview of key changes introduced by the Companies Act 2006

Provision and implementation date	Former position under Companies Act 1985	Private company (limited by shares)	Public company (traded and non-traded)	Action
Use of service addresses by directors (section 1142) From 1 October 2008 (to come into force with the relevant provisions of the Companies Act 2006)	Directors required to file residential address (unless they have obtained a confidentiality order).	Directors may use service addresses on all public documents to be filed with the Registrar of Companies.	Directors may use service addresses on all public documents to be filed with the Registrar of Companies.	Review and amend statutory books (from 1 October 2009) where necessary and maintain a separate list of directors' residential addresses.
Reduction of share capital (sections 641-644) From 1 October 2008 (Registration of resolutions and supporting documents to be lodged at Companies House within 15 days - to take effect from 1 October 2009)	All companies had to obtain a court order for a reduction of share capital.	A private company will be able to reduce its share capital by special resolution supported by a directors' statement of solvency.	A public company will still only be able to reduce its capital with the approval of the court.	No immediate action required.
Provision of financial assistance by a company for the acquisition of its own shares (sections 677 – 683) From 1 October 2008	Both public and private companies were prohibited from giving financial assistance.	The prohibition on private companies providing financial assistance for the acquisition of its own shares (or that of its private holding company) is repealed.	Public companies are still prohibited from giving financial assistance.	No immediate action required.

A1.7 Provisions implemented in October 2009

Provision and implementation date	Former position under Companies Act 1985	Private company (limited by shares)	Public company (traded and non-traded)	Action
Amendments to the memorandum of association of a company (section 17) From 1 October 2009	All companies must have a memorandum of association which sets out the company's objects.	The memorandum of association will no longer include an objects' clause and will be a simple document noting that the subscribers wish to incorporate the company and stating the shares that they wish to subscribe for. Transitional arrangements apply to companies that have already been incorporated.		Companies incorporated pre-Companies Act 2006 should decide whether to adopt new articles of association to reflect the new provisions
Re-registration of public company as private and unlimited (section 109) From 1 October 2009	Public company required to re-register as private before becoming unlimited.	Public companies can re-register as unlimited companies without the need to re-register as a private company first. A statement of compliance of the directors must accompany the application.		No immediate action required.
Single member companies (section 123) From 1 October 2009	Only private companies could have a single member.	Public, as well as private companies, can now have only one member		No immediate action required.
Re-denomination of share capital (sections 622-628) From 1 October 2009	A company could not redenominate its share capital.	A company can redenominate its share capital by ordinary resolution and can reduce its share capital by special resolution to achieve a 'round' nominal value for each share provided that the reduction is not in excess of 10% of the nominal value of the share capital.		No immediate action required.

Provision and implementation date	Former position under Companies Act 1985	Private company (limited by shares)	Public company (traded and non-traded)	Action
Purchase of own shares (sections 658 to 666 and 684 to 737). From October 2009.	Private and public companies would purchase own shares out of distributable profits or proceeds of fresh issue of shares. A private company could also find a purchase out of capital.	No longer requires authority in articles to purchase. Able to purchase out of distributable profits, fresh issue of shares or capital. Slightly simplified procedure for purchase out of capital.	As before but no authority required in the articles.	No action required.
A company's annual return (sections 854 - 859) From 1 October 2009.	Required by all companies.	Required by all companies. New forms will be required including a statement of capital.	Required by all companies For listed plcs no requirement to disclose members addresses unless hold 5% or more of shares.	No action required yet. New forms will be available in due course. If listed plc will need to review list of members to remove addresses of shareholders with less than 5% of shares.
Overseas companies (sections 1044-1059) From 1 October 2009	Separate regimes for registration and continuing obligations of branches and places of business.	Single regulatory regime for an overseas company with any kind of UK establishment.		No action required.

Overview of key changes introduced by the Companies Act 2006

Provision and implementation date	Former position under Companies Act 1985	Private company (limited by shares)	Public company (traded and non-traded)	Action
Business names (sections 1192-1208) From 1 October 2009	Name used by individual or group of individuals who wish to trade or be known other than his own name or, in the case or a company, the name of the company in the UK.	Extends application to all overseas companies carrying on business in the UK, not just those with a place of business in the UK.		No action required except for companies with places of business using business names who will need to comply with the existing provisions eg relating to disclosure of name.
Dissolution and restoration to the register (sections 1000 to 1034). From October 2009.	Only a private company can apply to be struck off the register. A company can be restored up to 20 years after the dissolution of the company.	Both public and private companies can apply to be struck off the register. A company can be restored up to six years after the dissolution of the company.		No action required.

Appendix 2

Implementation of the Takeovers Directive (2004/25/EE)

A2.1 Introduction A2001
    A2.1.1 What issues are covered by the Takeovers Directive? A2001
    A2.1.2 Background A2001
A2.2 What are the provisions of the Companies Act 2006 relating to
    the Panel? A2002
    A2.2.1 What is the Panel? A2002
    A2.2.2 What transactions does the Panel have power to
        regulate? A2002
    A2.2.3 What are the powers of the Panel pursuant to the
        Companies Act 2006? A2002
    A2.2.4 Can the information a company discloses to the Panel
        pursuant to a request under section 947 of the
        Companies Act 2006 be used against it in criminal
        proceedings? A2003
    A2.2.5 What are the consequences of failing to comply with
        Panel Rules relating to a takeover offer and response
        documents? A2003
    A2.2.6 Does a breach of the Panel Rules impact upon the
        validity of the takeover offer? A2004
A2.3 What are the provisions of the Companies Act 2006 relating to
    impediments to takeovers? A2004
    A2.3.1 What are 'break-through' provisions? A2004
    A2.3.2 What are the requirements for a company to opt in to
        the break-through provisions (i.e. a pre-bid defence) of
        the Takeovers Directive? A2005
    A2.3.3 Can a company opt out of the break-through
        provisions if it has passed an opting-in resolution? . . A2005
    A2.3.4 What are the requirements for an opting-in and
        opting-out resolution? A2005
    A2.3.5 What is the effect of passing an opting-in resolution? A2006
    A2.3.6 Is the company obliged to notify anyone that the
        opting-in/opting-out resolution has been passed? . . . A2006
A2.4 What are the provisions of the Companies Act 2006 relating to
    the compulsory acquisition of shares? A2006
    A2.4.1 When will a right or obligation to the compulsory
        offer to acquire shares arise? A2007
    A2.4.2 What is the meaning of a takeover offer in the context
        of the compulsory offer to acquire shares? A2007
    A2.4.3 When is an offer to acquire shares treated as being an
        offer on the same terms? A2008

A2.4.4 What if the offeror is unable to communicate an offer to shareholders? A2008

A2.4.5 What are squeeze-out rights? A2009

A2.4.6 When can a notice exercising an offeror's squeeze-out rights be given? A2009

A2.4.7 Is the offeror required to send a copy of the squeeze-out notice to the target? A2010

A2.4.8 What is the effect of a notice exercising the offeror's squeeze-out rights? A2010

A2.4.9 What are sell-out rights? A2010

A2.4.10 When can sell-out rights be exercised by shareholders? A2011

A2.4.11 What is the effect of a shareholder exercising his sell-out rights? A2011

A2.5 What are the provisions of the Companies Act 2006 relating to the directors' report? A2012

A2.5.1 What disclosure is required in the directors' report by the Takeovers Directive? A2012

A2.5.2 Are there any exceptions to disclosing this information in the directors' report? A2012

A2.5.3 What are the practical implications of these disclosure requirements? A2013

Implementation of the Takeovers Directive (2004/25/EE)

A2.1 Introduction

In this appendix we summarise Part 28[1] of the Companies Act 2006, which came into force on 6 April 2008 and which permanently implements the European Directive on Takeover Bids[2] (the 'Takeovers Directive').

A2.1.1 What issues are covered by the Takeovers Directive?

The Takeovers Directive, and the corresponding provisions of the Companies Act 2006, are important as they regulate the following four key areas:

(i)   the Panel on Takeovers and Mergers (the 'Panel');

(ii)   impediments to takeover offers;

(iii) the compulsory acquisition of minority shareholders, in relation to public and private companies; and

(iv)   financial reporting.

We discuss each of these areas in more detail below.

In addition to the provisions of the Companies Act 2006, listed companies will also need to have regard to the provisions of the City Code on Takeovers and Mergers (the 'Takeovers Code'), the Takeover Code Rules, the Listing Rules, and where applicable, the AIM Rules (all of which are outside of the scope of review of this Appendix).

A2.1.2 Background

The Takeovers Directive was adopted on 21 April 2004 and EU member states had until 20 May 2006 to transpose the provisions of the Takeovers Directive into domestic legislation. To comply with this deadline, the UK implemented the provisions of the Takeovers Directive on a temporary basis through the implementation of the Takeovers Directive (Interim Implementation) Regulations 2006[3] (the 'Interim Regulations'). The Interim Regulations were

---

[1]   Sections 942 – 992, Companies Act 2006.
[2]   (2004/25/EC).
[3]   SI 2006/1183.

repealed and replaced on 6 April 2007 by Part 28 of the Companies Act 2006, which implements the Takeovers Directive in the UK permanently.

As a result of the temporary implementation of the Takeovers Directive in the UK, during the period 20 May 2006 until 6 April 2007 there was a two tier approach to the governance of the compulsory acquisition of shares and takeover offers. For companies that were subject to the Takeovers Directive, namely companies listed on a regulated market (which would include companies listed on the main market of the London Stock Exchange but not the Alternative Investment Market ('AIM')), the Interim Regulations applied. For all other companies such matters were governed, in the case of the compulsory acquisition of shares, by the Companies Act 1985 and in the case of takeover offers (such as an offer for a company listed on AIM) by the provisions of the Takeover Code Rules and the Panel albeit on a non-statutory basis. The implementation of the relevant provisions of the Companies Act 2006 means that takeover offers and the compulsory acquisition of shares are now governed by a single regime.

A2.2   What are the provisions of the Companies Act 2006 relating to the Panel[4]?

A2.2.1   What is the Panel?

The Panel is an independent administrative body that administers the Takeovers Code. The objective of the Panel is to ensure fair treatment for all shareholders in takeover bids[5].

A2.2.2   What transactions does the Panel have power to regulate?

The Panel regulates takeover offers (and other merger transactions) that are made in respect of companies that have their registered offices in the UK, the Channel Islands or the Isle of Man provided that the target company has securities that are listed on a regulated market in the UK or on a stock exchange in the Channel Islands or the Isle of Man.

A2.2.3   What are the powers of the Panel pursuant to the Companies Act 2006?

The Companies Act 2006 has given the Panel the statutory power to regulate takeover offers, mergers and other transactions affecting (directly or indirectly) the ownership or control of companies[6].

---

[4]   Sections 942 – 965, Companies Act 2006.
[5]   http://www.thetakeoverpanel.org.uk/new/.
[6]   Section 943, Companies Act 2006.

As part of its statutory authority, the Panel may make rules (the 'Panel Rules') giving effect to the Takeovers Directive[7] and can give binding rulings on the interpretation or effect of such rules[8].

The Companies Act 2006 gives the Panel the power to require the disclosure of documents and information that are reasonably required by the Panel to discharge its functions under the Companies Act 2006[9]. Disclosure of such documents or information is not required where a claim of legal professional privilege could be maintained in legal proceedings in respect of such material.

A2.2.4 Can the information a company discloses to the Panel pursuant to a request under section 947 of the Companies Act 2006 be used against it in criminal proceedings?

No. The Companies Act 2006 details that a statement made by a person in response to a Panel request made under section 947, or an order made by the court under section 955, of the Companies Act 2006 cannot be used against that person in criminal proceedings other than proceedings relating to false statements made otherwise than on oath[10].

A2.2.5 What are the consequences of failing to comply with Panel Rules relating to a takeover offer and response documents?

The Companies Act 2006 introduces a criminal offence in the event that a takeover offer is made for a company listed on a regulated market in the UK and the offer document published in respect of the takeover offer does not comply with the applicable offer document rules[11]. The offence is committed by the person making the takeover offer (or the directors, officers or member who caused the document to be published where the entity making the offer is a body of persons) provided that such a person knew that the offer document did not comply or was reckless as to whether it complied and failed to take all reasonable steps to secure that it did comply.

A similar offence is also created when a response document published in respect of the takeover offer does not comply with response document rules[12]. Again, the offence is committed by any directors or other officer of the target who knew that the response document did not comply or was reckless as to whether it complied and failed to take all reasonable steps to secure that it did comply.

---

[7] Section 943(1), Companies Act 2006.
[8] Section 945, Companies Act 2006.
[9] Section 947, Companies Act 2006.
[10] Section 962, Companies Act 2006.
[11] Section 953(2), Companies Act 2006.
[12] Section 953(4), Companies Act 2006.

A2.2.6   Does a breach of the Panel Rules impact upon the validity of the takeover offer?

No. The Companies Act 2006 specifically states that a breach of a Panel Rule does not make any transaction void or unenforceable[13].

A2.3   What are the provisions of the Companies Act 2006 relating to impediments to takeovers[14]?

In principle, companies whose shares are admitted to trading on a regulated market can structure their share capital in a way that could provide an effective barrier to future takeovers, although in practice very few have done so. In light of this, the Takeovers' Directive does contain provisions (so-called break though provisions) that are designed to remove certain types of obstacles to takeovers (otherwise know as 'poison pill' provisions), which a member state may adopt if it so wishes.

The UK decided not to automatically adopt the break-through provisions of the Takeovers Directive. However, as required by the Takeovers Directive, the 2006 Act provides a regime under which shareholders can elect by special resolution to opt-in to apply the break-through provisions and in doing so disapply certain voting restrictions (or poison pills) in the context of a takeover bid.

A2.3.1   What are 'break-through' provisions?

One of the intentions of the Takeovers Directive was to introduce a regime[15] that prevented impediments to takeover offers (such as the use of enhanced voting rights or other poison pills) being utilised. To do this, the Takeovers Directive provided that once a takeover offer has been made public, the offeror will be able to 'break-through' any restrictions on the transfer of securities in the target's articles of association, any restrictions on the transfer of securities that is contained in any contractual relationships between the target and its shareholders and any restrictions on voting rights contained in the target's articles of association or contractual arrangement between the company and its shareholders.

In response to criticisms to these break-through provisions during the consultation period the Takeovers Directive does allow member states to opt-out of such provisions[16] provided they give companies registered in their jurisdiction the ability to apply or opt back in to the provisions if they so wish. The UK government decided not to automatically apply the break-through

---

[13]   Section 956, Companies Act 2006.
[14]   Sections 966 – 973, Companies Act 2006.
[15]   Article 11, Takeovers Directive.
[16]   Article 12, Takeovers Directive.

provisions to UK companies, giving UK companies the option to voluntarily opt back in to such provisions if they so wish.

A2.3.2   What are the requirements for a company to opt in to the break-through provisions (i.e. a pre-bid defence) of the Takeovers Directive?

A company may opt-in to the break-through provisions provided it satisfies the following three conditions[17]:

(i)   the company has voting shares admitted to trading on a regulated market;

(ii)   the company's articles of association cannot contain any share transfer restrictions during the time allowed for acceptance of a bid or restrictions on voting rights at general meetings to decide on any defence measures or, if they do, they must also contain a provision that such restrictions will not apply in the event of a takeover offer or such other transaction covered by the break through provisions; and

(iii)   no shares conferring special rights in the company are held by a UK governmental minister (or a Scottish or Northern Irish minister), a nominee of such minister or a company directly or indirectly controlled by such minister and no such rights are exercisable by or on behalf of a minster under any enactment.

A2.3.3   Can a company opt out of the break-through provisions if it has passed an opting-in resolution?

Yes, once a company has opted into the break-through provisions it can opt-out of them again by passing a special resolution to this effect[18].

A2.3.4   What are the requirements for an opting-in and opting-out resolution?

An opting-in/opting-out resolution must specify the date from which it is to have effect, which cannot be earlier than the date on which the resolution is passed[19].

An opting-in resolution can be passed before a company's shares are admitted to trading on a regulated market provided that instead of specifying an effective date the resolution is expressed to take effect from the date of listing.

The effective date of an opting-out resolution cannot be earlier than the first anniversary of the date on which a copy of the opting-in resolution was sent to the registrar of companies.

---

[17]   Section 966, Companies Act 2006.
[18]   Section 966(5), Companies Act 2006.
[19]   Section 967, Companies Act 2006.

A2.3.5   What is the effect of passing an opting-in resolution?

The effect of an opting-in resolution is that where a takeover offer has been made for an opted-in company any agreement entered into between shareholders of the company on or after 21 April 2004, or that is entered into at any time between a shareholder and the company, will be invalid so far as it places a restriction on:

(i)   the transfer of shares in the company to the offeror (or his nominee) during the offer;

(ii)   the transfer of shares in the company to any person during the offer period when the offeror holds shares of not less than 75% in the value of all voting shares in the company;

(iii) the right to vote at a general meeting of the company (or on a written resolution of the company) that decides whether to take any action that might result in the frustration of the bids (as determined by reference to Article 9 of the Takeover Directive) or

(iv)   the right to vote at a general meeting of the company that:

■   is the first such meeting to be held after the end of the offer period; and

■   is held at a time when the offeror holds shares of not less than 75% in value of the voting shares in the company[20].

If a takeover offer is made for an opted-in company, provided the offeror holds 75% or more of the value of the voting shares in the company the offeror can require the directors of the target to convene a general meeting of the company.

A2.3.6   Is the company obliged to notify anyone that the opting-in/opting-out resolution has been passed?

Yes. The Company must notify the Panel and, where the company has shares admitted to trading on a regulated market in an EEA state other than the UK (or has requested such admission), must notify the supervisory authority designated by the Takeovers Directive for such a market, within 15 days of the resolution being passed[21].

A2.4   What are the provisions of the Companies Act 2006 relating to the compulsory acquisition of shares[22]?

Prior to 6 April 2007, a two track regime applied to the compulsory acquisition of shares. The Companies Act 2006 has now introduced a single regime that

---

[20]   Section 968, Companies Act 2006.
[21]   Section 970, Companies Act 2006.
[22]   Sections 974 – 991, Companies Act 2006.

applies to the compulsory acquisition of shares (referred to in the Companies Act 2006 as 'squeeze-out' and 'sell-out' rights), which we set out below.

A2.4.1 When will a right or obligation to the compulsory offer to acquire shares arise?

The need to invoke the right to compulsorily offer to acquire shares in a company commonly arises in the following situations:

(i) where a public offer is made to acquire 30% of the issued share capital of a company that is regulated by the Takeover Code;

(ii) where the majority shareholders propose to sell their interests to a third party and wish to 'drag along' the minority shareholders;

(iii) where the minority shareholders wish to ensure that the third party can be required to acquire their shares; and

(iv) where a public or private company wishes to eliminate minority holdings for the purposes of administrative convenience or in the context of an acquisition where 100% ownership of the target is sought.

In many cases it is simply impracticable to obtain the consent of every minority shareholder to such a transfer. This is sometimes because shareholders cannot be traced; it may also be because a minority still object to the transfer. The Companies Act 2006 contains provisions under which a company can compel a minority to transfer their shares which are called 'squeeze-out rights' subject to satisfaction of a number of detailed protections. The Companies Act 2006 also contains provisions under which the minority shareholders can compel the acquisition of their shares, which are called 'sell-out' rights.

Private companies with minority shareholders (including holders of shares or options under employee share schemes) commonly have provisions in their articles under which a minority can be obliged by the majority to sell their shares to a third party purchaser of the majority interest ('drag along rights') or where a minority can require a third party purchaser of the majority to acquire their shares ('tag along rights'), in which case there will be no need to apply the statutory squeeze-out rights as the process will be governed entirely by the articles. Where the articles do not make such provision then the statutory 'squeeze-out' provisions will be of relevance.

A2.4.2 What is the meaning of a takeover offer in the context of the compulsory offer to acquire shares?

Squeeze-out and sell-out rights apply when a takeover offer has been made. In this context, a takeover offer is an offer to acquire shares in a company when the following two conditions are satisfied:

(i)   the offer is an offer to acquire all of the shares in a company (other than those already held by the offeror) or, where there is more than one class of shares in a company, all of the shares of one or more classes; and

(ii)   the terms of the offer are the same in relation to all the shares to which the offer relates or, where the shares to which the offer relates include shares of different classes, in relation to all the shares of each class.

A2.4.3   When is an offer to acquire shares treated as being an offer on the same terms?

As set out above, for an offer to acquire shares to constitute a takeover offer it has to be an offer to acquire shares on the same terms as each other (or on the same terms as shares of the same class). There are exceptions to this where[23]:

(i)   the shares, which are the subject of the offer, carry a differential dividend based on their date of allotment and where the difference in terms of the offer simply reflects the difference in entitlement to the dividend; and

(ii)   the laws of another country preclude the form of consideration offered or the attachment of conditions with which the offeror is unable to comply or which are unduly onerous, and the shareholders in such a jurisdiction are able to receive consideration in another form that is of substantially equivalent value, and the condition for an offer to be made on the same terms would be satisfied but for the fact that an offer of consideration on the same terms to those persons is precluded.

A2.4.4   What if the offeror is unable to communicate an offer to shareholders?

If there are shareholders in the target company to whom the offer to acquire shares cannot be communicated, the offer to acquire shares will still be considered to be a takeover offer (and therefore squeeze-out rights will still be triggered) provided that[24]:

(i)   those shareholders have no registered address in the UK;

(ii)   the offer was not communicated to those shareholders in order not to contravene the law of a country or territory outside of the UK; and

(iii) either:

- the offer is published in the *London Gazette*; or

- the offer can be inspected, or a copy of it obtained, at a place in an EEA State or on a website, and a notice is published in the *London Gazette* specifying the address of that place or website.

---

[23] Section 976, Companies Act 2006.
[24] Section 978, Companies Act 2006.

A2.4.5   What are squeeze-out rights?

Squeeze-out rights are, in general terms, the ability for an offeror to compulsorily acquire those shares in the target company that shareholders have not agreed to sell provided that the offeror has acquired (or unconditionally contracted to acquire) 90% of the issued share capital of the company. The structuring of a successful squeeze-out offer is a highly technical area of company law and one on which specialist advice should be sought.

The application of squeeze-out rights does vary slightly depending on whether the takeover offer relates to one or multiple classes of shares and we discuss each of these regimes below.

(i)   where a takeover offer is made for one class of shares, if the offeror has, by virtue of acceptances of the offer, acquired or unconditionally contracted to acquire not less than 90% in value of the shares to which the offer relates and, where such shares are voting shares, not less than 90% of the voting rights carried by those shares, the offeror may give notice to the holders of those shares that the offeror has not acquired that he desires to acquire those shares;

(ii) where a takeover offer is made for different classes of shares, if the offeror has, by virtue of acceptance of the offer, acquired or unconditionally contracted to acquire not less than 90% in value of the shares of any class to which the offer relates, and in a case where the shares of that class are voting shares, not less than 90% of the voting rights carried by those shares, the offeror may give notice to the holder of any shares of that class to which the offer relates which the offeror has not acquired or unconditionally contracted to acquire that he desires to acquire those shares.

A2.4.6   When can a notice exercising an offeror's squeeze-out rights be given?

Any notices to be given must respect certain deadlines. A notice exercising squeeze-out rights can only be given prior to the end of the period of three months beginning with the day after the last day on which the offer can be accepted or, if earlier (and provided the time for acceptance of the takeover offer is not governed by the rules of the Panel on Takeovers and Mergers that give effect to Article 7 of the Takeovers Directive), the period of six months beginning with the date of the offer[25].

---

[25] Section 980, Companies Act 2006.

A2.4.7 Is the offeror required to send a copy of the squeeze-out notice to the target?

Yes. The offeror must send a copy of the notice to the target together with a statutory declaration, in the prescribed form, signed by him stating that the conditions for the giving of the notice are satisfied[26].

A2.4.8 What is the effect of a notice exercising the offeror's squeeze-out rights?

The effect of a notice exercising the offeror's squeeze-out rights is that the offeror is entitled and bound to acquire the shares to which the notice relates on the terms of the offer[27].

A2.4.9 What are sell-out rights?

Sell-out rights are, in general terms, the right of a minority shareholder to be bought out by an offeror where the offeror has acquired, or has contracted to acquire (whether unconditionally or not) 90% of the issued share capital of the company.

Again, the rules relating to sell-out rights vary depending on whether the shares are voting, non-voting and whether it relates to more that one class of share.

The holder of any voting shares to which the offer relates and who has not accepted the takeover offer may require the offeror to acquire those shares if, at any time before the end of the period within which the offer can be accepted:

(i) the offeror has by virtue of acceptances of the offer acquired or unconditionally contracted to acquire some but not all of the shares to which the offer relates; and

(ii) those shares, with or without any other shares in the company which the offeror has acquired, or contracted to acquire (whether unconditionally or not):

- amount to 90% or more in value of all the voting shares in the company; and

- carry at least 90% of the voting rights in the company.

The holder of any non-voting shares to which the offer relates and who has not accepted the takeover offer may require the offeror to acquire those shares if, at any time before the end of the period within which the offer can be accepted:

---

[26] Section 980(4), Companies Act 2006.
[27] Section 981, Companies Act 2006.

(i)   the offeror has by virtue of acceptances of the offer acquired or unconditionally contracted to acquire some but not all of the shares to which the offer relates; and

(ii)   those shares, with or without any other shares in the company which the offeror has acquired, or contracted to acquire (whether unconditionally or not), amount to not less than 90% in value of all of the shares in the company.

If a takeover offer relates to shares of more than one class and at any time before the end of the period within which the offer can be accepted:

(i)   the offeror has by virtue of acceptances of the offer acquired or unconditionally contracted to acquire some but not all of the shares to which the offer relates; and

(ii)   those shares, with or without any other shares of that class which the offeror has acquired, or contracted to acquire (whether unconditionally or not):

- amount to 90% or more in value of all the shares of that class; and

- where the shares of that class are voting shares, carry at least 90% of the voting rights carried by the shares of that class.

A2.4.10   When can sell-out rights be exercised by shareholders?

A shareholder cannot exercise its sell-out rights after the end of the period of three months from[28]:

(i)   the end of the period within which the offer can be accepted; or

(ii)   if later, the date of the notice that must be given by the offeror to the shareholders of the target that have not accepted the offer (being the date one month after the thresholds of 90% of all target shares and 40% of the voting rights have been achieved), detailing that any shareholders who have not accepted the offer have sell-out rights that can be exercised and the timeframe for such exercise.

A2.4.11   What is the effect of a shareholder exercising his sell-out rights?

If a shareholder exercises his sell-out rights the offeror is entitled and bound to acquire those shares on the terms of the offer or on such other terms as may be agreed[29].

---

[28] Section 984, Companies Act 2006.
[29] Section 985, Companies Act 2006.

A2.5 What are the provisions of the Companies Act 2006 relating to the directors' report[30]?

The Companies Act 2006 requires a company, which has securities carrying voting rights admitted to trading on a regulated market at the end of that year, to publish in its annual report detailed information on its defence mechanisms to takeovers. This repeats the provisions which were introduced by statutory instrument in May 2006 in relation to years commencing on or after May 2006.

A2.5.1 What disclosure is required in the directors' report by the Takeovers Directive?

Amongst other matters a directors' report must include (in addition to other requirements)[31]:

(i) details of the structure of the company's capital, including rights and obligations attaching to shares or a class of shares;

(ii) any restrictions on the transfer of securities in the company;

(iii) details of each person with a significant direct or indirect holding of securities in the company;

(iv) in relation to any securities that carry special rights with regard to control of the company, who holds such securities and details of the rights;

(v) any restriction on voting rights;

(vi) the nature of any special rights attaching to securities;

(vii) any agreements between shareholders that are known to the company and that may result in restrictions on the transfer of securities or on voting rights;

(viii) any significant agreements to which the company is party that take effect, alter or terminate upon a change of control of the company following a takeover offer and the efforts of these agreements; and

(ix) any agreements between the company and its directors or employees providing for compensation for loss of office or employment that occurs because of a takeover offer.

A2.5.2 Are there any exceptions to disclosing this information in the directors' report?

Yes. A company is not required to disclose any significant agreements that alter or terminate upon a change of control of the company following a takeover bid where disclosure of such an agreement would be seriously prejudicial to the

---

[30] Section 992, Companies Act 2006.
[31] Section 992(2), Companies Act 2006.

company and the company is not under any other obligation to disclose the agreement.

A2.5.3   What are the practical implications of these disclosure requirements?

There have been significant concerns expressed in connection with the requirement for a company to "disclose any significant agreements to which the company is a party that take effect, alter or terminate upon a change of control of the company following a takeover bid, and the effects of any such agreements".

In practical terms, unless a company can rely on the exemption referred to above, this requirement necessitates a review of all agreements to which the company is a party (including those with subsidiaries) to identify any change of control provisions that apply in the event of a takeover offer. The company will then need to determine whether these agreements are 'significant' and therefore require disclosure. Once identified, the company will need to maintain a list of all such agreements, which will need to be updated to reflect any new agreements that the company enters into and that may require disclosure in future reports.

Appendix 3

Implementation timetable for secondary legislation

A3.1 Introduction A3001

    A3.1.1   The Companies Act 2006 (Commencement No. 1, Transitional Provisions & Savings) Order 2006 . . . . A3001

    A3.1.2   The Companies Act 2006 (Commencement No. 2, Consequential Amendments, Transitional Provisions & Savings) Order 2007 . . . . A3001

    A3.1.3   The Companies Act 2006 (Commencement No. 3, Consequential Amendments, Transitional Provisions & Savings) Order 2007 . . . . A3002

    A3.1.4   The Companies Act 2006 (Commencement No. 4 and Commencement No. 3 (Amendment)) Order 2007 . . . A3004

    A3.1.5   The Companies Act 2006 (Commencement No. 5, Transitional Provisions & Savings) Order 2007 . . . . . A3004

    A3.1.6   The Companies Act 2006 (Commencement No. 6, Saving and Commencement Nos 3 and 5 (Amendment)) Order 2008 . . . . A3006

    A3.1.7   The Companies Act 2006 (Consequential Amendments etc.) Order 2008 . . . . A3007

    A3.1.8   The Companies Act 2006 (Commencement No. 7 Transitional Provisional Savings) Order 2008 . . . . . . A3007

A3.2 Secondary legislation A3008

    A3.2.1   SI 2006/3429 The Companies (Registrar, Languages and Trading Disclosures) Regulations 2006 . . . . A3008

    A3.2.2   2007/318 The Companies Acts (Unregistered Companies) Regulations 2007 . . . . A3008

    A3.2.3   2007/2612 The Companies (Fees for Inspection and Copying of Company Records) Regulations 2007 . . . A3009

    A3.2.4   2007/3152 The Company and Business Names (Amendment) (No. 2) Regulations 2007 . . . . A3009

    A3.2.5   2007/3534 The Independent Supervisor Appointment Order 2007 . . . . A3009

    A3.2.6   2007/3535 The Companies (Fees for Inspection and Copying of Company Records) (No. 2) Regulations 2007 . . . . A3009

    A3.2.7   2007/2081 Companies (Political Expenditure Exemption) Order 2007 . . . . A3009

    A3.2.8   2007/3494 The Statutory Auditors and Third Country Auditors Regulations 2007 . . . . A3009

A3.2.9   2008/489 The Companies (Disclosure of Auditor
Remuneration and Liability Limitation Agreements)
Regulations 2008 .... A3010

A3.2.10   2008/496 The Statutory Auditors (Delegation of
Functions etc.) Order 2008 .... A3010

A3.2.11   2008/499 The Statutory Auditors and Third Country
Auditors (Amendment) Regulations 2008 .... A3010

A3.2.12   2008/495 The Companies (Trading Disclosures)
Regulations 2008 .... A3010

A3.2.13   2008/497 The Companies (Late Filing Penalties) and
Limited Liability Partnerships (Filing Periods and
Late Filing Penalties) Regulations 2008 .... A3010

A3.2.14   2008/729 The Companies (Authorised Minimum)
Regulations 2008 .... A3010

A3.2.15   2007/2541 The Companies (Tables A to F)
(Amendment) Regulations 2007 .... A3011

A3.2.16   2007/2826 The Companies (Tables A to F)
(Amendment) (No. 2) Regulations 2007 .... A3012

A3.2.17   2008/739 The Companies (Tables A to F)
(Amendment) Regulations 2008 .... A3012

A3.2.18   2008/373 The Companies (Revision of Defective
Accounts and Reports) Regulations 2008 .... A3012

A3.2.19   2008/374 The Companies (Summary Financial
Statement) Regulations 2008 .... A3012

A3.2.20   2008/393 The Companies Act 2006 (Amendment)
(Accounts and Reports) Regulations 2008 .... A3012

A3.2.21   2008/409 The Small Companies and Groups
(Accounts and Directors' Reports) Regulations 2008   A3013

A3.2.22   2008/410 The Large and Medium-sized Companies
and Groups (Accounts and Reports) Regulations
2008 .... A3013

A3.2.23   2008/565 The Insurance Accounts Directive
(Miscellaneous Insurance Undertakings) Regulations
2008 .... A3013

A3.2.24   2008/567 The Bank Accounts Directive
(Miscellaneous Banks) Regulations 2008 .... A3013

A3.2.25   2008/569 The Partnerships (Accounts) Regulations
2008 .... A3013

A3.2.26   2008/623 The Companies (Defective Accounts and
Directors' Reports) (Authorised Person) and
Supervision of Accounts and Reports (Prescribed
Body) Order 2008 .... A3013

A3.2.27   2008/651 The Accounting Standards (Prescribed
Body) Regulations 2008 .... A3014

A3.2.28   2008/690 Companies (Mergers and Divisions of Public
Companies) (Amendment) Regulations 2008 .... A3014

A3.2.29 2007/2242 The Companies (Interest Rate for
         Unauthorised Political Donation or Expenditure)
         Regulations 2007 .... A3014
A3.2.30 2008/719 The Companies (Reduction of Capital)
         (Creditor Protection) Regulations A3014
A3.2.31 Postscript: Further subordinate legislation coming
         into force on 1 October 2008 .... A3014
A3.3 Draft secondary legislation as at 30 June 2008 .... A3015

Appendix 3

Implementation timetable for secondary legislation

A3.1 Introduction

The implementation of the Act requires a series of secondary legislative measures. There follows a list of these measures which identifies the secondary legislation which is:

(i) already in force as at 30 June 2008;

(ii) comes into force on 1 October 2008; and

(iii) in draft form with proposed implementation dates.

A3.1.1 The Companies Act 2006 (Commencement No. 1, Transitional Provisions & Savings) Orders 2006

This order covered the provisions relating to the increase in facilities for e-communications with the Registrar of Companies on 1 January 2007.

However the main provisions that were dealt with under this order came into force on 20 January 2007 and covered provisions for communicating electronically with shareholders, the inclusion of an exemption for directors for liability for statements in the directors' report and directors' remuneration report in the accounts unless they are knowingly or recklessly incorrect and the inclusion of a new definition of major shareholding which is taken from the Transparency Directive[1].

A3.1.2 The Companies Act 2006 (Commencement No. 2, Consequential Amendments, Transitional Provisions and Savings) Order 2007

The second commencement order dealt with provisions of the Companies Act 2006 which came into force on 6 April 2007. Five sections of the Companies Act 2006 were implemented by this order: Firstly, Section 2 of the Act which deals with the definition of 'Companies Acts' used; secondly, the provisions relating to takeovers (Sections 942-992 and Schedule 2); thirdly, the provisions relating to unregistered companies in Section 1043; fourthly, Section 1170 dealing with the definition of EEA State and related expressions; and finally, Section 1284(1) which extends the application of the first three sections mentioned above to Northern Ireland.

---

[1] 2004/109/EC.

In addition, this order brought into force a number of provisions of the Companies Act 2006 only so far as required to implement the sections listed above[2]. The order also introduced some traditional provisions where required and appended a range of legislation as a consequence of the provisions implemented or repealed by the order.

A3.1.3   The Companies Act 2006 (Commencement No. 3, Consequential Amendments, Transitional Provisions and Savings) Order 2007

The third Commencement order dealt with provisions which came into force on 1 October 2007, 1 November 2007, 15 December 2007 and 1 October 2008.

On 1 October 2007 the following provisions came into force:

- Sections 29 & 30 relating to resolutions or agreements which affect the constitution of a company;

- Sections 116 to 119 relating to inspection of the register of members;

- Sections 145 to 153 relating to the exercise of rights of members;

- Section 154 relating to companies which are required to have directors;

- Section 160 relating to the requirement that the appointment of each director to a public company should be voted on individually

- Section 161 relating to the validity of acts of directors;

- Sections 168-169 relating to the removal of directors;

- Sections 170 to 181 relating to the general duties of directors (but not including Sections 175-177)

- Sections 188 to 226 relating to transactions with directors which require the approval of members;

- Sections 227 to 230 relating to the service contracts for directors;

- Section 231 relating to contracts which are made with a sole member who is also a director of the company;

- Sections 232 to 239 relating to director's liabilities;

- Sections 247 (subsequently amended to 248 by a later commencement order) to 259 relating to supplementary provisions concerning a company's directors;

- Sections 260 to 269 relating to derivate claims and proceedings by members;

- Sections 281 to 287 relating to general provisions about resolutions;

[2]   Sections 546, 558, 1121 to 1123, 1125 to 1133, 1134, 1135, 1138, 1139, 1140, 1168 and 1173, Companies Act 2006.

- Sections 288 to 300 relating to written resolutions;

- Sections 301 to 307, 310 to 326, 327(1), (2)(a) and (b) and 3, 328, 329, 330(1) to (5), (6)(a) and (b) and (7), 331, 332, 334 and 335 relating to resolutions at meetings;

- Sections 336 to 340 relating to the additional requirement for AGMs of public companies;

- Sections 341 to 354 relating to additional requirements for resolutions and meetings for quoted companies;

- Sections 355 to 359 relating to records of resolutions and meetings;

- Sections 360 and 361 relating to supplementary provisions for meetings and resolutions;

- Section 417 relating to the contents of the business review in the directors' report;

- Sections 485 to 488 relating to the appointment of auditors by private companies;

- Section 993 relating to fraudulent trading;

- Sections 994 to 999 relating to the protection of members against unfair prejudice;

- Sections 1035 to 1039, 1124 and Schedule 3 relating to company investigations and other amendments; and

- Sections 1121 to 1123 and 1125 to 1133 relating to offences under the Companies Act 2006 (only so far as they relate to Part XIV or Part XV of the Companies Act 1985).

Sections 362 to 379 relating to control of political donations and expenditure, with the exception of certain provisions of the order relating to independent election candidates.

A number of sections of the Companies Act 2006 were implemented in so far as was necessary to assist with the bringing into force of the above sections.[3]

On 1 November 2007 Sections 362 to 379 which relate to the control of political donations and expenditure came into force in Northern Ireland.[4]

On 15 December 2007, Section 1068, relating to the Registrar of Companies' authentication and manner of delivery of documents (except Subsection (5) which is already in force) and Sections 1168 and 1284, in so far as is necessary

---

[3] Sections 17, 385, 540(1) and 4, 545,546,548,629,1121,1122,1125,1127 to 1133, 1158,1168, 1173 and 1284, Companies Act 2006.

[4] Sections 546,1158,1173 and 1284, Companies Act 2006 were also implemented so far as necessary for the implementation of the main provisions coming into force on this date.

to implement directive 2005/56/EC on cross-border mergers of limited liability companies came into force.[5]

On 1 October 2008 certain provisions within the Act relating to the control of political donations and expenditure to independent election candidates are implemented[6].

A3.1.4 The Companies Act 2006 (Commencement No. 4 and Commencment No. 3) Order 2007

This order implemented Section 1137(1), (4), (5)(b) and (6) relating to the inspection of company records and Section 1167 setting out the definition of 'prescribed' and Section 1284 relating to extension of Companies Acts to Northern Ireland so far as necessary for the purposes of the foregoing provisions, from 30 September 2007. In addition, this commencement order made the following amendments to the Companies Act 2006 (Commencement No. 3, Consequential Amendments, Transitional Provisions and Savings) Order 2007:

- the substitution of '248' instead of '247' in article 2(1)(d);

- in Part 1 of Schedule 2 the substitution of '380(4)(a) and (c) to (m)' instead of '380(1) and (4) to (5)', the omission of 'Section 719' and the omission of '380(5)' in the reference to Schedule 24 to the Companies Act 1985;

- in Part 2 of Schedule 2 the substitution of '388(4)(a) and (c) to (m)' instead of '388(1) and (4) to (5)', the omission of 'Article 668' and '388(5)' from the reference to Schedule 23 to the Companies Act (Northern Ireland) Order 1986; and

- omit paragraph 18 from Schedule 3.

A3.1.5 The Companies Act 2006 (Commencement No. 5, Transitional Provisions and Savings) Order 2007

This order deals with provisions that came into force on 6 April 2008, 29 June 2008 and 1 October 2008 (together with some minor amendments that had come into force on force on 31 December 2007 and 14 January 2008).

On 6 April 2008 the following provisions came into force:

- Section 44 relating to the execution of documents;

---

[5] Sections 1168 and 1248, Companies Act 2006 also came into force on 15 December 2007 so far as was necessary to implement the main provisions brought into force on that date.
[6] Sections 362(a), 363(2)(a), 363(3), 364(3), 365(1)(a) and (b)(i), 366(1)(a), 367(3)(a) and 378(2), Companies Act 2006.

- Sections 121 and 128 relating to the removal of entries from the register of members and the time limit for claims;

- Section 270 to 274 and 280 relating to company secretaries;

- Sections 380 to 416, 418 to 462 and 464 to 474 relating to accounts and reports;

- Sections 475 to 484 and 489 to 539 relating to audit;

- Section 544 relating to the transferability of shares;

- Sections 738 to 754 relating to debentures;

- Sections 755 to 767 relating to private and public companies;

- Sections 768 to 790 relating to the certification and transfer of securities;

- Sections 811(4), 812 and 814 relating to the exercise of the right to inspect the register of interests disclosed;

- Sections 829 to 853 relating to distributions;

- Sections 895 to 901 relating to arrangements and reconstructions;

- Sections 902 to 941 relating to the mergers and divisions of public companies;

- Section 1126 relating to the consents required for certain prosecutions;

- Sections 1161 and 1162 and Schedule 7 relating to the meaning of 'undertaking' and related expressions;

- Section 1164 relating to the meaning of 'banking company' and 'banking group';

- Section 1165 relating to the meaning of 'insurance company' and related expressions;

- Section 1169 relating to dormant companies;

- Section 1172 relating to references to requirements of the Companies Act 2006;

- Section 1173 relating to the definitions of 'credit institution' and 'working day';

- Sections 1209 to 1241, 1245 to 1264 and Schedules 10, 11, 13 and 14 relating to statutory auditors; and

- Section 1282 relating to the payment of expenses of winding up.

A number of sections of the Companies Act 2006 were implemented insofar as was necessary to assist with the bringing into force of the above sections[7].

---

[7]   1117(1),(2) and (3), 17, 540(1) and (4), 545, 546, 548, 629, 1121 to 1123, 1125 and 1127 to 1133, 1139, 1140, 1168, 1173, 1159, 1160 and Schedule 6 and 1284, Companies Act 2006.

Sections 1242 to 1244 and Schedule 12 were implemented on 29 June 2008. These provisions relate to the information to be supplied by and the duties of third country auditors.

On 1 October 2008 the following provisions came into force:

- Sections 69 to 74 relating to objections to company names;

- Sections 82 to 85 relating to trading disclosures;

- Sections 155 to 159 relating to the appointment of directors;

- Sections 175 to 177 relating to the general duties of directors;

- Sections 182 to 187 relating to the duty of directors to declare an interest in an existing transaction or arrangement;

- Section 1157 relating to the power of the court to grant relief in certain cases; and

- Sections 1277 to 1280 relating to the information as to the exercise of voting rights by institutional investors.

Again, a number of provisions within the Companies Act 2006 come into force so far as is necessary to allow the implementation of the above listed provisions.[8]

The order also made some amendments to the first and third Commencement Orders made under the Companies Act 2006.

A3.1.6 The Companies Act 2006 (Commencement No. 6, Saving and Commencement Nos. 3 and 5 (Amendment)) Order 2008

This order concerns the implementation of provisions in the Act relating to the audit of small charitable companies.

The following provisions came into force on 1 April 2008:

Section 1175 and Section 1295 and Schedule 16 relating to the removal of special provisions about accounts and audit of charitable companies (so far as it relates to Part VII of the Companies Act 1985 and Part 1 of Schedule 9 and Sections 1295 and Schedule 16).

The order also made the some amendments to the third and fifth Commencement Orders made under the Companies Act 2006.

---

[8]   1295 and Schedule 16, 1121 to 1123, 1125 and 1127 to 1133, 1168,1173 and 1284, Companies Act 2006.

A3.1.7   The Companies Act 2006 (Consequential Amendments etc.) Order 2008

This order makes consequential amendments to UK legislation to take account of the provisions of the Companies Act that are effective from 6 April 2008 and 1 October 2008.

A3.1.8   The Companies Act 2006 (Commencement No. 7 Transitional Provisional and Savings) Order 2008

This order concerns the reduction of capital by private companies supported by a solvency statement and the treatment of reserves arising out of the reduction.

The following provisions come into force on 1 October 2008:

- Sections 641(1)(a) and (2) to (6) and 642 to 644 relating to private company reduction of share capital supported by solvency statement;

- Section 654 relating to the treatment of reserve arising from reduction of capital;

- Sections 610(2) to (4) relating to the application to share premium account as if it were paid up share capital;

- 652(1) and (3) relating to the liability of members following reduction of capital;

- 733(5) and (6) relating to the application to capital redemption reserve as if it were paid up share capital.

So far as relating to the provisions relating to reduction of capital under the Sections 641, 642 to 644 and 654:

- Section 1284(1) relating to the extension of Companies Acts to Northern Ireland so far as necessary for the purposes of the provisions mentioned in sub-paragraphs (a) to (c);

- Section 1286(1)(a) and (2)(a) relating to the extension to Northern Ireland of Great Britain enactments relating to limited liability partnerships, so far as relating to the application to limited liability partnerships of the subject matter of Part 15 (accounts and reports), Part 16 (audit) and Part 42 (statutory auditors);

- Section 1295 and Schedule 16 relating to repeals, so far as relating to the repeals of the second sentence of Section 141(4) of the Companies Act 1989 and of the second sentence of Article 75(4) of the Companies (No. 2) (Northern Ireland) Order 1990; and

- Paragraph 11(2) of Schedule 15 relating to the amendment of definition of "regulated market" in Section 103(1) of the Financial Services and Markets Act 2000.

A3.2 Secondary Legislation

In addition to the Statutory Instruments referred to above made in relation to the implementation timetable, further regulations have also been made pursuant to the Act.

A3.2.1 SI 2006/3429 The Companies (Registrar, Languages and Trading Disclosures) Regulations 2006

These Regulations came into force on 1 January 2007 and make changes in 5 main areas. Firstly, they confirm that an electronic signature attached to an electronic copy of a document by the Registrar of Companies can be confirmation that it is a certified copy of the original document. Secondly, the regulations extend the application of s1105 Companies Act 2006 to contracts relating to the allotment of shares under section 88(2)(b)ii of the 1985 Act and to voluntary filings of translation pursuant to s1106. Thirdly, they substitute new wording into s 188(1) of the Insolvency Act 1986 in order to comply with the provisions in the new Act. Fourthly, they make amendments to the provisions relating to trading disclosure under s349, 351 and 705(4) (a) of the 1985 Act relating to punishment of offences. Finally, the Regulations make amendments to Schedule 24 of the 1985 Act so as to comply with the provisions of the 2006 Act which have already come into force until Schedule 24 of the Act is repealed.

A3.2.2 2007/318 The Companies Acts (Unregistered Companies) Regulations 2007

This Regulation extends the application of the following provisions of the Companies Act 2006 to un-registered companies:

- Chapter 2 (Impediments to takeovers) and Chapter 3 (Squeeze out and sell out) of Part 28 (Take-overs);

- Section 546 (Issued and allotted share capital) and Section 558 (when shares are allocated) of Part 17 (a company's share capital);

- Section 1122 (liability of company as officer in default) and s1132 (production and inspection of documents where offence suspected) in Part 36 (offences);

- Sections 1134,1135 and 1138 (company records), s1139 (1) and (4) (service of documents on company) and s1140 (service of documents on directors, secretaries and others) in Part 37 (supplementary provisions);

- Section 1173 (minor definitions: general) in Part 38 (companies interpretation); and

- Parts 46 & 47 (general supplementary provisions and final provisions).

These changes came into force on 6 April 2007.

A3.2.3   2007/2612 The Companies (Fees for Inspection and Copying of Company Records) Regulations 2007

Following the implementation of these Regulations on 1 October 2007, the fees for inspecting the register of a company, obtaining copies of the register and copies of the company records have been amended.

A3.2.4   2007/3152 The Company and Business Names (Amendment) (No.2) Regulations 2007

These Regulations, which came into force on 6 November 2007, amend the list of specific words or expressions that will trigger the need for prior approval if seeking to register a company or trade under such a name.

A3.2.5   2007/3534 The Independent Supervisor Appointment Order 2007

These Regulations, which came into force on 6 April 2008, appoint the Professional Oversight Board as Independent Supervisor of the Auditors General when they carry out the functions of statutory auditors and sets out requirements and provisions concerning the exercise of that function.

A3.2.6   2007/3535 The Companies (Fees for Inspection and Copying of Company Records) (No.2) Regulations 2007

These Regulations, which came into force on 6 April 2008, amend the fees payable for inspecting and copying the register of debenture holders and obtaining a copy of any debenture trust deeds.

A3.2.7   2007/2081 Companies (Political Expenditure Exemption) Order 2007

This order came in to force in Great Britain on 1 October 2007 and provides for an exemption from the need for authorisation under Part 14 of the Companies Act 2006 if certain conditions set out in the Order can be met or apply to a company.

A3.2.8   2007/3494 The Statutory Auditors and Third Country Auditors Regulations 2007

These regulations were made in order to implement in Part Directive 2006/43/EC and provide for the necessary Sections of the Companies Act 2006 to be amended to comply with the directive. In addition the regulation provides for a register of Non-EEA auditors to be maintained.

A3.2.9 2008/489 The Companies (Disclosure of Auditor Remuneration and Liability Limitation Agreements) Regulations 2008

These regulations, which came into force on 6 April 2008, require companies to disclose information about amounts payable for the services they and their associates have purchased from their auditors and their associates in their annual accounts and to disclose whether they have entered into a liability limitation agreement with their auditors.

A3.2.10 2008/496 The Statutory Auditors (Delegation of Functions etc.) Order 2008

This Order, which came into full force on 29 June 2008, delegates certain functions of the Secretary of State under Part 42 of the Companies Act 2006 to the Professional Oversight Board.

A3.2.11 2008/499 The Statutory Auditors and Third Country Auditors (Amendment) Regulations 2008

These regulations came into force on 5 April 2008 and correct a number of errors in the Statutory Auditors and Third Country Auditors Regulations 2007.

A3.2.12 2008/495 The Companies (Trading Disclosures) Regulations 2008

These regulations which are in force on 1 October 2008 set out the instances when and the manner in which companies are to make trading disclosures at certain locations on company documentation and on company websites.

A3.2.13 2008/497 The Companies (Late Filing Penalties) and Limited Liability Partnerships (Filing Periods and Late Filing Penalties) Regulations 2008

These regulations, which are in force on 6 April 2008 amend, with effect from 1 February 2009, the penalties which are to be paid by limited companies and limited liability partnerships which file their accounts after the time period specified in the Companies Acts 1985 and 2006. The regulations also amend the time period within which limited liability partnerships are obliged to file their accounts.

A3.2.14 2008/729 The Companies (Authorised Minimum) Regulations 2008

These regulations, which came into force on 6 April 2008 detail the authorised minimum allotted share capital in euros and sterling for public companies.

A3.2.15   2007/2541 The Companies (Tables A to F) (Amendment) Regulations 2007

These regulations came into force on 1 October 2007 and amended Tables A and C in the following ways:

(i)   Amendments relating to all companies limited by shares

■   Regulation 1 of Table A is amended to incorporate a new definition of 'the Act';

■   Regulation 36 ceases to have effect;

■   Regulation 37 is amended so as to remove the reference to an extraordinary meeting and to make the date by which the general meeting is to be called 'in accordance with the provisions of the Act';

■   Regulation 53 ceases to have effect; and

■   Regulation 117 is amended to remove the reference to an extraordinary resolution and to replace it with a reference to special resolution.

(ii)   Amendments applicable to private companies limited by shares only

■   Regulation 38 of Table A is amended;

■   Regulation 40 is amended to address proceedings at general meetings;

■   Regulations 60 & 61 are amended to as to remove the words annual/extraordinary in voting proxy forms;

■   Regulations 73-75 cease to have effect; and

■   Regulation 76 is amended to incorporate the words 'other than a director retiring by rotation' after 'no person' in relation to appointment and retirement of directors.

(iii)   Amendments applicable to public companies limited by shares only

■   Regulation 38 is amended; and

■   Regulations 60 & 61 are amended to replace the words 'extraordinary' with 'any other' after the words 'our behalf at the annual' in relation to votes of members.

(iv)   Amendments applicable to companies limited by guarantee and not having a share capital

Before Article 1 of Table C the following words are to be inserted 'References in these Articles to Table A are to that Table so far as it relates to private companies limited by shares'.

A3.2.16   2007/2826 The Companies (Tables A to F) (Amendment) (No. 2) Regulations 2007

As from 1 October 2007:

- Regulation 50 of Table A relating to proceedings at general meetings ceases to have effect; and

- Regulation 54 of Table A is amended to include necessary references to proxies.

A3.2.17   2008/739 The Companies (Tables A to F) (Amendment) Regulations 2008

As from 6 April 2008:

- Article 8 of Table C in the Companies (Tables A to F) Regulations 1985 is amended by inserting the words 'or by proxy' after the words 'is present in person'; and

- Article 2 of Table E in the Companies (Tables A to F) Regulations 1985 ceases to have effect.

A3.2.18   2008/373 The Companies (Revision of Defective Accounts and Reports) Regulations 2008

These regulations, which came into force on 6 April 2008, set out how companies should revise their accounts and reports under the Act in the event the accounts and reports are defective.

A3.2.19   2008/374 The Companies (Summary Financial Statement) Regulations 2008

These regulations, which came into force on 6 April 2008, set out the instances when companies may prepare summary financial statements instead of full accounts and reports together with the form and content of the summary financial statements.

A3.2.20   2008/393 The Companies Act 2006 (Amendment) (Accounts and Reports) Regulations 2008

These regulations came into force on 6 April 2008 and, amongst other matters, implement provisions of Directive 2006/46/EC on company reporting, by amending Parts 15 and 16 of the Act which set out the conditions that determine whether a company or group qualifies as small or medium-sized (SMEs).

A3.2.21 2008/409 The Small Companies and Groups (Accounts and Directors' Reports) Regulations 2008

These regulations came into force on 6 April 2008 and set out the detailed format and content of the accounts and directors' report required for small and group companies.

A3.2.22 2008/410 The Large and Medium-sized Companies and Groups (Accounts and Reports) Regulations 2008

These regulations came into force 6 April 2008 and set out the detailed format and content of accounts and reports of large and medium-sized companies.

A3.2.23 2008/565 The Insurance Accounts Directive (Miscellaneous Insurance Undertakings) Regulations 2008

These regulations came into force on 6 April 2008 and ensure that insurance undertakings are subject to the same accounting requirements as insurance companies subject to the Companies Act 2006.

A3.2.24 2008/567 The Bank Accounts Directive (Miscellaneous Banks) Regulations 2008

These regulations came into force on 6 April 2008 and ensure certain banking undertakings are subject to the same accounting requirements as banking companies subject to the Companies Act 2006 in implementation of EU Directives.

A3.2.25 2008/569 The Partnerships (Accounts) Regulations 2008

These regulations came into force on 6 April 2008 and ensure certain partnerships whose members have limited liability are subject to the same accounting and audit requirements as companies subject to the Companies Act 2006.

A3.2.26 2008/623 The Companies (Defective Accounts and Directors' Reports) (Authorised Person) and Supervision of Accounts and Reports (Prescribed Body) Order 2008

This order came into force on 6 April 2008 and reflects administrative changes at the Financial Reporting Review Panel.

A3.2.27 2008/651 The Accounting Standards (Prescribed Body) Regulations 2008

These regulations came into force on 6 April 2008 and appointed the Accounting Standards Board as the prescribed body for the purposes of Section 464 of the Companies Act 2006 which deals with accounting standards.

A3.2.28 2008/690 Companies (Mergers and Divisions of Public Companies) (Amendment) Regulations 2008

These regulations came into force on 6 April 2008 and deal with the requirements for an independent expert's report on a merger of a public limited liability company implementing Directive 2007/63. They relax the requirement for an independent expert's report in the case of a company merger if all shareholders agree one is not necessary.

A3.2.29 2007/2242 The Companies (Interest Rate for Unauthorised Political Donation or Expenditure) Regulations 2007

These regulations came into force on 1 October 2007 in Great Britain and set out the level of interest on unauthorised donations or expenditure which directors are liable to make good to the company.

A3.2.30 2008/719 The Companies (Reduction of Capital) (Creditor Protection) Regulations

These regulations came into force on 6 April 2008 and amend the Act to require a creditor, who seeks to object to a reduction of capital application made to court, to show a real likelihood that the proposed capital reduction would result in the company being unable to pay his claim when it fell due.

A3.2.31 Postscript: Further subordinate legislation coming into force on 1 October 2008

Further subordinate legislation has been made after 30 June 2008 which comes into force on 1 October 2008 and is included below:

(i)   SI 2008/1659. The Companies Act 1985 (Annual Return) and Companies (Principal Business Activities) (Amendment) Regulations 2008.

(ii) SI 2008/1738. The Company Names Adjudication Rules 2008.

(iii) SI 2008/1915. The Companies (Reduction of Share Capital) Order 2008.

A3.3   Draft secondary legislation as at 30 June 2008

Name	Overview	Date of Draft	Date of coming into force
The Companies Act 2006 (Commencement No 8 Transitional Provision and Savings) Order 2008	This order lists sections that will come into force on 1 October 2009.	19 June 2008	1 October 2009
The Companies (Annual Return and Service Addresses) Regulations 2008	These regulations detail the information that is required on the annual return of a company and the conditions required for an address for service.	26 April 2008	1 October 2009
The Companies (Model Articles) Regulations 2008	These regulations set out model articles of association for a company to be used from 1 October 2009.	July 2007	1 October 2009
The Companies (Prescribed Particulars of Company Charges) Regulations 2008	These regulations detail the information to be provided to the Registrar of Companies on the registration of a charge.	10 December 2007	1 October 2009
The Companies (Registration) Regulations 2008	These regulations deal with certain aspects of company formation under the Act.	28 February 2008	1 October 2009
The Companies (Company and Business Names) (Miscellaneous Provisions) Regulations 2008	These regulations deal with company and business names under the Act.	April 2008	1 October 2009
The Companies Act 1985 (Annual Return) Regulations 2008	These regulations deal with the information to be provided on a company's annual return.	30 April 08	1 October 2008

Implementation timetable for secondary legislation

Name	Overview	Date of Draft	Date of coming into force
The Companies (Shares, Share Capital and Authorised Minimum) Regulations	These regulations deal with the euro equivalent of the minimum authorised share capital and makes provision in relation to shares and share capital for the purposes of various provisions of the Companies Act 2006.	31 March 2008	1 October 2009
The Companies (Company Records) Regulations 2008	These regulations deal with the location, inspection and copying of company records.	April 2008	1 October 2009
The Companies (Disclosure of Address) Regulations 2008	These regulations relate to applications under Sections 243 and 1088 for disclosure of an address.	1 July 2008	1 October 2009
The Non-Companies Act Companies Authorised to Register Regulations 2008	These regulations make provision for the registration of companies which are not formed under the Companies Act.	April 2008	1 October 2009
The Companies (Trading Disclosures) (Amendment) Regulations 2008	These regulations amend Companies (Trading Disclosures) Regulations 2008 (5.I 2008/495) and deals with the obligation of a company to display its registered name at its registered address.	19 July 2007	1 October 2008
The Companies (Registrar of Companies and Application for Striking off) Regulations 2008	These regulations relate to the functions and powers of the Registrar under Part 35 and 31 of the Act.	17 March 2008	1 October 2009

Name	Overview	Date of Draft	Date of coming into force
The Overseas Companies Regulations 2008	These regulations impose registration and filing obligations on foreign companies that establish a place of business or branch in the UK.	13 December 2007	1 October 2009
The Companies (fees for Inspection and copying of Company Records) Regulations	These regulations deal with the selling of fees for inspection and copying of Company Records.	April 08	
The Companies (Unregistered Companies) Regulations	These regulations extend certain provisions of the Act to unregistered companies	July 2007	1 October 2009

Glossary of terms

Term	Definition
Accounting Regulatory Committee (ARC)	A committee composed of representatives from Member States and chaired by the European Commission, set up in accordance with the requirements contained in Article 6 of the International Accounting Standards Regulation. The function of the Committee is a regulatory one and consists in providing an opinion on Commission proposals to adopt (endorse) an international accounting standard.
Accounting Standards Board (ASB)	UK accounting body appointed by statute to review and issue accounting standards, part of the Financial Reporting Council.
Accounts meeting	The general meeting of shareholders of a public company at which the annual accounts and reports are laid.
Accounts Modernisation Directive (AMD)	European Directive 2003/51/EC amending the Directives on the annual and consolidated accounts of certain types of companies, banks and other financial institutions and insurance undertakings to harmonise with EU-adopted IFRS.
Accounts regulations	(See chapter 5 for definition.)
Affirmative resolution procedure	A process of parliamentary approval for a statutory instrument that requires a draft of the regulations or order to be laid before Parliament and for a resolution of each House of Parliament to approve the draft statutory instrument. (See negative resolution procedure).
Alternative Investment Market (AIM)	AIM is the London Stock Exchange's international market for smaller growing companies. It is regulated by the LSE as an exchange-regulated market and not a regulated market governed by the requirements of the Financial Services and Markets Act 2000.

Glossary of terms

Term	Definition
Amendment regulations	Companies Act 2006 (Accounts and Reports) (Amendment) Regulations 2008 (SI 2008/393) that amend the size thresholds for small and medium-sized companies and groups and introduce the new disclosure requirements on related party transactions and off-balance sheet arrangements.
Annual accounts; annual accounts and reports	Annual accounts in relation to a financial year mean the company's individual accounts for that year and any group accounts prepared by the company for that year. [Companies Act 2006, section 471(1)]. An unquoted company's annual accounts and reports for a financial year are its annual accounts, the directors' report and the auditors' report on those accounts and directors' report (unless the company is exempt from audit). [Companies Act 2006, section 471(2)]. A quoted company's annual accounts and reports for a financial year are its annual accounts, the directors' remuneration report, the directors' report and the auditors' report on those accounts, on the auditable part of the directors' remuneration report and on the directors' report. [Companies Act 2006, section 471(3)].
Annual financial report	The term used by DTR4.1.5 to mean the annual audited financial statements, management report and responsibility statements.
Annual general meeting (AGM)	An annual meeting of the shareholders of a company. A public company is required to hold an AGM, but this is now optional for a private company.
Articles of association	Constitutional document governing the business of a company and its internal organisation. The articles of association create a contract between the company and its members.

Term	Definition
Associated company for capital gains tax purposes	Two or more companies are associated if, by themselves, they would form a group of companies for the purposes of capital gains taxation. This term is not to be confused with associated company or associate for company law purposes or associates as defined by accounting standards.
Audit committee	A committee of the board of a company, particularly a listed company and larger private committees, that deals with (amongst other matters): (i) the adoption of appropriate accounting policies; (ii) the review of accounts; (iii) the liaison with the company's auditor; and (iv) the review of internal audits.
Audit Inspection Unit (AIU)	The AIU of the Professional Oversight Board is responsible for the monitoring of the audits of all listed and other major public interest entities.
Audit Quality Forum	Forum involving investors, auditors, business and regulatory bodies designed to encourage parties to contribute ideas on how to improve the quality and transparency of auditing.
Audit Regulations	The Audit Regulations of the Recognised Supervisory Bodies set out the rules as to: (a) the eligibility of persons for appointment as a statutory auditor, and (b) the conduct of statutory audit work.
Auditing Practices Board (APB)	UK auditing body appointed by statute to review and issue auditing standards, part of the Financial Reporting Council.
Authorised Guarantee Agreement (AGA)	A guarantee which is given by an outgoing tenant to its landlord upon the assignment of a lease which guarantees the preference of the incoming tenant's obligations under the lease.
BERR	(See *Department for Business, Enterprise and Regulatory Reform.*)
Bona fide	In good faith, without deceit or fraud.
Bona vacantia	The principle that, in the event of a company being dissolved, the property it held prior to dissolution belongs to the Crown, subject to certain exceptions.

Term	Definition
Bushel v Faith clause	A clause in the articles of association or a shareholders' agreement which increases a director's voting rights in respect of a resolution for his removal.
Capital gains tax taper relief	A relief from Capital Gains Tax available to individuals, trustees and personal representatives, but not to companies, the effect of which is to reduce a chargeable capital gain.
Certificate of incorporation	A document issued by Companies House on the registration of a company signifying that the formalities for creation of the company have been completed.
Combined Code	The principal guide to corporate governance best practice for listed companies. The Code is maintained by the FRC. The Listing Rules require listed companies to disclose in their annual reports how they have implemented the recommendation of the Combined Code.
Committee of European Securities Regulators (CESR)	Committee with the principal purpose to encourage co-ordination between the European Union's securities regulators.
Common seal	A seal bearing the company's name for the execution of documents which require a seal, such as a deed.
Companies (Audit, Investigations and Community Enterprise) Act 2004 (CAICE)	An Act to amend the law relating to company auditors and accounts, to the provision that may be made in respect of certain liabilities incurred by a company's officers, and to company investigations; to make provision for community interest companies; and for connected purposes.
Companies (Disclosure of Auditor Remuneration and Liability Limitation Agreements) Regulations 2008	SI 2008/489 Regulations requiring companies, in their annual accounts, to disclose information about amounts payable for the services they and their associates have purchased from their auditors and their associates. It also stipulates the disclosures to make if the company enters into a liability limitation agreement with its auditors.

Term	Definition
Companies (Summary Financial Statement) Regulations 2008	SI 2008/374 Regulations setting out the circumstances in which companies may prepare summary financial statements (SFS) to send to members in place of the full accounts and reports. The regulations also provide for the form and content of the SFS for different sizes and types of companies.
Companies Act accounts; Companies Act individual accounts; Companies Act group accounts	A company's individual or group accounts prepared in accordance with the provisions of the Companies Acts and following the form and content stipulated in the Small Accounts or the Large and Medium-sized Accounts regulations. [Companies Act 2006, sections 395, 396 and 403].
Companies House	The registry for companies based in England and Wales.
Company Directors Disqualification Act 1986	An Act to consolidate the rules of disqualification of persons from being directors of companies.
Company Law Reform Bill (also known as Companies Bill)	The Parliamentary bill which preceded the Companies Act 2006.
Company Share Option Plan (CSOP)	A form of share option scheme, requiring the prior approval of the Inland Revenue, that allows the option-holder to benefit from income tax relief.
Consumer Protection Act 1987	An Act to enhance the protection of consumers in respect of defective products. The Act also includes provisions relating to price indication of products.
Corporate Reporting Directive	European Union Directive No. 2006/46/EC amending the Directives on the annual and consolidated accounts of certain types of companies, banks and other financial institutions and insurance undertakings to provide for the collective responsibility of board members, increase transparency in transactions with related parties and off-balance-sheet arrangements and improve disclosure about corporate governance practices applied in a company.

Glossary of terms

Term	Definition
Corporate Social Responsibility (CSR)	Government initiative to encourage companies to consider the economic, social and environmental impacts of its operations (now often referred to as 'CR' or corporate responsibility).
Corporate tax self assessment	The requirement for a company to determine its own tax liability before inspection by HMRC.
Credit transaction	An arrangement for the provision of credit by a public company, or a company associated with a public company, which requires prior shareholder approval.
Data Protection Act 1998	An Act to make provision for the regulation of the processing of information relating to individuals, including the obtaining, holding, use or disclosure of such information.
Debenture	A document executed by a company as a deed in favour of a creditor, providing the creditor with a charge over all, or most of, the company's assets.
Declaration of solvency	A statement made by a company's directors pertaining to the assets of the company exceeding its liabilities before an application for a members' voluntary liquidation can be made.
Deed	A written document that is signed, sealed and delivered. A deed is enforceable, despite a lack of consideration and the limitation period for a claim arising pursuant to a deed which is generally 12 years.
Defective Accounts Regulations	Companies (Revision of Defective Accounts and Reports) Regulations 2008 (SI 2008/373) set out the circumstances in which companies may voluntarily revise their annual accounts and reports or must revise their abbreviated Companies Act accounts or how the provisions are applied where a request to revise is made by the Secretary of State or the Financial Reporting Review Panel.
De minimis	A general legal principle that the law will not have regard to the most negligible of matters.
Department for Business, Enterprise and Regulatory Reform (BERR)	Government department responsible for business and enterprise (formerly the Department of Trade and Industry).

Term	Definition
Deregulation and Contracting Out Act 1994	An act now repealed by the Companies Act 2006, which introduced a number of changes to UK competition law.
Derivative claim	A claim brought by a shareholder of a company on behalf of the company in respect of a course of action that the company is entitled to.
Directors – de facto – natural – appointed – de jure – courtesy – alternate – non-executive – executive – shadow – associate	(See Chapter 1 for definitions.)
Disclosure and Transparency Rules (FSA DTR)	The rules, which are contained in the Disclosure and Transparency Rules Source Book that is part of the FSA Handbook, that apply to issuers whose financial instruments are admitted to trading on a regulated market in the UK. The rules cover such matters as the contents of periodic financial reporting, disclosure of substantial interests in shares and related derivatives.
Distribution in specie	A distribution made in assets and not cash.
Dormant company	A company that has not had a significant accounting transaction for a certain period of time.
Eighth Company Law Directive	European Union Directive No. 84/253/EEC on the approval of persons responsible for carrying out the statutory audits of accounting documents. Repealed by the Statutory Audit Directive.
Eleventh Company Law Directive	European Union Directive No. 89/666/EEC concerning disclosure requirements in respect of branches opened in a Member State by certain types of company governed by the law of another state.

Glossary of terms

Term	Definition
Emoluments, directors'	Payments or other benefits received by directors for the service provided to the company. These must be disclosed in the directors' remuneration report of a quoted company, and include benefits such as salary, fees and bonuses, sums paid by way of expenses allowance but not certain other benefits – for example, value of share option granted to him. All companies have to provide summarised disclosures in the notes to accounts.
Employee Benefit Trusts (EBTs)	A trust set up for the benefit of employees to incentivise and reward employees, and which enjoys tax advantages but is subject to strict legislative regulation provided by the Inheritance Tax Act 1984.
Enlightened shareholder value	The principle that directors will be more likely to achieve long-term success for shareholders if companies operate responsibly with regard to such matters as the interests of employees and the environment.
Enterprise Management Incentive options (EMI options)	An option scheme granted by qualifying companies which attract a lower tax rate up to a combined total amount of £3 million.
EU-adopted IAS or IFRS	The term used interchangeably to mean the international accounting standards and interpretations adopted by the EU in accordance with the procedure laid down in Article 6(2) of the IAS Regulation. [Article 4 of the IAS Regulation].
European Commission (EC)	The European Commission is the executive branch of the European Union. The body is responsible for proposing legislation, implementing decisions, upholding the Union's treaties and the general day-to-day running of the Union.
European Economic Area (EEA)	The economic area comprising the European Union, Iceland, Liechtenstein and Norway which brings the EEA territories under the governance of the EU in respect of the free movement of goods, services, capital and persons.

Term	Definition
Ex gratia	'By favour', a payment that is made where there is no obligation to do so, i.e. a severance payment.
Exchange-regulated market	A market regulated by a sponsoring recognised investment exchange and not by the FSA, such as the LSE's AIM and Plus Markets' PLUS-quoted. Such markets are not regulated markets that have been authorised in accordance with MiFID.
Exercise price	The price at which the holder of an option may buy or sell the underlying security.
Extra Statutory Concession	HMRC may allow relief on an extra-statutory basis if there is a specific set of circumstances to all businesses falling within the relevant conditions – for example, ESC/C16, which allows distributions made under an informal winding-up to be treated as if made under a formal winding-up procedure, and so treated as capital as opposed to an income dividend.
Extraordinary general meeting (EGM)	A general meeting of the company's shareholders other than the annual general meeting (this is no longer applicable under the Companies Act 2006).
Financial Reporting Council (FRC)	Independent regulatory body to promote corporate reporting and governance.
Financial Reporting Exposure Draft (FRED)	The name given to an exposure draft of a proposed UK FRS issued by the Accounting Standards Board.
Financial Reporting Review Panel (FRRP)	UK body appointed by statute to review the accounts of public companies and large private companies to ensure compliance with accounting standards.
Financial Reporting Standard (FRS)	The name given to UK accounting standards issued by the Accounting Standards Board.
Financial Services and Markets Act 2000 (FSMA 2000)	The Act that provides for the regulation of the financial services markets in the UK and which appointed the FSA as the regulator.
Financial Services Authority (FSA)	Non-governmental body appointed by statute to oversee and regulate the financial services markets in the UK.

Glossary of terms

Term	Definition
First Company Law Directive	European Union Directive No. 68/151/EEC on co-ordination of safeguards which, for the protection of the interests of members and others, are required by Member States of companies, with a view to making such safeguards equivalent throughout the Community.
Fourth Company Law Directive	European Union Directive No. 78/660/EEC on the annual accounts of certain types of companies.
Generally Accepted Accounting Practices UK (UK GAAP)	Compliance with UK accounting standards, company law and best practice.
Generally Accepted Accounting Principles US (US GAAP)	The US counterpart of UK GAAP.
The General Counsel 100	Forum for the General Counsels of FTSE 100 companies to provide their opinion on key areas of legislative and policy reform and to enable members to share advice in relation to other matters which characteristically affect large companies.
Good leaver/bad leaver	Term in an employee's contract (and also Shareholders' agreements) determining the status of an employee's departure from a company. A good leaver typically leaves the company for reason of illness or death and will entitle the leaver (or his estate) to a more favourable benefits package than would be the case if he left as a bad leaver, which usually means there was justification for his dismissal.
Half-yearly report	The term used by DTR4.2.3 to mean the condensed set of financial statements, interim management report, and responsibility statements in respect of the first six months of a financial year.
Her Majesty's Revenue and Customs (HMRC)	Government department that is responsible for the collection and administration of taxes.
Higgs Report	Review into the role of independent directors, many recommendations of which are included in the Combined Code.

Term	Definition
IAS accounts; IAS individual accounts; IAS group accounts	A company's individual or group accounts prepared in accordance with EU-adopted IAS or IFRS [Companies Act 2006, sections 395 and 403].
IAS Regulation	EC Regulation 1606/2002 of the European Parliament and of the Council of 19 July 2002 on the application of international accounting standards.
ICAEW	(See Institute of Chartered Accountants in England & Wales.)
ICAEW Technical Release Tech 1/08	A Technical Release from the ICAEW providing guidance on materiality in financial reporting by UK entities, whether using UK GAAP or EU-adopted IFRS.
ICAEW Technical Release Tech 3/08	A Technical Release from the ICAEW providing guidance on materiality in financial reporting by UK entities, whether using UK GAAP or EU-adopted IFRS.
ICAEW Technical Release Tech 6/06 (revised)	A Technical Release from the ICAEW providing answers to a series of frequently asked questions on the disclosure of auditors' remuneration under the previous 2005 regulations but which are relevant for the new ones that are virtually identical to their predecessor.
IFRS	International Financial Reporting Standard as issued by the IASB and as referred to in Article 2 of the IAS Regulation.
Income Taxes Act 1988 (ICTA)	Act that regulates income and corporation tax.
Indemnity	A promise by a party to meet a potential legal liability of another party. An indemnity entitles the person indemnified to a payment in the event the liability, without a need for the indemnified party to show that it has suffered a loss (an indemnity therefore offers more protection than a warranty).
Insolvency Act 1986	Act that that regulates the affairs of companies who are in financial difficulties or insolvent.

Glossary of terms

Term	Definition
Institute of Chartered Accountants in England & Wales (ICAEW)	One of the professional bodies for chartered accountants in the UK.
Inter alia	Amongst other things.
Interim management report	The interim management report must be included in a listed company's half-yearly report and must include at least: (1) an indication of important events that have occurred during the first six months of the financial year, and their impact on the condensed set of financial statements, and (2) a description of the principal risks and uncertainties for the remaining six months of the financial year. [DTR4.2.7]
Interim Management Statements (IMS)	An interim management statement is a statement to be published by a listed company during the first and second six months of a financial year, that is, effectively a first- and third-quarter report.
International Accounting Standards (IAS)	International Accounting Standards as issued or adopted by the IASB and as referred to in Article 2 of the IAS Regulation.
International Accounting Standards Board (IASB)	Independent board with the purpose of developing and maintaining high-quality accounting standards globally.
International Financial Reporting Interpretations Committee (IFRIC)	The IASB's interpretative body.
Investment Services Directive (ISD)	European Directive on 93/22/EEC on investment services in the securities market. The ISD established the requirements for authorised investment firms and banks could provide certain services in other EU member states. Now repealed by MiFID.
Joint and several	Two or more parties who accept liability both together and individually.
Key Management Personnel	Persons having authority and responsibility for planning, directing and controlling the activities of the company, directly or indirectly including but not limited to executive and non-executive directors.

Term	Definition
Key Performance Indicators (KPI)	Financial and non-financial factors to help measure and determine a company's achievement of certain objectives.
Landlord and Tenant (Covenants) Act 1995	An act to enable outgoing tenants to be released from certain covenants by which they are bound.
Large and Medium-sized Companies Accounts regulations	The Large and Medium-sized Companies and Groups (Accounts and Reports) Regulations 2008 (SI 2008/410) that provide the form and content of Companies Act accounts for all companies other than small companies. The regulations also deal with the content of the directors' report and a quoted company's directors' remuneration report. They replace Schedules 4, 4A, 5, 6, 7, 7A, 9 and 9A to the Companies Act 1985.
Legal personality	Upon incorporation, the company is a person legally distinct from its members or shareholders and can, for example, enter into and be liable for agreements in its own capacity.
Limitation Act 1980	Principal statute that governs the period in which time a claim can be brought.
Listed company	A company whose shares are admitted to the Official List maintained by the FSA and which are traded on a regulated market operated by a recognised investment exchange.
Listing Rules (FSA LR)	The rules, which are contained in the Listing Rules source book that is part of the FSA Handbook, that must be complied with for securities to be admitted to Listing and that Listed companies must continue to comply with.
London Stock Exchange (LSE)	The London Stock Exchange plc is one of the UK's recognised investment exchanges that operates a regulated market.
Long-term Incentive Plan (LTIP)	A scheme whereby a senior employee can be allotted shares in the company for free, subject to his continued employment for a minimum period and his achievement of certain performance goals.
Main Market	One of the UK's regulated market exchanges operated by the LSE and regulated by the FSA.

Glossary of terms

Term	Definition
Major audit	A statutory audit conducted in respect of a Listed company or any other person in whose financial condition there is a major public interest. The Public Oversight Board has published statutory guidance on those audits that fall into the latter category. (See Chapter 7.)
Markets in Financial Instruments Directive (MiFID)	European Union Directive No. 2004/39/EC on markets in financial instruments that has replaced the Investment Services Directive.
Members' Voluntary Liquidation (MVL)	Procedure for liquidation of a solvent company requiring a declaration of solvency by the directors and a special resolution by the shareholders.
Memorandum of association	The constitutional document that essentially regulates the company's interaction with the outside world and which sets out the status and the capacity of the company.
MiFID investment firm	An investment firm as described in section 474(1) of the Companies Act 2006.
Model articles of association	The Companies Act (Model Articles) Regulations 2008.
National Insurance Contributions (NICs)	Sums owed to HMRC by employees and their employers and by workers who are self-employed.
Negative resolution procedure	A process of parliamentary approval for a statutory instrument that requires the draft regulations or order to be laid before Parliament, and which does not require positive approval and is subject to annulment in pursuance of a resolution of either House of Parliament (see *Affirmative resolution procedure*).
Non-statutory accounts	Any document, other than the statutory accounts, that contains a profit and loss account and/or balance sheet of a company or group that purports to deal with a financial year of the company or group [Companies Act 2006, section 435(3)].

Term	Definition
Notes to the accounts	A company's annual accounts, or a balance sheet or profit and loss account, include notes to the accounts, which give additional information that is required by any provision of the Companies Act 2006 or by international accounting standards.
Official List	The main list of securities admitted to trading on recognised investment exchanges in the UK, regulated by the Financial Services Authority as the UKLA.
Operating and Financial Review (OFR)	A review by quoted companies to assist shareholders to make an informed assessment of a company's financial performance. OFRs are provided on a voluntary basis and follow the guidance provided by the Accounting Standards Board in its Reporting Statement 1. A lot of the material covered in an OFR is now a mandatory component on the extended business review required from quoted companies.
Ordinary resolution	A decision by the shareholders at a general meeting of the company that requires a simple majority.
Overseas Companies regulations	Regulations, currently in draft form, concerning the registration and delivery of accounts of overseas companies that have operations, a place of business or a branch in the UK.
'Parmalat'	A reference to the Italian company whose accounting scandal in 2003 was largely responsible for the changes made through the Corporate Reporting Directive to the definition of 'related party' and the new disclosures to be made about related-party transactions and off-balance-sheet arrangements.
Passporting rights	Under MiFID, investment firms that have already been authorised by their home state may transfer to other EU states without any further authorisation from the host state.
Pay as you earn (PAYE)	Payment of income tax where the sum owed by the employee is deducted by the employer from the employee's wage.

Term	Definition
Persons Discharging Managerial Responsibilities (PDMR)	For the purposes of the DTR, someone who is a director or a senior executive who has regular access to inside information and has the power to make decisions affecting the business prospects of the company.
Phoenix company	A company which has a director who, within the past five years, had also been a director in another company within 12 months prior of that company going into liquidation and where the latter company had used a sufficiently similar name to suggest an association between the two companies.
PLUS-listed	One of the UK's regulated markets operated by Plus Markets plc and regulated by the Financial Services Authority.
Plus Markets	Plus Markets plc one of the operators of the UK's recognised investment exchanges.
PLUS-quoted	The exchange-regulated market operated by Plus Markets plc that is similar to the LSE's AIM.
Prima facie	In the first instant.
Privity of contract	The principle of contract law that allows only parties to a contract to enforce the contractual obligations arising under that contract. The principle has been truncated by the Contract (Rights of Third Parties) Act 1999.
Professional Oversight Board (POB)	Part of the Financial Reporting Council that oversees the regulation of the accounting, auditing and actuarial professions.
Property Managing Subsidiary	For the purposes of corporation tax, a subsidiary of an issuing company the business of which consists wholly or mainly in the holding or managing of land or any property deriving its value from land.
Prospective Financial Information (PFI)	Statements relating to financial forecasts according to the guidance issued by the ICAEW.

Term	Definition
Prospectus Rules	The rules relating to the requirement of a prospectus for a company applying for admission to trading, or an offer to the public of, transferable securities on a regulated market in the UK.
Public limited company (plc)	Company limited by shares or guarantee, which states in its memorandum that it is a public limited company, and which complies with the additional requirements for the formation of a plc in the applicable Companies Act.
Public Offers of Securities Regulations 1995	The predecessor to the Prospectus Rules.
Publicly traded company	See *Traded company* below.
Qualifying Services	A person's services at any time while he is a director of the company for the purposes of a directors' remuneration report.
Quasi-loan	An arrangement by a public company, or a company associated with a public company, that requires prior shareholder approval and which is, in substance, a loan but does not involve the company (the lender) lending money directly to the borrower. It occurs, for example, where a director uses a company credit card to buy goods and does so on the understanding that the company will settle the liability to the credit card provider and will be reimbursed by the director at a later date. The formal definition is found at section 199 of the Companies Act 2006.
Quorum	The minimum number of people needed for a duly formed meeting of a company – for example, a general meeting of shareholders or a board meeting.
Quoted company	A company whose equity share capital has been included on the Official List, an official list in an EEA State or which is admitted to dealing on either the New York Stock Exchange or Nasdaq.
Ratify	The process whereby shareholders can approve an action that has been taken by a director of the company.

Term	Definition
Recital	A paragraph in the preface to a European Union directive that provides some history or explanation of an Article in the directive.
Recognised Supervisory Body (RSB)	A body established in the UK (whether a body corporate or an unincorporated association) that has been recognised by the Secretary of State for the supervision of statutory auditors. The accountancy institutes in the UK that have members involved in statutory auditors are RSBs. The body must maintain and enforce rules as to: (a) the eligibility of persons for appointment as a statutory auditor, and (b) the conduct of statutory audit work –rules which are binding on persons seeking appointment or acting as a statutory auditor because they are members of that body. These rules are known as the Audit Regulations.
Registrar of Companies	Person responsible for the overseeing of the registration and administration duties of Companies House.
Regulated market	A market that meets the definition in the MiFID (Article 4(1)(14)) for trading in financial instruments and which has been authorised as such in accordance with MiFID.
Regulatory Information Services (RIS)	An FSA approved information service that allows listed companies to disseminate information relating to the company to the public.
Retirement by rotation	A requirement under the 1985 Table A articles of association that one third of the directors at each AGM shall retire automatically.
'Safe harbour provision'	This is a reference to the statutory liability regime for directors in respect of narrative reporting. This regime includes a 'safe harbour' protection for information in directors' reports (including the business review) and directors' remuneration reports, unless the director knew or was reckless, or if an omission was a dishonest concealment. It covers such reports published on or after 20 January 2007. An explicit statement is not required in the annual report in order for the 'safe harbour' protection to be invoked.

Term	Definition
Save as you earn (SAYE)	A scheme for employees to make contributions from their salary into a savings plan which is tax free for a period, at the end of which the employees can, if they choose, use the money contributed and the interest to purchase shares in the company.
Scheme Interests	An interest in an Long-term Incentive Plan.
Secretary of State for BERR	Government minister responsible for the administration of BERR.
Securities and Exchange Commission (SEC)	The regulator of the US securities market.
Senior statutory auditor	The individual identified as the audit engagement leader by an audit firm appointed as the statutory auditor and who will sign the audit report in his own name.
Service Agreement, director's	An employment contract between a director and a company.
Seventh Company Law Directive	European Union Directive No. 83/349/EEC dealing with consolidated accounts of certain companies.
Share option	An agreement where one party pays a premium in return for the right (as opposed to the obligation) to buy a share from another party at an exercise price on a certain date.
Simple majority	More than 50 per cent of the votes cast.
Small Companies Accounts regulations	The Small Companies and Groups (Accounts and Directors' Report) Regulations 2008 (SI 2008/409) that provide the form and content of Companies Act accounts for small companies. The regulations also deal with the content of the directors' report. They replace Schedules 4, 4A, 5, 6, 7, 8 and 8A to the Companies Act 1985 for small companies.
Small companies exemption	The term given to the exemption from providing certain information (such as a business review) in the directors' report of a small company that either qualifies for the small companies regime or would have done so had it not been a member of an ineligible group [Companies Act 2006, section 415A].

Glossary of terms

Term	Definition
Small companies regime	The name given to the collection of provisions of the Companies Act 2006 that applies to companies that qualify as small, and which is designed to reduce their reporting and auditing burdens.
Smith Guidance	A report on audit committees that provides practical advice to implementing provisions of the Combined Code on corporate governance relating to audit committees.
Special resolution	A decision by the shareholders at a general meeting of the company that requires a majority of not less than 75 per cent of members.
Squeeze out	This is the right of an entity that has acquired, or has unconditionally contracted to acquire, 90 per cent of the issued share capital of a company to force the holders of the remaining 10 per cent of the issued share capital of the company to sell their shares to the acquirer.
Statutory accounts	A company's statutory accounts are its accounts for a financial year as required to be delivered to the Registrar of Companies under section 441 of the Companies Act 2006 [Companies Act 2006, section 434(3)].
Statutory Audit Directive (SAD)	European Union Directive No. 2006/43/EC on statutory audit of annual accounts and consolidated accounts and amending the Fourth and Seventh Company Law Directives. It replaces the Eighth Company Law Directive.
Statutory auditor	A person appointed as an auditor either under Part 16 of the Companies Act 2006 or under other prescribed legislation such as the Building Societies Act 1986, Friendly Societies Act 1992, as set out in section 1210 of the Companies Act 2006.
Striking-off	The process whereby a dormant company, not having traded for three months, is struck off the register of companies, either voluntarily or forcibly by the Registrar of Companies.

Term	Definition
Substantial property transaction	A transaction involving a non-cash asset between a director and the company that satisfies certain financial thresholds and which requires shareholder approval.
Table A articles of association	The default model articles for a company that does not adopt bespoke articles of association. The most recent default articles are contained in Companies (Tables A to F) Regulations 1985, as amended by the Companies (Tables A to F) (Amendment) Regulations 2007, S12007/2541, the Companies (Tables A to F) (amendment) (No. 2) Regulations 2007 SI 2007/2826 and the Companies (Tables A to F)(Amendment) Regulations 2008 SI 2008/739. These are to be replaced by the Companies (Model Articles)Regulations 2008 that are to come into force on1 October 2009.
Takeover Code	The City Code on Takeovers and Mergers that contains the rules and guiding principles maintained by the Takeover Panel for all takeover offers and other transactions to which the Code applies, typically those admitted to the Official List.
Takeover Directive	European Union Directive No. 2004/25/EC on takeover bids.
Takeover Panel	The body that administers the City Code on Takeovers and Mergers, and supervises takeovers, ensuring fair treatment for all shareholders.
Taxation and Chargeable Gains Act 1992	A consolidation act concerning capital gains tax.
Taxes Management Act 1970	A consolidation act concerning income tax, capital gains tax and corporation tax.
Third country	A reference to a non-EEA Member State.
Traded company	Companies whose shares are admitted to trading on a regulated market in the EEA.
Transfer of Undertakings (Protection of Employment) Regulations 2006	Regulations relating to the automatic transfer of employment on the transfer or merger of undertakings, businesses or parts of businesses.

Glossary of terms

Term	Definition
Transparency Obligations Directive (TOD)	European Union Directive No. 2004/109/EC to improve the quality, quantity and timeliness of periodic financial information produced by companies whose securities are traded on a regulated market.
Treasury Solicitor	Department that provides legal services to central government departments.
UCITS	Undertaking for Collective Investment in Transferable Securities, as defined in the Glossary forming part of the Handbook made by the Financial Services Authority under the FSMA 2000.
UKLA *List!*	The periodic newsletter issued by the FSA in its capacity as the UK Listing Authority (UKLA) which provides informal guidance to listed companies on new or topical issues connected to the Prospectus, Listing and Disclosure and Transparency Rules.
UK Listing Authority (UKLA)	The part of the FSA that maintains the Official List.
Ultra Vires	Beyond the power.
Underwater option	An employee share option that is priced higher than the current market value of the share.
Unquoted company	A company that is not a quoted company.
Urgent Issues Task Force (UITF)	The Accounting Standards Board's interpretive body.
Vest	Possession of a power or interest.

Table of cases

Anglo – Continental Supply Co Ltd, Re [1922] 2 Ch 723 .... 9.8.4.4
Aveling Barford Ltd v Perion Ltd [1989] BCLC 626 .... 9.6.2, 9.6.3

BDG Roof Bond Ltd v Douglas [2000] 1 BCLC 401 .... 9.4.5.12
Borough Commercial and Building Society, Re [1893] 2 Ch 242 .... 9.10.3
Brady v Brady [1989] AC 755 .... 9.9.5.1, 9.9.6
Bushell v Faith [1970] AC 1099 .... 1.14.3.2, 1.15.1.5

Dodds v Walker [1981] 1 WLR 1441 .... 6.4.3
Dorchester Finance Co Ltd v Stebbing [1989] BCLC 498 .... 1.2.13.6
Dorman Long & Co Ltd, Re [1934] 1 Ch 635 .... 9.8.4.4

Foss v Harbottle (1843) 2 Hare 461 .... 1.5.12

Hickman v Kent or Romney Marsh Sheep Breeders
Association [1915] 1 Ch 881 .... 8.1.1
Hydrodam (Corby) Ltd, Re [1994] BCC 161 .... 1.2.13.3

National Bank Ltd, Re [1966] 1 WLR 819 .... 9.8.4.3
Neilson v Stuart 1991 SC (HL) 22 .... 9.9.6

Panorama Developments Ltd v Fidelis Furnishing
Fabrics Ltd [1971] 2 QB 711 .... 3.9.6

Ratner Group plc, Re [1988] BCLC 685 .... 9.8.1

Tiessen v Henderson [1899] 1 Ch 681 .... 9.8.4.2

Table of legislation

Bankruptcy and Diligence etc. (Scotland)
Act 2007...................... 3.11.9, 3.11.10
Business Names Act 1985................. 3.12.4
Charities Act 2006........................... 3.2.1
Companies Act 1948
s. 19.. 3.6.3
Sch. 1, Table A........................... 4.4.1
Companies Act 1985
s. 2............................. 10.1.1, 10.2.2.4
s. 9–12.................................... 1.14.2.2
s. 10, 12................................. 1.14.2.1
s. 18.. 8.15.5
s. 23................... 8.16.2, 9.6.7.4, 10.4.2.2
s. 23(1)..................................... 8.16.6
s. 23(2)........................... 8.16.5, 10.1.1
s. 23(3)..................................... 8.16.5
s. 23(5)..................................... 8.16.6
s. 23(8)..................................... 8.16.3
s. 24.. 9.10.4
s. 28.. 9.2.2
s. 29, 30................................. 9.10.6.5
s. 80...................... 8.4, 10.1.1, 10.2.2.2
s. 80(A)........................... 8.4.1, 8.5.1
s. 80(2)(a)................................. 10.1.1
s. 80(4).................................... 8.4.1
s. 80(7).................................... 8.4.2
s. 80(8).................................... 8.4.4
s. 81...................................... 10.1.1
s. 84(1), (2), (3).......................... 8.10.8
s. 85....................................... 8.10.8
s. 88...................................... 8.6.2.1
s. 88(2)(b)ii.................... App. 3(A3.2.1)
s. 89–95................................. 10.2.2.2
s. 89................. 8.5.1, 10.1.1, 10.2.2.6
s. 89(1)..................................... 8.5.2
s. 89(2)................................. 10.2.2.6
s. 89(3)........................... 8.5.1, 8.5.5.1
s. 89(4)..................................... 8.5.1
s. 89(5).................................... 10.1.1
s. 90(5)................................... 8.5.5.1
s. 90(6)..................................... 8.5.3
s. 91..................................... 8.5.5.1
s. 92....................................... 8.5.6
s. 93(3)..................................... 8.5.1
s. 94....................................... 8.5.1
s. 94(3A)................................... 8.5.1
s. 95........................... 8.5.5.1, 10.1.1
s. 95(1)................................... 8.5.5.1
s. 95(3)................................... 8.5.5.1
s. 95(5)................................... 8.5.5.1
s. 97, 98......................... 8.12.1, 8.12.2
s. 99....................................... 8.10.1
s. 100................... 8.7.1, 10.1.1, 10.4.4.1
s. 101................... 8.10.1, 8.10.2, 10.4.4.1

Companies Act 1985—*cont.*
s. 101(1), (2)........................... 10.4.4.1
s. 102...................................... 8.10.1
s. 103...................................... 8.10.3
s. 103(2)................................... 8.10.4
s. 103(5)................................... 8.10.3
s. 103(6)................................. 8.10.7.2
s. 104...................................... 8.10.3
s. 104(1), (1)(a), (1)(b)................. 8.10.5
s. 104(3), (3)(a).......................... 8.10.5
s. 104(6).................................. 8.10.5
s. 105.................................... 8.10.7.3
s. 106...................................... 8.10.1
s. 110....................................... 9.11
s. 111...................................... 8.10.3
s. 111(1), (2)............................ 8.10.7.1
s. 112...................................... 8.11.1
s. 113........................... 8.10.2, 8.11.2
s. 119....................................... 8.7.5
s. 121–123............................... 10.2.2.4
s. 121...................................... 8.13.2
s. 121(2)(a)................................. 8.3
s. 121(3)................................... 8.13.2
s. 122....................................... 9.5.2
s. 125–129.................................. 8.15.1
s. 127...................................... 8.15.4
s. 128...................................... 8.15.5
s. 128(2)................................... 8.15
s. 129...................................... 8.15.5
s. 130....................................... 8.8.2
s. 131....................................... 8.8.5
s. 132....................................... 8.8.3
s. 135....................................... 9.3.3
s. 135(1)................................... 9.3.3
s. 136....................................... 9.3.3
s. 138....................................... 9.3.3
s. 138(2)................................... 9.3.3
s. 143...................................... 9.10.3
s. 146....................................... 8.7.4
s. 151–158.................................. 10.1.1
s. 151....................... 9.6.7.1, 10.2.2.7
s. 151(1)................................... 9.10.3
s. 152.................................... 10.4.4.2
s. 152(1)(a)(iii), (iv).................... 10.4.4.2
s. 153(3)(c), (d).......................... 9.10.3
s. 153(4)................................... 10.1.1
s. 153(4)(b)............................. 10.2.2.7
s. 153(4)(bb)............................ 10.2.2.7
Pt. VII.......... 5.1.2, 7.1.2, App. 3(A3.1.6)
s. 155–158............................... 10.2.2.7
s. 155..................................... 9.9.4.1
s. 156(7).................................. 9.9.4.2
s. 157..................................... 9.9.4.2
s. 159...................................... 8.1.9

Companies Act 1985—*cont.*
s. 159(A)............................ 8.1.9, 9.5.2
s. 159(1), (2)........................... 9.5.2
s. 159(3).......... 9.4.4, 9.4.5.13, 9.5.1, 9.5.2
s. 160....................................... 9.4.4
s. 160(4)................................... 9.4.4
s. 162....................................... 9.4.4
s. 162(3)................................. 9.4.5.15
s. 162A–162G.. 8.19, 9.4.12, 10.1.1, 10.4.1.3
s. 162A................................. 10.4.1.3
s. 162B................................. 10.4.1.3
s. 162C................................. 10.4.1.3
s. 162D................................. 10.4.1.3
s. 164............................ 9.4.2.2, 9.4.4
s. 164(5), (6)........................... 9.4.2.2
s. 165............................ 9.4.2.2, 9.4.4
s. 166....................................... 9.4.4
s. 166(1), (2)........................... 9.4.2.1
s. 170............................ 9.4.4, 9.4.8
s. 171....................................... 9.4.4
s. 171(3)................................. 9.4.7.2
s. 172................................... 9.4.7.2
s. 172(3), (6)........................... 9.4.7.2
s. 185(4), (4A)......................... 8.6.2.2
s. 186................................... 8.6.2.2
s. 198–211............................... 4.6.1
s. 212..................................... 4.6.2
s. 234B................................... 10.1.1
s. 238..................................... 6.3.4
s. 239..................................... 1.6.1
s. 247A(2)............................... 5.3.6
s. 251..................................... 6.3.4
s. 263..................................... 9.6.2
s. 263(1), (3)............................ 9.2.2
s. 264(1), (3)............................ 9.2.2
s. 268..................................... 9.10.3
s. 270–273............................... 9.2.2
s. 270(2)................................. 9.2.2
s. 272(4)................................. 9.2.2
s. 273(6)................................. 9.2.2
s. 276................................... 9.7.2.1
s. 277..................................... 9.2.2
s. 277(1), (2).......................... 11.4.10.2
s. 283(2)................................. 1.12.3
s. 285................................... 1.14.7
s. 288................................... 1.14.5
s. 288(6)............................... 1.2.13.2
s. 303................................... 1.15.1
s. 310................................... 7.6.1
s. 311............................ 10.1.1, 10.4.3
s. 317................................. 10.4.2.4
s. 323–327............................... 10.4.3
s. 323................................... 10.1.1
s. 324–329............................... 10.1.1
s. 330–342............................... 10.4.5
s. 330................................... 10.1.1
s. 349.......................... App. 3(A3.2.1)
s. 351.......................... App. 3(A3.2.1)
s. 352................................... 8.6.2.3
s. 355................................... 8.18.3
s. 369................................... 6.3.4
s. 380................................... 8.15.1

Companies Act 1985—*cont.*
s. 388..................................... 7.5.1
s. 391–391A............................... 7.5.1
s. 425–427A...................... 9.8.2, 10.7.1
s. 425...................... 9.11, 10.1.1, 11.4.2
s. 429................................... 10.1.1
Pt. XIV....................... App. 3(A3.1.3)
Pt. XV........................ App. 3(A3.1.3)
s. 459–461................................. 4.8
s. 652..................................... 11.4.1
s. 652A......... 11.3, 11.4.1, 11.4.4, 11.4.4.1,
                        11.4.4.3, 11.4.9, 11.4.11
s. 653C................................... 11.4.5
s. 654................................... 11.4.11
s. 705(4)(a)................... App. 3(A3.2.1)
s. 727..................................... 1.6.2
s. 736................................... 8.16.3
s. 738(2)........................ 8.7.5, 10.4.4.1
s. 743..... 10.1.1, 10.2.2.2, 10.2.2.7, 10.4.4.1
s. 744................................... 3.14.9
Sch. 4...................... 5.1.1, 5.3.10
Sch. 4, para. 88, 89................. 9.2.2
Sch. 4A................................. 5.1.1
Sch. 5................... 5.3.5, 5.3.10, 10.6.1.1
Sch. 6................... 5.3.5, 5.3.10, 10.6, 10.6.1.1
Sch. 7............................. 5.3.5, 10.6
Sch. 7A................................. 10.6
Sch. 8........... 5.1.1, 5.3.5, 5.3.10, 10.6.1.1
Sch. 8A........................ 5.1.1, 5.3.5
Sch. 9, 9A..................... 5.1.1, 5.1.5
Sch. 15B................................. 9.8.2
Sch. 24.................... App. 3(A3.2.1)

Companies Act 1989
See generally........................... 7.1.1
s. 141(4)...................... App. 3(A3.1.8)

Companies Act 2006
s. 2............................ App. 3(A3.1.2)
s. 2(5)(a)................................. 8.1.6
s. 3–6....................................... 3.2
Pt. 2..................... 10.2.2.1, 10.2.2.4
s. 7–16..................................... 3.3
s. 8..................................... 10.1.1
s. 9........................ 8.A.1.1, 10.2.2.4
s. 15..................................... 3.3.3
Pt. 3..................... 10.2.2.1, 10.2.2.4
s. 17–38................................... 3.4
s. 17... 1.2.3, App. 1(A1.7), App. 3(A3.1.3),
                                    App. 3(A3.1.5)
s. 18–28................................. 3.4.3
s. 18................................... 3.4.3
s. 22................................... 3.4.9
s. 28........................... 3.4.13, 10.1.1
s. 29................... 9.3.6.4, App. 3(A3.1.3)
s. 30................... 9.3.6.4, App. 3(A3.1.3)
s. 30(1)................................. 8.15.5
s. 31........................... 10.1.1, 10.2.2.1
s. 39–52................................... 3.5
s. 41................................... 3.5.3
s. 44.. 1.12.2, App. 1(A1.5), App. 3(A3.1.5)
s. 48................................... 3.5.9
s. 53–74................................... 3.6
s. 57................................... 3.6.2

Companies Act 2006—*cont.*

s. 69–74................ 3.6.4, App. 3(A3.1.5)
s. 77–81.................................... 3.6.6
s. 82–85...................... App. 3(A3.1.5)
s. 86–88...................................... 3.7
s. 88... 3.7
s. 88(3)...................................... 3.7
s. 89–111.................................... 3.8
s. 90–96................................... 3.8.1
s. 92(3)................................... 3.8.6
s. 97–101................................ 3.8.12
s. 102–104............................... 3.8.16
s. 102.................................... 3.8.16
s. 105–108............................... 3.8.18
s. 109–111............................... 3.8.19
s. 109.................... 9.10.2, App. 1(A1.7)
s. 112..................................... 8.1.5
s. 116–119..................... App. 3(A3.1.3)
s. 119.................................... 3.14.5
s. 121......................... App. 3(A3.1.5)
s. 122(1)(b), (4).......................... 8.18.4
s. 123......................... App. 1(A1.7)
s. 128......................... App. 3(A3.1.5)
s. 129–135............................... 3.14.11
s. 136–144............................... 8.16.2
s. 136.................... 9.6.7.4, 10.1.1
s. 136(1)................................... 8.16.6
s. 137.................................... 8.16.6
s. 138.................... 10.1.1, 10.4.2.2
s. 138(1), (2)............................. 8.16.5
s. 141(1), (2)............................. 8.16.5
Pt. 9.. 4.3
s. 145–153..................... App. 3(A3.1.3)
s. 145..... 4.3.1.1, 6.3.2, 6.3.9, App. 1(A1.4)
s. 146.... 4.3.2.1, 6.3.2, 6.3.10, App. 1(A1.4)
s. 146(2)(b)(ii)............................ 6.3.6
s. 147.................................... 6.3.10
s. 153.................................... 4.3.1.4
s. 154–161................................ 1.13.1
s. 154..... 1.12.1, 3.4.8, App. 1(A1.4), App.
                                        3(A3.1.3)
s. 154(1), (2)............................. 1.12.2
s. 155–159..................... App. 3(A3.1.5)
s. 155......................... App. 1(A1.6)
s. 155(1)................................... 1.13.5
s. 157–159..................... App. 1(A1.6)
s. 157(1)................................... 1.13.6
s. 159(2), (3)............................. 1.13.6
s. 160.......... 1.14.6, 4.8.5, App. 3(A3.1.3)
s. 161................... 1.14.7, App. 3(A3.1.3)
s. 162.................................... 1.14.5
s. 162(6).................................. 1.2.13.2
s. 168–169..................... App. 3(A3.1.3)
s. 168.................... 1.15.1, 1.15.1.5
s. 169(2)................................. 1.15.1.5
s. 170–181..................... App. 3(A3.1.3)
s. 170(1)................................... 1.2.14
s. 170(2)................................... 1.2.15
s. 170(3)................................... 1.2.11
s. 170(4)................................... 1.2.11
s. 170(5).................................. 1.2.13.2
s. 171–174..................... App. 1(A1.4)

Companies Act 2006—*cont.*

s. 171–177................................ 9.2.2
s. 171..................................... 1.2.3
s. 172............ 1.2.4, 1.2.4.6, 1.2.14, 1.5.4,
                                        1.5.9, 9.1
s. 172(1)(f)................................ 1.2.4.3
s. 172(2).................... 1.2.4.2, 1.2.4.3
s. 173..................................... 1.2.5
s. 174..................................... 1.2.6
s. 175–177.... App. 1 (A1.4), App. 1(A1.6),
                      App. 3(A3.1.3), App. 3(A3.1.5)
s. 175.............. 1.2.7, 1.2.15, 2.2.18
s. 175(4)................................... 1.2.7
s. 175(5)................................... 1.2.7.1
s. 175(7)................................... 1.2.7
s. 176.................... 1.2.8, 1.2.15
s. 176(2)................................... 1.2.8
s. 176(4)................................... 1.2.8
s. 177.............. 1.2.7, 1.2.9, 1.2.9.1
s. 177(2)................................... 1.2.9
s. 177(3)................... 1.2.9, 1.2.9.2
s. 178(1)................................... 1.4.1
s. 179.................................... 1.2.10
s. 182–187.... App. 1(A1.6), App. 3(A3.1.5)
s. 182................................... 1.2.9.1
s. 182(3)................................. 1.2.9.2
s. 188–226.................... App. 3(A3.1.3)
s. 188.................... 2.2.1, App. 1(A1.4)
s. 188(3)................................... 2.2.5
s. 188(6)................................... 2.2.8
s. 189.................................... 2.2.11
s. 190–196................................ 2.3.1
s. 190............ 2.3.2, 9.4.5.7, App. 1(A1.4)
s. 190(4)................................... 2.3.3
s. 190(5)................................... 2.3.5
s. 190(6)................................... 2.3.4
s. 191..................................... 2.3.2
s. 192.................................... 9.4.5.7
s. 192(a), (b)............................. 2.3.6
s. 193.................................... 2.3.6
s. 194.................... 2.3.6, 9.4.5.7
s. 195.................................... 2.3.12
s. 195(2)................................. 2.3.13
s. 195(3)................................. 2.3.14
s. 196.................... 2.3.13, 2.3.15
s. 197–214.............. 2.4.1, 10.1.1, 10.4.5
s. 197.................... 5.3.17, App. 1(A1.4)
s. 198................................... 5.3.17
s. 199.................................... 2.4.3
s. 200, 201............................... 5.3.17
s. 202.................................... 2.4.4
s. 203.................................... 2.4.7
s. 204–209............................... 5.3.17
s. 204................................... 2.4.9.1
s. 205................................... 2.4.9.2
s. 207(1)................................. 2.4.9.4
s. 207(2)................................. 2.4.9.4
s. 207(3)................................. 2.4.9.4
s. 209(1)................................. 2.4.9.6
s. 209(2)................................. 2.4.9.6
s. 209(3)................................. 2.4.9.6
s. 211................................... 2.4.9.1

Companies Act 2006—*cont.*

s. 213...................................... 2.4.11
s. 214.............................. 2.4.13, 5.3.17
s. 215(3).................................... 2.6.2
s. 218...................................... 2.6.2
s. 219...................................... 2.6.2
s. 220...................................... 2.6.4
s. 221...................................... 2.6.4
s. 222...................................... 2.6.5
s. 225...................................... 2.7
s. 227–230............. 2.2.1, App. 3(A3.1.3)
s. 227...................................... 2.2.2
s. 228..................................... 2.2.12
s. 228(3)................................... 2.2.13
s. 229.......................... 2.2.14, 2.2.16
s. 230..................................... 2.2.17
s. 231........................... App. 3(A3.1.3)
s. 232–238....................... App. 1(A1.4)
s. 232–239....................... App. 3(A3.1.3)
s. 232(1), (2)............................... 1.6.3
s. 233..................................... 1.6.3.1
s. 234(2), (3).............................. 1.6.3.2
s. 234(5).................................. 1.6.3.2
s. 235(2), (3).............................. 1.6.3.3
s. 236..................................... 1.6.3.4
s. 237..................................... 1.6.3.5
s. 238..................................... 1.6.3.5
s. 239........................... App. 1(A1.4)
s. 247–259....................... App. 3(A3.1.3)
s. 247...................................... 4.8.4
s. 248(2)..................................... 1.3
s. 250..................................... 1.2.13
s. 251(1)................................. 1.2.13.2
s. 251(3)................................. 1.2.13.3
s. 252–255........................ 5.1.3, 5.3.19
s. 252...................................... 2.3.9
s. 254..................................... 2.3.11
s. 254(4).................................. 2.3.11
s. 256.............................. 1.2.8, 2.4.8
s. 257...................................... 1.2.3
s. 260–264............... 1.5.2, App. 1(A1.4)
s. 260–269............... 1.5.4, App. 3(A3.1.3)
s. 261(2).................................... 1.5.7
s. 263(3).................................... 1.5.9
s. 265–269................................... 1.5.2
s. 270–274....................... App. 3(A3.1.5)
s. 270–280.................... 3.9, App. 1(A1.5)
s. 270........................... App. 1(A1.4)
s. 271........................... App. 1(A1.4)
s. 273...................................... 3.9.4
s. 275..................................... 3.9.10
s. 280........................... App. 3(A3.1.5)
s. 281–287....................... App. 3(A3.1.3)
s. 281–300.................. 1.14.3.2, 4.4.26
s. 281....................... 4.4.27, App. 1(A1.4)
s. 282.......................... 4.4.33, 11.5.2.3
s. 283.......................... 4.4.33, 11.5.2.3
Pt. 13, Ch. 2............ 4.4.31, App. 1(A1.4)
s. 288–300.... App. 1(A1.4), App. 3(A3.1.3)
s. 291..................................... 4.4.29
s. 292..................................... 4.4.30
s. 300..................................... 4.4.28

Companies Act 2006—*cont.*

s. 301–307....................... App. 3(A3.1.3)
s. 301........................... App. 1(A1.4)
s. 302...................................... 4.4.4
s. 303.............................. 4.4.4, 4.4.5
s. 304...................................... 4.4.5
s. 305...................................... 4.8.2
s. 306...................................... 4.4.5
s. 307.......................... 4.4.6, 11.5.2.3
s. 308–309.................................. 4.2.1
s. 309.............................. 4.4.8, 4.4.9
s. 310–326....................... App. 3(A3.1.3)
s. 310..................................... 4.4.10
s. 311.. 2.5
s. 312(4)................................... 4.4.34
s. 314–317.................................. 4.4.11
s. 314..................................... 4.4.11
s. 316..................................... 4.4.11
s. 318.............................. 3.4.8, 4.4.12
s. 319..................................... 4.4.13
s. 320..................................... 4.4.23
s. 321..................................... 4.4.24
s. 323(4)................................... 4.4.21
s. 324–331....................... App. 1(A1.4)
s. 324.......................... 4.4.15, 4.4.21
s. 325...................................... 4.4.7
s. 327..................................... 4.4.19
s. 327(1), (2)(a), (b), (3)...... App. 3(A3.1.3)
s. 328.......... 4.4.13, 4.4.18, App. 3(A3.1.3)
s. 329........................... App. 3(A3.1.3)
s. 330(1)–(5), (6)(a), (b), (7). App. 3(A3.1.3)
s. 331........................... App. 3(A3.1.3)
s. 332.................. 4.4.14, App. 3(A3.1.3)
s. 333...................................... 4.2.1
s. 334, 335....................... App. 3(A3.1.3)
s. 336–340....................... App. 3(A3.1.3)
s. 336........................... App. 1(A1.4)
s. 338...................................... 4.8.2
s. 341–354....................... App. 3(A3.1.3)
s. 341........................ 4.5.1, App. 1(A1.4)
s. 342–354....................... App. 1(A1.4)
s. 342...................................... 4.5.2
s. 344..................................... 4.5.2.2
s. 347..................................... 4.5.2.3
s. 348..................................... 4.5.2.4
s. 349..................................... 4.5.2.4
s. 351..................................... 4.5.2.5
s. 355–359....................... App. 3(A3.1.3)
s. 360–361....................... App. 3(A3.1.3)
Pt. 14...................................... 4.7.1
s. 362–379.......... 4.7, App. 1(A1.4), App.
                                        3(A3.1.3)
s. 362(a)....................... App. 3(A3.1.3)
s. 363(2)(a), (3)............... App. 3(A3.1.3)
s. 364...................................... 4.7.3
s. 364(3)....................... App. 3(A3.1.3)
s. 365...................................... 4.7.4
s. 365(1)(a), (b)(i)............ App. 3(A3.1.3)
s. 366–368.................................. 4.7.5
s. 366(1)(a)................... App. 3(A3.1.3)
s. 366(4)................................... 4.7.6
s. 367(5)................................... 4.7.7

Companies Act 2006—*cont.*
s. 367(3)(a)..................... App. 3(A3.1.3)
s. 369.. 4.8.2
s. 370.. 4.8.2
s. 378(2)........................ App. 3(A3.1.3)
s. 380–416..................... App. 3(A3.1.5)
Pt. 15.......... 5.1.1, 5.1.2, 5.1.3, 7.1.2, App.
3(A3.1.8), App. 3(A3.2.20)
s. 382(5)................................... 5.3.6
s. 383(5), (6)............................. 5.3.9
s. 384...................................... 5.3.6
s. 384(2)......................... 5.3.6, 7.2.2
s. 384(3)................................... 7.2.2
s. 385.......................... App. 3(A3.1.3)
s. 386...................................... 5.2.1
s. 393(1)................................... 5.3.2
s. 395...................................... 5.3.1
s. 395(4)(aa)............................. 5.3.1
s. 396..................................... 3.12.11
s. 399(2)........................ 5.3.11, 6.4.12
s. 404..................................... 3.12.11
s. 407...................................... 5.3.1
s. 408......................... 5.3.26, 6.4.12
s. 410A..................................... 5.3.20
s. 410A(1)–(3)........................... 5.3.22
s. 411...................................... 5.3.26
s. 412.. 10.6
s. 413...................................... 5.3.18
s. 414...................................... 7.2.2
s. 415A................. 5.4.4, 5.4.9, 6.4.8
s. 416.. 10.6
s. 417......... 5.1.3, 5.4.3, App. 3(A3.1.3)
s. 417(2)................................... 1.2.4.6
s. 417(7)......................... 5.4.4, 6.4.10
s. 418–462..................... App. 3(A3.1.5)
s. 418(2), (3)............................. 7.4.2
s. 420................... 10.1.1, 10.6, 10.6.3.1
s. 421...................................... 10.1.1
s. 423...................................... 6.3.1
s. 424...................................... 6.3.2
s. 430...................................... 6.3.11
s. 433...................................... 6.4.3
s. 435...................................... 6.3.8
s. 437(1)................................... 6.2.2
s. 439...................................... 4.8.4
s. 441...................................... 6.4.1
s. 442.............. 6.4.2, 6.4.4, App. 1(A1.5)
s. 444(1)(a)............................... 6.4.7
s. 444(7)........................ 6.4.14, 7.4.7
s. 444A(1)(a)............................. 6.4.8
s. 444A(1)(b)............................. 6.4.8
s. 444A(2)................................. 6.4.8
s. 444A(5)................................. 6.4.14
s. 445...................................... 6.4.8
s. 445(4)................................... 6.4.10
s. 445(6)................................... 6.4.14
s. 446...................................... 6.4.12
s. 446(3)................................... 6.4.14
s. 447(4)................................... 6.4.14
s. 449...................................... 6.4.10
s. 449(2)................................... 7.2.9
s. 449(3)................................... 7.2.9

Companies Act 2006—*cont.*
s. 449(4), (4A)........................... 6.4.14
s. 454...................................... 6.5.1
s. 455...................................... 6.5.2
s. 456...................................... 6.5.2
s. 463................. 5.1.3, 5.4.8, 6.6.11
s. 464–474..................... App. 3(A3.1.5)
s. 464..................... App. 3(A3.2.27)
s. 466(5), (6)............................. 5.3.9
s. 467...................................... 5.3.6
s. 467(2)................................... 5.3.6
s. 467(4)................. 5.4.4, 6.4.10, 6.4.11
s. 471...................................... 6.4.12
s. 472(2)................................... 6.4.7
s. 474...................................... 5.3.7
Pt. 16.... 7.1.1, 7.1.2, 7.1.3, App. 3(A3.1.8),
App. 3(A3.2.20)
s. 475–484..................... App. 3(A3.1.5)
s. 475...................................... 7.2.1
s. 475(2), (3), (4)....................... 7.2.2
s. 476...................................... 4.8.2
s. 477...................................... 7.2.2
s. 482...................................... 7.2.7
s. 485–488.............. 7.1.3, App. 3(A3.1.3)
s. 485........................ 4.8.4, 7.3.2
s. 485(2)................................... 7.3.2
s. 486...................................... 7.3.2
s. 487–488..................... App. 1(A1.4)
s. 487...................................... 7.3.2
s. 488........................ 4.8.2, 7.3.2
s. 488(3)................................... 7.3.2
s. 489–539..................... App. 3(A3.1.5)
s. 489(3)................................... 7.3.3
s. 491...................................... 7.3.3
s. 492...................................... 7.3.5
s. 493........................ 7.3.1, 7.3.3
s. 494...................................... 7.3.5
s. 495–497................................. 7.4.5
s. 496...................................... 7.4.5
s. 497...................................... 7.4.5
s. 498...................................... 7.4.12
s. 499–501................................. 7.4.1
s. 499...................................... 7.4.1
s. 500...................................... 7.4.1
s. 500(1)................................... 8.5.1
s. 503...................................... 7.4.6
s. 504...................................... 7.4.8
s. 507........................ 7.1.3, 7.4.12
s. 510–518................................. 7.5.1
s. 519–525................................. 7.1.3
s. 519................. 7.5.3, App. 1(A1.5)
s. 521...................................... 7.5.5
s. 522, 523................................. 7.5.6
s. 525...................................... 7.5.7
s. 527–531..................... App. 1(A1.5)
s. 527...................................... 4.8.2
s. 532..................... App. 1(A1.5)
s. 534...................................... 7.6.2
s. 536...................................... 4.8.4
s. 537...................................... 7.6.4
s. 540–657................................. 8.10
s. 540...................................... 9.9.3.1

Table of legislation

Companies Act 2006—*cont.*
s. 540(1), (4)................ App. 3(A3.1.3),
                               App. 3(A3.1.5)
s. 542(1)........................... 8.1.6, 8.1.7
s. 542(3)................................... 8.1.6
s. 544........................ App. 3(A3.1.5)
s. 545...... App. 3(A3.1.3), App. 3(A3.1.5)
s. 546 App. 3(A3.1.2), App. 3(A3.1.3), App.
               3(A3.1.5), App. 3(A3.2.2)
s. 548 App. 3(A3.1.3), App. 3(A3.1.5), App.
                              3(A3.2.2)
s. 549–551............. 8.4.5, 10.1.1, 10.2.2.5
s. 550................................. 10.2.2.5
s. 552.................................. 8.12.2
s. 553.................................. 8.12.2
s. 554–557............................... 8.6.1
s. 554................................... 8.6.1
s. 555............... 8.6.3.1, 8.A.1.1, 10.1.1
s. 555(3), (4)......................... 10.2.2.4
s. 556................................... 8.6.4
s. 558............... 8.2.3, App. 3(A3.1.2)
s. 560–577.............................. 8.5.1
s. 561........................ 10.1.1, 10.2.2.6
s. 561(1)................................ 8.5.1
s. 561(1)(a)............................. 8.5.2
s. 561(3)................................ 8.5.1
s. 562(3)............................... 8.5.5.1
s. 562(5)................................ 8.5.3
s. 563.................................. 8.5.6
s. 565.................................. 8.5.1
s. 566........................ 10.1.1, 10.2.2.6
s. 567................................. 8.5.5.2
s. 568................................. 8.5.5.2
s. 569................................. 8.5.5.2
s. 570............................ 4.8.5, 8.5.5.2
s. 570(1), (2)........................ 8.5.5.1
s. 570(3)............................. 8.5.5.1
s. 571................................. 8.5.5.2
s. 571(2), (3), (5)................... 8.5.5.1
s. 571(5), (6)........................ 8.5.5.2
s. 573............................. 4.8.5, 8.5.1
s. 578–579.............................. 8.10.8
s. 578(1)(a)............................ 8.10.8
s. 578(1)(b)............................ 8.10.8
s. 578(1)(b)(ii)........................ 8.10.8
s. 578(2), (3).......................... 8.10.8
s. 579................................. 8.10.8
s. 580.............. 8.7.1, 10.1.1, 10.4.4.1
s. 581............................ 8.7.3, 9.2.8
s. 583............................ 8.7.5, 10.4.4.1
s. 584................................. 8.10.1
s. 585................................. 8.10.1
s. 586.............. 8.10.1, 8.10.2, 10.4.4.1
s. 586(1), (2)........................ 8.5.5.1
s. 586(2)(a)........................... 8.10.2
s. 587................................. 8.10.1
s. 588................................. 8.11.1
s. 589............................ 8.10.2, 8.11.2
s. 589(1)(a)........................... 8.10.5
s. 593............................ 8.10.3, 8.10.4
s. 593(1)(a), (b), (c).................. 8.10.3
s. 593(3).............................. 8.10.7.2

Companies Act 2006—*cont.*
s. 594................................. 8.10.3
s. 595–603............................. 8.10.3
s. 595................................. 8.10.4
s. 597................................. 8.10.7.1
s. 597(1).............................. 8.10.3
s. 598(1), (4), (5).................... 8.10.5
s. 601.................................. 4.8.4
s. 602................................. 8.10.7.1
s. 603................................. 8.10.5
s. 604................................. 8.10.7.3
s. 605............... 8.10.7.4, 8.11.1, 8.11.2
Pt. 17, Ch. 7.......................... 8.8.1
s. 610................................. 8.8.2
s. 610(1)......................... 8.8.3, 8.8.6
s. 610(2)–(4)................. App. 3(A3.1.8)
s. 610(2), (3)......................... 8.8.6
s. 611............. 8.8.3, 8.8.4, 8.8.5, 8.8.6
s. 612............................ 8.8.5, 8.8.6
s. 613............................ 8.8.5, 8.8.6
s. 615............. 8.8.4, 8.8.5, 8.8.6
Pt. 17, Ch. 8.......................... 3.4.8
s. 618(3).............................. 8.13.3
s. 619........................... 8.14.5, 8.A.1.1
s. 619(1), (2)......................... 8.13.5
s. 621........................... 8.14.5, 8.A.1.1
s. 622–628.............. 8.14.3, App. 1(A1.7)
s. 622................................. 8.7.4
s. 622(1).............................. 8.14.3
s. 622(2)......................... 8.14.3, 8.A.1.1
s. 624................................. 8.14.3
s. 625........................... 8.14.5, 8.A.1.1
s. 626................................. 4.8.5
s. 626(6).............................. 8.14.4.4
s. 627................................. 8.A.1.1
s. 627(2).............................. 8.14.4.4
s. 627(5).............................. 8.14.4.1
s. 628................................. 8.14.4.5
s. 629–640............................. 8.15.1
s. 629..... 8.4.5, 8.15, App. 3(A3.1.3), App.
                             3(A3.1.5)
s. 630–640............................. 8.15.3
s. 630.................................. 4.8.5
s. 631............................ 4.8.5, 8.15.3
s. 633............................ 4.8.2, 8.15.4
s, 633(3).............................. 8.15.4
s. 634................................. 8.15.4
s. 640................................. 8.15.5
s. 641–644........................ App. 1(A1.6)
s. 641................ 9.3.3, App. 3(A3.1.8)
s. 641(1).............................. 9.3.3
s. 641(1)(a)...... 4.8.5, 9.3.2, App. 3(A3.1.8)
s. 641(1)(b)................ 4.8.5, 9.3.2
s. 641(2)–(6).... 4.8.5, 9.3.2, App. 3(A3.1.8)
s. 641(4).............................. 9.3.4
s. 642–644............. 9.3.2, App. 3(A3.1.8)
s. 642............................. 9.3.2, 9.3.7.1
s. 643................................. 9.3.7.2
s. 643(2).............................. 9.3.7.2
s. 643(4).......................... 9.3.7.2, 9.3.11
s. 644............................. 9.3.3, 9.3.7.3
s. 644(4).............................. 9.3.7.4

Companies Act 2006—*cont.*
s. 644(7), (8)............................ 9.3.11
s. 645–650............................... 9.3.2
s. 645.................................... 9.3.3
s. 646.................................... 9.3.3
s. 649.................................... 8.A.1.1
s. 649(3)................................. 9.3.3
s. 651.................................... 9.3.9
s. 652(1), (3)................. App. 3(A3.1.8)
s. 654.............. 9.3.10, App. 3(A3.1.8)
s. 658–666...................... App. 1(A1.7)
s. 658.................................... 9.10.3
s. 663.................................... 8.A.1.1
s. 677–683............. 9.9.1, 10.1.1, 10.2.2.7,
                                App. 1(A1.6)
s. 677.................................... 10.4.4.2
s. 677(1)................................. 9.9.3.2
s. 678.................................... 9.9.3
s. 678(1)................................. 9.9.3.1
s. 678(2)................................. 9.9.5.1
s. 678(3)................................. 9.9.3.1
s. 678(4)................................. 9.9.5.1
s. 679.................................... 9.9.3
s. 680.................................... 9.9.6
s. 681.................................... 9.9.5.2
s. 682........................... 9.9.5.2, 10.2.2.7
s. 683(2)................................. 9.9.3.1
s. 683(3), (4)............................ 9.9.5.2
s. 684–737...................... App. 1(A1.7)
s. 684.......................... 8.1.9, 9.5.2
s. 684(4)................................. 9.5.2
s. 685.................... 4.8.4, 8.1.9, 9.5.2
s. 685(1)................................. 8.16
s. 685(1)(a), (b)......................... 8.16
s. 685(3)(G).............................. 8.16
s. 685(4)................................. 8.16
s. 686(1)................................. 8.16
s. 686(2).................... 8.16, 9.5.1, 9.5.2
s. 687(1)................................. 8.16
s. 687(2)(b).............................. 8.16
s. 687(3), (4), (6)....................... 8.16
s. 689........................... 8.A.1.1, 9.5.2
s. 690–723................................ 9.4.3
s. 690(2)................................. 9.4.5.15
s. 691(1)................................. 9.4.5.13
s. 691(2).......................... 9.4.4, 9.5.1
s. 694............................ 4.8.5, 9.4.4
s. 694(5)................................. 9.4.4
s. 695(2)................................. 9.4.5.10
s. 697.................................... 4.8.5
s. 700.................................... 4.8.5
s. 701............................ 4.8.4, 9.4.4
s. 706.................................... 9.4.4
s. 706(b)................................. 9.4.4
s. 708........................... 8.A.1.1, 9.4.4
s. 709.................................... 9.4.4
s. 710.................................... 9.4.7.2
s. 712.................................... 9.4.7.2
s. 712(3)................................. 9.4.7.2
s. 712(6)................................. 9.4.7.2
s. 714.................................... 9.4.7.2
s. 716............................ 4.8.5, 9.4.7.2

Companies Act 2006—*cont.*
s. 717(3)................................. 9.4.7.2
s. 719.................................... 9.4.7.2
s. 723.................................... 9.4.7.2
s. 724–732.............. 8.19, 9.4.12, 10.1.1
s. 724.................................... 8.19.1
s. 725(1), (2), (3)....................... 8.19.2
s. 726(2), (3), (4)....................... 8.19.3
s. 727, 728............................... 8.19.4
s. 729(1), (2)............................ 8.19.5
s. 730.................................... 8.A.1.1
s. 730(1), (3), (4), (5).................. 8.19.5
s. 731(2), (4)............................ 8.19.6
s. 733............................ 9.4.4, 9.4.8
s. 733(5), (6)................. App. 3(A3.1.8)
s. 735(1)................................. 8.16.3
Pt. 19.................................... 3.14.9
s. 738–754...................... App. 3(A3.1.5)
s. 738.................................... 3.14.9
s. 747.................................... 3.14.9
s. 755–757................................ 8.9.1
s. 755–767...................... App. 3(3.1.5)
s. 755.................................... 10.1.1
s. 755(2)................................. 8.9.3
s. 755(3)................................. 8.9.4.1
s. 756.................................... 8.9.1
s. 756(5)................................. 8.9.1
s. 757.................................... 8.9.4.2
s. 757(3)................................. 8.9.4.3
s. 759.................................... 8.9.4.4
s. 760.................................... 8.9.4.5
s. 761–767................................ 3.3.5
s. 767.................................... 3.3.7
s. 768–770................................ 8.17.1
s. 768–790...................... App. 3(A3.1.5)
s. 770(1)................................. 8.17.3
s. 776(2)................................. 8.17.3
s. 779.................................... 8.18.1
Pt. 21, Ch. 2............................. 3.14.9
s. 793.... 3.14.7, 4.6.2, 4.6.4, 10.6.2.1, 10.6.6
s. 808.................................... 4.6.4
s. 811(4), 812, 814............ App. 3(A3.1.5)
s. 816.................................... 4.6.4
s. 817.................................... 4.6.4
s. 829–853.............. 9.2.1, App. 3(A3.1.5)
s. 829.................................... 11.4.10.2
s. 830............................. 9.2.2, 9.2.4
s. 831.................................... 9.2.3
s. 831(1).......................... 8.16, 9.2.2
s. 831(4)................................. 9.2.2
s. 836............................. 9.2.2, 9.2.5
s. 837–839................................ 9.2.2
s. 838.................................... 9.2.5
s. 838(6)................................. 9.2.2
s. 839.................................... 9.2.5
s. 839(7)................................. 9.2.2
s. 840.................................... 9.2.6
s. 845............................ 9.6.3, 9.7.2.1
s. 846............................ 9.2.4, 9.7.2.1
s. 847............................ 9.2.2, 9.2.11
s. 851.................................... 9.2.2
s. 853.................................... 9.2.4

Companies Act 2006—*cont.*
s. 854–859................. 3.10, App. 1(A1.7)
s. 856.. 8.A.1.1
s. 860–877...................................... 3.11
s. 860.. 3.11.1
s. 866.. 3.11.2
s. 867.. 3.11.3
s. 868.. 3.11.3
s. 869.. 3.11.8
s. 872.. 3.11.4
s. 874.. 3.11.5
s. 876.. 3.11.6
s. 878–892...................................... 3.11
s. 878–894...................................... 3.11.9
Pt. 26.......................... 4.8.5, 9.8.2, 9.9.5.2
s. 895–901.... 10.1.1, 10.7.1, App. 3(A3.1.5)
s. 895.. 11.4.2
s. 896.. 9.8.4.1
s. 897.. 9.8.4.2
s. 899.. 9.8.4.1
Pt. 27............................... 4.8.5, 9.8.2
s. 902–941...................... App. 3(A3.1.5)
s. 936.. 9.8.2
Pt. 28......... App. 2(A2.1), App. 2(A2.1.2)
s. 942–965...................... App. 2(A2.1.2)
s. 942–992...................... App. 3(A3.1.2)
s. 943............................ App. 2(A2.2.3)
s. 943(1)......................... App. 2(A2.2.3)
s. 945............................ App. 2(A2.2.3)
s. 947........ App. 2(A2.2.3), App. 2(A2.2.4)
s. 953(2), (4)................... App. 2(A2.2.5)
s. 955............................ App. 2(A2.2.4)
s. 956............................ App. 2(A2.2.3)
Pt. 28, Ch. 2................... App. 3(A3.2.2)
s. 966–973...................... App. 2(A2.3)
s. 966............................ App. 2(A2.3.2)
s. 966(5)......................... App. 2(A2.3.3)
s. 967............................ App. 2(A2.3.4)
s. 968............................ App. 2(A2.3.5)
s. 970............................ App. 2(A2.3.6)
Pt. 28, Ch. 3................... App. 3(A3.2.2)
s. 974–990...................... 10.7.1
s. 974–991...................... App. 2(A2.4)
s. 976............................ App. 2(A2.4.3)
s. 978............................ App. 2(A2.4.4)
s. 979–982...................... 10.1.1
s. 979............................ 4.8.5
s. 980............................ App. 2(A2.4.6)
s. 980(4)......................... App. 2(A2.4.7)
s. 981............................ App. 2(A2.4.8)
s. 983............................ 4.8.5
s. 984............................ App. 2(A2.4.10)
s. 985............................ App. 2(A2.4.11)
s. 992............................ 5.4.1, App. 2(A2.5)
s. 992(2)......................... App. 2(A2.5.1)
s. 993............................ 1.7.2, App. 3(A3.1.3)
Pt. 30............................ 4.8
s. 994–999...................... App. 3(A3.1.3)
s. 994............................ 4.8.1
s. 1000–1034................... App. 1(A1.7)
s. 1000........................... 6.4.5.2
s. 1003–1110................... 11.4.9

Companies Act 2006—*cont.*
s. 1013........................... 6.4.5.4
s. 1024–1025................... 11.4.7
s. 1024........................... 6.4.5.3
s. 1025........................... 6.4.5.3
s. 1035–1039................... App. 3(A3.1.3)
s. 1040–1043................... 3.2.3
s. 1043........................... App. 3(A3.1.2)
s. 1044–1059................... 3.12, App. 1(A1.7)
s. 1044........................... 3.12.1
s. 1060–1120................... 3.16
s. 1062........................... 3.16.1
s. 1068............... 6.4.15, App. 3(A3.1.3)
s. 1068(5)....................... App. 3(A3.1.3)
s. 1078........................... 6.4.15
s. 1083........................... 3.16.5
s. 1087........................... 3.16.7
s. 1104........................... 3.16.9
s. 1105................. 3.16.9, App. 3(A3.2.1)
s. 1106........................... App. 3(A3.2.1)
s. 1117(1), (2), (3)............ App. 3(A31.5)
s. 1121–1123.......... App. 3(A3.1.2), App.
3(A3.1.3), App. 3(A3.1.5)
s. 1121........................... App. 3(A3.1.3)
s. 1122...... App. 3(A3.1.3), App. 3(A3.2.2)
s. 1124........................... App. 3(A3.1.3)
s. 1125–1133.......... App. 3(A3.1.2), App.
3(A3.1.3)
s. 1125...... App. 3(A3.1.3), App. 3(A3.1.5)
s. 1126........................... App. 3(A3.1.5)
s. 1127–1133.......... App. 3(A3.1.3), App.
3(A3.1.5)
s. 1132........................... App. 3(A3.2.2)
s. 1134–1138............. 3.14, App. 1(A1.3)
s. 1134, 1135.......... App. 3(A3.1.2), App.
3(A3.2.2)
s. 1137(1), (4), (5)(b), (6).... App. 3(A3.1.4)
s. 1138...... App. 3(A3.1.2), App. 3(A3.2.2)
s. 1139–1142................... 3.15
s. 1139................... 3.7, App. 3(A3.1.2),
App. 3(A3.1.5)
s. 1139(1), (4)................. App. 3(A3.2.2)
s. 1140..... App. 3(A3.1.2), App. 3(A3.1.5),
App. 3(A3.2.2)
s. 1142........................... App. 1(A1.6)
s. 1143–1148................... 4.2.1
s. 1143........................... 4.2.4
s. 1145........................... 4.2.14, 6.3.6
s. 1147........................... 3.15.2
s. 1157........................... 1.6.2, App. 3(A3.1.5)
s. 1158........................... App. 3(A3.1.3)
s. 1159....... 8.16.3, 9.9.3.1, App. 3(A3.1.5)
s. 1160........................... App. 3(A3.1.5)
s. 1161, 1162................... App. 3(A3.1.5)
s. 1163........................... 2.3.2
s. 1164, 1165.................. App. 3(A3.1.5)
s. 1166........................... 10.1.1, 10.2.2.2
s. 1167........................... App. 3(A3.1.4)
s. 1168–1173................... 4.2.1
s. 1168.......... 4.2.1, App. 3(A3.1.2), App.
3(A3.1.3), App. 3(A3.1.5)
s. 1169........................... App. 3(A3.1.5)

Companies Act 2006—*cont.*
s. 1170.......................... App. 3(A3.1.2)
s. 1172.......................... App. 3(A3.1.5)
s. 1173........... 4.2.1, App. 3(A3.1.2), App.
     3(A3.1.3), App. 3(A3.1.5), App.
     3(A3.1.5), App. 3(A3.2.2)
s. 1173(1)................................. 6.4.5.4
s. 1175.................. 7.2.6, App. 3(A3.1.6)
s. 1177........................... 10.1.1, 10.4.3
s. 1192–1208.............. 3.13, App. 1(A1.7)
s. 1193...................................... 3.13.1
s. 1198...................................... 3.13.1
Pt. 42......... 7.1.1, 7.1.2, 7.1.3, 7.4.8, 7.7.1,
     7.7.2, App. 3(A3.1.8),
     App. 3(A3.2.10)
s. 1209–1241................... App. 3(A3.1.5)
s. 1210....................................... 7.7.3
s. 1214....................................... 9.8.2
s. 1241–1247.............................. 7.7.4
s. 1242–1244................... App. 3(A3.1.5)
s. 1245–1264................... App. 3(A3.1.5)
s. 1248.............................. App. 3(A3.1.3)
Pt. 43................................. 6.6.1, 6.6.9
s. 1277–1280................... App. 3(A3.1.5)
s. 1282.............................. App. 3(A3.1.5)
s. 1284..... App. 3(A3.1.3), App. 3(A3.1.4),
     App. 3(A3.1.5)
s. 1284(1)...................... App. 3(A3.1.2)
s. 1284(1)(a)–(c)............... App. 3(A3.1.8)
s. 1286(1)(a), (2)(a)........... App. 3(A3.1.8)
Pt. 46.............................. App. 3(A3.2.2)
s. 1295..... App. 3(A3.1.5), App. 3(A3.1.6),
     App. 3(A3.1.8)
Pt. 47.............................. App. 3(A3.2.2)
Sch. 2............................. App. 3(A3.1.2)
Sch. 3............................. App. 3(A3.1.3)
Sch. 4............................... 4.2.1, 4.3.4
Sch. 5...................... 4.2.1, 4.3.4, 4.6.3
Sch. 5, para. 9.............................. 6.3.4
Sch. 5, para. 10............................ 4.2.6
Sch. 5, para. 13............................ 6.3.4
Sch. 6............................. App. 3(A3.1.5)
Sch. 7............................. App. 3(A3.1.5)
Sch. 9....................................... 7.2.6
Sch. 9, Pt. 1.................... App. 3(A3.1.6)
Sch. 10, 11..................... App. 3(A3.1.5)
Sch. 12.................. 7.7.4, App. 3(A3.1.5)
Sch. 13, 14...................... App. 3(A3.1.5)
Sch. 15, para. 11(2)........... App. 3(A3.1.8)
Sch. 16..... App. 3(A3.1.5), App. 3(A3.1.6),
     App. 3(A3.1.8)
Companies (Audit, Investigations and
    Community Enterprise) Act 2004
See generally........................ 7.1.1, 7.4.1
s. 14.. 6.5.3
Company Directors Disqualification
    Act 1986
See generally............................ 1.13.2
s. 11.. 1.13.3

Consumer Protection Act 1987
s. 4.. 11.2.5
Data Protection Act 1998................... 6.5.2
Deregulation and
Contracting Out Act 1994................ 11.4.1
Finance Act 2003
Sch. 23................................. 10.7.2.3
Financial Services and Markets Act 2000
See generally.......... 8.2.2, 9.1, 9.4.5.1, 10.5.1
Pt. IV...................................... 5.3.6
s. 87A...................................... 8.2.2
s. 90A(1)................................... 6.6.11
s. 91(B)................................... 6.6.11
s. 103(1)...................... App. 3(A3.1.8)
Fraud Act 2006............................. 7.4.12
Income and Corporation Taxes Act 1988
s. 8(2)................................... 11.5.5.2
s. 12(7)................................. 11.5.5.2
Insolvency Act 1986
See generally 1.7, 3.16.1, 8.7.4, 9.9.2.2, 9.9.5.2,
     11.4.11.1, 11.5
s. 84... 11.5.1
s. 87(1)..................................... 11.5.5
s. 87(2)..................................... 11.5.5
s. 89–94..................................... 11.3
s. 89...................................... 11.5.2.2
s. 89(5)................................... 11.5.2.2
s. 90...................................... 11.5.2.2
s. 93...................................... 11.5.6.3
s. 94.. 11.5.8
s. 94(5)..................................... 11.5.8
s. 110........................... 9.7.2.3, 9.9.5.2
s. 111.................................... 9.7.2.3
s. 171(6)..................................... 11.5.9
s. 188(1)...................... App. 3(A3.2.1)
s. 213.. 1.7.2
s. 214.............................. 1.2.6, 1.7.1
s. 216...................................... 1.13.4
s. 238, 239............................... 9.6.7.2
s. 423, 424............................... 9.6.7.2
Sch. 4...................... 11.5.2.3, 11.5.6.1
Sch. 4, Pt. I, II, III..................... 11.5.6.1
Judgements Act 1838..................... 8.10.8
Landlord and Tenant (Covenants) Act
    1995.................................... 11.2.4.2
Limitation Act 1980
s. 2, 4(1), 8, 11, 19, 24.................. 11.2.5
Mental Health Act 1983................. 1.16.1.4
Parties, Elections and Referendums Act
    2000
s. 50–53...................................... 4.7
Pensions Act 2004............................. 9.1
Requirements of Writing (Scotland) Act
    1995....................................... 3.5.9
Stock Transfer Act 1963.................. 8.17.3
Taxation of Chargeable Gains Act 1992
s. 122................................... 11.4.11.1

Index

(all references are to section number)

Abbreviated accounts
generally, 7.2.9
revision, 6.5.4
Absence of directors from board meetings
vacation of office
Model articles, under, 1.16.2.5
Table A articles, under, 1.16.1.5
Accounting records
access for auditors, 7.4.1
adequacy, 5.2.2
introduction, 5.2.1
Accounting standards
subordinate legislation, A3.2.27
Accounts
See also **Annual accounts**
dividends, and, 9.2.5
overseas companies, and
annual, 3.12.11—3.12.12
group, 3.12.13
registration, on, 3.12.3
subordinate legislation
generally, A3.2.20
groups, A3.2.22
insurance companies, A3.2.23—A3.2.24
large and medium-sized companies, A3.2.22
partnerships, A3.2.25
small companies, A3.2.21
supervision, A3.2.26
Accounts meetings
generally, 6.2.2
members raising concerns, 6.2.5
Acquisition of company shares by third party
See also **Employee incentive share plans**
cash cancellation, 10.7.4
early vesting or exercise, 10.7.2.2
employee meeting any employer's NIC, 10.7.2.6
exercise of rights, 10.7.2.1
impact of share plans, 10.7.1
introduction, 10.7
issue of additional shares, 10.7.3
lapse date, 10.7.2.7
overall acquisition cost, 10.7.3
payment of exercise price, 10.7.2.4
performance conditions, 10.7.2.2
recovery of PAYE and NICs, 10.7.2.5
relevant provisions of share plans, 10.7.2—10.7.2.7
retention of 'key' employees, 10.7.5
rollover of rights, 10.7.4
securing support of rights holders, 10.7.6

Acquisition of company shares by third party—cont.
takeover-related vesting or exercise, 10.7.2.3
vesting of rights, 10.7.2.1
Acting honestly and reasonably
directors' duties, and, 1.6.2
Acts in accordance with company constitution
consequences of breach, 1.4.2
generally, 1.2.3
Acts within powers
consequences of breach, 1.4.2
generally, 1.2.3
Additional directors
appointment, 1.14.3.4—1.14.3.5
Address
company secretary, 3.9.7
directors, 3.3.1
directors of overseas companies, and, 3.12.8
registered office, 3.7
Adjournment
general meetings, and, 4.4.14
Affirmation
loans and credit transactions, and, 2.4.13
substantial property transactions, and, 2.3.15
Age of directors
maximum, 1.13.7
minimum, 1.13.6
Aggregation of transactions
substantial property transactions, and, 2.3.5
AIM companies
purchase by company of its own shares, and, 9.4.5.1
Allotment of shares
allowances on
CA 2006 changes, 8.12.2
current position, 8.12.1
checklists
private limited company, 8.A.2
public company, 8.A.3
commissions on
CA 2006 changes, 8.12.2
current position, 8.12.1
consideration payable for shares in public company
effect of breach of restrictions, 8.10.7—8.10.7.3
exemptions from valuation requirements, 8.10.4
interposition of new plc holding company, 8.10.6
introduction, 8.10
recently re-registered company, 8.10.5

Allotment of shares—*cont.*
consideration payable for shares in public
company—*cont.*
restrictions, 8.10.1
sanctions for breach of restrictions, 8.10.2
valuation requirements, 8.10.3—8.10.4
difference from issue, 8.2.3
discounts
CA 2006 changes, 8.12.2
current position, 8.12.1
meaning, 8.2.3
post-allotment steps
action on or after 1 October 2009,
8.6.3.1—8.6.3.3
CA 2006 changes, 8.6.1
filings, 8.6.2.1
issue of share certificates, 8.6.2.2
penalties for non-compliance, 8.6.5
summary of current and new position,
8.6.6
unlimited companies, and, 8.6.4
updating registers, 8.6.2.3
pre-emption rights
action prior to 1 October 2009, 8.5.7
beneficiaries, 8.5.2
exclusion or disapplication,
8.5.5.1—8.5.5.2
meaning, 8.5.1
notice of offer, 8.5.4
penalties for non-compliance, 8.5.7
summary of current and new position,
8.5.8
terms, 8.5.3
public company, in, 8.10.8
shareholder approval
action prior to 1 October 2009, 8.4.7
agreements before expiry, 8.4.2
CA 2006 changes, 8.4.5
current position, 8.4.1—8.4.4
filing, 8.4.4
introduction, 8.4
offers before expiry, 8.4.2
renewal, 8.4.3
revocation, 8.4.3
summary of current and new position,
8.4.6
variation, 8.4.3
Alternate directors
appointees, 1.11.3
appointment, 1.11.2—1.11.2.2
capacity to bind a company, and, 3.5.7
duration of appointment, 1.11.7
filings, 1.11.6
generally, 1.2.13.5
introduction, 1.11.1
liabilities, 1.11.5
minimum number of directors, and, 1.11.9
remuneration, 1.11.8.1—1.11.8.2
rights, 1.11.4
tenure, 1.11.7
Annual accounts
accounting framework, 5.3.1

Annual accounts—*cont.*
approval
accounts meetings, 6.2.2
generally, 6.2.1
laying accounts at AGM, 6.2.3
private companies, 6.2.3
public companies, 6.2.2
quoted companies, 6.2.5
time for holding AGM, 6.2.4
banks, and, 5.1.5
CA 2006 changes
commencement, 5.1.3
generally, 5.1.2
collective board responsibility, and, 5.3.25
connected persons, 5.1.3
directors' loans, 5.3.17—5.3.18
directors' transactions, 5.3.16
disclosure requirements, 5.3.12
employee costs and numbers, 5.3.26
fair value accounting, 5.3.24
GAAP accounts, and, 5.3.1
groups
changes to content of accounts, 5.3.27
form of accounts, 5.3.10—5.3.11
size limit, 5.3.9
IAS accounts, and, 5.3.1
insurance companies, and, 5.1.5
introduction, 5.1.1
large companies
generally, 5.3.6
MiFiD companies, 5.3.7
size limit, 5.3.8
legislative basis
banks, 5.1.5
generally, 5.1.1
insurance companies, 5.1.5
loans and credit transactions, 5.3.17—5.3.18
medium-sized companies
form of accounts, 5.3.11
generally, 5.3.6
off-balance-sheet arrangements, 5.3.21
size limit, 5.3.8
MiFiD companies, 5.3.7
off-balance-sheet arrangements
compliance guidance, 5.3.22
directors' obligations, 5.3.23
generally, 5.3.20
small and medium-sized companies, 5.3.21
overseas companies, and
contents, 3.12.12
generally, 3.12.11
group accounts, 3.12.13
'present fairly' requirement, 5.3.3
records, and
adequacy, 5.2.2
introduction, 5.2.1
regulatory framework
banks, 5.1.5
generally, 5.1.1
insurance companies, 5.1.5
related party transactions
GAAP accounts, and, 5.3.5

Annual accounts—*cont.*
  related party transactions—*cont.*
    generally, 5.3.13
    IAS accounts, and, 5.3.14
  role of preparer, 5.1.4
  safe harbour provision, 5.1.3
  small companies
    form of accounts, 5.3.10
    introduction, 5.1.2
    meaning, 5.3.6
    off-balance-sheet arrangements, 5.3.2
    size limit, 5.3.81
  'think small first' philosophy
    introduction, 5.1.2
    meaning, 5.3.5
  transitional arrangements, 5.3.19
  'true and fair' requirement, 5.3.2—5.3.4
Annual general meetings
  See also **General meetings**
  financial reporting, and
    laying accounts, 6.2.3
    time for holding, 6.2.4
  private companies, 4.4.1
  public companies, 4.4.2—4.4.3
Annual report
  financial reporting, and
    contents, 6.6.3
    time for publication, 6.6.2
Annual returns
  CA 2006 changes, 3.10.1
  contents, 3.10
  generally, 3.10
Appointment of auditors
  disclosure of terms, 7.3.4—7.3.5
  generally, 7.3.1
  private companies, 7.3.2
  public companies, 7.3.3
  terms, 7.3.4
Appointment of directors
  acceptance, 1.14.10
  additional appointees, 1.14.3.4—1.14.3.5
  Bushell v Faith clauses, 1.14.3.2
  casual vacancies, 1.14.3.3
  checklist of considerations, 1.14.9
  Combined Code, and, 1.14.6
  effects of defects, 1.14.7
  enhanced voting rights, 1.14.3.2
  first directors, 1.14.2.1—1.14.2.2
  informed consent, 1.14.1
  introduction, 1.14
  maximum number, and, 1.14.3.1
  notifications to Registrar of Companies,
    1.14.4
  registers requiring updating, 1.14.5
  residential address, 1.14.8
  restrictions
    age, 1.13.6
    CA 2006 provisions, 1.13.1
    Combined Code, and, 1.13.10
    companies, 1.13.5
    comparison table, 1.3.11

Appointment of directors—*cont.*
  restrictions—*cont.*
    disqualified directors, 1.13.2
    introduction, 1.13
    'phoenix' companies, and, 1.13.4
    qualifications, 1.13.8
    residence in UK, 1.13.9
    undischarged bankrupts, 1.13.3
  shareholders, by, 1.14.3.2
  subsequent directors, 1.14.3—1.14.3.5
  termination, 1.15.1—1.15.6
Arrangements
  substantial property transactions, and, 2.3.2
Articles of association
  absence of directors from board meetings
    Model articles, under, 1.16.2.5
    Table A articles, under, 1.16.1.5
  amendment, 3.4.10—3.4.12
  CA 2006 changes, 3.4.6
  changes to existing arrangements,
    3.4.13—3.4.14
  conflicts of interest, and, 1.2.17
  copies, 3.4.15
  directors, and, 1.0
  effect of amendments, 3.4.12
  electronic communications, and, 4.2.3
  entrenching provisions in, 3.4.9
  filing amendments, 3.4.11
  generally, 3.4.3
  introduction, 3.4
  liability limitation agreements, and, 7.6.3
  meaning, 4.4.3
  Model articles (2006)
    CA 2006 changes, 3.4.8
    generally, 3.4.7
    overview, 3.0
  overview, 3.0
  political donations and expenditures, and,
    4.7.6
  reduction of share capital, and, 9.3.5.1
  share capital, and, 8.1.4
  Table A articles
    CA 2006 changes, 3.4.6
    differences from Model articles, 3.4.8
    generally, 3.4.4
    overview, 3.0
  Tables B—F articles
    CA 2006 changes, 3.4.6
    generally, 3.4.5
  transitional Table A articles, 3.0
Associate directors
  directors' duties, and, 1.2.13.4
  transactions, and, 3.5.3
Attorneys
  execution of documents, and, 3.5.6
Audited accounts
  abbreviated CA accounts, 7.2.9
  dormant companies
    financial services sector, in, 7.2.5
    generally, 7.2.4
  financial services sector companies
    dormant companies, 7.2.5

Audited accounts—*cont.*
  financial services sector companies—*cont.*
    small companies, 7.2.3
    generally, 7.2.1
    medium-sized companies, 7.2.8
    public sector companies, 7.2.7
    small charitable companies, 7.2.6
  small companies
    financial services sector, in, 7.2.3
    generally, 7.2.2
Auditors
  access to accounting records and personnel,
    7.4.1
  appointment
    disclosure of terms, 7.3.4—7.3.5
    generally, 7.3.1
    private companies, 7.3.2
    public companies, 7.3.3
    terms, 7.3.4
  audited accounts
    abbreviated CA accounts, 7.2.9
    dormant companies, 7.2.4—7.2.5
    financial services sector companies, 7.2.3
    generally, 7.2.1
    medium-sized companies, 7.2.8
    public sector companies, 7.2.7
    small charitable companies, 7.2.6
    small companies, 7.2.2—7.2.3
  auditor's reports
    criminal offences, 7.4.12—7.4.13
    generally, 7.4.5
    signature, 7.4.6—7.4.11
  CA 2006 changes
    background, 7.1.1
    commencement, 7.1.3
    generally, 7.1.2
  cessation statements
    company's duties, 7.5.5
    deposit, 7.5.4
    generally, 7.5.3
    'major audit', 7.5.7
    notification to regulators, 7.5.6—7.5.9
  change of auditors, 7.5.10
  conclusion, 7.8
  directors' voluntary disclosures
    communication of relevant audit
      information, 7.4.3
    effect, 7.4.4
    generally, 7.4.2
  EU Company Law Directives, 7.1.1
  EU Statutory Audit Directive, 7.1.1
  functions
    access to accounting records and
      personnel, 7.4.1
    auditor's reports, 7.4.5—7.4.13
    directors' voluntary disclosures,
      7.4.2—7.4.4
  introduction, 7.1.1—7.1.3
  liability limitation agreements
    articles of association, and, 7.6.3
    authorisation, 7.6.3
    cap, 7.6.4

Auditors—*cont.*
  liability limitation agreements—*cont.*
    definition, 7.6.2
    directors' responsibilities, 7.6.2
    'fair and reasonable', 7.6.4
    generally, 7.6.1
    guidance on preparation, 7.6.5
    nature of arrangements, 7.6.6.1
    proportionality, 7.6.4
    SEC reaction, 7.6.6.3
  regulatory framework, 7.1.1
  removal
    cessation statements, 7.5.3—7.5.9
    generally, 7.5.1
    reporting, 7.5.2
  remuneration, 7.3.5
  resignation
    cessation statements, 7.5.3—7.5.9
    generally, 7.5.1
    reporting, 7.5.2
  signature of auditor's reports
    change of SSA during reporting period,
      7.4.9
    filed copies, and, 7.4.7
    generally, 7.4.6
    joint auditors, and, 7.4.10
    risk from violence or intimidation, 7.4.11
    'senior statutory auditor', 7.4.8
  statutory auditors
    generally, 7.7.2
    introduction, 7.7.1
    non-EU companies, 7.7.4
  subordinate legislation, A3.2.7
Auditor's reports
  criminal offences, 7.4.12—7.4.13
  generally, 7.4.5
  signature
    change of SSA during reporting period,
      7.4.9
    filed copies, and, 7.4.7
    generally, 7.4.6
    joint auditors, and, 7.4.10
    risk from violence or intimidation, 7.4.11
    'senior statutory auditor', 7.4.8
Authorised minimum share capital
  subordinate legislation, A3.2.14
Authorised share capital
  and see **Share capital**
  action prior to 1 October 2009, 8.3.2
  CA 2006 changes, 8.3.1
  employee incentive share plans, and, 10.2.2.4
Authority to allot shares
  employee incentive share plans, and, 10.2.2.5
Automatic vacation of office
  introduction, 1.16
  Model articles, under, 1.16.2—1.16.2.5
  Table A articles, under, 1.16.1—1.16.1.5

Balance sheets
  purchase by company of its own shares, and
    generally, 9.4.9
    purchase at premium, 9.4.9.2

Balance sheets—*cont.*
purchase by company of its own shares, and—*cont.*
purchase out of capital, 9.4.9.3
purchase out of distributable services, 9.4.9.1
signature, 6.4.14
Bankruptcy
vacation of office
Model articles, under, 1.16.2.3
Table A articles, under, 1.16.1.3
Banks
annual accounts, and, 5.1.5
BERR guidance
directors' duties, and, 1.2.16
Board minutes
directors' duties, and
disclosure in litigation, 1.3.3
impact of duties, 1.3.2
introduction, 1.3
status, 1.3.1
Bona vacantia
striking off, and, 11.4.11
Bonus issues
share capital, and, 8.7.6
'Box-ticking'
directors' duties, and, 1.2.17.1
Branches
And see **Overseas companies**
change of location, 3.12.7
definition, 3.12.1
generally, 3.12
registration, 3.12.2
Bushell v Faith clauses
directors, and, 1.14.3.2
Business expenditure to £50,000
loans and credit transactions, and, 2.4.9.1
Business names
introduction, 3.13
restrictions, 3.13.1
subordinate legislation, A3.2.4
Business review
CA 2006 changes
commencement, 5.1.3
generally, 5.1.2
competitively sensitive information, 5.4.15.1
contents, 5.4.11
contractual arrangements, 5.4.17
corporate social responsibility, 5.4.16
disclosure requirements, 5.4.3
employee issues, 5.4.16
environmental issues, 5.4.16
exemptions, 5.4.4
format, 5.4.7
future trends and factors
competitively sensitive information, 5.4.15.1
generally, 5.4.15
profit forecasts, 5.4.15.3
supportability of information, 5.4.15.2
interpretation of requirements, 5.4.9

Business review—*cont.*
key performance indicators
choice, 5.4.14
disclosure, 5.4.10
group, 5.4.13.3
'key', 5.4.13.1
number, 5.4.13.2
problem areas, 5.4.13
reliability, 5.4.13.5
segmental, 5.4.13.3
medium-sized companies, and, 5.4.4
principal risks
disclosure, 5.4.10
problem areas, 5.4.12
problem areas
employee issues, 5,4,16
environmental issues, 5.4.16
future trends and factors, 5.4.15
key performance indicators, 5.4.13
principal risks, 5.4.12
resources available to an entity, 5.4.14
significant contractual arrangements, 5.4.17
social issues, 5.4.16
profit forecasts, 5.4.15.3
purpose, 5.4.1.1
quoted companies, and, 5.4.5
resources available to an entity, 5.4.14
responsibility for preparation, 5.4.2
role of FRRP, 5.4.18
safe harbour provision, and, 5.4.8
sensitive information, 5.4.15.1
seriously prejudicial exemptions, 5.4.6
significant contractual arrangements, 5.4.17
small companies, and, 5.4.4
social issues, 5.4.16
Business transactions
loans and credit transactions, and, 2.4.9.4

Calling meetings
general powers, 4.4.4
members, by, 4.4.5
Cancellation of shares
purchase by company of its own shares, and, 9.4.5.17
Capacity to bind a company
alternate directors, and, 3.5.7
associate's transactions, 3.5.3
breach of limitation in constitution, 3.5.1
companies not incorporated at time of signature, 3.5.8
directors' transactions, 3.5.3
employee incentive share plans, and, 10.2.2.1
entering into contracts, 3.5.2
execution of documents
attorney, by, 3.5.6
companies not incorporated, where, 3.5.8
contracts, 3.5.4
deeds, as, 3.5.5
Scottish companies, by, 3.5.9
introduction, 3.5

Index

Capital maintenance
purchase by company of its own shares, and,
9.4.8
'Cash' payment
share capital, and, 8.7.5
Casual vacancies
directors, and, 1.14.3.3
Certificate of incorporation
generally, 3.3.3
Cessation statements
company's duties, 7.5.5
deposit, 7.5.4
generally, 7.5.3
'major audit', 7.5.7
notification to regulators, 7.5.6—7.5.9
Chairperson
general meetings, and, 4.4.13
Change management
benefits of integrated approach, 12.4
conclusion, 12.5
consequences of incomplete implementation,
12.3
introduction, 12.1
management control, 12.2
Change of auditors
notification to regulators, 7.5.10
Charges
directors' service contracts
copies, 2.2.16
inspection, 2.2.14
Charges over assets
consequences of failure to register, 3.11.5
copies, 3.11.6
introduction, 3.10
overseas companies, and, 3.11.1
property situate in another UK jurisdiction,
3.11.3
property situate outside UK, 3.11.2
property situate within UK, 3.11.1
register of charges
company's obligations, 3.11.6
consequences of failure to maintain, 3.11.7
obligations of Registrar of Companies,
3.11.8
release, 3.11.4
satisfaction, 3.11.4
Scottish charges, 3.11.9—3.11.10
Charitable donations
directors' report, and, 5.4.21
Circulation of accounts
electronic communication, 6.3.3
hard copy documents, 6.3.6
indirect investor's rights, 6.3.9—6.3.10
person entitled to receive, 6.3.1
quoted companies, 6.3.11
summary financial statements, 6.3.8
timing, 6.3.2
trading on regulated markets, 6.3.7
website communication, 6.3.4—6.3.5
City Code of Takeovers and Mergers
purchase by company of its own shares, and,
9.4.5.3

Class rights
variation
action prior to 1 October 2009, 8.15.6
CA 2006 changes, 8.15.1
current procedure, 8.15.2
filing requirements, 8.15.5
introduction, 8.15
new procedure, 8.15.3—8.15.5
objections by class, 8.15.4
Collective board responsibility
annual accounts, and, 5.3.25
Combined Code
introduction, 1.0
Commissions
allotment of shares, and
CA 2006 changes, 8.12.2
current position, 8.12.1
Common law
directors' duties, and, 1.2.11—1.2.12
Community interest companies
generally, 3.2.1
Companies
And see under individual headings
annual returns
CA 2006 changes, 3.10.1
contents, 3.10
generally, 3.10
articles of association
amendment, 3.4.10—3.4.12
CA 2006 changes, 3.4.6
changes to existing arrangements,
3.4.13—3.4.14
copies, 3.4.15
effect of amendments, 3.4.12
entrenching provisions in, 3.4.9
filing amendments, 3.4.11
generally, 3.4.3
introduction, 3.4
meaning, 4.4.3
Model articles, 3.4.7
Table A, 3.4.4
Tables B—F, 3.4.5
business names
introduction, 3.13
restrictions, 3.13.1
CA 2006 changes
background, 3.1.2
generally, 3.1.3
summary, 3.18
capacity to bind
alternate directors, and, 3.5.7
associate's transactions, 3.5.3
breach of limitation in constitution, 3.5.1
companies not incorporated at time of
signature, 3.5.8
directors' transactions, 3.5.3
entering into contracts, 3.5.2
execution of documents, 3.5.4—3.5.6
introduction, 3.5
change of status, and
And see **Re-registration**
generally, 3.8—3.8.19

Companies—*cont.*
charges over assets
 And see **Charges over assets**
 generally, 3.11—3.11.10
community interest companies, 3.2.1
companies not formed under companies
 legislation, 3.2.3
company secretary
 address, 3.9.7
 introduction, 3.9
 necessity of appointment, 3.9.1—3.9.3
 notification to Registrar of Companies,
  3.9.9
 private companies, and, 3.9.1
 qualifications, 3.9.4—3.9.5
 register, 3.9.10
 responsibilities, 3.9.6
 service address, 3.9.7
 vacancies, 3.9.8
constitution
 articles of association, 3.4.3—3.4.11
 changes to existing arrangements,
  3.4.13—3.4.14
 copies, 3.4.15
 effect of amendments, 3.4.12
 introduction, 3.4
 memorandum of association, 3.4.1
 objects clause, 3.4.2
directors, and, 1.13.5
execution of documents
 attorney, by, 3.5.6
 companies not incorporated, where, 3.5.8
 contracts, 3.5.4
 deeds, as, 3.5.5
 Scottish companies, by, 3.5.9
formation
 CA 2006 changes, 3.3—3.3.8
 capacity to bind, 3.5—3.5.9
 certificate, 3.3.3
 company secretary, 3.9—3.9.10
 constitution, 3.4—3.4.15
 date, 3.3.3
 directors, 3.3.1
 Forms 10 and 12, 3.3.1
 introduction, 3.1.1—3.1.3
 minimum number of members, 3.3.8
 name, 3.6—3.8
 officers, 3.3.1
 on-line, 3.3.2
 refusal by Registrar of Companies, 3.3.4
 registered office, 3.7
 service address, 3.3.1
 statement of capital, 3.3.1
 statement of guarantee, 3.3.1
 supporting documentation, 3.3.1
 trading requirements, 3.3.5—3.3.7
 types of company, 3.2—3.2.2
 unlawful purpose, and, 3.3.4
 validity, 3.3.3
guarantee companies
 definition, 3.2.2
 introduction, 3.2.1

Companies—*cont.*
letters patent, in pursuance of, 3.2.3
limited companies
 definition, 3.2.2
 introduction, 3.2.1
maintenance
 annual returns, 3.10—3.10.1
 business names, 3.13—3.13.1
 change of status, 3.8—3.8.19
 charges over assets and property,
  3.11—3.11.10
 company records, 3.14—3.14.13
 company secretary, 3.9—3.9.10
 compliance obligations, 3.17
 introduction, 3.1.1—3.1.3
 service of documents, 3.15—3.15.2
 types of company, 3.2—3.2.2
memorandum of association
 changes to existing arrangements, 3.4.13
 copies, 3.4.15
 generally, 3.4.1
 introduction, 3.4
name
 change, 3.6.5—3.6.7
 choice restrictions, 3.6.2
 disclosure, 3.6.8
 introduction, 3.6
 limited, 3.6.3
 objections, 3.6.4
 pre-decision checks, 3.6.1
 trade marks, and, 3.6.1
Northern Irish companies, 3.2.1
objects clause
 directors' duties, and, 3.4.2
 generally, 3.4.1
 need, 3.4.2
overseas companies
 And see **Overseas companies**
 generally, 3.12—3.12.13
 introduction, 3.2.1
pre-2 November 1862 companies, and, 3.2.3
private limited companies
 definition, 3.2.2
 introduction, 3.2.1
public limited companies
 definition, 3.2.2
 introduction, 3.2.1
 trading certificates, 3.3.5
Registrar of Companies, 3.16—3.16.12
registration of overseas companies,
 3.12—3.12.13
re-registration, and
 And see **Re-registration**
 generally, 3.8—3.8.19
trading certificates
 applications, 3.3.6
 consequences of failure to obtain, 3.3.7
 generally, 3.3.5
 purpose, 3.3.6
types, 3.2—3.2.2

Companies—*cont.*
unlimited companies
companies not registered under Companies
Acts, 3.2.3
definition, 3.2.2
introduction, 3.2.1
Companies Act 2006
commencement
introduction, A1.3
Order No.1, A3.1.1
Order No.2, A3.1.2
Order No.3, A3.1.3
Order No.4, A3.1.4
Order No.5, A3.1.5
Order No.6, A3.1.6
Order No.7, A3.1.8
consequential amendments, A3.1.2—A3.1.5,
A3.1.7—A3.1.8
derivation table, 1.7
destination table, 1.7
implementation timetable
April 2007, A1.2
April 2008, A1.4
generally, I.3
introduction, A1.1
January 2007, A1.2
October 2007, A1.3
October 2008, A1.5
October 2009, A1.6
introduction, I.1—I.2
origin table, 1.7
savings, A3.1.1—A3.1.3, A3.1.5—A3.1.6,
A3.1.8
subordinate legislation
drafts, A3.4
due 1 October 2008, A3.2.31
introduction, A3.2
list of regulations, A3.2.1—A3.2.30
Takeovers Directive, and, A2.1—A2.5
transitional provisions, A3.1.1—A3.1.3,
A3.1.5, A3.1.8
Company names
See also **Business names**
change
consequential effects, 3.6.7
generally, 3.6.6
misleading, where, 3.6.5
procedure, 3.6.6
choice restrictions, 3.6.2
disclosure, 3.6.8
introduction, 3.6
limited, 3.6.3
objections, 3.6.4
overseas companies, and, 3.12.4
pre-decision checks, 3.6.1
trade marks, and, 3.6.1
Company records
copying
generally, 3.14.1
rights, 3.14.4
debentures, 3.14.9
directors and secretaries, 3.14.6

Company records—*cont.*
directors' interests in shares, 3.14.8
electronic form, 3.14.3
inspection
generally, 3.14.1
rights, 3.14.4
introduction, 3.14
location, 3.14.2
members, 3.14.5
overseas branch register
discontinuance, 3.14.13
obligations to maintain, 3.14.11
requirements to maintain, 3.14.12
records of meetings and resolutions, 3.14.10
substantial interests in shares, 3.14.7
transfer of debentures, 3.14.9
Company secretary
address, 3.9.7
dispensing with
articles of association, and, 3.9.3
considerations, 3.9.2
introduction, 3.9.1
notification to Registrar of Companies,
3.9.9
generally, 1.12.3
introduction, 3.9
necessity of appointment, 3.9.1
notification to Registrar of Companies, 3.9.9
private limited companies, and
dispensing with appointment, 3.9.2—3.9.3
generally, 3.9.1
qualifications, 3.9.5
qualifications
private limited companies, 3.9.5
public companies, 3.9.4
register, 3.9.10
responsibilities, 3.9.6
service address, 3.9.7
vacancies, 3.9.8
Company shareholders
general meetings, and
attendance, 4.4.21
representatives, 4.4.22
Competitively sensitive information
business review, and, 5.4.15.1
Compulsory acquisition of shares
takeovers, and, A2.4—A2.4.11
Conduct of business
directors' duties, and, 1.1.3
Conflicts of interest
directors' duties, and
authorisation by company, 1.2.7.1
generally, 1.2.7
directors' service contracts, and, 2.2.18
Connected persons
annual accounts, and, 5.1.3
companies, 2.3.11
generally, 2.3.8
introduction, 2.3.2
members of director's family, 2.3.10
relevant persons, 2.3.9

Consideration
shares in public company, for
effect of breach of restrictions,
8.10.7—8.10.7.3
exemptions from valuation requirements,
8.10.4
interposition of new plc holding company,
8.10.6
introduction, 8.10
recently re-registered company, 8.10.5
restrictions, 8.10.1
sanctions for breach of restrictions, 8.10.2
valuation requirements, 8.10.3—8.10.4
subscription of shares, and
bonus issues, 8.7.6
'cash' payment, 8.7.5
different payment terms, 8.7.3
failure to pay outstanding instalments,
8.7.4
generally, 8.7.1
'nil paid' shares, 8.7.2
'part paid' shares, 8.7.2
scrip dividends, 8.7.6
shares in public company, 8.10—8.10.7
Consolidation of shares
CA 2006 changes, 8.13.2—8.13.3
filing requirements, 8.13.5
purpose, 8.13.1
restrictions, 8.13.4
Contracts
execution of documents, and, 3.5.4
Contractual arrangements
business review, and, 5.4.17
Convertible shares
share capital, and, 8.1.2
Copying
articles of association, 3.4.15
company records
generally, 3.14.1
rights, 3.14.4
fees, A3.2.3, A3.2.6
service contracts, 2.2.16
Corporate capacity
employee incentive share plans, and, 10.2.2.1
Corporate governance
Combined Code (2006), and, 6.6.10
generally, 6.6.9
penalties for breach, 6.6.11
Corporate simplification
conclusion, 11.7—11.7.1
dormant companies
latent issues remaining, 11.2.4—11.2.5
legal dormancy, 11.2.1
meaning, 11.2
members' voluntary liquidation,
11.5—11.5.9
methods of removal, 11.3
retention, 11.2.2
risks attendant on retention, 11.2.3
striking off, 11.4—11.4.11
introduction, 11.1

Corporate social responsibility (CSR)
business review, and, 5.4.16
Courtesy directors
directors' duties, and, 1.2.13.4
Credit transactions
affirmation by shareholders, 2.4.13
business transactions, for, 2.4.9.4
changes under CA 2006, 2.4.1
company business expenditure to £50,000,
for, 2.4.9.1
defending proceedings, for, 2.4.9.2
exemptions from approval
business transactions, 2.4.9.4
company business expenditure to £50,000,
2.4.9.1
defending proceedings, 2.4.9.2
introduction, 2.4.9
intra-group transactions, 2.4.9.5
minor transactions, 2.4.9.4
money-lending companies, 2.4.9.6
regulatory investigations or actions, 2.4.9.3
expenditure, for
company business up to £50,000, on,
2.4.9.1
defending proceedings, on, 2.4.9.2
intra-group transactions, for, 2.4.9.5
minor transactions, on, 2.4.9.4
regulatory investigations or actions, and,
2.4.9.3
failure to obtain approval, 2.4.11—2.4.12
home loans, and, 2.4.9.6
intra-group transactions, for, 2.4.9.5
introduction, 2.4
meaning, 2.4.4
minor transactions, for, 2.4.9.4
money-lending companies, and, 2.4.9.6
personal liability
defences, 2.4.12
generally, 2.4.11.2
public companies, and, 2.4.8
regulatory investigations or actions, and,
2.4.9.3
rescission, and, 2.4.11.1
shareholder approval
anti-avoidance provisions, 2.4.7
exemptions, 2.4.9
introduction, 2.4.2
procedure, 2.4.5
public companies, and, 2.4.8
relevant shareholders, 2.4.6
third party arrangements, 2.4.7
value of transaction, 2.4.10
Creditor protection
reduction of share capital, and, 9.3.6.3
Cross-holdings
share capital, and
CA 2006 changes, 8.16.2
consequences, 8.16.6
exemptions, 8.16.6
holding companies, and, 8.16.3
meaning, 8.16.1

Cross-holdings—*cont.*
share capital, and—*cont.*
shares in company holding shares in parent, 8.16.4
CSOP
employee incentive share plans, and, 10.3.7

Data protection
employee incentive share plans, and, 10.5.4
intra-group transactions, and, 9.6.7.4
Date of incorporation
generally, 3.3.3
De facto directors
directors' duties, and, 1.2.13.3
De jure directors
directors' duties, and, 1.2.13.1
Debentures
changes under CA 2006, 3.14.9
Declaration of solvency
members' voluntary liquidation, and, 11.5.2.2
Declaring interests in proposed transactions
existing transaction or arrangement, 1.2.9.1
generally, 1.2.9
updating information, 1.2.9.2
Deeds
execution of documents, and, 3.5.5
Defective accounts
subordinate legislation, A3.2.18
Defending proceedings
loans and credit transactions, and, 2.4.9.2
Deferred shares
share capital, and, 8.1.2
Definitions
glossary, Appendix 4
Demergers
indirect demerger, 9.7.2.2
introduction, 9.7
methods
distribution in specie, 9.7.2.1
indirect demerger, 9.7.2.2
introduction, 9.7.2
schemes of arrangement, 9.7.2.4
section 110 scheme, 9.7.2.3
three-cornered demerger, 9.7.2.2
reasons, 9.7.1
schemes of arrangement, 9.7.2.4
section 110 scheme, 9.7.2.3
three-cornered demerger, 9.7.2.2
Derivative claims
basis, 1.5.4
causes of action prior to 1 October 2007, 1.5.13
changes under CA 2006, 1.5.3
claimants, 1.5.5
continuation, 1.5.7
defendants, 1.5.6
examples, 1.5.11
factors determinative of permission, 1.5.9
future purchase of a company, 1.5.11
grounds, 1.5.4
implication of new regime, 1.5.10

Derivative claims—*cont.*
meaning, 1.5.1
practical steps, 1.5.14
pre-1 October 2007 regime, 1.5.12
provisions, 1.5.2
redundancy programme, 1.5.11
refusal of permission to continue, 1.5.8—1.5.9
sale of subsidiary, and, 1.5.11
wholly-owned subsidiaries, and, 1.5.11
Directors
absence from board meetings
vacation under Model articles, 1.16.2.5
vacation under Table A articles, 1.16.1.5
additional appointment, 1.14.3.4—1.14.3.5
age
maximum, 1.13.7
minimum, 1.13.6
alternate directors
appointees, 1.11.3
appointment, 1.11.2—1.11.2.2
duration of appointment, 1.11.7
filings, 1.11.6
generally, 1.2.13.5
introduction, 1.11.1
liabilities, 1.11.5
minimum number of directors, and, 1.11.9
remuneration, 1.11.8.1—1.11.8.2
rights, 1.11.4
tenure, 1.11.7
appointment
acceptance, 1.14.10
additional appointees, 1.14.3.4—1.14.3.5
Bushell v Faith clauses, 1.14.3.2
casual vacancies, 1.14.3.3
checklist of considerations, 1.14.9
Combined Code, and, 1.14.6
effects of defects, 1.14.7
enhanced voting rights, 1.14.3.2
first directors, 1.14.2.1—1.14.2.2
informed consent, 1.14.1
introduction, 1.14
maximum number, and, 1.14.3.1
notifications to Registrar of Companies, 1.14.4
registers requiring updating, 1.14.5
residential address, 1.14.8
restrictions, 1.13—1.13.11
shareholders, by, 1.14.3.2
subsequent directors, 1.14.3—1.14.3.5
termination, 1.15.1—1.15.6
appointment restrictions
age, 1.13.6
CA 2006 provisions, 1.13.1
Combined Code, and, 1.13.10
companies, 1.13.5
comparison table, 1.3.11
disqualified directors, 1.13.2
introduction, 1.13
'phoenix' companies, and, 1.13.4
qualifications, 1.13.8
residence in UK, 1.13.9

Directors—*cont.*
  appointment restrictions—*cont.*
    undischarged bankrupts, 1.13.3
  automatic vacation of office
    introduction, 1.16
    Model articles, under, 1.16.2—1.16.2.5
    Table A articles, under, 1.16.1—1.16.1.5
  bankruptcy
    vacation under Model articles, 1.16.2.3
    vacation under Table A articles, 1.16.1.3
  Bushell v Faith clauses, 1.14.3.2
  casual vacancies, 1.14.3.3
  changes under CA 2006, 1.17
  companies as, 1.13.5
  company records, 3.14.6
  disqualification from acting
    removal, 1.13.2
    vacation under Model articles, 1.16.2.1
    vacation under Table A articles, 1.16.1.1
  duties
    See also **Directors' duties**
    BERR guidance, 1.2.16
    derivative claims, and, 1.5.1—1.5.14
    documenting board decisions, 1.3—1.3.3
    effect on common law, 1.2.11—1.2.12
    former directors, 1.2.15
    generally, 1.2.2—1.2.9
    liability for breach, 1.4.1—1.4.3
    purpose, 1.2.1
    overlap, 1.2.10
    persons affected, 1.2.13
    persons owed duty, 1.2.14
    practical steps, 1.2.17
  employees, as, 1.8
  executive directors
    general role, 1.10.1
    generally, 1.2.13.6
    introduction, 1.10
  first directors, 1.14.2.1—1.14.2.2
  formation of companies, and, 3.3.1
  fraudulent trading, 1.7.2
  group companies, and
    direction of parent company, 1.9.2
    example, 1.9.3
    generally, 1.9
    UK subsidiary of overseas parent, 1.9.1
  introduction, 1.1.1—1.1.5
  letters of appointment, 2.2
  liability on insolvency of company
    fraudulent trading, 1.7.2
    wrongful trading, 1.7.1
  loss of mental capacity
    vacation under Model articles, 1.16.2.4
    vacation under Table A articles, 1.16.1.4
  maximum number
    appointment, and, 1.14.3.1
    generally, 1.12.4
    maximum number, and, 1.14.3.1
    notification to Registrar of Companies, 1.14.4
    registers requiring updating, 1.14.5
    restrictions, 1.13—1.13.11

Directors—*cont.*
  maximum number—*cont.*
    shareholders, by, 1.14.3.2
    subsequent directors, 1.14.3—1.14.3.5
  minimum number, 1.12.2
  managing risk of personal liability
    acting honestly and reasonably, 1.6.2
    indemnity by company. 1.6.3—1.6.3.6
    ratification of decisions by shareholders, 1.6.1
  minimum age, 1.13.6
  non-executive directors
    duties, 1.10.3
    general role, 1.10.2
    generally, 1.2.13.6
    introduction, 1.10
    liabilities, 1.10.3
  number
    alternate directors, and, 1.11.9
    Combined Code, and, 1.12.6
    insufficient, 1.12.5
    introduction, 1.12
    maximum, 1.12.4
    minimum, 1.12.2
  operation of law
    vacation under Model articles, 1.16.2.1
    vacation under Table A articles, 1.16.1.1
  'phoenix' companies, and, 1.13.4
  qualifications, 1.13.8
  reduction of share capital, and, 9.3.5.5
  registers, 3.14.6
  removal
    board, by, 1.15.1.4
    checklist of considerations, 1.15.6
    employee director, of, 1.15.2.1
    expiry of fixed term contract, 1.15.1.3
    methods, 1.15.1
    notification to Registrar of Companies, 1.15.4
    payments, 1.15.3
    registers requiring updating, 1.15.5
    resignation, by, 1.15.1.1
    rotation, by, 1.15.1.2
    shareholder director, of, 1.15.2.2
    shareholders, by, 1.15.1.15
  residence in UK, 1.13.9
  residential address, and, 1.14.81
  resignation
    Model articles, under, 1.16.2.2
    Table A articles, under, 1.16.1.2
  secretary of company, and, 1.12.3
  service contracts
    approval, 2.2.4—2.2.11
    changes under CA 2006, 2.2.1
    charges for inspection, 2.2.14
    conflicts of interest, and, 2.2.18
    contracts affected, 2.2.2
    copies, 2.2.16
    directors' duties, and, 2.2.3
    exemption from approval, 2.2.8
    failure to obtain approval, 2.2.11
    'guaranteed term', 2.2.5

Index

Directors—*cont.*
  service contracts—*cont.*
    inspection, 2.2.12—2.2.15
    introduction, 2.2
    pre-1 October 2007 contracts, 2.2.10
    shadow directors, and, 2.2.17
    shareholder approval, 2.2.4—2.2.11
    sole member also director, 2.2.19
    successive terms of less than two years,
      2.2.6
  termination of appointment
    automatic vacation of office, 1.16—1.16.2
    methods, 1.15.1
    removal, 1.15.1.1—1.15.6
  transactions with
    And see **Directors' transactions**
    approval, 2.7
    credit, 2.4—2.4.13
    disclosure of interests in shares, 2.8—2.9
    introduction, 2.1.1—2.1.5
    loans, 2.4—2.4.13
    payments for loss of office, 2.6—2.6.5
    service contracts, 2.2—2.2.19
    substantial property transactions,
      2.3—2.3.15
    summary of changes, 2.10
    tax-free payments, 2.5
  undischarged bankrupts, and, 1.13.3
  wrongful trading, 1.7.1
Directors' and officers' insurance
  generally, 1.6.3.1
  introduction, 1.2.17
Directors' duties
  act in accordance with company constitution,
    to
    consequences of breach, 1.4.2
    generally, 1.2.3
  act within powers, to
    consequences of breach, 1.4.2
    generally, 1.2.3
  acting honestly and reasonably, and, 1.6.2
  alternate directors, 1.2.13.5
  articles of association, and, 1.2.17
  associate directors, 1.2.13.4
  avoid conflicts of interest, to
    authorisation by company, 1.2.7.1
    generally, 1.2.7
  benefits from third parties, and, 1.2.8
  BERR guidance, 1.2.16
  board minutes, and
    disclosure in litigation, 1.3.3
    impact of duties, 1.3.2
    introduction, 1.3
    status, 1.3.1
  'box-ticking', and, 1.2.17.1
  breach of
    consequences, 1.4.1—1.4.3
    introduction, 1.4
  changes under CA 2006
    background, 1.1.2—1.1.4
    generally, 1.1.5
    scope, 1.1.1

Directors' duties—*cont.*
  codification
    effect on common law, 1.2.11—1.2.12
    introduction, 1.2
    overlap situations, 1.2.10
    persons affected, 1.2.13—1.2.13.6
    persons owed duty, 1.2.14
    purpose, 1.2.1
    statutory duties, 1.2.2—1.2.9
  common law, and, 1.2.11—1.2.12
  conduct of business, and, 1.1.3
  conflicts of interest, and
    authorisation by company, 1.2.7.1
    generally, 1.2.7
  courtesy directors, 1.2.13.4
  de facto directors, 1.2.13.3
  de jure directors, 1.2.13.1
  declare interests in proposed transactions
    existing transaction or arrangement,
      1.2.9.1
    generally, 1.2.9
    updating information, 1.2.9.2
  derivative claims
    basis, 1.5.4
    causes of action prior to 1 October 2007,
      1.5.13
    changes under CA 2006, 1.5.3
    claimants, 1.5.5
    continuation, 1.5.7
    defendants, 1.5.6
    examples, 1.5.11
    factors determinative of permission, 1.5.9
    future purchase of a company, 1.5.11
    grounds, 1.5.4
    implication of new regime, 1.5.10
    meaning, 1.5.1
    practical steps, 1.5.14
    pre-1 October 2007 regime, 1.5.12
    provisions, 1.5.2
    redundancy programme, 1.5.11
    refusal of permission to continue,
      1.5.8—1.5.9
    sale of subsidiary, and, 1.5.11
    wholly-owned subsidiaries, and, 1.5.11
  directions of parent company, and, 1.9.2
  directors affected
    alternate directors, 1.2.13.5
    associate directors, 1.2.13.4
    courtesy directors, 1.2.13.4
    de facto directors, 1.2.13.3
    de jure directors, 1.2.13.1
    executive directors, 1.2.13.6
    generally, 1.2.13
    non-executive directors, 1.2.13.6
    shadow directors, 1.2.13.2
    statutory directors, 1.2.13.1
  directors' and officers' insurance, and
    generally, 1.6.3.1
    introduction, 1.2.17
  directors' service contracts, and, 2.2.3
  dividends, and, 9.2.10

Directors' duties—*cont.*
documenting decisions
  disclosure in litigation, 1.3.3
  impact of duties, 1.3.2
  introduction, 1.3
  status, 1.3.1
executive directors, 1.2.13.6
exercise independent judgment, to, 1.2.5
exercise reasonable care, skill and diligence,
  to, 1.2.6
filing accounts, 6.4.1
financial assistance, and, 9.9.2.1
former directors, 1.2.15
fraudulent trading, and, 1.7.2
group companies, and
  direction of parent company, 1.9.2
  example, 1.9.3
  generally, 1.9
  UK subsidiary of overseas parent, 1.9.1
honest and reasonable behaviour, and, 1.6.2
indemnity by company
  changes under CA 2006, 1.6.3.6
  generally, 1.6.3
  insurance provision, 1.6.3.1
  qualifying pension scheme indemnities,
    1.6.3.3
  qualifying third party indemnities, 1.6.3.2
  summary, 1.6.3.6
independent judgment, and, 1.2.5
insolvency of company, and
  fraudulent trading, 1.7.2
  wrongful trading, 1.7.1
insurance, and
  generally, 1.6.3.1
  introduction, 1.2.17
interests in proposed transactions, and
  existing transaction or arrangement,
    1.2.9.1
  generally, 1.2.9
  updating information, 1.2.9.2
introduction, 1.1.1—1.1.5
liability for breach
  acting in accordance with company
    constitution, of, 1.4.2
  generally, 1.4.1
  introduction, 1.4
  other statutory duties, of, 1.4.3
managing risk of personal liability
  acting honestly and reasonably, 1.6.2
  indemnity by company. 1.6.3—1.6.3.6
  ratification of decisions by shareholders,
    1.6.1
non-executive directors, 1.2.13.6
not to accept benefits from third parties, 1.2.8
overlap of, 1.2.10
overview, 1.0
owner-managed companies, and, 1.1.4
pension scheme indemnities
  disclosure, 1.6.3.4
  generally, 1.6.3.3
  inspection, 1.6.3.5

Directors' duties—*cont.*
persons affected
  alternate directors, 1.2.13.5
  associate directors, 1.2.13.4
  courtesy directors, 1.2.13.4
  de facto directors, 1.2.13.3
  de jure directors, 1.2.13.1
  executive directors, 1.2.13.6
  generally, 1.2.13
  non-executive directors, 1.2.13.6
  shadow directors, 1.2.13.2
  statutory directors, 1.2.13.1
persons owed duty, 1.2.14
practical steps, 1.2.17—1.2.17.1
promote success of company, to
  'benefit for members as a whole', 1.2.4.3
  business review, and, 1.2.4.6
  charities, and, 1.2.4.2
  commercial company, of, 1.2.4.1
  common law duty, and, 1.2.12
  conflicting interests, and, 1.2.4.5
  factors to be considered, 1.2.4.4
  generally, 1.2.4
  non-commercial company, of, 1.2.4.2
  'success', 1.2.4.1—1.2.4.2
qualifying pension scheme indemnities
  disclosure, 1.6.3.4
  generally, 1.6.3.3
  inspection, 1.6.3.5
qualifying third party indemnities
  disclosure, 1.6.3.4
  generally, 1.6.3.2
  inspection, 1.6.3.5
ratification of decisions by shareholders,
  1.6.1
reasonable behaviour, and, 1.6.2
reasonable care, skill and diligence, and, 1.2.6
service contracts, and, 2.2.3
shadow directors, 1.2.13.2
statutory directors, 1.2.13.1
statutory duties
  act within powers, 1.2.3
  avoid conflicts of interest, 1.2.7—1.2.7.1
  declare interest in proposed transactions,
    1.2.9—1.2.9.2
  exercise independent judgment, 1.2.5
  exercise reasonable care, skill and
    diligence, 1.2.6
  introduction, 1.2.2
  not to accept benefits from third parties,
    1.2.8
  promote success of company,
    1.2.4—1.2.4.6
success of company, and
  'benefit for members as a whole', 1.2.4.3
  business review, and, 1.2.4.6
  charities, and, 1.2.4.2
  commercial company, of, 1.2.4.1
  common law duty, and, 1.2.12
  conflicting interests, and, 1.2.4.5
  factors to be considered, 1.2.4.4
  generally, 1.2.4

Directors' duties—*cont.*
  success of company, and—*cont.*
    non-commercial company, of, 1.2.4.2
    'success', 1.2.4.1—1.2.4.2
  third party indemnities
    disclosure, 1.6.3.4
    generally, 1.6.3.2
    inspection, 1.6.3.5
  wholly-owned subsidiaries, and, 1.1.4
  wrongful trading, and, 1.7.1
Directors' emoluments
  employee incentive share plans, and, 10.6.1
Directors' loans
  affirmation by shareholders, 2.4.13
  business transactions, for, 2.4.9.4
  changes under CA 2006, 2.4.1
  company business expenditure to £50,000,
    for, 2.4.9.1
  defending proceedings, for, 2.4.9.2
  exemptions from approval
    business transactions, 2.4.9.4
    company business expenditure to £50,000,
      2.4.9.1
    defending proceedings, 2.4.9.2
    introduction, 2.4.9
    intra-group transactions, 2.4.9.5
    minor transactions, 2.4.9.4
    money-lending companies, 2.4.9.6
    regulatory investigations or actions, 2.4.9.3
  expenditure, for
    company business up to £50,000, on,
      2.4.9.1
    defending proceedings, on, 2.4.9.2
    intra-group transactions, for, 2.4.9.5
    minor transactions, on, 2.4.9.4
    regulatory investigations or actions, and,
      2.4.9.3
  failure to obtain approval, 2.4.11—2.4.12
  home loans, and, 2.4.9
  intra-group transactions, for, 2.4.9.5
  introduction, 2.4
  meaning, 2.4.4
  minor transactions, for, 2.4.9.4
  money-lending companies, and, 2.4.9.6
  personal liability
    defences, 2.4.12
    generally, 2.4.11.2
  public companies, and, 2.4.8
  regulatory investigations or actions, and,
    2.4.9.3
  rescission, and, 2.4.11.1
  shareholder approval
    anti-avoidance provisions, 2.4.7
    exemptions, 2.4.9
    introduction, 2.4.2
    procedure, 2.4.5
    public companies, and, 2.4.8
    relevant shareholders, 2.4.6
  third party arrangements, 2.4.7
  value of transaction, 2.4.10
Directors' long-term incentives
  generally, 10.6.3.5

Directors' long-term incentives—*cont.*
  'long-term incentives', 10.6.7
Directors' remuneration report
  employee incentive share plans, and
    content, 10.6.3.1
    statement of policy, 10.6.3.2
  generally, 5.5.1
Directors' report
  business review
    contents, 5.4.11
    disclosure requirements, 5.4.3
    exemptions, 5.4.4
    format, 5.4.7
    interpretation of requirements, 5.4.9
    KPI disclosure, 5.4.10
    medium-sized companies, and, 5.4.4
    principal risks disclosure, 5.4.10
    problem areas, 5.4.12—5.4.17
    purpose, 5.4.1.1
    quoted companies, and, 5.4.5
    responsibility for preparation, 5.4.2
    role of FRRP, 5.4.18
    safe harbour provision, and, 5.4.8
    seriously prejudicial exemptions, 5.4.6
    small companies, and, 5.4.4
  CA 2006 changes
    commencement, 5.1.3
    generally, 5.1.2
  changes to content, 5.4.1
  charitable donations, 5.4.21
  conclusion, 5.6
  disclosure of directors' interests
    generally, 5.4.19
    listed companies, 5.4.20
  legislative framework
    generally, 5.1.1
    regulations, 5.1.6
  political donations, 5.4.21
  remuneration of directors, 5.5.1
  signature, 6.4.14
Directors' responsibility statements
  generally, 6.6.4
Directors' service contracts
  approval
    circumvention of, 2.2.6
    exemptions, 2.2.8
    failure to obtain, 2.2.11
    generally, 2.2.4
    'guaranteed term', 2.2.5
    pre-1 October 2007 contracts, 2.2.10
    procedure, 2.2.9
    relevant shareholders, 2.2.7
  changes under CA 2006, 2.2.1
  charges for inspection, 2.2.14
  conflicts of interest, and, 2.2.18
  contracts affected, 2.2.2
  copies, 2.2.16
  directors' duties, and, 2.2.3
  exemption from approval, 2.2.8
  failure to obtain approval, 2.2.11
  'guaranteed term', 2.2.4

Directors' service contracts—*cont.*
  inspection
    changes under CA 2006, 2.2.13
    charges, 2.2.14
    generally, 2.2.12
    refusal to allow, 2.2.5
  introduction, 2.2
  pre-1 October 2007 contracts, 2.2.10
  shadow directors, and, 2.2.17
  shareholder approval
    circumvention of, 2.2.6
    exemptions, 2.2.8
    failure to obtain, 2.2.11
    generally, 2.2.4
    'guaranteed term', 2.2.5
    pre-1 October 2007 contracts, 2.2.10
    procedure, 2.2.9
    relevant shareholders, 2.2.7
  sole member also director, 2.2.19
  substantial property transactions, and, 2.3.4
  successive terms of less than two years, 2.2.6
Directors' share options
  employee incentive share plans, and,
    10.6.3.3—10.6.3.4
Directors' shareholdings
  employee incentive share plans, and, 10.6.2
Directors' transactions
  annual accounts, and, 5.3.16
  approval under more than one provision, 2.7
  breach of rules, 2.1.4
  capacity to bind a company, and, 3.5.3
  changes under CA 2006
    background, 2.1.2
    generally, 2.1.5
    scope, 2.1.1
    summary, 2.10
  connected persons, 2.1.1
  credit transactions
    affirmation by shareholders, 2.4.13
    changes under CA 2006, 2.4.1
    exemption from approval, 2.4.9
    failure to obtain approval, 2.4.11—2.4.12
    introduction, 2.4
    meaning, 2.4.4
    personal liability, 2.4.11—2.4.12
    public companies, and, 2.4.8
    relevant transactions, 2.4.2
    shareholder approval, 2.4.2—2.4.7
    third party arrangements, 2.4.7
    value of transaction, 2.4.10
  disclosure of interests in company shares
    directors, by, 2.9
    generally, 2.8
    registers, 3.14.8
  failure to comply, 2.1.1
  introduction, 2.1.1—2.1.5
  loans
    affirmation by shareholders, 2.4.13
    changes under CA 2006, 2.4.1
    exemption from approval, 2.4.9
    failure to obtain approval, 2.4.11—2.4.12
    introduction, 2.4

Directors' transactions—*cont.*
  loans—*cont.*
    personal liability, 2.4.11—2.4.12
    public companies, and, 2.4.8
    relevant transactions, 2.4.2
    shareholder approval, 2.4.2—2.4.7
    third party arrangements, 2.4.7
    value of transaction, 2.4.10
  majority shareholders, and, 2.1.3
  payments for loss of office
    changes under CA 2006, 2.6.1
    exemption from approval, 2.6.4
    failure to obtain approval, 2.6.5
    introduction, 2.6
    meaning, 2.6.2
    shareholder approval, 2.6.3—2.6.5
  penalties for failure to comply, 2.1.1
  quasi-loans
    And see **Loans**
    meaning, 2.4.3
  service contracts
    approval, 2.2.4—2.2.11
    changes under CA 2006, 2.2.1
    charges for inspection, 2.2.14
    conflicts of interest, and, 2.2.18
    contracts affected, 2.2.2
    copies, 2.2.16
    directors' duties, and, 2.2.3
    exemption from approval, 2.2.8
    failure to obtain approval, 2.2.11
    'guaranteed term', 2.2.4
    inspection, 2.2.12—2.2.15
    introduction, 2.2
    pre-1 October 2007 contracts, 2.2.10
    shadow directors, and, 2.2.17
    sole member also director, 2.2.19
    shareholder approval, 2.2.4—2.2.11
    successive terms of less than two years,
      2.2.6
  substantial property transactions
    affirmation by shareholders, 2.3.15
    aggregation of transactions, 2.3.5
    approval, 2.3.3
    'arrangements', 2.3.2
    changes under CA 2006, 2.3.1
    'connected persons', 2.3.8—2.3.11
    directors affected, 2.3.7
    directors' service contracts, and, 2.3.4
    examples, 2.3.2
    exemption from approval, 2.3.6
    failure to obtain approval, 2.3.12—2.3.14
    introduction, 2.3
    meaning, 2.3.2
    'non-cash asset', 2.3.2
    payment for loss of office, and, 2.3.4
    personal liability for breach, 2.3.14
    rescission, 2.3.13
    series of transactions, 2.3.5
    shareholder approval, 2.3.3
    'substantial', 2.3.2
  summary of changes, 2.10
  tax-free payments, 2.5

Directors' voluntary disclosures
communication of relevant audit
information, 7.4.3
effect, 7.4.4
generally, 7.4.2
Disclosure
annual accounts, and, 5.3.12
annual returns, in
CA 2006 changes, 3.10.1
contents, 3.10
generally, 3.10
board minutes in litigation, of, 1.3.3
business review, and, 5.4.3
company name, of, 3.6.8
interests in company shares, of
directors, by, 2.9
generally, 2.8
pension scheme indemnities, of, 1.6.3.4
Disclosure of directors' interests
company shares, in, 2.9
directors' report, and
generally, 5.4.19
listed companies, 5.4.20
Disclosure of directors' remuneration
accounting standards requirements, 10.6.5
emoluments, 10.6.1
FSA Disclosure and Transparency Rules,
10.6.6
glossary, 10.6.7
introduction, 10.6
Listing Rules requirements, 10.6.4
long-term incentives, 10.6.3.5
remuneration report, 10.6.3
share options, 10.6.3.3—10.6.3.4
shareholdings, 10.6.2
Discounts
allotment of shares, and
CA 2006 changes, 8.12.2
current position, 8.12.1
Disqualification of directors
removal from office, 1.13.2
vacation of office
Model articles, under, 1.16.2.1
Table A articles, under, 1.16.1.1
Dissolution of dormant companies
introduction, 11.1
members' voluntary liquidation
advertisement, 11.5.4
appointment of liquidator, 11.5.3
comparison with striking-off, 11.6
date of dissolution, 11.5.9
dealing with creditor claims,
11.5.6.2—11.5.6.3
declaration of solvency, 11.5.2.2
effect on status, 11.5.5
final board meeting, 11.5.2.1
final meeting of members, 11.5.8
general meeting of members, 11.5.2.3
grounds, 11.5.1
introduction, 11.5
key elements, 11.5.2
liquidator's duties, 11.5.6.2

Dissolution of dormant companies—*cont.*
members' voluntary liquidation—*cont.*
liquidator's powers, 11.5.6.1
liquidator's role, 11.5.6
London Gazette notice, 11.5.4
publication, 11.5.4
realisation of assets, 11.5.6.2
seeking out creditor claims, 11.5.6.2
shareholdings, 11.5.5.3
statutory filing and compliance, 11.5.5.1
tax affairs, 11.5.5.2
timing of distribution, 11.5.7
striking off
applications, 11.4.4
balance sheet simplification, 11.4.3.2
bona vacantia property, 11.4.11
CA 2006 changes, 11.4.9
comparison with liquidation, 11.6
consultation with HMRC, 11.4.3.1
date of dissolution, 11.4.6
directors' liabilities, 11.4.8
distribution of assets, 11.4.10.2—11.4.11.1
ESC C16, 11.4.11.1
Form 652A, 11.4.4.1
introduction, 11.4
legislative framework, 1.4.1
London Gazette notice, 11.4.6
notification of application, 11.4.5
notification of intention, 11.4.3.1
pre-conditions, 1.4.2
preliminary actions, 11.4.3
procedure, 11.4.4
registration of application, 11.4.4.2
relationship with creditors, 11.4.10.1
suitability, 11.4.10
unlawful dividends, 11.4.10.2
Distributable profits
dividends, and, 9.2.4
Distributions
And see **Dividends**
accounting treatment, 9.2.9
unlimited companies, and, 9.10.8
Dividends
accounting treatment, 9.2.9
accounts, 9.2.5
available profits, 9.2.4
breach of procedures, 9.2.11
CA 2006 changes
generally, 9.2.1
summary table, 9.2.2
different amount paid to holders of same
class of share, 9.2.8
directors duties, and, 9.2.10
distributable profits, 9.2.4
distributions made after relevant accounts,
9.2.6
introduction, 9.2
realised profits, 9.2.4
requirements, 9.2.2
restrictions on amount, 9.2.3
relevant accounts, 9.2.5

Dividends—*cont.*
shareholder approval
final dividend, 9.2.7.1
interim dividend, 9.2.7.2
introduction, 9.2.7
non-cash dividend, 9.2.7.3
summary table, 9.2.2
unlimited companies, and, 9.10.8
Division of public companies
subordinate legislation, A3.2.28
Dormant companies
audited accounts, and
financial services sector, in, 7.2.5
generally, 7.2.4
CA 2006 changes, 11.1
commercial dormancy, 11.2.1
conclusion, 11.7—11.7.1
dissolution
introduction, 11.1
members' voluntary liquidation,
11.5—11.5.9
striking off, 11.4—11.4.11
internal transfer of trades, 11.2.4.1
introduction, 11.1
latent issues remaining
internal transfer of trades, 11.2.4.1
introduction, 11.2.4
leasehold properties, 11.2.4.2
leasehold properties, 11.2.4.2
legal dormancy, 11.2.1
limitation periods, 11.2.5
'long tail' liabilities, 11.2.5
meaning, 11.2
members' voluntary liquidation
advertisement, 11.5.4
appointment of liquidator, 11.5.3
comparison with striking-off, 11.6
date of dissolution, 11.5.9
dealing with creditor claims,
11.5.6.2—11.5.6.3
declaration of solvency, 11.5.2.2
effect on status, 11.5.5
final board meeting, 11.5.2.1
final meeting of members, 11.5.8
general meeting of members, 11.5.2.3
grounds, 11.5.1
introduction, 11.5
key elements, 11.5.2
liquidator's duties, 11.5.6.2
liquidator's powers, 11.5.6.1
liquidator's role, 11.5.6
London Gazette notice, 11.5.4
publication, 11.5.4
realisation of assets, 11.5.6.2
seeking out creditor claims, 11.5.6.2
shareholdings, 11.5.5.3
statutory filing and compliance, 11.5.5.1
tax affairs, 11.5.5.2
timing of distribution, 11.5.7
methods of removal, 11.3
personal injury claims, 11.2.5
restoration to register, 11.4.7

Dormant companies—*cont.*
retention, 11.2.2
risks attendant on retention, 11.2.3
striking off
applications, 11.4.4
balance sheet simplification, 11.4.3.2
bona vacantia property, 11.4.11
CA 2006 changes, 11.4.9
comparison with liquidation, 11.6
consultation with HMRC, 11.4.3.1
date of dissolution, 11.4.6
directors' liabilities, 11.4.8
distribution of assets, 11.4.10.2—11.4.11.1
ESC C16, 11.4.11.1
Form 652A, 11.4.4.1
introduction, 11.4
legislative framework, 1.4.1
London Gazette notice, 11.4.6
notification of application, 11.4.5
notification of intention, 11.4.3.1
pre-conditions, 1.4.2
preliminary actions, 11.4.3
procedure, 11.4.4
registration of application, 11.4.4.2
relationship with creditors, 11.4.10.1
suitability, 11.4.10
unlawful dividends, 11.4.10.2

Electronic communications
See also **Website communications**
application of provisions, 4.2.2
articles of association, and, 4.2.4
authorisation, 4.2.4
CA 2006 changes
background, 4.1.2
list, 4.9.1
summary, 4.1.3
circulation of accounts, 6.3.3
communicable documents, 4.2.3
conclusion, 4.9—4.9.1
filing accounts, 6.4.15
general meetings, and
circulation of resolutions, 4.4.30
circulation of statements, 4.4.25
polls, 4.2.25
proxies, 4.4.22
voting, 4.4.27
written resolutions, 4.4.31
introduction, 4.2.1
investigation of ownership of shares, and, 4.6.3
meaning, 4.2.3
nominees, and, 4.2.15
shareholder consent, 4.2.4
E-mail
website communications, and, 4.2.11
Employee benefit trusts
beneficiaries, 10.4.2.3
directors' meetings, 10.4.2.4
formation, 10.4.2.1
funding, 10.4.2.5
introduction, 10.4.2
trustees, 10.4.2.2

Employee incentive share plans
approved schemes and plans
company share option plan, 10.3.7
save as you earn option scheme, 10.3.8
share incentive plan, 10.3.9
acquisition of company assets by third party, and, 10.7.7
acquisition of company shares by third party, and
cash cancellation, 10.7.4
early vesting or exercise, 10.7.2.2
employee meeting any employer's NIC, 10.7.2.6
exercise of rights, 10.7.2.1
impact of share plans, 10.7.1
introduction, 10.7
issue of additional shares, 10.7.3
lapse date, 10.7.2.7
overall acquisition cost, 10.7.3
payment of exercise price, 10.7.2.4
performance conditions, 10.7.2.2
recovery of PAYE and NICs, 10.7.2.5
relevant provisions of share plans, 10.7.2—10.7.2.7
retention of 'key' employees, 10.7.5
rollover of rights, 10.7.4
securing support of rights holders, 10.7.6
takeover-related vesting or exercise, 10.7.2.3
vesting of rights, 10.7.2.1
authorised share capital, 10.2.2.4
authority to allot shares, 10.2.2.5
common issues
conclusion, 10.2.3
corporate capacity, 10.2.2.1
'employees' share scheme', 10.2.2.2
financial assistance 10.2.2.7
introduction, 10.2.2
shareholder approval, 10.2.2.3—10.2.2.6
company law considerations
example, 10.1.2
generally, 10.1.1
corporate capacity, 10.2.2.1
CSOP, 10.3.7
data protection, and, 10.5.4
directors' emoluments, 10.6.1
directors' long-term incentives
generally, 10.6.3.5
'long-term incentives', 10.6.7
directors' remuneration report
content, 10.6.3.1
statement of policy, 10.6.3.2
directors' share options, 10.6.3.3—10.6.3.4
directors' shareholdings, 10.6.2
disclosure of directors' remuneration
accounting standards requirements, 10.6.5
emoluments, 10.6.1
FSA Disclosure and Transparency Rules, 10.6.6
glossary, 10.6.7
introduction, 10.6
Listing Rules requirements, 10.6.4

Employee incentive share plans—*cont.*
disclosure of directors' remuneration—*cont.*
long-term incentives, 10.6.3.5
remuneration report, 10.6.3
share options, 10.6.3.3—10.6.3.4
shareholdings, 10.6.2
documentation
exercise notice, 10.2.1.3
option grant certificate, 10.2.1.2
plan rules, 10.2.1.1
employee benefit trusts
beneficiaries, 10.4.2.3
directors' meetings, 10.4.2.4
formation, 10.4.2.1
funding, 10.4.2.5
introduction, 10.4.2
trustees, 10.4.2.2
'employees' share scheme', 10.2.2.2
employment law, and, 10.5.4
enterprise management incentives
gross assets, 10.3.6.3
independence, 10.3.6.1
introduction, 10.3.6
material interest, 10.3.6.6
number of employees, 10.3.6.7
qualifying subsidiaries, 10.3.6.2
trading activities, 10.3.6.4
working time, 10.3.6.5
exercise notice, 10.2.1.3
financial assistance
generally, 10.2.2.7
partly paid shares, 10.4.4.2
free shares, 10.3.2
FSA Disclosure and Transparency Rules, 10.6.6
introduction, 10.1
Listing Rules requirements, 10.6.4
loans to directors, 10.4.5
long-term incentives
generally, 10.6.3.5
'long-term incentives', 10.6.7
meaning, 10.2.2.2
national insurance contributions, and, 10.5.2
option grant certificate, 10.2.1.2
partly paid shares
financial assistance, and, 10.4.4.2
introduction, 10.4.4
meaning, 10.4.4.1
PAYE, and, 10.5.2
phantom share options, 10.3.4
plan rules, 10.2.1.1
pre-emption rights, 10.2.2.6
remuneration of directors, and, 10.4.3
reporting obligations, 10.5.3
restricted shares, 10.3.3
SAYE scheme, 10.3.8
securities laws, and, 10.5.1
share incentive plan, 10.3.9
share options, 10.3.1
shareholder approval
authorised share capital, 10.2.2.4
authority to allot shares, 10.2.2.5

Employee incentive share plans—*cont.*
shareholder approval—*cont.*
generally, 10.2.2.3
statutory pre-emption rights, 10.2.2.6
source of shares for plans
introduction, 10.4.1
issue of new shares, 10.4.1.1
purchase of existing shares, 10.4.1.2
Treasury shares, 10.4.1.3
tax free payments to directors, 10.4.3
tax reporting obligations, 10.5.3
taxation issues
corporate tax, 10.5.4
generally, 10.1
tax-favoured plans, 10.3.5
types, 10.3.1—10.3.9
Employees
annual accounts, and, 5.3.26
business review, and, 5.4.16
enterprise management incentives, and,
10.3.6.7
directors, and, 1.8
Employment law
employee incentive share plans, and, 10.5.4
Enterprise management incentives
gross assets, 10.3.6.3
independence, 10.3.6.1
introduction, 10.3.6
material interest, 10.3.6.6
number of employees, 10.3.6.7
qualifying subsidiaries, 10.3.6.2
trading activities, 10.3.6.4
working time, 10.3.6.5
Entrenching provisions
formation of companies, and, 3.4.9
Environmental issues
business review, and, 5.4.16
EU Company Law Directives
auditors, and, 7.1.1
EU Statutory Audit Directive
auditors, and, 7.1.1
EU Transparency Obligations Directive
contents of annual report, 6.6.3
corporate governance, 6.6.9—6.6.10
directors' responsibility statements, 6.6.4
half yearly interim management reports, 6.6.7
half yearly reports, 6.6.6
impact, 6.6.1
interim management statements, 6.6.8
penalties for breach, 6.6.11
preliminary statements of results, 6.5.5
time for publication of annual report, 6.6.2
Execution of documents
attorney, by, 3.5.6
companies not incorporated, where, 3.5.8
contracts, 3.5.4
deeds, as, 3.5.5
Scottish companies, by, 3.5.9
Executive directors
general role, 1.10.1
generally, 1.2.13.6
introduction, 1.10

Exercise independent judgment
directors' duties, and, 1.2.5
Exercise notice
employee incentive share plans, and, 10.2.1.3
Exercise reasonable care, skill and diligence
directors' duties, and, 1.2.6
Extraordinary general meetings
generally, 4.4

Fair value accounting
annual accounts, and, 5.3.24
False statements
penalties, 6.6.11
Filing accounts
calculation of filing date, 6.4.3
directors' duties, 6.4.1
electronic communication, 6.4.15
first filing period, 6.4.4
fixed penalty fines, 6.4.5.1
large private companies, 6.4.13
late filing penalties
fixed penalty fines, 6.4.5.1
striking off, 6.4.5.2—6.4.5.4
medium-sized companies, 6.4.6, 6.4.9—6.4.12
publication of statutory accounts, 6.4.16
publication of non-statutory accounts, 6.4.17
quoted companies, 6.4.13
signature, 6.4.14
small companies, 6.4.6—6.4.8
striking off for failure to file
bona vacantia, 6.4.5.4
generally, 6.4.5.2
subsequent restoration, 6.4.5.3
timing, 6.4.2
takeovers, and, A2.5—A2.5.3
Financial assistance
CA 2006 changes, 9.9.1
consequences of breach, 9.9.6
contractual restrictions, 9.9.2.3
definition, 9.9.3.2
directors' duties, 9.9.2.1
employee incentive share plans, and
generally, 10.2.2.7
partly paid shares, 10.4.4.2
intra-group transactions, and, 9.6.7.1
introduction, 9.9
lawful exceptions, 9.9.5.2
meaning, 9.9.3.2
new position, 9.9.3
permitted transactions
introduction, 9.9.5
lawful exceptions, 9.9.5.2
purpose exemptions, 9.9.5.1
preliminary issues
contractual restrictions, 9.9.2.3
directors' duties, 9.9.2.1
introduction, 9.9.2
transactions at an undervalue, 9.9.2.2
prohibited assistance, 9.9.3.1
purpose exemptions, 9.9.5.1
summary flowchart
Companies Act 1985 procedure, 9.9.7

Financial assistance—*cont.*
summary flowchart—*cont.*
Companies Act 2006 procedure, 9.9.8
transactions at an undervalue, 9.9.2.2
'whitewash' procedure
common law, at, 9.9.4.3
Companies Act 1985, under, 9.9.4.1
Companies Act 2006, under, 9.9.4.2
Financial reporting
abbreviated accounts, 6.5.4
accounts meetings
generally, 6.2.2
members raising concerns, 6.2.5
annual general meetings
laying accounts, 6.2.3
time for holding, 6.2.4
annual report
contents, 6.6.3
time for publication, 6.6.2
approval of accounts
accounts meetings, 6.2.2
generally, 6.2.1
laying accounts at AGM, 6.2.3
private companies, 6.2.3
public companies, 6.2.2
quoted companies, 6.2.5
time for holding AGM, 6.2.4
balance sheet
signature, 6.4.14
CA 2006 changes
background, 6.1.1
generally, 6.1.2
implementation, 6.1.3
circulation of accounts
electronic communication, 6.3.3
hard copy documents, 6.3.6
indirect investor's rights, 6.3.9—6.3.10
person entitled to receive, 6.3.1
quoted companies, 6.3.11
summary financial statements, 6.3.8
timing, 6.3.2
trading on regulated markets, 6.3.7
website communication, 6.3.4—6.3.5
conclusion, 6.7
corporate governance
Combined Code (2006), and, 6.6.10
generally, 6.6.9
penalties for breach, 6.6.11
directors' duties
filing accounts, 6.4.1
directors' report
signature, 6.4.14
directors' responsibility statements, 6.6.4
electronic communication
circulation of accounts, 6.3.3
filing accounts, 6.4.15
EU Transparency Obligations Directive
contents of annual report, 6.6.3
corporate governance, 6.6.9—6.6.10
directors' responsibility statements, 6.6.4
half yearly interim management reports,
6.6.7

Financial reporting—*cont.*
EU Transparency Obligations Directive—
cont.
half yearly reports, 6.6.6
impact, 6.6.1
interim management statements, 6.6.8
penalties for breach, 6.6.11
preliminary statements of results, 6.5.5
time for publication of annual report, 6.6.2
false statements
penalties, 6.6.11
filing accounts
calculation of filing date, 6.4.3
directors' duties, 6.4.1
electronic communication, 6.4.15
first filing period, 6.4.4
large private companies, 6.4.13
late filing penalties, 6.4.5
medium-sized companies, 6.4.6,
6.4.9—6.4.12
publication of statutory accounts, 6.4.16
publication of non-statutory accounts,
6.4.17
quoted companies, 6.4.13
signature, 6.4.14
small companies, 6.4.6—6.4.8
timing, 6.4.2
half yearly reports
generally, 6.6.6
interim management reports, 6.6.7
review by FRRP, 6.5.3
hard copy documents, 6.3.6
indirect investor's rights
information rights, 6.3.10
shareholder rights, 6.3.9
interim management reports, 6.6.7
interim management statements, 6.6.8
introduction, 6.1.1—6.1.3
late filing penalties, 6.4.5
laying accounts at AGM, 6.2.3
medium-sized companies
filing accounts, 6.4.6, 6.4.9—6.4.12
revision of defective annual accounts and
reports, 6.5.4
misleading statements
penalties, 6.6.11
preliminary statements of results, 6.5.5
public companies
accounts meetings, 6.2.2
publication of accounts, 6.3.11
time for holding AGM, 6.2.4
publication of accounts
non-statutory, 6.4.17
quoted companies, 6.3.11
statutory, 6.4.16
quoted companies
approval of accounts, 6.2.5
filing accounts, 6.4.13
website communication, 6.3.11
revision of defective annual accounts and
reports
abbreviated accounts, 6.5.4

Financial reporting—*cont.*
revision of defective annual accounts and
 reports—*cont.*
 generally, 6.5.1
 half yearly reports, 6.5.3
 medium sized companies, 6.5.4
 request by FRRP, 6.5.2
 small companies, 6.5.4
 time of delivery, 6.5.5
signature, 6.4.14
small companies
 filing accounts, 6.4.6—6.4.8
 laying accounts at AGM, 6.2.3
 revision of defective annual accounts and
 reports, 6.5.4
summary financial statements, 6.3.8
trading on regulated markets, 6.3.7
website communication
 generally, 6.3.4—6.3.5
 quoted companies, 6.3.11
Financial Reporting Review Panel
business review, and, 5.4.18
Financial services sector companies
audited accounts, and
 dormant companies, 7.2.5
 small companies, 7.2.3
Formation of companies
articles of association
 amendment, 3.4.10—3.4.12
 CA 2006 changes, 3.4.6
 changes to existing arrangements,
 3.4.13—3.4.14
 copies, 3.4.15
 effect of amendments, 3.4.12
 entrenching provisions in, 3.4.9
 filing amendments, 3.4.11
 generally, 3.4.3
 introduction, 3.4
 meaning, 4.4.3
 Model articles, 3.4.7
 Table A, 3.4.4
 Tables B—F, 3.4.5
CA 2006 changes
 articles of association, 3.4.6
 generally, 3.3—3.3.8
capacity to bind, and
 See also **Capacity to bind a company**
 generally, 3.5—3.5.9
certificate, 3.3.3
company secretary, 3.9—3.9.10
constitution
 articles of association, 3.4.3—3.4.11
 changes to existing arrangements,
 3.4.13—3.4.14
 copies, 3.4.15
 effect of amendments, 3.4.12
 introduction, 3.4
 memorandum of association, 3.4.1
 objects clause, 3.4.2
date, 3.3.3
directors, 3.3.1
entrenching provisions, 3.4.9

Formation of companies—*cont.*
Forms 10 and 12, 3.3.1
introduction, 3.1.1—3.1.3
memorandum of association
 changes to existing arrangements, 3.4.13
 copies, 3.4.15
 generally, 3.4.1
 introduction, 3.4
minimum number of members, 3.3.8
Model articles
 CA 2006 changes, 3.4.8
 generally, 3.4.7
name
 change, 3.6.5—3.6.7
 choice restrictions, 3.6.2
 disclosure, 3.6.8
 introduction, 3.6
 limited, 3.6.3
 objections, 3.6.4
 pre-decision checks, 3.6.1
 trade marks, and, 3.6.1
objects clause
 directors' duties, and, 3.4.2
 generally, 3.4.1
 need, 3.4.2
officers, 3.3.1
on-line, 3.3.2
refusal by Registrar of Companies, 3.3.4
registered office, 3.7
re-registration, and
 And see **Re-registration**
 generally, 3.8—3.8.19
service address, 3.3.1
statement of capital, 3.3.1
statement of guarantee, 3.3.1
supporting documentation, 3.3.1
Table A articles
 CA 2006 changes, 3.4.6
 differences from Model articles, 3.4.8
 generally, 3.4.4
Tables B—F articles
 CA 2006 changes, 3.4.6
 generally, 3.4.5
trading certificates
 applications, 3.3.6
 consequences of failure to obtain, 3.3.7
 generally, 3.3.5
 purpose, 3.3.6
types of company, 3.2—3.2.2
ultra vires, and, 3.4.1
unlawful purpose, and, 3.3.4
validity, 3.3.3
Fixed penalties
late filing of accounts, 6.4.5.1
Former directors
directors' duties, and, 1.2.15
Forms 10 and 12
formation of companies, and, 3.3.1
Fraudulent trading
directors, and, 1.7.2
Free shares
employee incentive share plans, and, 10.3.2

FSA Disclosure and Transparency Rules
employee incentive share plans, and, 10.6.6
Fully paid-up shares
purchase by company of its own shares, and,
9.4.5.13
Future trends and factors
competitively sensitive information, 5.4.15.1
generally, 5.4.15
profit forecasts, 5.4.15.3
supportability of information, 5.4.15.2

GAAP
And see **Annual accounts**
generally, 5.3.1
General meetings
adjournment, 4.4.14
annual general meetings
private companies, 4.4.1
public companies, 4.4.2—4.4.3
appointment of chairperson, 4.4.13
attendance
companies, by, 4.4.21—4.4.22
generally, 4.4.15
CA 2006 changes
background, 4.1.2
list, 4.9.1
summary, 4.1.3
calling
general powers, 4.4.4
members, by, 4.4.5
chairperson, 4.4.13
circulation of statements, 4.4.11
class of shareholders, of, 4.4.25
companies, and
attendance, 4.4.21
representatives, 4.4.22
conclusion, 4.9
conduct, 4.4.13
electronic communications
circulation of resolutions, 4.4.30
circulation of statements, 4.4.25
polls, 4.2.25
proxies, 4.4.22
voting, 4.4.27
written resolutions, 4.4.31
introduction, 4.4
members' voluntary liquidation, and, 11.5.2.3
notice
contents, 4.4.7
electronic communication, 4.4.8
period, 4.4.6
persons entitled, 4.4.10
website communication, 4.4.9
quorum, 4.4.12
particular class of shareholders, of, 4.4.25
persons entitled to notice, 4.4.10
polls
generally, 4.4.24
quoted companies, and, 4.5.1—4.5.2
power to call
general, 4.4.4
members, 4.4.5

General meetings—*cont.*
proxies
appointment, 4.4.17
notification of appointment, 4.4.19
number, 4.4.16
powers, 4.4.18
termination of authority, 4.4.20
resolutions
generally, 4.4.23
ordinary resolutions, 4.4.33
polls, 4.4.24
procedure, 4.4.25
show of hands, and, 4.4.27
special resolutions, 4.4.33
types, 4.4.32
written resolutions, 4.4.28—4.4.31
show of hands, 4.4.27
special notice, 4.4.34
voting
attendance, and, 4.4.15
corporate shareholders, by, 4.4.21—4.4.22
proxies, 4.4.16—4.4.20
show of hands, 4.4.27
website notification, 4.4.9
written resolutions
electronic communications, and, 4.4.31
generally, 4.4.28
proposed by directors, 4.4.29
requisitioned by members, 4.4.30
Glossary
terms and definitions, Appendix 4
Group reconstruction relief
share capital, and, 8.8.3—8.8.4
Groups
annual accounts, and
changes to content of accounts, 5.3.27
form of accounts, 5.3.10—5.3.11
size limit, 5.3.9
directors, and
direction of parent company, 1.9.2
example, 1.9.3
generally, 1.9
UK subsidiary of overseas parent, 1.9.1
Guarantee companies
constitution
And see **Constitution of companies**
generally, 3.4.1—3.4.15
definition, 3.2.2
formation
And see **Formation of companies**
generally, 3.3.1—3.3.8
introduction, 3.2.1
'Guaranteed term'
directors' service contracts, and, 2.2.4

Half yearly reports
generally, 6.6.6
interim management reports, 6.6.7
review by FRRP, 6.5.3
Hard copy documents
financial reports, and, 6.3.6
website communications, and, 4.2.14

Higgs Report
introduction, 1.0
Home address
company secretary, and, 3.9.7
directors, and, 3.3.1
Home loans
loans and credit transactions, and, 2.4.9.6
Honest and reasonable behaviour
directors' duties, and, 1.6.2

IAS
And see **Annual accounts**
generally, 5.3.1
Incorporation of companies
articles of association
amendment, 3.4.10—3.4.12
CA 2006 changes, 3.4.6
changes to existing arrangements,
3.4.13—3.4.14
copies, 3.4.15
effect of amendments, 3.4.12
entrenching provisions in, 3.4.9
filing amendments, 3.4.11
generally, 3.4.3
introduction, 3.4
meaning, 4.4.3
Model articles, 3.4.7
Table A, 3.4.4
Tables B—F, 3.4.5
CA 2006 changes
articles of association, 3.4.6
generally, 3.3—3.3.8
capacity to bind, and
See also **Capacity to bind a company**
generally, 3.5—3.5.9
certificate, 3.3.3
company secretary, 3.9—3.9.10
constitution
articles of association, 3.4.3—3.4.11
changes to existing arrangements,
3.4.13—3.4.14
copies, 3.4.15
effect of amendments, 3.4.12
introduction, 3.4
memorandum of association, 3.4.1
objects clause, 3.4.2
date, 3.3.3
directors, 3.3.1
entrenching provisions, 3.4.9
Forms 10 and 12, 3.3.1
introduction, 3.1.1—3.1.3
memorandum of association
changes to existing arrangements, 3.4.13
copies, 3.4.15
generally, 3.4.1
introduction, 3.4
minimum number of members, 3.3.8
Model articles
CA 2006 changes, 3.4.8
generally, 3.4.7
name
change, 3.6.5—3.6.7

Incorporation of companies—*cont.*
name—*cont.*
choice restrictions, 3.6.2
disclosure, 3.6.8
introduction, 3.6
limited, 3.6.3
objections, 3.6.4
pre-decision checks, 3.6.1
trade marks, and, 3.6.1
objects clause
directors' duties, and, 3.4.2
generally, 3.4.1
need, 3.4.2
officers, 3.3.1
on-line, 3.3.2
refusal by Registrar of Companies, 3.3.4
registered office, 3.7
re-registration, and
And see **Re-registration**
generally, 3.8—3.8.19
service address, 3.3.1
statement of capital, 3.3.1
statement of guarantee, 3.3.1
supporting documentation, 3.3.1
Table A articles
CA 2006 changes, 3.4.6
differences from Model articles, 3.4.8
generally, 3.4.4
Tables B—F articles
CA 2006 changes, 3.4.6
generally, 3.4.5
trading certificates
applications, 3.3.6
consequences of failure to obtain, 3.3.7
generally, 3.3.5
purpose, 3.3.6
types of company, 3.2—3.2.2
ultra vires, and, 3.4.1
unlawful purpose, and, 3.3.4
validity, 3.3.3
Indemnity by company
changes under CA 2006, 1.6.3.6
generally, 1.6.3
insurance provision, 1.6.3.1
qualifying pension scheme indemnities,
1.6.3.3
qualifying third party indemnities, 1.6.3.2
summary, 1.6.3.6
Independent judgment
directors' duties, and, 1.2.5
Independent supervisor
subordinate legislation, A3.2.5
Indirect investors' rights
CA 2006 changes
background, 4.1.2
list, 4.9.1
summary, 4.1.3
commencement of provisions, 4.3.1
conclusion, 4.9
data protection, and, 4.3.3.3
financial reports, and
information rights, 6.3.10

Indirect investors' rights—*cont.*
  financial reports, and—*cont.*
    shareholder rights, 6.3.9
  information rights
    articles of association, and, 4.3.2.5
    application of, 4.3.2.2
    general right, 4.3.2.1
    limitations, 4.3.2.6
    operative date, 4.3.2.3
    relevant information, 4.3.2.2
    use of regime, 4.3.2.4
  introduction, 4.3
  nomination of third parties
    articles of association, and, 4.3.1.3
    general right, 4.3.1.1
    termination, 4.3.2.7
    use of regime, 4.3.1.2
  proxies, 4.3.2
  record of, 4.3.3.1
  shareholder rights
    limitations, 4.3.1.5
    nomination of third parties,
      4.3.1.1—4.3.1.4
Inherent rights
  shares, and, 8.1.3
Insolvency of company
  directors, and
    fraudulent trading, 1.7.2
    wrongful trading, 1.7.1
Inspection
  company records
    generally, 3.14.1
    rights, 3.14.4
  directors' service contracts
    changes under CA 2006, 2.2.13
    charges, 2.2.14
    generally, 2.2.12
    refusal to allow, 2.2.5
Inspection fees
  directors' service contracts, and, 2.2.14
  subordinate legislation, A3.2.3, A3.2.6
Insurance
  directors' and officers' insurance
    generally, 1.6.3.1
    introduction, 1.2.17
  directors' duties, and, 1.6.3.1
Insurance companies
  annual accounts, and, 5.1.5
Interest rate
  subordinate legislation, A3.2.29
Interests in company shares
  disclosure
    directors, by, 2.9
    generally, 2.8
Interests in proposed transactions
  existing transaction or arrangement, 1.2.9.1
  generally, 1.2.9
  updating information, 1.2.9.2
Interim management reports
  financial reports, and, 6.6.7
Interim management statements
  financial reports, and, 6.6.8

Internal transfer of trades
  dissolution of dormant companies, and,
    11.2.4.1
Intra-group transactions
  assets to be transferred, 9.6.7.4
  CA 2006 changes, 9.6.3
  changes in existing procedures, 9.6.8
  data protection, 9.6.7.4
  directors, with, 2.4.9.5
  directors' duties, 9.6.7.3
  downstream transfers, and, 9.6.5.3
  employees, 9.6.7.4
  financial assistance, 9.6.7.1
  general issues
    directors' duties, 9.6.7.3
    financial assistance, 9.6.7.1
    other, 9.6.7.4
    undervalue transactions, 9.6.7.2
  identity of parties, 9.6.7.4
  introduction, 9.6.1
  licences and consents, 9.6.7.4
  loans and credit transactions, and, 2.4.9
  memorandum of association, and, 9.6.7.3
  pensions, 9.6.7.4
  purposes, 9.6.1
  relevant circumstances, 9.6.1
  relevant transactions
    introduction, 9.6.5
    transfer between sister companies, 9.6.5.1
    transfer to parent company, 9.6.5.2
  transfer of asset for less than market value,
    9.6.2
  undervalue transactions, 9.6.7.2
  valuation
    methods, 9.6.6
    summary of rules, 9.6.4
  value at which assets can be transferred,
    9.6.3.1
Investigation of ownership of shares
  electronic communications, 4.6.3
  general power, 4.6
  introduction, 4.6
  notification of interests in shares by
    shareholders, 4.6.1
  register of requests for information, 4.6.4
  request for information concerning interest in
    shares, 4.6.2
Issue of shares
  and see **Share capital**
  accounting treatment, 8.8—8.8.6
  difference from allotment, 8.2.3
  employee incentive share plans, and, 10.4.1.1
  meaning, 8.2.3
  shareholder approval, 8.4—8.4.7

Key performance indicators
  choice, 5.4.14
  disclosure, 5.4.10
  group, 5.4.13.3
  'key', 5.4.13.1
  number, 5.4.13.2
  problem areas, 5.4.13

Key performance indicators—*cont.*
reliability, 5.4.13.5
segmental, 5.4.13.3

Languages
subordinate legislation, A3.2.2
Large companies
annual accounts, and
generally, 5.3.6
MiFiD companies, 5.3.7
size limit, 5.3.8
Late filing penalties
financial reports, and, 6.4.5
subordinate legislation, A3.2.13
Laying accounts at AGM
financial reports, and, 6.2.3
Leasehold properties
dissolution of dormant companies, and,
11.2.4.2
Letters patent
unlimited companies, and, 3.2.3
Liability limitation agreements
articles of association, and, 7.6.3
authorisation, 7.6.3
cap, 7.6.4
definition, 7.6.2
directors' responsibilities, 7.6.2
'fair and reasonable', 7.6.4
generally, 7.6.1
guidance on preparation, 7.6.5
nature of arrangements, 7.6.6.1
proportionality, 7.6.4
SEC reaction, 7.6.6.3
Licences and consents
intra-group transactions, and, 9.6.7.4
Limitation periods
dissolution of dormant companies, and,
11.2.5
Limited companies
constitution
And see **Constitution of companies**
generally, 3.4.1—3.4.15
definition, 3.2.2
formation
And see **Formation of companies**
generally, 3.3.1—3.3.8
introduction, 3.2.1
Liquidators
appointment, 11.5.3
duties, 11.5.6.2
powers, 11.5.6.1
role, 11.5.6
Listed companies
purchase by company of its own shares, and,
9.4.5.1
Listed convertible securities
purchase by company of its own shares, and,
9.4.5.2
Listing Rules requirements
employee incentive share plans, and, 10.6.4
Loans and credit transactions
intra-group transactions, and, 2.4.9.6

Loans to directors
affirmation by shareholders, 2.4.13
business transactions, for, 2.4.9.4
changes under CA 2006, 2.4.1
company business expenditure to £50,000,
for, 2.4.9.1
defending proceedings, for, 2.4.9.2
exemptions from approval
business transactions, 2.4.9.4
company business expenditure to £50,000,
2.4.9.1
defending proceedings, 2.4.9.2
introduction, 2.4.9
intra-group transactions, 2.4.9.5
minor transactions, 2.4.9.4
money-lending companies, 2.4.9.6
regulatory investigations or actions, 2.4.9.3
expenditure, for
company business up to £50,000, on,
2.4.9.1
defending proceedings, on, 2.4.9.2
intra-group transactions, for, 2.4.9.5
minor transactions, on, 2.4.9.4
regulatory investigations or actions, and,
2.4.9.3
failure to obtain approval, 2.4.11—2.4.12
home loans, and, 2.4.9
intra-group transactions, for, 2.4.9.5
introduction, 2.4
meaning, 2.4.4
minor transactions, for, 2.4.9.4
money-lending companies, and, 2.4.9.6
personal liability
defences, 2.4.12
generally, 2.4.11.2
public companies, and, 2.4.8
regulatory investigations or actions, and,
2.4.9.3
rescission, and, 2.4.11.1
shareholder approval
anti-avoidance provisions, 2.4.7
exemptions, 2.4.9
introduction, 2.4.2
procedure, 2.4.5
public companies, and, 2.4.8
relevant shareholders, 2.4.6
third party arrangements, 2.4.7
value of transaction, 2.4.10
London Gazette
members' voluntary liquidation, and, 11.5.4
striking off, and, 11.4.6
'Long tail' liabilities
dissolution of dormant companies, and,
11.2.5
Long-term incentives
generally, 10.6.3.5
'long-term incentives', 10.6.7
Loss of office payments
changes under CA 2006, 2.6.1
exemption from approval, 2.6.4
failure to obtain approval, 2.6.5

Loss of office payments—*cont.*
meaning, 2.6.2
introduction, 2.6
shareholder approval, 2.6.3—2.6.5

Major audit
cessation statements, and, 7.5.7
Managing risk of personal liability
acting honestly and reasonably, 1.6.2
indemnity by company. 1.6.3—1.6.3.6
ratification of decisions by shareholders,
1.6.1
Mandatory offers
purchase by company of its own shares, and,
9.4.5.3
Market purchases
purchase by company of its own shares, and,
9.4.2.1
Medium-sized companies
annual accounts, and
form of accounts, 5.3.11
generally, 5.3.6
off-balance-sheet arrangements, 5.3.21
size limit, 5.3.8
audited accounts, and, 7.2.8
business review, and, 5.4.4
financial reports, and
filing accounts, 6.4.6, 6.4.9—6.4.12
revision of defective annual accounts and
reports, 6.5.4
Meetings
annual general meetings
exceptions to date to be held, 4.4.3
generally, 4.4.1
notice periods, 4.4.6
public companies, and, 4.4.2
CA 2006 changes
background, 4.1.2
list, 4.9.1
summary, 4.1.3
conclusion, 4.9
extraordinary general meetings, 4.4
general meetings
adjournment, 4.4.14
annual general meetings, 4.4.1—4.4.3
appointment of chairperson, 4.4.13
attendance, 4.4.15
attendance by companies, 4.4.21—4.4.22
calling, 4.4.4—4.4.5
circulation of statements, 4.4.11
conduct, 4.4.13
electronic communications, 4.4.25
introduction, 4.4
notice, 4.4.6—4.4.10
polls, 4.4.24
proxies, 4.4.16—4.4.20
recipients entitled to notice, 4.4.10
resolutions, 4.4.25—4.4.31
voting, 4.4.15
records, 3.14.10

Members
minimum number, 3.3.8
registers, 3.14.5
share capital, and, 8.1.5
Members' voluntary liquidation
advertisement, 11.5.4
appointment of liquidator, 11.5.3
comparison with striking-off, 11.6
compliance, 11.5.5.1
date of dissolution, 11.5.9
dealing with creditor claims,
11.5.6.2—11.5.6.3
declaration of solvency, 11.5.2.2
effect on status
generally, 11.5.5
shareholdings, 11.5.5.3
statutory filing and compliance, 11.5.5.1
tax affairs, 11.5.5.2
final board meeting, 11.5.2.1
final meeting of members, 11.5.8
general meeting of members, 11.5.2.3
grounds, 11.5.1
introduction, 11.5
liquidator
appointment, 11.5.3
duties, 11.5.6.2
powers, 11.5.6.1
role, 11.5.6
London Gazette notice, 11.5.4
procedure
advertisement, 11.5.4
appointment of liquidator, 11.5.3
declaration of solvency, 11.5.2.2
final board meeting, 11.5.2.1
general meeting of members, 11.5.2.3
introduction, 11.5.2
publication, 11.5.4
realisation of assets, 11.5.6.2
seeking out creditor claims, 11.5.6.2
shareholdings, 11.5.5.3
statutory filings, 11.5.5.1
tax affairs, 11.5.5.2
timing of distribution, 11.5.7
Memorandum of association
changes to existing arrangements, 3.4.13
copies, 3.4.15
generally, 3.4.1
intra-group transactions, and, and, 9.6.7.3
introduction, 3.4
share capital, and, 8.1.4
Mental capacity
vacation of office
Model articles, under, 1.16.2.4
Table A articles, under, 1.16.1.4
Merger of public companies
subordinate legislation, A3.2.28
Merger relief
share capital, and, 8.8.5
MiFiD companies
annual accounts, and, 5.3.7
Minimum age
directors, and, 1.13.6

Minor transactions
loans and credit transactions, and, 2.4.9.4
Minority shareholders
CA 2006 changes
background, 4.1.2
list, 4.9.1
summary, 4.1.3
conclusion, 4.9—4.9.1
introduction, 4.8
miscellaneous statutory powers, 4.8.2
resolutions, and
matters requiring approval, 4.8.4—4.85
thresholds, 4.8.3
unfair prejudice, and, 4.8.1
Misleading statements
penalties, 6.6.11
Model Articles (2006)
and see under individual subject headings
directors, and, 1.0
generally, 3.4.7—3.4.8
Money-lending companies
loans and credit transactions, and, 2.4.9.4

Name of company
change
consequential effects, 3.6.7
generally, 3.6.6
misleading, where, 3.6.5
procedure, 3.6.6
choice restrictions, 3.6.2
disclosure, 3.6.8
introduction, 3.6
limited, 3.6.3
objections, 3.6.4
overseas companies, and, 3.12.4
pre-decision checks, 3.6.1
trade marks, and, 3.6.1
National insurance contributions
employee incentive share plans, and, 10.5.2
'Nil paid' shares
share capital, and, 8.7.2
No par value shares
share capital, and, 8.1.8
Nominal value of a share
and see **Share capital**
generally, 8.1.6
importance, 8.1.7
Nominees
electronic communications, and, 4.2.15
Non-cash assets
substantial property transactions, and, 2.3.2
Non-executive directors
duties, 1.10.3
general role, 1.10.2
generally, 1.2.13.6
introduction, 1.10
liabilities, 1.10.3
Northern Irish companies
generally, 3.2.1
Number of directors
maximum
appointment, and, 1.14.3.1

Number of directors—*cont.*
maximum—*cont.*
generally, 1.12.4
maximum number, and, 1.14.3.1
notification to Registrar of Companies, 1.14.4
registers requiring updating, 1.14.5
restrictions, 1.13—1.13.11
shareholders, by, 1.14.3.2
subsequent directors, 1.14.3—1.14.3.5
minimum, 1.12.2
Number of employees
annual accounts, and, 5.3.26
business review, and, 5.4.16
enterprise management incentives, and, 10.3.6.7

Objects clause
directors' duties, and, 3.4.2
generally, 3.4.1
need, 3.4.2
Off-balance-sheet arrangements
compliance guidance, 5.3.22
directors' obligations, 5.3.23
generally, 5.3.20
small and medium-sized companies, 5.3.21
Off-market purchases
purchase by company of its own shares, and, 9.4.2.2
Offer of securities
CA 2006 changes
de-criminalisation, 8.9.4.3
injunctive relief, 8.9.4.2
introduction, 8.9.4
offers in contemplation of re-registration as plc, 8.9.4.1
remedial orders, 8.9.4.4
validity of allotment, 8.9.4.5
introduction, 8.9
'offer to the public', 8.9.1
private companies, and, 8.9.1
relevant securities, 8.9.2
third party, via, 8.9.3
Office of Commercial Name Adjudication
generally, 3.6.4
On-line formation
generally, 3.3.2
Operation of law
vacation of office
Model articles, under, 1.16.2.1
Table A articles, under, 1.16.1.1
Option grant certificate
employee incentive share plans, and, 10.2.1.2
Ordinary resolutions
See also **Resolutions**
generally, 4.4.33
matters requiring approval, 4.8.4
thresholds, 4.8.3
Ordinary shares
share capital, and, 8.1.2
Overseas branch registers
discontinuance, 3.14.13

Index

Overseas branch registers—*cont.*
obligations to maintain, 3.14.11
requirements to maintain, 3.14.12
Overseas companies
accounts
annual, 3.12.11—3.12.12
group, 3.12.13
registration, on, 3.12.3
annual accounts
contents, 3.12.12
generally, 3.12.11
group accounts, 3.12.13
branches
change of location, 3.12.7
definition, 3.12.1
generally, 3.12
registration, 3.12.1—3.12.2
change of particulars, 3.12.6
charges on assets, and, 3.11.1
company names, 3.12.4
consequences of failure to register, 3.12.10
definition, 3.12.1
directors' addresses, 3.12.8
disclosures at trading address, 3.12.5
generally, 3.2.1
introduction, 3.12
listed on regulated market, 3.12.14
multiple branches, 3.12.9
names, 3.12.4
place of business, 3.12
registration, 3.12.2
Ownership of shares
electronic communications, 4.6.3
general power, 4.6
introduction, 4.6
notification of interests in shares by
shareholders, 4.6.1
register of requests for information, 4.6.4
request for information concerning interest in
shares, 4.6.2

Partly paid shares
employee incentive share plans, and
financial assistance, and, 10.4.4.2
introduction, 10.4.4
meaning, 10.4.4.1
share capital, and, 8.7.2
PAYE
employee incentive share plans, and, 10.5.2
Payments for loss of office
changes under CA 2006, 2.6.1
exemption from approval, 2.6.4
failure to obtain approval, 2.6.5
introduction, 2.6
meaning, 2.6.2
shareholder approval, 2.6.3—2.6.5
substantial property transactions, and, 2.3.4
Pension scheme indemnities
disclosure, 1.6.3.4
generally, 1.6.3.3
inspection, 1.6.3.5

Pensions
intra-group transactions, and, 9.6.7.4
Personal liability
loans and credit transactions, and
defences, 2.4.12
generally, 2.4.11.1
substantial property transactions, and, 2.3.14
Phantom share options
employee incentive share plans, and, 10.3.4
'Phoenix' companies
directors, and, 1.13.4
Plan rules
employee incentive share plans, and, 10.2.1.1
Political donations and expenditures
articles of association, and, 4.7.6
authorisation, 4.7.5
CA 2006 changes
background, 4.1.2
generally, 4.7.1
list, 4.9.1
operative date, 4.7.2
summary, 4.1.3
conclusion, 4.9
directors' report, and, 5.4.21
introduction, 4.7
legislation
exemption, A3.2.7
interest rate for unauthorised payments,
A3.2.29
'political donations', 4.7.3
'political expenditures', 4.7.4
resolutions, 4.7.7
Polls
challenges to results
assessor's rights, 4.5.2.4
contents of report, 4.5.2.3
'independent', 4.5.2.2
introduction, 4.5.2
notification of appointment of assessor,
4.5.2.5
preparation of report, 4.5.2.1
generally, 4.4.24
publication of result, 4.5.1
quoted companies, and
challenges to results, 4.5.2
publication, 4.5.1
Pre-emption rights
and see **Share capital**
action prior to 1 October 2009, 8.5.7
beneficiaries, 8.5.2
employee incentive share plans, and, 10.2.2.6
exclusion or disapplication, 8.5.5.1—8.5.5.2
meaning, 8.5.1
notice of offer, 8.5.4
penalties for non-compliance, 8.5.7
purchase by company of its own shares, and,
9.4.5.6
summary of current and new position, 8.5.8
terms, 8.5.3
Preference shares
share capital, and, 8.1.2

Preliminary statements of results
financial reports, and, 6.5.5
'Present fairly' requirement
annual accounts, and, 5.3.3
Principal risks
disclosure, 5.4.10
problem areas, 5.4.12
Private limited companies
annual general meetings, 4.4.1
company secretary
dispensing with appointment, 3.9.2—3.9.3
generally, 3.9.1
qualifications, 3.9.5
constitution
And see **Constitution of companies**
generally, 3.4.1—3.4.15
definition, 3.2.2
formation
And see **Formation of companies**
generally, 3.3.1—3.3.8
introduction, 3.2.1
public offer of securities, and, 8.9.1
reduction of share capital, and
applications to court, 9.3.8
court confirmation procedure,
9.3.5—9.3.6.6
solvency statement procedure,
9.3.7—9.3.7.4
re-registration as public company
allotments of shares for non-cash
consideration, 3.8.7
applications to Registrar of Companies,
3.8.9
articles of association, 3.8.2
company documentation, 3.8.4
company secretary, 3.8.3
effective date, 3.8.10
generally, 3.8.1
inability to meet requirements, 3.8.8
net assets, 3.8.6
procedure, 3.8.1
share capital, 3.8.5
stationery, 3.8.4
supporting documentation, 3.8.9
re-registration as unlimited company
generally, 3.8.16
procedure, 3.8.18
purpose, 3.8.17
Profit forecasts
business review, and, 5.4.15.3
Promotion of success of company
'benefit for members as a whole', 1.2.4.3
business review, and, 1.2.4.6
charities, and, 1.2.4.2
commercial company, of, 1.2.4.1
common law duty, and, 1.2.12
conflicting interests, and, 1.2.4.5
factors to be considered, 1.2.4.4
generally, 1.2.4
non-commercial company, of, 1.2.4.2
'success', 1.2.4.1—1.2.4.2

Proportionality
liability limitation agreements, and, 7.6.4
Proxies
appointment
generally, 4.4.17
notification, 4.4.19
CA 2006 changes
background, 4.1.2
list, 4.9.1
summary, 4.1.3
number, 4.4.16
powers, 4.4.18
termination of authority, 4.4.20
Public limited companies
And see **Quoted companies**
allotment of shares, 8.10.8
annual general meetings, 4.4.2—4.4.3
constitution
And see **Constitution of companies**
generally, 3.4.1—3.4.15
definition, 3.2.2
financial reports, and
accounts meetings, 6.2.2
time for holding AGM, 6.2.4
formation
And see **Formation of companies**
generally, 3.3.1—3.3.8
introduction, 3.2.1
loans and credit transactions, and, 2.4.8
public offer of securities
CA 2006 changes, 8.9.4—8.9.4.5
introduction, 8.9
'offer to the public', 8.9.1
private companies, and, 8.9.1
relevant securities, 8.9.2
third party, via, 8.9.3
purchase by company of its own shares, and,
9.4.5.3
reduction of share capital, and
court confirmation procedure,
9.3.5—9.3.6.6
re-registration as private company, 9.3.9
re-registration as private limited company
articles of association, 3.8.13
company documentation, 3.8.15
generally, 3.8.12
objections, 3.8.14
procedure, 3.8.12
stationery, 3.8.15
re-registration as unlimited company, 3.8.19
trading certificates
applications, 3.3.6
consequences of failure to obtain, 3.3.7
generally, 3.3.5
purpose, 3.3.6
Public offer of securities
CA 2006 changes
de-criminalisation, 8.9.4.3
injunctive relief, 8.9.4.2
introduction, 8.9.4
offers in contemplation of re-registration
as plc, 8.9.4.1

Public offer of securities—*cont.*
CA 2006 changes—*cont.*
  remedial orders, 8.9.4.4
  validity of allotment, 8.9.4.5
introduction, 8.9
'offer to the public', 8.9.1
private companies, and, 8.9.1
relevant securities, 8.9.2
third party, via, 8.9.3
Public sector companies
audited accounts, and, 7.2.7
Publication of accounts
financial reports, and
  statutory, 6.4.16
  non-statutory, 6.4.17
Purchase by company of its own shares
AIM companies, 9.4.5.1
balance sheets
  generally, 9.4.9
  purchase at premium, 9.4.9.2
  purchase out of capital, 9.4.9.3
  purchase out of distributable services,
    9.4.9.1
breach of requirements, 9.4.11
CA 2006 changes
  generally, 9.4.3
  summary table, 9.4.4
cancellation of shares on purchase, 9.4.5.17
capital maintenance, and, 9.4.8
City Code of Takeovers and Mergers, 9.4.5.3
determining factors, 9.4.6
financing
  generally, 9.4.5.12
  restrictions, 9.4.7—9.4.7.1
fully paid-up shares, 9.4.5.13
introduction, 9.4.1
listed companies, 9.4.5.1
listed convertible securities, 9.4.5.2
mandatory offers, 9.4.5.3
market purchases, 9.4.2.1
objections by creditors, 9.4.5.8
off-market purchases, 9.4.2.2
permissible methods
  introduction, 9.4.2
  market purchases, 9.4.2.1
  off-market purchases, 9.4.2.2
pre-emption rights, 9.4.5.6
preliminary issues
  AIM companies, 9.4.5.1
  City Code of Takeovers and Mergers,
    9.4.5.3
  disadvantaged shareholders, 9.4.5.9
  financing, 9.4.5.12
  fully paid-up shares, 9.4.5.13
  listed companies, 9.4.5.1
  listed convertible securities, 9.4.5.2
  mandatory offers, 9.4.5.3
  objections by creditors, 9.4.5.8
  pre-emption rights, 9.4.5.6
  price, 9.4.511
  public companies, 9.4.5.3

Purchase by company of its own shares—*cont.*
preliminary issues—*cont.*
  restrictions in third party agreements,
    9.4.5.6
  review of articles of association, 9.4.5.16
  sale of shares by directors, 9.4.5.7
  securities laws, 9.4.5.5
  shareholder holding shares, 9.4.5.15
  single member companies, 9.4.5.10
  stamp duty, 9.4.5.14
  takeover offers, 9.4.5.3
  variation of class rights, 9.4.5.4
price, 9.4.511
public companies, 9.4.5.3
purposes, 9.4.1
requirements, 9.4.4
review of articles of association, 9.4.5.16
sale of shares by directors, 9.4.5.7
securities laws, 9.4.5.5
shareholder approval
  market purchases, 9.4.2.1
  off-market purchases, 9.4.2.2
shareholder holding shares, 9.4.5.15
single member companies, 9.4.5.10
stamp duty, 9.4.5.14
summary table, 9.4.4
takeover offers, 9.4.5.3
third party agreements, 9.4.5.6
timetable, 9.4.10
Treasury shares, 9.4.12
unlimited companies, and
  generally, 9.10.7
  preliminary issues, 9.10.7.2
  procedure, 9.10.7.1
variation of class rights, 9.4.5.4

Qualifying pension scheme indemnities
disclosure, 1.6.3.4
generally, 1.6.3.3
inspection, 1.6.3.5
Qualifying third party indemnities
disclosure, 1.6.3.4
generally, 1.6.3.2
inspection, 1.6.3.5
Quasi-loans
affirmation by shareholders, 2.4.13
business transactions, for, 2.4.9.4
changes under CA 2006, 2.4.1
company business expenditure to £50,000,
  for, 2.4.9.1
defending proceedings, for, 2.4.9.2
exemptions from approval
  business transactions, 2.4.9.4
  company business expenditure to £50,000,
    2.4.9.1
  defending proceedings, 2.4.9.2
  introduction, 2.4.9
  intra-group transactions, 2.4.9.5
  minor transactions, 2.4.9.4
  money-lending companies, 2.4.9.6
  regulatory investigations or actions, 2.4.9.3

Quasi-loans—*cont.*
expenditure, for
company business up to £50,000, on,
2.4.9.1
defending proceedings, on, 2.4.9.2
intra-group transactions, for, 2.4.9.5
minor transactions, on, 2.4.9.4
regulatory investigations or actions, and,
2.4.9.3
failure to obtain approval, 2.4.11—2.4.12
home loans, and, 2.4.9
intra-group transactions, for, 2.4.9.5
introduction, 2.4
meaning, 2.4.4
minor transactions, for, 2.4.9.4
money-lending companies, and, 2.4.9.6
personal liability
defences, 2.4.12
generally, 2.4.11.2
public companies, and, 2.4.8
regulatory investigations or actions, and,
2.4.9.3
rescission, and, 2.4.11.1
shareholder approval
anti-avoidance provisions, 2.4.7
exemptions, 2.4.9
introduction, 2.4.2
procedure, 2.4.5
public companies, and, 2.4.8
relevant shareholders, 2.4.6
third party arrangements, 2.4.7
value of transaction, 2.4.10
Quoted companies
See also **Public limited companies**
accounts
approval of accounts, 6.2.5
filing accounts, 6.4.13
website communication, 6.3.11
business review, 5.4.5
challenges to poll results
assessor's rights, 4.5.2.4
contents of report, 4.5.2.3
'independent', 4.5.2.2
introduction, 4.5.2
notification of appointment of assessor,
4.5.2.5
preparation of report, 4.5.2.1
overseas companies, 3.12.14
polls
challenges to results, 4.5.2
publication, 4.5.1
public offer of securities
CA 2006 changes, 8.9.4—8.9.4.5
introduction, 8.9
'offer to the public', 8.9.1
private companies, and, 8.9.1
relevant securities, 8.9.2
third party, via, 8.9.3
publication of accounts, 6.3.11

Ratification of decisions by shareholders
directors, and, 1.6.1

Realised profits
dividends, and, 9.2.4
Reasonable behaviour
directors, and, 1.6.2
Reasonable care, skill and diligence
directors' duties, and, 1.2.6
Records
annual accounts, and
adequacy, 5.2.2
introduction, 5.2.1
copying
generally, 3.14.1
rights, 3.14.4
debentures, 3.14.9
directors and secretaries, 3.14.6
directors' interests in shares, 3.14.8
electronic form, 3.14.3
inspection
generally, 3.14.1
rights, 3.14.4
introduction, 3.14
location, 3.14.2
members, 3.14.5
overseas branch register
discontinuance, 3.14.13
obligations to maintain, 3.14.11
requirements to maintain, 3.14.12
records of meetings and resolutions, 3.14.10
substantial interests in shares, 3.14.7
transfer of debentures, 3.14.9
Redeemable shares
CA 2006 changes, 8.1.9
generally, 8.1.2
Redemption of redeemable shares
benefits, 9.5.1
CA 2006 changes, 9.5.2
introduction, 9.5.1
summary table, 9.5.2
Redenomination of shares
action prior to 1 October 2009, 8.14.6
CA 2006 changes, 8.14.3
current position, 8.14.2
fractions, and
filing requirements, 8.14.4.4
introduction, 8.14.4
maximum limit. 8.14.4.2
redenomination reserve, 8.14.4.5
special resolution, 8.14.4.1
time limit, 8.14.4.3
penalties for non-compliance, 8.14.5
purpose, 8.14.1
Reduction of share capital
accounting treatment, 9.3.10
applications to court, 9.3.8
articles of association, and, 9.3.5.1
breach of requirements, 9.3.11
CA 2006 changes
generally, 9.3.2
summary table, 9.3.3
court confirmation procedure
documentation, 9.3.6.2
effective date, 9.3.6.5

Reduction of share capital—*cont.*
court confirmation procedure—*cont.*
filing, 9.3.6.4
introduction, 9.3.6
protection of creditors, 9.3.6.3
requirements, 9.3.6.1
timetable, 9.3.13
creditor position, 9.3.5.4
creditor protection, 9.3.6.3
determining factors, 9.4.6
directors' duties, 9.3.5.5
documentation, 9.3.6.2
effective date, 9.3.6.5
filing, 9.3.6.4
introduction, 9.3.1
preliminary issues
creditor position, 9.3.5.4
directors' duties, 9.3.5.5
introduction, 9.3.5
restrictions in third party agreements,
9.3.5.2
review of articles of association, 9.3.5.1
variation of class rights, 9.3.5.3
private companies
applications to court, 9.3.8
court confirmation procedure,
9.3.5—9.3.6.6
solvency statement procedure,
9.3.7—9.3.7.4
procedure
court confirmation , 9.3.5—9.3.6.6
solvency statement, 9.3.7—9.3.7.4
protection of creditors, 9.3.6.3
public companies
court confirmation procedure,
9.3.5—9.3.6.6
re-registration as private company, 9.3.9
purposes, 9.3.1
relevant reserves, 9.3.4
solvency statement procedure
effective date, 9.3.7.4
filing, 9.3.7.3
form of statement, 9.3.7.2
introduction, 9.3.7
requirements, 9.3.7.1
timetable, 9.3.12
subordinate legislation, A3.2.30
summary table, 9.3.3
third party agreements, and, 9.3.5.2
timetables
court confirmation procedure, 9.3.13
solvency statement procedure, 9.3.12
unlimited companies, and
distributable reserves, 9.10.6.4
effective date, 9.10.6.6
filing requirements, 9.10.6.5
introduction, 9.10.6.1
methods, 9.10.6.2
preliminary issues, 9.10.6.3
variation of class rights, 9.3.5.3
Registered office
formation of companies, and, 3.7

Registers
charges on assets
company's obligations, 3.11.6
consequences of failure to maintain, 3.11.7
obligations of Registrar of Companies,
3.11.8
Scottish charges, 3.11.9—3.11.10
company secretaries
CA 2006 changes, 3.14.6
generally, 3.9.10
directors, 3.14.6
directors' interests in shares, 3.14.8
members, 3.14.5
overseas branches
discontinuance, 3.14.13
obligations to maintain, 3.14.11
requirements to maintain, 3.14.12
requests for information concerning interest
in shares, 4.6.2
substantial interests in shares, 3.14.7
Registrar of Companies
allocation and use of unique identifiers,
3.16.4
annual accounts, 3.17
annual compliance obligations, 3.17
annual returns, 3.17
certification of documents, 3.16.9
copies of filed documents, 3.16.6
delivery of documents to, 3.16.2
electronic communications, 3.16.12
enforcement of filing obligations, 3.16.11
false statements, 3.16.10
generally, 3.16
index of companies, 3.16.3
inspection of filed documents
exclusions, 3.16.7
generally, 3.16.6
language requirements, 3.16.9
obligations
keep register, 3.16.3
preservation of documents, 3.16.5
preservation of original documents, 3.16.5
rectification of material on register. 3.16.8
register of companies, 3.16.3
removal of material from register. 3.16.8
responsibilities, 3.16.1
verification of documents, 3.16.9
Regulatory change
benefits of integrated approach, 12.4
conclusion, 12.5
consequences of incomplete implementation,
12.3
introduction, 12.1
management control, 12.2
Regulatory investigations or actions
loans and credit transactions, and, 2.4.9.3
Related party transactions
GAAP accounts, and, 5.3.5
generally, 5.3.13
IAS accounts, and, 5.3.14
Removal of auditors
cessation statements, 7.5.3—7.5.9

Removal of auditors—*cont.*
  generally, 7.5.1
  reporting, 7.5.2
Removal of directors
  board, by, 1.15.1.4
  checklist of considerations, 1.15.6
  employee director, of, 1.15.2.1
  expiry of fixed term contract, 1.15.1.3
  methods, 1.15.1
  notification to Registrar of Companies,
    1.15.4
  payments, 1.15.3
  registers requiring updating, 1.15.5
  resignation, by, 1.15.1.1
  rotation, by, 1.15.1.2
  shareholder director, of, 1.15.2.2
  shareholders, by, 1.15.1.15
Remuneration
  auditors, and, 7.3.5
  employee incentive share plans, and, 10.4.3
Reporting obligations
  employee incentive share plans, and, 10.5.3
Re-registration
  change of status, and, 3.8
  generally, 3.8
  private limited company to public company,
    of
    allotments of shares for non-cash
      consideration, 3.8.7
    applications to Registrar of Companies,
      3.8.9
    articles of association, 3.8.2
    company documentation, 3.8.4
    company secretary, 3.8.3
    effective date, 3.8.10
    generally, 3.8.1
    inability to meet requirements, 3.8.8
    net assets, 3.8.6
    procedure, 3.8.1
    share capital, 3.8.5
    stationery, 3.8.4
    supporting documentation, 3.8.9
  private limited company to unlimited
    company, of
    generally, 3.8.16
    procedure, 3.8.18
    purpose, 3.8.17
  public company to private limited company,
    of
    articles of association, 3.8.13
    company documentation, 3.8.15
    generally, 3.8.12
    objections, 3.8.14
    procedure, 3.8.12
    stationery, 3.8.15
  public company to unlimited company, of,
    3.8.19
  relevant circumstances, 3.8
  statements of compliance, 3.8
Rescission
  loans and credit transactions, and, 2.4.11.1
  substantial property transactions, and, 2.3.13

Residence
  directors, and, 1.13.9
Residential address
  directors, and, 1.14.81
Resignation of auditors
  cessation statements, 7.5.3—7.5.9
  generally, 7.5.1
  reporting, 7.5.2
Resignation of directors
  Model articles, under, 1.16.2.2
  Table A articles, under, 1.16.1.2
Resolutions
  generally, 4.4.23
  matters requiring approval
    ordinary resolution, by, 4.8.4
    special resolution, by, 4.8.5
  minority shareholders, and
    matters requiring approval, 4.8.4—4.8.5
    thresholds, 4.8.3
  ordinary resolutions
    generally, 4.4.33
    matters requiring approval, 4.8.4
  political donations and expenditures, and,
    4.7.7
  polls, 4.4.24
  procedure, 4.4.25
  records, 3.14.10
  show of hands, and, 4.4.27
  special resolutions
    generally, 4.4.33
    matters requiring approval, 4.8.5
  types, 4.4.32
  written resolutions
    electronic communications, and, 4.4.31
    generally, 4.4.28
    proposed by directors, 4.4.29
    requisitioned by members, 4.4.30
Resources available to an entity
  business review, and, 5.4.14
Restricted shares
  employee incentive share plans, and, 10.3.3
Returning cash/assets to shareholders
  And see under individual headings
  demergers, 9.7
  dividends, 9.2
  financing acquisition of shares, 9.9
  intra group reorganisations, 9.6
  introduction, 9.1
  purchase of company's own shares, 9.4
  redemption of redeemable shares, 9.5
  reduction of share capital, 9.3
  reorganisations, 9.10
  schemes of arrangement, 9.8
  summary, 9.11
Revision of defective accounts
  subordinate legislation, A3.2.18
Rights of pre-emption
  and see **Share capital**
  action prior to 1 October 2009, 8.5.7
  beneficiaries, 8.5.2
  employee incentive share plans, and, 10.2.2.6
  exclusion or disapplication, 8.5.5.1—8.5.5.2

Rights of pre-emption—*cont.*
meaning, 8.5.1
notice of offer, 8.5.4
penalties for non-compliance, 8.5.7
purchase by company of its own shares, and, 9.4.5.6
summary of current and new position, 8.5.8
terms, 8.5.3

Safe harbour provision
annual accounts, and, 5.1.3
business review, and, 5.4.8
SAYE scheme
employee incentive share plans, and, 10.3.8
Schemes of arrangement
advantages, 9.8.3
CA 2006 changes, 9.8.2
demergers, and, 9.7.2.4
introduction, 9.8
relevant circumstances, 9.8.1
requirements
court approval, 9.8.4.4
court meeting, 9.8.4.1
explanatory statement, 9.8.4.2
members' meeting, 9.8.4.3
sample timetable, 9.8.5
Scottish companies
execution of documents, and, 3.5.9
Scottish charges
registration, 3.11.9—3.11.10
Scrip dividends
share capital, and, 8.7.6
Secretary of company
address, 3.9.7
dispensing with
articles of association, and, 3.9.3
considerations, 3.9.2
introduction, 3.9.1
notification to Registrar of Companies, 3.9.9
generally, 1.12.3
introduction, 3.9
necessity of appointment, 3.9.1
notification to Registrar of Companies, 3.9.9
private limited companies, and
dispensing with appointment, 3.9.2—3.9.3
generally, 3.9.1
qualifications, 3.9.5
qualifications
private limited companies, 3.9.5
public companies, 3.9.4
register, 3.9.10
responsibilities, 3.9.6
service address, 3.9.7
vacancies, 3.9.8
Section 110 scheme
demergers, and, 9.7.2.3
Securities
employee incentive share plans, and, 10.5.1
public offer
CA 2006 changes, 8.9.4—8.9.4.5
introduction, 8.9

Securities—*cont.*
public offer—*cont.*
'offer to the public', 8.9.1
private companies, and, 8.9.1
relevant securities, 8.9.2
third party, via, 8.9.3
purchase by company of its own shares, and, 9.4.5.5
Sell-out rights
takeovers, and, A2.4.9—A2.4.11
Sensitive information
business review, and, 5.4.15.1
Series of transactions
substantial property transactions, and, 2.3.5
Seriously prejudicial exemptions
business review, and, 5.4.6
Service address
company secretary, and, 3.9.7
directors, and, 3.3.1
Service contracts
approval
circumvention of, 2.2.6
exemptions, 2.2.8
failure to obtain, 2.2.11
generally, 2.2.4
'guaranteed term', 2.2.5
pre-1 October 2007 contracts, 2.2.10
procedure, 2.2.9
relevant shareholders, 2.2.7
changes under CA 2006, 2.2.1
charges for inspection, 2.2.14
conflicts of interest, and, 2.2.18
contracts affected, 2.2.2
copies, 2.2.16
directors' duties, and, 2.2.3
exemption from approval, 2.2.8
failure to obtain approval, 2.2.11
'guaranteed term', 2.2.4
inspection
changes under CA 2006, 2.2.13
charges, 2.2.14
generally, 2.2.12
refusal to allow, 2.2.5
introduction, 2.2
pre-1 October 2007 contracts, 2.2.10
shadow directors, and, 2.2.17
shareholder approval
circumvention of, 2.2.6
exemptions, 2.2.8
failure to obtain, 2.2.11
generally, 2.2.4
'guaranteed term', 2.2.5
pre-1 October 2007 contracts, 2.2.10
procedure, 2.2.9
relevant shareholders, 2.2.7
sole member also director, 2.2.19
successive terms of less than two years, 2.2.6
Service of documents
change of address, 3.15.1
deemed, 3.15.2
generally, 3.15

Shadow directors
directors' service contracts, and, 2.2.17
generally, 1.2.13.2
Share capital
accounting treatment on issue
  CA 2006 changes, 8.8.1—8.8.2
  group reconstruction relief, 8.8.3—8.8.4
  introduction, 8.8
  merger relief, 8.8.5
  summary of current and new position,
    8.8.6
allotment
  checklist, 8.6.1.2—8.6.1.3
  commissions, and, 8.12.1—8.12.2
  consideration payable for shares in public
    company, 8.10—8.10.7
  difference from issue, 8.2.3
  discounts, and, 8.12.1—8.12.2
  meaning, 8.2.3
  post-allotment steps, 8.6.1—8.6.6
  pre-emption rights, 8.5.1—8.5.8
  public company, in, 8.10.8
  shareholder approval, 8.4—8.4.7
allowances on allotment
  CA 2006 changes, 8.12.2
  current position, 8.12.1
articles of association, 8.1.4
authorised share capital
  action prior to 1 October 2009, 8.3.2
  CA 2006 changes, 8.3.1
bonus issues, 8.7.6
'cash' payment, 8.7.5
commissions on allotment
  CA 2006 changes, 8.12.2
  current position, 8.12.1
consideration on subscription
  bonus issues, 8.7.6
  'cash' payment, 8.7.5
  different payment terms, 8.7.3
  failure to pay outstanding instalments,
    8.7.4
  generally, 8.7.1
  'nil paid' shares, 8.7.2
  'part paid' shares, 8.7.2
  scrip dividends, 8.7.6
  shares in public company, 8.10—8.10.7
consideration payable for shares in public
  company
  effect of breach of restrictions,
    8.10.7—8.10.7.3
  exemptions from valuation requirements,
    8.10.4
  interposition of new plc holding company,
    8.10.6
  introduction, 8.10
  recently re-registered company, 8.10.5
  restrictions, 8.10.1
  sanctions for breach of restrictions, 8.10.2
  valuation requirements, 8.10.3—8.10.4
consolidation of shares
  CA 2006 changes, 8.13.2—8.13.3
  filing requirements, 8.13.5

Share capital—*cont.*
consolidation of shares—*cont.*
  purpose, 8.13.1
  restrictions, 8.13.4
convertible shares, 8.1.2
cross-holdings
  CA 2006 changes, 8.16.2
  consequences, 8.16.6
  exemptions, 8.16.6
  holding companies, and, 8.16.3
  meaning, 8.16.1
  shares in company holding shares in
    parent, 8.16.4
deferred shares, 8.1.2
discounts on allotment
  CA 2006 changes, 8.12.2
  current position, 8.12.1
failure to pay outstanding instalments, 8.7.4
filing requirements
  action on or after 1 October 2009, 8.6.3.1
  current position, 8.6.2.1
group reconstruction relief, 8.8.3—8.8.4
incorporation of company, and
  articles, 8.1.4
  introduction, 8.1.4
  memorandum, 8.1.4
  statement of capital, 8.1.4
  subscriber, 8.1.4
increase of
  allotment, and, 8.2.3
  company law issues, 8.2.1
  issue, and, 8.2.3
  regulatory issues, 8.2.2
inherent rights in a share, 8.1.3
introduction, 8.1.1
investigation of ownership
  electronic communications, 4.6.3
  general power, 4.6
  introduction, 4.6
  notification of interests in shares by
    shareholders, 4.6.1
  register of requests for information, 4.6.4
  request for information concerning interest
    in shares, 4.6.2
issue, and
  accounting treatment, 8.8—8.8.6
  difference from allotment, 8.2.3
  meaning, 8.2.3
  shareholder approval, 8.4—8.4.7
issue of share certificates
  action on or after 1 October 2009, 8.6.3.2
  current position, 8.6.2.2
members, and, 8.1.5
memorandum of association, 8.1.4
merger relief, 8.8.5
nature of rights in a share, 8.1.3
'nil paid' shares, 8.7.2
no par value shares, 8.1.8
nominal value of a share
  generally, 8.1.6
  importance, 8.1.7
ordinary shares, 8.1.2

Share capital—*cont.*
'part paid' shares, 8.7.2
post-allotment steps
action on or after 1 October 2009,
8.6.3.1—8.6.3.3
CA 2006 changes, 8.6.1
filings, 8.6.2.1
issue of share certificates, 8.6.2.2
penalties for non-compliance, 8.6.5
summary of current and new position,
8.6.6
unlimited companies, and, 8.6.4
updating registers, 8.6.2.3
pre-emption rights
action prior to 1 October 2009, 8.5.7
beneficiaries, 8.5.2
exclusion or disapplication,
8.5.5.1—8.5.5.2
meaning, 8.5.1
notice of offer, 8.5.4
penalties for non-compliance, 8.5.7
summary of current and new position,
8.5.8
terms, 8.5.3
preference shares, 8.1.2
public offer of securities
CA 2006 changes, 8.9.4—8.9.4.5
introduction, 8.9
'offer to the public', 8.9.1
private companies, and, 8.9.1
relevant securities, 8.9.2
third party, via, 8.9.3
purposes, 8.1
redenomination of
action prior to 1 October 2009, 8.14.6
CA 2006 changes, 8.14.3
current position, 8.14.2
fractions, and, 8.14.4—8.14.4.5
penalties for non-compliance, 8.14.5
purpose, 8.14.1
reduction of
And see **Reduction of share capital**
accounting treatment, 9.3.10
applications to court, 9.3.8
breach of requirements, 9.3.11
CA 2006 changes, 9.3.2—9.3.3
court confirmation procedure, 9.3.6
introduction, 9.3.1
preliminary issues, 9.3.5
purposes, 9.3.1
relevant reserves, 9.3.4
re-registration of public company as
private company, 9.3.9
solvency statement procedure, 9.3.7
timetables, 9.3.12—9.3.13
redeemable shares
CA 2006 changes, 8.1.9
generally, 8.1.2
regulatory issues, 8.2.2
rights in a share, 8.1.3
scrip dividends, 8.7.6

Share capital—*cont.*
share premiums
CA 2006 changes, 8.8.1—8.8.2
group reconstruction relief, 8.8.3—8.8.4
introduction, 8.8
merger relief, 8.8.5
summary of current and new position,
8.8.6
share warrants
issue from 1 October 2009, 8.18.4
issue prior to 1 October 2009, 8.18.3
meaning, 8.18.1
rights carried, 8.18.2
shareholder approval
action prior to 1 October 2009, 8.4.7
agreements before expiry, 8.4.2
CA 2006 changes, 8.4.5
current position, 8.4.1—8.4.4
filing, 8.4.4
introduction, 8.4
offers before expiry, 8.4.2
renewal, 8.4.3
revocation, 8.4.3
summary of current and new position,
8.4.6
variation, 8.4.3
shareholders, and, 8.1.5
shares
inherent rights, 8.1.3
no par value, 8.1.8
nominal value, 8.1.6—8.1.7
types, 8.1.2
statement of capital
circumstances in which filing required,
8.A.1
filing requirements, 8.6.3.1
generally, 8.1.4
sub-division of shares
CA 2006 changes, 8.13.2—8.13.3
filing requirements, 8.13.5
purpose, 8.13.1
restrictions, 8.13.4
subscriber, 8.1.4
subsequent purchasers from person in breach
of CA
introduction, 8.11
liability, 8.11.1
power to grant relief, 8.11.2
summary of CA 2006 changes, 8.19
transfer of shares
CA 2006 changes, 8.17.1
certificated shares, 8.17.3
methods, 8.17.2
uncertificated shares, 8.17.4
treasury shares
accounting for proceeds, 8.19.6
cancellation, 8.19.5
dealings, 8.19.4
exercise of shareholders' rights, 8.19.3
introduction, 8.19
limit on holding, 8.19.2
relevant shares, 8.19.1

Share capital—*cont.*
  types of shares, 8.1.2
  unlimited companies, and, 8.6.4
  updating registers
    action on or after 1 October 2009, 8.6.3.3
    current position, 8.6.2.3
  variation of class rights
    action prior to 1 October 2009, 8.15.6
    CA 2006 changes, 8.15.1
    current procedure, 8.15.2
    filing requirements, 8.15.5
    introduction, 8.15
    new procedure, 8.15.3—8.15.5
    objections by class, 8.15.4
Share incentive plans
  employee incentive share plans, and, 10.3.9
Share options
  employee incentive share plans, and, 10.3.1
Share premiums
  CA 2006 changes, 8.8.1—8.8.2
  group reconstruction relief, 8.8.3—8.8.4
  introduction, 8.8
  merger relief, 8.8.5
  summary of current and new position, 8.8.6
Share warrants
  issue from 1 October 2009, 8.18.4
  issue prior to 1 October 2009, 8.18.3
  meaning, 8.18.1
  rights carried, 8.18.2
Shareholder approval
  allotment of shares, and
    action prior to 1 October 2009, 8.4.7
    agreements before expiry, 8.4.2
    CA 2006 changes, 8.4.5
    current position, 8.4.1—8.4.4
    filing, 8.4.4
    introduction, 8.4
    offers before expiry, 8.4.2
    renewal, 8.4.3
    revocation, 8.4.3
    summary of current and new position,
      8.4.6
    variation, 8.4.3
  directors' service contracts, and
    circumvention of, 2.2.6
    exemptions, 2.2.8
    failure to obtain, 2.2.11
    generally, 2.2.4
    'guaranteed term', 2.2.5
    pre-1 October 2007 contracts, 2.2.10
    procedure, 2.2.9
    relevant shareholders, 2.2.7
  directors' transactions, and
    majority shareholders, 2.1.3
  dividends, and
    final dividend, 9.2.7.1
    interim dividend, 9.2.7.2
    introduction, 9.2.7
    non-cash dividend, 9.2.7.3
  electronic communications, and, 4.2.4
  employee incentive share plans, and
    authorised share capital, 10.2.2.4

Shareholder approval—*cont.*
  employee incentive share plans, and—*cont.*
    authority to allot shares, 10.2.2.5
    generally, 10.2.2.3
    statutory pre-emption rights, 10.2.2.6
  loans and credit transactions, and
    anti-avoidance provisions, 2.4.7
    exemptions, 2.4.9
    introduction, 2.4.2
    procedure, 2.4.5
    public companies, and, 2.4.8
    relevant shareholders, 2.4.6
  ordinary resolution, by, 4.8.4
  payments for loss of office, and, 2.6.3—2.6.5
  purchase by company of its own shares, and
    market purchases, 9.4.2.1
    off-market purchases, 9.4.2.2
  special resolution, by, 4.8.5
  substantial property transactions, and
    aggregated transactions, 2.3.5
    exemption, 2.3.6
    generally, 2.3.3
  website communications, and, 4.2.6
Shareholder relationship
  and see under individual headings
  annual general meetings
    exceptions to date to be held, 4.4.3
    generally, 4.4.1
    notice periods, 4.4.6
    public companies, and, 4.4.2
  CA 2006 changes
    background, 4.1.2
    list, 4.9.1
    summary, 4.1.3
  conclusion, 4.9—4.9.1
  electronic communications
    application of provisions, 4.2.2
    authorisation, 4.2.4
    introduction, 4.2.1
    meaning, 4.2.3
    nominees, and, 4.2.15
  extraordinary general meetings, 4.4
  general meetings
    adjournment, 4.4.14
    annual general meetings, 4.4.1—4.4.3
    appointment of chairperson, 4.4.13
    attendance, 4.4.15
    attendance by companies, 4.4.21—4.4.22
    calling, 4.4.4—4.4.5
    circulation of statements, 4.4.11
    conduct, 4.4.13
    electronic communications, 4.4.25
    introduction, 4.4
    notice, 4.4.6—4.4.10
    polls, 4.4.24
    proxies, 4.4.16—4.4.20
    recipients entitled to notice, 4.4.10
    resolutions, 4.4.25—4.4.31
    voting, 4.4.15
  indirect investors' rights
    general rules, 4.3.3
    information rights, 4.3.2

Shareholder relationship—*cont.*
  indirect investors' rights—*cont.*
    introduction, 4.3
    shareholder rights, 4.3.1
  introduction, 4.1.1—4.1.3
  investigation of ownership of shares
    electronic communications, 4.6.3
    general power, 4.6
    introduction, 4.6
    notification of interests in shares by
      shareholders, 4.6.1
    register of requests for information, 4.6.4
    request for information concerning interest
      in shares, 4.6.2
  minority shareholders
    introduction, 4.8
    matters requiring approval by ordinary
      resolution, 4.8.4
    matters requiring approval by special
      resolution, 4.8.5
    miscellaneous statutory powers, 4.8.2
    thresholds for resolutions, 4.8.3
    unfair prejudice, 4.8.1
  political donations and expenditures
    articles of association, and, 4.7.6
    authorisation, 4.7.5
    CA 2006 changes, 4.7.1
    introduction, 4.7
    operative date of changes, 4.7.2
    'political donations', 4.7.3
    'political expenditures', 4.7.4
    resolutions, 4.7.7
  polls
    generally, 4.4.24
    quoted companies, and, 4.5.1—4.5.2
  website communications
    application of provisions, 4.2.2
    authorisation, 4.2.6
    deeming provisions, 4.2.5—4.2.9
    delivery times, 4.2.13
    duration, 4.2.12
    hard copy documents, and, 4.2.14
    introduction, 4.2.1
    meaning, 4.2.5
    nominees, and, 4.2.15
    notification procedure, 4.2.10—4.2.11
    request for consent, 4.2.7
    revocation of consent, 4.2.9
    shareholder consent, 4.2.6
Shareholders
  approval by
    And see **Shareholder approval**
    directors' service contracts, 2.2.4—2.2.11
    loans and credit transactions, 2.4.5—2.4.9
    payments for loss of office, 2.6.3—2.6.5
    substantial property transactions,
      2.3.3—2.3.6
  management of relationship with
    And see **Shareholder relationship**
    communications, 4.2.1—4.2.15
    conclusion, 4.9—4.9.1
    general meetings, 4.4—4.4.31

Shareholders—*cont.*
  management of relationship with—*cont.*
    indirect investors' rights, 4.3.1—4.3.3
    introduction, 4.1.1—4.1.3
    minority shareholders, 4.8—4.85
    political donations and expenditures,
      4.7—4.7.7
    polls, 4.5.1—4.5.2
Shares
  and see **Share capital**
  inherent rights, 8.1.3
  no par value, 8.1.8
  nominal value, 8.1.6—8.1.7
  types, 8.1.2
Show of hands
  general meetings, and, 4.4.27
Signature
  auditor's reports, and
    change of SSA during reporting period,
      7.4.9
    filed copies, and, 7.4.7
    generally, 7.4.6
    joint auditors, and, 7.4.10
    risk from violence or intimidation, 7.4.11
    'senior statutory auditor', 7.4.8
  financial reports, and, 6.4.14
Significant contractual arrangements
  business review, and, 5.4.17
Single member companies
  purchase by company of its own shares, and,
    9.4.5.10
Small charitable companies
  audited accounts, and, 7.2.6
Small companies
  annual accounts, and
    form of accounts, 5.3.10
    introduction, 5.1.2
    meaning, 5.3.6
    off-balance-sheet arrangements, 5.3.2
    size limit, 5.3.8
  audited accounts, and
    financial services sector, in, 7.2.3
    generally, 7.2.2
  business review, and, 5.4.4
  financial reports, and
    filing accounts, 6.4.6—6.4.8
    laying accounts at AGM, 6.2.3
    revision of defective annual accounts and
      reports, 6.5.4
  subordinate legislation, A3.2.21
Smith Report
  introduction, 1.0
Social issues
  business review, and, 5.4.16
Sole members
  directors' service contracts, and, 2.2.19
Solvency statement procedure
  effective date, 9.3.7.4
  filing, 9.3.7.3
  form of statement, 9.3.7.2
  introduction, 9.3.7
  requirements, 9.3.7.1

Solvency statement procedure—*cont.*
timetable, 9.3.12
Special notice
general meetings, and, 4.4.34
Special resolutions
See also **Resolutions**
generally, 4.4.33
matters requiring approval, 4.8.5
thresholds, 4.8.3
Squeeze-out rights
takeovers, and, A2.4.5—A2.4.8
Stamp duty
purchase by company of its own shares, and,
9.4.5.14
Statements of capital
circumstances in which filing required, 8.A.1
filing requirements, 8.6.3.1
formation of companies, and, 3.3.1
generally, 8.1.4
Statements of compliance
formation of companies, and, 3.3.1
re-registration, and, 3.8
Statements of guarantee
formation of companies, and, 3.3.1
Statements of officers
formation of companies, and, 3.3.1
Statutory auditors
generally, 7.7.2
introduction, 7.7.1
non-EU companies, 7.7.4
Statutory directors
generally, 1.2.13.1
Striking off
applications, 11.4.4
balance sheet simplification, 11.4.3.2
bona vacantia property
failure to file accounts, and, 6.4.5.4
generally, 11.4.11
CA 2006 changes, 11.4.9
comparison with liquidation, 11.6
consultation with HMRC, 11.4.3.1
date of dissolution, 11.4.6
directors' liabilities, 11.4.8
distribution of assets
bona vacantia property, 11.4.11
ESC C16, 11.4.11.1
generally, 11.4.10.2
ESC C16, 11.4.11.1
failure to file accounts, and
bona vacantia, 6.4.5.4
generally, 6.4.5.2
subsequent restoration, 6.4.5.3
Form 652A, 11.4.4.1
introduction, 11.4
legislative framework, 1.4.1
London Gazette notice, 11.4.6
notification of application, 11.4.5
notification of intention, 11.4.3.1
pre-conditions, 1.4.2
preliminary actions
balance sheet simplification, 11.4.3.2
introduction, 11.4.3

Striking off—*cont.*
preliminary actions—*cont.*
notification of intention, 11.4.3.1
procedure
date of dissolution, 11.4.6
Form 652A, 11.4.4.1
introduction, 11.4.4
notification of application, 11.4.5
objection to application, 11.4.5
registration of application, 11.4.4.2
registration of application, 11.4.4.2
relationship with creditors, 11.4.10.1
restoration, and, 11.4.7
suitability
distribution of assets, 11.4.10.2—11.4.11.1
introduction, 11.4.10
relationship with creditors, 11.4.10.1
unlawful dividends, 11.4.10.2
Sub-division of shares
CA 2006 changes, 8.13.2—8.13.3
filing requirements, 8.13.5
purpose, 8.13.1
restrictions, 8.13.4
Subscriber
share capital, and, 8.1.4
Substantial interests in shares
registers, 3.14.7
Substantial property transactions
affirmation by shareholders, 2.3.15
aggregation of transactions, 2.3.5
approval
exemption, 2.3.6
generally, 2.3.3
'arrangements', 2.3.2
changes under CA 2006, 2.3.1
'connected persons'
companies, 2.3.11
generally, 2.3.8
introduction, 2.3.2
members of director's family, 2.3.10
relevant persons, 2.3.9
directors affected, 2.3.7
directors' service contracts, and, 2.3.4
examples, 2.3.2
exemption from approval, 2.3.6
failure to obtain approval
generally, 2.3.12
personal liability, 2.3.14
rescission, 2.3.13
introduction, 2.3
meaning, 2.3.2
'non-cash asset', 2.3.2
payment for loss of office, and, 2.3.4
personal liability for breach, 2.3.14
rescission, 2.3.13
series of transactions, 2.3.5
shareholder approval
aggregated transactions, 2.3.5
exemption, 2.3.6
generally, 2.3.3
'substantial', 2.3.2
terminology, 2.3.2

Success of company
'benefit for members as a whole', 1.2.4.3
business review, and, 1.2.4.6
charities, and, 1.2.4.2
commercial company, of, 1.2.4.1
conflicting interests, and, 1.2.4.5
factors to be considered, 1.2.4.4
generally, 1.2.4
non-commercial company, of, 1.2.4.2
'success', 1.2.4.1—1.2.4.2
Summary financial statements
financial reports, and, 6.3.8
Supporting documentation
formation of companies, and, 3.3.1

Table A articles (1985)
CA 2006 changes, 3.4.6
differences from Model articles, 3.4.8
generally, 3.4.4
directors, and, 1.0
subordinate legislation, A3.2.15—A3.2.17
Tables B—F articles
CA 2006 changes, 3.4.6
generally, 3.4.5
Takeovers Directive
background, A2.1.2
compulsory acquisition of shares,
    A2.4—A2.4.11
coverage, A2.1.1
directors' report, A2.5—A2.5.3
impediments to takeovers, A2.3—A2.3.6
introduction, A2.1
sell-out rights, A2.4.9—A2.4.11
squeeze-out rights, A2.4.5—A2.4.8
Takeover Panel, and, A2.2.1—A2.2.6
Takeover Panel
generally, A2.2.1—A2.2.6
Tax free payments
directors, and, 10.4.3
generally, 2.5
Tax reporting obligations
employee incentive share plans, and, 10.5.3
Taxation
employee incentive share plans, and
    corporate tax, 10.5.4
generally, 10.1
Tax-favoured plans
employee incentive share plans, and, 10.3.5
Terms and definitions
glossary, Appendix 4
'Think small first' philosophy
introduction, 5.1.2
meaning, 5.3.5
Third country auditors
subordinate legislation, A3.2.7
Third party arrangements
loans and credit transactions, and, 2.4.7
reduction of share capital, and, 9.3.5.2
Third party indemnities
disclosure, 1.6.3.4
generally, 1.6.3.2
inspection, 1.6.3.5

'Three-cornered demerger'
generally, 9.7.2.2
Trade marks
company names, and, 3.6.1
Trading certificates
applications, 3.3.6
consequences of failure to obtain, 3.3.7
generally, 3.3.5
purpose, 3.3.6
Trading disclosures
subordinate legislation, A3.2.2, A3.2.12
Trading on regulated markets
financial reports, and, 6.3.7
subordinate legislation, A3.2.19
Transactions at an undervalue
financial assistance, and, 9.9.2.2
intra-group transactions, and, 9.6.7.2
Transactions with directors
approval under more than one provision, 2.7
breach of rules, 2.1.4
capacity to bind a company, and, 3.5.3
changes under CA 2006
    background, 2.1.2
    generally, 2.1.5
    scope, 2.1.1
    summary, 2.10
connected persons, 2.1.1
credit transactions
    affirmation by shareholders, 2.4.13
    changes under CA 2006, 2.4.1
    exemption from approval, 2.4.9
    failure to obtain approval, 2.4.11—2.4.12
    introduction, 2.4
    meaning, 2.4.4
    personal liability, 2.4.11—2.4.12
    public companies, and, 2.4.8
    relevant transactions, 2.4.2
    shareholder approval, 2.4.2—2.4.7
    third party arrangements, 2.4.7
    value of transaction, 2.4.10
disclosure of interests in company shares
    directors, by, 2.9
    generally, 2.8
    registers, 3.14.8
failure to comply, 2.1.1
introduction, 2.1.1—2.1.5
loans
    affirmation by shareholders, 2.4.13
    changes under CA 2006, 2.4.1
    exemption from approval, 2.4.9
    failure to obtain approval, 2.4.11—2.4.12
    introduction, 2.4
    personal liability, 2.4.11—2.4.12
    public companies, and, 2.4.8
    relevant transactions, 2.4.2
    shareholder approval, 2.4.2—2.4.7
    third party arrangements, 2.4.7
    value of transaction, 2.4.10
majority shareholders, and, 2.1.3
payments for loss of office
    changes under CA 2006, 2.6.1
    exemption from approval, 2.6.4

Transactions with directors—*cont.*
payments for loss of office—*cont.*
failure to obtain approval, 2.6.5
introduction, 2.6
meaning, 2.6.2
shareholder approval, 2.6.3—2.6.5
penalties for failure to comply, 2.1.1
quasi-loans
And see **Loans**
meaning, 2.4.3
service contracts
approval, 2.2.4—2.2.11
changes under CA 2006, 2.2.1
charges for inspection, 2.2.14
conflicts of interest, and, 2.2.18
contracts affected, 2.2.2
copies, 2.2.16
directors' duties, and, 2.2.3
exemption from approval, 2.2.8
failure to obtain approval, 2.2.11
'guaranteed term', 2.2.4
inspection, 2.2.12—2.2.15
introduction, 2.2
pre-1 October 2007 contracts, 2.2.10
shadow directors, and, 2.2.17
shareholder approval, 2.2.4—2.2.11
sole member also director, 2.2.19
successive terms of less than two years,
2.2.6
substantial property transactions
affirmation by shareholders, 2.3.15
aggregation of transactions, 2.3.5
approval, 2.3.3
'arrangements', 2.3.2
changes under CA 2006, 2.3.1
'connected persons', 2.3.8—2.3.11
directors affected, 2.3.7
directors' service contracts, and, 2.3.4
examples, 2.3.2
exemption from approval, 2.3.6
failure to obtain approval, 2.3.12—2.3.14
introduction, 2.3
meaning, 2.3.2
'non-cash asset', 2.3.2
payment for loss of office, and, 2.3.4
personal liability for breach, 2.3.14
rescission, 2.3.13
series of transactions, 2.3.5
shareholder approval, 2.3.3
'substantial', 2.3.2
summary of changes, 2.10
tax-free payments, 2.5
Transfer of debentures
registers, 3.14.9
Transfer of shares
CA 2006 changes, 8.17.1
certificated shares, 8.17.3
methods, 8.17.2
uncertificated shares, 8.17.4
Treasury shares
accounting for proceeds, 8.19.6
cancellation, 8.19.5

Treasury shares—*cont.*
dealings, 8.19.4
employee incentive share plans, and, 10.4.1.3
exercise of shareholders' rights, 8.19.3
introduction, 8.19
limit on holding, 8.19.2
purchase by company of its own shares, and,
9.4.12
relevant shares, 8.19.1
'True and fair' requirement
annual accounts, and, 5.3.2—5.3.4

Ultra vires
formation of companies, and, 3.4.1
Undervalue transactions
financial assistance, and, 9.9.2.2
intra-group transactions, and, 9.6.7.2
Undischarged bankrupts
directors, and, 1.13.3
Unfair prejudice
minority shareholders, and, 4.8.1
Unlawful purpose
formation of companies, and, 3.3.4
Unlimited companies
change of status by private limited company
generally, 3.8.16
procedure, 3.8.18
purpose, 3.8.17
change of status by public company, 3.8.19
companies not registered under Companies
Acts, 3.2.3
constitution
And see **Constitution of companies**
generally, 3.4.1—3.4.15
definition, 3.2.2
distributions, 9.10.5
financial assistance, 9.10.8
formation
And see **Formation of companies**
generally, 3.3.1—3.3.8
introduction, 3.2.1
letters patent, in pursuance of, 3.2.3
pre-2 November 1862 companies, 3.2.3
purchase by company of its own shares
generally, 9.10.7
preliminary issues, 9.10.7.2
procedure, 9.10.7.1
reduction of share capital
distributable reserves, 9.10.6.4
effective date, 9.10.6.6
filing requirements, 9.10.6.5
introduction, 9.10.6.1
methods, 9.10.6.2
preliminary issues, 9.10.6.3
share capital, and, 8.6.4
use in reorganisations, and
CA 2006 changes, 9.10.2
comparison table, 9.10.3
distributions, 9.10.5
purchase by company of its own shares,
9.10.7
purpose, 9.10.1

Unlimited companies—*cont.*
use in reorganisations, and—*cont.*
reduction of share capital, 9.10.6
risks, 9.10.4
summary table, 9.11
Unregistered companies
subordinate legislation, A3.2.2

Valuations
intra-group transactions, and
methods, 9.6.6
summary of rules, 9.6.4
Variation of class rights
action prior to 1 October 2009, 8.15.6
CA 2006 changes, 8.15.1
current procedure, 8.15.2
filing requirements, 8.15.5
introduction, 8.15
new procedure, 8.15.3—8.15.5
objections by class, 8.15.4
purchase by company of its own shares, and,
9.4.2.2
Voluntary liquidation (members')
advertisement, 11.5.4
appointment of liquidator, 11.5.3
comparison with striking-off, 11.6
compliance, 11.5.5.1
date of dissolution, 11.5.9
dealing with creditor claims,
11.5.6.2—11.5.6.3
declaration of solvency, 11.5.2.2
effect on status
generally, 11.5.5
shareholdings, 11.5.5.3
statutory filing and compliance,
11.5.5.1
tax affairs, 11.5.5.2
final board meeting, 11.5.2.1
final meeting of members, 11.5.8
general meeting of members, 11.5.2.3
grounds, 11.5.1
introduction, 11.5
liquidator
appointment, 11.5.3
duties, 11.5.6.2
powers, 11.5.6.1
role, 11.5.6
London Gazette notice, 11.5.4
procedure
advertisement, 11.5.4
appointment of liquidator, 11.5.3
declaration of solvency, 11.5.2.2
final board meeting, 11.5.2.1
general meeting of members, 11.5.2.3
introduction, 11.5.2
publication, 11.5.4
realisation of assets, 11.5.6.2
seeking out creditor claims, 11.5.6.2

Voluntary liquidation (members')—*cont.*
shareholdings, 11.5.5.3
statutory filings, 11.5.5.1
tax affairs, 11.5.5.2
timing of distribution, 11.5.7
Voting rights
attendance, and, 4.4.15
corporate shareholders, by, 4.4.21—4.4.22
proxies, 4.4.16—4.4.20
show of hands, 4.4.27

Website communications
See also **Electronic communications**
application of provisions, 4.2.2
authorisation, 4.2.6
deemed consent
disadvantages, 4.2.8
generally, 4.2.6
introduction, 4.2.5
revocation, 4.2.9
deemed delivery times, 4.2.13
duration, 4.2.12
financial reports, and
generally, 6.3.4—6.3. 5
quoted companies, 6.3.11
general meetings, and, 4.4.9
hard copy documents, and, 4.2.14
introduction, 4.2.1
meaning, 4.2.5
nominees, and, 4.2.15
notification procedure
e-mail, 4.2.11
generally, 4.2.10
request for consent
generally, 4.2.7
timing, 4.2.6
revocation of consent, 4.2.9
shareholder consent
generally, 4.2.6
request, 4.2.7
revocation, 4.2.9
timing of request, 4.2.6
'Whitewash' procedure
common law, at, 9.9.4.3
Companies Act 1985, under, 9.9.4.1
Companies Act 2006, under, 9.9.4.2
employee share plans, and, 10.2.2.7
Wholly-owned subsidiaries
directors, and, 1.1.4
Words and phrases
glossary, Appendix 4
Written resolutions
electronic communications, and, 4.4.31
generally, 4.4.28
proposed by directors, 4.4.29
requisitioned by members, 4.4.30
Wrongful trading
directors, and, 1.7.1